DECLARATION OF INDEPENDENCE

THE CENTURY OF INDEPENDENCE:

EMBRACING A COLLECTION, FROM OFFICIAL SOURCES, OF THE MOST IMPORTANT

Documents and Statistics

CONNECTED WITH THE

POLITICAL HISTORY OF AMERICA;

ALSO,

A Chronological Record of the Principal Events, from its Discovery to the Present Time;

WITH

BIOGRAPHICAL AND HISTORICAL SKETCHES.

J. R. HUSSEY & CO.,
INDIANAPOLIS, IND.
1876.

Stereotyped at
FRANKLIN TYPE FOUNDRY,
Cincinnati.

WILSTACH, BALDWIN & Co.,
Printers, Bookbinders, and Stationers,
Cincinnati, Ohio.

CONTENTS.

CONFEDERATION OF THE ORIGINAL STATES.

On Monday, the 5th of September, 1774, there were assembled at Carpenter's Hall, in the city of Philadelphia, a number of men who had been chosen and appointed by the several colonies in North America to hold a Congress for the purpose of discussing certain grievances imputed against the mother country. This Congress resolved, on the next day, that each colony should have one vote only. On Tuesday, the 2d July, 1776, the Congress resolved, "That these United Colonies are, and of right ought to be, Free and Independent States," etc., etc.; and on Thursday, the 4th July, the whole Declaration of Independence having been agreed upon, it was publicly read to the people. Shortly after, on the 9th September, it was resolved that the words "United Colonies" should be no longer used, and that the "UNITED STATES OF AMERICA" should thenceforward be the style and title of the Union. On Saturday, the 15th November, 1777, "Articles of Confederation and Perpetual Union of the United States of America" were agreed to by the State delegates, subject to the ratification of the State legislatures severally. Eight of the States ratified these articles on the 9th July, 1778; one on the 21st July; one on the 24th July; one on the 26th November of the same year; one on the 22d February, 1779; and the last one on the 1st March, 1781. Here was a bond of union between thirteen independent States, whose delegates in Congress legislated for the general welfare, and executed certain powers so far as they were permitted by the articles aforesaid. The following are the names of the Presidents of the Continental Congress from 1774 to 1788:

Peyton Randolph, Virginia.............5th Sept., 1774.
Henry Middleton, South Carolina.......22d Oct., 1774.
Peyton Randolph, Virginia............10th May, 1775.

John Hancock, Massachusetts..........24th May, 1776.
Henry Laurens, South Carolina........1st Nov., 1777.
John Jay, New York..................10th Dec., 1778.
Samuel Huntington, Connecticut.......28th Sept., 1779.
Thomas McKean, Delaware...........10th July, 1781.
John Hanson, Maryland..............5th Nov., 1781.
Elias Boudinot, New Jersey...........4th " 1782.
Thomas Mifflin, Pennsylvania..........3d " 1783.
Richard Henry Lee, Virginia..........30th " 1784.
Nathaniel Gorham, Massachusetts......6th Jan., 1786.
Arthur St. Clair, Pennsylvania.........2d Feb., 1787.
Cyrus Griffin, Virginia................22d Jan., 1788.

The seat of government was established as follows: At Philadelphia, Pa., commencing September 5, 1774, and May 10, 1775; at Baltimore, Md., December 20, 1776; at Philadelphia, Pa., March 4, 1777; at Lancaster, Pa., September 27, 1777; at York, Pa., September 30, 1777; at Philadelphia, Pa., July 2, 1778; at Princeton, N. J., June 30, 1783; at Annapolis, Md., November 26, 1783; at Trenton, N. J., November 1, 1784; and at New York City, N. Y., January 11, 1785.

On the 4th March, 1789, the present Constitution, which had been adopted by a convention and ratified by the requisite number of States, went into operation.

WASHINGTON'S ACCEPTANCE OF THE COMMAND OF THE ARMY.

There were not many occasions during his public career that Washington was called upon to exercise his abilities as a writer or an orator; but when such occasion did occur, he always acquitted himself with a degree of perspicuity and modesty which may be said to have been characteristic of himself alone. The addresses which follow mark, as it were, four distinct epochs in the history of this unexampled man: the first, when he accepted the command of the armies by which our national independence was achieved; the second, when he surrendered his commission, after having driven the foes of freedom from his beloved country; the third, when he assumed the responsible duties of President, in which office his high qualities for civil government were as conspicuous as had been his military talents in the field; and fourth, when he resigned his great trust and took leave of the people in his imperishable "Farewell Address," an inestimable legacy, which can not be too frequently conned by every American who values his birthright.

WASHINGTON'S ELECTION AS COMMANDER-IN-CHIEF.

On the 15th of June, 1775, Washington was unanimously elected by Congress to "command all the Continental forces raised, or to be raised, for the defense of American liberty," and when he appeared in his place the next day, the President of that body acquainted him with his election, in a well-timed address, "and requested that he should accept of that employment;" to which Washington replied as follows:

"MR. PRESIDENT: Though I am truly sensible of the high honor done me, in this appointment, yet I feel great distress, from consciousness that my abilities and military experience may not be equal to the extensive and important trust: However, as the Congress desire it, I will enter upon the momentous duty, and exert every power I possess in their service, and for support of the glorious cause. I beg they will accept my most cordial thanks for this distinguished testimony of their approbation.

"But lest some unlucky event should happen, unfavorable to my reputation, I beg it may be remembered, by every gentleman in the room, that I, this day, declare, with the utmost sincerity, I do not think myself equal to the command I am honored with.

"As to pay, sir, I beg leave to assure the Congress, that, as no pecuniary consideration could have tempted me to accept this arduous employment, at the expense of my domestic ease and happiness, I do not wish to make any profit from it. I will keep an exact account of my expenses. Those, I doubt not, they will discharge, and that is all I desire."

DECLARATION OF INDEPENDENCE.

IN CONGRESS, TUESDAY, JULY 4, 1776.

Agreeably to the order of the day, the Congress resolved itself into a committee of the whole, to take into their further consideration the Declaration; and, after some time, the President resumed the chair, and Mr. Harrison reported that the Committee had agreed to a Declaration, which they desired him to report. (The committee consisted of Jefferson, Franklin, John Adams, Sherman, and R. R. Livingston.)

The Declaration, being read, was agreed to as follows:

A DECLARATION

BY THE REPRESENTATIVES OF THE UNITED STATES OF AMERICA, IN CONGRESS ASSEMBLED.

When, in the course of human events, it becomes necessary for one people to dissolve the political bands which have connected them with another, and to assume among the powers of the earth the separate and equal station to which the laws of nature and of nature's God entitle them, a decent respect for the opinions of mankind requires that they should declare the causes which impel them to the separation.

We hold these truths to be self-evident: that all men are created equal; that they are endowed by their Creator with certain inalienable rights; that among these are life, liberty, and the pursuit of happiness. That, to secure these rights, governments are instituted among men, deriving their just powers from the consent of the governed; that, whenever any form of government becomes destructive of these ends, it is the right of the people to alter or to abolish it, and to institute a new government, laying its foundation on such principles, and organizing its powers in such form, as to them shall seem most likely to effect their safety and happiness. Prudence, indeed, will dictate that governments long established should not be changed for light and transient causes; and, accordingly, all experience hath shown that mankind are more disposed to suffer, while evils are sufferable, than to right themselves by abolishing the forms to which they are accustomed. But, when a long train of abuses and usurpations, pursuing invariably the same object, evinces a design to reduce them under absolute despotism, it is their right, it is their duty, to throw off such government, and to provide new guards for their future security. Such has been the patient sufferance of these colonies, and such is now the necessity which constrains them to alter their former systems of government. The history of the present King of Great Britain is a history of repeated injuries and usurpations, all having in direct object the establishment of an absolute tyranny over these States. To prove this, let facts be submitted to a candid world:

He has refused his assent to laws the most wholesome and necessary for the public good.

He has forbidden his Governors to pass laws of immediate and pressing importance, unless suspended in their operation till his assent should be obtained; and, when so suspended, he has utterly neglected to attend to them.

He has refused to pass other laws for the accommodation of large districts of people unless those people would relinquish the right of representation in the legislature — a right inestimable to them, and formidable to tyrants only.

He has called together legislative bodies at places unusual, uncomfortable, and distant from the depository of their public records, for the sole purpose of fatiguing them into compliance with his measures.

He has dissolved representative houses repeatedly for opposing, with manly firmness, his invasions on the rights of the people.

He has refused, for a long time after such dissolutions, to cause others to be elected; whereby the legislative powers, incapable of annihilation, have returned to the people at large for their exercise, the State remaining, in the mean time, exposed to all the danger of invasion from without, and convulsions within.

He has endeavored to prevent the population of these States; for that purpose, obstructing the laws for naturalization of foreigners; refusing to pass others to encourage their emigration hither, and raising the conditions of new appropriations of lands.

He has obstructed the administration of justice, by refusing his assent to laws for establishing judiciary powers.

He has made judges dependent on his will alone for the tenure of their offices and the amount and payment of their salaries.

He has erected a multitude of new offices, and sent hither swarms of officers to harass our people, and eat out their substance.

He has kept among us, in times of peace, standing armies, without the consent of our legislature.

He has affected to render the military independent of, and superior to, the civil power.

He has combined, with others, to subject us to a jurisdiction foreign to our constitution, and unacknowledged by our laws; giving his assent to their acts of pretended legislation:

For quartering large bodies of armed troops among us;

For protecting them, by mock trial, from punishment, for any murders which they should commit on the inhabitants of these States;

For cutting off our trade with all parts of the world;

For imposing taxes on us without our consent;

For depriving us, in many cases, of the benefits of trial by jury;

For transporting us beyond seas to be tried for pretended offenses;

For abolishing the free system of English laws in a neighboring province, establishing therein an arbitrary government, and enlarging its boundaries, so as to render it at once an example and fit instrument for introducing the same absolute rule into these colonies;

For taking away our charters, abolishing our most valuable laws, and altering, fundamentally, the powers of our governments;

For suspending our own legislature, and declaring themselves invested with power to legislate for us in all cases whatsoever.

He has abdicated government here, by declaring us out of his protection, and waging war against us.

He has plundered our seas, ravaged our coast, burnt our towns, and destroyed the lives of our people.

He is, at this time, transporting large armies of foreign mercenaries to complete the works of death, desolation, and tyranny, already begun, with circumstances of cruelty and perfidy, scarcely paralleled in the most barbarous ages, and totally unworthy the head of a civilized nation.

He has constrained our fellow-citizens, taken captive on the high seas, to bear arms against their country, to become the executioners of their friends and brethren, or to fall themselves by their hands.

He has excited domestic insurrections amongst us, and has endeavored to bring on the inhabitants of our frontiers the merciless Indian savages, whose known rule of warfare is an undistinguished destruction, of all ages, sexes, and conditions.

In every stage of these oppressions, we have petitioned for redress, in the most humble terms; our repeated petitions have been answered only by repeated injury. A prince, whose character is thus marked by every act which may define a tyrant, is unfit to be the ruler of a free people.

Nor have we been wanting in attention to our British brethren. We have warned them, from time to time, of attempts made by their legislature to extend an unwarrantable jurisdiction over us. We have reminded them of the circumstances of our emigration and settlement here. We have appealed to their native justice and magnanimity, and we have conjured them by the ties of our common kindred, to disavow these usurpations, which would inevitably interrupt our connections and correspondence. They, too, have been deaf to the voice of justice and consanguinity. We must, therefore, acquiesce in the necessity, which denounces our separation, and hold them, as we hold the rest of mankind, enemies in war — in peace, friends.

We, therefore, the representatives of the UNITED STATES OF AMERICA, in GENERAL CONGRESS assembled, appealing to the Supreme Judge of the World for the rectitude of our intentions, do in the name, and by the authority of the good people of these colonies, solemnly publish and declare, That these United Colonies are, and of right ought to be, FREE AND INDEPENDENT STATES; that they are absolved from all allegiance to the British crown, and that all political connections between them and the State of Great Britain is, and ought to be, totally dissolved; and that, as *FREE AND INDEPENDENT STATES*, they have full power to levy war, conclude peace, contract alliances, establish commerce, and to do all other acts and things which INDEPENDENT STATES may of right do. And for the support of this Declaration, with a firm reliance on the protection of DIVINE PROVIDENCE, we mutually pledge to each other, our lives, our fortunes, and our sacred honor.

The foregoing Declaration was, by order of Congress, engrossed, and signed by the following members:

JOHN HANCOCK.

New Hampshire.

JOSIAH BARTLETT,
WILLIAM WHIPPLE,
MATTHEW THORNTON.

Massachusetts Bay.

SAMUEL ADAMS,
JOHN ADAMS,
ROBERT TREAT PAYNE,
ELBRIDGE GERRY.

Rhode Island.

STEPHEN HOPKINS,
WILLIAM ELLERY.

New York.

WILLIAM FLOYD,
PHILIP LIVINGSTON,
FRANCIS LEWIS,
LEWIS MORRIS.

Connecticut.

Roger Sherman,
Samuel Huntington,
William Williams,
Oliver Wolcott.

Pennsylvania.

Robert Morris,
Benjamin Rush,
Benjamin Franklin,
John Morton,
George Clymer,
James Smith,
George Taylor,
James Wilson,
George Ross.

Delaware.

Cæsar Rodney,
George Read,
Thomas M'Kean.

Maryland.

Samuel Chase,
William Paca,
Thomas Stone,
Charles Carroll, of Carrollton.

New Jersey.

Richard Stockton,
John Witherspoon,
Francis Hopkinson,
John Hart,
Abraham Clark.

Virginia.

George Wythe,
Richard Henry Lee,
Thomas Jefferson,
Benjamin Harrison,
Thomas Nelson, Jun.,
Francis Lightfoot Lee,
Carter Braxton.

North Carolina.

William Hooper,
Joseph Hewes,
John Penn.

South Carolina.

Edward Rutledge,
Thomas Heyward, Jun.,
Thomas Lynch, Jun.,
Arthur Middleton.

Georgia.

Button Gwinnett,
Lyman Hall,
George Walton.

ARTICLES OF CONFEDERATION

AND

PERPETUAL UNION BETWEEN THE STATES.

The Articles of Confederation reported July 12, '76, and debated from day to day, and time to time, for two years; were ratified July 9, '78, by ten States; by New Jersey, on the 26th of November of the same year; and by Delaware, on the 23d of February following. Maryland, alone, held off two years more, acceding to them March 1, '81, and thus closing the obligation. The following are the Articles:

To all whom these Presents shall come, We, the undersigned Delegates of the States affixed to our names, send greeting— Whereas, the Delegates of the United States of America, in Congress assembled, did, on the 15th day of November, in the year of our Lord, 1777, and in the Second Year of the Independence of America, agree to certain Articles of Confederation and Perpetual Union between the States of New Hampshire, Massachusetts Bay, Rhode Island and Providence Plantations, Connecticut, New York, New Jersey, Pennsylvania, Delaware, Maryland, Virginia, North Carolina, South Carolina, and Georgia, in the words following, viz.:

"*Articles of Confederation and Perpetual Union between the States of New Hampshire, Massachusetts Bay, Rhode Island and Providence Plantations, Connecticut, New York, New Jersey, Pennsylvania, Delaware, Maryland, Virginia, North Carolina, South Carolina, and Georgia.*

ARTICLE 1. The style of this Confederacy shall be "The United States of America."

ARTICLE 2. Each State retains its sovereignty, freedom, and independence, and every power, jurisdiction, and right, which is not by this confederation expressly delegated to the United States in Congress assembled.

ARTICLE 3. The said States hereby severally enter into a firm league of friendship with each other for their common defense, the security of their liberties, and their mutual and general welfare, binding themselves to assist each other against all force offered to, or attacks made upon them, or any of them, on account of religion, sovereignty, trade, or any other pretense whatever.

ARTICLE 4. The better to secure and perpetuate mutual friendship and intercourse among the people of the different States in this Union, the free inhabitants of each of these States—paupers, vagabonds, and fugitives from justice excepted—shall be entitled to all privileges and immunities of free citizens in the several States; and the people of each State shall have free ingress and regress to and from any other State, and shall enjoy therein all the privileges of trade and commerce, subject to the same duties, impositions, and restrictions, as the inhabitants thereof respectively, provided that such restriction shall not extend so far as to prevent the removal of property, imported into any State, to any other State of which the owner is an inhabitant; provided, also, that no imposition, duties or restriction shall be laid by any State on the property of the United States, or either of them.

If any person guilty of or charged with treason, felony, or other high misdemeanor in any State, shall flee from justice, and be found in any of the United States, he shall, upon demand of the Governor, or executive power of the State from which he fled, be delivered up and removed to the State having jurisdiction of his offense.

Full faith and credit shall be given in each of these States, to the records, acts, and judicial proceedings of the courts and magistrates of every other State.

ARTICLE 5. For the more convenient management of the general interest of the United States, Delegates shall be annually appointed, in such manner as the legislature of each State shall direct, to meet in Congress on the first Monday in November, in every year, with a power reserved to each State, to recall its Delegates, or any of them, at any time within the year, and to send others in their stead, for the remainder of the year.

No state shall be represented in Congress by less than two, nor by more than seven members; and no person shall be capable of being a Delegate for more than three years in any term of six years; nor shall any person, being a Delegate, be capable of holding any office under the United States, for which he, or another for his benefit, receives any salary, fees, or emolument of any kind.

Each State shall maintain its own Delegates in any meeting of the States, and while they act as members of the Committee of the States.

In determining questions in the United States, in Congress assembled, each State shall have one vote.

Freedom of speech and debate in Congress shall not be impeached or questioned in any court or place, out of Congress, and the members of Congress shall be protected in their persons from arrests and imprisonments, during the time of their going to and from, and attendance on Congress, except for treason, felony, or breach of the peace.

ARTICLE 6. No State, without the consent of the United States in Congress assembled, shall send an embassy to, or receive an embassy from, or enter into any conference, agreement, alliance, or treaty with any King, Prince, or State; nor shall any person holding any office of profit or trust under the United States, or any of them, accept of any present, emolument, office or title of any kind whatever from any King, Prince, or Foreign State; nor shall the United States in Congress assembled, or any of them, grant any title of nobility.

No two or more States shall enter into any treaty, confederation or alliance whatever between them, without the consent of the United States in Congress assembled, specifying accurately the purposes for which the same is to be entered into, and how long it shall continue.

No State shall lay any imposts or duties which may interfere with any stipulations in treaties, entered into by the United States in Congress assembled, with any King, Prince or State, in pursuance of any treaties already proposed by Congress, to the Courts of France and Spain.

No vessels of war shall be kept up in time of peace by any State except such number only, as shall be deemed necessary by the United States in Congress assembled, for the defense of such State, or its trade; nor shall any body of forces be kept up by any State, in time of peace, except such number only, as in the judgment of the United States in Congress assembled, shall be deemed requisite to garrison the forts necessary for the defense of such State; but every State shall always keep up a well regulated and disciplined militia, sufficiently armed and accoutred, and shall provide and have constantly ready for use, in public stores, a due number of field-pieces and tents, and a proper quantity of arms, ammunition, and camp equipage.

No State shall engage in any war without the consent of the United States in Congress assembled, unless such State be actually invaded by enemies, or shall have received certain advice of a resolution being formed by some nation of Indians to invade such a State, and the danger is so imminent as not to admit of a delay, till the United States in Congress assembled can be consulted: nor shall any State grant commissions to any ships or vessels of war, nor letters of marque or reprisal, except it be after a declaration of war by the United States in Congress assembled, and then only against the Kingdom or State, and the subjects thereof, against which war has been so declared, and under such regulations as shall be established by the United States in Congress assembled, unless such State be infested by pirates, in which case vessels of war may be fitted out for that occasion, and kept so long as the danger shall continue, or until the United States in Congress assembled shall determine otherwise.

Article 7. When land forces are raised by any State for the common defense, all officers of, or under the rank of colonel, shall be appointed by the legislature of each State respectively, by whom such forces shall be raised, or in such manner as such State shall direct, and all vacancies shall be filled up by the State which first made the appointment.

Article 8. All charges of war, and all other expenses that shall be incurred for the common defense or general welfare, and allowed by the United States in Congress assembled, shall be defrayed out of a common treasury, which shall be supplied by the several States, in proportion to the value of all land within each State, granted to or surveyed for any person, as such land and the buildings and improvements thereon shall be estimated according to such mode as the United States in Congress assembled, shall, from time to time, direct and appoint. The taxes for paying that proportion shall be laid and levied by the authority and direction of the legislatures of the several States within the time agreed upon by the United States in Congress assembled.

ARTICLE 9. The United States in Congress assembled shall have the sole and exclusive right and power of determining on peace and war, except in the cases mentioned in the 6th article—of sending and receiving embassadors—entering into treaties and alliances, provided that no treaty of commerce shall be made whereby the legislative power of the respective States shall be restrained from imposing such imposts and duties on foreigners, as their own people are subjected to, or from prohibiting the exportation or importation of any species of goods or commodities whatsoever—of establishing rules for deciding in all cases what captures on land or water shall be legal, and in what manner prizes taken by land or naval forces in the service of the United States shall be divided or appropriated—of granting letters of marque and reprisal in times of peace—appointing courts for the trial of piracies and felonies committed on the high seas and establishing courts for receiving and determining finally appeals in all cases of captures; provided that no member of Congress shall be appointed a judge of any of the said courts.

The United States in Congress assembled shall also be the last resort on appeal in all disputes and differences now subsisting or that hereafter may arise between two or more States concerning boundary, jurisdiction, or any other cause whatever; which authority shall always be exercised in the manner following:—Whenever the legislative or executive authority or lawful agent of any State in controversy with another shall present a petition to Congress, stating the matter in question, and praying for a hearing, notice thereof shall be given by order of Congress, to the legislative or executive authority of the other State in controversy, and a day assigned for the appearance of the parties by their lawful agents, who shall then be directed to appoint, by joint consent, commissioners or judges to constitute a court for hearing and determining the matter in question: but if they can not agree, Congress shall name three persons out of each of the United States, and from the list of such persons each party shall alternately strike out one, the petitioners beginning, until the number shall be reduced to thirteen; and from that number not less than seven, nor more than nine names, as Congress shall direct, shall in the presence of Congress be drawn out by lot, and the persons whose names shall be so drawn or any five of them, shall be commissioners or judges, to hear and finally determine the controversy, so always as a major part of the judges who shall hear the cause shall agree in the determination: and if either party shall neglect to attend at the day appointed, without showing reasons which Congress shall judge sufficient, or being present shall refuse to strike, the Congress shall proceed to nominate three persons out of each State, and the Secretary of Congress shall strike in behalf of such party absent or refusing; and the judgment and sentence of the court to be appointed, in the manner above prescribed, shall be final and conclusive; and if any of the parties shall refuse to submit to the authority of such court, or to appear or defend their claim or cause, the court shall, nevertheless, proceed to pronounce sentence or judgment, which shall in like manner be final and decisive, the judgment or sentence and other proceedings being in either case transmitted to Congress and lodged among the acts of Congress for the security of the parties concerned: provided that every commissioner, before he sits in judgment, shall take an oath, to be administered by one of the judges of the Supreme or Superior Court of the State where the cause shall be tried, "well and truly to hear and determine the matter in question, according to the best of his judgment, without favor, affection, or hope of reward:" provided also that no State shall be deprived of territory for the benefit of the United States.

All controversies concerning the private right of soil claimed under different grants of two or more States, whose jurisdictions as they may respect such lands, and the States which passed such grants, are adjusted; the said grants or either of them being at the same time claimed to have originated antecedent to such settlement of jurisdiction, shall, on the petition of either party to the Congress of the United States, be finally determined as near as may be in the same manner as is before prescribed for deciding disputes respecting territorial jurisdiction between different States.

The United States in Congress assembled shall also have the sole exclusive right and power of regulating the alloy and value of coin struck by their own authority, or by that of the respective States—fixing the standard of weights and measures throughout the United States—regulating the trade and managing all affairs with the Indians, not members of any of the States; provided that the legislative right of any State within its own limits be not infringed or violated—establishing or regulating post-offices from one State to another, throughout all the United States, and exacting such postage on the papers passing through the same as may be requisite to defray the expenses of the said office—appointing all officers of the land forces, in the service of the United States, excepting regimental officers—appointing all the officers of the naval forces, and commissioning all officers whatever in the service of the United States—making rules for the government and regulation of the said land and naval forces, and directing their operations.

The United States in Congress assembled shall have authority to appoint a committee, to sit in the recess of Congress, to be denominated "A Committee of the States," and to consist of one delegate from each State; and to appoint such other committees and civil officers as may be necessary for managing the general affairs of the United States, under their direction—to appoint one of their number to preside; provided that no person be allowed to serve in the office of president more than one year in any term of three years—to ascertain the necessary sums of money to be raised for the service of the United States, and to appropriate and apply the same for defraying the public expenses—to borrow money, or emit bills on the credit of the United States, transmitting every half year to the respective States an account of the sums of money so borrowed or emitted—to build and equip a navy—to agree upon the number of land forces, and to make requisitions from each State for its quota, in proportion to the number of white inhabitants in such State; which requisition shall be binding; and thereupon the legislatures of each State shall appoint the regimental officers, raise the men, and clothe, arm, and equip them in a soldier-like manner, at the expense of the United States; and the officers and men so clothed, armed, and equipped, shall march to the place appointed, and within the time agreed on by the United States in Congress assembled; but if the United States in Congress assembled shall, on consideration of circumstances, judge proper that any State should not raise men, or should raise a smaller number than its quota, and that any other State should raise a greater number of men than the quota thereof, such extra number shall be raised, officered, clothed, armed, and equipped in the same manner as the quota of such State, unless the legislature of such state shall judge that such extra number can not be safely spared out of the same; in which case they shall raise, officer, clothe, arm, and equip as many of such extra number as they judge can be safely spared. And the officers and men so clothed, armed, and equipped, shall march to the place appointed, and within the time agreed on by the United States in Congress assembled.

The United States in Congress assembled shall never engage in a war, nor grant letters of marque and reprisal in time of peace, nor enter into any treaties or alliances, nor coin money, nor regulate the value thereof, nor ascertain the sums and expenses necessary for the defense and welfare of the United States, or any of them, nor emit bills, nor borrow money on the credit of the United States, nor appropriate money, nor agree upon the number of vessels of war to be built or purchased, or the number of land or sea forces to be raised, nor appoint a commander-in-chief of the army or navy unless nine States assent to the same; nor shall a question on any other point, except for adjourning from day to day, be determined, unless by the votes of a majority of the United States in Congress assembled.

The Congress of the United States shall have power to adjourn to any time within the year, and to any place within the United States, so that no period of adjournment be for a longer duration than the space of six months, and shall publish the journal of their proceedings monthly, except such parts thereof relating to treaties, alliances, or military operations, as in their judgment require secresy; and the yeas and nays of the delegates of each State on any question shall be entered on the journal when it is desired by any delegate; and the delegates of a State, or any of them, at his or their request, shall be furnished with a transcript of the said journal, except such parts as are above excepted, to lay before the legislatures of the several States.

ARTICLE 10. The committee of the States, or any nine of them shall be authorized to execute, in the recess of Congress, such of the powers of Congress as the United States in Congress assembled, by the consent of nine States, shall, from time to time, think expedient to vest them with; provided that no power be delegated to the said committee; for the exercise of which, by the Articles of Confederation, the voice of nine States in the Congress of the United States assembled is requisite.

ARTICLE 11. Canada, acceding to this confederation and joining in the measures of the United States, shall be admitted into, and entitled to all the advantages of this union; but no other colony shall be admitted into the same unless such admission be agreed to by nine States.

ARTICLE 12. All bills of credit emitted, moneys borrowed, and debts contracted by, or under the authority of Congress, before the assembling of the United States, in pursuance of the present confederation, shall be deemed and considered as a charge against the United States—for payment and satisfaction whereof, the said United States and the public faith are hereby solemnly pledged.

ARTICLE 13. Every State shall abide by the determinations of the United States in Congress assembled on all questions which, by this confederation, are submitted to them. And the articles of this confederation shall be inviolably observed by every State, and the union shall be perpetual; nor shall any alteration at any time hereafter be made in any of them, unless such alteration be agreed to in a Congress of the United States, and be afterward confirmed by the legislatures of every State.

And Whereas, It hath pleased the Great Governor of the

3

World to incline the hearts of the legislatures we respectively represent in Congress, to approve of and to authorize us to ratify the said Articles of Confederation and perpetual union. Know Ye that we, the undersigned delegates, by virtue of the power and authority to us given for that purpose, do, by these presents, in the name and in behalf of our respective constituents, fully and entirely ratify and confirm each and every of the said Articles of Confederation and perpetual Union, and all and singular the matters and things therein contained. And we do further solemnly plight and engage the faith of our respective constituents, that they shall abide by the determinations of the United States in Congress assembled on all questions which, by the said confederation, are submitted to them. And that the articles thereof shall be inviolably observed by the States we respectively represent, and that the union shall be perpetual. In witness whereof we have hereunto set our hands in Congress. Done at Philadelphia, in the State of Pennsylvania, the 9th day of July, in the year of our Lord 1778, and in the 3d year of the Independence of America.

ORDINANCE OF 1787.

IN CONGRESS, JULY 13, 1787.

An Ordinance for the government of the territory of the United States, north-west of the river Ohio.

Be it ordained, by the United States in Congress assembled, that the said Territory, for the purpose of temporary government, be one district; subject, however, to be divided into two districts, as future circumstances may, in the opinion of Congress, make it expedient.

Be it ordained, by the authority aforesaid, that the estates both of resident and non-resident proprietors in the said Territory, dying intestate, shall descend to, and be distributed among their children, and the descendants of a deceased child in equal parts; the descendants of a deceased child or grand-child, to take the share of their deceased parent, in equal parts, among them, and where there shall be no children or descendants, then in equal parts to the next of kin, in equal degree; and among collaterals, the children of a deceased brother or sister of the intestate shall have, in equal parts, among them, their deceased parent's share; and there shall in no case be a distinction between kindred of the whole and half blood; saving in all cases to the widow of the intestate her third part of the real estate for life, and one-third part of the personal estate; and this law relative to descents and dower shall remain in full force until altered by the Legislature of the district. And until the Governor and judges shall adopt laws as hereinafter mentioned, estates in the said territory may be devised or bequeathed by wills in writing, signed and sealed by him or her, in whom the estate may be (being of full age), and attested by three witnesses; and real estates may be conveyed by lease or release, or bargain and sale, signed, sealed, and delivered by the person, being of full age, in whom the estate may, and attested by two witnesses, provided such wills be duly proved, and such conveyances be acknowledged, or the execution thereof duly proved, and be recorded within one year after proper magistrates, courts, and registers shall be appointed for that purpose, and personal property may be transferred by delivery, saving, however, to the French and Canadian inhabitants, and other settlers of the Kaskaskias, Saint Vincents, and the neighboring villages, who have heretofore professed themselves citizens of Virginia, their laws and customs now in force among them, relative to descent and conveyance of property.

Be it ordained, by the authority aforesaid, that there shall be appointed, from time to time, by Congress, a Governor, whose commission shall continue in force for the term of three years, unless sooner revoked by Congress; he shall reside in the district and have a freehold estate therein, in one thousand acres of land, while in the exercise of his office. There shall be appointed, from time to time, by Congress, a Secretary, whose commission shall continue in force for four years, unless sooner revoked; he shall reside therein, and have a freehold estate therein, in five hundred acres of land, while in the exercise of his office; it shall be his duty to keep and preserve the acts and laws passed by the Legislature, and the public records of the district, and the proceedings of the Governor in his executive department, and transmit authentic copies of such acts and proceedings, every six months, to the Secretary of Congress. There shall also be appointed a court, to consist of three judges, any two of whom to form a court, who shall have a common law jurisdiction, and reside in the district, and have each therein a freehold estate in five hundred acres of land, while in the exercise of their offices; and their commissions shall continue in force during good behavior.

The Governor and judges, or a majority of them, shall adopt and publish in the district such laws of the original States, criminal and civil, as may be necessary, and best suited to the circumstances of the district, and report them to Congress, from time to time, which laws shall be in force in the district until the organization of the General Assembly therein, unless disapproved by Congress; but afterward, the Legislature shall have authority to alter them as they shall think fit.

The Governor, for the time being, shall be commander-in-chief of the militia, appoint and commission all officers in the same, below the rank of general officers. All general officers shall be appointed and commissioned by Congress.

Previous to the organization of the General Assembly, the Governor shall appoint such magistrates and other civil officers, in each county or township, as he shall find necessary for the preservation of the peace and good order in the same. After the General Assembly shall be organized, the powers and duties of magistrates and other civil officers shall be regulated and defined by the said Assembly; but all magistrates and other civil officers, not herein otherwise directed, shall, during the continuance of this temporary government, be appointed by the Governor.

For the prevention of crimes and injuries, the laws to be adopted or made, shall have force in all parts of the district, and for the execution of process, criminal and civil, the Governor shall make proper divisions thereof; and shall proceed, from time to time, as circumstances may require, to lay out the parts of the district in which the Indian titles shall have been extinguished, into counties and townships, subject, however, to such alterations as may hereafter be made by the Legislature.

So soon as there shall be five thousand free male inhabitants, of full age, in the district, upon giving proof thereof to the Governor, they shall receive authority, with time and place, to elect representatives from their counties or townships, to represent them in the General Assembly; *Provided*, That for every five hundred free male inhabitants there shall be one representative, and so on progressively with the number of free male inhabitants, shall the right of representation increase, until the number of representatives shall amount to twenty-five, after which the number and proportion of representatives shall be regulated by the Legislature; *Provided*, That no person be eligible or qualified to act as a representative, unless he shall have been a citizen of one of the United States three years and be a resident in the district, or unless he shall have resided in the district three years, and in either case shall likewise hold in his own right, in fee simple, two hundred acres of land within the same; *Provided*, also, that a freehold in fifty acres of land in the district, having been a citizen of one of the States, and being resident in the district, or the like freehold and two years' residence in the district, shall be necessary to qualify a man as an elector of a representative.

The representative thus elected, shall serve for the term of two years, and in case of the death of a representative, or removal from office, the Governor shall issue a writ to the county or township for which he was a member, to elect another in his stead, to serve for the residue of the term.

The General Assembly, or Legislature, shall consist of the Governor, Legislative Council, and a House of Representatives. The Legislative Council shall consist of five members, to continue in office five years, unless sooner removed by Congress, any three of whom to be a quorum, and the members of the Council, shall be nominated and appointed in the following manner, to wit: as soon as representatives shall be elected, the Governor shall appoint a time and place for them to meet together, and, when met, they shall nominate ten persons, residents in the district, and each possessed of a freehold in five hundred acres of land, and return their names to Congress, five of whom Congress shall appoint and commission to serve as aforesaid; and whenever a vacancy shall happen in the Council, by death or removal from office, the House of Representatives shall nominate two persons qualified as aforesaid, for each vacancy, and return their names to Congress, one of whom Congress shall appoint and commission for the residue of the term; and every five years, four months at least before the expiration of the time of service of the Council, the said House shall nominate ten persons qualified as aforesaid, and return their names to Congress, five of whom Congress shall appoint and commission to serve as members of the Council five years, unless sooner removed. And the Governor, Legislative Council, and House of Representatives, shall have authority to make laws in all cases for the good government of the district, not repugnant to the principles and articles in this ordinance established and declared. And all bills having passed by a majority in the House, and by a majority in the Council, shall be referred to the Governor for his assent; but no bill or legislative act whatever, shall be of any force without his assent. The Governor shall have power to convene, prorogue, and dissolve the assembly, when in his opinion it shall be expedient.

The Governor, Judges, Legislative Council, Secretary, and such other officers as Congress shall appoint in the district, shall take an oath or affirmation of fidelity, and of office—the Governor before the President of Congress, and all other officers before the Governor. As soon as a Legislature shall be formed in the District, the Council and House, assembled in one room, shall have authority, by joint ballot, to elect a delegate to Congress, who shall have a seat in Congress, with the right of debating, but not of voting, during this temporary government.

And for extending the fundamental principles of civil and religious liberty, which form the basis whereon these republics, their laws and constitutions, are elected; *to fix and establish those principles as the basis of all laws, constitutions, and governments, which* FOREVER *hereafter shall be formed in the said Territory;* to provide also for the establishment of States, and for their admission to a share in the Federal Council on an equal footing with the original States, at as early periods as may be consistent with the general interest:

It is hereby ordained and declared, by the authority aforesaid, that the following articles shall be considered as articles of compact between the original States and the people and States in the said Territory, and forever remain unalterable, unless by common consent; viz.:

ARTICLE I. No person, demeaning himself in a peaceable and orderly manner, shall ever be molested on account of his mode of worship or religious sentiments in the said Territory.

ART. II. The inhabitants of the said Territory shall always be entitled to the benefit of the writ of *habeas corpus* and of the trial by jury; of a proportionate representation of the people in the Legislature, and of judicial proceedings according to the course of the common law; all persons shall be bailable unless for capital offenses, where the proof shall be evident, or the presumption great; all fines shall be moderate, and no cruel or unusual punishments shall be inflicted; no man shall be deprived of his liberty or property but by the judgment of his peers or the law of the land; and should the public exigencies make it necessary for the common preservation to take any person's property, or to demand his particular services, full compensation shall be made for the same; and, in the just preservation of rights and property, it is understood and declared, that no law ought ever to be made, or have force in the said territory, that shall, in any manner whatever, interfere with or affect private contracts or engagements, *bona fide*, and, without fraud, previously formed.

ART. III. Religion, morality, and knowledge being necessary to good government and the happiness of mankind, schools and the means of education shall forever be encouraged. The utmost good faith shall always be observed toward the Indians; their lands and property shall never be taken from them without their consent; and in their property, rights, and liberty, they never shall be invaded or disturbed, unless in just and lawful wars authorized by Congress; but laws founded in justice and humanity shall, from time to time, be made, for preventing wrongs being done to them, and for preserving peace and friendship with them.

ART. IV. The said Territory, and the States which may be formed therein, shall forever remain a part of this Confederacy of the United States of America, subject to the Articles of Confederation,* and to such alterations therein as shall be constitutionally made; and to all the acts and ordinances of the United States in Congress as-

* This ordinance was drawn up before the Constitution was formed

sembled, conformable thereto. The inhabitants and settlers in the said Territory shall be subject to pay a part of the Federal debts contracted, or to be contracted, and a proportional part of the expenses of government, to be apportioned on them by Congress, according to the same common rule and measure by which apportionments thereof shall be made on the other States; and the taxes for paying their proportion shall be laid and levied by the authority and direction of the Legislatures of the District, or Districts, or new States, as in the original States, within the time agreed upon by the United States in Congress assembled. The Legislatures of those Districts, or new States, shall never interfere with the primary disposal of the soil by the United States in Congress assembled, nor with any regulations Congress may find necessary for securing the title in such soil to the *bona fide* purchasers. No tax shall be imposed on lands the property of the United States; and in no case shall non-resident proprietors be taxed higher than residents. The navigable waters leading into the Mississippi and St. Lawrence, and the carrying places between the same, shall be common highways, and forever free, as well to the inhabitants of the said Territory as to the citizens of the United States, and those of any other States that may be admitted into the confederacy, without any tax, impost, or duty therefor.

Art. V. There shall be formed in the said Territory not less than three, nor more than five States; and the boundaries of the States, as soon as Virginia shall alter her act of session and consent to the same, shall become fixed and established as follows, to wit: The western State shall be bounded by the Mississippi, the Ohio, and Wabash Rivers; a direct line drawn from the Wabash and Post Vincents due north to the territorial line between the United States and Canada, and by the said territorial line to the Lake of the Woods and Mississippi. The middle State shall be bounded by the said direct line, the Wabash from Post Vincents to the Ohio, by the Ohio, by direct line drawn due north from the mouth of the Great Miami to the said territorial line, and by said territorial line. The eastern State shall be bounded by the last mentioned direct line, the Ohio, Pennsylvania, and the said territorial line; *Provided*, however, and it is further understood and declared, that the boundaries of these three States shall be subject so far to be altered, and, if Congress shall hereafter find it expedient, they shall have authority to form one or two States in that part of the said Territory which lies north of an east and west line drawn through the southerly bend or extreme of Lake Michigan; and whenever any of the said States shall have sixty thousand free inhabitants therein, such States shall be admitted, by their delegates, into the Congress of the United States, on an equal footing with the original States in all respects whatsoever; and shall be at liberty to form a permanent constitution and State government; *Provided*, the constitution and government so to be formed shall be republican, and in conformity to the principles contained in these articles; and, so far as it can be consistent with the general interest of the confederacy, such admission shall be allowed at an earlier period, and when there may be a less number of free inhabitants in the State than sixty thousand.

ART VI. There shall be neither slavery nor involuntary servitude in the said Territory, otherwise than in the punishment of crimes whereof the party shall have been duly convicted; *Provided*, always, that any person escaping into the same, from whom labor or service is lawfully claimed in any of the original States, such fugitive may be lawfully reclaimed and conveyed to the person claiming his or her labor or service as aforesaid.

Be it ordained, by the authority aforesaid, that the resolutions of the 23d of April, 1784, relative to the subject of this ordinance, be, and the same are hereby repealed, and declared null and void.

NOTE.—By this ordinance, Virginia ceded to the United States the territory now composing the States of Ohio, Indiana, Illinois, Wisconsin, and Michigan, making the ordinance the fundamental law of these States

CONSTITUTION

OF THE

UNITED STATES OF AMERICA.

We, the People of the United States, in order to form a more perfect Union, establish justice, insure domestic tranquillity, provide for the common defense, promote the general welfare, and secure the blessings of liberty to ourselves and our posterity, do ordain and establish this Constitution for the United States of America:

ARTICLE I.

SECTION 1. All the legislative powers herein granted shall be vested in a Congress of the United States, which shall consist of a Senate and House of Representatives.

SEC. 2. The House of Representatives shall be composed of members chosen every second year by the people of the several States; and the electors in each State shall have the qualifications requisite for electors of the most numerous branch of the State Legislature.

No person shall be a Representative who shall not have attained to the age of twenty-five years, and been seven years a citizen of the United States, and who shall not, when elected, be an inhabitant of that State in which he shall be chosen.

Representatives and direct taxes shall be apportioned among the several States which may be included within this Union, according to their respective numbers, which shall be determined by adding to the whole number of free persons, including those bound to service for a term of years, and excluding Indians not taxed, three-fifths of all other persons. The actual enumeration shall be made within three years after the first meeting of the Congress of the United States, and within every subsequent term of ten years, in such manner as they shall by law direct. The number of Representatives shall not exceed one for every thirty thousand, but each State shall have at least one Representative; and until such enumeration shall be made, the State of New Hampshire shall be entitled to choose three, Massachusetts eight, Rhode Island and Providence Plantations one, Connecticut five, New York six, New Jersey four, Pennsylvania eight, Delaware one, Maryland six, Virginia ten, North Carolina five, South Carolina five, and Georgia three.

When vacancies happen in the representation from any State, the Executive authority thereof shall issue Writs of Election to fill such vacancies.

The House of Representatives shall choose their Speaker and other officers; and shall have the sole power of impeachment.

SEC. 3. The Senate of the United States shall be composed of two Senators from each State, chosen by the Legislature thereof, for six years; and each Senator shall have one vote.

Immediately after they shall be assembled in consequence of the first election, they shall be divided as equally as may be into three classes. The seats of the Senators of the first class shall be vacated at the expiration of the second year, of the second class at the expiration of the fourth year, and of the third class at the expiration of the sixth year, so that one-third may be chosen every second year; and if vacancies happen by resignation, or otherwise, during the recess of the Legislature of any State, the Executive thereof may make temporary appointments until the next meeting of the Legislature, which shall then fill such vacancies.

No person shall be a Senator who shall not have attained to the age of thirty years, and been nine years a citizen of the United States, and who shall not, when elected, be an inhabitant of that State for which he shall be chosen.

The Vice-President of the United States shall be President of the Senate, but shall have no vote, unless they be equally divided.

The Senate shall choose their other officers, and also a President *pro tempore*, in the absence of the Vice-President, or when he shall exercise the office of President of the United States.

The Senate shall have the sole power to try all impeachments. When sitting for that purpose, they shall be on oath or affirmation. When the President of the United States is tried, the Chief Justice shall preside; and no person shall be convicted without the concurrence of two-thirds of the members present.

Judgment in cases of impeachment shall not extend further than to removal from office, and disqualification to hold and enjoy any office of honor, trust or profit under the United States; but the party convicted shall nevertheless be liable and subject to indictment, trial, judgment and punishment, according to law.

SEC. 4. The times, places, and manner of holding elections for Senators and Representatives, shall be prescribed in each State by the Legislature thereof; but the Congress may, at any time, by law make or alter such regulations, except as the places of choosing Senators.

The Congress shall assemble at least once in every year, and such meeting shall be on the first Monday in December, unless they shall by law appoint a different day.

SEC. 5. Each House shall be the judge of the elections, returns, and qualifications of its own members, and a majority of each shall constitute a quorum to do business; but a smaller number may adjourn from day to day, and may be authorized to compel the attendance of absent members, in such manner and under such penalties as each House may provide.

Each House may determine the Rules of its Proceedings, punish its members for disorderly behavior, and with the concurrence of two-thirds, expel a member.

Each House shall keep a Journal of its Proceedings, and from time to time publish the same, excepting such parts as may, in their judgment, require secrecy; and the yeas and nays of the members of either House on any question shall, at the desire of one-fifth of those present, be entered on the journal.

Neither House, during the session of Congress, shall, without the consent of the other, adjourn for more than three days, nor to any other place than that in which the two Houses shall be sitting.

Sec. 6. The Senators and Representatives shall receive a compensation for their services, to be ascertained by law and paid out of the treasury of the United States. They shall in all cases, except treason, felony, and breach of the peace, be privileged from arrest during their attendance at the session of their respective Houses, and in going to and returning from the same; and for any speech or debate in either House, they shall not be questioned in any other place.

No Senator or Representative shall, during the time for which he was elected, be appointed to any civil office under the authority of the United States, which shall have been created, or the emoluments whereof shall have been increased during such time, and no person holding any office under the United States shall be a member of either House during his continuance in office.

Sec. 7. All bills for raising revenue shall originate in the House of Representatives; but the Senate may propose or concur with amendments as on other bills.

Every bill which shall have passed the House of Representatives and the Senate, shall, before it becomes a law, be presented to the President of the United States: If he approve, he shall sign it; but if not, he shall return it, with his objections, to that House in which it shall have originated, who shall enter the objections at large on their Journal, and proceed to reconsider it. If, after such reconsideration, two-thirds of that House shall agree to pass the bill, it shall be sent, together with the objections, to the other House, by which it shall likewise be reconsidered, and if approved by two-thirds of that House, it shall become a law. But in all such cases the votes of both Houses shall be determined by yeas and nays, and the names of the persons voting for and against the bill shall be entered on the Journal of each House respectively. If any bill shall not be returned by the President within ten days (Sundays excepted) after it shall have been presented to him, the same shall be a law, in like manner as if he had signed it, unless the Congress, by their adjournment, prevent its return, in which case it shall not be a law.

Every order, resolution, or vote to which the concurrence of the Senate and House of Representatives may be necessary (except on a question of adjournment) shall be presented to the President of the United States; and before the same shall take effect, shall be approved by him; or, being disapproved by him, shall be repassed by two-thirds of the Senate and House of Representatives, according to the rules and limitations prescribed in the case of a bill.

SEC. 8. The Congress shall have Power—

To lay and collect Taxes, Duties, Imposts and Excises, to pay the debts and provide for the common defense and general welfare of the United States; but all Duties, Imposts and Excises shall be uniform throughout the United States;

To borrow money on the credit of the United States;

To regulate commerce with foreign nations, and among the several States, and with the Indian tribes;

To establish an uniform rule of naturalization, and uniform laws on the subject of bankruptcies throughout the United States;

To coin money, regulate the value thereof and of foreign coin, and fix the standard of weights and measures;

To provide for the punishment of counterfeiting the securities and current coin of the United States;

To establish post-offices and post-roads;

To promote the progress of science and useful arts, by securing for limited times to authors and inventors the exclusive right to their respective writings and discoveries;

To constitute tribunals inferior to the Supreme Court;

To define and punish piracies and felonies committed on the high seas, and offenses against the law of nations;

To declare war, grant letters of marque and reprisal, and make rules concerning captures on land and water;

To raise and support armies, but no appropriation of money to that use shall be for a longer term than two years;

To provide and maintain a navy;

To make rules for the government and regulation of the land and naval forces;

To provide for calling forth the militia to execute the laws of the Union, suppress insurrections, and repel invasions;

To provide for organizing, arming, and disciplining the militia, and for governing such part of them as may be employed in the service of the United States, reserving to the States respectively the appointment of the officers, and the authority of training the militia according to the discipline prescribed by Congress;

To exercise exclusive legislation, in all cases whatsoever, over such district (not exceeding ten miles square) as may, by cession of particular States, and the acceptance of Congress, become the Seat of the Government of the United States, and to exercise like authority over all places purchased by the consent of the Legislature of the State in which the same shall be, for the erection of forts, magazines, arsenals, dock-yards, and other needful buildings; and

To make all laws which shall be necessary and proper for carrying into execution the foregoing powers, and all other powers vested by this Constitution in the Government of the United States, or in any department or officer thereof.

SEC. 9. The migration or importation of such persons as any of the States now existing shall think proper to admit, shall not be prohibited by the Congress prior to the year one thousand eight hundred and eight, but a tax or duty may be imposed on such importation, not exceeding ten dollars for each person.

The privilege of the Writ of Habeas Corpus shall not be suspended, unless when, in cases of rebellion or invasion, the public safety may require it.

No bill of attainder or ex post facto law shall be passed.

No capitation, or other direct tax shall be laid, unless in proportion to the census or enumeration hereinbefore directed to be taken.

No tax or duty shall be laid on articles exported from any State.

No preference shall be given by any regulation of commerce or revenue to the ports of one State over those of another; nor shall vessels bound to or from one State, be obliged to enter, clear, or pay duties in another.

No money shall be drawn from the treasury but in consequence of appropriations made by law; and a regular statement and account of the receipts and expenditures of all public money shall be published from time to time.

No title of nobility shall be granted by the United States: And no person holding any office of profit or trust under them shall, without the consent of the Congress, accept of any present, emolument, office, or title, of any kind whatever, from any king, prince, or foreign State.

SEC. 10. No State shall enter into any treaty, alliance, or confederation; grant letters of marque or reprisal; coin money; emit bills of credit; make any thing but gold and silver coin a tender in payment of debts; pass any bill of attainder, ex post facto law, or law impairing the obligation of contracts, or grant any title of nobility.

No State shall, without the consent of the Congress, lay any imposts or duties on imports or exports, except what may be absolutely necessary for executing its inspection laws; and the net produce of all duties and imposts, laid by any State on imports or exports, shall be for the use of the treasury of the United States; and all such laws shall be subject to the revision and control of the Congress.

No State shall, without the consent of Congress, lay any duty of tonnage, keep troops, or ships of war in time of peace, enter into any agreement or compact with another State, or with a foreign power, or engage in war, unless actually invaded, or in such imminent danger as will not admit of delay.

ARTICLE II.

SECTION 1. The Executive Power shall be vested in a President of the United States of America. He shall hold his office during the term of four years, and, together with the Vice-President, chosen for the same term, be elected as follows:

Each State shall appoint, in such manner as the Legislature thereof may direct, a number of electors equal to the number of Senators and Representatives to which the State may be entitled in the Congress; but no Senator or Representative, or person holding an office of trust or profit under the United States, shall be appointed an elector.

[The electors shall meet in their respective States, and vote by ballot for two persons—of one at least shall not be an inhabitant of the same State with themselves. And they shall make a list of all the persons voted for, and of the number of votes for each; which list they shall sign and certify, and transmit, sealed, to the seat of the Government of the United States, directed to the President of the Senate. The President of the Senate shall, in the presence of the Senate and House of Representatives, open all the certificates, and the votes shall then be counted. The person having the greatest number of votes shall be the President, if such number be a majority of the whole number of electors appointed; and if there be more than one who have such majority, and have an equal number of votes, then the House of Representatives shall immediately choose by ballot one of them for President; and if no person have a majority, then from the five highest on the list the said House shall, in like manner, choose the President. But, in choosing the President, the votes shall be taken by States, the representation from each State having one vote. A quorum for this purpose shall consist of a member or members from two-thirds of the States, and a majority of all the States shall be necessary to a choice. In every case, after the choice of the President, the person having the greatest number of votes of the electors shall be the Vice-President. But if there should remain two or more who have equal votes, the Senate shall choose from them by ballot the Vice-President.*]

The Congress may determine the time of choosing the electors, and the day on which they shall give their votes; which day shall be the same throughout the United States.

No person, except a natural born citizen, or a citizen of the United States at the time of the adoption of this Constitution, shall be eligible to the office of President; nei-

* This clause has been repealed and annuled by the 12th amendment.

ther shall any person be eligible to that office who shall not have attained to the age of thirty-five years, and been fourteen years a resident within the United States.

In case of the removal of the President from office, or of his death, resignation, or inability to discharge the powers and duties of the said office, the same shall devolve on the Vice-President; and the Congress may by law provide for the case of removal, death, resignation, or inability, both of the President and Vice-President, declaring what officer shall then act as President; and such officer shall act accordingly until the disability be removed, or a President shall be elected.

The President shall, at stated times, receive for his services a compensation, which shall neither be increased nor diminished during the period for which he shall have been elected; and he shall not receive within that period any other emolument from the United States, or any of them.

Before he enter on the execution of his office, he shall take the following oath or affirmation:

"I do solemnly swear (or affirm) that I will faithfully execute the office of President of the United States, and will, to the best of my ability, preserve, protect, and defend the Constitution of the United States."

SEC. 2. The President shall be Commander-in-Chief of the Army and Navy of the United States, and of the militia of the several States when called into the actual service of the United States; he may require the opinion, in writing, of the principal officer in each of the Executive Departments, upon any subject relating to the duties of their respective offices; and he shall have power to grant reprieves and pardons for offenses against the United States, except in cases of impeachment.

He shall have power, by and with the advice and consent of the Senate, to make treaties, provided two-thirds of the Senate present concur; and he shall nominate, and by and with the advice and consent of the Senate, shall appoint Embassadors, other public Ministers and Consuls, Judges of the Supreme Court, and all other officers of the United States whose appointments are not herein otherwise provided for, and which shall be established by law; but the Congress may by law vest the appointment of such inferior officers as they think proper in the President alone, in the Courts of Law, or in the Heads of Departments.

The President shall have power to fill up all vacancies that may happen during the recess of the Senate, by granting commissions, which shall expire at the end of their next session.

SEC. 3. He shall, from time to time, give to the Congress information of the state of the Union, and recommend to their consideration such measures as he shall judge necessary and expedient; he may, on extraordinary occasions, convene both Houses, or either of them; and, in case of disagreement between them with respect to the time of adjournment, he may adjourn them to such time as he shall think proper; he shall receive Embassadors and other public Ministers; he shall take care that the laws be faithfully executed, and shall commission all the officers of the United States.

SEC. 4. The President, Vice-President, and all Civil Officers of the United States, shall be removed from office on impeachment for, and conviction of, Treason, Bribery, or other high Crimes and Misdemeanors.

ARTICLE III.

SECTION 1. The judicial power of the United States shall be vested in one Supreme Court, and in such inferior Courts as the Congress may from time to time ordain and establish. The Judges, both of the Supreme and inferior courts, shall hold their offices during good behavior, and shall, at stated times, receive for their services a compensation, which shall not be diminished during their continuance in office.

SEC. 2. The judicial power shall extend to all cases, in Law and Equity, arising under this Constitution, the Laws of the United States, and Treaties made, or which shall be made, under their authority; to all cases affecting Embassadors, other public Ministers, and Consuls; to all cases of admiralty and maritime jurisdiction; to controversies to which the United States shall be a party; to controversies between two or more States; between a State and citizens of another State; between citizens of different States; between citizens of the same State claiming lands under grants of different States; and between a State, or the citizens thereof, and foreign States, citizens, or subjects.

In all cases affecting Embassadors, other public Ministers and Consuls, and those in which a State shall be a party, the Supreme Court shall have original jurisdiction. In all the other cases before mentioned, the Supreme Court shall have appellate jurisdiction, both as to law and fact, with such exceptions and under such regulations as the Congress shall make.

The trial of all crimes, except in cases of Impeachment, shall be by jury; and such trial shall be held in the State where the said crimes shall have been committed; but when not committed within any State, the trial shall be at such place or places as the Congress may by law have directed.

SEC. 3. Treason against the United States shall consist only in levying war against them, or adhering to their enemies, giving them aid and comfort. No person shall be convicted of treason unless on the testimony of two witnesses to the same overt act, or on confession in open Court.

The Congress shall have power to declare the punishment of treason, but no Attainder of Treason shall work corruption of blood, or forfeiture, except during the life of the person attainted.

ARTICLE IV.

SECTION 1. Full faith and credit shall be given in each State to the public acts, records, and judicial proceedings of every other State. And the Congress may by general laws prescribe the manner in which such acts, records, and proceedings shall be proved, and the effect thereof.

SEC. 2. The citizens of each State shall be entitled to all privileges and immunities of citizens in the several States.

A person charged in any State with treason, felony, or other crime, who shall flee from justice, and be found in another State, shall, on demand of the executive authority of the State from which he fled, be delivered up, to be removed to the State having jurisdiction of the crime.

No person held to service or labor in one State, under the laws thereof, escaping into another, shall, in consequence of any law or regulation therein, be discharged from such service or labor, but shall be delivered up on claim of the party to whom such service or labor may be due.

SEC. 3. New States may be admitted by the Congress into this Union; but no new State shall be formed or erected within the jurisdiction of any other State; nor any State be formed by the junction of two or more States or parts of States without the consent of the Legislatures of the States concerned, as well as of the Congress.

The Congress shall have power to dispose of and make all needful rules and regulations respecting the territory or other property belonging to the United States; and nothing in this Constitution shall be so construed as to prejudice any claims of the United States, or any particular State.

SEC. 4. The United States shall guarantee to every State in this Union a republican form of Government, and shall protect each of them against invasion; and on application of the Legislature, or of the Executive (when the Legislature can not be convened), against domestic violence.

ARTICLE V.

The Congress, whenever two-thirds of both Houses shall deem it necessary, shall propose amendments to the Constitution, or, on the application of the Legislatures of two-thirds of the several States, shall call a convention for proposing amendments, which, in either case, shall be valid to all intents and purposes, as part of this Constitution, when ratified by the Legislatures of three-fourths of the several States, or by conventions in three-fourths thereof, as the one or the other mode of ratification may be proposed by the Congress; *Provided*, that no amendment which may be made prior to the year one thousand eight hundred and eight shall in any manner affect the first and fourth clauses in the ninth section of the first article; and that no State, without its consent, shall be deprived of its equal suffrage in the Senate

ARTICLE VI.

All debts contracted and engagements entered into before the adoption of this Constitution, shall be as valid against the United States, under this Constitution, as under the Confederation.

This Constitution and the laws of the United States which shall be made in pursuance thereof, and all Treaties made, or which shall be made, under the authority of the United States, shall be the supreme law of the land; and the Judges in every State shall be bound thereby, any thing in the Constitution or laws of any State to the contrary notwithstanding.

The Senators and Representatives before mentioned, and the members of the several State Legislatures, and all executive and judicial officers, both of the United States and of the several States, shall be bound by oath or affirmation to support this Constitution; but no religious test shall ever be required as a qualification to any office or public trust under the United States.

ARTICLE VII.

The ratification of the conventions of nine States shall be sufficient for the establishment of this Constitution between the States so ratifying the same.

DONE in convention, by the unanimous consent of the States present, the seventeenth day of September, in the year of our Lord one thousand seven hundred and eighty-seven, and of the Independence of the United States of America the twelfth. In Witness whereof, we have hereunto subscribed our names.

GEO. WASHINGTON,
Pres't and Deputy from Virginia.

New Hampshire.

JOHN LANGDON, NICHOLAS GILMAN

Massachusetts.

NATHANIEL GORHAM, RUFUS KING.

Connecticut.

WM. SAML. JOHNSON, ROGER SHERMAN.

New York.

Alexander Hamilton.

New Jersey.

Wil. Livingston, David Brearley,
Wm. Paterson, Jona. Dayton.

Pennsylvania.

B. Franklin, Thomas Mifflin,
Robt. Morris, Geo. Clymer,
Tho. Fitzsimons, Jared Ingersoll,
James Wilson, Gouv. Morris.

Delaware.

Geo. Read, Gunning Bedford, Jun'r,
John Dickinson, Richard Bassett.
Jaco. Broom,

Maryland.

James M'Henry, Dan. of St. Thos. Jenifer.
Danl. Carroll,

Virginia.

John Blair, James Madison, Jr.

North Carolina.

Wm. Blount, Rich'd Dobbs Spaight.
Hu. Williamson,

South Corolina.

J. Rutledge, Charles Cotesworth Pinckney
Charles Pinckney, Pierce Butler.

Georgia.

William Few, Abr. Baldwin.

Attest: WILLIAM JACKSON, *Secretary.*

ARTICLES,

In addition to, and amendment of, the Constitution of the United States of America, proposed by Congress, and ratified by the Legislatures of the several States, pursuant to the fifth article of the original Constitution.

ARTICLE I.

Congress shall make no law respecting an establishment of religion, or prohibiting the free exercise thereof; or abridging the freedom of speech or of the press; or the right of the people peaceably to assemble, and to petition the Government for a redress of grievances.

ARTICLE II.

A well-regulated Militia being necessary to the security of a free State, the right of the people to keep and bear arms shall not be infringed.

ARTICLE III.

No soldier shall, in time of peace, be quartered in any house, without the consent of the owner, nor in time of war, but in a manner to be prescribed by law.

ARTICLE IV.

The right of the people to be secure in their persons, houses, papers, and effects, against unreasonable searches and seizures, shall not be violated, and no warrant shall issue but upon probable cause, supported by oath or affirmation, and particularly describing the place to be searched, and the persons or things to be seized.

ARTICLE V.

No person shall be held to answer for a capital, or otherwise infamous crime, unless on a presentment or indictment of a Grand Jury, except in cases arising in the land or naval forces, or in the militia, when in actual service in time of war or public danger; nor shall any person be subject for the same offense to be twice put in jeopardy of life or limb; nor shall be compelled in any criminal case to be a witness against himself, nor be deprived of life, liberty, or property, without due process of law; nor shall private property be taken for public use without just compensation.

ARTICLE VI.

In all criminal prosecutions, the accused shall enjoy the right to a speedy and public trial, by an impartial jury of the State and district wherein the crime shall have been committed, which district shall have been previously ascertained by law and to be informed of the nature and cause of the accusation to be confronted with the witnesses against him; to have compulsory process for obtaining witnesses in his favor, and to have the assistance of counsel for his defense.

ARTICLE VII.

In suits at common law, where the value in controversy shall exceed twenty dollars, the right of trial by jury shall be preserved, and no fact tried by a jury shall be otherwise reëxamined in any Court of the United States, than according to the rules of the common law.

ARTICLE VIII.

Excessive bail shall not be required, nor excessive fines imposed, nor cruel and unusual punishments inflicted.

ARTICLE IX.

The enumeration in the Constitution of certain rights, shall not be construed to deny or disparage others retained by the people.

ARTICLE X.

The powers not delegated to the United States by the Constitution, nor prohibited by it to the States, are reserved to the States respectively, or to the people.

ARTICLE XI.

The judicial power of the United States shall not be construed to extend to any suit in law or equity, commenced or prosecuted against one of the United States by citizens of another State, or by citizens or subjects of any foreign State.

ARTICLE XII.

The Electors shall meet in their respective States, and vote by ballot for President and Vice-President, one of whom, at least, shall not be an inhabitant of the same State with themselves; they shall name in their ballot the person voted for as President, and in distinct ballots the person voted for as Vice-President, and they shall make distinct lists of all persons voted for as President, and all persons voted for as Vice-President, and of the number of votes for each, which lists they shall sign and certify, and transmit sealed to the seat of government of the United States, directed to the President of the Senate:—The President of the Senate shall, in presence of the Senate and House of Representatives, open all the certificates, and the votes shall then be counted; The person having the greatest number of votes for President shall be the President, if such number be a majority of the whole number of Electors appointed; and if no person have such majority, then from the persons having the highest numbers, not exceeding three, on the list of those voted for as President, the House of Representatives shall choose immediately by ballot the President. But in choosing the President, the votes shall be taken by States, the representation from each State having one; a quorum for this shall consist of a member or members from two-thirds of the States, and a majority of all the States shall be necessary to a choice. And if the House of Representatives shall not choose a President, whenever the right of choice shall devolve upon them, before the fourth day of March next following, then the Vice-President shall act as President, as in the case of the death or other constitutional disability of the President. The person having the greatest number of votes as Vice-President, shall be the Vice-President, if such number be a majority of the whole number of electors appointed; and if no person have a majority, then, from the two highest numbers on the list, the Senate shall choose the Vice-President; a quorum for the purpose shall consist of two-thirds of the whole number of Senators, and a majority of the whole number shall be necessary to a choice. But no person constitutionally ineligible to the office of President, shall be eligible to that of Vice-President of the United States.

ARTICLE XIII.

"SECTION 1. Neither slavery nor involuntary servitude, except as a punishment for crime, whereof the party shall have been duly convicted, shall exist within the United States, or any place subject to their jurisdiction.

"SEC. 2. Congress shall have power to enforce this Article by appropriate legislation, approved February 1, 1863."

ARTICLE XIV.

SECTION 1. All persons born or naturalized in the United States, and subject to the jurisdiction thereof, are citizens of the United States and of the State wherein they reside. No State shall make or enforce any law which shall abridge the privileges or immunities of citizens of the United States; nor shall any State deprive any person of life, liberty, or property, without due process of law, nor deny to any person within its jurisdiction the equal protection of the laws.

SEC. 2. Representatives shall be apportioned among the several States according to their respective numbers, counting the whole number of persons in each State, excluding Indians not taxed. But when the right to vote at any election for the choice of electors for President and Vice-President of the United States, representatives in Congress, the executive and judicial officers of a State, or the members of the legislature thereof, is denied to any of the male inhabitants of such State, being twenty-one years of age, and citizens of the United States, or in any way abridged, except for participation in rebellion or other crime, the basis of representation therein shall be reduced in the proportion which the number of such male citizens shall bear to the whole number of male citizens twenty-one years of age in such State.

SEC. 3. No person shall be a senator or representative

in Congress, or elector of President and Vice-President, or hold any office, civil or military, under the United States, or under any State, who, having previously taken an oath, as a member of Congress, or as an officer of the United States, or as a member of any State legislature, or as an executive or judicial officer of any State, to support the Constitution of the United States, shall have engaged in insurrection or rebellion against the same, or given aid or comfort to the enemies thereof. But Congress may, by a vote of two-thirds of each house, remove such disability.

SEC. 4. The validity of the public debt of the United States, authorized by law, including debts incurred for the payment of pensions and bounties for services in suppressing insurrection or rebellion, shall not be questioned. But neither the United States nor any State shall assume or pay any debt or obligation incurred in aid of insurrection or rebellion against the United States, or any claim for the loss or emancipation of any slave; but all such debts, obligations and claims shall be held illegal and void.

SEC. 5. The Congress shall have power to enforce, by appropriate legislation, the provisions of this Article.

The Amendment passed the Senate by a vote of 33 yeas to 11 nays, and the House by a vote of 138 yeas to 36 nays.

ARTICLE XV.

SECTION 1. The right of citizens of the United States to vote shall not be denied or abridged by the United States or by any State on account of race, color, or previous condition of servitude.

SEC. 2. The Congress shall have power to enforce this article by appropriate legislation.

The Constitution was adopted on the 17th of September, 1787, by the convention appointed in pursuance of the Resolution of the Congress of the Confederation, of the 21st February, 1787, and ratified by the conventions of the several States, as follows:

By Convention of	Delaware	....	7th December, 1787
" "	Pennsylvania	....	12th December, 1787
" "	New Jersey	.....	18th December, 1787
" "	Georgia	....	2d January, 1788
" "	Connecticut	....	9th January, 1788
" "	Massachusetts	.....	6th February, 1788
" "	Maryland	....	28th April, 1788
" "	South Carolina	....	28th May, 1788
" "	New Hampshire	......	21st June, 1788
" "	Virginia	....	26th June, 1788
" "	New York	....	26th July, 1788
" "	North Carolina	...	21st November, 1789
" "	Rhode Island	....	29th May, 1790

The first ten of the Amendments were proposed on the 25th September, 1789, and ratified by the constitutional number of States on the 15th December, 1791; the eleventh, on the 8th January, 1798; the twelfth, on the 25th September, 1804; the thirteenth, on the 1st February, 1863; the fourteenth, on the 21st July, 1868; and the fifteenth, on the 30th March, 1870.

WASHINGTON'S RESIGNATION OF HIS COMMISSION.

The War of the Revolution having terminated auspiciously, Washington took leave of his officers and army at New York, and repaired to Annapolis, Md., where Congress was then in session. On the 20th of December, 1783, he transmitted a letter to that body apprising them of his arrival, with the intention of resigning his commission, and desiring to know whether it would be most agreeable to receive it in writing or at an audience. It was immediately resolved that a public entertainment be given him on the 22d, and that he be admitted to an audience on the 23d, at 12 o'clock. Accordingly, he attended at that time, and, being seated, the President informed him that Congress were prepared to receive his communications. Whereupon he arose, and spoke as follows:

"Mr. President: — The great events on which my resignation depended having at length taken place, I have now the honor of offering my sincere congratulations to Congress, and of presenting myself before them, to surrender into their hands the trust committed to me, and to claim the indulgence of retiring from the service of my country.

"Happy in the confirmation of our independence and sovereignty, and pleased with the opportunity afforded the United States of becoming a respectable nation, I resign with satisfaction the appointment I accepted with diffidence: a diffidence in my abilities to accomplish so arduous a task; which, however, was superseded by a confidence in the rectitude of our cause, the support of the supreme power of the Union, and the patronage of Heaven.

"The successful termination of the war has verified the most sanguine expectations; and my gratitude for the interposition of Providence, and the assistance I have received from my countrymen, increases with every review of the momentous contest.

"While I repeat my obligations to the army in general, I should do injustice to my own feelings not to acknowledge, in this place, the peculiar services and distinguished merits of the gentlemen who have been attached to my person during the war. It was impossible the choice of confidential officers to compose my family should have been more fortunate. Permit me, sir, to recommend, in particular, those who have continued in the service to the present moment, as worthy of the favorable notice and patronage of Congress.

"I consider it an indispensable duty to close this last act of my official life by commending the interests of our dearest country to the protection of Almighty God, and those who have the superintendence of them to his holy keeping.

"Having now finished the work assigned me, I retire from the great theater of action, and bidding an affectionate farewell to this august body, under whose orders I have so long acted, I here offer my commission, and take my leave of all the employments of public life."

WASHINGTON'S INAUGURAL ADDRESS.

In accordance with previous arrangements, General Washington met Congress in New York, on the 30th of April, 1789, for the purpose of being inaugurated as the first President of the United States. The oath of office having been administered by the Chancellor of the State of New York, in presence of the Senate and House of Representatives, the President delivered the following Inaugural Address:

"*Fellow-citizens of the Senate and of the House of Representatives:*

"Among the vicissitudes incident to life, no event could have filled me with greater anxieties than that of which the notification was transmitted by your order, and received on the 14th day of the present month. On the one hand, I was summoned by my country, whose voice I can never hear but with veneration and love, from a retreat which I had chosen with the fondest predilection, and, in my flattering hopes, with an immutable decision, as the asylum of my declining years — a retreat which was rendered every day more necessary, as well as more dear to me, by the addition of habit to inclination, and of frequent interruptions in my health, to the gradual waste committed on it by time. On the other hand, the magnitude and difficulty of the trust to which the voice of my country called me, being sufficient to awaken, in the wisest and most experienced of her citizens, a distrustful scrutiny into his qualifications, could not but overwhelm with despondency one who, inheriting inferior endowments from nature, and unpracticed in the duties of civil administration, ought to be peculiarly conscious of his own deficiencies. In this conflict of emotion, all I dare aver is, that it has been my faithful study to collect my duty from a just appreciation of every circumstance by which it might be affected. All I dare hope is, that if, in executing this task, I have been too much swayed by a grateful remembrance of former instances, or by an affectionate sensibility to this transcendent proof of the confidence of my fellow-citizens, and have thence too little consulted my incapacity as well as disinclination for the weighty and untried cares before me, my error will be palliated by the motives which misled me, and its consequences be judged by my country, with some share of the partiality in which they originated.

"Such being the impressions under which I have, in obedience to the public summons, repaired to the present station, it would be peculiarly improper to omit, in this first official act, my fervent supplications to that Almighty Being who rules over the universe — who presides in the councils of nations—and whose providential aids can supply every human defect, that his benediction may consecrate to the liberties and happiness of the people of the United States — a government instituted by themselves for these essential purposes — and may enable every instrument employed in its administration to execute with success the functions allotted to his charge. In tendering this homage to the Great Author of every public and private good, I assure myself that it expresses your sentiments not less than my own; nor those of my fellow-citizens at large, less than either. No people can be bound to acknowledge and adore the invisible hand which conducts the affairs of men more than the people of the United States. Every step by which they have advanced to the character of an independent nation seems to have been distinguished by some token of providential agency; and in the important revolution just accomplished in the system of their united government, the tranquil deliberations, and voluntary consent of so many distinct communities, from which the event has resulted, can not be compared with the means by which most governments have been established without some return of pious gratitude, along with an humble anticipation of the future blessings which the past seem to presage. These reflections, arising out of the present crisis, have forced themselves too strongly on my mind to be suppressed. You will join with me, I trust, in thinking that there are none under the influence of which the proceedings of a new and free government can more auspiciously commence.

"By the article establishing the executive department, it is made the duty of the President 'to recommend to your consideration such measures as he shall judge necessary and expedient.' The circumstances under which I now meet you, will acquit me from not entering into that subject farther than to refer to the great constitutional charter under which you are assembled, and which, in defining your powers, designates the objects to which your attention is to be given. It will be more consistent with those circumstances, and far more congenial with the feelings which actuate me, to substitute in place of a recommendation of particular measures, the tribute that is due to the talents, the rectitude, and the patriotism which adorn the characters selected to advise and adopt them. In these honorable qualifications I behold the surest pledges that as, on one side, no local prejudices or attachments, no separate views, nor party animosities, will misdirect the comprehensive and equal eye which ought to watch over this great assemblage of communities and interests; so, on another, that the foundations of our national policy will be laid in the pure and immutable principles of private morality; and the preëminence of free government be exemplified by all the attributes which can win the affections of its citizens, and command the respect of the world. I dwell on this prospect with every satisfaction which an ardent love for my country can inspire; since there is no truth more thoroughly established than that there exists in the economy and course of nature an indissoluble union between virtue and happiness — between duty and advantage — between the genuine maxims of an honest and magnanimous policy and the solid rewards of public prosperity and felicity; since we ought to be no less persuaded that the propitious smiles of Heaven can never be expected on a nation that disregards the eternal rules of order and right, which Heaven itself has ordained; and since the preservation of the sacred fire of liberty and the destiny of the republican model of government are justly considered as deeply, perhaps as finally, staked on the experiment intrusted to the hands of the American people.

"Besides the ordinary objects submitted to your care, it will remain with your judgment to decide how far an exercise of the occasional power delegated by the fifth article of the Constitution is rendered expedient at the present juncture by the nature of objections which have been urged against the system, or by the degree of inquietude which has given birth to them. Instead of undertaking particular recommendations on this subject, in which I could be guided by no lights derived from official opportunities, I shall again give way to my entire confidence in your discernment and pursuit of the public good; for, I assure myself, that while you carefully avoid every alteration which might endanger the benefits of an united and effective government, or which ought to await the future lessons of experience, a reverence for the characteristic rights of freemen, and a regard for the public harmony, will sufficiently influence your deliberations on the question, how far the former can be more impregnably fortified, or the latter be safely and advantageously promoted.

"To the preceding observations I have one to add, which will be most properly addressed to the House of Representatives. It concerns myself, and will, therefore, be as brief as possible: When I was first honored with a call into the service of my country, then on the eve of an arduous struggle for its liberties, the light in which I contemplated my duty required that I should renounce every pecuniary compensation. From this resolution I have in no instance departed, and, being still under the impressions which produced it, I must decline, as inapplicable to myself, any share in the personal emoluments which may be indispensably included in a permanent provision for the executive department, and must accordingly pray that the pecuniary estimates for the station in which I am placed may, during my continuance in it, be limited to such actual expenditures as the public good may be thought to require.

"Having thus imparted to you my sentiments, as they have been awakened by the occasion which brings us together, I shall take my present leave, but not without resorting once more to the benign Parent of the human race, in humble supplication, that since he has been pleased to favor the American people with opportunities for deliberating in perfect tranquillity, and dispositions for deciding with unparalleled unanimity on a form of government for the security of their Union and the advancement of their happiness, so his Divine blessing may be equally conspicuous in the enlarged views, the temperate consultations, and the wise measures, on which the success of this government must depend."

WASHINGTON'S FAREWELL ADDRESS.

Friends and Fellow-Citizens:

The period for a new election of a citizen to administer the Executive Government of the United States being not far distant, and the time actually arrived when your thoughts must be employed in designating the person who is to be clothed with that important trust, it appears to me proper especially as it may conduce to a more distinct expression of the public voice, that I should now apprise you of the resolution I have formed, to decline being considered among the number of those out of whom a choice is to be made.

I beg you, at the same time, to do me the justice to be assured that this resolution has not been taken without a strict regard to all the considerations appertaining to the relation which binds a dutiful citizen to his country; and that, in withdrawing the tender of service, which silence in my situation might imply, I am influenced by no diminution of zeal for your future interest; no deficiency of grateful respect for your past kindness, but am supported by a full conviction that the step is compatible with both.

The acceptance of, and continuance hitherto in, the office to which your suffrages have twice called me, have been a uniform sacrifice of inclination to the opinion of duty, and to a deference for what appeared to be your desire. I constantly hoped that it would have been much earlier in my power, consistently with motives which I was not at liberty to disregard, to return to that retirement from which I had been reluctantly drawn. The strength of my inclination to do this, previous to the last election, had even led to the preparation of an address to declare it to you; but mature reflection on the then perplexed and critical posture of our affairs with foreign nations, and the unanimous advice of persons entitled to my confidence impelled me to abandon the idea.

G. Washington

I rejoice that the state of your concerns, external as well as internal, no longer renders the pursuit of inclination incompatible with the sentiment of duty or propriety; and am persuaded, whatever partiality may be retained for my services, that, in the present circumstances of our country, you will not disapprove my determination to retire.

The impressions with which I undertook the arduous trust were explained on the proper occasion. In the discharge of this trust, I will only say that I have with good intentions contributed toward the organization and administration of the Government the best exertions of which a very fallible judgment was capable. Not unconscious in the outset of the inferiority of my qualifications, experience, in my own eyes—perhaps still more in the eyes of others—has strengthened the motives to diffidence of myself; and every day the increasing weight of years admonishes me more and more, that the shade of retirement is as necessary to me as it will be welcome. Satisfied that if any circumstances have given peculiar value to my services, they were temporary, I have the consolation to believe that, while choice and prudence invite me to quit the political scene, patriotism does not forbid it.

In looking forward to the moment which is intended to terminate the career of my public life, my feelings do not permit me to suspend the deep acknowledgment of that debt of gratitude which I owe to my beloved country for the many honors it has conferred upon me; still more for the steadfast confidence with which it has supported me; and for the opportunities I have thence enjoyed of manifesting my inviolable attachment, by services faithful and persevering, though in usefulness unequal to my zeal. If benefits have resulted to our country from these services, let it always be remembered to your praise, and as an instructive example in our annals that, under circumstances in which the passions, agitated in every direction, were liable to mislead; amid appearances sometimes dubious, vicissitudes of fortune often discouraging; in situations in which, not unfrequently, want of success has countenanced the spirit of criticism—the constancy of your support was the essential prop of the efforts, and a guarantee of the plans, by which they were effected. Profoundly penetrated with this idea, I shall carry it with me to my grave, as a strong incitement to unceasing vows, that Heaven may continue to you the choicest tokens of its beneficence; that your union and brotherly affection may be perpetual; that the free Constitution, which is the work of your hands, may be sacredly maintained; that its administration, in every department, may be stamped with wisdom and virtue; that, in fine, the happiness of the people of these States, under the auspices of liberty, may be made complete by so careful a preservation and so prudent a use of this blessing as will acquire to them the glory of recommending it to the applause, the affection, and the adoption of every nation which is yet a stranger to it.

Here, perhaps, I ought to stop; but a solicitude for your welfare, which can not end but with my life, and the apprehension of danger natural to that solicitude, urge me, on an occasion like the present, to offer to your solemn contemplation, and to recommend to your frequent review, some sentiments which are the result of much reflection, of no inconsiderable observation, and which appear to me all-important to the permanency of our felicity as a people. These will be afforded to you with the more freedom, as you can only see in them the disinterested warnings of a parting friend, who can possibly have no personal motive to bias his counsel; nor can I forget, as an encouragement to it, your indulgent reception of my sentiments on a former and not dissimilar occasion.

Interwoven as is the love of liberty with every ligament of your hearts, no recommendation of mine is necessary to fortify or confirm the attachment.

The unity of government which constitutes you one people, is also now dear to you. It is justly so; for it is a main pillar in the edifice of your real independence—the support of your tranquillity at home, your peace abroad, of your safety, of your prosperity, of that very liberty which you so highly prize. But as it is easy to foresee that, from different causes and from different quarters, much pains will be taken, many artifices employed, to weaken in your minds the conviction of this truth; as this is the point in your political fortress against which the batteries of internal and external enemies will be most constantly and actively (though often covertly and insidiously) directed, it is of infinite moment that you should properly estimate the immense value of your National Union to your collective and individual happiness; that you should cherish a cordial, habitual, and immovable attachment to it; accustoming yourselves to think and speak of it as of the palladium of your political safety and prosperity; watching for its preservation with jealous anxiety; discountenancing whatever may suggest even a suspicion that it can, in any event, be abandoned; and indignantly frowning upon the first dawning of every attempt to alienate any portion of our country from the rest, or to enfeeble the sacred ties which now link together the various parts.

For this you have every inducement of sympathy and interest. Citizens by birth or choice, of a common country, that country has a right to concentrate your affections. The name of *American*, which belongs to you in your national capacity, must always exalt the just pride of patriotism, more than any appellation derived from local discriminations. With slight shades of difference, you have the same religion, manners, habits, and political principles. You have, in a common cause, fought and triumphed together; the independence and liberty you possess are the work of joint counsels and joint efforts—of common dangers, sufferings and successes.

But these considerations, however powerfully they address themselves to your sensibility, are greatly outweighed by those which apply more immediately to your interest; here every portion of our country finds the most commanding motives for carefully guarding and preserving the union of the whole.

The North, in an unrestrained intercourse with the South, protected by the equal laws of a common government, finds, in the productions of the latter, great additional resources of maritime and commercial enterprise, and precious materials of manufacturing industry. The South, in the same intercourse, benefiting by the agency of the North, sees its agriculture grow and its commerce expand. Turning partly into its own channels the seamen of the North, it finds its particular navigation invigorated; and while it contributes, in different ways, to nourish and increase the general mass of the national navigation, it looks forward to the protection of a maritime strength to which itself is unequally adapted. The East, in like intercourse with the West, already finds—and in the progressive improvement of interior communication by land and water, will more and more find—a valuable vent for the commodities which it brings from abroad or manufactures at home. The West derives from the East supplies requisite to its growth and comfort; and what is, perhaps, of still greater consequence, it must, of necessity, owe the secure enjoyment of indispensable outlets for its own productions, to the weight, influence, and the future maritime strength of the Atlantic side of the Union, directed by an indissoluble community of interest as one nation. Any other tenure by which the West can hold this essential advantage, whether derived from its own separate strength, or from an apostate and unnatural connection with any foreign power, must be intrinsically precarious.

While, then, every part of our country thus feels an immediate and particular interest in UNION, all the parts combined can not fail to find, in the united mass of means and efforts, greater strength, greater resource, proportionately greater security from external danger, a less frequent interruption of their peace by foreign nations; and what is of inestimable value, they must derive from union an exemption from those broils and wars between themselves, which so frequently afflict neighboring countries, not tied together by the same government; which their own rivalship alone would be sufficient to produce, but which opposite foreign alliances, attachments, and intrigues would stimulate and embitter. Hence, likewise, they will avoid the necessity of those overgrown military establishments, which, under any form of government, are inauspicious to liberty, and which are to be regarded as particularly hostile to republican liberty; in this sense it is that your union ought to be considered as a main prop of your liberty, and that the love of the one ought to endear to you the preservation of the other.

These considerations speak a persuasive language to every reflecting and virtuous mind, and exhibit the continuance of the Union as a primary object of patriotic desire. Is there a doubt, whether a common government can embrace so large a sphere? Let experience solve it. To listen to mere speculation, in such a case, were criminal. We are authorized to hope, that a proper organization of the whole, with the auxiliary agency of governments for the respective subdivisions, will afford a happy issue to the experiment. It is well worth a fair and full experiment. With such powerful and obvious motives to Union, affecting all parts of our country, while experience shall not have demonstrated its impracticability, there will always be reason to distrust the patriotism of those who, in any quarter, may endeavor to weaken its bands.

In contemplating the causes which may disturb our Union, it occurs, as a matter of serious concern, that any ground should have been furnished for characterizing parties by geographical discriminations—Northern and Southern, Atlantic and Western—whence designing men may endeavor to excite a belief that there is a real difference of local interests and views. One of the expedients of party to acquire influence within particular districts, is to misrepresent the opinions and aims of other districts. You can not shield yourself too much against the jealousies and heart-burnings which spring from these misrepresentations; they tend to render alien to each other those who ought to be bound together by fraternal affection. The inhabitants of our western country have lately had a useful lesson on this head; they have seen in the negotiation of the Executive, and in the unanimous ratification by the Senate, of the treaty with Spain, and in the universal satisfaction at that event throughout the United States, a decisive proof how unfounded were the suspicions propagated among them of a policy in the General Government, and in the Atlantic States, unfriendly to their interests in regard to the Mississippi; they have been witnesses to the formation of two treaties—that with Great Britain, and that with Spain—which secure to them every thing they could desire in respect to our foreign relations, toward confirming their prosperity. Will it not be their wisdom to rely for the preservation of these advantages on the Union by which they were procured? Will they not henceforth be deaf to those advisers, if such there be, who would sever them from their brethren, and connect them with aliens?

To the efficacy and permanency of your Union, a Government for the whole is indispensable. No alliance, however strict between the parts, can be an adequate substitute; they must inevitably experience the infractions and interruptions which all alliances, in all time, have experienced. Sensible of this momentous truth, you have improved upon your first essay, by the adoption of a Constitution of Government better calculated than your former for an intimate Union, and for the efficacious management of your common concerns. This Government, the offspring of our own choice, uninfluenced and unawed, adopted upon full investigation and mature deliberation, completely free in its principles, in the distribution of its powers, uniting security with energy, and containing within itself a provision for its own amendment, has a just claim to your confidence and your support. Respect its authority, compliance with its laws, acquiescence in its measures, are duties enjoined by the fundamental maxims of true liberty. The basis of our political systems, is the right of the people to make and to alter their constitutions of Government; but the Constitution which at any time exists, till changed by an explicit and authentic act of the whole people, is sacredly obligatory upon all. The very idea of the power and the right of the people to establish Government, presupposes the duty of every individual to obey the established Government.

All obstructions to the execution of the laws, all combinations and associations, under whatever plausible character, with the real design to direct, control, counteract, or awe the regular deliberation and action of the constituted authorities, are destructive to this fundamental principle, and of fatal tendency. They serve to organize faction, to give it an artificial and extraordinary force, to put in the place of the delegated will of the nation the will of a party, often a small but artful and enterprising minority of the community; and, according to the alternate triumphs of different parties, to make the public administration the mirror of the ill-concerted and incongruous projects of faction, rather than the organ of consistent and wholesome plans, digested by common counsels, and modified by mutual interests.

However combinations and associations of the above description may now and then answer popular ends, they are likely, in the course of time and things, to become potent engines, by which cunning, ambitious, and unprincipled men, will be enabled to subvert the power of the people, and to usurp for themselves the reins of Government; destroying, afterward, the very engines which had lifted them to unjust dominion.

Toward the preservation of your Government, and the permanency of your present happy state, it is requisite, not only that you steadily discountenance irregular oppositions, to its acknowledged authority, but also that you resist, with care, the spirit of innovation upon its principles, however specious the pretexts. One method of assault may be to effect, in the forms' Constitution, alterations which will impair the energy of the system, and thus to undermine what can not be directly overthrown. In all the changes to which you may be invited, remember that time and habit are at least as necessary to fix the true character of Governments as of other human institutions; that experience is the surest standard by which to test the real tendency of the existing constitution of a country; that facility in changes, upon the credit of mere hypothesis and opinion, exposes to perpetual change, from the endless variety of hypothesis and opinion; and remember, especially, that for the efficient management of your common interests, in a country so extensive as ours, a Government of as much vigor as is consistent with the perfect security of liberty, is indispensable. Liberty itself will find in such a Government, with powers properly distributed and adjusted, its surest guardian. It is, indeed, little else than a name, where the Government is too feeble to withstand the enterprises of faction, to confine each member of the society within the limits prescribed by the laws, and to maintain all in the secure and tranquil enjoyment of the rights of person and property.

I have already intimated to you the danger of parties in the State, with particular reference to the founding of them on geographical discriminations. Let me now take a more comprehensive view, and warn you, in the most solemn manner, against the baneful effects of the spirit of party generally.

This spirit, unfortunately, is inseparable from our nature, having its root in the strongest passions of the human mind. It exists under different shapes, in all Governments, more or less stifled, controlled, or repressed; but in those of the popular form it is seen in its greatest rankness, and is truly their worst enemy.

The alternate domination of one faction over another, sharpened by the spirit of revenge, natural to party dissension, which, in different ages and countries, has perpetrated the most horrid enormities, is itself a frightful despotism. But this leads, at length, to a more formal and permanent despotism. The disorders and miseries which result, gradually incline the minds of men to seek security and repose in the absolute power of an individual; and, sooner or later, the chief of some prevailing faction, more able or more fortunate than his competitors, turns this disposition to the purposes of his own elevation on the ruins of public liberty.

Without looking forward to an extremity of this kind, (which, nevertheless, ought not to be entirely out of sight,) the common and continual mischiefs of the spirit of party are sufficient to make it the interest and duty of a wise people to discourage and restrain it.

It serves always to distract the public counsels, and enfeeble the public administration. It agitates the community with ill-founded jealousies and false alarms; kindles the animosities of one part against another; foments, occasionally, riot and insurrection. It opens the door to foreign influence and corruption, which find a facilitated access to the Government itself, through the channels of party passions. Thus the policy and the will of one country are subjected to the policy and will of another.

There is an opinion that parties, in free countries, are useful checks upon the administration of the Government, and serve to keep alive the spirit of liberty. This, within certain limits, is probably true; and in Governments of a monarchical cast, patriotism may look with indulgence, if not with favor, upon the spirit of party. But in those of the popular character, in Governments purely elective, it is a spirit not to be encouraged. From their natural tendency, it is certain there will always be enough of that spirit for every salutary purpose. And there being constant danger of excess, the effort ought to be, by force of public opinion, to mitigate and assuage it. A fire not to be quenched, it demands a uniform vigilance to prevent its bursting into a flame, lest, instead of warming, it should consume.

It is important, likewise, that the habits of thinking, in a free country, should inspire caution in those intrusted with its administration to confine themselves within their respective constitutional spheres, avoiding in the exercise of one department, to encroach upon another. The spirit of encroachment tends to consolidate the powers of all the departments in one, and thus to create, whatever the form of Government, a real despotism. A just estimate of that love of power, and proneness to abuse it which predominates in the human heart, is sufficient to satisfy us of the truth of this position. The necessity of reciprocal checks in the exercise of political power, by dividing and distributing it into different depositories, and constituting each the guardian of public weal, against invasions by the others, has been evinced by experiments, ancient and modern, some of them in our own country, and under our own eyes. To preserve them must be as necessary as to institute them. If, in the opinion of the people, the distribution or modification of the constitutional powers be, in any particular, wrong, let it be corrected by an amendment in the way which the Constitution designates. But let there be no change by usurpation; for though this, in one instance, may be the instrument of good, it is the customary weapon by which free Governments are destroyed. The precedent must always greatly overbalance, in permanent evil, any partial or transient benefit which the use can, at any time, yield.

Of all the dispositions and habits which lead to political prosperity, religion and morality are indispensable supports. In vain would that man claim the tribute of patriotism, who should labor to subvert these great pillars of human happiness, these firmest props of the duties of men and citizens. The mere politician, equally with the pious man, ought to respect and to cherish them. A volume could not trace all their connections with private and public felicity. Let it simply be asked, Where is the security for property, for reputation, for life, if the sense of religious obligation *desert* the oaths which are the instruments of investigation in the courts of justice? And let us with caution indulge the supposition, that morality can be maintained without religion. Whatever may be conceded to the influence of refined education on minds of peculiar structure, reason and experience both forbid us to expect that national morality can prevail in exclusion of religious principles.

It is substantially true, that virtue or morality is a necessary spring of popular Government. The rule, indeed, extends with more or less force to every species of free Government. Who, that is a sincere friend to it, can look with indifference upon attempts to shake the foundation of the fabric?

Promote, then, as an object of primary importance, institutions for the general diffusion of knowledge. In proportion as the structure of a Government gives force to public opinion, it is essential that public opinion should be enlightened.

As a very important source of strength and security, cherish public credit. One method to preserve it is to use it as sparingly as possible; avoiding occasions of expense by cultivating peace, but remembering also that timely disbursements, to prepare for danger, frequently prevent much greater disbursements to repel it; avoiding, likewise, the accumulation of debt, not only by shunning occasion of expense, but by vigorous exertions in time of peace to discharge the debts which unavoidable wars may have occasioned, not ungenerously throwing upon posterity the burden which we ourselves ought to bear. The execution of these maxims belong to your representatives, but it is necessary that public opinion should coöperate. To facilitate to them the performance of their duty, it is essential that you should practically bear in mind, that toward the payment of debts there must be revenue; that to have revenue there must be taxes; that no taxes can be devised which are not more or less inconvenient and unpleasant; that the intrinsic embarrassment inseparable from the selection of the proper objects (which is always a choice of difficulties) ought to be a decisive motive for a candid construction of the conduct of the Government in making it, and for a spirit of acquiescence in the measures for obtaining revenue, which the public exigencies may at that time dictate.

Observe good faith and justice toward all nations; cultivate peace and harmony with all; religion and morality enjoin this conduct: and can it be that good policy does not equally enjoin it? It will be worthy of a free, enlightened, and, at no distant period, a great nation, to give to mankind the magnanimous and too novel example of a people always guided by an exalted justice and benevolence. Who can doubt that, in the course of time and things, the fruits of such a plan would richly repay any temporary advantages which might be lost by a steady adherence to it? Can it be that Providence has not connected the permanent felicity of a nation with its virtue? The experiment, at least, is recommended by every sentiment which ennobles human nature. Alas! is it to be rendered impossible by its vices?

In the execution of such a plan, nothing is more essential than that permanent inveterate antipathies against particular nations, and passionate attachment for others, should be excluded; and that, in place of them, just and amicable feelings toward all should be cultivated. The nation which indulges toward another an habitual hatred, or an habitual fondness, is, in some degree, a slave. It is a slave to its animosity or its affection, either of which is sufficient to lead it astray from its duty and its interest. Antipathy in one nation against another, disposes each more readily to offer insult and injury, to lay hold of slight causes of umbrage, and to be haughty and intractable when accidental or trifling occasions of dispute occur. Hence frequent collisions, obstinate, envenomed, and bloody contests. The nation, prompted by ill-will and resentment, sometimes impels to war the Government contrary to the best calculations of policy. The Government sometimes participates in the national propensity, and adopts, through passion, what reason would reject; at other times it makes the animosity of the nation subservient to projects of hostility, instigated by pride, ambition, and other sinister and pernicious motives. The peace often, sometimes perhaps the liberty, of nations has been the victim.

So, likewise, a passionate attachment of one nation to another produces a variety of evils. Sympathy for the favorite nation, facilitating the illusion of an imaginary common interest, in cases where no real common interest exists, and infusing into one the enmities of the other, betrays the former into a participation in the quarrels and wars of the latter, without adequate inducement or justification. It leads also to concessions to the favorite nation of privileges denied to others, which is apt doubly to injure the nation making the concessions; by unnecessarily parting with what ought to have been retained, and by exciting jealousy, ill-will, and a disposition to retaliate in the parties from whom equal privileges are withheld; and it gives to ambitious, corrupted, or deluded citizens (who devote themselves to the favorite nation) facility to betray, or sacrifice the interest of their own country, without odium, sometimes even with popularity; gilding with the appearance of virtuous sense of obligation, a commendable deference for public opinion, or a laudable zeal for public good the base or foolish compliances of ambition, corruption, or infatuation.

As avenues to foreign influence, in innumerable ways, such attachments are particularly alarming to the truly enlightened and independent patriot. How many opportunities do they afford to tamper with domestic factions, to practice the art of seduction, to mislead public opinion, to influence or awe the public councils! Such an attachment of a small or weak, toward a great and powerful nation, dooms the former to be the satellite of the latter.

Against the insidious wiles of foreign influence (I conjure you to believe me, fellow-citizens) the jealousy of a free people ought to be *constantly* awake; since history and experience prove that foreign influence is one of the most baneful foes of Republican Government. But that jealousy, to be useful, must be impartial, else it becomes the instrument of the very influence to be avoided, instead of a defense against it. Excessive partiality for one foreign nation, and excessive dislike for another, cause those whom they actuate to see danger only on one side, and serve to veil, and even second the arts of influence on the other. Real patriots, who may resist the intrigues of the favorite, are liable to become suspected and odious; while its tools and dupes usurp the applause and confidence of the people to surrender their interests.

The great rule of conduct for us, in regard to foreign nations, is, in extending our commercial relations, to have with them as little political connection as possible. So far as we have already formed engagements, let them be fulfilled with perfect good faith. Here let us stop.

Europe has a set of primary interests, which to us have none, or a very remote relation. Hence she must be engaged in frequent controversies, the causes of which are essentially foreign to our concerns. Hence, therefore, it must be unwise in us to implicate ourselves, by artificial ties, in the ordinary vicissitudes of her politics, or the ordinary combinations and collisions of her friendships or enmities.

Our detached and distant situation invites and enables us to pursue a different course. If we remain one people, under an efficient Government, the period is not far off when we may defy material injury from external annoyance; when we may take such an attitude as will cause the neutrality we may at any time resolve upon, to be scrupulously respected; when belligerent nations, under the impossibility of making acquisitions upon us, will not lightly hazard the giving us provocation; when we may choose peace or war, as our interest, guided by justice, shall counsel.

Why forego the advantages of such a peculiar situation? Why quit our own to stand upon foreign ground? Why, by interweaving our destiny with that of any part of Europe, entangle our peace and prosperity in the toils of European ambition, rivalship, interest, humor, or caprice?

It is our true policy to steer clear of permanent alliances with any portion of the foreign world; so far, I mean, as we are now at liberty to do it; for let me not be understood as capable of patronizing infidelity to existing engagements. I hold the maxim no less applicable to public than to private affairs, that honesty is always the best policy. I repeat it, therefore, let those engagements be observed in their genuine sense. But, in my opinion, it is unnecessary, and would be unwise to extend them.

Taking care always to keep ourselves, by suitable establishments, on a respectable defensive posture, we may safely trust to temporary alliances for extraordinary emergencies.

Harmony and a liberal intercourse with all nations, are recommended by policy, humanity, and interest. But even our commercial policy should hold an equal and impartial hand; neither seeking nor granting exclusive favors or preferences; consulting the natural course of things; diffusing and diversifying, by gentle means, the streams of commerce, but forcing nothing; establishing, with powers so disposed, in order to give trade a stable course, to define the rights of our merchants, and to enable the Government to support conventional rules of intercourse, the best that present circumstances and mutual opinions will permit, but temporary, and liable to be, from time to time, abandoned or varied, as experience and circumstances shall dictate; constantly keeping in view, that it is folly in one nation to look for disinterested favors from another; that it must pay, with a portion of its independence, for whatever it may accept under that character; that by such acceptance it may place itself in the condition of having given equivalents for nominal favors, and yet of being reproached with ingratitude for not giving more. There can be no greater error than to expect, or calculate upon, real favors from nation to nation. It is an illusion which experience must cure, which a just pride ought to discard.

In offering to you, my countrymen, these counsels of an old and affectionate friend, I dare not hope they will make the strong and lasting impression I could wish—that they will control the usual current of the passions, or prevent our nation from running the course which has hitherto marked the destiny of nations—but if I may even flatter myself that they may be productive of some partial benefit, some occasional good, that they may now and then recur to moderate the fury of party spirit, to warn against the mischief of foreign intrigues, to guard against the impostures of pretended patriotism, this hope will be a full recompense for the solicitude for your welfare by which they have been dictated.

How far, in the discharge of my official duties, I have been guided by the principles which have been delineated, the public records, and other evidences of my conduct, must witness to you and the world. To myself the assurance of my own conscience is, that I have at least believed myself to be guided by them.

In relation to this still subsisting war in Europe, my proclamation of the 22d of April, 1793, is the index to my plan. Sanctioned by your approving voice, and by that of your Representatives in both Houses of Congress, the spirit of that measure has continually governed me, uninfluenced by any attempts to deter or divert me from it.

After deliberate examination, with the aid of the best lights I could obtain, I was well satisfied that our country, under all the circumstances of the case, had a right to take—and was bound in duty and interest to take—a neutral position. Having taken it, I determined, as far as should depend upon me, to maintain it with moderation, perseverance, and firmness.

The considerations which respect the right to hold this conduct, it is not necessary on this occasion to detail. I will only observe that, according to my understanding of the matter, that right, so far from being denied by any of the belligerent powers, has been virtually admitted by all.

The duty of holding a neutral conduct may be inferred, without any thing more, from the obligation which justice and humanity impose on every nation, in cases in which it is free to act, to maintain inviolate the relations of peace and amity toward other nations.

The inducements of interest, for observing that conduct, will best be referred to your own reflections and experience. With me, a predominant motive has been to endeavor to gain time to our country to settle and mature its yet recent institutions, and to progress, without interruption, to that degree of strength and consistency which is necessary to give it, humanly speaking, the command of its own fortunes.

Though in reviewing the incidents of my administration, I am unconscious of intentional error, I am, nevertheless, too sensible of my defects not to think it probable that I may have committed many errors. Whatever they may be, I fervently beseech the Almighty to avert or mitigate the evils to which they may tend. I shall also carry with me the hope, that my country will never cease to view them with indulgence; and that, after forty-five years of my life dedicated to its service with an upright zeal, the faults of incompetent abilities will be consigned to oblivion, as myself must soon be to the mansions of rest.

Relying on its kindness in this, as in other things, and actuated by that fervent love toward it which is so natural to a man who views in it the native soil of himself and his progenitors, I anticipate, with pleasing expectation, that retreat in which I promise myself to realize, without alloy, the sweet enjoyment of partaking, in the midst of my fellow-citizens, the benign influence of good laws under a free Government—the ever-favorite object of my heart—and the happy reward, as I trust, of our mutual cares, labors, and dangers.

GEORGE WASHINGTON.

UNITED STATES, 17th September, 1796.

MISSOURI SLAVERY COMPROMISE OF 1820.

When Missouri applied for admission into the Union, a proposition was started in Congress to prohibit the introduction of slavery into the new State. This had the effect of arraying the South against the North—the slaveholding against the non-slaveholding States—and the whole subject of slavery became the exciting topic of debate throughout the country. The question was finally settled by a *Compromise*, which tolerated slavery in Missouri, but otherwise prohibited it in all the territory of the United States north and west of the northern limits of Arkansas.

As the principle then settled has often since been the prolific source of much sectional controversy and angry debate, and as it is desirable that every one should be familiar with the *real* provisions of the act by which Missouri was admitted, we have concluded to insert here so much of the law as is necessary to a full understanding of the subject. All the sections, except the following, relate entirely to the formation of the Missouri territory, in the usual form of territorial bills:

"Sec. 8. That in all that territory ceded by France to the United States, under the name of Louisiana, which lies north of thirty-six degrees and thirty minutes north latitude, not included within the limits of the State contemplated by this act, slavery and involuntary servitude, otherwise than in the punishment of crimes, whereof the parties shall be duly convicted, shall be, and is hereby, forever prohibited. *Provided always*, That any person escaping into the same, from whom labor or service is lawfully claimed, in any State or Territory of the United States, such fugitive may be lawfully reclaimed and conveyed to the person claiming his or her labor or service as aforesaid.

JACKSON'S PROCLAMATION TO THE SOUTH CAROLINA NULLIFIERS.

The President of the United States to the nullifiers of South Carolina:

WHEREAS, A convention assembled in the State of South Carolina have passed an ordinance, by which they declare, "that the several acts and parts of acts of the Congress of the United States, purporting to be laws for the imposing of duties and imposts on the importation of foreign commodities, and now having actual operation and effect within the United States, and more especially," two acts for the same purposes passed on the 29th of May, 1828, and on the 14th of July, 1832, "are unauthorized by the Constitution of the United States, and violate the true meaning and intent thereof, and are null and void, and no law," nor binding on the citizens of that State or its officers; and by the said ordinance, it is further declared to be unlawful for any of the constituted authorities of the State or of the United States to enforce the payment of the duties imposed by the said acts with the same State, and that it is the duty of the Legislature to pass such laws as may be necessary to give full effect to the said ordinance:

AND, WHEREAS, By the said ordinance, it is further ordained that in no case of law or equity decided in the courts of said State, wherein shall be drawn in question the validity of the said ordinance, or of the acts of the Legislature that may be passed to give it effect, or of the said laws of the United States, no appeal shall be allowed to the Supreme Court of the United States, nor shall any copy of the record be permitted or allowed for that purpose; and that any person attempting to take such appeal shall be punished as for a contempt of court:

And, finally, the said ordinance declares that the people of South Carolina will maintain the said ordinance at every hazard; and that they will consider the passage of any act, by Congress, abolishing or closing the ports of the said State, or otherwise obstructing the free ingress or egress of vessels to and from the said ports, or any other act of the Federal Government to coerce the State, shut up her ports, destroy or harass her commerce, or to enforce the said act otherwise than through the civil tribunals of the country, as inconsistent with the longer continuance of South Carolina in the Union, and that the people of the said State will thenceforth hold themselves absolved from all further obligation to maintain or preserve their political connection with the people of the other States, and will forthwith proceed to organize a separate government and do all other acts and things which sovereign and independent States may of right do.

AND, WHEREAS, The said ordinance prescribes to the people of South Carolina a course of conduct in direct violation of their duty as citizens of the United States, contrary to the laws of their country, subversive of its Constitution, and having for its object the destruction of the Union—that Union, which, coeval with our political existence, led our fathers, without any other ties to unite them than those of patriotism and a common cause, through a sanguinary struggle to a glorious independence—that sacred Union, hitherto inviolate, which, perfected by our happy Constitution, has brought us, by the favor of Heaven, to a state of prosperity at home, and high consideration abroad, rarely, if ever, equaled in the history of nations. To preserve this bond of our political existence from destruction, to maintain inviolate this state of national honor and prosperity, and to justify the confidence my fellow-citizens have reposed in me, I, ANDREW JACKSON, President of the United States, have thought proper to issue this, my PROCLAMATION, stating my views of the Constitution and laws applicable to the measures adopted by the Convention of South Carolina, and to the reasons they have put forth to sustain them, declaring the course which duty will require me to pursue, and, appealing to the understanding and patriotism of the people, warn them of the consequences that must inevitably result from an observance of the dictates of the convention.

Strict duty would require of me nothing more than the exercise of those powers with which I am now, or may hereafter be invested, for preserving the peace of the Union, and for the execution of the laws. But the imposing aspect which opposition has assumed in this case, by clothing itself with State authority, and the deep interest which the people of the United States must all feel in preventing a resort to stronger measures, while there is a hope that any thing will be yielded to reasoning and remonstrance, perhaps demand, and will certainly justify, a full exposition to South Carolina and the nation of the views I entertain of this important question, as well as a distinct enunciation of the course which my sense of duty will require me to pursue.

The ordinance is founded, not on the indefeasible right of resisting acts which are plainly unconstitutional, and too oppressive to be endured; but on the strange position that any one State may not only declare an act void, but prohibit its execution—that they may do this consistently with the Constitution—that the true construction of that instrument permits a State to retain its place in the Union, and yet be bound by no other of its laws than those it may choose to consider as constitutional. It is true, they add, that to justify this abrogation of law, it must be palpably contrary to the Constitution; but it is evident, that to give the right of resisting laws of that description, coupled with the uncontrolled right to decide what laws deserve that character, is to give the power of resisting all laws. For, as by the theory, there is no appeal, the reasons alleged by the State, good or bad, must prevail. If it should be said that public opinion is a sufficient check against the abuse of this power, it may be asked why it is not deemed a sufficient guard against an unconstitutional act of Congress? There is, however, a restraint in this last case, which makes the assumed power of a State more indefensible, and which does not exist in the other. There are two appeals from an unconstitutional act passed by Congress—one to the judiciary, the other to the people and the States. There is no appeal from the State decision in theory, and the practical illustration shows that the courts are closed against an application to revise it.

both judges and jurors being sworn to decide in its favor. But reasoning on this subject is superfluous, when our social compact, in express terms, declares that the laws of the United States, its Constitution, and treaties made under it, are the supreme law of the land; and, for the greater caution, adds "that the judges in every State shall be bound thereby, any thing in the Constitution or laws of any State to the contrary notwithstanding." And it may be asserted, without fear of refutation, that no Federal Government could exist without a similar provision. Look for a moment to the consequence. If South Carolina considers the revenues unconstitutional, and has a right to prevent their execution in the port of Charleston, there would be a clear constitutional objection to their collection in every other port, and no revenue could be collected anywhere; for all imposts must be equal. It is no answer to repeat, that an unconstitutional law is no law, so long as the question of its legality is to be decided by the State itself; for every law operating injuriously upon any local interest will be, perhaps, thought, and certainly represented, as unconstitutional; and, as has been shown, there is no appeal.

If this doctrine had been established at an earlier day, the Union would have been dissolved in its infancy. The excise law in Pennsylvania, the embargo and non-intercourse law in the eastern States, the carriage tax in Virginia, were all deemed unconstitutional, and were more unequal in their operation than any of the laws now complained of; but fortunately none of those States discovered that they had the right now claimed by South Carolina. The war into which we were forced to support the dignity of the nation and the rights of our citizens, might have ended in defeat and disgrace instead of victory and honor, if the States who supposed it a ruinous and unconstitutional measure, had thought they possessed the right of nullifying the act by which it was declared, and denying supplies for its prosecution. Hardly and unequally as those measures bore upon several members of the Union, to the legislatures of none did this efficient and peaceable remedy, as it is called, suggest itself. The discovery of this important feature in our Constitution was reserved to the present day. To the statesmen of South

Carolina belongs the invention, and upon the citizens of that State will unfortunately fall the evils of reducing it to practice.

If the doctrine of a State veto upon the laws of the Union carries with it internal evidence of its impracticable absurdity, our constitutional history will also afford abundant proof that it would have been repudiated with indignation had it been proposed to form a feature in our Government.

In our colonial state, although dependent on another power, we very early considered ourselves as connected by common interest with each other. Leagues were formed for common defense, and, before the Declaration of Independence, we were known in our aggregate character as the United Colonies of America. That decisive and important step was taken jointly. We declared ourselves a nation by a joint, not by several acts, and when the terms of our Confederation were reduced to form, it was that of a solemn league of several States, by which they agreed that they would collectively form one nation for the purpose of conducting some certain domestic concerns and all foreign relations. In the instrument forming that Union is found an article which declares that "every State shall abide by the determination of Congress on all questions which, by that Confederation, should be submitted to them."

Under the Confederation, then, no State could legally annul a decision of the Congress, or refuse to submit to its execution; but no provision was made to enforce these decisions. Congress made requisitions, but they were not complied with. The Government could not operate on individuals. They had no judiciary, no means of collecting revenue.

But the defects of the Confederation need not be detailed. Under its operation we could scarcely be called a nation. We had neither prosperity at home nor consideration abroad. This state of things could not be endured, and our present happy Constitution was formed, but formed in vain, if this fatal doctrine prevails. It was formed for important objects that are announced in the preamble made in the name and by the authority of the people of the United States, whose delegates framed, and whose conventions approved it. The most important among those objects, that which is placed first in rank, on which all others rest, is, "to form a more perfect Union." Now, is it possible that even if there were no express provision giving supremacy to the Constitution and laws of the United States—can it be conceived, that an instrument made for the purpose of "forming a more perfect Union" than that of the Confederation, could be so constructed by the assembled wisdom of our country as to substitute for that Confederation a form of government dependent for its existence on the local interest, the party spirit of a State, or of a prevailing faction in a State? Every man of plain, unsophisticated understanding, who hears the question, will give such an answer as will preserve the Union. Metaphysical subtlety, in pursuit of an impracticable theory, could alone have devised one that is calculated to destroy it.

I consider, then, the power to annul a law of the United States, assumed by one State, incompatible with the existence of the Union, contradicted expressly by the letter of the Constitution, unauthorized by its spirit, inconsistent with every principle on which it was founded, and destructive of the great object for which it was formed.

After this general view of the leading principle, we must examine the particular application of it which is made in the ordinance.

The preamble rests its justification on these grounds: It assumes, as a fact, that the obnoxious laws, although they purport to be laws for raising revenue, were in reality intended for the protection of manufactures, which purpose it asserts to be unconstitutional; that the operation of these laws is unequal; that the amount raised by them is greater than is required by the wants of the Government; and, finally, that the proceeds are to be applied to objects unauthorized by the Constitution. These are the only causes alleged to justify an open opposition to the laws of the country, and a threat of seceding from the Union, if any attempt should be made to enforce them. The first virtually acknowledges that the law in question was passed under a power expressly given by the Constitution to lay and collect imposts; but its constitutionality is drawn in question from the motives of those who passed it. However apparent this purpose may be in the present case, nothing can be more dangerous than to admit the position that an unconstitutional purpose, entertained by the members who assent to a law enacted under constitutional power, shall make the law void: for how is that purpose to be ascertained? How often may bad purposes be falsely imputed—in how many cases are they concealed by false professions—in how many is no declaration of motive made? Admit this doctrine, and you give to the States an uncontrolled right to decide, and every law may be annulled under this pretext. If, therefore, the absurd and dangerous doctrine should be admitted, that a State may annul an unconstitutional law, or one that it deems such, it will not apply to the present case.

The next objection is, that the laws in question operate unequally. This objection may be made with truth to every law that has been or may be passed. The wisdom of man never yet contrived a system of taxation that would operate with perfect equality. If the unequal operation of a law makes it unconstitutional, and if all laws of that description may be abrogated by any State for that cause, then indeed is the Federal Constitution unworthy the slightest effort for its preservation. We have hitherto relied on it as the perpetual bond of our Union. We have received it as the work of the assembled wisdom of the nation. We have trusted to it as the sheet anchor of our safety in the stormy, times of conflict with a foreign or domestic foe. We have looked to it with sacred awe as the palladium of our liberties, and with all the solemnities of religion have pledged to each other our lives and fortunes here, and our hopes of happiness hereafter, in its defense and support. Were we mistaken, my countrymen, in attaching this importance to the Constitution of our country? Was our devotion paid to the wretched, inefficient, clumsy, contrivance which this new doctrine would make it? Did we pledge ourselves to the support of an airy nothing—a bubble, that must be blown away by the first breath of dissatisfaction? Was this self-destroying, visionary theory, the work of the profound statesmen, the exalted patriots, to whom the task of constitutional reform was intrusted? Did the name of Washington sanction, did the States deliberately ratify such an anamoly in the history of fundamental legislation? No. We were not mistaken. The letter of this great instrument is free from this radical fault; its language directly contradicts the imputation; its spirit--its evident intent, contradicts it. No, we did not err! Our Constitution does not contain the absurdity of giving power to make laws, and another power to resist them. The sages whose memory will always be reverenced, have given us a practical, and, as they hoped, a permanent constitutional compact. The Father of his Country did not affix his revered name to so palpable an absurdity. Nor did the States, when they severally ratified it, do so under the impression that a veto on the laws of the United States, was reserved to them, or that they could exercise it by implication. Search the debates in all their conventions, examine the speeches of the most zealous opposers of federal authority, look at the amendments that were proposed; they are all silent—not a syllable uttered, not a vote given, not a motion made, to correct the explicit supremacy given to the laws of the Union over those of the States, or to show that implication, as is now contended, could defeat it. No, we have not erred! The Constitution is still the object of our reverence, the bond of our Union, our defense in danger, the source of our prosperity in peace; it shall descend as we received it, uncorrupted, by sophistical construction, to our posterity, and the sacrifices of local interest, of State prejudices, of personal animosities, that were made to bring it into existence, will again be patriotically offered for its support.

The two remaining objections made by the ordinance to these laws, are that the sums intended to be raised by them are greater than are required, and that the proceeds will be unconstitutionally employed.

The Constitution has given, expressly, to Congress the right of raising revenue, and of determining the sum the public exigencies will require. The States have no control over the exercise of this right, other than that which results from the power of changing the representatives who abuse it, and thus procure redress. Congress may, undoubtedly, abuse this discretionary power; but the same may be said of others with which they are vested. Yet this discretion must exist somewhere. The Constitution has given it to the representatives of all the people, checked by the representatives of the States and by the executive power. The South Carolina construction gives it to the legislature or the convention of a single State, where neither the people of the different States, nor the States in their separate capacity, nor the chief magistrate elected by the people, have any representation. Which is the most discreet disposition of the power? I do not ask you, fellow-citizens, which is the constitutional disposition; that instrument speaks a language not to be misunderstood. But if you were assembled in general convention, which would you think the safest depository of this discretionary power in the last resort? Would you add a clause giving it to each of the States, or would you sanction the wise provisions already made by your Constitution? If this should be the result of your deliberations when providing for the future, are you, can you be ready to risk all that we hold dear to establish, for a temporary and a local purpose, that which you must acknowledge to be destructive, and even absurd, as a general provision? Carry out the consequences of this right vested in the different States, and you must perceive that the crisis your conduct presents at this day would recur whenever any law of the United States displeased any of the States, and that we should soon cease to be a nation.

The ordinance, with the same knowledge of the future that characterizes a former objection, tells you that the proceeds of the tax will be unconstitutionally applied. If this could be ascertained with certainty, the objection would, with more propriety, be reserved for the law so applying the proceeds, but surely can not be urged against the laws levying the duty.

These are the allegations contained in the ordinance. Examine them seriously, my fellow-citizens; judge for yourselves. I appeal to you to determine whether they are so clear, so convincing, as to leave no doubt of their correctness; and even if you should come to this conclusion, how far they justify the reckless, destructive course which you are directed to pursue. Review these objections, and the conclusions drawn from them, once more. What are they? Every law, then, for raising revenue, according to the South Carolina ordinance, may be rightfully annulled, unless it be so framed as no law ever will or can be framed. Congress has the right to pass laws for raising a revenue, and each State has a right to oppose their execution—two rights directly opposed to each other; and yet is this absurdity supposed to be contained in an instrument drawn for the express purpose of avoiding collisions between the States and the General Government, by an assembly of the most enlightened statesmen and purest patriots ever embodied for a similar purpose.

In vain have these sages declared that Congress shall have power to lay and collect taxes, duties, imposts, and excises; in vain have they provided that they shall have power to pass laws which shall be necessary and proper to carry those powers into execution; that those laws and that Constitution shall be the "supreme law of the land, and that the judges in every State shall be bound thereby, any thing in the Constitution or laws of any State to the contrary notwithstanding." In vain have the people of the several States solemnly sanctified these provisions, made them their paramount law, and individually sworn to support them whenever they were called on to execute any office. Vain provision! ineffectual restrictions! vile profanation of oaths! miserable mockery of legislation! if the bare majority of the voters in any one State may, on a real or supposed knowledge of the intent with which a law has been passed, declare themselves free from its operation—say here it gives too little, there too much, and operates unequally—here it suffers articles to be free that ought to be taxed—there it taxes those that ought to be free—in this case the proceeds are intended to be applied to purposes which we do not approve—in that the amount raised is more than is wanted. Congress, it is true, is invested by the Constitution with the right of deciding these questions according to their sound discretion; Congress is composed of the representatives of all the States, and of all the people of all the States; but we, part of the people of one State, to whom the Constitution has given no power on the subject, from whom it has expressly taken it away—we, who have solemnly agreed that this Constitution shall be our law—we, most of whom have sworn to support it—we now abrogate this law, and swear, and force others to swear that it shall not be obeyed; and we do this, not because Congress have no right to pass such laws—this we do not allege—but because they have passed them with improper views. They are unconstitutional from the motives of those who passed them, which we can never with certainty know; from their unequal operation, although it is impossible, from the nature of things, that they should be equal; and from the disposition which we presume may be made of their proceeds, although that disposition has not been declared. This is the plain meaning of the ordinance, in relation to laws which it abrogates for alleged unconstitutionality. But it does not stop there. It repeals, in express terms, an important part of the Constitution itself, and of laws passed to give it effect, which have never been alleged to be unconstitutional. The Constitution declares that the judicial powers of the United States extend to cases arising under the laws of the United States; and that such laws, the Constitution and treaties, shall be paramount to the State Constitutions and laws. The judiciary act prescribes the mode by which the case may be brought before a court of the United States by appeal, when a State tribunal shall decide against this provision of the Constitution. The ordinance declares that there shall be no appeal, makes the State law paramount to the Constitution and laws of the United States, forces judges and jurors to swear that they will disregard their provisions, and even makes it penal in a suit to attempt relief by appeal. It further declares that it shall not be lawful for the authorities of the United States, or of that State, to enforce the payment of duties imposed by the revenue laws within its limits.

Here is a law of the United States, not even pretended

to be unconstitutional, repealed by the authority of a small majority of the voters of a single State. Here is a provision of the Constitution, which is solemnly abrogated by the same authority.

On such expositions and reasonings, the ordinance grounds not only an assertion of the right to annul the laws, of which it complains, but to enforce it by a threat of seceding from the Union, if any attempt is made to execute them.

This right to secede is deduced from the nature of the Constitution, which they say is a compact between sovereign States, who have preserved their whole sovereignty, and therefore are subject to no superior; that because they made the compact, they can break it, when, in their opinion, it has been departed from by other States. Fallacious as this course of reasoning is, it enlists State pride, and finds advocates in the honest prejudices of those who have not studied the nature of our government sufficiently to see the radical error on which it rests.

The people of the United States formed the Constitution, acting through the State Legislatures in forming the compact, to meet and discuss its provisions, and acting in separate conventions when they ratified those provisions; but the terms used in its construction show it to be a government in which the people of all the States collectively are represented. We are *one people* in the choice of President and Vice-President. Here the States have no other agency than to direct the mode in which the votes shall be given. The candidates having a majority of all the votes are chosen. The electors of a majority of States may have given their votes for one candidate, and yet another may be chosen. The people, then, and not the States, are represented in the executive branch.

In the House of Representatives there is this difference: that the people of one State do not, as in the case of President and Vice-President, all vote for the same officers. The people of all the States do not vote for all the members, each State electing only its own Representatives. But this creates no national distinction. When chosen, they are all Representatives of the United States, not representatives of the particular State from whence they come. They are paid by the United States, not by the State; nor are they accountable to it for any act done in the performance of their legislative functions; and however they may, in practice, as it is their duty to do, consult and prefer the interests of their particular constituents, when they come in conflict with any other partial or local interest, yet it is the first and highest duty of a Representative of the United States to promote the general good.

The Constitution of the United States, then, forms a *government*, not a league; and whether it be formed by compact between the States, or in any other manner, its character is the same. It is a government in which all the people are represented, which operates directly on the people individually, not upon the States; they retained all the power they did not grant. But each State having expressly parted with so many powers, as to constitute jointly with the other States a single nation, can not, from that period, possess any right to secede, because such secession does not break a league, but destroys the unity of a nation; and any injury to that unity is not only a breach, which would result from the contravention of a compact, but it is an offense against the whole Union. To say that any State may at pleasure secede from the Union, is to say that the United States are not a nation; because it would be a solecism to contend, that any part of a nation might dissolve its connection with the other parts, to their injury or ruin, without committing any offense. Secession, like any other revolutionary act, may be morally justified by the extremity of oppression; but to call it a constitutional right is confounding the meaning of the terms; and can only be done through gross error, or to deceive those who are willing to assert a right, but would pause before they made a revolution, or incur the penalties consequent on a failure.

Because the Union was formed by compact, it is said the parties to that compact may, when they feel themselves aggrieved, depart from it; but it is precisely because it is a compact that they can not. A compact is an agreement or binding obligation. It may, by its terms, have a sanction or penalty for its breach, or it may not. If it contains no sanction, it may be broken, with no other consequences than moral guilt; if it have a sanction, then the breach incurs the designated or implied penalty. A league between independent nations generally has no sanction other than a moral one; or, if it should contain a penalty, as there is no common superior, it can not be enforced. A government, on the contrary, always has a sanction, express or implied; and, in our case, it is both necessarily implied and expressly given. An attempt, by force of arms, to destroy a government, is an offense, by whatever means the constitutional compact may have been formed; and such government has the right, by the law of self-defense, to pass acts for punishing the offender, unless that right is modified, restrained, or resumed by the constitutional act. In our system, although it is modified in the case of treason, yet authority is expressly given to pass all laws necessary to carry its powers into effect; and, under this grant, provision has beeen made for punishing acts which obstruct the due administration of the laws.

It would seem superfluous to add any thing to show the nature of that Union which connects us; but as erroneous opinions on this subject are the foundation of doctrines the most destructive to our peace, I must give further development to my views on this subject. No one, fellow-citizens, has a higher reverence for the reserved rights of the States than the magistrate who now addresses you; no one would make greater personal sacrifices or official exertion to defend them from violation; but equal care must be taken to prevent, on their part, an improper interference with, or resumption of, the rights they have vested in the nation. The line has not been so distinctly drawn as to avoid doubts, in some cases, of the exercise of power. Men of the best intentions and soundest views may differ in their construction of some parts of the Constitution; but there are others on which dispassionate reflection can leave no doubt. Of this nature appears to be the assumed right of secession. It rests, as we have seen, on the alleged undivided sovereignty of the States, and on their having formed, in this sovereign capacity, a compact, which is called the Constitution, from which, because they made it, they have the right to secede. Both of these positions are erroneous, and some of the arguments to prove them so have been anticipated.

The States severally have not retained their entire sovereignty. It has been shown that, in becoming parts of a nation, not members of a league, they surrendered many of their essential parts of sovereignty. The right to make treaties, declare war, levy taxes, exercise exclusive judicial and legislative powers, were, all of them, functions of sovereign power. The States, then, for all these purposes, were no longer sovereign. The allegiance of their citizens was transferred, in the first instance, to the Government of the United States; they became American citizens, and owed obedience to the Constitution of the United States, and to laws made in conformity with the powers it vested in Congress. This last position has not been, and can not be, denied. How, then, can that State be said to be sovereign and independent whose citizens owe obedience to laws not made by it, and whose magistrates are sworn to disregard those laws when they come in conflict with those passed by another? What shows conclusively that the States can not be said to have reserved an undivided sovereignty is, that they expressly ceded the right to punish treason—not treason against their separate power, but treason against the United States. Treason is an offense against sovereignty, and sovereignty must reside with the power to punish it. But the reserved rights of the States are not less sacred because they have, for their common interest, made the General Government the depository of these powers.

The unity of our political character (as has been shown for another purpose) commenced with its very existence. Under the royal government we had no separate character; our opposition to its oppressions began as *united colonies.* We were the United States, under the Confederation, and the name was perpetuated, and the Union rendered more perfect by the Federal Constitution. In none of these stages did we consider ourselves in any other light than as forming one nation. Treaties and alliances were made in the name of all. Troops were raised for the joint defense. How, then, with all these proofs, that, under all changes of our position, we had, for designated purposes, and with defined powers, created national governments; how is it that the most perfect of those several modes of union should now be considered as a mere league, that may be dissolved at pleasure? It is from an abuse of terms. "Compact" is used as synonymous with "league," although the true term is not employed, because it would at once show the fallacy of the reasoning. It would not do to say that our Constitution was only a league; but it is labored to prove it a compact (which in one sense it is), and then to argue that, as a league is a compact, every compact between nations must, of course, be a league, and that from such an engagement every sovereign power has a right to recede. But it has been shown that, in this sense, the States are not sovereign, and that even if they were, and the national Constitution had been formed by compact, there would be no right in any one State to exonerate itself from its obligations.

So obvious are the reasons which forbid this secession, that it is necessary only to allude to them. The Union was formed for the benefit of all. It was produced by mutual sacrifices of interests and opinions. Can those sacrifices be recalled? Can the States, who magnanimously surrender their title to the territories in the West, recall the grant? Will the inhabitants of the inland States agree to pay the duties that may be imposed, without their assent, by those on the Atlantic or the Gulf for their own benefit? Shall there be a free port in one State, and onerous duties in another? No one believes that any right exists, in a single State, to involve the others in these and countless other evils contrary to the engagements solemnly made. Every one must see that the other States, in self-defense, must oppose it, at all hazards.

These are the alternatives that are presented by the convention: A repeal of all the acts for raising revenue, leaving the Government without the means of support, or an acquiescence in the dissolution of our Union by the secession of one of its members. When the first was proposed, it was known that it could not be listened to for a moment. It was known, if force was applied to oppose the execution of the laws, that it must be repelled by force; that Congress could not, without involving itself in disgrace and the country in ruin, accede to the proposition; and yet, if this is not done on a given day, or if any attempt is made to execute the laws, the State is, by the ordinance, declared to be out of the Union. The majority of a convention, assembled for the purpose, have dictated these terms, or rather this rejection of all terms, in the name of the people of South Carolina. It is true that the Governor of the State speaks of the submission of their grievances to a convention of all the States, which, he says, they "sincerely and anxiously seek and desire." Yet this obvious and constitutional mode of obtaining the sense of the other States, on the construction of the Federal compact, and amending it if necessary, has never been attempted by those who have urged the State on to this destructive measure. The State might have proposed to call for a general convention of the other States; and Congress, if a sufficient number of them concurred, must have called it. But the first magistrate of South Carolina, when he expressed a hope that, "on a review by Congress and the functionaries of the General Government of the merits of the controversy," such a convention will be accorded to them, must have known that neither Congress, nor any functionary of the General Government, has authority to call such a convention, unless it be demanded by two-thirds of the States. This suggestion, then, is another instance of the reckless inattention to the provisions of the Constitution with which this crisis has been madly hurried on; or of the attempt to persuade the people that a constitutional remedy has been sought and refused. If the Legislature of South Carolina "anxiously desire" a general convention to consider their complaints, why have they not made application for it in the way the Constitution points out? The assertion that they "earnestly seek" it is completely negatived by the omission.

This, then, is the position in which we stand. A small

majority of the citizens of one State in the Union have elected delegates to a State convention; that convention has ordained that all the revenue laws of the United States must be repealed, or that they are no longer a member of this Union. The Governor of that State has recommended to the Legislature the raising of an army to carry the secession into effect, and that he may be empowered to give clearances to vessels in the name of the State. No act of violent opposition to the laws has yet been committed, but such a state of things is hourly apprehended; and it is the intent of this instrument to proclaim, not only that the duty imposed on me by the Constitution "to take care that the laws be faithfully executed," shall be performed to the extent of the powers already vested in me by law, or of such others as the wisdom of Congress shall devise and intrust to me for that purpose, but to warn the citizens of South Carolina, who have been deluded into an opposition to the laws, of the danger they will incur by obedience to the illegal and disorganizing ordinance of the convention; to exhort those who have refused to support it to persevere in their determination to uphold the Constitution and laws of their country; and to point out to all the perilous situation into which the good people of that State have been led, and that the course they are urged to pursue is one of ruin and disgrace to the very State whose rights they affect to support.

Fellow-citizens of my native State, let me not only admonish you, as the First Magistrate of our common country, not to incur the penalty of its laws, but use the influence that a father would over his children whom he saw rushing to certain ruin. In that paternal language, with that paternal feeling, let me tell you, my countrymen, that you are deluded by men who are either deceived themselves, or wish to deceive you. Mark under what pretenses you have been led on to the brink of insurrection and treason, and on which you stand! First, a diminution of the value of your staple commodity, lowered by over-production in other quarters, and the consequent diminution in the value of your lands, were the sole effect of the tariff laws.

The effect of those laws was confessedly injurious, but the evil was greatly exaggerated by the unfounded theory you were taught to believe, that its burdens were in proportion to your exports, not to your consumption of imported articles. Your pride was roused by the assertion that a submission to those laws was a state of vassalage, and that resistance to them was equal, in patriotic merit, to the opposition our fathers offered to the oppressive laws of Great Britain. You were told that this opposition might be peaceably—might be constitutionally made; that you might enjoy all the advantages of the Union, and bear none of its burdens. Eloquent appeals to your passions, to your State pride, to your native courage, to your sense of real injury, were used, to prepare you for the period when the mask, which concealed the hideous features of disunion, should be taken off. It fell, and you were made to look with complacency on objects which, not long since, you would have regarded with horror. Look back to the arts which have brought you to this state—look forward to the consequences to which it must inevitably lead! Look back to what was first told you as an inducement to enter into this dangerous course. The great political truth was repeated to you, that you had the revolutionary right of resisting all laws that were palpably unconstitutional and intolerably oppressive; it was added that the right to nullify a law rested on the same principle, but that it was a peaceable remedy! This character which was given to it, made you receive, with too much confidence, the assertions that were made of the unconstitutionality of the law and its oppressive effects. Mark, my fellow-citizens, that, by the admission of your leaders, the unconstitutionality must be *palpable*, or it will not justify either resistance or nullification! What is the meaning of the word *palpable*, in the sense in which it is here used? that which is apparent to every one; that which no man of ordinary intellect will fail to perceive. Is the unconstitutionality of these laws of that description? Let those among your leaders who once approved and advocated the principle of protective duties, answer the question; and let them choose whether they will be considered as incapable, then, of perceiving that which must have been apparent to every man of common understanding, or as imposing on your confidence, and endeavoring to mislead you now. In either case, they are unsafe guides in the perilous path they urge you to tread. Ponder well on this circumstance, and you will know how to appreciate the exaggerated language they address to you. They are not champions of liberty, emulating the fame of our revolutionary fathers; nor are you an oppressed people, contending, as they repeat to you, against worse than colonial vassalage.

You are free members of a flourishing and happy Union. There is no settled design to oppress you. You have, indeed, felt the unequal operation of laws which may have been unwisely, not unconstitutionally passed; but that inequality must necessarily be removed. At the very moment when you were madly urged on to the unfortunate course you have begun, a change in public opinion had commenced. The nearly approaching payment of the public debt, and the consequent necessity of a diminution of duties, had already produced a considerable reduction, and that, too, on some articles of general consumption in your State. The importance of this change was underrated, and you are authoritatively told that no further alleviation of your burdens were to be expected at the very time when the condition of the country imperiously demanded such a modification of the duties as should reduce them to a just and equitable scale. But, as if apprehensive of the effect of this change in allaying your discontents, you were precipitated into the fearful state in which you now find yourselves.

I have urged you to look back to the means that were used to hurry you on to the position you have now assumed, and forward to the consequences it will produce. Something more is necessary. Contemplate the condition of that country of which you still form an important part. Consider its Government, uniting in one bond of common interest and general protection so many different States—giving to all their inhabitants the proud title of American citizens; protecting their commerce; securing their literature and their arts; facilitating their intercommunication;

defending their frontiers, and making their names respected in the remotest parts of the earth. Consider the extent of its territory; its increasing and happy population; its advance in arts, which render life agreeable; and the sciences, which elevate the mind! See education spreading the lights of religion, morality, and general information into every cottage in this wide extent of our Territories and States! Behold it as the asylum where the wretched and the oppressed find a refuge and support! Look on this picture of happiness and honor, and say: "*We, too, are citizens of America!* Carolina is one of these proud States—her arms have defended—her best blood has cemented this happy Union!" And then add, if you can, without horror and remorse, "this happy Union we will dissolve; this picture of peace and prosperity we will deface; this free intercourse we will interrupt; these fertile fields we will deluge with blood; the protection of that glorious flag we renounce; the very name of Americans we discard." And for what, mistaken men—for what do you throw away these inestimable blessings? for what would you exchange your share in the advantages and honor of the Union? For the dream of separate independence—a dream interrupted by bloody conflicts with your neighbors, and a vile dependence on a foreign power. If your leaders could succeed in establishing a separation, what would be your situation? Are you united at home—are you free from the apprehension of civil discord, with all its fearful consequences? Do our neighboring republics, every day suffering some new revolution, or contending with some new insurrection—do they excite your envy? But the dictates of a high duty obliges me solemnly to announce that you can not succeed. The laws of the United States must be executed. I have no discretionary power on the subject—my duty is emphatically pronounced in the Constitution. Those who told you that you might peaceably prevent their execution, deceived you—they could not have been deceived themselves. They know that a forcible opposition could alone prevent the execution of the laws, and they know that such opposition must be repelled. Their object is disunion; but be not deceived by names; disunion, by armed force, is *treason.*

Are you really ready to incur its guilt? If you are, on the heads of the instigators of the act be the dreadful consequences—on their heads be the dishonor, but on yours may fall the punishment; on your unhappy State will inevitably fall all the evils of the conflict you force upon the government of your country. It can not accede to the mad project of disunion, of which you would be the first victims—its First Magistrate can not, if he would, avoid the performance of his duty; the consequences must be fearful to you, distressing to your fellow-citizens here, and to the friends of good government throughout the world. Its enemies have beheld our prosperity with a vexation they could not conceal—it was a standing refutation of their slavish doctrines, and they will point to our discord with the triumph of malignant joy. It is yet in your power to disappoint them. There is yet time to show that the descendants of the Pinckneys, the Sumters, the Rutledges, and of the thousand other names, which adorn the pages of your revolutionary history, will not abandon that Union, to support which so many of them fought, and bled, and died.

I adjure you, as you honor their memory—as you love the cause of freedom, to which they dedicated their lives—as you prize the peace of your country, the lives of its best citizens, and your own fair fame, to retrace your steps. Snatch from the archives of your State the disorganizing edict of its convention—bid its members to re-assemble, and promulgate the decided expressions of your will to remain in the path which alone can conduct you to safety, prosperity, and honor. Tell them that, compared to disunion, all other evils are light, because that brings with it an accumulation of all. Declare that you will never take the field unless the star-spangled banner of your country shall float over you; that you will not be stigmatized when dead, and dishonored and scorned while you live, as the authors of the first attack on the Constitution of your country. Its destroyers you can not be. You may disturb its peace—you may interrupt the course of its prosperity—you may cloud its reputation for stability; but its tranquillity will be restored, its prosperity will return, and the stain upon its national character will be transferred, and remain an eternal blot on the memory of those who caused the disorder.

Fellow-citizens of the United States! The threat of unhallowed disunion—the names of those once respected, by whom it is uttered—the array of military force to support it—denotes the approach of a crisis in our affairs, on which the continuance of our unexampled prosperity, our political existence, and perhaps that of all free governments, may depend. The conjuncture demanded a free, a full, and explicit enunciation, not only of my intentions, but of my principles of action: and as the claim was asserted of a right by a State to annul the laws of the Union, and even to secede from it at pleasure, a frank exposition of my opinions in relation to the origin and form of our government, and the construction I give to the instrument by which it was created, seemed to be proper. Having the fullest confidence in the justness of the legal and constitutional opinion of my duties, which has been expressed, I rely, with equal confidence, on your undivided support in my determination to execute the laws—to preserve the Union by all constitutional means—to arrest, if possible, by moderate but firm measures, the necessity of a recourse to force; and, if it be the will of Heaven, that the recurrence of its primeval curse on man for the shedding of a brother's blood should fall upon our land, that it be not called down by any offensive act on the part of the United States.

Fellow-citizens! the momentous case is before you. On your undivided support of your Government depends the decision of the great question it involves, whether your sacred Union will be preserved, and the blessings it secures to us as one people shall be perpetuated. No one can doubt that the unanimity with which that decision will be expressed, will be such as to inspire new confidence in republican institutions, and that the prudence, the wisdom, and the courage which it will bring to their defense will transmit them unimpaired and invigorated to our children.

May the Great Ruler of Nations grant that the signal blessings with which He has favored ours, may not, by the madness of party or personal ambition, be disregarded and lost; and may His wise providence bring those who have produced this crisis to see their folly, before they feel the misery of civil strife, and inspire a returning veneration for that Union, which, if we may dare to penetrate His designs, He has chosen as the only means of attaining the high destinies to which we may reasonably aspire.

In testimony whereof, I have caused the seal of the United States to be hereunto affixed, having signed the same with my hand.

Done at the city of Washington, this 10th day of December, in the year of our Lord one thousand eight hundred and thirty-two, and of the Independence of the United States the fifty-seventh.

By the President: ANDREW JACKSON.

EDWD. LIVINGSTON, *Secretary of State.*

FUGITIVE SLAVE LAW OF 1850.

An Act to amend, and supplementary to, the Act entitled, "An Act respecting Fugitives from Justice, and persons escaping from the Service of their Masters," and approved February 12, 1793.

Be it enacted by the Senate and House of Representatives of the United States of America in Congress assembled, That the persons who have been, or may hereafter be, appointed Commissioners, in virtue of any Act of Congress, by the Circuit Courts of the United States, and who, in consequence of such appointment, are authorized to exercise the powers that any justice of the peace, or other magistrate of any of the United States, may exercise in respect to offenders for any crime or offense against the United States, by arresting, imprisoning, or bailing the same, under, and by virtue of, the thirty-third section of the act of the twenty-fourth of September, seventeen hundred and eighty-nine, entitled, "An Act to establish the judicial courts of the United States," shall be, and are hereby, authorized and required to exercise and discharge all the powers and duties conferred by this Act.

SEC. 2. That the Superior Court of each organized Territory of the United States shall have the same power to appoint Commissioners to take acknowledgments of bail and affidavits, and to take depositions of witnesses in civil causes, which is now possessed by the Circuit Court of the United States; and all Commissioners who shall hereafter be appointed for such purposes by the Superior Court of any organized Territory of the United States shall possess all the powers, and exercise all the duties, conferred by law upon the Commissioners appointed by the Circuit Courts of the United States for similar purposes, and shall moreover exercise and discharge all the powers and duties conferred by this Act.

SEC. 3. That the Circuit Courts of the United States,

and the Superior Courts of each organized territory of the United States, shall, from time to time, enlarge the number of Commissioners with a view to afford reasonable facilities to reclaim fugitives from labor, and to the prompt discharge of the duties imposed by this Act.

SEC. 4. That the Commissioners above named shall have concurrent jurisdiction with the Judges of the Circuit and District Courts of the United States, in their respective circuits and districts within the several States, and the Judges of the Superior Courts of the territories severally and collectively, in term time and vacation; and shall grant certificates to such claimants, upon satisfactory proof being made, with authority to take and remove such fugitives from service or labor, under the restrictions herein contained, to the State or Territory from which such persons may have escaped or fled.

SEC. 5. That it shall be the duty of all marshals and deputy marshals to obey and execute all warrants and precepts issued under the provisions of this act when to them directed; and should any marshal or deputy marshal refuse to receive such warrant, or other process, when tendered, or to use all proper means diligently to execute the same, he shall, on conviction thereof, be fined in the sum of one thousand dollars, to the use of such claimant, on the motion of such claimant, by the Circuit or District Court for the district of such marshal; and after the arrest of such fugitive, by such marshal or his deputy, or while at any time in his custody, under the provisions of this act, should such fugitive escape, whether with or without the assent of such marshal or his deputy, such marshal shall be liable, on his official bond, to be prosecuted, for the benefit of such claimant, for the full value of the service or labor of said fugitive in the State, Territory, or district whence he escaped; and, the better to enable said Commissioners, when thus appointed, to execute their duties faithfully and efficiently, in conformity with the requirements of the Constitution of the United States, and of this Act, they are hereby authorized and empowered, within their counties respectively, to appoint, in writing under their hands, any one or more suitable persons, from time to time, to execute all such warrants and other process as may be issued by them in the lawful performance of their respective duties; with authority to such Commissioners, or the persons to be appointed by them, to execute process as aforesaid, to summon and call to their aid the bystanders, or *posse commitatus* of the proper county, when necessary to insure a faithful observance of the clause of the Constitution referred to, in conformity with the provisions of this Act; and all good citizens are commanded to aid and assist in the prompt and efficient execution of this law whenever their services may be required, as aforesaid, for that purpose; and said warrants shall run, and be executed by said officers, anywhere in the State within which they are issued.

SEC. 6. That when a person held to service or labor in any State or Territory of the United States has heretofore or shall hereafter escape into another State or Territory of the United States, the person or persons to whom such service or labor may be due, or his, her, or their agent or attorney, duly authorized by power of attorney, in writing acknowledged and certified under the seal of some legal officer or Court of the State or Territory in which the same may be executed, may pursue and reclaim such fugitive person, either by procuring a warrant from some one of the Courts, Judges, or Commissioners aforesaid, of the proper circuit, district, or county, for the apprehension of such fugitive from service or labor, or by seizing and arresting such fugitive where the same can be done without process, and by taking or causing such person to be taken forthwith before such Court, Judge, or Commissioner, whose duty it shall be to hear and determine the case of such claimant in a summary manner; and, upon satisfactory proof being made, by deposition or affidavit in writing, to be taken and certified by such Court, Judge, or Commissioner, or by other satisfactory testimony, duly taken and certified by some Court, Magistrate, Justice of the Peace, or other legal officer authorized to administer an oath and take depositions under the laws of the State or Territory from which such person owing service or labor may have escaped, with a certificate of such magistracy, or other authority as aforesaid, with the seal of the proper Court or officer thereto attached, which seal shall be sufficient to establish the competency of the proof, and with proof, also by affidavit, of the identity of the person whose service or labor is claimed to be due as aforesaid, that the person so arrested does in fact owe service or labor to the person or persons claiming him or her, in the State or Territory from which such fugitive may have escaped as aforesaid, and that said person escaped, to make out and deliver to said claimant, his or her agent or attorney, a certificate setting forth the substantial facts as to the service or labor due from such fugitive to the claimant, and of his or her escape from the State or Territory in which such service or labor was due to the State or Territory in which he or she was arrested, with authority to such claimant, or his or her agent or attorney, to use such reasonable force and restraint as may be necessary, under the circumstances of the case, to take and remove such fugitive person back to the State or Territory whence he or she may have escaped as aforesaid. In no trial or hearing under this Act shall the testimony of such alleged fugitive be admitted in evidence; and the certificates in this and the first [fourth] section mentioned shall be conclusive of the right of the person or persons in whose favor granted to remove such fugitive to the State or Territory from which he escaped, and shall prevent all molestation of such person or persons by any process issued by any Court, Judge, Magistrate, or other person whomsoever.

SEC. 7. That any person who shall knowingly and willingly obstruct, hinder, or prevent such claimant, his agent or attorney, or any person or persons lawfully assisting him, her, or them, from arresting such a fugitive from service or labor, either with or without process as aforesaid, or shall rescue or attempt to rescue such fugitive from service or labor from the custody of such claimant, his or her agent or attorney, or other person or persons lawfully assisting as aforesaid, when so arrested pursuant to the authority herein given and declared, or shall aid, abet, or assist such person so owing service or labor as aforesaid, directly or indirectly to escape from such claimant, his agent or attorney, or other person or persons legally authorized as aforesaid; or shall harbor or conceal such fugitive so as to prevent the discovery and arrest of such person, after notice or knowledge of the fact that such person was a fugitive from service or labor as aforesaid, shall, for either of said offenses, be subject to a fine not exceeding one thousand dollars, and imprisonment not exceeding six months, by indictment and conviction before the District Court of the United States for the district in which such offense may have been committed, or before the proper court of criminal jurisdiction, if committed within any one of the organized Territories of the United States, and shall moreover forfeit and pay, by way of civil damages to the party injured by such illegal conduct, the sum of one thousand dollars for each fugitive so lost as aforesaid, to be recovered as aforesaid, to be recovered by action of debt in any of the District or Territorial Courts aforesaid, within whose jurisdiction the said offense may have been committed.

SEC. 8. That the marshals, their deputies, and the clerks of the said District and Territorial Courts, shall be paid for their services the like fees as may be allowed to them for similar services in other cases; and where such services are rendered exclusively in the arrest, custody, and delivery of the fugitive to the claimant, his or her agent or attorney, or where such supposed fugitive may be discharged out of custody for the want of sufficient proof as aforesaid, then such fees are to be paid in the whole by such claimant, his agent or attorney; and in all cases where the proceedings are before a Commissioner, he shall be entitled to a fee of ten dollars in full for his services in each case, upon the delivery of the said certificate to the claimant, his or her agent or attorney; or a fee of five dollars in cases where the proof shall not, in the opinion of such Commissioner, warrant such certificate and delivery, inclusive of all services incident to such arrest and examination, to be paid in either case by the claimant, his or her agent or attorney. The person or persons authorized to execute the process to be issued by such Commissioner for the arrest and detention of fugitives from service or labor as aforesaid shall also be entitled to a fee of five dollars each for each person he or they may arrest and take before any such Commissioner, as aforesaid, at the instance and request of such claimant, with such other fees as may be deemed reasonable by such Commissioners for such other additional services as may be necessarily performed by him or them, such as attending at the examination, keeping the fugitive in custody, providing him with food and lodging during his detention and until the final determination of such Commissioner; and, in general, for performing such other duties as may be required by such claimant, his or her attorney or agent, or Commissioner in the premises. Such fees to be made up in conformity with the fees usually charged by the officers of the courts of justice within the proper district or county, as near as may be practicable, and paid by such claimants, their agents or attorneys, whether such supposed fugitives from service or labor be ordered to be delivered to such claimants by the final determination of such Commissioner or not.

Sec. 9. That, upon affidavit made by the claimant of such fugitive, his agent or attorney, after such certificate has been issued, that he has reason to apprehend that such fugitive will be rescued by force from his or her possession before he can be taken beyond the limits of the State in which the arrest is made, it shall be the duty of the officer making the arrest to retain such fugitive in his custody, and to remove him to the State whence he fled, and there to deliver him to said claimant, his agent or attorney. And, to this end, the officer aforesaid is hereby authorized and required to employ so many persons as he may deem necessary to overcome such force, and to retain them in his service so long as circumstances may require. The said officer and his assistants, while so employed, to receive the same compensation and to be allowed the same expenses as are now allowed by law for transportation of criminals, to be certified by the Judge of the district within which the arrest is made, and paid out of the treasury of the United States.

Sec. 10. That when any person held to service or labor in any State or Territory, or in the District of Columbia, shall escape therefrom, the party to whom such service or labor may be due, his, her, or their agent or attorney, may apply to any court of record therein, or Judge thereof in vacation, and make satisfactory proof to such court, or Judge in vacation, of the escape aforesaid, and that the person escaping owed service or labor to such party. Whereupon the court shall cause a record to be made of the matters so proved, and also a general description of the person so escaping, with such convenient certainty as may be; and a transcript of such record authenticated by the attestation of the clerk and of the seal of the said court, being produced in any other State, Territory, or District in which the person so escaping may be found, and, being exhibited to any Judge, Commissioner, or other officer authorized by the law of the United States to cause persons escaping from service or labor to be delivered up, shall be held and taken to be full and conclusive evidence of the fact of the escape, and that the service or labor of the person escaping is due to the party in such record mentioned. And upon the production, by the said party, of other and further evidence, if necessary, either oral or by affidavit, in addition to what is contained in the said record of the identity of the person escaping, he or she shall be delivered up to the claimant. And the said Court, Commissioner, Judge, or other person authorized by this Act to grant certificates to claimants of fugitives, shall, upon the production of the record and other evidences aforesaid, grant to such claimant a certificate of his right to take any such person identified and proved to be owing service or labor as aforesaid, which shall authorize such claimant to seize or arrest and transport such person to the State or Territory from which he escaped: *Provided*, That nothing herein contained shall be construed as requiring the production of a transcript of such record as evidence as aforesaid. But, in its absence, the claim shall be heard and determined upon other satisfactory proofs competent in law.

Approved September 18, 1850.

[The above law was repealed by the 38th Congress, 1864.]

KANSAS AND NEBRASKA TERRITORIAL ACT OF 1854.

An Act to Organize the Territories of Nebraska and Kansas.

Be it enacted by the Senate and House of Representatives of the United States of America in Congress assembled, That all that part of the territory of the United States included within the following limits, except such portions thereof as are hereinafter expressly exempted from the operations of this Act, to wit: beginning at a point on the Missouri River where the fortieth parallel of north latitude crosses the same; thence west on said parallel to the east boundary of the Territory of Utah on the summit of the Rocky Mountains; thence on said summit northward to the forty-ninth parallel of north latitude; thence east on said parallel to the western boundary of the Territory of Minnesota; thence southward on said boundary to the Missouri River; thence down the main channel of said river to the place of beginning, be, and the same is hereby, created into a temporary government by the name of the Territory of Nebraska; and when admitted as a State or States, the said Territory, or any portion of the same, shall be received into the Union with or without slavery, as their Constitution may prescribe at the time of their admission: *Provided,* That nothing in this Act contained shall be construed to inhibit the Government of the United States from dividing said Territory into two or more Territories, in such manner and at such times as Congress shall deem convenient and proper, or from attaching any portion of said Territory to any other State or Territory of the United States: *Provided, further,* That nothing in this Act contained shall be construed to impair the rights of person or property now pertaining to the Indians in said Territory, so long as such rights shall remain unextinguished by treaty between the United States and such Indians, or to include any Territory which, by treaty with any Indian tribe, is not, without the consent of said tribe, to be included within the Territorial limits or jurisdiction of any State or Territory; but all such Territory shall be excepted out of the boundaries, and constitute no part of the Territory of Nebraska, until said tribe shall signify their assent to the President of the United States to be included within the said Territory of Nebraska, or to affect the authority of the Government of the United States to make any regulations respecting such Indians, their lands, property or other rights, by treaty, law, or otherwise, which it would have been competent to the Government to make if this Act had never passed.

SEC. 2. That the executive power and authority in and over said Territory of Nebraska shall be vested in a Governor, who shall hold his office for four years, and until his successor shall be appointed and qualified, unless sooner removed by the President of the United States. The Governor shall reside within said Territory, and shall be commander-in-chief of the militia thereof. He may grant pardons and respites for offenses against the laws of said Territory, and reprieves for offenses against the laws of the United States, until the decision of the President can be made known thereon; he shall commission all officers who shall be appointed to office under the laws of the said Territory, and shall take care that the laws be faithfully executed.

SEC. 3. That there shall be a Secretary of said Territory, who shall reside therein, and hold his office for five years, unless sooner removed by the President of the United States; he shall record and preserve all the laws and proceedings of the Legislative Assembly hereinafter constituted, and all the acts and proceedings of the Governor in his executive department; he shall transmit one copy of the laws and journals of the Legislative Assembly within thirty days after the end of each session, and one copy of the executive proceedings and official correspondence semi-annually, on the first days of January and July in each year, to the President of the United States, and two copies of the laws to the President of the Senate and to the Speaker of the House of Representatives, to be deposited in the libraries of Congress; and, in case of the death, removal, resignation, or absence of the Governor from the Territory, the Secretary shall be, and he is hereby duly authorized and required to execute and perform all the powers and duties of the Governor during such vacancy or absence, or until another Governor shall be duly appointed and qualified to fill such vacancy.

SEC. 4. That the legislative power and authority of said Territory shall be vested in the Governor and a Legislative Assembly. The Legislative Assembly shall consist of a Council and House of Representatives. The Council shall consist of thirteen members, having the qualifications of voters, as hereinafter prescribed, whose term of service shall continue two years. The House of Representatives shall, at its first session, consist of twenty-six members, possessing the same qualifications as prescribed for members of the Council, and whose term of service shall continue one year. The number of Representatives may be increased by the Legislative Assembly, from time to time, in proportion to the increase of qualified voters: *Provided*, That the whole number shall never exceed thirty-nine; an apportionment shall be made as nearly equal as practicable, among the several counties or districts, for the election of the Council and Representatives, giving each section of the Territory representation in the ratio of its qualified voters as nearly as may be. And the members of the Council and of the House of Representatives shall reside in, and be inhabitants of, the district or county, or counties, for which they may be elected respectively. Previous to the first election, the Governor shall cause a census or enumeration of the inhabitants and qualified voters of the several counties and districts of the Territory, to be taken by such persons and in such mode as the Governor shall designate and appoint; and the persons so appointed shall receive a reasonable compensation therefor. And the first election shall be held at such times and places, and be conducted in such manner, both as to the persons who shall superintend such election and the returns thereof, as the Governor shall appoint and direct; and he shall at the same time declare the number of members of the Council and House of Representatives to which each of the counties or districts shall be entitled under this Act. The persons having the highest number of legal votes in each of said Council districts for members of the Council, shall be declared by the Governor to be duly elected to the Council; and the persons having the highest number of legal votes for the House of Representatives, shall be declared by the Governor to be duly elected members of said House: *Provided*, That, in case two or more persons voted for shall have an equal number of votes, and in case a vacancy shall otherwise occur in either branch of the Legislative Assembly, the Governor shall order a new election; and the persons thus elected to the Legislative Assembly shall meet at such place and on such day as the Governor shall appoint; but thereafter, the time, place, and manner of holding and conducting all elections by the people, and the apportioning the representation in the several counties or districts to the Council and House of Representatives, according to the number of qualified voters, shall be prescribed by law, as well as the day of the commencement of the regular sessions of the Legislative Assembly: *Provided*, That no session in any one year shall exceed the term of forty days, except the first session, which may continue sixty days.

SEC. 5. That every free white male inhabitant, above the age of twenty-one years, who shall be an actual resident of said Territory, and shall possess the qualifications hereinafter prescribed, shall be entitled to vote at the first election, and shall be eligible to any office within the said Territory; but the qualifications of voters, and of holding office, at all subsequent elections, shall be such as shall be prescribed by the Legislative Assembly: *Provided*, That the right of suffrage and of holding office shall be exercised only by citizens of the United States and those who shall have declared on oath their intention to become such, and shall have taken an oath to support the Constitution of the United States and the provisions of this act: *And provided, further*, That no officer, soldier, seaman, or marine, or other person in the army or navy of the United States, or attached to troops in the service of the United States, shall be allowed to vote or hold office in said Territory, by reason of being on service therein.

SEC. 6. That the legislative power of the Territory shall extend to all rightful subjects of legislation consistent with the Constitution of the United States and the provisions of this Act; but no law shall be passed interfering with the primary disposal of the soil; no tax shall be imposed upon the property of the United States; nor shall the lands or other property of non-residents be taxed higher than the lands or other property of residents. Every bill which shall have passed the Council and House of Representatives of said Territory, shall, before it become a law, be presented to the Governor of the Territory; if he approve, he shall sign it; but if not, he shall return it, with his objections, to the House in which it originated, who shall enter the objections at large on their journal, and proceed to reconsider it. If, after such reconsideration, two-thirds of that House shall agree to pass the bill, it shall be sent, together with the objections, to the other House, by which it shall likewise be reconsidered, and if approved by two-thirds of that House, it shall become a law. But in all such cases the votes of both Houses shall be determined by yeas and nays, to be entered on the journal of each House respectively. If any bill shall not be returned by the Governor within three days (Sundays excepted) after it shall have been presented to him, the same shall be a law in like manner as if he had signed it, unless the Assembly, by adjournment, prevent its return, in which case it shall not be a law.

SEC. 7. That all township, district, and county officers, not herein otherwise provided for, shall be appointed or elected, as the case may be, in such manner as shall be provided by the Governor and Legislative Assembly of the Territory of Nebraska. The Governor shall nominate, and, by and with the advice and consent of the Legislative Council, appoint all officers not herein otherwise provided for; and in the first instance the Governor alone may appoint all said officers, who shall hold their offices until the end of the first session of the Legislative Assembly; and shall lay off the necessary districts for members of the Council and House of Representatives, and all other officers.

SEC. 8. That no member of the Legislative Assembly

shall hold, or be appointed to any office which may have been created, or the salary or emoluments of which shall have been increased, while he was a member, during the term for which he was elected, and for one year after the expiration of such term; but this restriction shall not be applicable to members of the first Legislative Assembly; and no person holding a commission or appointment under the United States, except postmasters, shall be a member of the Legislative Assembly, or shall hold any office under the government of said Territory.

SEC. 9. That the judicial power of said Territory shall be vested in a Supreme Court, District Courts, Probate Courts, and in Justices of the Peace. The Supreme Court shall consist of a Chief Justice and two Associate Justices, any two of whom shall constitute a quorum, and who shall hold a term at the seat of government of said Territory annually, and they shall hold their offices during the period of four years, and until their successors shall be appointed and qualified. The said Territory shall be divided into three judicial districts, and a District Court shall be held in each of said districts by one of the Justices of the Supreme Court, at such times and places as may be prescribed by law; and the said Judges shall, after their appointments, respectively reside in the district which be assigned them. The jurisdiction of the several courts herein provided for—both appellate and original—and that of the Probate Courts and of Justices of the Peace, shall be limited by law: *Provided*, That Justices of the Peace shall not have jurisdiction of the matter in controversy when the title or boundaries of lands may be in dispute, or where the debt or sum claimed shall exceed one hundred dollars; and the said Supreme and District Courts, respectively, shall possess chancery as well as common law jurisdiction. Each District Court, or the judge thereof, shall appoint its clerk, who shall also be the register in chancery, and shall keep his office at the place where the Court may be held. Writs of error, bills of exception, and appeals, shall be allowed in all cases from the final decisions of said District Courts to the Supreme Court, under such regulations as may be prescribed by law; but in no case removed to the Supreme

Court shall trial by jury be allowed by said Court. The Supreme Court, or the Justices thereof, shall appoint its own clerk, and every clerk shall hold his office at the pleasure of the Court for which he shall have been appointed. Writs of error and appeals from the final decision of said Supreme Court shall be allowed, and may be taken to the Supreme Court of the United States in the same manner and under the same regulations as from the Circuit Courts of the United States, where the value of the property, or the amount in controversy, to be ascertained by the oath or affirmation of either party, or other competent witness, shall exceed one thousand dollars; except only that in all cases involving title to slaves, the said writs of error or appeals shall be allowed and decided by the said Supreme Court, without regard to the value of the matter, property, or title in controversy; and except also that a writ of error or appeal shall also be allowed to the Supreme Court of the United States, from the decisions of the said Supreme Court created by this act, or of any judge thereof, or of the District Courts created by this Act, or of any judge thereof, upon any writ of *habeas corpus*, involving the question of personal freedom: *Provided*, That nothing herein contained shall be construed to apply to or affect provisions of the "Act respecting fugitives from justice, and persons escaping from the service of their masters," (approved February 12, 1793,) and the "Act to amend and supplementary to the aforesaid Act," (approved September 18, 1850;) and each of the said District Courts shall have and exercise the same jurisdiction in all cases arising under the Constitution and laws of the United States as is vested in the Circuit and District Courts of the United States; and the said Supreme and District Courts of the said Territory, and the respective judges thereof, shall and may grant writs of *habeas corpus* in all cases in which the same are granted by the judges of the United States in the District of Columbia; and the first six days of every term of said courts, or so much thereof as shall be necessary, shall be appropriated to the trial of causes arising under the said Constitution and laws; and writs of error and appeal in all such cases shall be made to the Supreme Court of said Territory, the same as in other cases. The said clerk shall receive, in all such cases, the same fees which the clerks of the District Courts of Utah Territory now receive for similar services.

SEC. 10. That the provisions of an Act entitled "an Act respecting fugitives from justice, and persons escaping from the service of their masters," (approved February 12, 1793,) and the provisions of the Act entitled "an Act to amend, and supplementary to the aforesaid Act," (approved September 18, 1850,) be, and the same are hereby, declared to extend to and be in full force within the limits of said Territory of Nebraska.

SEC. 11. That there shall be appointed an attorney for said Territory, who shall continue in office for four years, and until his successor shall be appointed and qualified, unless sooner removed by the President, and who shall receive the same fees and salary as the attorney of the United States for the present Territory of Utah. There shall also be a marshal for the Territory appointed, who shall hold his office for four years, and until his successor shall be appointed and qualified, unless sooner removed by the President, and who shall execute all processes issuing from the said courts when exercising their jurisdiction as Circuit and District Courts of the United States; he shall perform the duties, be subject to the same regulations and penalties, and be entitled to the same fees as the marshal of the District Court of the United States for the present Territory of Utah, and shall, in addition, be paid two hundred dollars annually as a compensation for extra services.

SEC. 12. That the Governor, Secretary, Chief Justice, and Associate Justices, Attorney, and Marshal, shall be nominated, and—by and with the advice and consent of the Senate—appointed by the President of the United States. The Governor and Secretary, to be appointed as aforesaid, shall, before they act as such, respectively take an oath or affirmation before the District Judge or some Justice of the Peace in the limits of said Territory, duly authorized to administer oaths and affirmations by the laws now in force therein, or before the Chief Justice or some Associate Justice of the Supreme Court of the United States, to support the Constitution of the United States, and faithfully discharge the duties of their respective offices, which said oaths, when so taken, shall be certified by the person by whom the same shall have been taken; and such certificates shall be received and recorded by the said Secretary among the executive proceedings; and the Chief Justice, and Associate Justices, and all other civil officers in said Territory, before they act as such, shall take a like oath or affirmation before the said Governor or Secretary, or some Judge or Justice of the Peace of the Territory, who may be duly commissioned and qualified, which said oath or affirmation shall be certified and transmitted by the person taking the same to the Secretary, to be by him recorded as aforesaid; and afterward, the like oath or affirmation shall be taken, certified, and recorded in such manner and form as may be prescribed by law. The Governor shall receive an annual salary of two thousand five hundred dollars. The Chief Justice and Associate Justices shall receive an annual salary of two thousand dollars. The Secretary shall receive an annual salary of two thousand dollars. The said salaries shall be paid quarter-yearly, from the dates of the respective appointments, at the treasury of the United States; but no such payment shall be made until said officers shall have entered upon the duties of their respective appointments. The members of the Legislative Assembly shall be entitled to receive three dollars each per day during their attendance at the sessions thereof, and three dollars each for every twenty miles' travel in going to and returning from the said sessions, estimated according to the nearest usually traveled route; and an additional allowance of three dollars shall be paid to the presiding officer of each House for each day he shall so preside. And a chief clerk, one assistant clerk, a sergeant-at-arms, and door-keeper may be chosen for each House; and the chief clerk shall receive four dollars per day, and the said other officers three dollars per day, during the session of the Legislative Assembly; but no other officer shall be paid by the United States: *Provided*, That there shall be but one session of the Legislature annually, unless, on an extraordinary occasion, the Governor shall think proper to call the Legislature together. There shall be appropriated, annually, the usual sum, to be expended by the

Governor, to defray the contingent expenses of the Territory, including the salary of a Clerk of the Executive Department; and there shall also be appropriated, annually, a sufficient sum, to be expended by the Secretary of the Territory, and upon an estimate to be made by the Secretary of the Treasury of the United States, to defray the expenses of the Legislative Assembly, the printing of the laws, and other incidental expenses; and the Governor and Secretary of the Territory shall, in the disbursement of all moneys intrusted to them, be governed solely by the instructions of the Secretary of the Treasury of the United States, and shall, semi-annually, account to the said Secretary for the manner in which the aforesaid moneys shall have been expended; and no expenditure shall be made by said Legislative Assembly for objects not specially authorized by the Acts of Congress making the appropriations, nor beyond the sums thus appropriated for such objects.

SEC. 13. That the Legislative Assembly of the Territory of Nebraska shall hold its first session at such time and place in said Territory as the Governor thereof shall appoint and direct; and at said first session, or as soon thereafter as they shall deem expedient, the Governor and Legislative Assembly shall proceed to locate and establish the seat of government for said Territory at such place as they may deem eligible; which place, however, shall thereafter be subject to be changed by the said Governor and Legislative Assembly.

SEC. 14. That a delegate to the House of Representatives of the United States, to serve for the term of two years, who shall be a citizen of the United States, may be elected by the voters qualified to elect members of the Legislative Assembly, who shall be entitled to the same rights and privileges as are exercised and enjoyed by the delegates from the several other Territories of the United States to the said House of Representatives; but the delegate first elected shall hold his seat only during the term of the Congress to which he shall be elected. The first election shall be held at such time and places, and be conducted in such manner as the Governor shall appoint and direct; and at all subsequent elections the times, places, and manner of holding the elections shall be prescribed by law. The person having the greatest number of votes shall be declared by the Governor to be duly elected, and a certificate thereof shall be given accordingly. That the Constitution, and all the laws of the United States which are not locally inapplicable, shall have the same force and effect within the said Territory of Nebraska as elsewhere within the United States, except the eighth section of the act preparatory to the admission of Missouri into the Union, (approved March 6, 1820,) which, being inconsistent with the principle of non-intervention by Congress with slavery in the States and Territories—as recognized by the legislation of 1850, commonly called the Compromise Measures—is hereby declared inoperative and void; it being the true intent and meaning of this act not to legislate slavery into any Territory or State, nor to exclude it therefrom, but to leave the people thereof perfectly free to form and regulate their domestic institutions in their own way, subject only to the Constitution of the United States: *Provided*, That nothing herein contained shall be construed to revive or put in force any law or regulation which may have existed prior to the act of March 6, 1820, either protecting, establishing, prohibiting, or abolishing slavery.

SEC. 15. That there shall hereafter be appropriated, as has been customary for the territorial governments, a sufficient amount, to be expended under the direction of the said Governor of the Territory of Nebraska, not exceeding the sums heretofore appropriated for similar objects, for the erection of suitable public buildings at the seat of government, and for the purchase of a library, to be kept at the seat of government, for the use of the Governor, Legislative Assembly, Judges of the Supreme Court, Secretary, Marshal, and Attorney of said Territory, and such other persons, and under such regulations, as shall be prescribed by law.

SEC. 16. That when the lands in said Territory shall be surveyed under the direction of the Government of the United States, preparatory to bringing the same into market, sections numbered sixteen and thirty-six, in each township in said Territory, shall be, and the same are hereby, reserved for the purpose of being applied to schools in said Territory, and in the States and Territories hereafter to be erected out of the same.

SEC. 17. That, until otherwise provided by law, the Governor of said Territory may define the judicial districts of said Territory, and assign the judges who may be appointed for said Territory to the several districts; and also appoint the times and places for holding courts in the several counties or subdivisions in each of said judicial districts by proclamation, to be issued by him; but the Legislative Assembly, at their first or any subsequent session, may organize, alter, or modify such judicial districts, and assign the judges, and alter the times and places of holding the courts, as to them shall seem proper and convenient.

SEC. 18. That all officers to be appointed by the President, by and with the advice and consent of the Senate, for the Territory of Nebraska, who, by virtue of the provisions of any law now existing, or which may be enacted during the present Congress, are required to give security for moneys that may be intrusted with them for disbursements, shall give security, at such time and place, and in such manner as the Secretary of Treasury may prescribe.

SEC. 19. That all that part of the territory of the United States included within the following limits, except such portions thereof as are hereinafter expressly exempted from the operations of this act, to wit: beginning at a point on the western boundary of the State of Missouri, where the thirty-seventh parallel of north latitude crosses the same; thence west on said parallel to the eastern boundary of New Mexico; thence north on said boundary to latitude thirty-eight; thence following said boundary westward to the east boundary of the Territory of Utah, on the summit of the Rocky Mountains; thence northward on said summit to the fortieth parallel of latitude; thence east on said parallel to the western boundary of the State of Missouri; thence south with the western boundary of said State to the place of beginning, be, and the same is hereby, created into a temporary government by the name of the Territory of Kansas; and when admitted as a State or States, the said Territory, or any portion of the same, shall be received into the Union with or without slavery, as the Constitution may prescribe at the time of their admission: *Provided*, That nothing in this Act contained shall be construed to inhibit the Government of the United States from dividing said Territory into two or more Territories, in such manner and at such times as Congress shall deem convenient and proper, or from attaching any portion of said Territory to any other State or Territory of the United States: *Provided, further*, That nothing in this Act contained shall be so construed as to impair the rights of persons or property now pertaining to the Indians in said Territory, so long as such rights shall remain unextinguished by treaty between the United States and such Indians, or to include any Territory which, by treaty with any Indian tribe, is not, without the consent of said tribe, to be included within the territorial limits or jurisdiction of any State or Territory; but all such territory shall be excepted out of the boundaries, and constitute no part of the Territory of Kansas, until said tribe shall signify their assent to the President of the United States to be included within the said Territory of Kansas, or to affect the authority of the Government of the United States to make any regulation respecting such Indians, their lands, property, or other rights, by treaty, law, or otherwise, which it would have been competent to the government to make if this act had never passed.

[With the single exception of the location of the seat of government for Kansas at Fort Leavenworth, provided for in section 31, the ensuing sixteen sections, relative to the organization and government of the Territory, are precisely similar to the sections already recited, providing for the government of Nebraska Territory. The final section of the act, which has a general reference to both Territories, is as follows:]

SEC. 37. *And be it further enacted*, That all treaties, laws, and other engagements made by the Government of the United States with the Indian tribes inhabiting the Territories embraced within this act, shall be faithfully and rigidly observed, notwithstanding any thing contained in this act; and that the existing agencies and superintendencies of said Indians be continued, with the same powers and duties which are now prescribed by law, except that the President of the United States may, at his discretion, change the location of the office of superintendent.

HISTORY OF EACH OF THE STATES.

VIRGINIA.

"The Old Dominion," so distinguished as being the native State of the Father of American Liberty, and the "Mother of Presidents," really seemed at one time, to be peculiarly favorable to the birth and development of statesmen. It has furnished no less than five Presidents, among whom are Washington, Monroe, Madison, and Jefferson. It was the first Colony, on the Continent, settled by the English. In 1607, a company formed under the patronage of James I, obtained a grant to make settlements in America, between the 34th and 38th degrees of north latitude. In May, 1607, a colony of one hundred and five persons, under direction of this company, arrived off the coast of South Virginia. Their intention had been to form a settlement on Roanoke, now in North Carolina; but being driven north by a violent storm, they discovered and entered the mouth of Chesapeake Bay. Passing up this bay they named its capes—Henry and Charles—in honor of the king's two sons. They were commanded by Capt. Christopher Newport, an experienced and distinguished navigator. Passing up James River, they arrived at a peninsula, upon which they landed and established Jamestown.

After promulgating a code of laws which had been formed by the London company, Capt. Newport sailed for England, leaving the colony under the care of Capt. John Smith, whose subsequent relations to the settlement became so important, and without whose efforts the enterprise would doubtless have proved a failure. The colonists seem to have been very poorly adapted to the labor required at their hands. Too many of them were *gentlemen*, and came, it appears, only to enrich themselves by gathering gold, which, they had heard, was very abundant.

Through a series of difficulties, which it is rarely the lot of man to encounter, this colony progressed; the settlers awhile quarreling among themselves, and awhile contending against savages and famine, for bare existence, until the period of the Revolution, in which it was one of the first colonies to take active part, furnishing to the young republic many of its most efficient military chieftains and statesmen. It ratified the Constitution June 26, 1788. After the Revolution its course was for many years one of great prosperity. But, unfortunately, the year 1861 found the majority of its statesmen arrayed against the Government, on the side of secession, and on the 15th of April, 1861, she seceded from the Union. On the 17th of June, 1861, all the counties lying between the Alleghany Mountains and the Ohio River, were, by a convention held at Wheeling, declared independent of the old State government, and were organized into a new State, called West Virginia, which remains loyal. The capital of the old State was selected as the seat of government of the so-called Confederate States of America.

MASSACHUSETTS.

Massachusetts was settled in the year 1620, by the Puritans. These people, having been severely persecuted in England, had previously taken refuge in Holland; but for various reasons they determined, after remaining in Holland a season, to emigrate to the New World. Unfortunately, they started at a very unpropitious season of the year, arriving at New England in the winter. The severity of the climate, their scarcity of food at times, operated seriously against their comfort and progress. It is said that they were frequently threatened with starvation. At one time the entire company had but one pint of Indian corn, which being divided equally among them, allowed to each person eight grains. But, unlike the early settlers of Virginia, they were all working men, and good economists. From the time of the landing at Plymouth, up to 1691, this first settlement was known as the Plymouth Colony. Meantime, another settlement had been formed, styled the Massachusetts Colony. Both were for some years under the control of a London company. In 1691, Massachusetts and Plymouth Colonies were united, and thenceforward their history is one. The people of Massachusetts were, during the early part of their colonial existence, sorely vexed, at times, by the Indians, especially by the Pequods. They, unfortunately, had imbibed, during their own persecutions, too much of the spirit of conscription, and, although themselves refugees from religious bigotry, sullied much of their history prior to the Revolution by punishing what they called heresy in the Quakers and Baptists. During 1774 and 1775, Massachusetts took a very prominent part in favor of colonial rights, and was the first State to manifest the spirit of resentment toward Great Britain. Its history during the War for Independence is one of glory. It adopted the Constitution June 6, 1788.

NEW HAMPSHIRE.

This State was a part of Massachusetts up to the year 1680. It was, however, settled in 1624, the first settlement being formed at Dover by the English. In 1680, it was erected into a separate colony, and its first legislative assembly met this year. John Mason was its first Governor. It suffered severely from Indian wars, and its progress, during the first years of its existence, was slow. In 1742 it contained only six hundred persons liable to taxation. Its first Constitution was formed in 1683. It suffered from the effects of an insurrection in 1686, although prior and subsequent to this affair, it seems to have been one of the most peaceful and quiet of the colonies. It is distinguished for its excellent pastures, towering hills, and fine cattle. The White Mountains are the highest in New England. It took a prominent and active part in the Revolution. It ratified the Constitution June 21, 1788, since which time it has been highly prosperous. Its present population is 326,073. Its course during the rebellion has been highly commendable.

MARYLAND.

In 1632, Sir George Calvert (Lord Baltimore) visited

America, explored a tract of country lying on the Chesapeake Bay, belonging to what was then called South Virginia, and returned to England to procure a grant for it. But before the patent was made out, he died, and it was given to his son Cecil. The province was named by King Charles I, in the patent, in honor of his Queen, Henrietta Maria. A part of the province appears to have been included in the grant made some time afterward to William Penn, and to have caused much contention between the successors of Penn and Baltimore.

In March, 1634, Leonard Calvert, the brother of Cecil, arrived at the mouth of the Potomac River, bringing with him two hundred emigrants, most of whom were Roman Catholic gentlemen. Leaving the vessel, he ascended in a pinnace as far as Piskataqua, an Indian village nearly opposite Mount Vernon. The Indian Sachem gave him full liberty to settle there if he chose; but not deeming it safe, he began a settlement lower down on a branch of the Potomac, at the Indian town of Yoacomoco. The settlement was called St. Mary's.

Maryland made a very fortunate beginning. The colonists arrived in time to make a crop for that year. Their neighbors in Virginia supplied them with cattle, and protected them in great part from the Indians, while their own kind and consistent course materially promoted their happy relations with the savages.

The charter which had been granted them was very liberal—ceding to them the full power of legislation, without any interference on the part of the Crown. In 1635, they made laws for their government, which were somewhat modified in 1639. In 1650, they had an upper and lower legislative assembly, as had their Virginia neighbors.

Ten or twelve years after its settlement, Maryland was disturbed by an insurrection, headed by one Clayborne; but this difficulty was soon settled. It played a conspicuous part in the Revolution, and adopted the Constitution April 28, 1788. Its progress has been fair, its present population being 687,049. Its geographical position and the mixed political character of its people caused it to assume a rather dubious attitude at the commencement of the rebellion of 1861. Some of its best statesmen, however, were among the most uncompromising friends of the Union.

NEW YORK.

Captain Henry Hudson, the famous voyager, discovered what is now New York, together with a considerable extent of territory contiguous to it, in the year 1609. Although an Englishman by nativity, Hudson was at this time employed by the Dutch, (Hollanders) who, consequently, claimed the territory. Meantime the English set up a claim to it, as being part of North Virginia. They also claimed it on account of Hudson being an Englishman. The Dutch, however, determined to hold it, and in 1610 opened a trade with the natives at Manhattan Island, on the spot where the city of New York now stands. They erected a fort on or near the site of Albany, named the country in general, New Netherlands, and the station at Manhattan, New Amsterdam. The Dutch retained the country until the year 1664.

It seems that, up to this time, they claimed not only the present territory of New York, but also that of Connecticut and New Jersey. The liberal governments of the surrounding colonies stood in great contrast with the despotic one imposed by the Dutch Government upon their American colonists. And when, in 1664, the English squadron dispatched by James, Duke of York, with instructions to take possession of the province of New Netherlands, appeared before New Amsterdam, the inhabitants were willing to capitulate without resistance. Peter Stuyvesant, their Governor, and an able executive, made vain efforts to rouse them to defense, and was forced to surrender. The English Government was now acknowledged over the whole of New Netherlands, the capital receiving the name of New York, as well as the province. From this time forward to the Revolutionary War, New York remained in the hands of the English, and was under the control of a very arbitrary succession of Governors. The progress of the colony was steady, in numbers, wealth, and civilization. It took an active part in the Revolution, and adopted its Constitution July 26, 1788. After this it outstripped every other State in the Union in every thing pertaining to wealth and greatness, save education, in which matter no State can compare with Massachusetts. At the commencement of the great Rebellion, this noble State showed herself truly worthy to be ranked as the Empire State. She has furnished the Government more money than any other State. Her population is 3,880,735.

CONNECTICUT.

In the year 1633, the Puritans of Massachusetts, having heard very flattering reports of the valley of Connecticut, resolved to make an effort to settle it. Accordingly, a company of them sailed for the Connecticut River, taking with them the frame of a house. Meantime the Dutch, claiming the territory as theirs, built a fort on the river where Hartford now stands, to prevent the emigrants from passing up. The Yankees, however, with that steady perseverance which has always marked their course, proceeded on their way, paying no attention to the Dutch fort, whose only demonstration was an unexecuted threat to fire on the emigrants if they passed it. Landing where Farmington River enters the Connecticut, they founded the town of Windsor. Other settlements were subsequently formed at Westerfield, Hartford, and Watertown. The first general court was held at Hartford, in the year 1636. The province suffered severely from the depredations of the Pequod Indians, with which tribe a great and decisive battle was ultimately fought on the river Mystic, in the year 1636.* During this year the towns of Windsor, Hartford, and Wethersfield, met in convention and formed a Government, electing John Haynes the first Governor of the colony.

Its course from this period forward was one of great prosperity. It stood in the front rank during the war for Independence, and in no case was ever known to flinch from duty. It ratified the Constitution June 9, 1788. Its present population is 460,147.

* This battle resulted in the destruction of the Pequod tribe.

At the commencement of the Rebellion, in 1861, its voice was for the Union and the Government of the Fathers. Its aid in behalf of freedom has been earnest and efficient.

RHODE ISLAND.

In June, 1636, Roger Williams, an earnest, enthusiastic advocate of religious liberty in the broadest sense, having been banished by the Puritans of Massachusetts from that colony, went to what is now known as Rhode Island, purchased the present site of Providence of the Narragansett Indians, and founded a colony, of which he was at once pastor, teacher, and father. He donated land to any whom he thought worthy, and Providence Plantation, as it was long called, became an asylum for persecuted Christians of all denominations, especially the Baptists. The first settlement in Rhode Island proper, was formed by William Codington, in the year 1636. Up to 1640, the citizens of Rhode Island made their own laws in general convention. But, in 1644, Roger Williams, with the aid of Gov. Vane, of Massachusetts, procured a charter for two settlements, under the name of Rhode Island and Providence Plantations. The Constitution framed under this charter was a good one; and lasted until the year 1818. For many years the legislative assembly of this colony met twice a year.

Rhode Island is distinguished as the smallest State in the Union. It did noble service in the war for Independence, but did not, for some reason, adopt the Constitution till the 29th of May, 1790. It has been a highly prosperous State; is distinguished for its good schools and large manufactories.

At the breaking out of the Rebellion in 1861, it stepped nobly forward in defense of the Government, sending its own Governor to Washington at the head of a regiment of volunteers. Its population is 174,620.

NEW JERSEY,

At first, formed a part of the Dutch province of New Netherlands. But soon after the latter came into the hands of the English, the Territory of New Jersey was transferred to Lord Berkley and Sir George Carteret, by the Duke of York. The first permanent settlement was formed at Elizabethtown, in 1664, by emigrants from Long Island. Philip Carteret arrived in the colony in 1665, and became its first Governor. The province had very little trouble with the Indians. Many emigrants from New England and New York soon arrived, and for a series of years the colony advanced in prosperity. It enjoyed the blessings flowing from a liberal form of government.

In the year 1685, the Duke of York became the King of England, under the title of James II, and disregarding his former pledges, assumed, in 1688, the government of New Jersey, placing it under the control of Sir Edmund Andros, whom he had already made Governor of New York and New England. This state of things was terminated by the revolution in England, but left New Jersey for years in a very precarious condition. In 1702, its proprietors having resigned their claims, it became a royal province, and was united to New York. In 1738 it became again a separate province, and so continued until the Revolution, in which it took a very active part in favor of liberty. It ratified the Constitution December 18, 1787. Thenceforward its career has been a highly prosperous one. Its strength has been put forth to aid in crushing the great Rebellion. Population 672,075.

DELAWARE.

Gustavus Adolphus, King of Sweden, formed a plan of establishing colonies in America as early as the year 1626. But as he died on the field of Leutzen, during the German war in 1633, without carrying his scheme into effect, his minister took it up, and employed Peter Minuets, the first Governor of New Netherlands, to carry it into effect. In 1638, a small Swedish colony arrived under the direction of Minuets, and settled on Christian Creek, near the present town of Wilmington. Notwithstanding the remonstrances of the Dutch Government of New Netherlands, who claimed the territory, the Swedes continued to extend their settlements from this time until they preëmpted all the territory from Cape Henlopen to the falls of the Delaware. At this time the colony was called New Sweden. In 1651, Governor Stuyvesant, to check the aggressive movements of the Swedes, built a fort near the present site of New Castle, of which the Swedes afterward obtained possession by stratagem. Enraged at this movement, the Government of Holland ordered Stuyvesant to reduce the Swedes to submission, which he speedily accomplished with six hundred men, in 1655. The province was soon after annexed to New Netherlands. Delaware was, after it fell into the hands of the English, included in the grant made to William Penn, in 1692. It remained attached to Pennsylvania till 1691, when it was allowed a separate government. It was reunited to Pennsylvania in 1692. In 1703, it was again separated, having its own legislature, though the same Governor presided over both colonies. The ancient forms of the government were preserved through the revolutionary struggle. It ratified the Constitution December 7, 1787.

Its position, at the commencement of the rebellion of 1861, was somewhat dubious. It being a northerly slave State, was somewhat divided as to where its interests lay. It, however, finally came out somewhat decidedly for the Union, although its entire strength has not been exerted against the rebellion. Its population is 112,216.

THE CAROLINAS.

In the year 1563, the coast of Carolina was explored, and named after Charles IX, of France. The first attempt to settle it was made by the celebrated and accomplished Sir Walter Raleigh, in 1585, twenty-two years before the settlement of Jamestown, and thirty-five years before the Puritans landed at Plymouth. This effort failed, on account of the incapacity of the Governor appointed by Raleigh, and the ill-behavior of the colonists toward the natives.

The first successful attempt was made sometime between 1640 and 1650, under the direction of Governor Berkley. The settlement was made in Albemarle County, by a few Virginia planters. In 1663, a large tract of land, lying between the 30th and 36th degrees of north latitude, having the Atlantic Ocean for its eastern boundary, was conveyed by Charles II, to Lord Clarendon and associates, under whose auspices a settlement was made near the mouth of Cape Fear River, in the year 1665, by emigrants from Barbadoes. Sir James Yeomans was appointed Governor. A settlement was made at Port Royal, South Carolina, in 1670; and in 1671, a few persons located at what was then called Old Charleston, which place was abandoned in 1680, and the foundation of the present city of Charleston laid, several miles nearer the sea.

All the various settlements here mentioned went under the general name of Carolina, until 1571, when a division was made, and the northern and southern portions were called by their distinctive names, North and South Carolina. These States were the scenes of many revolutionary tragedies. South Carolina, in particular, although the home of Sumter, and Marion, and Rutledge, was replete with tories, (royalists) who spared no efforts to annoy the infant Republic, and play into the hands of the British Government. South Carolina ratified the Constitution May 23, 1788, but threatened to break the compact in 1832, and was only prevented by the stern will of President Jackson. After this the State did nothing worthy of note until December 20, 1860, when it seceded from the Union, taking the lead in the great Rebellion. Present population 703,708.

North Carolina ratified the Constitution November 21, 1789, and seceded from the Union May 21, 1861. Population 992,622.

PENNSYLVANIA.

The Old Keystone State, and one of the most wealthy and prosperous in the Union, was settled by the Quakers, under the direction of Wm. Penn, at Philadelphia, in the year 1682. The founder of this colony showed himself a philosopher, a philanthropist, a thorough political economist, at the very commencement of his labors. He put the province under the government of a Council of Three and a House of Delegates, chosen by the freemen, who, according to his arrangement, were all those who acknowledged the existence of one God. He pursued such a course with the natives as won their confidence and esteem. No Quaker was ever murdered by an Indian; and to this day the "sons of Wm. Penn" are every-where respected by the savage. The treaty Penn made with the Indians was never violated. In framing the colonial government, he provided for the largest religious liberty, allowing every one to worship according to the dictates of his own conscience. Up to 1684, Delaware, as before mentioned, was included in Penn's grant. But about this time he procured a new charter, more strictly defining the rights and limits of Pennsylvania, and Delaware was detached. For seventy years prosperity smiled upon this colony, during much of which time Penn was, according to the historian, its governor, magistrate, preacher and teacher. It was troubled with no Indian wars till 1754, when Penn's example and teachings began to be forgotten. The population, owing to a considerable influx from Sweden, Germany, and some other countries, began, at a later date, to assume a more varied aspect; and when the colonies rebelled against the mother country, Pennsylvania contained sufficient "fighting" material to lend valuable assistance to the cause of liberty.

She adopted the Constitution December 12th, 1787, since which time her increase in wealth, and advancement in general improvement has been almost without a parallel. Her vast coal fields and rich iron mines constitute a source of eternal wealth. Upon the breaking out of the rebellion of 1861, her position in favor of the Union was well defined.

Her population is 2,906,115.

GEORGIA.

General James Oglethorpe, and a company of twenty-one others, received, in the year 1732, from George II, of England, a grant for all the land between the Savannah and the Altamaha Rivers. In January, 1733, a company of one hundred and fourteen men, women, and children, arrived at Charleston, S. C., destined for Georgia. They were kindly treated by the Charlestonians, and were greatly assisted by them in their labor of forming a colony. The first laws made for the province by the twenty-two grantees, prohibited the importation of rum, trade with the Indians, and the use of negroes. They also provided that lands should go back to the original owners in case the purchaser had no male heirs. Although the first, second, and third of these provisions were undoubtedly wholesome, the fourth was highly objectionable, and tended very much to retard the progress of the colony. In the year 1740, General Oglethorpe, as commander-in-chief of the forces in Georgia, at the head of two thousand men, invaded Florida with the intention of forcibly annexing it to Georgia; but he was soon repelled from the the territory, and returned home bootless. The Spanish, in turn, with two sail of vessels and three thousand men, invaded Georgia in 1742, and were likewise forced to return home thwarted. The progress of this colony was for many years very slow; the people manifesting that indolence and indifference which is still too prominent a characteristic of Georgians. It was mainly on the side of freedom during the revolution.

It ratified the Constitution January 9th, 1788. Since the Revolution, the State has manifested but little life as compared with its sisters, and its secession from the Union, May 19th, 1861, was followed by speedy ruin.

VERMONT.

The territory of which this State is composed began to be settled in the year 1731, but was for some years considered as a part of New Hampshire. It was also claimed at one time by New York, and a contest arose between that State and New Hampshire, which was adjusted by the King of England in a manner by no means satisfactory to the settlers. The result was a quarrel between Vermont and the Crown, in which the Green Mountain Boys, led by Col. Ethan Allen, resisted the officers of justice, as well as the New York militia, who were called out to sustain them.

The province appears not to have had even a territorial government until 1777, at which time a convention of delegates met at Westminster, and declared themselves an independent State, under the name of New Connecticut. Previous to this time, however, they had rendered material aid to the Revolution. In May, 1755, Col. Allen, at the head of two hundred and seventy men, reduced Fort Ticonderoga and Crown Point, and thus became complete masters of Lake Champlain. During the whole period of the Revolution the State did good service in the cause of liberty, although it remained independent. Some time subsequent to its declaration of independence its name was changed to Vermont. As it was not one of the original States, it did not ratify the Constitution, but, upon application, was admitted to the Union during the second session of Congress, in the year 1791. It has been a highly prosperous State, and added much to the luster of the Union in its palmy days of peace. It fully sustained its Revolutionary reputation at the commencement of the Rebellion of 1861. Its population is 315,098.

KENTUCKY

Was settled, in the year 1775, by Daniel Boone and a number of associates from North Carolina. The trials and adventures of these hardy pioneers, and especially those of Boone, constitute one of the most romantic leaves in the history of the West. For over two years, previous to 1775, Boone was busily employed in surveying Kentucky, building roads and forts. One of the latter he erected at Boonsborough; to which place he removed his family, in 1775. Boone said that his wife and daughter were the first white women who ever stood on the banks of the Kentucky River. For a number of years after Boone's settlement, he and his associates experienced many difficulties with the natives—Boone's daughter being at one time captured by the Indians, though shortly afterward rescued by her father. But, notwithstanding the difficulties with the savages, the young territory grew rapidly in population and wealth, and on June 1st, 1792, was admitted to the Union. Having a fertile soil, and affording excellent pasturage, she has far outstripped most of her slave-holding sisters in general improvement.

Her position for some time after the commencement of the Rebellion was by no means promotive of her prosperity.

Owing to her attempt to observe strict neutrality, she became the scene of many guerrilla outrages, and has suffered, perhaps, more than any other State during the struggle.

Her population is 1,115,684.

TENNESSEE.

Was, for some time, a part of North Carolina. It was made a territorial government in the year 1790, and was admitted into the Union in 1796. The first permanent white inhabitants of Tennessee went there, in the year 1775, and built Fort Louden, now in Blount County. They were, in 1760, attacked by the savages, and two hundred persons mere massacred. But, in 1767, the natives were reduced to submission by Colonel Grant, and a treaty was made with them, which encouraged emigration. Settlements were formed on Holston River in 1765, which, although frequently attacked by the Indians, made very fair progress. Colonel John Sevier, with the Tennessee militia and a few Virginia soldiers, gained a decisive victory over the savages, and, from this time forward, though more or less harassed by the Indians, the progress of the State, in population and improvement, was rapid. North Carolina gave up the Territory in 1789, and, in 1790, Congress recognized it as a separate province. It has great extent of territory, and, up to 1861, was considered as among the greatest of the agricultural States. At this time, however, it was seduced by the voice of the siren, Secession, and on the 24th of June, 1861, formally seceded from the Union. It should be stated, however, in justice to the State, that the eastern portion of it was generally loyal, and was only dragged out of the Union by force. It has, since the Rebellion, been readmitted into the Union.

OHIO.

Ohio was admitted to the Union on the 29th of November, 1802, the State containing, at the time, 72,000 inhabitants—2,000 more than was required in order to its admission. It was settled in the spring of 1788, one year after it, with a vast additional extent of North-western territory, had been ceded, by Virginia, to the United States.

The year 1788 was a famous year for emigration. It witnessed the passage of no less than 20,000 persons down the Ohio River. The company which settled Ohio consisted of forty persons, under General Rufus Putnam. They built a stockade fort at Marietta, of sufficient strength to resist the attacks of the natives, cleared several acres of ground, and planted a crop. They were joined by twenty additional families in the autumn. Both these companies were New England people.

For a number of years they were not troubled by the savages, nor did any of their number trouble the Indians, except in one or two instances. The earliest settlers of Cincinnati arrived there, about twenty in number in 1790. Until the year 1795, the attempts made to settle most parts of Ohio were attended with great difficulties, on account of Indian wars: Marietta, however, formed an exception to this rule. After the great victory which General Wayne achieved over the savages during Washington's administration, the population increased rapidly. Unembarrassed by any centralizing or aristocratic institutions, possessed of the finest natural resources, and vitalized by an enterprising population, Ohio, after its admission into the Union, made an advancement of which any State might well be proud. In population it is the third State in the Union, numbering 2,390,502.

At the breaking out of the Rebellion, Ohio took its position staunchly for the Union, and has done much during the war for the restoration of the authority of the Government over the seceded States.

LOUISIANA.

Was ceded by Spain to France in the year 1802, and was bought by the United States of the latter power, in 1803, at a cost of $15,000,000. Governor Clayborne took possession of it the same year. It was settled by the French, at Iberville, in 1699, and was admitted into the Union April 8th, 1812. It is an important State, in that it holds the keys of entrance to the mouth of the Mississippi. In the year 1860, nearly one-half of its population was slave. It seceded from the Union on the 26th of January, 1861. Its population in 1860 was 708,002. It has been a very forward State in the great Rebellion.

INDIANA.

About the year 1690, a French settlement, the first in Indiana, was made at Vincennes, that place being within the territory claimed, at that time, by the French, upon priority of discovery by La Salle. Indiana was long the residence of various Indian tribes, and the theater of Indian wars. By the terms of the treaty of the peace of 1763, it, with the rest of the North-western Territory, was ceded to Great Britain. It was still claimed by the Indians, but, by various treaties, extensive tracts were obtained for settlement. The Indians, however, retained possession of many parts of the State up to the year 1812, and to that portion known as the Indian Reserve, even later. It was erected into a Territory in 1809, and on the 11th of December, 1816, was admitted into the Union. Its population—1,350,428, in the year 1860—is an indication of its progress. In the matter of education, Indiana is somewhat behind some of her Western sisters, but her efforts in behalf of the Government during the great Rebellion shall halo her future with glory.

MISSISSIPPI.

The territory comprising the present States of Mississippi and Alabama having been divided, that portion lying next the river was, in 1817, admitted into the Union as a State, under the name Mississippi, while the eastern portion was organized as a Territory, and named Alabama. The whole of this territorry was explored, first by Ferdinand De Soto, and afterward by La Salle. It suffered greatly during the wars of the Natchez Indians. The Choctaws, for a long time, retained possession of the northern portion of it, and were, to some extent, civilized. Mississippi was settled by the French, in 1716, at Natchez. Its population—791,305 —shows fair progress. On the 9th of January, 1861, it went the way of the seceding States, since which time, its course, like theirs, has been downward.

ILLINOIS.

This most thriving and prosperous State came into the Union on the 3d of December, 1818. Until 1809 it was a part of Indiana, at which time it became a separate territory, and so remained till received into the Union. This State has been little disturbed by civil divisions or by Indian wars. Its most serious troubles arose from the appearance, within its borders, of the Mormons, in 1838, and from attempts made to curb their irregularities. This singular people, believing themselves to be ill-treated, assembled to the number of 700, under their leaders, in a remote part of the State, and proposed fighting for their rights. But a body of three hundred troops marched against and captured them. The whole sect was ultimately reduced to submission, and banished the State. It was explored by La Salle, and settled by the French at Kaskaskia,* in 1720. Its growth has been immense. Its population, in 1860, was 1,711,951. Its history has been one of the most glorious of the loyal States during the great Rebellion.

ALABAMA

Was admitted to the Union on the 14th of December, 1819. It has a deep, rich soil, and in many places a healthful climate. It remained till the Revolution a mere hunting-ground of the savages. From the peace of 1783 to 1802 it was claimed by Georgia, and lands were sold to settlers and speculators accordingly. In the year 1802, Georgia ceded all her western territory to the United States for $1,250,000. In 1800, the present State of Alabama became a part of Mississippi Territory, from which it was

* Kaskaskia, the first capital of Illinois, is located on Kaskaskia River, and is the present site of Vandalia.

separated when Mississippi became a State. It was settled, in 1711, at Mobile, by the French, being a part of the territory explored by La Salle in his Mississippi tour. It formally seceded from the Union, January 11, 1861.

MAINE.

In the year 1638, the same year in which New Haven was settled, Ferdinand Gorges procured a charter of the King of England for all the lands from the borders of New Hampshire, on the south-west, to Sagadahoc, on the Kennebeck River, on the north-east, under the name of the Province of Maine. It remained a separate province till 1652, when it became a part of Massachusetts. Various attempts were made, between 1785 and 1802 to form it into an independent State; but these efforts failed. In 1819 a large majority of the people were in favor of separating from Massachusetts. A convention was called, a Constitution prepared and adopted, and, in 1820, Maine was received into the Union. It is, by no means, an agricultural State, but its extensive fisheries and great lumber trade have greatly enriched it, and its progress in morality has, perhaps, been superior to that of any other State. It is the only State in the Union that has an efficient prohibitory liquor law. It proved itself true to the Government in 1861, and there is no danger of its ever ceasing to be so.

It was settled in 1625, at Bristol, by the English. Its population is 628,279.

MISSOURI.

This great, though crippled, State was admitted into the Union on the 10th of August, 1821. It, with all the territory then belonging to the United States, west of the Mississippi, was included in the purchase of Louisiana, made in 1803. Louisiana afterward was divided into Orleans Territory, Louisiana proper, and Missouri Territory. In 1819, Missouri Territory was divided into Arkansas, on the south, and Missouri on the north; and it was about this time that the latter took the requisite steps toward framing a State Constitution. It will be remembered that this is the State, the discussion of the propriety of the admission of which raised such a storm in Congress in 1820.

Being a border slave State, it was nearly equally divided on the question of secession in 1861, and thus, like Kentucky, has been overrun by both Southern and Northern troops during the Rebellion, and has been the scene of much bloodshed and ruin. It was settled in 1764, at St. Louis, by the French. Its population is 1,182,012.

FLORIDA.

The Peninsular States, discovered and explored by Ponce de Leon, a voyager with Columbus, and whose name was suggested to the discoverer by the abundance and beauty of its wild flora, was, from 1512 to 1819, with the exception of the interval between 1763 and 1783, a province of Spain. The first attempt to settle it was made in the year 1565, at St. Augustine, which is said to be the oldest town in America, by the Spaniards. This effort was attended with many difficulties, the colonists contending, for the first few years, alternately with the horrors of savage warfare and famine, at times being forced to subsist on roots and acorns. In 1819 it was transferred to the United States by treaty, which treaty was, after much delay, ratified by Spain, and with still more delay by the United States. Possession of the colony was granted the Government in July, 1821. The territory contained, in 1840, a population of 54,477, and on the 3d of March, 1845, became a State, and was received into the Union. Florida was the theater of the Seminole war, which cost the United States so much blood and treasure. It went the way of the seceding States, January 7th, 1861. Florida, like the Indian's gun, has "cost more than she has come to." Her population in 1860, was 140,425.

ARKANSAS.

This State lies South of Missouri, and was once attached to it. It has a fine climate and prolific soil. The first settlement of whites within its limits was made at Arkansas Post, in the year 1685. The earlier inhabitants were French. Its progress, for many years, was very slow. It was not till about the year 1829 that the tide of emigration began to flow from the Atlantic States in that direction. Little Rock, the early seat of government and the present capital, was laid out in the year 1820, during which year the first steamboat ascended the Arkansas River. The boat was eight days in going from New Orleans to the village of Arkansas—a distance of scarcely one hundred miles above the mouth of the Arkansas River. The State once contained the remnants of several powerful tribes of Indians. By a treaty made between the Cherokees and the United States, the former agreed to give up all their lands east of the Mississippi River, and to retire to a region guaranteed to them in the present State of Arkansas.

The State was admitted into the Union on the 15th of June, 1836. It seceded May 6th, 1861, and has since been the retreat of guerrillas, and the scene of some sanguinary battles.

MICHIGAN.

Was admitted into the Union January 26th, 1837. It had the requisite population (60,000) before this, but there were some difficulties in the way of its admission. In 1837 it contained 200,000; in 1840, 212,267, and in 1850, 851,470. The territory, when first discovered by the whites, contained a tribe of Indians called Hurons by the French, and Iroquois by the Indians themselves. Many of them were converted to Christianity, by the untiring labors of Catholic missionaries, as early as 1648. It was not, however, till 1670 that the French took possession of the territory. It was a portion of the extensive tract explored by the assiduous, daring La Salle. Its progress, while it belonged to the French, was very slow. It was not until 1763, when, by treaty, it was ceded to Great Britain, that much was done in the way of civilizing and improving it. Comparatively little, in fact, was done until 1783, when the territory was ceded by England to the United States. Until 1800 it was, for purposes of Government, considered a part of the Great North-western Territory. After Ohio, Indiana, and Illinois had been severally detached, the remainder, in 1805, became a distinct territory, the first Governor of which was General Hull, by appointment of President Jefferson. Michigan suffered much from the war of 1812. For about two years nearly the whole territory was the theater of sanguinary conflicts. It was exposed to the barbarity of the enemy and their Indian allies. Since then, however, its enterprising inhabitants have brought it up to a degree of improvement which few States of its age can boast. Its strength was offered the Government in 1861, and it continues as well as it began. Its population, in 1860, was 749,113.

IOWA.

This State derives its name from the Indians. It was included in the Louisiana purchase. It was first settled at Dubuque, by the French, in the year 1686. This settlement, however, does not seem to have been permanent, nor productive of any real good to the territory. In 1833 Burlington was settled by emigrants from the eastern States. It formed a part of Missouri from 1804 to 1821, when it was included in Michigan Territory. It subsequently belonged to Wisconsin Territory. It was admitted into the Union March 3d, 1845. It is a highly prosperous State, having a vast extent of rich soil and excellent pasturage. It is faithful to the Union; placed itself in the front rank at the commencement of the Rebellion.

TEXAS.

The territory of Texas was explored by Ponce de Leon and La Salle. After Mexico became independent of Spain, a grant which had been made to Moses Austin, a native of Connecticut, comprising a large tract of this province, was confirmed by the new Republic; and, being transferred by Moses Austin, at his death, to his son, Stephen, was subsequently enlarged by a further grant. Emigration from the United States was encouraged, and in 1830 nearly ten thousand Americans were settled in Texas. The prosperity of these inhabitants excited the jealousy of Mexico, and under the administration of Santa Anna, an unjust, oppressive policy was adopted toward Texas. Remonstrance proving useless, the people of the territory declared themselves independent. The revolution began in 1835, by a battle at Gonzales, in which five hundred Texans defeated over one thousand Mexicans. Other engagements followed, the result of which was the dispersion of the Mexican army. Santa Anna now redoubled his efforts, and appearing in March, 1835, with a force of eight thousand men, several bloody battles followed. On the 21st of April, having under his immediate command one thousand and five hundred men, he was met by General Sam. Houston, with eight hundred men, and totally defeated, on the banks of the San Jacinto. Santa Anna himself was captured the next day in the woods, when he acknowledged the independence of Texas, though the Mexican Congress refused to ratify the act. Active hostilities, however, were now abandoned, and the independence of Texas was acknowledged by the United States, Great Britain, and other European countries. It was in this condition of things that Texas was annexed to the United States. On the 24th of December, 1845, it was admitted into the Union, which act was ratified by the Texan Legislature, July 4th, 1846. But Mexico, still regarding Texas as a revolted province, refused to acknowledge the validity of this measure. The result was a war between Mexico and the United States, which terminated on the 2d of February, 1848, in a treaty by which the latter power, in consideration of the payment of a debt of $3,500,000, due from Mexico to the citizens of Texas, acquired New Mexico, Texas, and California. The progress of Texas from this time till the eve of the great Rebellion, was almost unprecedented, no less than twenty-five thousand Germans having emigrated to that State in five years' time. These, however, owing to the jealousy aroused against them by their having demonstrated the superiority of free labor, even in a slave State, were obliged to migrate to Mexico in the year 1860. By this and other oppressive acts on the part of the advocates of slavery, Texas, purchased by the blood and treasure of the United States, was driven into the whirlpool of secession, March 4th, 1861. Its population, in 1860, was 604,215. The first settlement within its borders was made by the Spaniards, at St. Antonia de Bexar, in 1690.

WISCONSIN

Was admitted into the Union May 29th, 1848. It was a part of the extensive territory ceded by France to Great Britain in the treaty of 1763. At the close of the Revolution it was given up by Great Britain to the United States. It was erected into a territory in 1836, the portion now forming the State of Iowa being detached in 1838. Its natural resources are extraordinary, the climate being very healthful, and the soil unsurpassed in fertility. It was settled in the year 1669, at Green Bay, by the French. It is thoroughly loyal to the Union. In 1860, it had a population of 775,881.

MINNESOTA

Lies north of Iowa, and extends to the Canadian boundary. On the north-east it touches Lake Superior, and, to the west, is bounded by Dakotah Territory. It comprises the head waters of the Mississippi, and abounds in rivers and lakes, teeming with fish. Its soil is highly prolific, and its forests are among the finest in the world. Its name is derived from Minnisotah, the Indian name of St. Peter's River. Primarily discovered by La Salle, it, for some years, belonged to the French, and at a very early period was traversed by their traders and soldiers. It was ceded to Great Britain by the treaty of 1763, and to the United States at the peace of 1783. It received a territorial government in 1849, and was admitted into the Union in May, 1858. It has still, within its borders, several bands of the Chippewas, with whom considerable trouble has been experienced since the breaking out of the rebellion. It is, however, a thrifty, growing State, and is thoroughly loyal. It was settled in 1846, at St. Paul, by emigrants from the eastern States.

OREGON

Was admitted into the Union in the year 1859. It, primarily, included Washington Territory, and, with the latter, comprised the extensive tract lying between the British Possessions, on the north, and California, on the south; the Rocky Mountains, on the east, and the Pacific Ocean, on the west. The coasts of this region were discovered by the Spaniards in the 16th century. In 1792, Capt. Grey, of Boston, discovered and entered the Columbia River, and thus the United States acquired the right of sovereignty over the territory. The exploration of the country from the Missouri to the Columbia, by Lewis and Clark, government appointees, in 1804–5–6, strengthened this claim. The British, however, laid claim to the northern part of the territory, which gave rise to a threatening dispute between Great Britain and the United States. But the difficulty was adjusted by a treaty in 1846, establishing the boundary of 49°, north latitude. The State still contains the Flathead, Pend Oreille, Spokane, Shoshane, and other tribes of Indians, who are, for the most part, in the savage state, though the Christian missionaries have done much in the way of civilizing a portion of them. The furs of this region, those of the badger, beaver, bear, fisher-fox, lynx, martin, mink, muskrat, etc., have long been a great source of revenue.

The American fur companies established trading posts in Oregon at an early period, that of Astoria being founded in 1810, under the auspices of the late John Jacob Astor, of New York. It was settled, at Astoria, by emigrants from the Eastern States, in the year 1811. Its population amounted to 52,465 in 1860.

KANSAS.

About the development of this young State cluster some of the most important events of American history. Its territorial organization, by the passage of the Kansas-Nebraska Bill, in 1854, re-opened the agitation of the slavery question, which seeming to have acquired fresh vigor and virulence from the sleep it had enjoyed under the Missouri Compromise, thoroughly aroused the old animosities between the pro and antislavery elements of our national politics. From 1854 to 1857 it was the theater of political tragedies, the bare mention of which may well put the blush of shame upon even the most fool-hardy partisan; and the historian has well said that these dire afflictions might have been expected when the bill organizing Kansas Territory was passed. No sooner was it decided that this territory was open alike to the abolitionist and the slave-holder, than the Emigrant Aid Societies of New England and the pro-slavery organizations of the South began pouring streams of settlers into it of opposite political views, entertaining the most hostile feelings, each party toward the other; and, as the legitimate result, came a civil war, which lasted about two years, and which, in some of its incidents would have shamed even savages.

The Territory made application to Congress, in 1857, for a place in the Union, but the Constitution under which it asked admission (the one framed at Lecompton) was known to be a fraudulent affair, and hence Kansas was rejected. The discussion of this Constitution caused a permanent division of the Democratic party. The Constitution was rejected by the people of Kansas by a majority of 10,000. Kansas was, however received into the Union, in 1861, under a free State Constitution, formed at Topeka.

CALIFORNIA

Was admitted into the Union on the 7th of September, 1850. The alarming discussion which occured upon the question of admission was what gave rise to the compromise measures of 1850, popularly styled the *Omnibus Bill*. The measures are presented in detail in another part of this work.

General Fremont, with a small but dauntless band of rangers, conquered California in 1846, having defeated, on frequent occasions, vastly superior forces of Mexicans. Its resources as a farming country early attracted attention. But when, in February, 1848, it was published that gold in quantities had been found on a branch of the Sacramento, the swarm of emigrants which rushed in, comprising representatives from every State in the Union, and from nearly all the nations of Europe, was almost incalculable. From a small village, San Francisco was rapidly inflated to a large city. In many places towns sprang up like mushrooms. Owing to the fact that its population had been thrown hastily together, from so many places, and in consequence of the want of a government, California was, for some time, the scene of many dark crimes and hideous outrages. Never was the want of wholesome legal restraint more keenly felt than here. The Constitution of California was framed by a convention of delegates in 1849. It took a firm stand for the Union in 1861. The first settlement, within its limits, was made at San Diego, by the Spanish, in 1764. It furnishes annually to the Government, seventy to eighty millions of dollars in gold.

WEST VIRGINIA.

On Virginia's passing the ordinance of secession, mass meetings were immediately held in West Virginia, to take into consideration the best means of preserving their allegiance to the United States. A convention of nearly five hundred delegates assembled there early in May, 1861, which declared the ordinance of secession to be null and void, and elected delegates to a general convention, to meet at Wheeling, to devise such measures as the welfare of the people might demand. On the 20th of August, 1861, the convention passed an ordinance to provide for the formation of a new State out of a portion of the territory of Virginia. In compliance with its provisions, delegates were elected to a constitutional convention, which assembled at Wheeling, November 26, 1861, which proceeded to draft a Constitution, which was submitted to the people on the first Thursday of April, 1862. The vote in favor was 18,862; that against 514. On the 31st of December, 1862, Congress passed an act admitting West Virginia into the Union on an equal footing with the original States, in all respects whatever, allowing them three members in the House of Representatives of the United States. On the 1st of November, 1862, the State had furnished to the Federal Army nearly 20,000 men.

NEVADA.

This Territory having formed a State Constitution, under an enabling act previously passed by Congress, was admitted as a member of the Federal Union, on an equal footing with the original States. The State convention was held at so late a period of the year, that it was necessary to telegraph the Constitution to Washington, in order that it might be received there in time to secure the admission of the State previous to the Presidential election. Immediately upon its reception, President Lincoln issued a proclamation, dated October 31st, A. D. 1864, in which he "declared and proclaimed that the said State of Nevada is admitted into the Union, on an equal footing with the original States," etc. The vote of the State at the Presidential election, in 1864, was 16,420—of which Mr. Lincoln received 9,826, and General McClellan 6,594. Majority for Mr. Lincoln, 3,232. This new State is probably the richest in the Union in respect to mineral resources. No region in the world is richer in argentiferous leads. Her silver mines are her great source of wealth. The Washoe region maintains the preëminence in these mineral resources.

NEBRASKA.

Nebraska was organized into a Territory in 1850. The first settlers were Americans. In the last few years it has increased in wealth and population more rapidly than any of the adjoining States or Territories, Probably the chief cause of this has been occasioned by the Pacific Railroad passing directly through the State from east to west. It is impossible, at the present time, to estimate the advantage it will be to the State in developing its resources. The value of its minerals in the western portion of the State is incalculable. It has fair prospects of becoming one of the richest mineral and agricultural States in the Union. Omaha, the capital, is a city of considerable commercial importance, being located at the junction of the Missouri River and the Pacific Railroad. In 1866, the Territory applied for admission into the Union, but, on account of the word "white" being used in its Constitution, it was rejected. The word was then stricken out, after which it was admitted, February, 1867—the bill for admission having been passed over the President's veto.

COLORADO.

Colorado was organized as a Territory March 2, 1861, from parts of Kansas, Nebraska, and Utah.

March 3, 1875, it was admitted into the Union of States — the thirty-eighth.

It is situated on each side of the Rocky Mountains, and has an area of 106,475 square miles. It is a superior grazing and cattle producing region, with a healthy climate and rich soil. An extensive coal-bed, and also gold, iron, and other minerals abound. Its population is rapidly increasing. Several growing towns serve as centers of supply and trade, and offer fine facilities for schools and churches. The "Colorado Springs," near Denver, are much resorted to, especially by asthmatics. The scenery at Pike's Peak and many of the canyons is sublimely grand and beautiful.

PROPOSED CRITTENDEN COMPROMISE.

At the commencement of the Congressional session of 1860, the portentous clouds of civil war, gathering and blackening in the southern horizon of our national sky, filled the hearts of the stoutest patriots with the most gloomy apprehensions, and cast a melancholy shadow over every Union-loving soul throughout the country, somewhat akin to that which hovers over an affectionate son or daughter, upon the approaching dissolution of a cherished, devoted mother. The following compromise, offered by Senator Crittenden, December 19, 1860, is one of the many measures proposed in Congress for adjusting the difficulties of that period:

Resolved, *By the Senate and House of Representatives*, That the following articles be proposed and submitted as an amendment to the Constitution, which shall be valid as a part of the Constitution, when ratified by the conventions of three-fourths of the people of the States:

1st. In all the territory now or hereafter acquired, north of 36° 30′, slavery, or involuntary servitude, except for the punishment of crime, is prohibited; while in all the territory south of that, slavery is hereby recognized as existing, and shall not be interfered with by Congress, but shall be protected as property by all the departments of the territorial government during its continuance. All the territory north or south of said line, within such boundaries as Congress may prescribe, when it contains a population necessary for a member of Congress, with a Republican form of government, shall be admitted into the Union on an equality with the original States, with or without slavery, as the Constitution of the State shall prescribe.

2d. Congress shall have no power to abolish slavery in the State permitting it.

3d. Congress shall have no power to abolish slavery in the District of Columbia while it exists in Virginia and

Maryland, or either; nor shall Congress at any time prohibit the officers of Government, or members of Congress, whose duties require them to live in the District of Columbia, bringing slaves there and using them as such.

4th. Congress shall have no power to hinder the transportation of slaves from one State to another, whether by land, navigable river, or sea.

5th. Congress shall have the power, by law, to pay any owner the full value of any fugitive slave, in all cases where the marshal is prevented from discharging his duty by force or rescue, made after arrest. In all such cases the owner shall have the power to sue the county in which the rescue or violence was made; and the county shall have the right to sue the individuals who committed the wrong, in the same manner as the owner would sue.

6th. No future amendment or amendments shall affect the preceding article; and Congress shall never have power to interfere with slavery within the States where it is permitted.

LINCOLN'S EMANCIPATION PROCLAMATION.

Whereas, On the twenty-second day of September, in the year of our Lord, one thousand eight hundred and sixty-two, a proclamation was issued by the President of the United States, containing among other things the following, to wit:

That, on the first day of January, in the year of our Lord, one thousand eight hundred and sixty-three, all persons held as slaves within any State, or designated part of a State, the people whereof shall then be in rebellion against the United States, shall be then, thenceforth and forever free, and the Executive Government of the United States, including the military and naval authorities thereof, will recognize and maintain the freedom of such persons, or any of them, in any efforts they may make for their actual freedom.

That the Executive will, on the first day of January aforesaid, by proclamation, designate the States and parts of States, if any, in which the people therein respectively shall then be in rebellion against the United States, and the fact that any State, or the people thereof, shall on that day be in good faith represented in the Congress of the United States by members chosen thereto, at elections wherein a majority of the qualified voters of such States shall have participated, shall, in the absence of strong countervailing testimony, be deemed conclusive evidence that such State and the people thereof are not then in rebellion against the United States.

Now, therefore, I, Abraham Lincoln, President of the United States, by virtue of the power in me vested as Commander-in-Chief of the Army and Navy of the United States, in time of actual armed rebellion against the authority and Government of the United States, and as a fit

A. Lincoln

necessary war measure for suppressing said rebellion, do, on this first day of January, in the year of our Lord, one thousand eight hundred and sixty-three, and in accordance with my purpose so to do, publicly proclaimed for the full period of one hundred days from the day of the first above-mentioned order, and designate, as the States and parts of States wherein the people thereof respectively are this day in rebellion against the United States, the following, to wit: Arkansas, Texas, Louisiana, except the parishes of St. Bernard, Plaquemines, Jefferson, St. John, St. Charles, St. James, Ascension, Assumption, Terre Bonne, Lafourche, St. Mary, St. Martin and Orleans, including the city of New Orleans. Mississippi, Alabama, Florida, Georgia, South Carolina, North Carolina, and Virginia, except the forty-eight counties designated as West Virginia, and also the counties of Berkeley, Accomac, Northampton, Elizabeth City, York, Princess Ann, and Norfolk, including the cities of Norfolk and Portsmouth, and which excepted parts are, for the present, left precisely as if this proclamation were not issued.

And by virtue of the power, and for the purpose aforesaid, I do order and declare that all persons held as slaves within said designated States and parts of States are, and henceforward, shall be free; and that the Executive Government of the United States, including the military and naval authorities thereof, will recognize and maintain the freedom of said persons.

And I hereby enjoin upon the people so declared to be free to abstain from all violence, unless in necessary self-defense; and I recommend to them that, in all cases, when allowed, they labor faithfully for reasonable wages.

And I further declare and make known that such persons of suitable condition will be received into the armed service of the United States, to garrison forts, positions, stations, and other places, and to man vessels of all sorts in said service.

And upon this, sincerely believed to be an act of justice, warranted by the Constitution upon military necessity, I invoke the considerate judgment of mankind and the gracious favor of Almighty God.

In witness whereof I have hereunto set my hand and caused the seal of the United States to be affixed.

Done at the City of Washington, this first day of January, in the year of our Lord one thousand eight hundred and sixty-three, and of the Independence of the United States of America the eighty-seventh.

By the President: ABRAHAM LINCOLN.

WILLIAM H. SEWARD, *Secretary of State.*

LETTER FROM THE PRESIDENT EXPLAINING THE EMANCIPATION PROCLAMATION.

The following letter, written in August, 1863, in answer to an invitation to attend a meeting of unconditional Union men held in Illinois, gives at length the President's views at that time on his Emancipation Proclamation:

EXECUTIVE MANSION, WASHINGTON, August 26th, 1863.

MY DEAR SIR: Your letter inviting me to attend a mass-meeting of unconditional Union men, to be held at the capitol of Illinois on the third day of September, has been received. It would be very agreeable to me to thus meet my old friends at my own home, but I can not just now be absent from this city so long as a visit there would require. The meeting is to be of all those who maintain unconditional devotion to the Union; and I am sure my old political friends will thank me for tendering, as I do, the nation's gratitude to those other noble men whom no partisan malice or partisan hope can make false to the nation's life. There are those who are dissatisfied with me. To such I would say, You desire peace, and you blame me that you do not have it. But how can we attain it? There are but three conceivable ways: First, to suppress the rebellion by force of arms. This I am trying to do. Are you for it? If you are, so far we are agreed. If you are not for it, a second way is to give up the Union. I am against this. If you are, you should say so, plainly. If you are not for force, nor yet for dissolution, there only remains some imaginable compromise. I do not believe that any compromise, embracing the maintenance of the Union, is now possible. All that I learn leads to a directly opposite belief. The strength of the rebellion is its military—its army. The army dominates all the country and all the people within its range. Any offer of any terms made by any man or men within that range, in opposition to that army, is simply nothing for the present, because such man or men have no power whatever to enforce their side of a compromise, if one were made with them. To illustrate: Suppose refugees from the South and peace men of the North get together in convention, and frame and proclaim a compromise embracing a restoration of the Union; in what way can that compromise be used to keep General Lee's army out of Pennsylvania? General Meade's army can keep Lee's army out of Pennsylvania, and, I think, can ultimately drive it out of existence. But no paper compromise, to which the controllers of Lee's army are not agreed, can at all affect that army. In an effort at such compromise we would waste time, which the enemy would improve to our disadvantage, and that would be all. A compromise, to be effective, must be made either with those who control the rebel army, or with the people, first liberated from the domination of that army by the success of our army. Now, allow me to assure you that no word or intimation from the rebel army, or from any of the men controlling it, in relation to any peace compromise, has ever come to my knowledge or belief. All charges and intimations to the contrary are deceptive and groundless. And I promise you that if any such proposition shall hereafter come, it shall not be rejected and kept secret from you. I freely acknowledge myself to be the servant of the people, according to the bond of service, the United States Constitution, and that, as such, I am responsible to them. But, to be plain: You are dissatisfied with me about the negro. Quite likely there is a difference of opinion between you and myself upon that subject. I certainly wish that all men could be free, while you, I suppose, do not. Yet I have neither adopted nor proposed any measure which is not consistent with even your view, provided you are for the Union. I suggested compensated emancipation; to which you replied that you wished not to be taxed to buy negroes. But I have not asked you to be taxed to buy negroes, except in such way as to save you from greater taxation, to save the Union exclusively by other means.

You dislike the Emancipation Proclamation, and perhaps would have it retracted. You say it is unconstitutional. I think differently: I think that the Constitution invests the Commander-in-Chief with the law of war in time of war. The most that can be said, if so much, is, that the slaves are property. Is there—has there ever been—any question that, by the law of war, property, both of enemies and friends, may be taken when needed? And is it not needed whenever taking it helps us, or hurts the enemy? Armies, the world over, destroy enemies' property when they can not use it; and even destroy their own to keep it from the enemy. Civilized belligerents do all in their power to help themselves or hurt the enemy, except a few things regarded as barbarous or cruel. Among the exceptions are the massacre of vanquished foes and non-combatants, male and female. But the proclamation, as law, is valid, or is not valid. If it is not valid, it needs no retraction; if it is valid, it can not be retracted, any more than the dead can be brought to life. Some of you profess to think that its retraction would operate favorably for the Union. Why better after the retraction than before the issue? There was more than a year and a half of trial to suppress the rebellion before the proclamation was issued, the last one hundred days of which passed under an explicit notice that it was coming, unless averted by those in revolt returning to their allegiance. The war has certainly progressed as favorably for us since the issue of the proclamation as before. I know as fully as one can know the opinion of others, that some of the commanders of our armies in the field, who have given us our most important victories, believe the emancipation policy and the aid of colored troops to be the heaviest blows yet dealt to the rebellion, and that at least one of these important successes could not have been achieved when it was but for the aid of black soldiers. Among the commanders holding these views are some who have never had any affinity with what is called abolitionism or with "Republican party politics," but who hold them purely as military opinions. I submit their opinions as being entitled to some weight against the objections often urged, that emancipation and arming the blacks are unwise as military measures, and were not adopted as such in good faith. You say that you will not fight to free negroes. Some of them seem to be willing to fight for you—but no matter. Fight you, then, exclusively, to save the Union. I issued the proclamation on purpose to aid you in saving the Union. Whenever you shall have conquered all resistance to the Union, if I shall urge you to continue fighting, it will be an apt time then for you to declare that you will not fight to free negroes. I thought that, in your struggle for the Union, to whatever extent the negroes should cease helping the enemy, to that extent it weakened the enemy in his resistance to you. Do you think differently? I thought that whatever negroes can be got to do as soldiers, leaves just so much less for white soldiers to do in saving the Union. Does it appear otherwise to you? But negroes, like other people, act upon motives. Why should they do any thing for us if we will not do any thing for them? If they stake their lives for us, they must be prompted by the strongest motive, even the promise of freedom. And, the promise being made, must be kept. The signs look better. The Father of Waters again goes unvexed to the sea. Thanks to the great North-west for it. Not yet wholly to them. Three hundred miles up they met New England, Empire, Keystone, and Jersey, hewing their way right and left. The Sunny South, too, in more colors than one, also lent a hand. On the spot, their part of the history was jotted down in black and white. The job was a great national one, and let none be blamed who bore an honorable part in it; and, while those who have cleared the great river may well be proud, even that is not all. It is hard to say that any thing has been more bravely or better done than at Antietam, Murfreesboro', Gettysburg, and on many fields of less note. Nor must Uncle Sam's web-fleet be forgotten. At all the waters' margins they have been present—not only on the deep sea, the broad bay, and the rapid river, but also up the narrow, muddy bayou; and, wherever the ground was a little damp, they have been, and made their tracks. Thanks to all. For the great republic—for the principles by which it lives and keeps alive—for man's vast future—thanks to all. Peace does not appear so far distant as it did. I hope it will come soon, and come to stay; and so come as to be worth keeping in all future time. It will then have proved that among freemen there can be no successful appeal from the ballot to the bullet, and that they who take such appeal are sure to lose their case and pay the cost. And then there will be some black men who can remember that, with silent tongue, and clenched teeth, and steady eye, and well-poised bayonet, they have helped mankind on to this great consummation; while I fear that there will be some white men unable to forget that, with maglignant heart and deceitful speech, they have striven to hinder it. Still, let us not be over-sanguine of a speedy final triumph. Let us be quite sober. Let us diligently apply the means, never doubting that a just God, in His own good time, will give us the rightful result.

Yours, very truly, A. LINCOLN.

JOHNSON'S AMNESTY PROCLAMATION.

By the President of the United States of America:

WHEREAS, The President of the United States, on the 8th day of December, 1863, and on the 26th day of March, 1864, did, with the object of suppressing the existing rebellion, to induce all persons to return to their loyalty and to restore the authority of the United States, issued Proclamations offering amnesty and pardon to certain persons who had directly or by implication engaged in said rebellion, and

WHEREAS, Many persons who had so engaged in the said rebellion, have, since the issue of said Proclamation, failed or neglected to take the benefits offered thereby; and whereas, many persons who have been justly deprived of all claim to amnesty and pardon thereunder by reason of their participation directly or by implication in said rebellion, and continued hostile to the Government of the United States since the date of said Proclamation, now desire to apply for and obtain amnesty and pardon; to the end, therefore, that the authority of the Government of the United States may be restored, and that peace, order, and freedom may be established.

I, Andrew Johnson, President of the United States, do proclaim and declare that I hereby grant to all persons who have directly or indirectly participated in the existing rebellion, except as hereinafter excepted, amnesty and pardon, with the restoration of all the rights of property, except as to slaves, except in cases where legal proceedings under the laws of the United States, providing for the confiscation of property of persons engaged in the rebellion, have been instituted; but on the condition, nevertheless, that every such person shall take and subscribe the following oath, which shall be registered for permanent preservation, and shall be the tenor and effect of the following, to wit:

"I do solemnly swear or affirm, in the presence of Almighty God, that I will henceforth faithfully defend the Constitution of the United States and the Union of the States thereunder; and that I will in like manner abide by and faithfully support all laws and proclamations which have been made during the existing rebellion, with reference to the emancipation of slavery, so help me God."

The following classes of persons are excepted from the benefits of this proclamation:

First—All who are, or shall have been, pretended civil or diplomatic officers or otherwise, domestic or foreign agents of the pretended Confederate Government.

Second—All who left judicial stations under the United States to aid the rebellion.

Third—All who shall have been military or naval officers of said pretended Confederate Government above the rank of Colonel in the Army, or Lieutenant in the Navy.

Fourth—All who left seats in the Congress of the United States to aid the rebellion.

Fifth—All who resigned or tendered the resignation of their commissions in the Army or Navy of the United States, to evade the duty in resisting the rebellion.

Sixth—All who have engaged in any way in treating otherwise than lawfully as prisoners of war, persons found in the United States service, as officers, soldiers, seamen, or in other capacities.

Seventh—All persons who have been or are absentees from the United States for the purpose of aiding the rebellion.

Eighth—All military or naval officers in the rebel service who were educated by the Government in the military academy at West Point, or in the United States Naval Academy.

Ninth—All persons who hold the pretended offices of Governors of States in insurrection against the United States.

Tenth—All persons who left their homes within the jurisdiction and protection of the United States and passed beyond the Federal military lines into the so-called Confederate States for the purpose of aiding the rebellion.

Eleventh—All persons who have engaged in the destruction of the commerce of the United States upon the high seas, and all persons who have made raids into the United States from Canada, or been engaged in destroying the commerce of the United States upon the lakes and rivers that separate the British Provinces from the United States.

Twelfth—All persons who, at the time when they seek to obtain the benefits hereof, by taking the oath prescribed, are in military, naval or civil confinement or custody, or under bond of the military or naval authorities, or agents of the United States, as prisoners of war, or persons detailed for offenses of any kind, either before or after the conviction.

Thirteenth—All persons who have voluntarily participated in said rebellion, and the estimate value of whose taxable property is over $20,000.

Fourteenth—All persons who have taken the oath of Amnesty as prescribed in the President's Proclamation, December 28th, 1863, or the Oath of Allegiance to the Government of the United States since the date of said Proclamation, and who have not thenceforward kept and maintained the same inviolate. Provided that special application may be made to the President for pardon by any person belonging to the excepted class, and such clemency will be liberally extended as may be consistent with the facts, and the peace and dignity of the United States. The Secretary of State will establish rules and regulations for administering and recording said Amnesty Oath, so as to insure its benefits to the people, and guard the Government against fraud.

IN TESTIMONY WHEREOF, I have hereunto set my hand and caused the Seal of the United States to be affixed. Done at the City of Washington, this 29th day of May, A. D. 1865, and of the Independence of the United States, the eighty-ninth.

SEAL

(Signed.)

By the President: ANDREW JOHNSON.

W. H. SEWARD, *Secretary of State.*

IMPEACHMENT TRIAL OF ANDREW JOHNSON.

THE events which led to the impeachment of President Johnson, may be briefly stated as follows: On the 21st of February, 1868, the President issued an order to Mr. Stanton, removing him from office as Secretary of War, and another to General Lorenzo Thomas, Adjutant-General of the Army, appointing him Secretary of War *ad interim*, directing the one to surrender and the other to receive, all the books, papers, and public property belonging to the War Department. As these orders fill an important place in the history of the impeachment, we give them here. The order to Mr. Stanton reads:

"By virtue of the power and authority vested in me as President by the Constitution and laws of the United States, you are hereby removed from office as Secretary for the Department of War, and your functions as such will terminate upon the receipt of this communication. You will transfer to Brevet Major-General Lorenzo Thomas, Adjutant-General of the Army, who has this day been authorized and empowered to act as Secretary of War *ad interim*, all records, books, papers, and other public property now in your custody and charge."

The order to General Thomas reads:

"The Hon. Edwin M. Stanton having been this day removed from office as Secretary for the Department of War, you are hereby authorized and empowered to act as Secretary of War *ad interim*, and will immediately enter upon the discharge of the duties pertaining to that office. Mr. Stanton has been instructed to transfer to you all the records, books, and other public property now in his custody and charge."

These orders having been officially communicated to the Senate, that body, after an earnest debate, passed the following resolution:

"*Resolved by the Senate of the United States*, That under the Constitution and laws of the United States the President has no power to remove the Secretary of War and designate any other officer to perform the duties of that office."

The President, upon the 24th, sent a message to the Senate, arguing at length that not only under the Constitution, but also under the laws as now existing, he had the right of removing Mr. Stanton and appointing another to fill his place. The point of his argument is: That by a special proviso in the Tenure-of-Office Bill the various Secretaries of Departments "shall hold their offices respectively for and during the term of the President by whom they may have been appointed, and for one month thereafter, subject to removal by and with the advice of the Senate." The President affirms that Mr. Stanton was appointed not by him, but by his predecessor, Mr. Lincoln, and held office only by the sufferance, not the appointment, of the present Executive; and that therefore his tenure is, by the express reading of the law excepted from the general provision, that every person duly appointed to office "by and with the advice and consent of the Senate," etc., shall be "entitled to hold office until a successor shall have been in like manner appointed and duly qualified, except as herein otherwise provided." The essential point of the President's argument, therefore, is that, as Mr. Stanton was not appointed by him, he had, under the Tenure-of-Office Bill, the right at any time to remove him; the same right which his own successor would have, no matter whether the incumbent had, by sufferance, not by appointment of the existing Executive, held the office for weeks or even years. "If," says the President, "my successor would have the power to remove Mr. Stanton, after permitting him to remain a period of two weeks, because he was not appointed by him, I who have tolerated Mr. Stanton for more than two years, certainly have the same right to remove him, and upon the same ground, namely, that he was not appointed by me but by my predecessor."

In the meantime General Thomas presented himself at the War Department and demanded to be placed in the position to which he had been assigned by the President. Mr. Stanton refused to surrender his post, and ordered General Thomas to proceed to the apartment which belonged to him as Adjutant-General. This order was not obeyed, and so the two claimants to the Secretaryship of War held their ground. A sort of legal by-play then ensued. Mr. Stanton entered a formal complaint before Judge Carter, Chief Justice of the Supreme Court of the District of Columbia, charging that General Thomas had illegally exercised and attempted to exercise the duties of Secretary of War; and had threatened to "forcibly remove the complainant from the buildings and apartments of the Secretary of War in the War Department, and forcibly take possession and control thereof under his pretended appointment by the President of the United States as Secretary of War *ad interim;*" and praying that he might be arrested and held to answer this charge. General Thomas was accordingly arrested, and held to bail in the sum of $15,000 to appear before the court on the 24th. Appearing on that day he was discharged from custody and bail; whereupon he entered an action against Mr. Stanton for false imprisonment, laying his damages at $150,000.

On the 22d of February the House Committee on Reconstruction, through its Chairman, Mr. Stevens, presented a brief report, merely stating the fact of the attempted removal by the President of Mr. Stanton, and closing as follows:

"Upon the evidence collected by the Committee, which is hereafter presented, and in virtue of the powers with which they have been invested by the House, they are of the opinion that Andrew Johnson, President of the United States, should be impeached of high crimes and misdemeanors. They, therefore, recommend to the House the adoption of the following resolution:

"*Resolved*, That Andrew Johnson, President of the United States be impeached of high crimes and misdemeanors."

After earnest debate, the question on the resolution was adopted, on the 24th, by a vote of 126 to 47. A committee of two members—Stevens and Bingham—were to notify the Senate of the action of the House; and another committee of seven—Boutwell, Stevens, Bingham, Wilson, Logan, Julian, and Ward—to prepare the articles of impeachment. On the 25th (February) Mr. Stevens thus announced to the Senate the action which had been taken by the House:

"In obedience to the order of the House of Representatives we have appeared before you, and in the name of the House of Representatives and of all the people of the United States, we do impeach Andrew Johnson, President of the United States, of high crimes and misdemeanors in office. And we further inform the Senate that the House of Representatives will in due time exhibit particular articles of impeachment against him, to make good the same; and in their name we demand that the Senate take due order for the appearance of the said Andrew Johnson to answer to the said impeachment."

The Senate thereupon, by a unanimous vote, resolved that this message from the House should be referred to a select Committee of Seven, to be appointed by the chair, to consider the same and report thereon. This Committee subsequently made a report laying down the rules of procedure to be observed on the trial.

On the 29th of February the Committee of the House appointed for that purpose presented the articles of impeachment which they had drawn up. These, with slight modification, were accepted on the 2d of March. They comprise nine articles, eight of which are based upon the action of the President in ordering the removal of Mr. Stanton, and the appointment of General Thomas as Secretary of War. The general title to the impeachment is:

"Articles exhibited by the House of Representatives of the United States, in the name of themselves and all the people of the United States, against Andrew Johnson, President of the United States, as maintenance and support of their impeachment against him for high crimes and misdemeanors in office."

Each of the articles commences with a preamble to the effect that the President, "unmindful of the high duties of his office, of his oath of office, and of the requirements of the Constitution that he should take care that the laws be faithfully executed, did unlawfully and in violation of the laws and Constitution of the United States, perform the several acts specified in the articles respectively;" closing with the declaration: "Whereby the said Andrew Johnson, President of the United States, did then and there commit and was guilty of a high misdemeanor in office." The phraseology is somewhat varied. In some cases the offense charged is designated as a "misdemeanor," in others as a "crime." The whole closes thus:

"And the House of Representatives, by protestation, saving to themselves the liberty of exhibiting at any time hereafter any further articles or other accusation or impeacement against the said Andrew Johnson, President of the United States, and also of replying to his answers which he shall make to the articles herein preferred against him, and of offering proof to the same and every part thereof, and to all and every other article, accusation, or impeachment which shall be exhibited by them as the case shall require, do demand that the said Andrew Johnson may be put to answer the high crimes and misdemeanors in office herein charged against him, and that such proceedings, examinations, trials, and judgments may be thereupon had and given as may be agreeable to law and justice."

The following is a summary in brief of the points in the articles of impeachment, legal and technical phraseology being omitted:

Article 1. Unlawfully ordering the removal of Mr. Stanton as Secretary of War, in violation of the provisions of the Tenure-of-Office Act.—*Article* 2. Unlawfully appointing General Lorenzo Thomas as Secretary of War *ad interim*.—*Article* 3 is substantially the same as Article 2, with the addition that there was at the time of the appointment of General Thomas no vacancy in the office of Secretary of War.—*Article* 4 charges the President with "conspiring with one Lorenzo Thomas and other persons, to the House of Representatives unknown," to prevent, by intimidation and threats, Mr. Stanton, the legally-appointed Secretary of War, from holding that office.—*Article* 5 charges the President with conspiring with General Thomas and others to hinder the execution of the Tenure-of-Office Act; and, in pursuance of this conspiracy, attempting to prevent Mr. Stanton from acting as Secretary of War.—*Article* 6 charges that the President conspired with General Thomas and others to take forcible possession of the property in the War Department.—*Article* 7 repeats the charge, in other terms, that the President conspired with General Thomas and others to hinder the execution of the Tenure-of-Office Act, and to prevent Mr. Stanton from executing the office of Secretary of War.—*Article* 8 again charges the President with conspiring with General Thomas and others to take possession of the property in the War Department.—*Article* 9 charges that the President called before him General Emory, who was in command of the forces in the Department of Washington, and declared to him that a law, passed on the 30th of June, 1867, directing that "all orders and instructions relating to military operations, issued by the President or Secretary of War, shall be issued through the Gen eral of the Army, and, in case of his inability, through the next in rank," was unconstitutional, and not binding upon General Emory; the intent being to induce General Emory to violate the law, and to obey orders issued directly from the President.

The foregoing articles of impeachment were adopted on the 2d of March, the votes upon each slightly varying, the average being 125 ayes to 40 nays. The question then came up of appointment of managers on the part of the House to conduct the impeachment before the Senate. Upon this question the Democratic members did not vote; 118 votes were cast, 60 being necessary to a choice. The following was the result, the number of votes cast for each elected manager being given: Stevens, of Penn., 105; Butler, of Mass., 108; Bingham, of Ohio, 114; Boutwell, of Mass., 113; Wilson, of Iowa, 112; Williams, of Penn., 107; Logan, of Ill., 106. The foregoing seven Representatives were, therefore, duly chosen as Managers of the Bill of Impeachment. The great body of the Democratic members of the House entered a formal protest against the whole course of proceedings involved in the impeachment of the President. They claimed to represent "directly or in principle more than one-half of the people of the United States." This protest was signed by forty-five Representatives.

On the 3d the Board of Managers presented two additional articles of impeachment, which were adopted by the House. The first charges, in substance, that

"The President, unmindful of the high duties of his office and of the harmony and courtesies which ought to be maintained between the executive and legislative branches of the Government of the United States, designing to set aside the rightful authority and powers of Congress, did attempt to bring into disgrace the Congress of the United States and the several branches thereof, to impair and destroy the regard and respect of all the good people of the United States for the Congress and legislative power thereof, and to excite the odium and resentment of all the good people of the United States against Congress and the laws by it enacted; and in pursuance of his said design openly and publicly, and before divers assemblages convened in divers parts thereof to meet and receive said Andrew Johnson as the Chief Magistrate of the United States, did on the 18th day of August, in the year of our Lord 1866, and on divers other days and times, as well before as afterward, make and deliver with a loud voice certain intemperate, inflammatory, and scandalous harangues, and did therein utter loud threats and bitter menaces as well against Congress as the laws of the United States duly enacted thereby."

To this article are appended copious extracts from speeches of Mr. Johnson. The second article is substantially as follows:

"The President did, on the 18th day of August, 1866, at the City of Washington, by public speech, declare and affirm in substance that the Thirty-ninth Congress of the United States was not a Congress of the United States, authorized by the Constitution to exercise legislative power under the same, but, on the contrary, was a Congress of only a part of the States, thereby denying and intending to deny that the legislation of said Congress was valid or obligatory upon him, except in so far as he saw fit to approve the same, and did devise and contrive means by which he might prevent Edwin M. Stanton from forthwith resuming the functions of the office of Secretary for the Department of War; and, also, by further unlawfully devising and contriving means to prevent the execution of an act entitled 'An act making appropriations for the support of the army for the fiscal year ending June 30, 1868, and for other purposes,' approved March 2, 1867; and also to prevent the execution of an act entitled 'An act to provide for the more efficient government of the rebel States,' passed March 2, 1867, did commit and was guilty of a high misdemeanor in office."

On the 4th of March the Senate notified the House that they were ready to receive the Managers of the Impeachment. They appeared, and the articles were formally read. The Senate had meanwhile adopted the rules of procedure. Chief Justice Chase sent a communication to the Senate to the effect that this body, when acting upon an impeachment, was a Court presided over by the Chief Justice, and that all orders and rules should be framed by the Court. On the 5th the Court was formally organized. An exception was taken to the eligibility of Mr. Wade as a member of the Court, on the ground that he was a party interested, since, in the event of the impeachment being sustained, he, as President of the Senate, would become Acting President of the United States. This objection was withdrawn, and Mr. Wade was sworn as a member of the Court. On the 7th the summons for the President to appear was formally served upon him. On the 13th the Court was again formally reopened. The President appeared by his counsel, Hon. Henry Stanbery, of Ohio; Hon. Wm. M. Evarts, of New York; Hon. Wm. S. Groesbeck, of Ohio; Hon. Benjamin R. Curtis, of Massachusetts; Hon. Thomas A. R. Nelson, of Tennessee, who asked for forty days to prepare an answer to the indictment. This was refused, and ten days granted; it being ordered that the proceedings should reopen on the 23d. Upon that day the President appeared by his counsel, and presented his answer to the articles of impeachment. This reply was in substance as follows:

The first eight articles in the Bill of Impeachment, as briefly summed up in our last record, are based upon the action of the President in ordering the removal of Mr. Stanton, and the temporary appointment of General Thomas as Secretary of War. The gist of them is contained in the first article, charging the unlawful removal of Mr. Stanton; for, this failing, the others would fail also. To this article a considerable part of the President's answer is devoted. It is mainly an amplification of the points put forth in the Message of February 24th, in which he gave his reasons for his orders. The President cites the laws by which this department of the administration was created, and the rules laid down for the duties pertaining to it; prominent among which are: that the Secretary shall "conduct the business of the department in such manner as the President of the United States shall from time to time order and instruct;" and that he should "hold the office during the pleasure of the President;" and that Congress had no legal right to deprive the President of the power to remove the Secretary. He was, however, aware that the design of the Tenure-of-Office Bill was to vest this power of removal, in certain cases, jointly in the Executive and the Senate; and that, while believing this act to be unconstitutional, yet it having been passed over his veto by the requisite majority of two-thirds, he considered it to be his duty to ascertain in how far the case of Mr. Stanton came within the provisions of this law; after consideration, he came to the conclusion that the case did not come within the prohibitions of the law, and that, by that law he still had the right of removing Mr. Stanton; but that, wishing to have the case decided by the Supreme Court, he, on the 12th of August, issued the order merely suspending, not removing, Mr. Stanton, a power expressly granted by the Tenure-of-Office Act, and appointed General Grant Secretary of War *ad interim*. The President then recites the subsequent action in the case of Mr. Stanton; and, as he avers, still believing that he had the constitutional power to remove him from office, issued the order of February 21st, for such removal, designing to thus bring the matter before the Supreme Court. He then proceeds formally to deny that at this time Mr. Stanton was in lawful possession of the office of Secretary of War; and that, consequently, the order for his removal was in violation of the Tenure-of-Office Act; and that it was in violation of the Constitution or of any law; or that it constituted any official crime or misdemeanor.

In regard to the seven succeeding articles of impeachment the President, while admitting the facts of the order appointing General Thomas as Secretary of War *ad interim*, denies all and every of the crimnal charges therein set forth. So of the ninth article, charging an effort to induce General Emory to violate the law, the President denies all such intent, and calls attention to the fact that while, for urgent reasons, he signed the bill prescribing that orders to the army should be issued only through the General, he at the same time declared it to be, in his judgment, unconstitutional; and affirms that in his interview with General Emory he said no more than he had before officially said to Congress—that is, that the law was unconstitutional.

As to the tenth article, the first of the supplementary ones, the President, while admitting that he made certain public speeches at the times and places specified, does not admit that the passages cited are fair reports of his remarks; denies that he has ever been unmindful of the courtesies which ought to be maintained between the executive and legislative departments; but he claims the perfect right at all times to express his views as to all public matters.

The reply to the eleventh article, the second supplementary one, is to the same general purport, denying that he ever affirmed that the Thirty-ninth Congress was not a valid Congress of the United States, and its acts obligatory only as they were approved by him; and denying that he had, as charged in the article, contrived unlawful means for preventing Mr. Stanton from resuming the functions of Secretary of War, or for preventing the execution of the act making appropriations for the support of the army, or that to provide for the more efficient government of the rebel States. In his answer to this article the President refers to his reply to the first article, in which he sets forth at length all the steps, and the reasons therefor, relating to the removal of Mr. Stanton. In brief, the answer of the President to the articles of impeachment is a general denial of each and every criminal act charged in the articles of impeachment.

The counsel for the President then asked for a delay of thirty days after the replication of the managers of the impeachment should have been rendered, before the trial should formally proceed. This was refused, and the managers of the impeachment stated that their replication would be presented the next day: it was that,

"The Senate will commence the trial of the President upon the articles of impeachment exhibited against him on Monday, the 30th day of March, and proceed therein with all dispatch under the rules of the Senate, sitting upon the trial of an impeachment."

The replication of the House of Representatives was a simple denial of each and every averment in the answer of the President, closing thus:

"The House of Representatives .... do say that the said Andrew Johnson, President of the United States, is guilty of the high crimes and misdemeanors mentioned in the said articles, and that the said House of Representatives are ready to prove the same."

The trial began, as appointed, on March 30. There being twenty-seven States represented, there were fifty-four Senators, who constituted the Court, presided over by Chief Justice Salmon P. Chase, of Ohio. SENATORS: *California*, Cole, Conness; *Connecticut*, Dixon, Ferry; *Delaware*, Bayard, Saulsbury; *Indiana*, Hendricks, Morton; *Illinois*, Trumbull, Yates; *Iowa*, Grimes, Harlan; *Kansas*, Pomeroy, Ross; *Kentucky*, Davis, McCreery; *Maine*, Fessenden, Morrill (Lot M.); *Maryland*, Johnson, Vickers; *Massachusetts*, Sumner, Wilson; *Michigan*, Chandler, Howard; *Minnesota*, Norton, Ramsay; *Missouri*, Drake, Henderson; *Nebraska*, Thayer, Tipton; *Nevada*, Nye, Stewart; *New Hampshire*, Cragin, Patterson (J. W.); *New Jersey*, Cattell, Frelinghuysen; *New York*, Conklin, Morgan; *Ohio*, Sherman, Wade; *Oregon*, Corbett, Williams; *Pennsylvania*, Buckalew, Cameron; *Rhode Island*, Anthony, Sprague; *Tennessee*, Fowler, Patterson (David);

Vermont, Edmunds, Morrill (J. S.); *West Virginia*, Van Winkle, Willey; *Wisconsin*, Doolittle, Howe.

Managers for the Prosecution: Messrs. Bingham, Boutwell, Butler, Logan, Stevens, Williams, Wilson.

Counsel for the President: Messrs. Curtis, Evarts, Groesbeck, Nelson, Stanbery.

The following was the order of procedure: The Senate convened at 11 or 12 o'clock, and was called to order by the president of that body, who, after prayer, would leave the chair, which was immediately assumed by the Chief Justice, who wore his official robes. The prosecution was mainly conducted by Mr. Butler, who examined the witnesses, and, in conjunction with the others, argued the points of law which came up. The defense, during the early part of the trial, was mainly conducted by Mr. Stanbery, who had resigned the office of Attorney-General for this purpose, but, being taken suddenly ill, Mr. Evarts took his place. According to the rule at first adopted, the trial was to be opened by one counsel on each side, and summed up by two on each side; but this rule was subsequently modified so as to allow as many of the managers and counsel as chose to sum up, either orally or by filing written arguments.

THE PROSECUTION.

The whole of the first day (March 30) was occupied by the opening speech of Mr. Butler. After touching upon the importance of the case, and the wisdom of the framers of the Constitution in providing for its possible occurrence, he laid down the following proposition, supporting it by a copious array of authorities and precedents:

"We define, therefore, an impeachable high crime or misdemeanor to be one, in its nature or consequences, subversive of some fundamental or essential principle of government, or highly prejudicial to the public interest, and this may consist of a violation of the Constitution, of law, of an official oath, or of duty, by an act committed or omitted, or, without violating a positive law, by the abuse of discretionary powers from improper motives, or for any improper purpose."

He then proceeded to discuss the nature and functions of the tribunal before which the trial is held. He asked: "Is this proceeding a trial, as that term is understood, so far as relates to the rights and duties of a court and jury upon an indictment for crime? Is it not rather more in the nature of an inquest?" The Constitution, he urged, "seems to have determined it to be the latter, because, under its provisions, the right to retain and hold office is the only subject to be finally adjudicated; all preliminary inquiry being carried on solely to determine that question, and that alone." He then proceeded to argue that this body now sitting to determine the accusation, is the Senate of the United States, and not a court. This question is of consequence, he argued, because, in the latter case, it would be bound by the rules and precedents of common-law statutes; the members of the court would be liable to challenge on many grounds; and the accused might claim that he could only be convicted when the evidence makes the fact clear beyond reasonable doubt, instead of by a preponderance of the evidence. The fact that in this case the Chief Justice presides, it was argued, does not constitute the Senate thus acting a court for in all cases of impeachment, save that of the President, its regular presiding officer presides. Moreover, the procedures have no analogy to those of an ordinary court of justice. The accused merely receives a notice of the case pending against him. He is not required to appear personally, and the case will go on without his presence. Mr. Butler thus summed up his position in this regard:

"A constitutional tribunal solely, you are bound by no law, either statute or common, which may limit your constitutional prerogative. You consult no precedents save those of the law and custom of parliamentary bodies. You are a law unto yourselves, bound only by the natural principles of equity and justice, and that *salus populi suprema est lex.*"

Mr. Butler then proceeded to consider the articles of impeachment. The first eight, he says, "set out, in several distinct forms, the acts of the President in removing Mr. Stanton and appointing General Thomas, differing, in legal effect, in the purposes for which, and the intent with which, either or both of the acts were done, and the legal duties and rights infringed, and the Acts of Congress violated in so doing." In respect to all of these articles, Mr. Butler says, referring to his former definition of what constituted an impeachable high crime:

"All the articles allege these acts to be in contravention of his oath of office, and in disregard of the duties thereof. If they are so, however, the President might have the power to do them under the law. Still, being so done, they are acts of official misconduct, and, as we have seen, impeachable. The President has the legal power to do many acts which, if done in disregard of his duty, or for improper purposes, then the exercise of that power is an official misdemeanor. For example, he has the power of pardon; if exercised, in a given case, for a corrupt motive, as for the payment of money, or wantonly pardoning all criminals, it would be a misdemeanor."

Mr. Butler affirmed that every fact charged in the first article, and substantially in the seven following, is admitted in the reply of the President; and also that the general intent to set aside the Tenure-of-Office Act is therein admitted and justified. He then proceeded to discuss the whole question of the power of the President for removals from office, and especially his claim that this power was imposed upon the President by the Constitution, and that it could not be taken from him, or be vested jointly in him and the Senate, partly or in whole. This, Mr. Butler affi ied, was the real question at issue before the Senate and the Am ican people. He said·

"Has the President, under the Constitution, the m re than royal prerogative at will to remove from office, or to suspend from office, all executive officers of the United States, either civil, military or naval, and to fill the vacancies, without any restraint whatever, or possibility of restraint, by the Senate or by Congress, through laws duly enacted? The House of Representatives, in behalf of the people, join issue by affirming that the exercise of such powers is a high misdemeanor in office. If the affirmative is maintained by the respondent, then, so far as the first eight articles are concerned—unless such corrupt purposes are shown as will of themselves make the exercise of a legal power a crime—the respondent must go, and ought to go, quit and free."

This point as to the legal right of the President to make removals from office, which constitutes the real burden of the articles of impeachment, was argued at length. Mr. Butler assumed that the Senate, by whom, in conjunction with the House, the Tenure-of-Office Act had been passed over the veto of the President, would maintain the law to be constitutional. The turning point was whether the special case of the removal of Mr. Stanton came within the provisions of this law. This rested upon the proviso of that law, that—

"The Secretaries shall hold their office during the term of the President by whom they may have been appointed, and for one month thereafter, subject to removal by and with the advice and consent of the Senate."

The extended argument upon this point, made by Mr. Butler, was to the effect that Mr. Stanton having been appointed by Mr. Lincoln, whose term of office reached to the 4th of March, 1869, that of Mr. Stanton existed until a month later, unless he was previously removed by the concurrent action of the President and Senate. The point of the argument is, that Mr. Johnson is merely serving out the balance of the term of Mr. Lincoln, cut short by his assassination, so that the Cabinet officers appointed by Mr. Lincoln held their places, by this very proviso, during that term and for a month thereafter; for, he argued, if Mr. Johnson was not merely serving out the balance of Mr. Lincoln's term, then he is entitled to the office of President for four full years, that being the period for which a President is elected. If, continues the argument, Mr. Stanton's commission was vacated by the Tenure-of-Office Act, it ceased on the 4th of April, 1865; or, if the act had no retroactive effect, still, if Mr. Stanton held office merely under his commission from Mr. Lincoln, then his functions would have ceased upon the passage of the bill, March 2, 1867; and, consequently, Mr. Johnson, in "employing" him after that date as Secretary of War, was guilty of a high misdemeanor, which would give ground for a new article of impeachment.

After justifying the course of Mr. Stanton in holding on to the secretaryship in opposition to the wish of the President, on the ground that "to desert it now would be to imitate the treachery of his accidental chief," Mr. Butler proceeded to discuss the reasons assigned by the President in his answer to the articles of impeachment for the attempt to remove Mr. Stanton. These, in substance, were that the President believed the Tenure-of-Office Act was unconstitutional, and, therefore, void and of no effect, and that he had the right to remove him and appoint another person in his place. Mr. Butler urged that, in all of these proceedings, the President professed to act upon the assumption that the act was valid, and that his action was in accordance with its provisions. He then went on to charge that the appointment of General Thomas as Secretary of War *ad interim*, was a separate violation of law. By the act of February 20, 1863, which repealed all previous laws inconsistent with it, the President was authorized, in case of the "death, resignation, absence from the seat of Government, or sickness of the head of an executive department," or in any other case where these officers could not perform their respective duties, to appoint the head of any other executive department to fulfill the duties of the office "until a successor be appointed, or until such absence or disability shall cease." Now, urged Mr. Butler, at the time of the appointment of General Thomas as Secretary of War *ad interim*, Mr. Stanton "had neither died nor resigned, was not sick nor absent," and, consequently, General Thomas, not being the head of a department, but only of a bureau of one of them, was not eligible to this appointment, and that, therefore, his appointment was illegal and void.

The ninth article of impeachment, wherein the President is charged with endeavoring to induce General Emory to take orders directly from himself, is dealt with in a rather slight manner. Mr. Butler says, "If the transaction set forth in this article stood alone, we might well admit that doubts might arise as to the sufficiency of the proof;" but, he adds, the surroundings are so pointed and significant as to leave no doubt in the mind of an impartial man as to the intents and purposes of the President"—these intents being, according to Mr. Butler, "to induce General Emory to take orders directly from himself, and thus to hinder the execution of the Civil Tenure Act, and to prevent Mr. Stanton from holding his office of Secretary of War."

As to the tenth article of impeachment, based upon various speeches of the President, Mr. Butler undertook to show that the reports of these speeches, as given in the article, were substantially correct; and accepted the issue made thereupon as to whether they are "decent and becoming the President of the United States, and do not tend to bring the office into ridicule and disgrace."

After having commented upon the eleventh and closing article, which charges the President with having denied the authority of the Thirty-ninth Congress, except so far as its acts were approved by him, Mr. Butler summed up the purport of the articles of impeachment in these words:

"The acts set out in the first eight articles are but the culmination of a series of wrongs, malfeasances, and usurpations committed by the respondent, and, therefore, need to be examined in the light of his precedent and concomitant acts to grasp their scope and design. The last three articles presented show the perversity and malignity with which he acted, so that the man as he is known may be clearly spread upon record, to be seen and known of all men hereafter. . . . . . We have presented the facts in the constitutional manner; we have brought the criminal to your bar, and demand judgment for his so great crimes."

The remainder of Monday, and a portion of the following day, were devoted to the presentation of documentary evidence as to the proceedings involved in the order for the removal of Mr. Stanton and the appointment of General Thomas. The prosecution then introduced witnesses to testify to the interviews between Mr. Stanton and General Thomas. They then brought forward a witness to show that General Thomas had avowed his determination to take forcible possession of the War Office. To this Mr. Stanbery, for the defense, objected. The Chief Justice decided the testimony to be admissible. Thereupon Senator Drake took exception to the ruling, on the ground that this question should be decided by the Senate—not by the presiding officer. The Chief Justice averred that, in his judgment, it was his duty to decide, in the first instance, upon any question of evidence, and then, if any Senator desired, to submit the decision to the Senate. Upon this objection and appeal arose the first conflict in the Senate as to the powers of its presiding officer. Mr. Butler argued at length in favor of the exception. Although, in this case, the decision was in favor of the prosecution, he objected to the power of the presiding officer to make it. This point was argued at length by the managers for the impeachment, who denied the right of the Chief Justice to make such decision. It was then moved that the Senate retire for private consultation on this point. There was a tie vote—25 ayes and 25 nays. The Chief Justice gave his casting vote in favor of the motion for consultation. The Senate, by a vote of 31 to 19, sustained the Chief Justice, deciding that "the presiding officer may rule on all questions of evidence and on incidental questions, which decision will stand as the judgment of the Senate for decision, or he may, at his option in the first instance, submit any such question to a vote of the members of the Senate." In the further progress of the trial the Chief Justice, in most important cases, submitted the question directly to the Senate, without himself giving any decision. Next morning (April 1) Mr. Sumner offered a resolution to the effect that the Chief Justice, in giving a casting vote, "acted without authority of the Constitution of the United States." This was negatived by a vote of 27 to 21, thus deciding that the presiding officer had the right to give a casting vote. The witness (Mr. Burleigh, delegate from Dakotah), who had been called to prove declarations of General Thomas, was then asked whether, at an interview between them, General Thomas had said any thing as "to the means by which he intended to obtain, or was directed by the President to obtain, possession of the War Department." To this question Mr. Stanbery objected, on the ground that any statements made by General Thomas could not be used as evidence against the President. Messrs. Butler and Bingham argued that the testimony was admissible, on the ground that there was, as charged, a conspiracy between the President and General Thomas, and that the acts of one conspirator were binding upon the other; and, also, that in these acts General Thomas was the agent of the President. The Senate, by 39 to 11, decided that the question was admissible. Mr. Burleigh thereupon testified substantially that General Thomas informed him that he had been directed by the President to take possession of the War Department; that he was bound to obey his superior officer; that, if Mr. Stanton objected, he should use force, and if he bolted the doors they would be broken down. The witness was then asked whether he had heard General Thomas make any statement to the clerks of the War Office, to the effect that, when he came into control, he would relax or rescind the rules of Mr. Stanton. To this question objection was made by the counsel of the President on the ground of irrelevancy. The Chief Justice was of opinion that the question was not admissible, but, if any Senator demanded, he would submit to the Senate whether it should be asked. The demand having been made, the Senate, by a vote of 28 to 22, allowed the question to be put, whereupon Mr. Burleigh testified that General Thomas, in his presence, called before him the heads of the divisions, and told them that the rules laid down by Mr. Stanton were arbitrary, and that he should relax them—that he should not hold them strictly to their letters of instruction, but should consider them as gentlemen who would do their duty—that they could come in or go out when they chose. Mr. Burleigh further testified that, subsequently, General Thomas had said to him that the only thing which prevented him from taking possession of the War Department was his arrest by the United States marshal. Other witnesses were called to prove the declarations of General Thomas. Mr. Wilkeson testified that General Thomas said to him that he should demand possession of the War Department, and, in case Mr. Stanton should refuse to give it up, he should call upon General Grant for a sufficient force to enable him to do so, and he did not see how this could be refused. Mr. Karsener, of Delaware, testified that he saw General Thomas at the President's house, told him that Delaware, of which State General Thomas is a citizen, expected him to stand firm; to which General Thomas replied that he was standing firm, that he would not disappoint his friends, but that, in a few days, he would "kick that fellow out," meaning, as the witness supposed, Mr. Stanton.

Thursday, April 2d.—Various witnesses were introduced to testify to the occurrences when General Thomas demanded possession of the War Department. After this General Emory was called to testify to the transactions which form the ground of the ninth article of impeachment. His testimony was to the effect that the President, on the 22d of February, requested him to call; that, upon so doing, the President asked respecting any changes that had been made in the disposition of the troops around Washington; that he informed the President that no important changes had been made, and that none could be made without an order from General Grant, as provided for in an order founded upon a law sanctioned by the President. The President said that this law was unconstitutional. Emory replied that the President had approved of it, and that it was not the prerogative of the officers of the army to decide upon the constitutionality of a law, and in that opinion he was justified by the opinion of eminent counsel, and thereupon the conversation ended.

The prosecution then endeavored to introduce testimony as to the appointment of Mr. Edmund Cooper, the Private Secretary of the President, as Assistant Secretary of the Treasury, in support of the eighth and eleventh articles of impeachment, which charge the President with an unlawful attempt to control the disposition of certain public funds. This testimony, by a vote of 27 to 22, was ruled out.

The prosecution now, in support of the tenth and eleventh articles of impeachment, charging the President with endeavoring to "set aside the rightful authority of Congress," offered a telegraphic dispatch from the President to Mr. Parsons, at that time (January 17, 1867) Provisional Governor of Alabama, of which the following is the essential part:

"I do not believe the people of the whole country will sustain any set of individuals in the attempt to change the whole character of our Government by enabling acts in this way. I believe, on the contrary, that they will eventually uphold all who have patriotism and courage to stand by the Constitution, and who place their confidence in the people. There should be no faltering on the part of those who are honest in their determination to sustain the several coördinate departments of the Government in accordance with its original design."

The introduction of this was objected to by the counsel for the President, but admitted by the Senate, the vote being 27 to 17.

The whole of Friday, and a great part of Saturday, (April 3d and 4th,) were occupied in the examination of the persons who reported the various speeches of the President which form the basis of the tenth article, the result being that the reports were shown to be either substantially or verbally accurate. Then, after some testimony relating to the forms in which commissions to office were made out, the managers announced that the case for the prosecution was substantially closed. The counsel for the President thereupon asked that three working days should be granted them to prepare for the defense. This, after some discussion, was granted by the Senate by a vote of 37 to 9, and the trial was adjourned to Thursday, April 9th.

THE DEFENSE.

The opening speech for the defense, occupying the whole of Thursday, and a part of Friday, was made by Mr. Curtis. Reserving, for a time, a rejoinder to Mr. Butler's argument as to the functions of the Senate when sitting as a Court of Impeachment, Mr. Curtis proceeded to a consideration of the articles of impeachment, in their order, his purpose being "to ascertain, in the first place, what the substantial allegations in each of them are, what is the legal proof and effect of these allegations, and what proof is necessary to be adduced in order to sustain them." The speech is substantially an elaboration of and argument for the points embraced in the answer of the President. The main stress of the argument related to the first article, which, as stated by Mr. Curtis, when stripped of all technical language, amounts exactly to these things:

"*First.* That the order set out in the article for the removal of Mr. Stanton, if executed, would have been a violation of the Tenure-of-Office Act.

"*Second.* That it was a violation of the Tenure-of-Office Act.

"*Third.* That it was an intentional violation of the Tenure-of-Office Act.

"*Fourth.* That it was in violation of the Constitution of the United States.

"*Fifth.* That it was intended by the President to be so.

"Or, to draw all these into one sentence, which I hope may be intelligible and clear enough, I suppose the substance of this first article is that the order for the removal of Mr. Stanton was, and was intended to be, a violation of the Constitution of the United States. These are the allegations which it is necessary for the honorable managers to make out in order to support that article."

Mr. Curtis proceeded to argue that the case of Mr. Stanton did not come within the provisions of the Tenure-of-Office Act, being expressly excepted by the proviso that Cabinet officers should hold their places during the term of the President by whom they were appointed, and for one month thereafter, unless removed by the consent of the Senate. Mr. Stanton was appointed by Mr. Lincoln, whose term of office came to an end by his death. He argued at length against the proposition that Mr. Johnson was merely serving out the remainder of Mr. Lincoln's term. The object of this exception, he said, was evident. The Cabinet officers were to be "the immediate confidential assistants of the President, for whose acts he was to be responsible, and in whom he was expected to repose the gravest honor, trust, and confidence; therefore it was that this act has connected the tenure of office of these officers with that of the President by whom they were appointed." Mr. Curtis gave a new interpretation to that clause in the Constitution which prescribes that the President "may require the opinion, in writing, of the principal officer in each of the executive departments upon any subject relating to the duties of their several offices." He understood that the word "their" included the President, so that he might call upon Cabinet officers for advice "relating to the duties of the office of these principal officers, or relating to the duties of the President himself." This, at least, he affirmed, had been the practical interpretation put upon this clause from the beginning. To confirm his position as to the intent of the Tenure-of-Office Act in this respect, Mr. Curtis quoted from speeches made in both houses at the time when the act was passed. Thus, Senator Sherman said that the act, as passed—

"Would not prevent the present President from removing the Secretary of War, the Secretary of the Navy, or the Secretary of State; and, if I supposed that either of these gentlemen was so wanting in manhood, in honor, as to hold his place after the politest intimation from the President of the United States that his services were no longer needed, I certainly, as a Senator, would consent to his removal at any time, and so would we all."

Mr. Curtis proceeded to argue that there was really no removal of Mr. Stanton; he still held his place, and so there was "no case of removal within the statute, and, therefore, no case of violation by removal." But, if the Senate should hold that the order for removal was, in effect, a removal, then, unless the Tenure-of-Office Act gave Mr. Stanton a tenure of office, this removal would not have been contrary to the provisions of this act. He proceeded to argue that there was room for grave doubt whether Mr. Stanton's case came within the provisions of the Tenure-of-Office Act, and that the President, upon due consideration, and having taken the best advice within his power, considering that it did not, and acting accordingly, did not, even if he was mistaken, commit an act "so willful and wrong that it can be justly and properly, and for the purposes of this prosecution, termed a high misdemeanor." He argued at length that the view of the President was the correct one, and that "the Senate had nothing whatever to do with the removal of Mr. Stanton, whether the Senate was in session or not."

Mr. Curtis then went on to urge that the President, being sworn to take care that the laws be faithfully executed, must carry out any law, even though passed over his veto, except in cases where a law which he believed to be unconstitutional has cut off a power confided to him, and in regard to which he alone could make an issue which would bring the matter before a court, so as to cause "a judicial decision to come between the two branches of the Government, to see which of them is right." This, said he, is what the President has done. This argument, in effect, was an answer to the first eight articles of impeachment.

The ninth article, charging the President with endeavoring to induce General Emory to violate the law by receiving orders directly from him, was very briefly touched upon, it being maintained that, as shown by the evidence, "the reason why the President sent for General Emory was not that he might endeavor to seduce that distinguished officer from his allegiance to the laws and Constitution of his country, but because he wished to obtain information about military movements which might require his personal attention."

As to the tenth article, based upon the President's speeches, it was averred that they were in no way in violation of the Constitution, or of any law existing at the time when they were made, and were not, therefore, impeachable offenses.

The reply to the eleventh article was very brief. The managers had "compounded it of the materials which they had previously worked up into others," and it "contained nothing new that needed notice." Mr. Curtis concluded his speech by saying that—

"This trial is and will be the most conspicuous instance that has ever been, or even can be expected to be found, of American justice or of American injustice; of that justice which is the great policy of all civilized States; of that injustice which is certain to be condemned, which makes even the wisest man mad, and which, in the fixed and unalterable order of God's providence, is sure to return and plague the inventor."

At the close of this opening speech for the defense, General Lorenzo Thomas was brought forward as a witness. His testimony, elicited upon examination and cross-examination, was to the effect that, having received the order appointing him Secretary of War *ad interim*, he presented it to Mr. Stanton, who asked, "Do you wish me to vacate the office at once, or will you give me time to get my private property together?" to which Thomas replied, "Act your pleasure." Afterward Stanton said, "I don't know whether I will obey your instructions." Subsequently Thomas said that he should issue orders as Secretary of War. Stanton said he should not do so, and afterward gave him a written direction, not to issue any order except as Adjutant-General. During the examination of General Thomas a question came up which, in many ways, recurred upon the trial. He was asked to tell what occurred at an interview between himself and the President. Objection was made by Mr. Butler, and the point was argued. The question was submitted to the Senate, which decided, by a vote of 42 to 10, that it was admissible. The testimony of General Thomas, from this point, took a wide range, and, being mainly given in response to questions of counsel, was, apparently, somewhat contradictory. The substance was that he was recognized by the President as Secretary of War; that, since the impeachment, he had acted as such only in attending Cabinet meetings, but had given no orders; that, when he reported to the President that Mr. Stanton would not vacate the War Department, the President directed him to "take possession of the office;" that, without orders from the President, he had intended to do this by force, if necessary; that, finding that this course might involve bloodshed, he had abandoned this purpose, but that, after this, he had, in several cases, affirmed his purpose to do so, but that these declarations were "merely boast and brag." On the following day General Thomas was recalled as a witness, to enable him to correct certain points in his testimony. The first was the date of an unimportant transaction; he had given it as taking place on the 21st of February, whereas it should have been the 22d. The second was that the words of the President were that he should "take charge," not "take possession" of the War Department. In explanation of the fact that he had repeatedly sworn to the words "take possession," he said that these were "put into his mouth." Finally, General Thomas, in reply to a direct question from Mr. Butler, said that his testimony on these points was "all wrong."

Lieutenant-General Sherman was then called as a witness. After some unimportant questions, he was asked in reference to an interview between himself and the President which took place on the 14th of January: "At that interview what conversation took place between the President and you in reference to the removal of Mr. Stanton?" To this question objection was made by Mr. Butler, and the point was elaborately argued. The Chief Justice decided that the question was admissible within the vote of the Senate of the previous day; the question then was as to the admissibility of evidence as to a conversation between the President and General Thomas; the present question was as to a conversation between the President and General Sherman. "Both questions," said the Chief Justice, "are asked for the purpose of procuring the intent of the President in the attempt to remove Mr. Stanton." The question being submitted to the Senate, it was decided, by a vote of 28 to 23, that it should not be admitted. The examination of General Sherman was continued, the question of the conversation aforesaid being frequently brought forward, and as often ruled out by the Senate. The only important fact elicited was that the President had twice, on the 25th and 30th of January, tendered to General Sherman the office of Secretary of War *ad interim.*

On Monday, April 13th, after transactions of minor importance, the general matter of the conversations between the President and General Sherman again came up, upon a question propounded by Senator Johnson—"When the President tendered to you the office of Secretary of War *ad interim*, did he, at the very time of making such tender, state to you what his purpose in so doing was?" This was admitted by the Senate, by a vote of 26 to 22. Senator Johnson then added to his question, "If he did, what did he state his purpose was?" This was admitted, by a vote of 25 to 26. The testimony of General Sherman, relating to several interviews, was to the effect that the President said that the relations between himself and Mr. Stanton were such that he could not execute the office of President without making provision to appoint a Secretary of War *ad interim*, and he offered that office to him (General Sherman), but did not state that his purpose was to bring the matter directly into the courts. Sherman said that, if Mr. Stanton would retire, he might, although against his own wishes, undertake to administer the office *ad interim*, but asked what would be done in case Mr. Stanton would not yield. To this the President replied, "He will make no opposition; you present the order, and he will retire. I know him better than you do; he is cowardly." General Sherman asked time for reflection, and then gave a written answer, declining to accept the appointment, but stated that his reasons were mostly of a personal nature.

On the 14th the Senate adjourned, on account of the sudden illness of Mr. Stanbery. It re-assembled on the 15th, but the proceedings touched wholly upon formal points of procedure and the introduction of unimportant documentary evidence. On the 16th Mr. Sumner moved that all evidence not trivial or obviously irrelevant shall be admitted, the Senate to judge of its value. This was negatived by a vote of 23 to 11.

The 17th was mainly taken up by testimony as to the reliability of the reports of the President's speeches. Mr. Welles, Secretary of the Navy, was then called to testify to certain proceedings in Cabinet Council at the time of the appointment of General Thomas. This was objected to. The Chief Justice decided that it was admissible, and his decision was sustained by a vote of 26 to 23 The defense then endeavored to introduce several members of the Cabinet, to show that, at meetings previous to the removal of Mr. Stanton, it was considered whether it was not desirable to obtain a judicial determination of the unconstitutionality of the Tenure-of-Office Act. This question was raised in several shapes, and its admission, after thorough argument on both sides, as often refused, in the last instance by a decisive vote of 30 to 19. The defense considered this testimony of the utmost importance, as going to show that the President had acted upon the counsel of his constitutional advisers, while the prosecution claimed that he could not plead in justification of a violation of the law that he had been advised by his cabinet, or any one else, that the law was unconstitutional. His duty was to execute the laws, and, if he failed to do this, or violated them, he did so at his own risk of the consequences. With the refusal of this testimony, the case, except the final summings up and the verdict of the Senate, was virtually closed.

The case had been so fully set forth in the opening speeches of Messrs. Butler and Curtis, and in the arguments which came up upon points of testimony, that there remained little for the other counsel except to restate what had before been said.

After the evidence had been closed the case was summed up, on the part of the managers by Messrs. Boutwell, Williams, Stevens, and Bingham in oral arguments, and Mr. Logan, who filed a written argument, and on the part of the President by Messrs. Nelson, Groesbeck, Stanbery, and Evarts. Many of these speeches were distinguished by great brilliancy and power, but, as no new points were presented, we omit any summary.

The Court decided to take a vote upon the articles on Tuesday, the 12th of May, at 12 o'clock, M. A secret session was held on Monday, during which several Senators made short speeches, giving the grounds upon which they expected to cast their votes. On Tuesday the Court agreed to postpone the vote until Saturday, the 16th. Upon that day, at 12 o'clock, a vote was taken upon the eleventh article, it having been determined to vote on that article first. The vote resulted in 35 votes for conviction, and 19 for acquittal.

The question being put to each Senator, "How say you, is the respondent, Andrew Johnson, President of the United States, guilty or not guilty of a high misdemeanor as charged in the article?"—those who responded guilty were Senators Anthony, Cameron, Cattell, Chandler, Cole, Conkling, Conness, Corbett, Cragin, Drake, Edmunds, Ferry, Frelinghuysen, Harlan, Howard, Howe, Morgan, Morrill, of Vermont, Morrill, of Maine, O. P. Morton, Nye, Patterson, N. H. Pomeroy, Sherman, Sprague, Stewart, Sumner, Thayer, Tipton, Wade, Willey, Williams, Wilson, and Yates.

Those who responded not guilty were Senators Bayard, Buckalew, Davis, Dixon, Doolittle, Fessenden, Fowler, Grimes, Henderson, Hendricks, Johnson, M'Creery, Norton, Patterson, of Tennessee, Ross, Saulsbury, Trumbull, Van Winkle, and Vickers.

The Constitution requiring a vote of two-thirds to convict, the President was acquitted on this article. After taking this vote the Court adjourned until Tuesday, May 26th, when votes were taken upon the second and third articles, with precisely the same result as on the eleventh, the vote in each case standing 35 for conviction and 19 for acquittal. A verdict of acquittal on the second, third, and eleventh articles was then ordered to be entered on the record, and, without voting on the other articles, the Court adjourned *sine die.* So the trial was ended, and the President acquitted.

CHRONOLOGICAL RECORD

OF THE

CENTURY OF INDEPENDENCE.

FIRST PERIOD:

FROM DISCOVERY OF AMERICA TO AMERICAN REVOLUTION

1492. San Salvador, the first land discovered in America by Christopher Columbus, Oct. 12; Cuba, Oct. 27; Hispaniola, Dec. 6.

1493. A Spanish Colony at Hispaniola.
Second voyage of Columbus.

1495. May 3.—Jamaica discovered by Columbus.

1496. Sebastian Cabot discovers Newfoundland for Henry VII. of England, and by him called Prima Vista.
Third voyage of Columbus.

1498. The eastern coast of North America found by Americus Vespucius, after whom America was finally named.

1502. The continent of America discovered by Columbus.
Fourth voyage of Columbus.
Coast of North America explored by Cortereal, a Portuguese.

1506. May 15.—Columbus died at Valladolid.

1507. The New World first called America, after Amerigo Vespucci, by Waldseemuller, of Fribourg.
Board of American Trade established at Seville.

1508. The Spaniards colonize Cuba, Jamaica, and Porto Rico.
Negro slaves imported into Hispaniola.

1510. Settlement at Darien.

1511. Cuba conquered by 300 Spaniards.

1512. Florida discovered by Ponce de Leon.

1517. First patent for importing negroes into America granted by Spain.

Mexico discovered by Francisco Fernandez.

1521. Mexico conquered by the Spanish, under Cortez.

1524. Verazzanni, a Florentine navigator, in the service of France, explores the coast of America from the Carolinas to Newfoundland.

1527. The Bermudas discovered by Juan Bermudas, a Spaniard.

1534. James Cartier discovered the St. Lawrence River, and took possession of the whole country in the name of the King of France.

1535. The mint of Mexico, the richest in the world, begun.

1536. California discovered by Cortez.

Ferdinand de Soto, with a fleet of 10 vessels and a gay company of 600 men, land at Tampa Bay and commence their march into the interior.

1541. Mississippi River discovered by De Soto.

1542. De Soto dies, and is buried in the Mississippi River.

1553. New Mexico discovered by the Spaniards.

1564. Coligny sends a colony of Huguenots to Florida; they are destroyed by the Spaniards.

1565. St. Augustine, Fla., settled by the Spaniards.

1576. Greenland visited by Frobisher.

1583. Tobacco first carried from Virginia to England.

1584. Virginia visited by Sir Walter Raleigh.

Miles Standish born—a military leader of the Pilgrims in New England. He died in 1656.

1585. Davis' Strait discovered by the English navigator whose name it bears.

John Cotton, a learned divine of Boston, born. He died in 1652.

First English colony in America, founded at Roanoke.

1587. John Winthrop, Governor of the Colony of Massachusetts, born. Died in 1649.

1588. William Bradford, second Governor of Plymouth Colony, born. Died in 1657.

1594. Edward Winslow, Governor of Plymouth Colony, born. Died in 1643.

1601. Roger Williams born. He founded Rhode Island. Died in 1683.

Acadia colonized by the French.

1602. Cape Cod discovered by Bartholomew Gosnold.

1603. Martin Pring, an English navigator, examines the shores and large rivers of Maine, and the coast as far as Martha's Vineyard.

1604. John Eliot, "The Apostle to the Indians," born. Died in 1690.
1605. Quebec founded by the French.
1606. Martin Pring makes a second and more accurate survey of the coast of Maine.
The London and Plymouth Companies receive Charters.
1607. Virginia, sometimes called the Old Dominion, settled in April, at Jamestown, on the James River, by the London Company—the first white settlement in the United States.
A settlement commenced at the mouth of the Kennebec River, Maine, by the Plymouth Company.
1609. Sir John Sommers cast away on the Burmuda Islands.
Plot of the Indians disclosed by Pocahontas.
Hudson's Bay discovered by Henry Hudson.
1610. The Virginia Colony reduced from nearly 500 to 60.
1613. Pocahontas married to Mr. John Rolf.
The Dutch erect some trading posts at the mouth of the Hudson River.
1614. New York City founded by the Dutch.
North Virginia called New England by Prince Charles.
24 natives of New England carried off and sold by Hunt.
Capt. John Smith explores the coast of New England.
1616. Baffin's Bay discovered by Wm. Baffin, an Englishman
Settlement of Virginia by Walter Raleigh.
1617. Most of the inhabitants from Narragansett to Penobscot swept away by war and pestilence.
1620. The first negro slaves in the English colonies of North America were brought to Virginia in a Dutch vessel-of-war.
Dec. 21 (Dec. 11, O. S.).—First settlement in New England, at Plymouth, Mass.
1621. A treaty made with Massasoit.
1622. March 27.—Massacre of 347 Virginians by the Indians.
1623. New Hampshire settled at Little Harbor and Dover.
Albany, Capital of New York, settled by the Dutch, and called Beaverwyck.
1624. New Jersey settled.
1628. John Endicott settles at Salem, Mass.
Massachusetts Bay Colony founded.
Charlestown, Mass., founded.
1629. First church in Massachusetts formed at Salem.
First permanent settlement of the Dutch at Manhattan.
1630. Arrival of Governor Winthrop at Boston, with about 1,500 emigrants.
Dorchester, Roxbury, and Cambridge founded.

1631. First vessel built in Massachusetts, called the "Blessing of the Bay," launched July 4.
John Smith, celebrated in Virginia history, dies. Aged 52 years.
1633. Connecticut settled at Windsor by Holmes, from Mass.
1634. Maryland settled at St. Mary's, on the Potomac, by 200 Catholics.
1635. The Saybrook Colony, Conn., established.
1636. Providence, R. I., settled by Roger Williams.
1637. War with the Pequot Indians—Connecticut.
First Synod at Newtown, occasioned by Ann Hutchinson.
1638. Delaware settled by the Swedes, near Christian Creek.
The New Haven Colony established.
Harvard College, the first college in the United States, established at Cambridge, Mass., by John Harvard.
1639. Settlements on the Connecticut united as the Connecticut Colony.
First printing in America, at Cambridge, Mass.
"The Freeman's Oath" and an almanac printed.
1640. Number of emigrants to America to this date—20,000.
1641. New Hampshire united with Massachusetts.
1643. Confederacy formed, under the name of United Colonies of New England, for mutual defense.
1644. The Connecticut and Saybrook Colonies unite.
The second Indian massacre occurs in Virginia.
The two settlements in Rhode Island united under the name of Rhode Island.
1645. Clayborne's rebellion in Maryland.
1646. Act of Massachusetts Legislature for carrying the Gospel to the Indians.
John Eliot preaches to the Indians.
Second Synod of Massachusetts.
Thomas Mayhew, preacher to the Indians, shipwrecked.
1647. Epidemic through America.
1650. North and South Carolina settled.
Conversion of the Indians on Martha's Vineyard, Mass.
1651. The Navigation Act passed by the English Parliament.
1652. Voluntary submission of Maine to Massachusetts.
Gorton and Roger Williams make a decree against slavery in Rhode Island.
1655. Law in Massachusetts requiring that "All hands not necessarily employed on other occasions, such as women, boys, and girls, should spin according to their skill and ability."
A civil war occurs in Maryland.
1656. Persecution of the Quakers in Massachusetts.

1656. Ann Hibbins, of Boston, executed for witchcraft.
1663. Carolina granted to Lord Clarendon and seven other noblemen of England by Charles II.
The Albemarle County Colony formed.
1664. New Netherlands taken by the English from the Dutch, and named New York.
New Jersey granted to Lord Berkely and Geo. Carteret.
First settlement at Elizabethtown (now Elizabeth).
J. Eliot's Indian Bible, one of the first books printed in America at Cambridge.
1665. The Clarendon County Colony established.
The Connecticut and New Haven Colonies united.
Six towns of Christian Indians in Massachusetts.
1667. The ceding of New York to the English confirmed by the peace of Breda.
1670. Bees first introduced into New England by the English.
South Carolina settled, on the Ashley River.
Conclusion of the American Treaty between England and Spain.
1672. White slaves bought in England, and brought to Virginia. Average price for five years' service, £5; while a negro was worth £25.
1673. Virginia ceded to Culpepper and Arlington.
1675. War with Philip, King of the Wampanoags, in New England.
Indian War in Virginia.
1676. King Philip killed, and his tribe destroyed.
Bacon's rebellion breaks out in Virginia.
Jamestown burned.
1677. Virginia becomes a proprietary Government, with Culpepper as Governor.
1679. New Hampshire made a royal province (first time).
1680. Settlement begun at Charleston, S. C.
1681. Pennsylvania granted by James II, to William Penn.
1782. Philadelphia founded by William Penn.
The Duke of York grants Delaware to William Penn.
1686. Sir Edmund Andros appointed Royal Governor of New England.
1687. The Connecticut Charter hid in the "Charter Oak."
1688. New York and New Jersey added to the jurisdiction of New England.
War with the Indians in New England, which continued several years.
1689. King William's war commenced, and continued 8 years.
1690. Port Royal captured by the English, under Sir Wm. Phipps.

1690. An expedition against Canada unsuccessful.
English settlements of Schenectady, N. Y.; Casco, Me.; and Salmon Falls, N. H., destroyed by the French.
1693. The Salem witchcraft delusion prevailed.
William and Mary's College, the second in the United States, founded in Virginia.
Episcopacy introduced into New York.
1696. 30 Indian churches in New England.
1697. The Treaty of Ryswick ends King William's war.
1698. Number of Indians in Massachusetts—about 4,000.
1700. Yale College founded at New Haven, Conn.
1702. Queen Anne's war begun.
1704. Capt. Church's expedition against the Indians.
"Boston News Letter"—first American periodical.
1709. First paper-money in New Jersey.
1710. Port Royal captured a second time by the English.
First post-office in New York.
1712. 137 people in the vicinity of Roanoke murdered by Tuscaroras.
1713. The Treaty of Utrecht ended Queen Anne's war.
Acadia (Nova Scotia) ceded to the English by the French. (See Longfellow's "Evangeline.")
1715. Indian War in South Carolina.
The Tuscaroras driven out of North Carolina, after 3 years' war.
1717. The city of New Orleans founded by the French.
1719. First Philadelphia newspaper.
1721. First New York newspaper.
1724. Vermont settled by Massachusetts colonists.
Trenton, N. J., founded.
1727. Earthquake in New England.
1729. Carolina separated into North and South Carolina.
Massacre of French at Fort Rosalie (Natchez).
Baltimore founded, and named in honor of Lord Baltimore.
1732. Feb. 22.—Geo. Washington born, at Pope's Creek, Virginia.
Franklin's "Poor Richard's Almanac"—Philadelphia—the first of any note in the United States.
1733. Georgia settled by Gen. Oglethorpe, at Savannah.
1734. First lodge of Freemasons in America, at Boston.
1735. Ravages of throat distemper in New Hampshire and Massachusetts.
1738. Nassau Hall College, Princeton, N. J., founded.
1740. Tennessee first explored.
1741. New Hampshire becomes a separate royal province.

1744. King George's war commenced.
1745. Louisburg and Cape Breton, taken by the English from the French.
1747. David Brainard and Benjamin Coleman die.
1748. Treaty of Aix-la-Chapelle ends King George s war.
1753. Georgia becomes a royal province.
Oct. 31.—Washington sent with a letter from Gov. Dinwiddie, of Virginia, to the French.
1754. May 28.—Washington defeats the French at Great Meadows.
July 4.—Washington capitulated at Fort Necessity, with permission to return to Virginia.
The Quakers abolish slavery among themselves.
1755. Moncton expels the French from Nova Scotia.
July 9.—Battle of the Monongahela—Braddock defeated, and mortally wounded.
Sept. 8.—Dieshau defeats the English near Lake George. He is afterward defeated, and mortally wounded.
War declared between England and France.
Aug. 14.—The French, under Montcalm, capture Oswego.
Armstrong defeats the Indians at Fort Kittanning.
1757. Aug. 9.—Fort William Henry surrendered by Webb to Montcalm.
1758. July 8.—Abercrombie repulsed by Montcalm at Ticonderoga.
July 26.—The English take Louisburg.
Aug. 27.—English, under Bradstreet, capture Fort Frontenac.
Fort Du Quesne captured by the English.
1759. The English, under Johnson, capture Fort Niagara.
July 31.—Wolfe defeated at the battle of Montmorenci.
Montcalm defeated by Wolfe on the plains of Abraham.
Sept. 13.—Wolfe killed.
Sept. 18.—Quebec surrenders to the English.
1760. All Canada surrendered to the English.
1762. Severest drought ever known in America.
1763. Feb. 10.—Treaty of Paris ends the French and Indian war.
1764. Pontiac's war with the Indians.
1765. Mar. 8.—Parliament passes the Stamp Act.
Oct. 7.—Colonial Congress met at New York.
1766. March 18.—Stamp Act repealed.
1767. June 29.—Bill passed taxing tea, glass, paper, etc., in the American colonies.
Expulsion of Jesuits from Mexico.

1768. Massachusetts assembly petition the King against the late tax.

Oct. 1.—A body of British troops land at Boston.

1769. Daniel Boone explores Kentucky.

1770. March 5.—Affray, known as the "Boston Massacre," occurs.

1771. May 16.—Battle of Almansee. North Carolinians defeated by Gov. Tryon.

1773. Dec. 16—The inhabitants of Boston throw 342 chests of the taxed tea into the sea.

1774. March 31.—The Boston Port Bill passed by Parliament.

Sept. 5.—The first Continental Congress meets at Philadelphia.

SECOND PERIOD:

FROM THE AMERICAN REVOLUTION TO THE GREAT REBELLION.

1775. April 19.—The war for American Independence commences with the Battle of Lexington.

May 10.—Allen and Arnold capture Ticonderoga.

May 25.—Reinforcements arrive at Boston, under Howe, Burgoyne, and Clinton.

June 15.—Washington elected Commander-in-Chief of the American army.

June 17.—Battle of Bunker Hill—Gen. Warren killed.

Sept. 10.—American forces, under Montgomery, invade Canada.

Nov. 13.—Montreal surrendered to Montgomery.

Dec. 31.—Montgomery defeated and slain at Quebec.

1776. March 17.—British troops evacuate Boston.

Boston occupied by Washington.

June 18.—Evacuation of Canada by the Americans.

June 28.—The British repulsed at Ft. Moultrie, Charleston.

July 4.—America is declared "free, sovereign, and independent"—a declaration which is signed by the following States: New Hampshire, Massachusetts, Rhode Island, Connecticut, Delaware, Maryland, Virginia, North Carolina, South Carolina, New York, New Jersey, Pennsylvania, and Georgia.

Nov. 16.—Fort Washington captured by the English.

Nov. 28.—Washington crosses the Delaware.

1777. April 26.—Gen. Tryon burns the town of Danbury, Conn.

1777. May 23.—Col. Meigs destroys the British shipping at Sag Harbor.
June 16.—Gen. Burgoyne invades New York.
July 5.—Ticonderoga captured by Burgoyne.
July 10.—Gen. Prescott, commander at Long Island, tured.
July 31.—The Marquis de La Fayette joins the American army.
Aug. 3.—Fort Schuyler besieged by St. Leger.
Oct. 17.—Burgoyne surrenders his army to Gates at Saratoga.
Nov. 15.—Congress adopts a Federal Government.
Dec. 11.—American army goes into winter quarters at Valley Forge.
Dec. 16.—France acknowledges the independence of the United States.

1778. Feb. 6.—Treaties of Amity and Commerce adopted between the United States and France.
Nov. 11—Massacre at Cherry Valley by Tories and Indians.
Dec. 29.—Campbell captured Savannah.

1779. May 13.—Siege of Charleston, S. C.
Aug. 29.—Gen. Sullivan defeats the Indians.
Sept. 23.—Paul Jones gained a victory off the coast of England.

1780. May 12.—Lincoln surrendered Charleston to Clinton.
Aug. 18.—Arnold plotted to betray West Point to the British.
Oct. 2.—Maj. Andre, a British officer, executed as a spy.

1781. Jan. 1.—Pennsylvania troops revolt.
Jan. 18.—New Jersey troops revolt.
Feb.—Articles of Confederation ratified by the States.
Oct. 19.—Surrender of Cornwallis at Yorktown.

1782. Oct. 8.—Independence of United States acknowledged by Holland.
Nov. 3.—Temporary Treaty of Peace signed at Paris.

1783. July 11.—Savannah evacuated by the British.
Sept. 3.—Treaty of Peace signed at Paris.
Nov. 3.—American army disbanded.
Nov 25.—New York evacuated by the British.
Dec. 19.—Charleston evacuated by the British.
Dec. 23.—Washington resigns his commission to Congress.

1785. June 1.—John Adams, first Minister from U. S. to London.

1786. Nov.—Shay's insurrection broke out in Massachusetts.
Major-General Greene died.

1787. July 20.—James Whittaker, first Shaker preacher, died

at Enfield, Conn., aged 36 years. Born at Oldham, Eng.; came to this country with the celebrated Mother Ann Lee, in 1774. Elder Whittaker may be considered the John Wesley of American Shakers.

1787. First Colonial See of the Anglican Church, erected in Nova Scotia.

Sept 17.—Constitution of the United States adopted by all the States, except Rhode Island.

1788. Cotton planted in Georgia.

1789. March 3.—First Congress, under the new Constitution, meets.

April 14.—George Washington declared the first President of the United States.

Ethan Allen and Gen. Knyphausen died this year.

1790. First census of the United States taken—population, 3,929,326.

Treaty concluded with the Creeks.

The territory South of the Ohio River ceded to the United States.

Oct. 17, 22.—Indians defeat Gen. Harmer, near Ft. Wayne, Ind.

1791. First United States Bank established at Philadelphia.

Nov. 4.—St. Clair defeated by the Indians in Western Ohio.

1792. United States mint established.

1793. March 3.—Washington again inaugurated President.

Neutrality declared in regard to France.

John Hancock, Roger Sherman, and John Manly, died this year.

1794. Aug. 20.—Gen. Wayne defeats the Indians on the Maumee.

Nov. 19.—Commercial Treaty concluded with Great Britain.

The Whisky Insurrection in Pennsylvania.

Gen. Sullivan, Richard Henry Lee, and Dr. Witherspoon, died.

1795. June 24.—Jay's Treaty with Great Britain ratified.

Gen. Francis Marion and President Ezra Stiles, of Yale College, died.

1796. Death of Anthony Wayne and David Rittenhouse this year.

Washington resigns.

1797. July.—Congress declares the treaties with France annulled.

1798. May.—Congress passes an Act for raising a regular army.

June.—Washington appointed Lieutenant-General and Commander-in-Chief.

1799. American navy consists of 42 vessels, with 950 guns.

Pennsylvania seat of government removed to Lancaster.

1799. Dec. 14.—Washington dies at Mount Vernon, Va.
1800. Aug.—United States seat of Government removed from Philadelphia to Washington.
Treaty of Peace concluded with France.
1801. June 10.—Tripoli declared war against the United States
Exports of the United States—$93,000,000.
1802. Louisiana ceded to France by Spain.
Gen. Daniel Morgan died. Aged 66 years.
1803. March 2.—Samuel Adams, distinguished statesman, died Aged 81.
April 30.—Louisiana purchased of France for $15,000,000.
Commodore Preble sent against Tripoli.
United States frigate "Philadelphia" taken by the Tripolitans.
1804. Brown University, R. I., founded.
Feb. 15.—Decatur recaptures and destroys the "Philadelphia."
Commodore Preble bombards Tripoli.
April 29.—Eaton captured Derne, a Tripolitan city.
June 3.—Treaty of Peace concluded with Tripoli.
July 11.—Aaron Burr kills Alexander Hamilton in a duel.
Pennsylvania Academy of Fine Arts founded.
1807. Jan. 27.—Aaron Burr arrested for conspiracy.
June 22.—British Frigate "Leopard" attacks the United States frigate "Chesapeake."
July 2.—British armed vessels ordered to leave the U. S.
Dec. 22.—Congress lays an embargo on American ships.
Com. Barron, of the "Chesapeake," suspended for 5 years.
1808. Jan. 1.—The African slave-trade abolished.
1809. March 1.—Congress interdicted commerce with England and France.
1811. May 16.—U. S. frigate "President" defeats the "Little Belt."
Nov. 7.—Gen. Harrison defeats the Indians at Tippecanoe.
Population of the United States—7,239,903.
1812. Jan. 11.—An additional force of 10,000 men authorized.
June 18.—War declared against Great Britain.
July 12.—Gen. Hull invades Canada.
July 17.—Fort Mackinaw surrendered to the British.
Aug. 5.—Americans defeated near Brownstown.
" 9.—Americans defeat the British near Brownstown.
" 16.—Gen. Hull surrenders Detroit to Gen. Brock.
Sept.—Gen. Harrison takes command of the Northwestern army.
1813. Jan. 22.—Gen. Winchester defeated at Frenchtown.
April 27.—York (now Toronto) captured by the Americans.

1813. May 1—Ft. Meigs besieged by the British—Gen. Clay defeated.
" 5.—Proctor defeated at Ft. Meigs by Harrison and Clay.
" 27.—Capture of Ft. George, Canada, by the Americans.
" 29.—The British repulsed by Brown at Sackett's Harbor.
Aug. 2.—The British repulsed at Ft. Stephenson by Maj. Croghan.
" 30.—Creek war begins by the massacre at Ft. Mims.
Oct. 5.—Battle of the Thames—Proctor defeated by Harrison. Tecumseh killed.

1814. March 27.—Battle of Tohopeka, which ended the Creek war.
" 30.—The British defeat Gen. Wilkinson at La Colle.
July 3.—Fort Erie captured by Gen. Brown.
Aug. 15.—British repulsed at Fort Erie.
" 24.—Gen. Ross enters Washington and burns the Capitol.
Sept. 12.—Battle of Baltimore, or North Point.
" 13.—British fleet repulsed at Fort McHenry.
" 17.—Gen. Brown attacks the British works at Fort Erie.
Nov. 7.—Gen. Jackson drives the British out of Pensacola.
Dec. 14.—United States flotilla captured on Lake Borgne.
" 15.—Delegates to the Hartford Convention meet. They oppose the war.
Dec. 24.—Treaty of Peace between the United States and England signed at Ghent.

1815. Jan. 1.—The British defeated at New Orleans.
March 2.—The United States declared war against Algiers.
May 21.—Commodore Decatur sent with a squadron against Algiers.

1816. April 10.—United States Bank chartered for 20 years.

1817. Jan. 1.—United States Bank opened at Philadelphia.
Commencement of the Seminole war.

1818. April.—The Seminoles defeated and dispersed by Gen. Jackson.

1819. Feb.—Treaty of Amity for the cession of Florida to the United States.
May.—The "Savannah"—the first steamer from New York to Liverpool.
Aug. 23.—Commodore Perry dies in the West Indies.

1820. March 3.—Missouri Compromise passed.

1822. Florida made a territory.

1824. Aug. 15.—The Marquis de La Fayette visits the U. S.
1826 Feb. 13.—American Temperance Society instituted at Boston.
July 4.—Ex-Presidents John Adams and Thomas Jefferson died.
1830. May 7.—Treaty between the United States and the Ottoman Porte.
The ports of the United States again opened to British commerce.
1832. The Black Hawk war commences.
Cholera in New York.
Nov. 24.—South Carolina declares the doctrine of nullification.
Gen. Jackson issues his celebrated proclamation.
1833. March 4.—Andrew Jackson commences his second administration.
Gen. Santa Anna elected President of Mexico.
1834. President Jackson censured by Congress for removing Government deposits.
1835. War with the Seminoles commenced.
Great fire in New York.
1837. Dec. 25.—Gen. Taylor defeats the Indians at Okeechobee.
" 28.—Steamer "Caroline" burned by Canadian royalists.
The Independence of Texas acknowledged.
1838. Rebellion of the "Sons of Liberty," in Canada.
President prohibits American citizens aiding the Canadians.
Nov. 7.—Battle of Prescott, U. C.—the rebellion suppressed.
National debt of United States paid—surplus revenue divided among the States.
Mexico declares war against France.
1839. March 9.—Peace concluded between France and Mexico.
Oct. 9.—United States Bank suspends payment.
Disturbances on the north-eastern boundary of Maine.
1841. Upper and Lower Canada united into one province.
April 4.—President Harrison dies and John Tyler succeeds him.
May 31.—Congress meets in extra session.
Aug. 9.—The Sub-Treasury Act repealed.
" 18.—Bankrupt Act passed.
1842. The Dorr Insurrection in Rhode Island.
The Seminole war terminated.
Treaty with England settling North-eastern Boundary Question.

1843. June 9.—Washington Allston, painter, died at Cambridge. Aged 64.

1845. Anti-rent riots in New York.

Mexico declares war against the United States.

1846. April 24.—Hostilities commence with Mexico.

May.—The Mexicans bombard Fort Brown.

" 18.—Taylor crosses the Rio Grande and takes Matamoras.

July 6.—Com. Sloat takes possession of California.

Aug. 22.—New Mexico annexed to the United States.

Nov. 14.—Tampico, Mexico, occupied by United States troops.

1847. Jan.—Mexicans massacre Americans in New Mexico.

March 29.—Vera cruz surrenders to Gen. Scott.

Sept. 12–14.—Chepultepec stormed, and city of Mexico taken by assault, by the Americans, under Gen. Scott.

1848. Feb. 2.—Upper California ceded to the United States.

" 22.—Treaty of Peace with Mexico signed at Guadaloupe, Hidalgo.

Cultivation of the tea-plant commenced in South Carolina.

Dec. 8.—First deposit of California gold in the Mint.

1849. April 25.—Parliament House at Montreal burned by insurgents.

1850. July 9.—Death of President Taylor.

" 10.—Inauguration of Millard Fillmore.

Sept. 18.—The Fugitive Slave Act passed.

Texas Boundary settled by payment of $10,000,000 to Texas.

New Mexico and Utah admitted as Territories.

Slave-trade abolished in the District of Columbia.

1851. April 16.—The light-house in Boston Harbor carried away.

May 8.—Southern Right's Convention at Charleston, S. C.

Nov.—The frigate "Mississippi" sent to Turkey for Kossuth.

Dec.—Kossuth arrives in New York.

" 14.—Principal room of the Congressional library burned.

1852. Jan.—The Ohio State House burned.

1853. May 30.—Dr. Kane sails on his Arctic expedition.

July 8.—Com. Perry's expedition arrived at Japan.

Dec. 16.—Santa Anna elected Dictator of Mexico for life.

1854. Jan. 5.—Steamer "San Francisco" foundered at sea—240 U. S. troops lost.

Mar. 8.—Commercial Treaty concluded with Japan.

April 20.—Miss Dix's Bill favoring the indigent insane vetoed.

1854. April 28.—U. S. announces neutrality in the Eastern Question.
May 31.—Kansas-Nebraska Bill passed by Congress.
June 7.—Reciprocity concluded with England.
July 13.—Bombardment of Greytown, Central America, by a United States man-of-war.
Dec.—Death of J. Harrington, last survivor of the battle of Lexington.

1855. Feb. 1.—U. S. steamer "Waterwitch" fired on, on the Paraguay.
Nov. 3.—Passmore Williamson released from 3 months' imprisonment in the Wheeler Slave Case.
Dec. 8.—Abdication of Santa Anna, Dictator of Mexico.

1856. Feb. 2.—N. P. Banks elected Speaker of U. S. House of Representatives.
April 17.—Quebec made the seat of Canadian government.
May 22.—Senator Sumner, of Mass., assaulted by Brooks, of S. C.
" 28.—The British Envoy ordered to quit Washington.
June 24.—Gen. Walker recognized as President of Nicaragua.
July 13.—J. W. Geary confirmed as Governor of Kansas.
Aug. 30.—Extra session of Congress adjourns.

1857. Mar. 6.—The Dred Scott Decision delivered by C. J. Taney.
" 26.—R. J. Walker appointed Governor of Kansas.
Aug. 24.—General financial panic begins.
Sept. 8.—Loss of the "Central America" and 450 lives.
" 23.—Commencement of the great religious revival.
Dec.—Commercial failures this year, 5,123; liabilities, $291,757,000.

1858. Feb.—Juarez declared President of Mexico—war ensues.
" 14.—U. S. army defeats the Mormons in Utah.
Mar. 28.—Nicaragua seeks the protection of the United States.
April 30.—The "English Kansas Bill" passes Congress.
May 23.—Minnesota State Government organized.
June 10.—Atlantic Telegraph fleet land.
" 13.—Treaty of Amity with China signed.
Aug. 5.—Completion of the Atlantic Telegraph.
" 7.—Ottawa made the Capital of Canada.
Oct. 5.—Crystal Palace, New York, burned.

1859. April 4.—Mr. McLane reorganizes the Juarez Gov., Mex.
Oct. 3.—J. Y. Mason, Minister to France, dies at Paris.
" 17.—John Brown's raid at Harper's Ferry, Va.

1860. Feb. 1.—Pennington, of N. J., elected Speaker U. S. House Rep.

May 14.—Japanese Embassy arrives at Washington.

June 3.—Terrible tornado in Illinois and Iowa.

" 28.—Steamer "Great Eastern" arrives at New York.

July 24.-Sept. 20.—Visit of Prince of Wales to U. S. and Canada.

Nov. 6.—Abraham Lincoln elected President.

" 7.—The "Palmetto Flag" hoisted in Charleston harbor.

" 10.—South Carolina Legislature proposes secession.

" 11.—Senator Hammond, of South Carolina, resigns.

" 18.—Georgia appropriates $1,000,000 to arm the State.

Maj. Anderson sent to Ft. Moultrie.

Dec. 1.—Great secession meeting at Memphis.

" 3.—Congress met.

" 10.—Howell Cobb, Secretary of the Treasury, resigns.

" 13.—The President opposes reinforcing Ft. Moultrie.

" 14.—Gen. Cass, Secretary of State, resigns.

" 18.—Crittenden Compromise introduced into U. S. Senate.

" 20.—South Carolina adopts Secession Ordinance.

" 22.—Crittenden Compromise defeated in Com. of 13.

" 25.—Members of Congress from South Carolina resign.

" 26.—Maj. Anderson, with 111 men, takes possession of Sumter.

" 27.—Rev'e cutter "Wm. Aiken" surrendered to S. C. authorities.

" 28.—S. C. authorities take Castle Pinckney and Ft. Moultrie.

" 29.—John B. Floyd, Secretary of War, resigns.

1861 Jan. 2.—Gov. Ellis, of N. C., takes possession of Ft. Macon.

" 4.—Gov. Moore, of Alabama, seizes Ft. Morgan, and United States arsenal at Mobile.

National Fast Day, by order of the President.

Jan. 8.—Jacob Thompson, Secretary of Interior, resigns.

" 9.-Feb. 1.—Mississippi, Florida, Alabama, Georgia, Louisiana, and Texas passed secession ordinances.

Steamer "Star of the West" fired on in Charleston harbor.

Jan. 11.—John A. Dix appointed Sec. of Treasury, *vice* Thomas, resigned.

" 13.—Florida troops take possession of Pensacola Navy-yard.

" 18.—Virginia appropriates $1,000,000 for State defense.

1861. Jan. 21.—Jeff. Davis resigns his seat in the U. S. Senate.
" 24.—U. S. arsenal at Augusta, Ga., seized.
Feb. 1.—Mint and custom house, N. O., seized by La. authorities.
" 4.—Southern Confederacy formed at Montgomery, Ala.
Peace Cong. meets at Wash'n—Ex-Pres. Tyler, Pres.
Feb. 9.—Jeff. Davis elected President of Southern Confederacy.
" 19.—Fort Kearney, Kansas, seized by the Confederates.
Mar. 1.—Gen. Twiggs expelled from the army for treason.
Peace Congress adjourned, after a stormy session—accomplished nothing.
Mar. 5.—Beauregard takes command at Charleston, S. C.
" 7.—Beauregard stops all intercourse between Ft. Sumter and Charleston.

THIRD PERIOD:

FROM THE GREAT REBELLION TO A. D. 1872.

1861. April 12.—Bombardment of Fort Sumter commenced.
" 13.—Maj. Anderson capitulates, and sails for New York.
" 15.—President Lincoln calls for 75,000 volunteers.
" 17.—Jeff. Davis offers letters of marque to privateers.
" 18.—Arsenal at Harper's Ferry destroyed by the Commander.
Col. Coke and 400 men, from Penn., arrive at Washington.
April 19.—The 6th Massachusetts regiment fired on in Baltimore—2 soldiers and 11 of the mob killed.
Pres. Lincoln declares the Southern ports in a state of Blockade.
" 20.—Gosport Navy-yard and 8 war-vessels destroyed.
The 4th Massachusetts Regiment arrives at Fortress Monroe.
April 25.—Virginia proclaimed a member of Southern Confederacy.
May 4.—McClellan placed in command of the Dep'm't of Ohio.
" 5.—Gen. Butler takes possession of the Relay House, Maryland.
" 6.—Arkansas secedes.

1861. May 11.—Charleston, S. C., blockaded.
" 13.—England acknowledges the insurgent states as belligerents.
" 16.—Gen. Scott orders the fortification of Arlington Heights.
" 18.—Gen. Butler takes command of the Department of Virginia—head-quarters, Fortress Monroe.
" 20.—North Carolina secedes; Kentucky declares neutrality.
" 21.—Tennessee secedes.
" 22.—Fortifications at Ship Island destroyed by Unionists.
" 24.—Federal troops cross the Potomac; Alexandria occupied; Col. Ellsworth shot.
" 26.—All postal services in the seceded States suspended.
June 3.—Hon. S. A. Douglas dies at Chicago.
Beauregard takes command of Confederates at Manassas Junction.
" 10.—Maj. Winthrop killed at Big Bethel.
" 14.—Confederates evacuate Harper's Ferry.
" 15.—The captured privateer "Savannah" arrives at N. Y.
" 17.—Gen. Lyon defeats the Confederates at Booneville, Mo.
" 20.—Gen. McClellan assumes command in West Virginia.
" 29.—The Wheeling Government, Virginia, acknowledged by the President.
" The privateer "Sumter" escapes from New Orleans.
July.—First United States war loan—$250,000,000.
" 4.—Congress meets in extra session.
" 6.—Fremont appointed to command of Western Department.
" 11.—Nine Southern members expelled from the U. S. Senate.
" 16.—The President authorized to call out 500,000 men.
" 22.—McClellan takes command of Army of the Potomac.
Aug. 3.—Confiscation Bill passed.
" 5.—Com. Alden bombards Galveston.
" 6.—Congress adjourns.
" 10.—Gen. Lyon killed at Wilson Creek.
" 14.—Gen. Fremont declares martial-law in St. Louis.
Mutiny of the 79th New York Regiment at Washington.
" 16.—Gen. Wool takes command at Fortress Monroe.

1861. Aug. 16.—President suspends all commerce with seceded States.

" 23.—A large body of Cherokee Indians join Confederates.

" 26.—The Hatteras Expedition sailed from Fortress Monroe.

" 29.—Capture of Forts Hatteras and Clarke.

Sept. 6.—Gen. Grant takes possession of Paducah, Ky.

" 11.—Pres. Lincoln orders Gen. Fremont to modify his emancipation proclamation.

" 18.—Secession members of Maryland Legislature sent to Ft. McHenry.

" 20.—Lexington, Mo., surrendered to the Confederates.

" 21.—Ex-Vice-Pres. Breckinridge joins the Confederates.

Oct. 11.—Confed. steamer "Nashville" escapes from Charleston.

" 29.—Naval expedition, under Com. Dupont and Gen. Sherman, leaves Fortress Monroe.

Nov. 1.—Gen. Scott resigns as Commander-in-Chief; Gen. McClellan succeeds him.

" 7.—Halleck assigned to the command of Department of the West.

" 8.—Mason and Slidell taken from a British steamer.

" 18.—C. S. Congress convened at Richmond, Va.

" 24.—Mason and Slidell placed in Ft. Warren, Boston harbor.

Dec. 4.—Breckinridge expelled from U. S. Senate for treason.

" 6.—Occupation of Beaufort, S. C., by U. S. forces.

" 11.—All the islands adjacent to Port Royal occupied by Union forces.

" 21.—17 stone vessels sunk in the harbor at Charleston, S. C.

" 30.—N. Y. and Boston banks suspend specie payment.

1862. Jan. 1.—Mason and Slidell delivered to the British Minister.

" 12.—The Burnside Expedition sailed from Ft. Monroe.

" 13.—E. M. Stanton app. Sec. of War, *vice* Cameron, resigned.

Cameron nominated Minister to Russia, *vice* Clay, resigned.

" 18.—Death of Ex-President Tyler, at Richmond, Va.

Feb. 5.—Jesse D. Bright expelled from the U. S. Senate.

" 6.—Ft. Henry, on Tenn. River, surren. to Com. Foote.

1862. Feb. 8.—Gen. Burnside captures 6 forts on Roanoke Island.

" 22.—Jefferson Davis inaugurated President of the Southern Confederacy.

Mar. 3.—Brigham Young elected Governor of Deseret, Utah.

" 8.—The "Merrimac" destroys 2 U. S. vessels.

" 9.—U. S. Battery "Monitor" defeats the "Merrimac."

" 11.—Gen. McClellan removed from the supreme command of the army and appointed to the command of the Army of the Potomac.

April 2.—Pres. Lincoln's Emancipation Resolution passed the Senate.

" 8.—National Tax Bill passed U. S. House of Rep.

" 24.—Destruction of Dismal Swamp canal completed.

" 27.—Stars and Stripes raised over U. S. mint in N. O. Gen. Butler landed his troops near Fort St. Philip.

April 28.—Forts Jackson and St. Philip surrender.

May 7.—Pres. Lincoln visits Fortress Monroe and the fleet.

" 9.—Confederates evacuate Pensacola and destroy the navy-yard.

" 11.—Confederates blow up the "Merrimac."

" 12.—Natchez surrendered to Com. Farragut.

" 25.—Gen. Banks retreats from Winchester to Martinsburg.

" 26.—Additional troops called for by Government. Gen. Banks' army crosses the Potomac. Confiscation Act passed the House of Representatives.

June 6.—Tax Bill passed U. S. Senate.

" 20.—Porter, with 10 mortar-boats, arrived off Vicksburg.

" 26.—Gen. Pope assigned to command of the Virginia army.

" 27.—Bombardment of Vicksburg commenced. Fremont relieved of his command, at his own request.

July 1.—President Lincoln calls for 600,000 volunteers.

" 11.—Gen. Halleck appointed commander of all land forces.

" 22.—Siege of Vicksburg abandoned.

" 27.—Steamer "Golden Gate," from San Francisco burned—230 passengers, and 1½ million treasure lost.

Aug. 4.—Draft ordered for 300,000 militia.

" 5.—Gen. Robt. McCook murdered, riding in an ambulance.

" 20.—Sioux Indians repulsed at Ft. Ridgely, Minn.

1862. Sept. 2.—Martial-law declared in Cincinnati.
" 5.—Confederate army commences crossing into Maryland.
" 7.—McClellan takes command in person of Potomac Army.
" 17.—Cumberland Gap evacuated by the Federals.
" 22.—Pres. Lincoln issues his Emancipation Proclamation.
" 24.—Convention of loyal Governors at Altoona, Penn.
" 25.—*Habeas Corpus* suspended by the U. S. Government.
" 29.—Gen. J. C. Davis kills Gen. Nelson at Louisville. Gen. Thomas succeeds Gen. Buell in command.
Oct. 10.—Confed. Gen. Stuart's cavalry reaches Chambersburg, Penn.
" 30.—Gen. Mitchel died of yellow fever, at Beaufort, S. C.
Nov. 5.—Gen. Burnside succeeds Gen. McClellan.
" 15.—Gen. A. G. Hamilton app. Military Gov. of Texas.
" 16.—Pres. Lincoln enjoins the observance of the Sabbath.
" 18.—The "Alabama" escapes from Martinique.
" 22.—All political state prisoners released.
Dec. 6.—Gen. Banks' expedition sails from N. Y., for New Orleans.
" 16.—Gen. Banks succeeds Gen. Butler at New Orleans.
" 17.—Union troops occupy Baton Rouge.
" 31.—West Virginia admitted as a State.

1863. Jan. 1.—Pres. Lincoln declares all the slaves in the Confederate States free.
" 9.—Exchange of 20,000 prisoners effected.
" 10.—Bombardment of Galveston begun.
" 11.—Gun-boat "Hatteras" sunk by the "Alabama."
Feb. 12.—National Currency Bill passes the Senate.
Mar. 21.—Death of Maj.-Gen. E. V. Sumner.
April 7.—Ship "Morning Star" captured by the "Alabama."
" 22–May 2.—Grierson's raid.
May 8.—Col. Streight's command (1,700) captured. Confederate Gen. Van Dorn killed by Dr. Peters.
" 10.—Death of "Stonewall" Jackson.
" 13.—Yazoo City captured by Union gun-boats.
" 18.—Commencement of the battles before Vicksburg.
" 25.—Confederate navy-yard destroyed at Yazoo City.
" 28.—First colored regiment from the North leaves Boston.

1863. June 1.—Gen. Gilmore succeeds Gen. Hunter in the South.
" 2.—3,000 Confederate prisoners arrive at Indianapolis.
" 17.—Kilpatrick defeats Fitzhugh Lee's cavalry brigade.
" 21.—Lee makes his second invasion of Maryland.
" 26.—Rear-Admiral Foote died in New York.
" 28.—Meade succeeds Hooker in command of Potomac army.
July 4.—Vicksburg surrendered to the Union army.
" 8.—Port Hudson, with 7,000 prisoners, surrendered to Banks.
Gen. Morgan invades Indiana and captures Corydon.
July 13–16.—Great riot in New York.
" 31.—Martial-law in Kentucky.
Aug. 21.—Lawrence, Kan., pillaged and burned by Quantrell's guerrillas—many citizens murdered.
" 23.—Shells thrown into Charleston—nearly 6 miles range. Fort Fisher, near Wilmington, bombarded.
Sept. 1.—Gen. Burnside occupied Knoxville, Tenn.
" 10.—General Burnside captures Cumberland Gap.
" 15.—Pres. Lincoln suspends the *Habeas Corpus* Act.
Nov. 5.—Brownsville, Texas, captured.
Dec. 4.—Gen. Longstreet raises the siege of Knoxville.

1864. Feb. 1.—Pres. Lincoln orders a draft for 500,000 men.
Kilpatrick and Dahlgren's raid on Richmond.
May 8.—Gen. Grant commissioned as Lieutenant-General.
" 12.—Gen. Grant appointed to command U. S. armies.
" 25.—Gen. Forrest captures and fires Paducah, Ky.
April 26.—Gov. accepts the service of 100-days' men.
May 5.—Gen. Butler lands on the south side of the James.
" 7.—Sherman begins his march against Atlanta.
" 13.—Sheridan reaches Hanover Junction in rear of the enemy.
June 19.—The "Kearsarge" sinks the "Alabama."
" 30.—Sec. Chase resigns; Hon. W. P. Fessenden appointed his successor.
July 5.—Confederates, under Early, invade Maryland.
" 30.—Chambersburg, Penn., partially burned.
Explosion of a mine at Petersburg.
Aug. 5.—Com. Farragut gains a victory in Mobile Bay.
" 18.—Weldon R. R. seized by Gen. Grant.
" 23.—Fort Morgan surrendered.
Sept. 19.—Gen. Sheridan's victory in the Shenandoah Valley.

1864. Oct. 7.—Pirate vessel "Florida" captured by the "Wachusett."

Nov. 3.—The "Albemarle" destroyed by Lieut. Cushing

" 16.—Gen. Sherman commences his march to the sea

Dec. 21.—Gen. Sherman enters Savannah, Ga.

1865. Jan. 15.—Union troops and fleet capture Fort Fisher.

Feb. 4.—Illinois black laws repealed.

" 18.—Gen. Gilmore takes possession of Charleston, S. C., and hoists the Old Flag over Fort Sumter

Feb. 19.—Fort Anderson, N. C., taken.

" 23.—Raleigh, N. C., captured.

Mar. 2.—Gen. Sheridan captures Gen. Early and his army.

" 10.—Gen. Sherman occupies Fayetteville, N. C.

" 17.—Confederate Congress adjourned "*sine die.*"

April 1.—New and higher tariff comes in force.

" 2.—Gen. Lee's line at Petersburg carried.

" 9.—Gen. Lee surrendered with his whole army.

" 14.—Pres. Lincoln assassinated by J. Wilkes Booth.

" 15.—Death of Lincoln; Andrew Johnson becomes President.

" 26.—Gen. Johnston surrendered.

" 27.—Booth, the assassin, mortally wounded and captured.

May 4.—Gen. Dick Taylor surrenders.

" 10.—Jeff. Davis captured.

" 22.—Proclamation opening southern ports, and exceptional amnesty.

May 24—Grand review of Gen. Sherman's army at Washington.

Jeff. Davis indicted for treason.

May 26.—Kirby Smith surrendered.

" 31.—Gen. Hood and staff surrendered.

End of the rebellion.

July 7.—The assassins of Pres. Lincoln hung.

Nov. 2.—National thanksgiving.

" 10.—Execution of Wirz, the Southern prison-keeper.

Dec. 18.—Slavery declared constitutionally abolished.

1866. May 3.—Colorado Bill vetoed.

June 7.—Pres. Johnson's address against the Fenian movement.

July 16.—Cong. passed second F.'s Bureau Bill over veto.

Sept. 6.—Corner-stone of Douglas Monument laid at Chicago.

Dec. 20.—Suffrage given to colored men in District of Columbia.

1867. Feb. 9.—Nebraska admitted as a State.
Mar. 2.—Tenure of Office Bill passed.
Reconstruction Bill passed over President's veto.
April 10.—Russian American Treaty approved by the Senate.
May 13.—Jeff. Davis released on bail.
July 1.—Congress meets in extra session.
" 19.—Supplementary Reconstruction Bill passed, over veto.
" 20.—Congress adjourns until November.
Aug. 12.—Pres. Johnson suspends Sec. Stanton from office.

1868. Jan. 1.—Gen. A. D. McCook succeeds Gen. McKenzie in the Sub-district of the Rio Grande.
Jan. 5.—U. S. Military Asylum at Augusta, Me., burned.
" 6.—Congress meets—Pres. censured for removing Sheridan.
Sec. Seward announced that 21 States had ratified the 14th amendment to the Constitution.
Jan. 11.—Chinese Government appoints Anson Burlingame (former U. S. Minister) Special Envoy. Salary, $40,000.
Jan. 13.—The Senate non-concurred in Stanton's suspension.
" 29.—Death of Bishop Hopkins, of Vermont. Aged 76.
Feb. 18.—Senate bill passed for the reduction of the army.
" 21.—The President declares Gen. Thomas in Stanton's place.
" 24.—The House of Representatives impeach the President.
Mar. 12.—Bill passed to abolish tax on manufactures.
" 18.—Admiral Farragut received by the Pope of Rome.
" 30.—Impeachment Trial commenced in the Senate.
May 22.—Arrival of the Chinese Embassy in New York.
" 23.—Kit Carson, the noted trapper, died. Aged 58.
" 26.—Impeachment Trial ends—Pres. Johnson acquitted.
Sec. Stanton resigns.
" 29.—G. A. of the Republic decorated Union soldiers' graves.
Ex-Gov. Lincoln of Massachusetts, dies. Aged 75.
Heavy shocks of earthquake at Sacramento.
" 30.—Treaty concluded with the Osage Nation.

1868. June 4.—Ex-Pres. Buchanan buried at Wheatland, Penn.
" 5.—The Chinese Embassy received by the President.
" 10.—Bill passed Senate for admission of S. States.
" 12.—Reverdy Johnson confirmed as Minister to England.
" 16.—Gov. Humphreys removed, and Gen. Ames appointed Governor of Mississippi.
" 20.—Commencement of difficulties between U. S. Embassador and the Government of Paraguay.
" 24.—The Senate ratifies the Chinese Treaty.
" 25.—Freedman's Bureau Bill passed, over veto.
July 4.—Pres. Johnson issues his proc. of amnesty to all engaged in the rebellion, except those already indicted.
" 15.—Wm. M. Evarts confirmed as Attorney-General.
" 16.—Laws of United States extended over Alaska.
Riot at Millican, Texas—45 persons killed.
" 17.—Senate appropriates $7,200,000 for payment for Alaska.
" 21.—Congress declares the 14th Amendment ratified.
" Bill passed organizing Wyoming Territory.
Aug. 3.—Mr. Washburn denies the charge of conspiracy against Lopez.
Failure of the Atlantic Cable of 1866.
Charles G. Halpine (Miles O'Reily) dies. Aged 39.
" 11.—Thaddeus Stevens, M. C. from Pennsylvania, dies. Aged 75.
" 14.—Encke's comet discovered at Naval Observatory Washington..
" 17.—National Teachers' Ass'n, at Nashville, Tenn.
" 20.—Chinese Embassy in Boston.
Death of Gen. B. F. Smith at Fort Reno. Aged 37.
Sept. 3.—Ga. Legis. declares negroes ineligible to seats.
" 18.—General Hindman assassinated at Helena, Ark.
Oct. 21.—Serious earthquakes in California.
James Hind, M. C. from Arkansas, assassinated.
" 25.—Colonel Carpenter defeats the Cheyennes and Arrapahoes.
Dec. 6.—Ku-Klux outrages in Tennessee.
" 20.—Augustus S. Mitchell, Amer. geographer, dies.
" 25.—President Johnson issues a universal amnesty proclamation.
" Mosby Clarke, a Revolutionary soldier, dies at Richmond, Virginia. Aged 121 years.
" General Sheridan captured the Indian chiefs Son tanta and Lone Wolf.

1869. Jan. 1.—New suspension bridge at Niagara Falls opened.

1869. Feb. 1.—United States Supreme Court decides Internal Revenue Laws constitutional.
" 19.—Jefferson Davis and his sureties released.
" 24.—The Copper Tariff Bill passed, over veto.
" 26.—Capital of West Virginia located at Charleston.
Constitutional Amendment passed, over the veto.
Passage of Bill to strengthen the public credit.
Mar. 4.—Hon. J. G. Blaine, of Maine, elected Speaker of the United States House of Representatives.
April 5.—United States Supreme Court decides the State taxation of national bank stock legal.
" 9.—Passage of the Reconstruction Bill.
" 10.—100 lodges Arrapahoe Indians surrender.
" 17.—Arrival of first cargo of tea at Chicago *via* Pacific Railroad.
May 10.—Central Pacific Railroad completed.
" 17.—Gen. D. E. Sickles appointed Minister to Spain.
" 29–30.—Decoration of Union Soldiers' graves.
June 1.—Corner-stone of the Atlanta (Ga.) Univ'ty laid.
" 10.—200 acres of the Mount Vernon estate sold.
" 15–18.—Great Peace Jubilee Concerts in Boston.
" 18.—Death of Honorable H. G. Raymond, of the New York "Times."
Dedication of Monument in Gettysburg Cemetery.
July 3.—Equestrian Statue of Washington unveiled in Boston.
" 8.—Monument to Fitz Greene Halleck dedicated at Guilford, Conneticut.
" 14.—Frightful accident and loss of life on the Erie Railroad.
National Convention of Y. M. C. A. at Portland, Me.
" 22.—Commodore S. S. Lee died in Virginia.
" 23.—Death of Ex-Governor Crapo, of Michigan.
Arrival of steamers laying the French Cable, at Duxbury, Massachusetts.
" 30.—Death of Hon. Isaac Toucey, of Connecticut.
Aug. 8.—Total eclipse of the sun, visible in the U. S.
" 12.—Com. Jarvis, U. S. N., died at Geneva, Illinois.
" 18.—Nat. Educational Convention, at Trenton, N. J.
Sept. 6.—Disastrous fire in a coal shaft near Scranton, Pennsylvania.
Secretary John A. Rawlins died at Washington.
Destructive gale in Massachusetts and Maine.
" 12.—Large meeting in Quebec favoring annexation to United States.
" 24.—Unparalleled gold excitement in New York.

1869. Oct. 1.—Boiler exp. at Ind. State Fair. 25 persons killed.
" 4.—Violent tornado on the coast of Maine.
" 5.—60th annual session of the A. B. C. F. M. at Pittsburg.
" 8.—Death of Ex-Pres. Franklin Pierce. Aged 64.
" 13.—Gen. W. W. Belknap, of Iowa, app. Sec. of War.
" 20.—C. W. Eliot installed Pres't of Harvard College.
" 27.—Remarkable meteor exp. near Forest Station, O.
" 28.—Steamer "Stonewall" burned below St. Louis. More than 200 lives lost.
Nov. 1.—Cincinnati School Board forbid reading the Bible in the Public Schools.
" 4.—George Peabody died at his residence in London.
" 8.—Rear-Admiral Stewart died at Bordentown, New Jersey. Aged 92.
" 11.—Death of Robert J. Walker in Washington.
" 12.—Amos Kendall, Ex-Post-master-General died. Aged 80.
" 23.—Indiana Supreme Court decide National Bank Currency taxable.
" 25.—A. D. Richardson mortally wounded in New York Tribune office, by Daniel McFarland.
Dec. 6.—Fem. Suff. Bill passed by Wyoming Legislature.
" 20.—E. M. Stanton confirmed as Judge of U. S. S. C.

1870. Jan. 8.—Death of Major-General J. A. Mower at N. O.
" 14.—Bill passed for the re-admission of Virginia.
" 21.—Prince Arthur, of England, arrived in N. Y.
" 25.—Peabody funeral fleet arrives at Portland, Me.
" 28.—U. S. corvette Oneida sunk by British steamer Bombay, near Yokohama, Japan. Many lives lost.
Feb. 7.—Legal Tender Act declared unconstitutional by Chief Justice Chase.
" 8.—Funeral of George Peabody at Peabody, Mass.
" 15.—Superior Court of Cincinnati decide against the authority of the School Board to exclude the Bible from the Public Schools.
Ohio River bridge at Louisville formally opened.
Mar. 5.—Forty families massacred by Indians in Texas.
" 7.—Women serve as jurors in Wyoming Territory.
" 8.—Governor Austin, of Minnesota, vetoed the Woman's Suffrage Bill.
" 26.—Pierre Soule died at New Orleans.
" 30.—Ratification of the 15th Amendment officially proclaimed.
Apr. 2.—Great earthquakes it San Francisco.
" 12.—The Saint Thomas treaty expires by limitation.

1870. Apr. 19.—The U. S. Senate pass the Georgia bill.

" 27.—The floor of the Court-house at Richmond, Virginia, falls. Nearly 200 persons killed and wounded.

May 6.—Return of General T. Jordan, the Cuban Commander, to New York.

" 23.—Beginning of the Fenian raid into Canada.

" 24.—Proclamation of President Grant against the Fenian raid.

" 26.—The North Pacific R. R. Bill becomes a law.

" 30.—Decoration of Union soldiers' graves.

June 6.—Reception of Red Cloud and the Sioux chiefs at Washington.

" 11.—Death of William Gilmore Simms, at Charleston, South Carolina.

" 21.—Bill to abolish the franking privilege defeated.

" 29.—The San Dom. treaty rejected by the Senate.

July 3.—The new Constitution of Illinois adopted.

" 12.—Serious riot between the Catholics and Orangemen in New York.

" 14.—Congress grants $3,000 per an. to Mrs. Lincoln.

" 15.—General Starr and other Fenians sentenced to two years imprisonment.

" 21.—International Convention of Young Men's Christian Association at Indianapolis.

Aug. 14.—Death of Ad. Farragut at Portsmouth, N. H.

Sept. 8.—The U. S. recognized the French Republic.

" 9.—Death of Dr. N. Lord, Ex-pres. of Dart. College.

" 30.—Great floods in Va. Richmond partially sub.

Oct. 1.—Yellow Fever raging on Governor's Island, N. Y.

" 8.—Second neutrality proclamation by the Pres.

" 20.—Severe shock of an earthquake in the Northeast and Middle States.

" 21.—Thomas Hughes, M. P., lectures in New York.

Nov. 7.—Bloody Riots in Donaldson, Louisiana.

" 14.—Minister Motley peremptorily recalled from England.

" 24.—Army of the Cumberland meets at Cleveland.

Dec. 1.—The S. Court of Mass. decides that a contract carried into effect on Sunday can not be repudiated.

" 4.—Arrest of General Jordan, the Cuban commander, in New York.

" 6.—Death of Gen. Hiram Walbridge in New York.

" 20.—Articles of impeachment preferred against Governor Holden of North Carolina.

1871 Jan. 1.—Terrific gales on the entire Atlantic coast.

" 2.—Reception at the President's White House

omitted. A custom never before departed from since Washington's day.

1871. Jan. 2.—Council of Indian nations at Ocmulgee, and a constitution adopted by a vote of 52 to 3.

" 3.—Celebration of the 8th anniversary of President Lincoln's Proclamation of Emancipation.

" 4.—Trial of Cadet Smith and others at West Point.

" 7.—Twenty car-loads of tea arrive at New York 23 days from Hong Kong *via* San Francisco.

" 8.—Alarming spread of hoof and mouth disease in New England.

" 9.—Correspondence between Secretary Fish and Minister Motley submitted to Congress.

The Cincinnati Clergy resolve against the license of prostitution in that city.

" 10.—The great coal mine strike begins in Penn.

The Mint Bill passed by the U. S. Senate.

In Kansas women made clerks in both Houses, and a girl appointed a page.

" 7–12.—The Hornet lands men on the coast of Cuba, who are attacked by Spaniards, and 17 men killed or captured.

" 11.—The United States Senate passes the San Domingo Commission Bill.

Fourteen mariners desert from the Pensacola Navy yard and all are drowned in trying to escape.

" 12.—The famous Ohio Liquor Bill becomes a law.

" 13.—The $300,000,000 five per cent. Refunding Bill, passed by the House.

Woman suffrage defeated in Congress; 3,000 women having memorialized Congress against it.

" 14–16.—Heavy and disastrous snow storm over the Western states.

" 14.—Steamer T. L. McGill exploded her boilers on the Mississippi, 58 persons perished.

" 15.—First arrival of teas at N. Y. *via* Suez Canal.

" 17.—Sailing of the Tennessee with San Domingo Commissioners.

" 18.—Fourteen Japanese nobles arrive at San Francisco to attend college in the United States.

At Laconia and Lake Village, New Hampshire, several earthquake shocks are felt.

" 19.—The first car load of California cotton sent to New England.

" 24.—Annual session of the Workingmen's assembly at Albany, New York.

1871. Jan. 25.—Vinnie Ream's statue of Lincoln unveiled at Washington.

" 28.—British America joins the Dominion of Canada. Steamer W. R. Arthur exploded her boilers near Island No. 40 on the Mississippi and burnt. 87 lives lost.

Feb. 1.—Congress admits the Georgia Senators, and the South is now all represented.

Sixty Indians killed in a fight on the Colorado River.

" 3.—The U. S. Senate pensions the soldiers of 1812.

" 5.—The New Hamburg, New York, Railway catastrophe killed and roasted or drowned 22 human beings, and cost the company hundreds of thousands of dollars.

" 6.—Congress votes $20,000 to defray expenses of investigating Ku Klux outrages.

" 7.—Committee of Ways and Means agree to report a bill for the repeal of the Income Tax.

" 8.—New Jersey ratifies the 15th Amendment.

" 10.—Messrs. Fish, Hoar, Schenck, and Williams confirmed as High Commissioners, for the settlement of the Anglo-American difficulties.

" 11.—Two steamers leave New York with provisions for France.

" 19.—The Chief Jus. of S. Court of Ark. impeached. The Governor and Lieutenant-Governor before, imp.

" 20-21.—Unparalleled tropical storm in San Fran.

" 23.—Dead lock in Indiana Legis., 34 Rep. resign.

" 26.—Arrival of 26 Japanese Nobles and Princes in New York.

March 1.—To this date, 6,000 women have memorialized Congress against granting Woman Suffrage.

A tidal wave swept through Long Island Sound.

" 2.—Boston Post Office Appropriation Bill passed in the Senate—cost not to exceed $1,500,000.

Severe earthquake shock in Eureka, California.

" The Boston, Hartford, and Erie Railroad Company declared bankrupt.

" 4.—The Forty-first Congress expires, and the Forty-second Congress is organized.

Treaty of Com. formed between Italy and the U. S.

Riot and murder at the Pennsylvania coal mines.

" 5.—Reign of terror in S. C. by Ku-Klux outrages.

A bloody Chinese fight in San Francisco.

" 6.—Horrible scene in court at Meridian, Miss. Judge Bramlette shot dead by a negro and ten negroes shot and killed

1871. March 8.—A terrible tornado swept every thing before it from Helena, Arkansas, to Fayette, Illinois.

" 9.—New York Chamber of Commerce propose a Pacific Ocean cable of 6,515 miles.

" 14.—Election in New Hampshire—Dem. victory.

" 17.—Project for a Congregational House in Boston, to cost $200,000.

" 19.—The Legislature of Illinois, after ten weeks' hard labor, passed three bills, and one of these was vetoed by the Governor.

" 23.—The New York City Viaduct Railway Bill passed by the Senate of New York.

" 25.—A meteor, so brilliant as to cast a shadow, seen at New York. On the same day, a fire destroys $250,000 worth of property in the city.

" 26.—The Tennessee reaches Charleston with the San Domingo Commissioners.

Great American Project set on foot to explore Palestine and Jerusalem.

" 31.—Magnificent aurora; a great cloud of blood-red in the north-east sky; the sight "to be remembered a life-time." During the month, a sun spot of 2,300,000 square miles was visible.

April 2.—Two sharp earthquake shocks at San Francisco, California.

" 3-4.—Elections in Rhode Island and Connecticut—Republican victories.

" 8.—Roger Williams' statue unveiled at Washingt'n.

" 11.—Equal Rights Bill passed the Mississippi Legislature.

" 14.—The Ku-Klux Bill passes the U. S. Senate.

" 17.—Nebraska State Insane Asylum at Lincoln, burnt, and two inmates perish.

" 18.—A United States captain and 14 soldiers killed by Indians in Texas.

" 20.—Ku-Klux Enforcement Bill passed by Congress and signed by the President.

" 27.—Indians massacre whites in Dakota.

A new line of steamers projected from New York to Rome.

" 28.—U. S. troops shoot 85 Arizona Indians.

May 3.—Indian battle in the Pinal Mountains, Arizona, 28 Apaches killed.

" 4.—Pres. Grant issues a Ku-Klux Proclamation.

" 7.—The Joint High Commission announce a treaty prepared.

1871. May 8.—U. S. troops kill or wound nearly 300 Indians in a battle near Laramie.

" 11.—Williamson's road steamer tried on Erie Canal.

" 12.—The Anglo-American treaty made public.

" 15.—New territorial government for Washington and the District of Columbia inaugurated.

" 20.—Arizona people report 200 citizens murdered by the Apaches.

" 21.—A twelve pound aerolite fell at Searsport, Me.

" 25.—The Mountain Indians of Arizona declare war against the whites.

" 27.—Twenty-one men killed and six more wounded, in a coal mine at Pittston, Pennsylvania.

June 1.—National Ins. Cong. at Washington adjourned. The Rhea sunk, and eight persons drowned near New York.

" 2.—Governor Butler of Nebraska impeached and removed from office.

Extraordinary sulphurous cyclone near Macon, Ill.

" 3.—Ex-Cong. Bowen found guilty of bigamy.

" 4.—U. S. Army reduced to peace footing, 35,284.

" 6.—Grand reception to Indian Chiefs at Boston.

" 10.—Unveiling of the Morse statue in Central Park, New York.

" 11.—Immense forest fires in Maine.

" 12.—The Gregorian Calendar adopted in Alaska to bring Sunday right.

Inauguration day in New Hampshire.

" 16.—A telegram from Hong Kong reaches New York, 15,000 miles, and is published in the daily papers next morning.

" 19.—National Musical Congress in Boston.

Earthquake at Long Island and in New Jersey.

Singular sinking of a canal bottom in Morris, N. J.

" 23.—Terrific thunder storm at Chicago.

" 25.—Alabama Claims, footed up to be $12,830,384.

" 24–25.—Government teamsters attacked by 250 Cheyennes at Fort Hill; eight killed, and three more burnt at the stake.

" 29.—Captain Hall leaves New York in the Polaris for the North Pole.

July 3.—The missionary ship Morning Star arrives at Honolulu.

" 5.—The Great Washington Treaty proclaimed by the President.

" 8.—Tidal wave on Lake Superior—cause unknown.

1871. July 11.—Superintendent Kelso, of N. Y., forbids the Orange display, and Gov. Hoffman revokes his order.

" 12.—Terrible conflict in New York between the Roman Catholic Irish, and the National Guards and Police. 62 persons killed, and 137 wounded.

" 13.—Amherst confers LL. D. upon Horace Greeley.

" 19.—Earthquake in all New England.

" 22.—The most remarkable aurora ever witnessed, observed at Springfield, Mass., and elsewhere.

" 24.—United States Scientific expedition to Brazil leaves New York.

" 28.—The Polaris heard from at Newfoundland.

" 30.—The "Westfield" explodes her boilers at New York. Of the 400 persons on board, 106 were killed, and 111 more or less injured. Com.'s loss $500,000.

Tidal wave 5 feet high on Lake Winnepisseogee, New Hampshire. It was the first ever seen there.

Aug. 1.—Women admitted to Burlington, Vermont, University.

" 3.—Fraudulent sale of $9,000,000, Rockford and St. Louis bonds in Frankfort.

" 4.—Formidable Indian raids in Montana.

" 8.—Nitro-glycerine exploded in Hoosac Tunnel by lightning. Three men killed.

" 15.—Doctor Hall heard from, at Holsteinburg, Sweden (July 31).

" 16.—Twentieth annual meeting of the American Science Association at Indianapolis, Indiana.

It is decided to prosecute the "Tammany" thieves.

" 24.—Great Pension frauds discovered at Wash.

" 25.—Duluth Canal opening.

" 26.—Terrific hurricane in the Gulf and along the Atlantic coast.

Alarming fires in Michigan.

Railroad Horrors. 33 persons killed and 50 injured at Revere, near Boston. 20 killed or wounded at Westport, Pennsylvania. 6 killed and 20 wounded at Williamsport, Pennsylvania.

" 27.—Steamer Ocean Wave exploded boilers at Mobile, Alabama. 70 persons killed or badly injured.

" 29.—Great losses by floods in Central New York and Maine.

" 30.—Deadly conflict between soldiers and citizens at Meridian, Mississippi.

Sept. 3.—Iron and Nail Works burnt at Wheeling West Virginia.

1871. Sept. 4.—Destructive hurricane at Windem, Minnesota.

" 6.—American Pomological Society meets at Richmond, Virginia.

" 8.—Mooshillock Mountain, N. H., 5,050 feet high, made a United States signal service observatory.

" 9.—The 116th new planet discovered by America.

" 1-10.—Appalling disaster to an American whaling fleet in the Arctic Ocean—33 vessels destroyed and abandoned.

" 19.—Nebraska votes on a new constitution.

" 20.—Tidal wave alarm on all the south Atlantic coast.

" 28.—National Commercial convention at Baltimore.

" 29.—The committee of "Seventy" sue the Tammany ring.

" 30.—Prof. Wilbur fell from his balloon at the height of a mile, at Paoli, Indiana.

Oct. 1.—International money order system goes into operation.

" 2.—Brigham Young indicted and arrested.

" 3.—Sixty-second annual session of A. B. C. F. M., at Salem, Massachusetts.

" 3.—Protestant Episcopal Triennial convention at Baltimore.

" 5.—Terrible forest fires raging in Wisconsin, Wyoming, Arizona, etc.

" 8.—Election riots in Philadelphia—many injured.

" 9-10.—The greatest conflagration on record occurred at Chicago. About 18,000 buildings of all descriptions were consumed, and the loss put at from $250,000,000 to $300,000,000, and from 100 to 500 persons perished in the flames, while 90,000 persons were made houseless and suffering.

" 9-12.—Awful forest fires in Wisconsin and Michigan, and whole towns destroyed. The Chicago *Tribune* says in Wisconsin and Michigan alone at least 90,000 people have lost all their possessions by fire. In all these western fires it is estimated that 3,000 persons perished in one week.

" 12.—Pre-historic skeletons 8 or 9 feet high found in Virginia.

" 13.—Encke's comet seen by New Haven astronomers.

" 14.—Chicago relief fund reaches $3,000,000.

" 16.—Martial-law in Texas.

" 17, 18.—Celebration of the completion of European and N. A. R. R., at Bangor, Me., Pres. Grant present.

1871. Oct. 21.—Mormon Hawkins convicted of adultery.
" 23.—National Police convention at St. Louis.
" 24.—National Insurance convention at New York.
" 24.—2,500 Mormon Women petition Congress in favor of Polygamy.
Terrible riot in Los Angeles, Cal.—19 Chinese killed.
" 23, 24.—Extensive forest fires in western New York.
" 27.—Tweed arrested and released on $2,000,000 bail.
" 28.—Brigham Young and his son indicted for murder.
" 29.—Day of fasting and prayer at Chicago.
" 30.—Gov. Bullock, of Georgia, disaffected, resigns.
Nov. 4.—$500,000 fraud discovered in the Indian Bounty Department at Washington.
" 6.—New York orders four regiments under arms for to-morrow's election.
" 7.—Election day in 9 States—Republican victories.
" 9.—An Aurora so bright in New York as to "cast shadows."
" 9.—A meteor fell and rolled along the ground beside a moving carriage, in South Easton, Massachusetts.
" 12.—Fred. W. Loring and six others killed on a stage coach in Arizona.
" 14.—Extraordinary storm from Europe to California—many Atlantic cities flooded.
" 15.—American and British Claims Commissioners meet at the National Capitol.
" 15.—Gloucester fishing season ends. It has been the most destructive to life and property of any for many years.
" 16.—The "Auk," an Arctic bird, visits New England for the first time.
" 17.—Gen. Sherman and staff leave in the Wabash for Europe.
" 18.—The Russian fleet with the Duke Alexis arrives in New York.
" 23.—Duke Alexis visits the Capitol and the President.
" 25.—Catacazy dismissed and Gen. Orloff made Charge d'Affaires of the Russian legation.
" 28.—The Supreme Court of New York pronounces mock marriages legal.
" 30.—National Thanksgiving day.
Dec. 2.—United States and England threaten to interfere in Cuban affairs.
" 2.—Sec. Boutwell reports a decrease in the National debt of $94,327,708.84, during the fiscal year.

1871. Dec. 5.—Agricultural congress at Selma, Alabama.
" 6.—National Board of Trade meets at St. Louis.
" 11.—Expense of the United States Census reported to be $3,287,600.
" 14.—The Apportionment Bill passed by Congress, the House to consist of 283 members.
" 18.—Bill introduced into Congress to incorporate a Company who are to girdle the earth with a telegraph.
" 20.—Gold $108\frac{3}{4}$; the lowest since 1862.
" 27.—Tweed, of the New York Ring, disappears.
" 30.—The New York Ring entirely broken up. Some imprisoned.
1872. Feb. 2.—Congress reports a bill for carrying into effect the treaty with Great Britain.
March 28.—The Tariff Bill passes the United States Senate. The income tax is abolished.
April 2.—Death of Prof. S. F. B. Morse, aged 81 years.
June 4.—Passage of the Tax and Tariff Bill, causing a diminution in the revenue of $53,000,000.
" 17.—Grand Musical Festival and Peace Jubilee at Boston; 2000 instruments, 20,000 singers.
" 20.—Indirect claims ruled out by Geneva Board. United States Government assents.
July 29.—Geneva Tribunal decides in favor of the United States in the Florida case.
" 31.—Two new asteroids discovered by Dr. Peters at Utica.
Aug. 23.—First vessel of Japan to an American port reaches San Francisco.
Sept. 6.—The Geneva Board conclude their arbitrament.
" 14.—Geneva award announced—$15,500,000 in gold.
Oct. 21.—Verdict of Emperor William of Germany on the San Juan question, in favor of the United States.
" 9–10.—The great fire in Boston. 80 acres burned over. Loss $80,000,000.
Nov. 29.—Death of Horace Greeley, aged 61 years.
1873. Jan. 2.—Militia preparing to attack the Modocs in Oregon.
" 6.—Opening of testimony in Credit Mobilier trial.
" 7.—Stokes sentenced to be hung Feb. 28.
" 27.—First repeal of the Franking Privilege.
Feb. 6.—Discovery of a planet of the tenth magnitude by Dr. Peters, of Clinton, N. Y.
March 2.—Passage of "Salary Grab."

1873. April 1.—Steamship "Atlantic" wrecked off Nova Scotia; 546 lives lost.

April 11.—Gen. E. R. S. Canby and Rev. E. Thomas, D. D., treacherously murdered by the Modoc Indians at a peace conference in Northern California.

" 30.—Three acres of the business part of Boston burned.

May 9.—Loss of the steamer Polaris, and death of Capt. Hall.

June 5.—Arrival of the Polaris' survivors in Washington.

Sept. 18.—Suspension of Jay Cooke & Co.

" 19.—Failure of nineteen banking firms in New York and eleven in Philadelphia.

Oct. 31.—Capture of the Steamer Virginius by the Spanish gun-boat Tornado, near Jamaica.

Nov. 4–7.—Massacre of many of the officers and passengers of the Virginius.

" 14.—United States war steamers sailed for Cuban waters.

" 27.—The Hoosic Tunnel opened.

Dec. 8.—Repeal of the Iron-clad Oath in the United States House of Representatives.

" 11.—Sen. Carpenter, of Wisconsin, elected *pro tem.* President of the United States Senate.

" 14.—Death of Prof. Agassiz.

1874. Jan. 10.—The miners' revolt at Pottsville, Pa. 9000 men protest against the monopolists.

" 13.—Political excitements in Louisiana.

Feb. 7.—Women's temperance crusade begins in Ohio.

" 11.—Grangers' National Convention at St. Louis.

March 8.—Ex-president Millard Fillmore died.

" 11.—Death of Sen. Sumner.

April 15.—Destructive floods in the Cumberland and Tennessee Rivers.

" 21.—Grant vetoes the Finance Bill.

" " —A pitched battle fought between the Brooks and Baxter forces in Arkansas.

May 5.—Two hundred thousand people made homeless by the Louisiana floods.

" 8.—Devout Catholics, of New York, prepare for a pilgrimage.

" 17.—Bursting of Goshen (Mass.) reservoir. 150 lives lost; $1,500,000 worth of property destroyed.

" 22.—United States Senate passes the Civil Rights Bill.

1874. June 10.—Military ordered to scene of Hocking Valley (Ohio) coal strikers.

" 24.—Fall of church in Syracuse, N. Y. 20 killed, 150 wounded.

July 1.—Abduction of Charlie Ross at Germantown.

" 4.—Opening of the Great Bridge at St. Louis.

" 7.—Serious outbreak of Comanches and Cheyennes in Indian Territory.

" 14.—Second great conflagration in Chicago.

" 27.—Great flood in Pittsburg. Immense loss of life.

Aug. 22.—Serious riot between the whites and blacks at Lancaster, Ky.

Sept. 14.—Insurrection in Louisiana. Attempt to overthrow the State Government. 20 persons killed.

Oct. 15.—Unveiling of Lincoln Statue at Sprinfield, Ill.

" 24.—Heavy mercantile failures in Boston.

Nov. 1.—Riot at Pottsville, Pa.

" 17.—Terrible fires raging in the coal mines under Pittsburg, Pa.

" 29.—Arrival of King Kalakaua in San Francisco.

Dec. 7.—Vicksburg is attacked by 700 negroes who are defeated, with 20 killed.

" 9.—The transit of Venus.

1875. Jan. 4.—Louisiana Legislature taken possession of by United States troops.

" 5.—Opening of Beecher–Tilton trial.

" 26.—Attempt to burn the Navy Department at Washington.

Feb. 6.—Civil Rights Bill passed by United States House of Representatives.

" 24.—Colorado admitted as a State.

" 26.—Ann Eliza Young obtains a divorce from Brigham Young, with alimony.

March 15.—Archbishop McCloskey created a Cardinal.

" 16.—Virginius matter settled with Spain for $80,000 in gold.

" 28.—The fifth anniversary of the American Tract Society, celebrated in New York.

April 23.—Lieut. Henley fights the Red Skins in Kansas. 27 killed.

" 26.—Fifty-sixth anniversary of "I. O. O. F."

May 10.—Gigantic whisky frauds brought to light by Secretary Bristow.

June 10.—The new cable of the "Direct United States Cable Co." completed.

1875. June 17.—Great demonstration in Boston at anniversary of Battle of Bunker Hill.

" 18.—Slight shock of earthquake through parts of Ohio and Indiana.

July 2.—Disagreement of jury in Beecher trial. Nine for acquittal; three for conviction.

PRESIDENTS AND VICE PRESIDENTS OF THE UNITED STATES.

FIRST ADMINISTRATION. 1789–97. 8 YEARS.

1789. George Washington, Virginia, President.
John Adams, Massachusetts, Vice President.

SECOND ADMINISTRATION. 1797–1801. 4 YEARS.

1797. John Adams, Massachusetts, President.
Thomas Jefferson, Virginia, Vice President.

THIRD ADMINISTRATION. 1801–9. 8 YEARS.

1801. Thomas Jefferson, Virginia, President.
Aaron Burr, New York, Vice President.
1805. George Clinton, New York, Vice President.

FOURTH ADMINISTRATION. 1809–17. 8 YEARS.

1809. James Madison, Virginia, President.
George Clinton, New York, Vice President.
1813. Elbridge Gerry, Massachusetts, Vice President.

FIFTH ADMINISTRATION. 1817–25. 8 YEARS.

1817. James Monroe, Virginia, President.
Daniel D. Tompkins, New York, Vice President.

SIXTH ADMINISTRATION. 1825–29. 4 YEARS.

1825. John Q. Adams, Massachusetts, President.
John C. Calhoun, South Carolina, Vice President.

SEVENTH ADMINISTRATION. 1829–37. 8 YEARS.

1829. Andrew Jackson, Tennessee, President.
John C. Calhoun, South Carolina, Vice President.
1833. Martin Van Buren, New York, Vice President.

EIGHTH ADMINISTRATION. 1837–41. 4 YEARS.

1837. Martin Van Buren, New York, President.
Richard M. Johnson, Kentucky, Vice President.

NINTH ADMINISTRATION. 1841–45. 4 YEARS.

1841. William H. Harrison, Ohio, President.
John Tyler, Virginia, Vice President. Became Pres't.

TENTH ADMINISTRATION. 1845–49. 4 YEARS.

1845. James K. Polk, Tennessee, President.
George M. Dallas, Pennsylvania, Vice President.

ELEVENTH ADMINISTRATION. 1849–53. 4 YEARS.

1849. Zachary Taylor, Louisiana, President.
1850. Millard Fillmore, New York, Vice Prest. Became Prest.

TWELFTH ADMINISTRATION. 1853–57. 4 YEARS.

1853. Franklin Pierce, New Hampshire, President.
Wm. R. King, Alabama, Vice Pres't. (Died April 18.)

THIRTEENTH ADMINISTRATION. 1857–61. 4 YEARS.

1857. James Buchanan, Pennsylvania, President.
John C. Breckinridge, Kentucky, Vice President.

FOURTEENTH ADMINISTRATION. 1861–69. 8 YEARS.

1861. Abraham Lincoln, Illinois, Pres't. (Assassinated 1865.)
Hannibal Hamlin, Maine, Vice President.
1865. Andrew Johnson, Tennessee, Vice Prest. Became Prest.

FIFTEENTH ADMINISTRATION. 1869–77. 8 YEARS.

1869. Ulysses S. Grant, Illinois, President.
Schuyler Colfax, Indiana, Vice President.
1873. Henry Wilson, Massachusetts, Vice President.

BATTLES OF THE SEVERAL WARS OF THE UNITED STATES.

NAVAL BATTLES OF THE SECOND WAR WITH ENGLAND.

DATES.	WHERE FOUGHT.	VESSELS.	
		AMERICAN.	BRITISH.
1812.			
August 13	Off Newfoundland	**Essex.*	Alert.
August 19	Off Massachusetts	*Constitution.*	Guerriere.
October 18	Off North Carolina	*Wasp.*	Frolic.
October 25	Near Canary Islands	*United States.*	Macedonian.
December 29	Off San Salvador	*Constitution.*	Java.
1813.			
February 24	Off Demarara	*Hornet.*	Peacock.
June 1	Massachusetts Bay	Chesapeake.	*Shannon.*
August 14	British Channel	Argus.	*Pelican.*
September 5	Off Coast of Maine	*Enterprise.*	Boxer.
September 10	Lake Erie	9 *Vessels.*	6 Vessels.
1814.			
March 28	Harbor of Valparaiso	Essex.	*Phebe.*
April 29	Off Coast of Florida	*Peacock.*	Epervier.
June 28	Near British Channel	*Wasp.*	Reindeer.
September 1	Near Africa	*Wasp.*	Avon.
September 11	Lake Champlain	14 *Vessels.*	17 Vessels.
December 14	Lake Borgne	5 Gunboats.	40 *Barges.*
1815.			
January 15	Off New Jersey	President.	*Squadron.*
February 20	Off Island of Maderia	*Constitution.*	Cyone.
March 23	Off Brazil	*Hornet.*	Penguin.

* *Name of the successful vessel in italics.*

IMPORTANT BATTLES OF U. S.

Principal Battles of the French and Indian War.

F. French victorious.
B. British victorious.

1754.

B. Great Meadows, May 28.
F. Fort Necessity, July 4.

1755.

F. Monongahela, July 9.
F. Lake George, Sept. 8.

1756.

F. Oswego, Aug. 14.
F. Kittanning, Sept. 8.

1757.

F. Fort William Henry, Aug. 9.

1758.

F. Ticonderoga, July 8.
B. Louisburg, July 26.
B. Fort Frontenac, Aug. 27.
B. Fort Duquesne, Nov. 25.

1759.

B. Fort Niagara, July 25.
F. Montmerenci, July 31.
B. Plains of Abraham, Sept. 13.
B. Quebec, Sept. 18.

1760.

B. Silleny, April 28.
B. Montreal, Sept. 8.

Principal Battles of the American Revolution.

A. Americans victorious.
B. British victorious.

1775.

B. Lexington, April 19.
B. Bunker Hill, June 17.
B. Quebec, Dec. 31.

1776.

A. Fort Moultrie, June 28.
B. Long Island, Aug. 27.
B. White Plains, Oct. 28.
B. Fort Washington, Nov. 16.
A. Trenton, Dec. 16.

1777.

A. Princeton, Jan. 3.
B. Ticonderoga, July 5.
A. Bennington, Aug. 16.
B. Brandywine, Sept. 11.
A. Stillwater, Sept. 19.
B. Paoli, Sept. 20.
B. Germantown, Oct. 4.
B. Fort Clinton, Oct. 6.
B. Fort Montgomery, Oct. 6.
A. Saratoga, Oct. 7.
A. Fort Mercer, Oct. 22.
A. Fort Mifflin, Oct. 22.
B. Fort Mifflin, Nov. 16.

1778.

A. Monmouth, June 28.
B. Wyoming, July 3.
A. Rhode Island, Aug. 29.
B. Savannah, Dec. 29.

1779.

A. Kettle Creek, Feb. 14.
B. Brier Creek, March 3.
B. Stone Ferry, June 20.
A. Stony Point, July 15.
B. Penobscot, Aug. 13.
B. Savannah, Oct. 9.

1780.

B. Charleston, May 12.
A. Springfield, N. J., June 23.
B. Rocky Mount, July 30.
A. Hanging Rock, Aug. 6.
B. Sander's Creek, Aug. 16.
B. Fishing Creek, Aug. 18.
A. King's Mountain, Oct. 7.

1781.

A. Cowpens, Jan. 17.
B. Guilford Court House, March 15.
B. Fort Griswold, Sept. 6.

B. Eutaw Springs, Sept. 8.
A. Yorktown, Oct. 19.

Principal Battles of the Second War with England.

A. Americans victorious.
B. British victorious.

1812.

B. Brownstown, Aug. 5.
A. Brownstown (second), Aug. 9.
B. Queenstown, Oct. 13.

1813.

B. Frenchtown, Jan. 22.
A. York, April 27.
A. Fort Meigs, May 5.
A. Sacket's Harbor, May 29.
A. Fort Stephenson, Aug. 2.
A. Thames, Oct. 5.
A. Chrysler's Field, Nov. 11.

1814.

B. La Colle, March 30.
A. Chippewa, July 5.
A. Lundy's Lane, July 25.
A. Fort Erie, Aug. 15.
B. Bladensburg, Aug. 24.
A. Plattsburg, Sept. 11.
B. North Point, Sept. 12.
A. Fort McHenry, Sept. 13.
A. Fort Bowyer, Sept. 15.
A. Fort Erie, Sept. 17.
A. Near New Orleans, Dec. 23.

1815.

A. New Orleans, Jan. 7.

Principal Battles of the War with Mexico.

Americans victorious in every battle.

1846.

Palo Alto, May 8.
Resaca de la Palma, May 9.
Monterey, Sept. 23.
Bracito, Dec. 25.

1847.

Beuna Vista, Feb. 23.
Vera Cruz, Feb. 27.
Sacramento, Feb. 28.
Cerro Gordo, April 18.
Contreras, Aug. 20.
Churubusco, Aug. 20.
Molino del Rey, Sept. 8.
Chepultepec, Sept. 12, 13.

Battles of the Great Rebellion.

U. Union army victorious.
C. Confederate army victorious.

1861.

U. Fairfax C. H., Va., June 3.
C. Big Bethel, June 10.
C. Carthage, Mo., July 5.
U. Laurel Hill, Va., July 10.
U. Rich Mountain, July 11.
U. Carrick's Ford, Va., July 13.
C. Scragtown, Va., July 13.
C. Blackburn Ford, July 18.
C. Bull Run, July 21.
C. Wilson Creek, Mo., Aug. 10.
U. Boone C. H., Va., Sept. 1.
U. Carnifex Ferry, Va., Sept. 10.
U. Cheat Mountain, Va., Sept. 12.
U. Papinsville, Mo., Sept. 21.
U. Romney, Va., Sept. 24.
U. Santa Rosa Island, Fla., Oct. 9.
U. Fredericktown, Mo., Oct. 21.
C. Ball's Bluff, Oct. 21.
U. Wild Cat, Ky., Oct. 21.
U. Romney, Va., Oct. 25.
U. Springfield, Mo., Oct. 26.
U. Gauly Bridge, Va., Nov. 1.
U. Forts Walker and Beauregard, at Port Royal, Nov. 7—captured.
C. Belmont, Mo., Nov. 7.
U. Piketon, Ky., Nov. 11.
U. Camp Allegheny, Dec. 13.
Drawn. Mumfordville, Kentucky, Dec. 17.
U. Drainsville, Va., Dec. 20.

1862.

U. Port Royal Island, Jan. 2.
U. Huntsville, Mo., Jan. 4.

U. Prestonburg, Ky., Jan. 10.
U. Mill Springs, Ky., Jan. 19.
U. Fort Henry, Ky., Feb. 6.
U. Fort Donelson, Feb. 16.
C. Ft. Craig, New Mexico, Feb. 21.
U. Pittsburg Landing, March 2.
U. Pea Ridge, Ark., March 8.
U. Newbern, N. C., March 14.
U. Winchester, Va., March 23.
U. Valle's Ranch, New Mexico, March 28.
U. Putnam's Ferry, Ark., April 1.
U. Shiloh, April 6, 7.
U. Island No. 10, April 8—surrendered.
U. Fort Pulaski, April 11.
U. Camden, N. C., April 19.
U. Parotta, N. M., April 23.
U. New Orleans, April 25—captured.
U. Monterey, Tenn., May 3.
U. Williamsburgh, Va., May 5.
U. West Point, Va., May 7.
U. McDowell, Va., May 8.
C. Farmington, Miss., May 9.
U. Louisburgh, Va., May 23.
C. Front Royal, Va., May 23.
U. Bottom Bridge, Va., May 24.
U. Corinth, May 27.
U. Fair Oaks, Va., May 31, June 1.
U. Memphis, June 6—gunboats.
U. Union Church, Va., June 7.
U. Cross Keys, Va., June 8.
C. Port Republic, Va., June 9.
C. James Island, S. C., June 14.
U. Battles before Richmond, June 25—July 1.
C. Murfreesboro, Tenn., July 13.
U. Fayetteville, Ark., July 14.
U. Moore's Hill, July 28.
U. Baton Rouge, Aug. 5.
U. Cedar Mountain, Aug. 9.
U. Williamsport, Tenn., Aug. 11.
U. Yellow Creek, Mo., Aug. 13.
U. Centreville, Va., Aug. 28.
C. Bull Run (second), Aug. 30.
C. Richmond, Ky., Aug. 30.
U. Weldon, Va., Aug. 31.
C. Chantilly, Va., Sept. 1.
U. Bretton's Lane, Tenn., Sept. 1.
U. South Mountain, Md., Sept. 14.
C. Harper's Ferry, Sept. 15.
U. Antietam, Sept. 17.
C. Munfordsville, Sept. 17.
U. Iuka, Miss., Sept. 19.
C. Augusta, Ky., Sept. 27.
U. Corinth, Miss., Oct. 4.
U. Perryville, Ky., Oct. 8, 9.
U. Maysville, Ark., Oct. 22.
U. Fayetteville, Ark., Oct. 28.
U. Cone Hill, Ark., Nov. 28.
U. Prairie Grove, Ark., Dec. 7.
C. Fredericksburg, Va., Dec. 13.
U. Kingston, N. C., Dec. 14.
U. Dumfries, Va., Dec. 23.
U. Van Buren, Ark., Dec. 28.
C. Vicksburg, Dec. 28, 29.
U. Murfreesboro, Dec. 31—Jan. 4, 1863.

1863.

U. Arkansas Post, Jan. 10.
U. Deserted House, Va., Jan. 30.
U. Kelley's Ford, Va., March 17.
U. Milton, Tenn., March 20.
U. Cottage Grove, Tenn., March 21.
U. Franklin, Tenn., April 8.
U. Fayetteville, Ark., April 18.
C. Beverly, Va., April 24.
C. Fairmount, W. Va., April 30
U. Port Gibson, May 1.
C. Fredericksburg, May 3–5.
U. Farnden's Creek, Miss., May 12.
U. Jackson, Miss., May 14.
U. Baker's Creek, Miss., May 16.
U. Big Black River Bridge, Miss., May 17.
U. Belle Plain, La., May 21.
C. Port Hudson, May 27.
U. Triune, Tenn., June 11.
U. Gettysburg, Penn., July 1–3.
U. Helena, Ark., July 4.
C. Fort Wagner, July 18.
U. Kelly's Ford, Aug. 1.
U. Grenada, Miss., Aug. 17.
U. Fort Smith, Ark., Sept. 1.
C. Chickamauga, Sept. 19, 20.
U. Madison C. H., Va., Sept. 22.
U. Chattanooga, Nov. 25.
U. Knoxville, Nov. 29.

1864.

C. Olustee, Feb. 20.
U. Shreveport, La., April 8.
C. Fort Pillow—massacre, April 12.
U. The Wilderness, May 5, 6.

U. Spottsylvania, May 12.
C. Newmarket, Va., May 15.
U. Dallas, Ga., May 28.
U. Cold Harbor, Va., June 3.
U. Piedmont, June 5.
U. Bottom Bridge, Va., June 12.
U. Lost Mountain, June 16.
C. Monocacy, July 9.
U. Atlanta, Ga., July 20.
U. Morefield, Va., Aug. 7.
U. Dalton, Ga., Aug. 15.
U. Winchester, Va., Sept. 19.
U. Fisher's Hill, Sept. 22.
U. Cedar Creek, Oct. 19.
U. Blue River, Mo., Oct. 23.
U. Hatcher's Run, Oct. 27.
U. Franklin, Tenn., Nov. 30.
U. Nashville, Dec. 16.

1865.

U. Wilmington, Feb. 22.
U. Kingston, N. C., March 10.
U. Averyboro, N. C., March 16.
U. Bentonville, N. C., March 19.
U. Five Forks, Va., April 1.
U. Before Richmond, April 1-3.

POPULATION OF THE UNITED STATES AT DECENNIAL PERIODS.

Census Years.	White Persons.	Colored Persons.			Total Population.
		Free.	Slave.	Total.	
1790..	3,172,464	59,466	697,897	757,363	3,929,827
1800..	4,304,489	108,359	893,041	1,001,436	5,305,925
1810..	5,862,004	186,446	1,191,364	1,377,810	7,239,814
1820..	7,861,937	238,156	1,538,038	1,776,194	9,638,131
1830..	10,537,378	319,599	2,009,043	2,328,642	12,866,020
1840..	14,195,695	386,303	2,487,455	2,873,758	17,069,453
1850..	19,553,068	434,495	3,204,313	3,638,808	23,191,876
1860..	26,964,930	487,970	3,953,760	4,441,730	31,443,322
1870..	33,592,245	4,886,387		4,886,387	38,925,598

EMINENT MEN AND WOMEN OF AMERICA.

	BORN	DIED
Adams, Abigail, *Author*	1744	1818
Adams, Charles Francis, *Statesman*	1817	——
Adams, Hannah, *Author*	1755	1831
Adams, Isaac, *Inventor*	1803	——
Adams, John, *Second President*	1735	1826
Adams, John Quincy, *Sixth President*	1767	1848
Adams, Nehemiah, *Author*	1806	——
Adams, Samuel, *Statesman*	1722	1803
Agassiz, Louis John Rudolph, *Naturalist*	1807	1873
Akers, Benjamin Paul, *Sculptor*	1825	1861
Alcott, Amos Bronson, *Educator*	1799	——
Alcott, Louisa May, *Author*	——	——
Alcott, William Alexander, *Physician*	1798	1859
Alden, James, *Naval officer*	1810	——
Aldrich, Thomas Bailey, *Author*	1836	——
Alexander, Archibald, *Clergyman*	1772	1851
Alexander, James Waddell, *Clergyman*	1804	1859
Alexander, John Henry, *Chemist and Physicist*	1812	1867
Alexander, William, *Officer and Astronomer*	1726	1783
Alger, William Rounseville, *Clergyman and Author*	1822	——
Allen, Ethan, *Military officer*	1737	1789
Allibone, Samuel Austin, *Author*	1816	——
Allston, Washington, *Painter*	1779	1843
Ames, Fisher, *Statesman*	1758	1808
Anderson, Robert, *Military officer*	1805	1871
Andrew, John Albion, *Statesman*	1818	1867
Appleton, Samuel, *Philanthropist*	1766	1853
Arnold, Benedict, *Military officer*	1741	1801
Audubon, John James, *Ornithologist*	1780	1851
Babbitt, Isaac, *Inventor*	1799	1862
Bache, Alexander Dallas, *Physicist*	1806	1867
Bacon, Leonard, *Clergyman and Author*	1802	——
Bainbridge, William, *Naval officer*	1774	1833
Baird, Spencer Fullerton, *Naturalist*	1823	——
Ball, Thomas, *Sculptor*	1819	——
Ballou, Hosea, *Clergyman*	1771	1852
Bancroft, George, *Author*	1800	——
Banks, Nathaniel Prentiss, *Statesman*	1816	——
Barlow, Joel, *Poet*	1755	1812
Barnard, Henry, *Educator*	1811	——
Barnes, Albert, *Clergyman*	1798	1870
Barney, Joshua, *Naval officer*	1759	1818
Barry, John, *Naval officer*	1745	1803
Bateman, Kate Josephine, *Actor*	1842	——
Bates, Joshua, *Philanthropist*	1788	1864
Bayard, James Ashton, *Statesman*	1767	1815
Beach, Moses Yale, *Inventor*	1800	1868
Beaumont, William, *Physician*	1785	1853
Beecher, Catherine Esther, *Author*	1800	——
Beecher, Henry Ward, *Clergyman and Author*	1813	——
Beecher, Lyman, *Clergyman*	1775	1863
Bell, John, *Statesman*	1797	1869
Bellows, Henry Whitney, *Clergyman and Author*	1814	——
Benjamin, Park, *Journalist*	1809	1864
Bennett, James Gordon, *Journalist*	1800	1871

	BORN	DIED
Benton, Thomas Hart, *Statesman*	1782	1858
Bierstadt, Albert, *Painter*	1829	——
Bigelow, Jacob, *Physician and Author*	1787	
Bigelow, John, *Author and Editor*	1817	——
Blair, Francis Preston, *Journalist and Politician*	1791	1875
Boker, George Henry, *Poet*	1823	——
Bond, William Cranch, *Astronomer*	1789	1859
Boone, Daniel, *Pioneer*	1735	1820
Booth, Edwin F., *Actor*	1833	——
Booth, Junius Brutus, *Actor*	1796	1852
Bowditch, Nathaniel, *Mathematician and Astronomer*	1773	1838
Bowdoin, James, *Statesman*	1727	1790
Bowen, Francis, *Author*	1811	——
Bowles, Samuel, *Journalist*	1826	——
Brace, Charles Loring, *Author*	1826	1875
Bradford, William, *Pilgrim*	1588	1657
Bradstreet, Anne, *Poet*	1612	1672
Breckinridge, John Cabell, *Statesman*	1821	1875
Brewster, William, *Pilgrim*	1566	1644
Brooks, Charles Timothy, *Clergyman and Author*	1813	——
Brown, Charles Brockden, *Novelist*	1771	1810
Brown, George L., *Painter*	1814	——
Brown, Goold, *Grammarian*	1791	1857
Brown, John, *of Ossawottomie*	1800	1859
Brown, Samuel Gilman, *Educator*	1813	——
Browne, Charles F., *Humorist*	1834	1867
Bryant, William Cullen, *Poet and Journalist*	1794	——
Buchanan, James, *Fifteenth President*	1791	1868
Buckingham, Joseph Tinker, *Journalist*	1779	1861
Buckminster, Joseph Stevens, *Clergyman*	1784	1812
Bullions, Peter, *Grammarian*	1791	1864
Burges, Tristam, *Orator and Jurist*	1770	1853
Burlingame, Anson, *Statesman and Diplomatist*	1822	1870
Burnside, Ambrose Everett, *Military officer*	1824	——
Burr, Aaron, *Statesman*	1756	1836
Burritt, Elihu, *Reformer*	1811	——
Burton, William Evans, *Comedian and Author*	1802	1860
Bushnell, Horace, *Clergyman and Author*	1802	——
Butler, Benjamin Franklin, *Lawyer and Politician*	1818	——
Byles, Mather, *Clergyman*	1706	1788
Calhoun, John Caldwell, *Statesman*	1782	1850
Calvert, George Henry, *Author*	1803	——
Cameron, Simon, *Statesman*	1799	——
Carey, Matthew, *Political writer*	1760	1839
Carroll, Charles, *of Carrollton, Patriot*	1737	1832
Carson, Christopher, *Mountaineer and Guide*	1809	1868
Carver, John, *Pilgrim*	——	1621
Cary, Alice, *Poet*	1820	1871
Cass, Lewis, *Statesman*	1782	1866
Cassin, John, *Ornithologist*	1813	1869
Channing, William Ellery, *Clergyman*	1780	1842
Chase, Samuel Portland, *Statesman*	1808	1873
Chauncey, Charles, *Clergyman*	1592	1672
Cheever, George Bauell, *Clergyman and Author*	1807	——
Chickering, Jonas, *Philanthropist*	1798	1853
Child, Lydia Maria, *Author*	1802	——
Choate, Rufus, *Lawyer and Orator*	1799	1859
Clarke, George Rogers, *Military officer*	1752	1818
Clarke, James Freeman, *Clergyman and Author*	1810	——
Clay, Henry, *Orator and Statesman*	1777	1852
Clemens, Samuel Langhorne, *Humorist*	1835	——
Clinton De Witt, *Statesman*	1769	1828

	BORN	DIED
Cogswell, Joseph Green, *Scholar*	1786	1871
Colburn, Warren, *Mathematician*	1793	1833
Cole, Thomas, *Painter*	1801	1847
Coleman, William, *Journalist*	1766	1829
Collyer, Robert, *Clergyman*	1823	——
Colt, Samuel, *Inventor*	1814	1862
Colton, Calvin, *Clergyman and Author*	1789	1857
Cooper, James Fenimore, *Novelist*	1789	1851
Cooper, Peter, *Philanthropist*	1791	——
Copley, John Singleton, *Painter*	1737	1813
Cotton, John, *Clergyman*	1585	1682
Crawford, Thomas, *Sculptor*	1814	1857
Crittenden, John Jordan, *Lawyer and Senator*	1786	1863
Curtis, Benjamin Robbins, *Jurist*	1809	1874
Curtis, George Ticknor, *Jurist and Author*	1812	——
Curtis, George William, *Author*	1824	——
Cushing, Caleb, *Politician and Jurist*	1800	——
Cushman, Charlotte Saunders, *Actor*	1816	——
Dahlgren, John A., *Naval officer*	1809	1870
Dallas, Alexander James, *Statesman and Financier*	1759	1817
Dallas, George Mifflin, *Statesman*	1792	1864
Dalton, John C., *Physiologist*	1825	——
Dana, James Dwight, *Physicist*	1813	——
Dana, Richard Henry, *Poet and Essayist*	1787	——
Dana, Richard Henry, Jr., *Lawyer and Writer*	1815	——
Dane, Nathan, *Jurist and Statesman*	1752	1835
Darley, Felix O. C., *Artist*	1822	——
Davies, Charles, *Mathematician*	1798	——
Davis, Charles Henry, *Mathematician and Naval officer*	1807	——
Davis, John, *Statesman*	1787	1854
Deane, Silas, *Diplomatist*	1737	1789
De Borr, James D. B., *Journalist and Statistician*	1820	1867
Decatur, Stephen, *Naval officer*	1779	1820
Dexter, Samuel, *Lawyer and Statesman*	1761	1816
Dickinson, Anna Elizabeth, *Orator and Reformer*	1842	——
Dickinson, John, *Statesman*	1732	1808
Dix, John A., *Soldier, Lawyer and Statesman*	1798	——
Dixon, Joseph, *Inventor*	1798	1869
Dodge, Mary Abigail, *Author*	1838	——
Douglass, Frederick, *Orator and Journalist*	1817	——
Douglas, Stephen Arnold, *Statesman*	1813	1861
Downing, Andrew Jackson, *Horticulturist*	1815	——
Drake, Joseph Rodman, *Poet*	1895	1820
Drake, Samuel Gardner, *Historical writer*	1798	——
Draper, John William, *Chemist and Physiologist*	1811	——
Duchi, Jacob, *Clergyman*	1739	1798
Dunglison, Robley, *Physician and Author*	1798	1869
Dunlap, William, *Painter and Author*	1766	1839
Dupont, Samuel Francis, *Naval officer*	1803	1865
Durant, Asher Brown, *Painter and Engraver*	1796	——
Duyckinck, Evert Augustus, *Author*	1816	——
Dwight, Timothy, *Clergyman and Scholar*	1752	1817
Edwards, Jonathan, *Metaphysician*	1703	1758
Eliot, John, *Apostle to the Indians*	1603	1690
Eliot, Samuel, *Author*	1821	——
Ellis, George Edward, *Clergyman and Author*	1814	——
Ellsworth, Oliver, *Jurist*	1745	1807
Emerson, George Barrell, *Educator*	1797	——
Emerson, Ralph Waldo, *Essayist*	1803	——
Emory, William Helmsley, *Military officer*	1812	——
Ericsson, John, *Inventor*	1803	——

	BORN	DIED
Everett, Alexander Hill, *Scholar and Diplomatist*	1790	1847
Everett, Edward, *Scholar and Orator*	1794	1865
Faneuil, Peter, *Merchant*	1700	1743
Farragut, David Glascoe, *Naval officer*	1801	1870
Felton, Cornelius Conway, *Scholar and Author*	1807	1862
Fessenden, William Pitt, *Lawyer and Senator*	1806	1869
Fillmore, Millard, *Thirteenth President*	1800	1874
Fitch, John, *Inventor*	1743	1798
Flint, Austin, *Physician*	1812	—
Foote, Andrew Hull, *Naval officer*	1806	1863
Force, Peter, *Historian*	1790	1868
Forney, John Weiss, *Journalist*	1817	—
Forrest, Edwin, *Tragedian*	1806	1872
Fowler, Orson Squire, *Phrenologist*	1809	—
Franklin, Benjamin, *Philosopher and Statesman*	1706	1790
Fremont, John Charles, *Explorer*	1813	—
Freneau, Philip, *Poet*	1752	1832
Frothingham, Richard, Jr., *Historian and Journalist*	1812	—
Fuller, Sarah Margaret, *Author*	1810	1850
Fulton, Robert, *Inventor*	1765	1815
Gallagher, William D., *Poet and Journalist*	1808	—
Gallatin, Albert, *Statesman*	1761	1849
Garrison, William Lloyd, *Anti-Slavery Agitator*	1804	—
Gerry, Elbridge, *Statesman*	1744	1814
Girard, Stephen, *Merchant and Banker*	1750	1831
Godwin, Parke, *Journalist and Author*	1816	—
Goodrich, Samuel Griswold, *Author*	1793	1860
Goodyear, Charles, *Inventor*	1800	1860
Gough, John B., *Temperance lecturer*	1817	—
Gould, Augustus Addison, *Naturalist*	1805	—
Grant, Ulysses Simpson, *Eighteenth President*	1822	—
Gray, Asa, *Botanist*	1810	—
Greeley, Horace, *Journalist*	1811	1872
Greene, Nathaniel, *Military officer*	1742	1786
Greenleaf, Simon, *Jurist*	1783	1853
Greenough, Horatio, *Sculptor*	1805	1852
Griswold, Rufus Wilmot, *Author*	1815	1857
Hale, Edward Everett, *Clergyman and Author*	1822	—
Halleck, Fitzgreene, *Poet*	1790	1867
Halleck, Henry Wagner, *Military officer*	1814	1872
Hamilton, Alexander, *Statesman*	1757	1804
Hamlin, Hannibal, *Statesman*	1809	—
Hancock, John, *Patriot*	1737	1793
Harding, Chester, *Painter*	1792	1866
Hare, Robert, *Chemist*	1781	1858
Harris, Thaddeus William, *Entomologist*	1795	1856
Harrison, William Henry, *Ninth President*	1773	1841
Hawks, Francis Lister, *Clergyman and Author*	1798	1866
Hawthorne, Nathaniel, *Author*	1804	1864
Hayne, Robert Young, *Statesman*	1791	1839
Headley, Joel Tyler, *Author*	1814	—
Henry, Joseph, *Physicist*	1797	—
Henry, Patrick, *Orator and Statesman*	1736	1799
Herbert, Henry William, *Author*	1807	1858
Higginson, Thomas Wentworth, *Author*	1823	—
Hildreth, Richard, *Author and Journalist*	1807	1865
Hill, Thomas, *Clergyman*	1818	1874
Hillard, George Stillman, *Lawyer and Author*	1808	—
Hitchcock, Edward, *Geologist*	1793	1864

	BORN	DIED
Hoar, Ebenezer Rockwood, *Jurist*	1816	——
Hoffman, Charles Fenno, *Author*	1806	——
Holland, Josiah Gilbert, *Author and Journalist*	1819	——
Holmes, Oliver Wendell, *Physician, Poet and Essayist*	1809	——
Holt, Joseph, *Statesman*	1807	——
Hooker, Joseph, *Military officer*	1815	——
Hosmer, Harriet G., *Sculptor*	1830	——
Houston, Samuel, *Soldier and Statesman*	1793	1863
Howe, Elias, Jr., *Inventor*	1819	1867
Howells, William Dean, *Author*	1837	——
Hughes, Robert Ball, *Sculptor*	1806	1868
Hull, Isaac, *Naval officer*	1775	1843
Humphreys, David, *Soldier, Diplomatist and Poet*	1752	1818
Huntington, Daniel, *Painter*	1816	——
Hutchinson, Thomas, *Governor of Mass*	1711	1780
Irving, Washington, *Author*	1783	1859
Jackson, Andrew, *Seventh President*	1767	1845
Jackson, Charles Thomas, *Chemist and Geologist*	1805	——
Jackson, James, *Physician*	1777	1867
Jackson, Thomas Jonathan, *Military officer*	1824	1863
Jay, John, *Statesman*	1745	1829
Jefferson, Joseph, *Comedian*	1829	——
Jefferson, Thomas, *Third President*	1743	1826
Johnson, Andrew, *Seventeenth President*	1808	1875
Johnson, *Sir* William, *Military officer*	1715	1774
Jones, John Paul, *Naval officer*	1747	1792
Kane, Elisha Kent, *Arctic explorer*	1820	1857
Kearny, Philip, *Military officer*	1815	1862
Kellogg, Clara Louise, *Vocalist*	1842	——
Kemble, Frances Anne, *Actor and Author*	1811	——
Kendall, Amos, *Politician and Publicist*	1789	1869
Kennedy, John Pendleton, *Author*	1795	1870
Kensett, John Frederick, *Artist*	1818	1872
Kent, James, *Jurist*	1763	1847
Kenton, Simon, *Pioneer*	1755	1836
King, Rufus, *Statesman and Diplomatist*	1755	1827
King, Thomas Starr, *Clergyman and Author*	1824	1864
Kirkland, Caroline Matilda, *Author*	1801	1864
Knuland, Samuel, *Naturalist*	1821	——
Knox, Henry, *Military officer*	1750	1806
Laurens, Henry, *Statesman*	1724	1792
Lawrence, Amos, *Philanthropist*	1786	1852
Lawrence, James, *Naval officer*	1781	1813
Ledyard, John, *Traveller*	1751	1789
Lee, Arthur, *Diplomatist*	1740	1792
Lee, Charles, *Military officer*	1731	1782
Lee, Henry, *Military officer*	1756	1818
Lee, Richard Henry, *Statesman*	1732	1794
Lee, Robert Edmund, *Military officer*	1807	1870
Leslie, Charles Robert, *Painter*	1794	1859
Lieber, Francis, *Publicist*	1800	1872
Lincoln, Abraham, *Sixteenth President*	1809	1865
Lincoln, Benjamin, *Military officer*	1733	1810
Livermore, May Ashton, *Reformer*	1821	——
Livingston, Edward, *Jurist and Statesman*	1764	1836

	BORN	DIED
Livingston, Philip, *Statesman*	1716	1778
Livingston, Robert R., *Statesman*	1747	1813
Livingston, William, *Statesman*	1723	1790
Longfellow, Henry Wadsworth, *Poet*	1807	——
Lossing, Benson John, *Author*	1813	——
Lowell, James Russell, *Poet*	1819	——
McClellan, George Brinton, *Military officer*	1826	——
Madison, James, *Fourth President*	1751	1836
Mann, Horace, *Educationist*	1796	1859
Marion, Francis, *Military officer*	1732	1795
Marshall, John, *Jurist*	1755	1835
Mason, George, *Statesman*	1726	1792
Mather, Cotton, *Clergyman*	1633	1728
Mather, Increase, *Clergyman*	1639	1723
Maury, Matthew Fontaine, *Naval officer*	1806	1873
Meade, George Gordon, *Military officer*	1816	1872
Mifflin, Thomas, *Military officer*	1744	1800
Mitchell, Donald Grant, *Author*	1822	——
Mitchell, Maria, *Astronomer*	1818	——
Mitchell, Ormsby MacKnight, *Astronomer*	1810	1862
Monroe, James, *Fifth President*	1758	1831
Morgan, Daniel, *Military officer*	1736	1802
Morris, George P., *Poet and Journalist*	1802	1864
Morris, Gouverneur, *Statesman*	1752	1816
Morse, Samuel Finley Breese, *Inventor*	1791	1872
Morton, Samuel George, *Naturalist*	1799	1851
Morton, William Thomas Green, *Physician*	1819	1868
Motley, John Lathrop, *Historian*	1814	——
Mott, Valentine, *Surgeon*	1785	1865
Moultrie, William, *Military officer*	1731	1805
Mowatt, Anna Cora, *Actor and Author*	1819	1870
Murray, John, *Clergyman*	1741	1815
Murray, Lindley, *Grammarian*	1745	1826
Nast, Thomas, *Artist*	1840	——
Neal, John, *Author and Poet*	1793	——
Olmstead, Denison, *Astronomer*	1791	1859
Otis, James, *Orator and Patriot*	1725	1783
Owen, Robert, *Philanthropist*	1771	1858
Paine, Thomas, *Political and Deistical writer*	1737	1809
Palfrey, John Gorham, *Author*	1796	——
Parker, Theodore, *Clergyman and Author*	1810	1860
Parkman, Francis, *Author*	1823	——
Parsons, Theophilus, *Jurist*	1750	1813
Parton, James, *Author*	1822	——
Paulding, James Kirke, *Author and Politician*	1779	1860
Payne, John Howard, *Actor and Dramatist*	1792	1852
Peabody, Andrew Preston, *Clergyman and Scholar*	1811	——
Peabody, George, *Philanthropist*	1795	1869
Peale, Charles Wilson, *Painter*	1741	1827
Peirce, Benjamin, *Mathematician*	1809	——
Percival, James Gates, *Poet*	1795	1856
Perkins, Thomas Handaryd, *Philanthropist*	1764	1854
Perry, Oliver Hazard, *Naval officer*	1785	1819
Phillips, Wendell, *Orator and Reformer*	1811	——
Phips, Sir William, *Governor of Mass.*	1651	1695
Physic, Phillip Syng, *Physician and Surgeon*	1768	1837
Pickens, Andrew, *Military officer*	1739	1817

	BORN	DIED
Pickering, Timothy, *Soldier and Statesman*	1745	1829
Pierce, Franklin, *Fourteenth President*	1804	1869
Pierpont, John, *Clergyman and Poet*	1785	1866
Pinckney, Charles Cotesworth, *Soldier and Statesman*	1746	1825
Poe, Edgar Allan, *Poet*	1811	1849
Polk, James Knox, *Eleventh President*	1795	1849
Porter, David, *Naval officer*	1780	1843
Powers, Hiram, *Sculptor*	1805	1873
Preble, Edward, *Naval officer*	1761	1807
Prentice, George Denison, *Poet and Journalist*	1802	1870
Prentiss, Seargeant Smith, *Lawyer and Orator*	1808	1850
Prescott, William, *Military officer*	1726	1795
Prescott, William Hickling, *Historian*	1796	1859
Priestley, Joseph, *Philosopher, Chemist and Theologian*	1733	1804
Prince, Thomas, *Minister and Chronologist*	1687	1758
Putnam, Israel, *Military officer*	1718	1790
Quincy, Josiah, Jr., *Patriot*	1744	1775
Quincy, Josiah, *Statesman and Scholar*	1772	1864
Randolph, John, *Orator*	1773	1833
Raymond, Henry Jarvis, *Journalist*	1820	1869
Read, Thomas Buchanan, *Painter and Poet*	1822	1872
Reed, Henry, *Author*	1808	1854
Reed, Joseph, *Statesman*	1741	1785
Revere, Paul, *Engraver and Patriot*	1735	1818
Rittenhouse, David, *Mathematician and Astronomer*	1732	1796
Rodgers, John, *Naval officer*	1771	1838
Rosecrans, William Starke, *Military officer*	1819	——
Rowson, Susanna, *Author*	1762	1824
Rumford, Sir Benjamin Thompson, *Physicist*	1753	1814
Rush, Benjamin, *Physician*	1745	1813
Rush, Richard, *Statesman and Diplomatist*	1780	1859
Rutledge, John, *Statesman and Jurist*	1739	1800
St. Clair, Arthur, *Military officer*	1734	1818
Sargent, Epes, *Author and Journalist*	1812	——
Saxe, John Godfrey, *Poet*	1816	——
Say, Thomas, *Naturalist*	1787	1834
Schoolcraft, Henry Rowe, *Author*	1793	1864
Schurtz, Carl, *Orator and Politician*	1829	——
Schuyler, Philip, *Military officer*	1733	1804
Scott, Winfield, *Military officer*	1786	1866
Seaton, William Winston, *Journalist*	1785	1866
Sedgwick, Catherine Maria, *Author*	1789	1867
Sedgwick, John, *Military officer*	1813	1864
Sewall, Samuel, *Jurist*	1652	1730
Seward, William Henry, *Statesman*	1801	1872
Shaw, Lemuel, *Jurist*	1781	1861
Sheridan, Philip Henry, *Military officer*	1831	——
Sherman, Roger, *Statesman*	1721	1793
Sherman, William Tecumseh, *Military officer*	1820	——
Sigourney, Lydia Howard Huntley, *Author*	1791	1865
Silliman, Benjamin, *Physicist*	1779	1864
Silliman, Benjamin, Jr., *Physicist*	1816	——
Simms, William Gilmore, *Author*	1806	1870
Sparks, Jared, *Historian*	1789	1866
Sprague, Charles, *Poet*	1791	1874
Sprague, William Buell, *Clergyman and Author*	1795	——
Spring, Gardiner, *Clergyman and Author*	1785	1873
Standish, Miles, *Pilgrim*	1584	1656
Stanton, Edwin McMasters, *Lawyer and Statesman*	1814	1869

	BORN	DIED
Stark, John, *Military officer*	1728	1822
Stedman, Edmund Clarence, *Poet*	1833	—
Stephens, Alexander Hamilton, *Statesman*	1812	—
Stephens, John Lloyd, *Traveller*	1805	187
Stevens, Thaddeus, *Political Leader*	1793	1868
Stewart, Charles, *Naval officer*	1778	1869
Stewart, Alexander T., *Merchant*	1803	—
Stiles, Ezra, *Clergyman and Scholar*	1727	1795
Stoddard, Richard Henry, *Poet*	1825	—
Story, Joseph, *Jurist*	1779	1845
Story, William Wetmore, *Poet and Sculptor*	1819	—
Stowe, Harriet Elizabeth Beecher, *Author*	1812	—
Stuart, Gilbert Charles, *Painter*	1754	1828
Sullivan, James, *Statesman and Jurist*	1744	1808
Sullivan, John, *Military officer*	1740	1795
Sully, Thomas, *Painter*	1783	1872
Sumner, Charles, *Orator and Statesman*	1811	1874
Sumter, Thomas, *Military officer*	1734	1832
Taney, Roger Brooke, *Jurist*	1777	1864
Taylor, James Bayard, *Traveller and Author*	1825	—
Taylor, Zachary, *Twelfth President*	1784	1850
Thoreau, Henry David, *Naturalist and Scholar*	1817	1862
Ticknor, George, *Scholar and Author*	1791	1871
Trowbridge, John Townsend, *Author*	1827	—
Trumbull, John, *Poet*	1750	1831
Trumbull, John, *Painter*	1756	1843
Tuckerman, Henry Theodore, *Poet and Essayist*	1813	1871
Tudor, William, *Scholar and Diplomatist*	1779	1830
Tyler, John, *Tenth President*	1790	1862
Van Buren, Martin, *Eighth President*	1782	1862
Warren, John, *Physician*	1753	1815
Warren, John Collins, *Surgeon and Author*	1778	1856
Warren, Joseph, *Physician and Patriot*	1741	1775
Warren, William, *Comedian*	1812	—
Washington, George, *First President*	1732	1799
Wayland, Francis, *Scholar and Clergyman*	1796	1865
Wayne, Anthony, *Military officer*	1745	1796
Webster, Daniel, *Statesman, Lawyer and Orator*	1782	1852
Webster, Noah, *Philologist and Publicist*	1758	1843
Weed, Thurlow, *Journalist and Politician*	1797	—
Weir, Robert Walter, *Painter*	1803	—
West, Benjamin, *Painter*	1738	1820
Wheaton, Henry, *Jurist and Diplomatist*	1785	1848
Whipple, Edwin Percy, *Essayist*	1819	—
White, Andrew Dickson, *Educator*	1832	—
White, Richard Grant, *Philologist and Scholar*	1822	—
Whitney, Eli, *Inventor*	1765	1825
Whitney, William Dwight, *Philologist*	1827	—
Whittier, John Greenleaf, *Poet*	1807	—
Wilkes, Charles, *Naval officer*	1801	—
Willard, Emma C., *Teacher and Author*	1787	1870
Williams, Roger, *Founder of R. I.*	1599	1683
Willis, Nathaniel Parker, *Poet and Journalist*	1807	1867
Wilson, Alexander, *Ornithologist*	1766	1813
Wilson, Henry, *Statesman*	1812	—
Winslow, Edward, *Pilgrim*	1595	1655
Winthrop, John, *Governor of Mass*	1588	1649
Woolsey, Theodore Dwight, *Scholar*	1801	—
Worcester, Joseph Emerson, *Lexicographer*	1784	1865

GEORGE WASHINGTON,

THE FIRST PRESIDENT OF THE UNITED STATES.

The most exemplary character, perhaps, that ever adorned any era in history, and who received in his life-time the noble appellations of "the Founder of a Republic," and "the Father of his Country," was born in the county of Westmoreland, Virginia, on the 22d of February, 1732. His early instruction was domestic and scanty, but full of good discipline and sound principles; and as his father died when he was only ten years old, he had no subsequent opportunities for acquiring a thorough literary or scientific education. However, as his mind was naturally mathematical and philosophical, he prepared himself to be useful to his fellow-citizens as a civil engineer; and as the country was wild, and much of it then unsurveyed, he occasionally found agreeable and profitable employment in surveying different parts of his native State. He also directed much of his attention to the science of arms, in the use of which every young man was instructed, in order to repel the incursions of the Indians, who were often led on by skillful Frenchmen. At the age of nineteen, he was appointed one of the adjutant-generals of Virginia, which gave him the rank of major, and soon after he was advanced to a colonelcy, and sent by Governor Dinwiddie to the Ohio with dispatches to the French commander, who was erecting fortifications from Canada to New Orleans, in violation of existing treaties. The Governor was so much pleased with the faithful discharge of this duty, that he ordered his journal, which extended to only eighty days, to be printed; but, small as it was, it afforded evidence of great sagacity, fortitude, and a sound judgment, and firmly laid the foundation of his future fame.

In the spring of 1755, Washington was persuaded to accompany General Braddock as an aid, with the rank of Colonel, in his disastrous expedition against Fort DuQuesne; and had his advice been followed on that occasion, the result would have been different.

Three years afterward (1758) Washington commanded the

Virginians in another expedition against the fort, which terminated successfully. At the close of this campaign he left the army, and was soon after married to Mrs. Martha Custis (the widow of Colonel Daniel Parke Custis), whose maiden name was Dandridge, and whose intelligent and patriotic conduct, as wife and widow, will ever be gratefully remembered in American annals.

In 1759, he was elected to the House of Burgesses, and continued to be returned to that body, with the exception of occasional intervals, until 1774, when he was sent to represent Virginia in the Continental Congress. His well-tempered zeal and military skill, which enabled him to suggest the most proper means for national defense, if the country were urged to extremities, soon fixed all eyes upon him, as one well qualified to direct in the hour of peril; and accordingly, after the first scene of the revolutionary drama was opened at Lexington and Concord, and an army had concentrated at Cambridge, he was, on the 15th of June, 1775, unanimously appointed Commander-in-Chief of the American forces. The self-sacrificing spirit which governed his future course is too well known to require any elucidation.

After bringing the war to a successful termination, he hastened to Annapolis, where Congress was then in session, and on the 23d of December, 1783, formally resigned his commission.

In May, 1787, he was elected to the Convention which met at Philadelphia for the purpose of forming a Constitution, and was at once called upon to preside over its deliberations. After that admirable instrument was adopted by the people, he was unanimously elected the first President of the United States for four years; at the expiration of which he was unanimously reëlected for a second term.

On the 12th of December, 1799, he was seized with an inflammation in the throat, which grew worse the next day, and terminated his life on the 14th, in the 68th year of his age.

ELECTORAL VOTES

FOR

PRESIDENT AND VICE-PRESIDENT OF THE UNITED STATES.

Election for the First Term, commenciug March 4, 1789, *and terminating March* 3, 1793.

No. of Electors from each State.	STATES.	George Washington, of Virginia.	John Adams, of Massachusetts.	Samuel Huntington, of Connecticut.	John Jay, of New York.	John Hancock, of Massachusetts.	R. H. Harrison, of Maryland.	George Clinton, of New York.	John Rutledge, of South Carolina.	John Milton, of Georgia.	James Armstrong, of Georgia.	Edward Telfair, of Georgia.	Benjamin Lincoln, of Massachusetts.
5	New Hampshire	5	5										
10	Massachusetts	10	10										
7	Connecticut	7	5	2									
6	New Jersey	6	1		5								
10	Pennsylvania	10	8			2							
3	Delaware	3			3								
6	Maryland	6					6						
10	Virginia	10	5		1	1		3					
7	South Carolina	7				1			6				
5	Georgia	5								2	1	1	1
69	Whole No. Electors	69	34	2	9	4	6	3	6	2	1	1	1
	Majority												

The first Congress under the Constitution was convened at the "Federal Hall," situated at the head of Broad, fronting on Wall street (where the Custom House now stands), in the city of New York, on the first Wednesday, being March 4, 1789—Senators and Representatives having been elected from the eleven States which had ratified the Constitution; but, owing to the absence of a quorum, the House was not organized till the 1st of April, and, for a like reason, the Senate was not organized till the 6th; when the latter body "proceeded by ballot to the choice of a President, for the sole purpose of opening and counting the [electoral] votes for President of the United States. John Langdon, of New Hampshire, was chosen President *pro tem.* of the Senate, and Samuel Alyne Otis, of Massachusetts, Secretary; after which, proper measures were taken to notify the successful individuals of their election.

George Washington took the oath of office, as President, and entered upon his duties April 30, 1789. (For his Inaugural Address, see p. 43.)

John Adams, Vice-President, entered upon his duties in the Senate April 21, 1789, and took the oath of office June 3, 1789.

Election for the Second Term, commencing March 4, 1793, *and terminating March* 3, 1797.

No. of Electors from each State.	STATES.	George Washington, of Virginia.	John Adams, of Massachusetts.	George Clinton, of New York.	Thomas Jefferson, of Virginia.	Aaron Burr, of New York.
6	New Hampshire	6	6	....	....	....
16	Massachusetts	16	16	....	....	....
4	Rhode Island	4	4	....	....	....
9	Connecticut	9	9	....	....	....
3	Vermont	3	3	....	....	....
12	New York	12	....	12	....	....
7	New Jersey	7	7	....	....	....
15	Pennsylvania	15	14	1	....	....
3	Delaware	3	3	....	....	....
8	Maryland	8	8	....	....	....
21	Virginia	21	....	21	....	....
4	Kentucky	4	....	....	4	....
12	North Carolina	12	....	12	....	....
8	South Carolina	8	7	....	....	1
4	Georgia	4	....	4	....	....
132	Whole No. of Electors	132	77	50	4	1
	Majority 67					

George Washington, re-elected President, took the oath of office for a second term, and entered upon his duties March 4, 1793.

John Adams, re-elected Vice President, took the oath of office, and entered upon his duties in the Senate December 2, 1793.

After the expiration of his second Presidential term, Washington retired to the tranquil shades of Mount Vernon, fondly indulging the hope that the remainder of his days would be peacefully enjoyed in his much cherished home; but these pleasing anticipations were not allowed to remain long undisturbed. In 1798 the conduct of the French Directory and its emissaries led to frequent difficulties with this country, which were calculated to provoke a war; and the opinion was universally entertained that he who had formerly so well acquitted himself, must be again called to the command of our armies. Accordingly, early in July, the rank and title of Lieutenant-General and Commander-in-Chief of all the armies raised, or to be raised, in the United States," was conferred upon him; and the Secretary of War, Mr. McHenry, immediately waited upon him to tender the commission. In a letter to President Adams, accepting this "new proof of public confidence," he makes a reservation that he shall not be called into the field until the army is in a situation to require his presence, and adds: "I take the liberty also to mention, that I must decline having my acceptance considered as drawing after it any immediate charge upon the public, and that I cannot receive any emoluments annexed to the appointment, before entering into a situation to incur expense."

JOHN ADAMS,

THE SECOND PRESIDENT OF THE UNITED STATES,

And whose fame as a patriot and statesman is imperishable, was born at Braintree, Massachusetts, October 19, 1735. He early displayed superior capacity for learning, and graduated at Cambridge College with great credit. After qualifying himself for the legal profession, he was admitted to practice in 1761, and soon attained that distinction to which his talents were entitled. From the commencement of the troubles with Great Britain, in 1769, he was among the most active in securing the freedom of his country. Being elected to the first Continental Congress, he took a prominent part in all the war measures that were then originated, and, subsequently, suggested the appointment of Washington as commander-in-chief of the army. He was one of the committee which reported the Declaration of Independence, in 1776, and the next year visited France, as commissioner, to form a treaty of alliance and commerce with that country. Although the object had been accomplished before his arrival, his visit had, otherwise, a favorable effect on the existing position of affairs; and he was afterward appointed to negotiate a treaty of peace with Great Britain, which, after many laborious and fruitless efforts, was finally accomplished in 1783. In 1785, he was sent to England as the first minister from this country, and, on his return, was elected first Vice-President, in which office he served two terms, and was then, in 1797, elected to succeed Washington as President. Many occurrences tended to embarrass his administration and to render it unpopular; but it is now generally admitted to have been characterized by patriotism and vigor equal to the emergencies which then existed. His political opponents, however, managed to defeat his reëlection, and he was succeeded in the Presidency by Mr. Jefferson, in 1801; after which he retired to his farm at Quincy, where his declining years were passed in the gratification of his unabated love for reading and contemplation, and where he was constantly cheered by an interesting circle of friendship and affection. The semi-centennial anniversary of American

Independence (July 4, 1826) was remarkable, not merely for the event which it commemorated, but for the decease of two of the most active participants in the measures by which independence was achieved. On that day, Adams and Jefferson were both gathered to their fathers, within about four hours of each other, "cheered by the benediction of their country, to whom they left the inheritance of their fame and the memory of their bright example."

As has been noticed elsewhere, Mr. Adams deemed it prudent, in the early part of his administration, when impending difficulties with France seemed to render war inevitable, to offer Washington the commission of Lieutenant-General and Commander-in-Chief of the army, which he accepted as a matter of duty, and held until his death, but fortunately never found it necessary to take the field.

Election for the Third Term, commencing March 4, 1797, *and. terminating March* 3. 1801.

No. of Electors from each State.	STATES.	John Adams, of Massachusetts.	Thomas Jefferson, of Virginia.	Thos. Pinckney, of South Carolina.	Aaron Burr, of New York.	Samuel Adams, of Massachusetts.	Oliver Ellsworth, of Connecticut.	John Jay, of New York.	George Clinton, of New York.	S. Johnston, of North Carolina.	James Iredell, of North Carolina.	Geo. Washington, of Virginia.	C. C. Pinckney, of South Carolina.	John Henry, of Maryland.
6	New Hampshire	6	....	....	....	....	6	....	....	....	....	....	....	....
16	Massachusetts..	16	....	13	....	....	1	....	....	2	....	....	....	....
4	Rhode Island..	4	....	....	....	....	4	....	....	....	....	....	....	..
9	Connecticut ...	9	....	4	....	....	....	5	....	....	....	....	....	....
4	Vermont	4	....	4	....	....	....	....	....	....	....	....	....	....
12	New York	12	....	12	. .	....	....	....	...	....	....	....	....	....
7	New Jersey....	7	....	7	....	....	....	....	....	....	....	....	....	....
15	Pennsylvania..	1	14	2	13	....	....	....	....	....	....	....	....	....
3	Delaware......	3	....	3	....	....	....	....	....	....	....	....	....	...
11	Maryland......	7	4	4	3	....	....	....	....	....	....	....	....	2
21	Virginia	1	20	1	1	15	....	....	3	....	....	1	....	...
4	Kentucky	....	4	....	4	....	....	....	....	....	....	....	....	....
12	North Carolina.	1	11	1	6	....	....	....	....	....	3	1	....	....
8	South Carolina.	....	8	8	....	....	....	....	....	....	....	....	1	....
4	Georgia........	....	4	....	....	....	....	....	4	....	....	....	....	....
3	Tennessee......	....	3	....	3	....	....	....	....	....	....	....	....	....
139	No. of Electors. Majority.....70	71	68	59	30	15	11	5	7	2	3	2	1	2

John Adams, elected President, took the oath of office, and entered upon his duties, March 4, 1797.

Thomas Jefferson, elected Vice President, took the oath of office, and entered upon his duties in the Senate, March 4, 1797.

The administration of Mr. Adams encountered the most virulent opposition, both domestic and foreign. France, still in the confusion following her revolution, made improper demands on our country, which not being complied with, she commenced seizing American property on the high seas. Our people, taking different sides, were about equally divided—some approving and others deprecating the course pursued by France. Letters of marque and reprisal were issued by our government, and a navy was raised with surprising promptitude. This had the desired effect, peace being thereby secured; and the aggressor was taught that the Americans were friends in peace, but were not fearful of war when it could not be honorably averted.

The Indians on our western frontiers also caused much trouble; but at length, being severely chastised by General Wayne, they sued for peace, which was granted in 1795.

In 1800 the seat of government was removed from Philadelphia to Washington City, which had been designated by Washington, under a law of Congress, as the most central situation.

THOMAS JEFFERSON,

THE THIRD PRESIDENT OF THE UNITED STATES,

Was born at Shadwell, Albemarle County, Virginia (near Monticello, the seat where he died), April 13, 1743. He was educated at William and Mary's College, and graduated with distinction when quite young. He was a great lover of learning, and particularly of natural philosophy. With the celebrated George Wythe, he commenced the study of the law, and became a favorite pupil. Mr. Jefferson was never distinguished as an advocate, but was considered a good lawyer. Soon after he came to the bar he was elected a member of the House of Burgesses, and, in that body, was duly appreciated for his learning and aptitude for business. He at once took fire at British oppression, and, in 1774, he employed his pen in discussing the whole course of the British ministry. The work was admired, and made a text-book by his countrymen. In June, 1775, he took his seat in the Continental Congress, from Virginia. In that body he soon became conspicuous, and was considered a firm friend of American liberty. In 1776, he was chosen chairman of the committee that drafted the Declaration of Independence. This instrument is nearly all his own, and was sanctioned by his coadjutors, with few alterations. In 1778, Mr. Jefferson was appointed embassador to France, to form a treaty with that government, but ill-health prevented his accepting this office. He succeded Patrick Henry, in 1779, as Governor of Virginia, and continued in that station two years. In 1781 he composed his notes on Virginia. In 1783 he was sent to France to join the ministers of our country, Mr. Adams and Dr. Franklin. In 1785 he succeeded Dr. Franklin as embassador, and continued performing the duties of that office for two years, when he retired, and returned home. In 1789 he was made Secretary of State, under Washington, in which situation he was highly distinguished for his talents. This station he resigned in 1793, and retired to private life. In 1797 he was elected Vice-President of the United States, and took his seat as President of the Senate, on the following 4th of March. In 1801, he was President of the United States, which office he held for eight years. After completing his second term, he retired to private life, in which he spent his days in philosophical pursuits, until the 4th of July, 1826, when he expired, just fifty years after penning the Declaration of Independence. His course was one of his own. Never lived there a politician who did more than Thomas Jefferson to bring his fellow-citizens to his own opinions.

Election for the Fourth Term, commencing March 4, 1801, *and terminating March* 3, 1805.

No. of Electors from each State.	STATES.	Thomas Jefferson, of Virginia.	Aaron Burr, of New York.	John Adams, of Massachusetts.	C. C. Pinckney, of South Carolina.	John Jay, of New York.
6	New Hampshire	....	....	6	6	....
16	Massachusetts	....	....	16	16	....
4	Rhode Island	....	....	4	3	1
9	Connecticut	....	....	9	9	....
4	Vermont	....	....	4	4	....
12	New York	12	12	....	....	....
7	New Jersey	....	....	7	7	....
15	Pennsylvania	8	8	7	7	....
3	Delaware	....	....	3	3	....
10	Maryland	5	5	5	5	....
21	Virginia	21	21	....	....	....
4	Kentucky	4	4	....	....	....
12	North Carolina	8	8	4	4	....
3	Tennessee	3	3	....	....	....
8	South Carolina	8	8	....	....	....
4	Georgia	4	4	....	....	....
138	No. of Electors	73	73	65	64	1
	Majority 70					

The electoral vote for Thos. Jefferson and Aaron Burr being equal, no choice was made by the people, and on the 11th of February, 1601, the House of Representatives proceeded to the choice of President in the manner prescribed by the Constitution. On the first ballot eight States voted for Thos. Jefferson, six for Aaron Burr, and the votes of two States were divided. The balloting continued till the 17th of February, when the thirty-fifth ballot, as had all previously, resulted the same as the first. After the thirty-sixth ballot, the Speaker declared that the votes of ten States had been given for Thos. Jefferson, the votes of four States for Aaron Burr, and the votes of two States in blank; and that, consequently, Thomas Jefferson had been elected for the term of four years.

Thomas Jefferson, thus elected President, took the oath of office, and entered upon his duties, March 4, 1801.

In his inaugural address, Mr. Jefferson used the following memorable expression: "We have called by different names brethren of the same principle. We are all republicans: we are all federalists. If there be any among us who would wish to dissolve this Union, or to change its republican form, let them stand, undisturbed, as monuments of the safety with which ERROR OF OPINION MAY BE TOLERATED, WHERE REASON IS LEFT FREE TO COMBAT IT."

Aaron Burr, elected Vice-President, took the oath of office, and entered upon his duties in the Senate, March 4, 1801.

Election for the Fifth Term, commencing March 4, 1805, *and terminating March* 3, 1809.

No. of Electors from each State.	STATES.	PRESID'T. Thomas Jefferson, of Virginia.	PRESID'T. Charles C. Pinckney, of South Carolina.	V. PRES'T. George Clinton of New York.	V. PRES'T. Rufus King, of New York.
7	New Hampshire	7	....	7	....
19	Massachusetts	19	....	10	....
4	Rhode Island	4	....	4	....
9	Connecticut	....	9	....	9
6	Vermont	6	....	6	...
19	New York	19	....	19	....
8	New Jersey	8	....	8	....
20	Pennsylvania	20	....	20	....
3	Delaware	....	3	....	3
11	Maryland	9	2	9	2
24	Virginia	24	....	24	....
14	North Carolina	14	....	14	....
10	South Carolina	10	....	10	....
6	Georgia	6	....	6	....
5	Tennessee	5	....	5	....
8	Kentucky	8	....	8	....
3	Ohio	3	....	3	....
176	Whole No. of Electors	162	14	162	14
	Majority 89				

Thomas Jefferson, elected President, took the oath of office for a second term, and entered upon his duties March 4, 1805.

George Clinton, elected Vice-President, took the oath of office, and entered upon his duties in the Senate, March 4, 1805.

Among the most important acts of Mr. Jefferson's administration was the purchase of Louisiana from France for $15,000,000, which territory was surrendered to our Government in December, 1803.

In November, 1808, the celebrated "ORDERS IN COUNCIL" were issued by the British Government, which prohibited all trade with France and her allies; and, as a retaliatory measure, in December following Bonaparte issued his "MILAN DECREE," interdicting all trade with England and her colonies—thus subjecting almost every American vessel on the ocean to capture. In requital for these tyrannous proceedings, and that England and France might both feel their injustice, Congress decreed an embargo; but as this failed to obtain from either power an acknowledgment of our rights, and was also ruinous to our commerce with other nations, it was repealed in March, 1809.

JAMES MADISON,

THE FOURTH PRESIDENT OF THE UNITED STATES,

Was born in Orange County, Virginia, March 16, 1751. His studies, preparatory to entering Princeton College, were pursued under the most favorable circumstances, he being provided with the most accomplished instructors, and he graduated with high honor in 1771. On returning to Virginia, he zealously commenced the study of the law, which he subsequently abandoned for political life.

In 1776, he was elected to the General Assembly of Virginia, and from this period, for more than forty years, he was continually in office, serving his State and his country in various capacities, from that of a State Legislator to that of President.

In 1778, he was elected by the Legislature to the executive council of the State, where he rendered important aid to Henry and Jefferson, Governors of Virginia, during the time he held a seat in the council; and by his probity of character, faithfulness in the discharge of duty, and amiableness of deportment, he won the approbation of these great men. In the winter of 1779–80, he took his seat in the Continental Congress, and became immediately an active and leading member, as the journal of that body abundantly testifies.

In 1784–5–6, he was a member of the Legislature of Virginia. In 1787, he became a member of the Convention held in Philadelphia, for the purpose of preparing a Constitution for the Government of the United States. Perhaps no member of that body had more to do with the formation of that noble instrument, the Constitution of the United States of America, than Mr. Madison.

It was during the recess between the proposition of the Constitution by the Convention of 1787, and its adoption by the States, that that celebrated work, "The Federalist," made its appearance. This is known to be the joint production of Alexander Hamilton, John Jay, and James Madison. The same year he was elected to Congress, and held his seat until the Continental Congress passed away among the things that were. He was a member of the

State Convention of Virginia which met to adopt the Constitution, and on the establishment of the new Congress under the Constitution, he was chosen a member, retaining his seat until the close of Washington's administration.

In 1801, as one of the presidential electors, he had the gratification of voting for his illustrious friend Jefferson, who immediately offered him a place in his cabinet, which was accepted. Accordingly, he entered on the discharge of his duties as Secretary of State, which duties he continued to perform during the whole of Mr. Jefferson's administration, and on the retirement of that great statesman, in 1809, he succeeded to the Presidency, in which office he served two terms.

Mr. Madison then retired to his peaceful home in Virginia, where he passed the remainder of his days in favorite pastimes, loved by the many and respected by all, until the 28th of June, 1826, when the last survivor of the framers of our Constitution was gathered to his fathers, full of years and glory.

Election for the Sixth Term, commencing March 4, 1809, *and terminating March* 3, 1813.

No. of Electors from each State.	STATES.	PRESIDENT.			VICE-PRESIDENT.				
		James Madison, of Virginia.	George Clinton of New York.	C. C. Pinckney, of South Carolina.	George Clinton, of New York.	James Madison, of Virginia.	James Monroe, of Virginia.	John Langdon, of New Hampshire.	Rufus King, of New York.
7	New Hampshire	....	....	7	....	....	....	....	7
19	Massachusetts	....	....	19	....	....	....	....	19
4	Rhode Island	....	....	4	....	....	....	....	4
9	Connecticut	....	....	9	....	....	....	....	9
6	Vermont	6	....	....	....	....	....	6	....
19	New York	13	6	....	13	3	3	....	....
8	New Jersey	8	....	....	8	....	....	....	....
20	Pennsylvania	20	....	....	20	....	....	....	....
3	Delaware	....	....	3	....	....	....	....	3
11	Maryland	9	....	2	9	....	....	....	2
24	Virginia	24	....	....	24	....	....	....	....
14	North Carolina	11	....	3	11	....	....	....	3
10	South Carolina	10	....	....	10	....	....	....	....
6	Georgia	6	....	....	6	....	....	....	....
7	Kentucky	7	....	....	7	....	....	....	....
5	Tennessee	5	....	....	5	....	....	....	....
3	Ohio	3	....	....	....	....	....	3	....
175	Whole No. of Electors Majority ... 88	122	6	47	113	3	3	9	47

James Madison took the oath of office, as President, and entered upon his duties March 4, 1809.

George Clinton, elected Vice President, took the oath of office, and attended in the Senate, March 4, 1809.

Our national position, especially in regard to England and France, was certainly a very perplexing one when Mr. Madison came to the Presidency. We were not only threatened by enemies abroad, but were harassed by a savage foe on our western frontier, probably urged on by British influence, and led by the famous chief Tecumseh and his brother the Prophet. These last were finally subdued in 1811; but our European foes were more troublesome. After all peaceful means had failed to check the aggressions of England, and when at length "patience had ceased to be a virtue," war was declared against that country, June 19, 1812. The events of that war it is not within our province to record; and it is sufficient to say, that they greatly elevated the American character in the estimation of both friends and enemies.

Election for the Seventh Term, commencing March 4, 1813, *and terminating March* 3, 1817.

No. of Electors from each State.	STATES.	PRESID'T. James Madison, of Virginia.	PRESID'T. De Witt Clinton, of New York.	V. PRES'T. Elbridge Gerry, of Massachusetts.	V. PRES'T. Jared Ingersoll, of Pennsylvania.
8	New Hampshire	....	8	1	7
22	Massachusetts	....	22	2	20
4	Rhode Island	....	4	....	4
9	Connecticut	....	9	....	9
8	Vermont	8	....	8	....
29	New York	. ..	29	....	29
]8	New Jersey	....	8	....	8
25	Pennsylvania	25	....	25	....
14	Delaware	....	4	....	4
11	Maryland	6	5	6	5
25	Virginia	25	....	25	....
15	North Carolina	15	....	15	....
11	South Carolina	11	....	11	....
8	Georgia	8	....	8	.. .
12	Kentucky	12	....	12	....
8	Tennessee	8	....	8	....
7	Ohio	7	....	7	....
3	Louisiana	3	....	3	....
217	Whole No. of Electors	128	89	131	86
	Majority ... 109				

James Madison, elected President for a second term. [There is no notice on the Journals of Congress of his having taken the oath.]

Elbridge Gerry, elected Vice-President, attended in the Senate on the 24th of May, 1813, and exhibited a certificate of his having taken the oath of office prescribed by law, which was read.

The war into which the country had been forced was brought to a close by the treaty of Ghent, which was signed December 24, 1814; but this treaty had scarcely been ratified, when it became necessary to commence another war for the protection of American commerce and seamen against Algerine piracies. In May, 1815, a squadron under Commodore Decatur sailed for the Mediterranean, where the naval force of Algiers was cruising for American vessels. After capturing two of the enemy's best frigates in that sea, Decatur proceeded to the Bay of Algiers, and there dictated a treaty which secured the United States from any further molestation from that quarter. Similar treaties were also concluded with the other Barbary powers.

JAMES MONROE,

THE FIFTH PRESIDENT OF THE UNITED STATES,

One of the few exalted characters that served his country in both a civil and military capacity, was born in Westmoreland county, Virginia, April 26, 1758, and was educated at William and Mary's College, whence he graduated in 1776, and commenced the study of the law. Anxious to aid in the struggle for independence, which had then just began, he abandoned his studies, and entered the army as a cadet—joining a corps under the gallant General Mercer. He soon distinguished himself in several well-fought battles, and rapid promotion followed, until he reached the rank of captain. He was at Harlem Heights, and White Plains, and shared the perils and fatigues of the distressing retreat of Washington through New Jersey, as well as the glory of the victory over the Hessians at Trenton, where he received a musket-ball in the shoulder; notwithstanding which, he valiantly "fought out the fight." He subsequently accepted the post of an aid to Lord Stirling, with the rank of Major, in which position he saw much hard service—being engaged in almost every conflict for the two succeeding campaigns, and displaying great courage and coolness at the bloody battles of Brandywine, Germantown, and Monmouth.

Aspiring to a separate command, he obtained permission to raise a regiment in his native State; for which purpose he left the army, and returned to Virginia, where he encountered so many unexpected and discouraging obstacles, that he finally relinquished the enterprise, and resumed his law studies in the office of Mr. Jefferson.

In 1780, he was elected to the Virginia Legislature, and in the following year was made one of Governor Jefferson's council, in which he continued until 1783, when, at the age of twenty-four years, he became a member of the Continental Congress. After serving three years in that body, he was again returned to the State Legislature.

In 1788, while a member of the Convention to decide upon the adoption of the new Constitution, he voted in the minority against that instrument; but this vote did not at all affect his popularity. Two years afterward he was elected United States Senator, and in 1794 he was sent envoy extraordinary and minister plenipotentiary to the Court of Versailles. After settling the cession of Louisiana to the United States, he went to England to succeed Mr. King as minister at the court of St. James. The affair of the frigate Chesapeake placing him in an uncomfortable situation, he returned to the United States, and, in 1810, was once more elected to the Virginia Legislature. He was soon after chosen Governor of that State, in which office he remained until Mr. Madison called him to assume the duties of Secretary of State in his cabinet. In 1817, he was elected President of the United States, and in 1821 was unanimously reëlected, with the exception of a single vote in New Hampshire. His administration was a prosperous and quiet one.

He united with Jefferson and Madison in founding the University of Virginia; and when the convention was formed for the revision of the Constitution of his State, he was called to preside over its action. Not long after this, he went to reside with a beloved daughter (the wife of Samuel L. Gouverneur, Esq.) in New York City, where he lived until the anniversary of Independence, in 1831, when, "amidst the pealing joy and congratulations of that proud day, he passed quietly and in glory away."

Election for the Eighth Term, commencing March 4, 1817, *and terminating March* 3, 1821.

No. of Electors from each State.	STATES.	PRESID'T.		VICE-PRESIDENT.				
		James Monroe, of Virginia.	Rufus King, of New York.	D. D. Tompkins, of New York.	John E. Howard, of Maryland.	James Ross, of Pennsylvania.	John Marshall, of Virginia.	Rob't G. Harper, of Maryland.
8	New Hampshire	8	....	8	....	....	....	....
22	Massachusetts	....	22	....	22	....	....	....
4	Rhode Island	4	....	4	....	....	....	....
9	Connecticut	....	9	....	....	5	4	....
8	Vermont	8	....	8	....	....	....	....
29	New York	29	....	29	....	....	....	....
8	New Jersey	8	....	8	....	....	....	....
25	Pennsylvania	25	....	25	....	....	....	....
3	Delaware	....	3	....	....	....	....	3
8	Maryland	8	....	8	....	....	....	....
25	Virginia	25	....	25	....	....	....	....
15	North Carolina	15	....	15	....	....	....	....
11	South Carolina	11	....	11	....	....	....	....
8	Georgia	8	....	8	....	....	....	....
12	Kentucky	12	....	12	....	....	....	....
8	Tennessee	8	....	8	....	....	....	....
8	Ohio	8	....	8	....	....	....	....
3	Louisiana	3	....	3	....	....	....	....
3	Indiana	3	....	3	....	....	....	....
217	Whole No. of Electors	183	34	183	22	5	4	3
	Majority 109							

James Monroe took the oath of office, as President, and entered upon his duties March 4, 1817.

Daniel D. Tompkins, elected Vice-President, took the oath of office, and attended in the Senate, March 4, 1817.

The Seminole and a few of the Creek Indians commenced depredations on the frontiers of Georgia and Alabama towards the close of 1817, for which they were severely chastised by a force under General Jackson, and gladly sued for peace.

In February, 1819, a treaty was negotiated at Washington, by which Spain ceded to the United States East and West Florida and the adjacent Islands. In the same year the southern portion of Missouri Territory was set off under the name of Arkansas, for which a territorial government was formed; and Alabama was constituted a State, and admitted into the Union.

Early in 1820 the province of Maine, which had been connected with Massachusetts since 1652, was separated from it and was admitted into the Union as an independent State.

Election for the Ninth Term, commencing March 4, 1821, *and terminating March* 3, 1825.

No. of Electors from each State.	STATES.	PRESID'T.		VICE PRESIDENT.				
		James Monroe, of Virginia.	John Quincy Adams, of Massachusetts.	Daniel D. Tompkins, of New York.	Richard Stockton, of New Jersey.	Robert C. Harper, of Maryland.	Richard Rush, of Pennsylvania.	Daniel Rodney, of Delaware.
8	New Hampshire	7	1	7	....	....	1	....
15	Massachusetts	15	....	7	8	....	....	....
4	Rhode Island	4	....	4	....	....	....	....
9	Connecticut	9	....	9	....	....	....	....
8	Vermont	8	....	8	....	....	....	....
29	New York	29	....	29	....	....	....	....
9	New Jersey	8	....	8	....	....	....	....
25	Pennsylvania	24	....	24	....	....	....	....
4	Delaware	4	....	....	....	....	....	4
11	Maryland	11	....	10	....	1	....	....
25	Virginia	25	....	25	....	....	....	....
15	North Carolina	15	....	15	....	....	....	....
11	South Carolina	11	....	11	....	....	....	....
8	Georgia	8	....	8	....	....	....	....
12	Kentucky	12	....	12	....	....	....	....
8	Tennessee	7	....	7	....	....	....	....
8	Ohio	8	....	8	....	....	....	....
3	Louisiana	3	....	3	....	....	....	....
3	Indiana	3	....	3	....	....	....	....
3	Mississippi	2	....	2	....	....	....	....
3	Illinois	3	....	3	....	....	....	....
3	Alabama	3	....	3	....	....	....	....
9	Maine	9	....	9	....	....	....	....
3	Missouri	3	....	3	....	....	....	....
235	No. of Electors Majority 118	231	1	218	8	1	1	4

James Monroe was re-elected President, but there is no notice on the Journals of Congress that he again took the oath of office.

Daniel D. Tompkins was re-elected Vice President, but there is no record of his having taken the oath of office.

Public attention was much occupied in 1824–5 by a visit from the venerable General Lafayette, who, after the lapse of nearly half a century from the period of his military career, was again welcomed with every token of respect that could be devised for honoring the "Nation's Guest." He landed in New York in August, 1824, and after remaining there a short time, set out on a tour through all the States. Upwards of a year was taken up in accomplishing this gratifying object; and in September, 1825, he sailed from Washington in the frigate Brandywine for his native home.

JOHN QUINCY ADAMS,

THE SIXTH PRESIDENT OF THE UNITED STATES,

Was born at Quincy, Massachusetts, July 11, 1767, and received the advantages of a pretty thorough education before entering Harvard College, which was not until the year 1786. After graduating with marked credit, he commenced the study of law at Newburyport, in the office of the Hon. Theophilus Parsons, for many years Chief Justice of Massachusetts. While pursuing his studies he found leisure to write several newspaper essays, which attracted much attention, and displayed a maturity of taste and judgment seldom attained so early in life. In 1794, Washington appointed him minister to the Netherlands, and subsequently transferred him to Portugal. He was afterward, at different periods, minister to Prussia, Russia, and England; and was one of the commissioners who negotiated the treaty of peace with Great Britain, at Ghent, in 1815. In 1817, he was appointed Secretary of State, in which office he continued during Mr. Monroe's administration, eight years; when he was elected by the House of Representatives President of the United States—the people having failed in making a choice. Like his father, he encountered strong opposition, and only served one term in this office, being defeated in a reëlection by General Jackson. He then retired to his farm at Quincy, but did not remain long in private life; for, two years afterward, he was chosen Representative in Congress, and continued to be reëlected until his death, which occurred in the Capitol, at Washington, February 23, 1848. Two days previous to this sad event, while engaged in his duties in the House of Representatives, he received a paralytic stroke, which apparently deprived him of all consciousness. He was borne to the Speaker's room, where he received every attention that could be bestowed by anxious and devoted friends, but all in vain—his hour was come. The last words he was heard to utter were, "This is the last of earth."

Mr. Adams was a man of rare gifts and rich acquisitions. A diligent student, and economical of his time, he found opportunity, amid all his public cares, to cultivate his tastes for literature and the sciences. He was one of the finest classical and belles-lettres scholars of his time, and filled the chair of Professor of Rhetoric and Belles-lettres in Harvard College for several years. Even in his old age, he often astonished his hearers with the elegant classical allusions and rhetorical tropes with which he enriched and embellished his own productions.

Election for the Tenth Term, commencing March 4. 1825, *and terminating March* 3, 1829.

No. of Electors from each State.	STATES.	PRESIDENT.				VICE PRESIDENT.					
		Andrew Jackson, of Tennessee.	John Quincy Adams, of Massachusetts.	Wm. H. Crawford, of Georgia.	Henry Clay, of Kentucky.	John C. Calhoun, of South Carolina.	Nathan Sanford, of New York.	Nathaniel Macon, of North Carolina.	Andrew Jackson, of Tennessee.	Henry Clay, of Kentucky.	Martin Van Buren, of New York.
8	New Hampshire	....	8	....	....	7	. .	....	1	....	....
15	Massachusetts	....	15	....	....	15	....	....	....	....	....
4	Rhode Island	....	4	....	....	3	....	....	....	....	....
8	Connecticut	....	8	....	....	....	....	....	8	....	....
7	Vermont	....	7	....	....	7	....	....	....	....	....
36	New York	1	26	5	4	29	7	....	....	....	....
8	New Jersey	8	....	....	....	8	....	....	....	....	....
28	Pennsylvania	28	....	....	....	28	....	....	....	....	....
3	Delaware	....	1	2	....	1	....	....	....	....	2
11	Maryland	7	3	1	....	10	....	....	1	....	....
24	Virginia	....	....	24	....	....	....	24	....	....	....
15	North Carolina	15	....	....	....	15	....	....	....	....	....
11	South Carolina	11	....	....	....	11	....	....	....	....	....
9	Georgia	....	....	9	....	....	....	....	....	9	....
14	Kentucky	....	....	....	14	7	7	....	....	....	....
11	Tennessee	11	....	....	....	11	....	....	....	....	....
16	Ohio	....	....	....	16	....	16	....	....	....	....
5	Louisiana	3	2	....	....	5	....	....	....	....	....
5	Indiana	5	....	....	....	5	....	....	....	....	....
3	Mississippi	3	....	....	....	3	....	....	....	....	....
3	Illinois	2	1	....	....	3	....	....	....	....	....
5	Alabama	5	....	....	....	5	....	....	....	....	....
9	Maine	....	9	....	....	9	....	....	....	....	....
3	Missouri	....	....	....	3	....	....	....	3	....	....
261	Whole No. of Electors... Majority.......... 131	99	84	41	37	182	30	24	13	9	2

Neither candidate for the Presidency having received a majority of the electoral votes, it devolved upon the House of Representatives to choose a President from the three highest on the list of those voted for, which three were Andrew Jackson, John Quincy Adams, and William H. Crawford. Twenty-four tellers (one member from each State) were appointed, who, after examining the ballots, announced that the votes of thirteen States had been given for John Quincy Adams; the votes of seven States for Andrew Jackson; and the votes of four States for William H. Crawford. The Speaker then declared that John Quincy Adams, having received a majority of the votes of all the States, was duly elected President of the United States for four years, commencing on the 4th of March, 1825; on which day Mr. Adams took the oath of office, and entered upon his duties.

John C. Calhoun, having been elected Vice President, took the oath of office, and attended in the Senate, March 4, 1825.

ANDREW JACKSON,

THE SEVENTH PRESIDENT OF THE UNITED STATES,

A statesman of rare integrity, and a general of invincible skill and courage, was born at Waxhaw, Lancaster County, South Carolina, in 1767, and while yet a mere lad, did something toward achieving the independence of his country. It is said that he commenced his military career at the age of fourteen years, and was soon after taken prisoner, together with an elder brother. During his captivity, he was ordered by a British officer to perform some menial service, which he promptly refused, and for this refusal was "severely wounded with the sword which the Englishman disgraced." He was educated for the bar, and commenced practice at Nashville, Tennessee, but relinquished his legal pursuits to "gain a name in arms." In the early part of the war of 1812, Congress, having voted to accept fifty thousand volunteers, General Jackson appealed to the militia of Tennessee, when twenty-five hundred enrolled their names, and presented themselves to Congress, with General Jackson at their head. They were accepted, and ordered to Natchez, to watch the operations of the British in lower Mississippi. Not long after, he received orders from headquarters to disband his men and send them to their homes. To obey, he foresaw, would be an act of great injustice to his command, and reflect disgrace on the country, and he resolved to disobey. He accordingly broke up his camp, and returned to Nashville, bringing all his sick with him, whose wants on the way he relieved with his private means, and there disbanded his troops in the midst of their homes.

He was soon called to the field once more, and his commission marked out his course of duty on the field of Indian warfare. Here for years he labored, and fought, and diplomatized, with the most consummate wisdom and undaunted courage. It was about this time that the treaty of the "Hickory Gound" occurred, which gave him the familiar sobriquet of "Old Hickory."

The crowning glory of his whole military career was the battle of New Orleans; which will ever occupy one of the brightest pages in American history.

At the close of the war he returned to his home in Nashville; but in 1818 was again called on by his country to render his military services in the expulsion of the Seminoles. His conduct during this campaign has been both bitterly condemned and highly applauded. An attempt in the House of Representatives to inflict a censure on the old hero for the irregularities of this campaign, after a long and bitter debate, was defeated by a large majority.

In 1828, and again in 1832, General Jackson was elected to fill the Presidential chair; thus occupying that elevated position for eight successive years. He then retired to his hospitable mansion ("the Hermitage"), near Nashville, "loaded with wealth and honors bravely won," where he continued to realize all the enjoyments that are inseparable from a well-spent life, until death translated him to those higher rewards, which "earth can neither give nor take away." He died June 8, 1845, and his last hours were soothed by a trustful reliance on the Savior of the world for salvation.

Election for the Eleventh Term, commencing March 4, 1829, *and terminating March* 3, 1833.

No. of Electors from each State.	STATES.	PRESID'T.		VICE PRESID'T.		
		Andrew Jackson, of Tennessee.	John Quincy Adams, of Massachusetts.	John C. Calhoun, of South Carolina.	Richard Rush, of Pennsylvania.	William Smith, of South Carolina.
9	Maine	1	8	1	8	....
8	New Hampshire	....	8	....	8	....
15	Massachusetts	....	15	....	15	....
4	Rhode Island	....	4	....	4	....
8	Connecticut	....	8	....	8	....
7	Vermont	....	7	....	7	....
36	New York	20	16	20	16	....
8	New Jersey	....	8	....	8	....
28	Pennsylvania	28	....	28	....	....
3	Delaware	....	3	....	3	....
11	Maryland	5	6	5	6	....
24	Virginia	24	....	24	....	....
15	North Carolina	15	....	15	....	....
11	South Carolina	11	....	11	....	....
9	Georgia	9	....	2	....	7
14	Kentucky	14	....	14	....	.
11	Tennessee	11	....	11	....	....
16	Ohio	16	....	16	....	....
5	Louisiana	5	....	5	....	....
3	Mississippi	3	....	3	....	....
5	Indiana	5	....	5	....	....
3	Illinois	3	....	3	....	....
5	Alabama	5	....	5	....	....
3	Missouri	3	....	3	....	....
261	Whole No. of Eelectors	178	83	171	83	7
	Majority 131					

Andrew Jackson took the oath of office, as President, and entered upon his duties March 4, 1829.

John C. Calhoun took the oath of office, as Vice President, and presided in the Senate March 4, 1829.

A series of unfortunate political and social occurrences soon led to a rupture of that cordiality which had formerly existed between these two distinguished individuals, the consequences of which were peculiarly disastrous to the political aspirations of Mr. Calhoun, who was never afterwards regarded with much favor beyond the immediate limits of his own State.

NOTE.—It was during this administration that the doctrine of State's rights was so strongly urged by Calhoun, and to this period may be dated the origin of the great rebellion of 1861.

Election for the Twelfth Term, commencing March 4, 1833, *and terminating March* 3, 1837.

No. of Electors from each State.	STATES.	PRESIDENT.				VICE PRESIDENT.				
		Andrew Jackson, of Tennessee.	Henry Clay, of Kentucky.	John Floyd, of Virginia.	William Wirt, of Maryland.	Martin VanBuren of New York.	John Sergeant, of Pennsylvania.	William Wilkins, of Pennsylvania.	Henry Lee, of Massachusetts.	Amos Ellmaker, of Pennsylvania.
10	Maine	10				10				
7	New Hampshire	7				7				
14	Massachusetts		14				14			
4	Rhode Island		4				4			
8	Connecticut		8				8			
7	Vermont				7					7
42	New York	42				42				
8	New Jersey	8				8				
30	Pennsylvania	30								
3	Delaware		3				3	30		
10	Maryland	3	5			3	5			
23	Virginia	23				23				
15	North Carolina	15				15				
11	South Carolina			11					11	
11	Georgia	11				11				
15	Kentucky		15				15			
15	Tennessee	15				15				
21	Ohio	21				21				
5	Louisiana	5				5				
4	Mississippi	4				4				
9	Indiana	9				9				
5	Illinois	5				5				
7	Alabama	7				7				
4	Missouri	4				4				
288	Whole No. of Electors.. Majority 145	219	49	11	7	189	49	30	11	7

Andrew Jackson, re-elected President, took the oath of office, and continued his duties, March 4, 1833.

Martin Van Buren, having been elected Vice President, took the oath of office, and attended in the Senate, March 4, 1833.

Early in June, 1833, the President left Washington on a tour through the Northern States, and was everywhere received with an enthusiasm that evinced the cordial approval of his administration by the people. One of his first measures, on returning to the seat of government, was the removal of the public moneys from the United States Bank, for which act he encountered the most virulent hostility of a small majority of the Senate, who passed resolutions censuring his course. But this injustice has not been perpetuated; for on the 16th of January, 1837, these partisan resolutions were expunged from the records by order of a handsome majority.

MARTIN VAN BUREN,

THE EIGHTH PRESIDENT OF THE UNITED STATES,

Was born in the flourishing town of Kinderhook, New York, September 5, 1782, and early received the best education that could then be obtained in the schools in his immediate vicinity. Having sufficiently prepared himself for the study of law, he entered the office of Francis Sylvester, in his native town, where he remained about six years. But law did not engross his whole time: he found leisure occasionally to peer into the mysteries of political economy, and finally arrived at the conclusion that his chances for fame and fortune were at least equal in the arena of politics to any thing he might accomplish by a strict adherence to legal pursuits. Fully impressed with this idea, he early set about cultivating what little popularity could be gained in his limited sphere, and so won upon the confidence of his neighbors and friends as to be appointed, while yet in his *teens*, a delegate to a convention in his native county, in which important political measures were to be acted upon.

In 1808, he was appointed Surrogate of Columbia County, the first public office he ever held; and in 1812 and 1816 he was elected to the State Senate, in which body he became a distinguished leader of the Madison party, and one of its most eloquent supporters.

In 1821, he was elected to the United States Senate, in which he held his seat for nearly eight years, and became remarkable not only for his close attention to business, but also for his devotion to the great principles of the Democratic party.

In 1828, he was elected Governor of his native State, and entered upon the duties of that office, on the first of January, 1829; but he filled the gubernatorial chair for only a few weeks. In March following, when General Jackson was elevated to the Presidency, he tendered Mr. Van Buren the post of Secretary of State, which was accepted. At the expiration of two years he resigned his seat in the Cabinet, and was immediately appointed minister to England; but when his nomination was submitted to the Senate (June 25, 1831) it was rejected by the casting vote of the Vice-President (Mr. Calhoun), and, of course, he was recalled. As his friends attributed his rejection to personal and political rancor, it only served to raise Mr. Van Buren in the estimation of his political adherents, and the result was that, in May following, he was nominated, with great unanimity, for the Vice-Presidency, by the Democratic Convention, at Baltimore. His triumphant election was regarded not merely as a high compliment to himself, but as a wholesome rebuke to his opponents.

In 1836, he was put in nomination for the chief magistracy, to which he was elected, by a large majority, over General Harrison; but, at the next Presidential election, the tables were turned, and he only received sixty votes out of two hundred and ninety-four.

After his defeat, he returned to Kinderhook, where he remained some time, and then visited Europe, with one of his sons, whose restoration to health was the principal object of his journey. Not long after his return he consented to become once more a candidate for the Presidency, and, in 1848, received the nomination of the Free-soil party, but did not secure a single electoral vote.

Election for the Thirteenth Term, commencing March 4, 1837 *and terminating March* 3, 1841.

No. of Electors from each State.	STATES.	PRESIDENT. Martin Van Buren of New York.	Wm. H. Harrison, of Ohio.	Hugh L. White, of Tennessee.	Daniel Webster, of Massachusetts.	Willie P. Mangum of North Carolina.	VICE PRESIDENT. Rich'd M Johnson of Kentucky.	Francis Granger, of New York.	John Tyler, of Virginia.	William Smith, of Alabama.
10	Maine	10	....	....	....	....	10	....	....	....
7	New Hampshire	7	....	....	....	....	7	....	....	....
14	Massachusetts	....	....	....	14	....	....	14	....	....
4	Rhode Island	4	....	....	....	....	4	....	....	....
8	Connecticut	8	....	....	....	....	8	....	....	....
7	Vermont	....	7	....	....	....	....	7	....	....
42	New York	42	....	....	....	....	42	....	....	....
8	New Jersey	....	8	....	....	....	....	8	....	....
30	Pennsylvania	30	....	....	....	....	30	....	....	....
3	Delaware	....	3	....	....	....	....	3	....	....
10	Maryland	....	10	....	....	....	....	....	10	....
23	Virginia	23	....	....	....	....	....	....	....	23
15	North Carolina	15	....	....	....	....	15	....	....	....
11	South Carolina	....	....	....	....	11	....	....	11	....
11	Georgia	....	....	11	....	....	....	....	11	....
15	Kentucky	....	15	....	....	....	....	15	....	....
15	Tennessee	....	....	15	....	....	....	....	15	....
21	Ohio	....	21	....	....	....	....	21	....	....
5	Louisiana	5	....	....	....	....	5	....	....	....
4	Mississippi	4	....	....	....	....	4	....	....	....
9	Indiana	....	9	....	....	....	....	9	....	....
5	Illinois	5	....	....	....	....	5	....	....	....
7	Alabama	7	....	....	....	....	7	....	....	....
4	Missouri	4	....	....	....	....	4	....	....	....
3	Arkansas	3	....	....	....	....	3	....	....	....
3	Michigan	3	....	....	....	....	3	....	....	....
294	Whole No. of Electors	170	73	26	14	11	147*	77	47	23
	Majority.....148									

Martin Van Buren, elected President, took the oath of office, and entered upon his duties, March 4, 1837.

Richard M. Johnson, elected Vice President, took the oath of office, and attended in the Senate, March 4, 1837.

Urged by the unprecedented financial embarrassments which were experienced in every branch of industry, and especially by the mercantile class, Mr. Van Buren's first measure was to convene a special meeting of Congress early in September, '37, which continued in session forty days, but accomplished very little. A bill authorizing the issue of $10,000,000 in treasury notes was passed; but the Independent Treasury bill (the great financial measure of the administration) was then rejected, although afterwards (in 1840) adopted.

*Elected by the Senate.

WILLIAM HENRY HARRISON,

THE NINTH PRESIDENT OF THE UNITED STATES,

Was born in Charles City County, Virginia, February 9, 1773, and was educated for the medical profession at Hampden Sydney College. He graduated at a time when our north-western frontier was suffering much from the neighboring Indians, and, believing that he could be of greater service in repelling the savage invaders than in pursuing his studies, he accepted an ensign's commission from President Washington, and joined the army. He was promoted to a lieutenancy in 1792, and his skill and bravery were highly commended by General Wayne, under whose command he was engaged in several actions. After the bloody battle of Miami Rapids, he was rewarded with the rank of captain, and immediately placed in command of Fort Washington. In 1797, he resigned his commission for the purpose of accepting the office of Secretary of the North-west Territory, from which he was elected a delegate to Congress in 1799.

When a territorial government was formed for Indiana, he was appointed the first Governor, and continued in that office till 1813. To his civil and military duties he added those of Commissioner and Superintendent of Indian Affairs; and, in the course of his administration, he concluded thirteen important treaties with the different tribes. On the 7th of November, 1811, he gained the celebrated battle of Tippecanoe, the news of which was received throughout the country with a burst of enthusiasm. During the war of 1812, he was made commander of the North-western army of the United States, and he bore a conspicuous part in the leading events in the campaign of 1812–13—the defense of Fort Meigs, and the victory of the Thames. In 1814, he was appointed, in conjunction with his companions in arms, Governor Shelby and General Cass, to treat with the Indians in the North-west, at Greenville; and, in the following year, he was placed at the head of a commission to treat with various other important tribes.

In 1816, he was elected a member of Congress from Ohio, and, in 1828, he was sent minister plenipotentiary to the republic of Colombia. On his return, he took up his residence at North Bend, on the Ohio, where he lived upon his farm, in comparative retirement, till 1836, when he became a candidate for the Presidency; and, although defeated on the first trial, four years afterward he was elected by a large majority, and inaugurated in 1841. But he did not long survive this crowning honor, as he died on the 4th of April, just one month after entering upon his duties. His funeral obsequies were performed on the 7th, and an immense concourse assembled to pay their testimony of respect. Funeral services and processions also took place in most of the principal cities throughout the country. As General Harrison was the first President who died while in office, his successor, Mr. Tyler, recommended that the 14th of May be observed as a day of fasting and prayer, and accordingly it was so observed.

Election for the Fourteenth Term, commencing March 4, 1841, *and terminating March* 3, 1845.

No. of Electors from each State.	STATES.	PRESID'T.		VICE PRESIDENT.			
		Wm. H. Harrison, of Ohio.	Martin Van Buren of New York.	John Tyler, of Virginia.	Rich'd M. Johnson of Kentucky.	L. W. Tazewell, of Virginia.	James K. Polk, of Tennessee.
10	Maine	10	....	10	....	....	....
7	New Hampshire	....	7	....	7	....	....
14	Massachusetts	14	....	14	....	....	....
4	Rhode Island	4	....	4	....	....	....
8	Connecticut	8	....	8	....	....	....
7	Vermont	7	....	7	....	....	....
42	New York	42	....	42	....	....	....
8	New Jersey	8	....	8	....	....	....
30	Pennsylvania	30	....	30	....	....	....
3	Delaware	3	....	3	....	....	....
10	Maryland	10	....	10	....	....	....
23	Virginia	....	23	....	22	....	1
15	North Carolina	15	....	15	....	....	....
11	South Carolina	....	11	....	....	....	....
11	Georgia	11	....	11	....	11	....
15	Kentucky	15	....	15	....	....	....
15	Tennessee	15	....	15	....	....	....
21	Ohio	21	....	21	....	....	....
5	Louisiana	5	....	5	....	....	....
4	Mississippi	4	....	4	....	....	....
9	Indiana	9	....	9	....	....	....
5	Illinois	....	5	....	5	....	....
7	Alabama	....	7	....	7	....	....
4	Missouri	....	4	....	4	....	....
3	Arkansas	....	3	....	3	....	....
3	Michigan	3	....	3	....	....	....
294	No. of Electors	234	60	234	48	11	1
	Majority 148						

William H. Harrison, elected President, took the oath of office, and entered upon his duties, March 4, 1841.

John Tyler, elected Vice President, took the oath of office, and attended in the Senate, March 4, 1841.

Soon after his inauguration, President Harrison issued a proclamation, convening Congress for an extra session on the 31st of May, to consider "sundry weighty and important matters, chiefly growing out of the state of the revenue and finances of the country." But he did not live to submit his remedial plans —dying, after a very brief illness, on the 4th of April, exactly one month after coming into office. He was the first President who had died during his official term, and a messenger was immediately dispatched with a letter, signed by all the members of the Cabinet, conveying the melancholy intelligence to the

Vice President, then at Williamsburg, Va. By extraordinary means he reached Washington at five o'clock on the morning of the 6th, and at twelve o'clock the Heads of Departments waited upon him, to pay their official and personal respects. After signifying his deep feeling of the public calamity sustained by the death of President Harrison, and expressing his profound sensibility of the heavy responsibilities so suddenly devolved upon himself, he made known his wishes that the several Heads of Departments would continue to fill the places which they then respectively occupied, and his confidence that they would afford all the aid in their power to enable him to carry on the administration of the government successfully. Mr. Tyler afterwards took and subscribed the following oath of office:

"I do solemnly swear, that I will faithfully execute the office of President of the United States, and will, to the best of my ability, preserve, protect, and defend the Constitution of the United States. JOHN TYLER.
"April 6, 1841."

Pursuant to the proclamation of President Harrison, Congress met on the 31st of May, and continued in session until the 13th of September. On the 27th of July a bill for the establishment of "The Fiscal Bank of the United States," passed the Senate by a vote of 26 to 23, and was concurred in by the House of Representatives on the 6th of August—128 to 91. President Tyler, however, returned the bill on the 16th, with his objections, and it was lost for lack of a constitutional majority. But the friends of a national bank were not to be deterred from their purpose by a single repulse: another bill (about the same in substance) was immediately hurried through both Houses, under the title of "The Fiscal Corporation of the United States," but this shared the fate of its predecessor.

A Senate bill for the establishment of a uniform system of bankruptcy throughout the United States, was concurred in by the House on the 18th of August, and became a law; but, meeting with very general condemnation, it was soon after repealed.

A bill was also passed at this extra session for the distribution of the proceeds of the sales of the public lands among the several States, in proportion to population.

In 1842 an important treaty, adjusting the north-eastern boundary of the United States, was negotiated at Washington between Mr. Webster, on the part of this country, and Lord Ashburton, on the part of Great Britain.

During the last year of Mr. Tyler's administration much excitement prevailed on the proposed annexation of Texas to the Union, which was strongly resisted at the North, on the ground that the South and southern institutions would thereby gain increased power in the national councils. A treaty of annexation, signed by the President, was rejected by the Senate, but measures were taken by which Texas was admitted the year following.

JOHN TYLER,

THE SUCCESSOR OF GENERAL HARRISON AS PRESIDENT,

Was born at Williamsburg, Virginia, March 29, 1790, and at the age of twelve years entered William and Mary's College, where he graduated with distinguished merit five years afterward. Few have commenced life at so early a period as Mr. Tyler—he having been admitted to the bar when only nineteen, and elected to the Virginia Legislature before attaining his twenty-second year. In 1816, he was sent to Congress; in 1825, elected Governor of Virginia; and in 1827, became United States Senator; in which capacity he firmly supported the administration of General Jackson—voting against the tariff bill of 1828, and against rechartering the United States Bank. Notwithstanding this last vote, the friends of the bank, presuming upon his well-known conservatism, at the special session of Congress called by his predecessor, introduced a bill for the establishment of the "Fiscal Bank of the United States," which passed both Houses by small majorities, and which Mr. Tyler felt bound to veto. But this did not dishearten the friends of the measure, who modified and rechristened their financial plan, which, under the name of "Fiscal Corporation of the United States," again passed both houses of Congress, and was again vetoed by the President. Of course, a large portion of the party that elected him were greatly dissatisfied with his course, and their denunciation of his alleged faithlessness were "loud and deep." To add to the embarrassments which were accumulating around him, all the members of his Cabinet, with the exception of Mr. Webster, resigned their places; but even this implied rebuke did not shake his integrity of purpose. An equally efficient phalanx of talent was called to his aid, and he had the satisfaction of seeing that his views were indorsed by a large number of leading statesmen. It has often been asserted that Mr. T. had pledged himself to sustain the financial schemes of the bank and its friends; but this has always been denied, and circumstances certainly warrant the conclusion that the assertion is unfounded. So gross and bitter were the assaults made upon him, that he felt called upon to defend himself from their violence; and, after declaring his determination to do his duty, regardless of party ties, he said, "I appeal from the vituperation of the present day to the pen of impartial history, in confidence that neither my motives nor my acts will bear the interpretation which, for sinister motives, has been placed upon them." On the expiration of his official term, he retired to his estate at Williamsburg.

JAMES KNOX POLK,

THE TENTH PRESIDENT OF THE UNITED STATES,

Was born at Mecklenberg, North Carolina, November 2, 1795, and there received the rudiments of his early education. In 1806, his father removed to Nashville, Tennessee, taking his family with him, and here it was that Mr. Polk pursued those preliminary studies which were requisite to qualify him for the legal profession. After due preparation, he entered the office of Hon. Felix Grundy, under whose able instruction he made such rapid progress, that he was admitted to practice in 1820. His duties at the bar did not prevent him from taking part in the political affairs of the day; and in this sphere his comprehensive views and zealous devotion to Democracy soon secured him a widely-extended popularity, which resulted in his election to the Legislature of Tennessee, in 1823. In 1825, while yet in his thirtieth year, he was chosen a member of Congress, in which body he remained fourteen years—being honored with the Speakership for several sessions. So well satisfied were his constituents with his congressional course, that he was elected Governor by a large majority, but some questions of local policy subsequently defeated his reëlection.

In 1844, he was unexpectedly nominated for the office of President of the United States by the Democratic Convention at Baltimore; and, having received sixty-five electoral votes more than his rival candidate, Mr. Clay, he was inaugurated on the 4th of March, 1845.

Soon after Mr. Polk assumed the reins of government, the country became involved in a war with Mexico, which was little more than a series of victories wherever the American banner was displayed, and which resulted in important territorial acquisitions. The ostensible ground for this war, on the part of Mexico, was the admission of Texas into the Union, which was one of the first acts of Mr. Polk's administration. The Mexicans, however, paid dearly for asserting their frivolous claim to Texas as a revolted province, and the prompt and energetic course pursued by Mr.

Polk was sanctioned and sustained by a large majority of the people.

But notwithstanding the advantageous issue of the war, the acquisition of Texas, and the satisfactory settlement of several vexed questions of long standing, Mr. Polk was not nominated for a second term—various extraneous matters leading to the selection of another candidate. Perhaps it was fortunate for the country and for himself that he was permitted to retire to the more congenial enjoyment of private life; for his health had become very much impaired, and he did not long survive after reaching his home in Nashville. He died June 15, 1849.

Election for the Fifteenth Term, commencing March 4, 1845, *and terminating March* 3, 1849.

No. of Electors from each State.	STATES.	PRES'T. James K. Polk, of Tennessee.	PRES'T. Henry Clay, of Kentucky.	V. PRES'T. George M. Dallas, of Pennsylvania.	V. PRES'T. T. Frelinghuysen, of New Jersey.
9	Maine	9	....	9	...
6	New Hampshire	6	....	6	...
12	Massachusetts	....	12	....	12
4	Rhode Island	....	4	....	4
6	Connecticut	....	6	....	6
6	Vermont	....	6	....	6
36	New York	36	....	36	...
7	New Jersey	....	7	....	7
26	Pennsylvania	26	....	26	....
3	Delaware	....	3	....	3
8	Maryland	....	8	....	8
17	Virginia	17	....	17	...
11	North Carolina	....	11	....	11
9	South Carolina	9	....	9	....
10	Georgia	10	....	10	....
12	Kentucky	....	12	....	12
13	Tennessee	....	13	....	13
23	Ohio	....	23	....	22
6	Louisiana	6	....	6	...
6	Mississippi	6	....	6	....
12	Indiana	12	....	12	....
9	Illinois	9	....	9	....
9	Alabama	9	....	9	....
7	Missouri	7	....	7	....
3	Arkansas	3	....	3	....
5	Michigan	5	....	5	....
275	Whole No. of Electors	170	105	170	105
	Majority 138				

James K. Polk took the oath of office, as President, and entered upon his duties March 4, 1845.

George M. Dallas took the oath of office, as Vice President, and attended in the Senate, March 4, 1845.

The most important incidents of Mr. Polk s administration were the admission of Texas and the consequent war with Mexico, the latter of which resulted in extending our territorial boundaries to the Pacific Ocean, embracing regions of incalcu lable value.

ZACHARY TAYLOR,

THE ELEVENTH PRESIDENT OF THE UNITED STATES,

Was born in Orange County, Virginia, November 24, 1790, and, after receiving an indifferent education, passed a considerable portion of his boyhood amid the stirring scenes which were being enacted at that time on our western border. In 1808, he was appointed a lieutenant in the United States infantry, and subsequently was promoted to a captaincy for his efficient services against the Indians. Soon after the declaration of war, in 1812, he was placed in command of Fort Harrison, which he so gallantly defended with a handful of men against the attack of a large body of savages, as to win the brevet rank of major. So familiar did he become with the Indian character, and with the mode of warfare of that wily foe, that his services at the West and South were deemed indispensable in the subjugation and removal of several hostile tribes. While effecting these desirable objects, he was occasionally rewarded for his toils and sacrifices by gradual promotion, and in 1840 attained the rank of brigadier-general. At the commencement of the troubles with Mexico, in 1845, he was ordered to occupy a position on the American side of the Rio Grande, but not to cross that river unless attacked by the Mexicans. He was not, however, allowed to remain long in repose: the enemy, by attacking Fort Brown, which he had built on the Rio Grande, opposite Matamoras, soon afforded him an opportunity to display his skill and valor, and gloriously did he improve it. The brilliant battles of Palo Alto and Resaca de la Palma, where he contended successfully against fearful odds, were precursors to a series of victories which have few parallels in military annals. The attack on Matamoras, the storming of Monterey, the sanguinary contest at Buena Vista, and the numerous skirmishes in which he was engaged, excited universal admiration; and on his return home, after so signally aiding to "conquer a peace" with Mexico, he was every-where received with the most gratifying demonstrations of respect and affection. In 1848, General Taylor received the nomination of the Whig party for the office of President of the United States, and, being elected, was inaugurated the year following. But the cares and responsibilities of this position were greater than his constitution could endure, hardened as it had been both in Indian and civilized warfare. After the lapse of little more than a year from the time he entered upon his new career, he sunk under its complicated trials, and his noble spirit sought refuge in a more congenial sphere, July 9, 1850.

Election for the Sixteenth Term, commencing March 4, 1849, *and terminating March* 3, 1851.

No. of Electors from each State.	STATES.	PRES'T.		V. PRES'T	
		Zachary Taylor, of Louisiana.	Lewis Cass, of Michigan.	Millard Fillmore, of New York.	William O. Butler, of Kentucky.
9	Maine	....	9	....	9
6	New Hampshire	....	6	....	6
12	Massachusetts	12	....	12	....
4	Rhode Island	4	....	4	....
6	Connecticut	6	....	6	....
6	Vermont	6	....	6	....
36	New York	36	....	36	....
7	New Jersey	7	....	7	....
26	Pennsylvania	26	....	26	....
3	Delaware	3	....	3	....
8	Maryland	8	....	8	....
17	Virginia	....	17	....	17
11	North Carolina	11	....	11	....
9	South Carolina	....	9	....	9
10	Georgia	10	....	10	....
12	Kentucky	12	....	12	....
13	Tennessee	13	....	13	....
23	Ohio	....	23	....	23
6	Louisiana	6	....	6	....
6	Mississippi	....	6	....	6
12	Indiana	....	12	....	12
9	Illinois	....	9	....	9
9	Alabama	....	9	....	9
7	Missouri	....	7	....	7
3	Arkansas	....	3	....	3
5	Michigan	....	5	....	5
3	Florida	3	....	3	....
4	Texas	....	4	....	4
4	Iowa	....	4	....	4
4	Wisconsin	....	4	....	4
290	Whole No. of Electors	163	127	163	127
	Majority 146				

Zachary Taylor took the oath of office, as President, and entered upon his duties March 4, 1849. He did not, however, long enjoy his honors—death suddenly closing his earthly career, July 9, 1850.

Millard Fillmore took the oath of office, as Vice President, and entered upon his duties March 4, 1849. Congress being in session at the time President Taylor died, the Vice President sent a message to both houses on the 10th of July, in which he feelingly announced the melancholy event. On the same day he took the requisite oath, and entered on the execution of the office of President.

Willie P. Mangum, of N. C., President *pro tem* of the Senate, acted as Vice President, *ex officio*, during the remainder of the term

MILLARD FILLMORE,

THE SUCCESSOR OF GENERAL TAYLOR AS PRESIDENT,

Was born at Summer Hill, Cayuga County, New York, January 7, 1800, and did not enjoy the advantages of any other education than what he derived from the then inefficient common schools of the county. At an early age he was sent into the wilds of Livingston County to learn a trade, and here he soon attracted the attention of a friend, who placed him in a lawyer's office—thus opening a new, and what was destined to be a most honorable and distinguished career. In 1827, he was admitted as an attorney, and two years afterward as counselor in the Supreme Court. Soon attracting attention, he established himself at Buffalo, where his talents and buisness habits secured him an extended practice.

His first entrance into public life was in January, 1829, when he took his seat as a member of the Assembly from Erie County. At this time he distinguished himself for his untiring opposition to imprisonment for debt, and to this are the people indebted in a great degree for the expunging of this relic of barbarism from the statute book. Having gained a high reputation for legislative capacity, in 1833, he was elected a member of the National House of Representatives; and on the assembling of the Twenty-seventh Congress, to which he was reëlected by a larger majority than was ever given to any person in his district, he was placed in the arduous position of Chairman of the Committee of Ways and Means. The measures which he brought forward and sustained with matchless ability, speedily relieved the government from its existing pecuniary embarrassments. In 1847, he was elected Comptroller of the State of New York by a larger majority than had ever been given to any State officer for many years. In 1848, he was selected as a candidate for Vice-President, General Taylor heading the ticket. On his election to that high office, he resigned his position as Comptroller, and entered upon his duties as President of the United States Senate. The courtesy, ability, and dignity exhibited by him, while presiding over the deliberations of that body, received general commendation. Upon the sudden death of Gen. Taylor, he became President, and promptly selected a cabinet, distinguished for its ability, patriotism, and devotion to the Union, and possessing, in an eminent degree, the confidence of the country.

After serving out the constitutional term, Mr. Fillmore returned to Buffalo, and again resumed those pursuits which had prepared the way to the elevated position from which he had just retired. He was welcomed home by troops of friends, with whom he still continues to enjoy an unabated popularity.

It should be borne in mind by every aspiring young man, that Mr. Fillmore is entirely indebted to his own exertions for his success in life. From a very humble origin, he attained the highest office in the world, climbing the rugged steep of fame step by step, with indefatigable industry and untiring perseverance, until he at length gained the summit, where he is long likely to enjoy his well-earned position.

FRANKLIN PIERCE,

THE TWELFTH PRESIDENT OF THE UNITED STATES,

Was born at Hillsborough, N. H., November 23, 1804, and early received the advantage of a liberal education. After going through a regular collegiate course at Bowdoin College, which he entered at the age of sixteen, he became a law student in the office of Judge Woodbury, at Portsmouth, whence he was transferred to the law school at Northampton, where he remained two years, and then finished his studies with Judge Parker, at Amherst. Although his rise at the bar was not rapid, by degrees he attained the highest rank as a lawyer and advocate.

In 1829, he was elected to represent his native town in the State Legislature, where he served four years, during the two last of which he held the speakership, and discharged the duties of the office with universal satisfaction.

From 1833 to 1837, he represented his State in Congress, and was then elected to the United States Senate, having barely reached the requisite age to qualify him for a seat in that body.

In 1834, he married Miss Jane Means, daughter of the Rev. Dr. Appleton, formerly President of Bowdoin College, soon after which he removed to Concord, where he still holds a residence. He was reëlected at the expiration of his senatorial term, but resigned his seat the year following, for the purpose of devoting himself exclusively to his legal buisness, which had become so extensive as to require all his attention.

In 1846, he declined the office of Attorney-General, tendered him by President Polk; but when the war with Mexico broke out, he was active in raising the New England regiments of volunteers; and afterward accepted the commission of Brigadier-General, with which he at once repaired to the field of operations, where he distinguished himself in several hard-fought battles. At Cerro Gordo and Chapultepec he displayed an ardor in his country's cause which extorted praise from his most inveterate political opponents; and on his return home he was everywhere received with gratifying evidences that his services were held in grateful remembrance by the people.

At the Democratic Convention, held in Baltimore in 1852, after trying in vain to concentrate their votes on a more prominent candidate, that body unexpectedly nominated General Pierce for the office of President of the United States, to which he was elected by an unprecedented majority over his rival, General Scott—receiving 254 votes out of 296. He was duly inaugurated on the 4th of March, 1853, and his administration was more remarkable for its futile attempts to reconcile conflicting interests, than for the achievement of any particular measure of great public utility. However, it will better become his future than his present biographer to "speak of him as he is; nor aught extenuate, nor aught set down in malice."

Election for the Seventeenth Term, commencing March 4, 1853, and terminating March 3, 1857.

No. of Electors from each State.	STATES.	PRES'T.		V. PRES'T	
		Franklin Pierce, of New Hampshire.	Winfield Scott, of New Jersey.	William R. King, of Alabama.	Wm. A. Graham, of North Carolina.
8	Maine	8	....	8	....
5	New Hampshire	5	....	5	....
13	Massachusetts	....	13	....	13
4	Rhode Island	4	....	4	....
6	Connecticut	6	....	6	....
5	Vermont	....	5	....	5
35	New York	35	....	35	....
7	New Jersey	7	....	7	....
27	Pennsylvania	27	....	27	....
3	Delaware	3	....	3	....
8	Maryland	8	....	8	....
15	Virginia	15	....	15	....
10	North Carolina	10	....	10	....
8	South Carolina	8	....	8	....
10	Georgia	10	....	10	....
12	Kentucky	....	12	....	12
12	Tennessee	....	12	....	12
23	Ohio	23	....	28	....
6	Louisiana	6	....	6	....
7	Mississippi	7	....	7	....
13	Indiana	13	....	13	...
11	Illinois	11	....	11	...
9	Alabama	9	....	9	...
9	Missouri	9	....	9	...
4	Arkansas	4	....	4	...
6	Michigan	6	....	6	....
3	Florida	3	....	3	....
4	Texas	4	....	4	....
4	Iowa	4	....	4	....
5	Wisconsin	5	....	5	....
4	California	4	....	4	....
296	Whole No. of Electors	254	42	254	42
	Majority 149				

Franklin Pierce took the oath of office, as President, and entered upon his duties March 4, 1853.

The oath of office was administered to William R. King by a commission while he was on a visit to Cuba for the benefit of his health; but he died soon after his return home, and Jesse D. Bright, of Indiana, then President of the Senate, acted as Vice President, *ex officio*, during the remainder of the term.

John P. Hale, of N. H., and George W. Julian, of Ind., were nominated by the "Free Democracy" for President and Vice President, but they did not receive a single electoral vote

JAMES BUCHANAN,

THIRTEENTH PRESIDENT OF THE UNITED STATES.

For the high position he so long maintained in the political affairs of this country, Mr. Buchanan is not alone indebted to his early and thorough education, but his entire devotion to whatever he undertook, and his perseverance in surmounting obstacles which would have intimidated less determined minds, had a large share in promoting his advancement. He is of Irish parentage, and was born at Stony Batter, Franklin County, Pennsylvania, April 23, 1791. At the age of seven years, he removed with his father's family to Mercersburg, and there received an education that fitted him for entering Dickinson College, in 1805, where he graduated two years afterward with the highest honors. He then studied law with James Hopkins, of Lancaster, and in 1812 was admitted to the bar, at which he attained a high rank and commanded an extensive practice.

In 1814, he commenced political life as a member of the Pennsylvania State Legislature, and in 1820 was sent as a Representative to Congress, where he remained for ten years—at the expiration of which he declined a re-nomination.

In 1831, he was appointed minister to Russia by President Jackson, of whom he was always the consistent friend and supporter, and he negotiated a commercial treaty which proved of great advantage to American commerce.

In December, 1834, having been elected to the United States Senate, he took his seat in that body, and continued one of its most efficient members until 1845, when he accepted the office of Secretary of State, under Mr. Polk. He held this responsible place until the expiration of Mr. Polk's term of service, when he returned home to repose awhile. But he did not, by any means, become an idle spectator in passing events; his letters and speeches show that he was no less vigilant as a private citizen, than as a counselor in the Cabinet, or a Representative and Senator in Congress.

On the accession of Mr. Pierce to the Presidency, in 1853, Mr. Buchanan was appointed minister to England, with which country questions were then pending that required great prudence and discrimination for their satisfactory adjustment.

In his intercourse with the British diplomatists he was not only discreet, but displayed sound sense, courtly forbearance, a just assertion of our rights, and the true dignity of the American character. So entirely unexceptionable was his whole course while abroad, that, on his return to this country, in April, 1856—he landed in New York on the sixty-fifth anniversary of his birthday—he was received with an enthusiasm seldom accorded to political men.

In June, 1856, Mr. Buchanan was nominated by the Democratic Convention at Cincinnati, as a candidate for the Presidency; and although there were powerful political elements arrayed against him in the succeeding campaign, he was triumphantly elected to that responsible and honorable office.

His administration was attended with unusual difficulties—difficulties which it would seem he was not fully able to meet. The troubles in Kansas, arising from the repeal of the Missouri Compromise, and the opposition made to his views touching the admission of Kansas with the Lecompton Constitution, by the Douglas wing of the Democratic party, were matters of sore vexation to him, and tended greatly to unpopularize the latter part of his public life. But these were considerations of small moment as compared to the embarrassment which the Government suffered in consequence of the treacherous intrigues of some of the members of his Cabinet. His Secretary of War and Secretary of the Treasury, afterward so conspicuous in the great Rebellion, were particularly instrumental in crippling the pecuniary and military resources of the country, and turning them to the benefit of the South. When treason began to assume a threatening attitude, Buchanan declared against the right of secession, but at the same time denied the right of coercion by the Government. This, perhaps, is the most inconsistent, inexplicable position ever taken by any of the nation's chief rulers. On the 4th of March, 1861, Mr. Buchanan retired from the Presidency, leaving to his successor the highly perplexing task of setting to right the machinery of a government crippled and weakened in all its parts, and fully ripe for the most gigantic civil war known to history.

It was, at one time, presumed by many that Mr. Buchanan was not only encouraging the rebellion by his weak, indecisive policy toward armed traitors, and by winking at the thieving proceedings of some of his Cabinet officers, but that he was himself leagued with the leaders of the secession movement, and secretly acted in unison with them.

While it is true that the unhindered appropriation of millions of treasure to the furtherance of rebellious schemes, and the large deposit of choice arms made in Southern arsenals, would indicate an affiliation of the President with the chief rebels of the South, yet there has never been adduced any direct proof of such affiliation; and nothing said or done by Mr. Buchanan since his retirement shows active sympathy with the Rebellion. There is, however, evidence on every hand of weakness—an element of character he never manifested prior to his executive career—of that negative disposition which will, under circumstances such as surrounded him during the latter part of his administration, wholly unfit a man for the performance of his duties.

The subject of the present sketch would, doubtless, have been a very good executive at a period when the country was undisturbed by sectional agitation; at a time when there were no conflicting local interests to stir up and embitter South against North. But the exigencies of the period during which he sat at the helm of state demanded a man who could take hold with a strong hand; a man of Jacksonian character, who, with the loftiest political integrity and most devoted loyalty, combined a Napoleonic will; a man who, foreseeing the certain results of the pursuits of a conciliatory course with rebellion, would have given it a decisive blow in its very infancy.

But it seems that Mr. Buchanan proposed to deal with secessionists as an over-fond, weak-minded mother deals with a spoiled child—scolding and coaxing alternately, satisfied to exhibit her authority by the former, and confident that she can reform her fondling by the latter. Perhaps he may be partially excused by some in consideration of the debt of gratitude he felt he owed to the Southern States, for the valuable services they had rendered him in his election. But a truly great executive never allows his feelings to interfere with the performance of duty. The life of the nation was in jeopardy; that grand superstructure, the American Government, whose foundation stones had been cemented by the sacred blood of the Revolutionary sires, whose columns had been reared by the wisest, purest statesmen the world ever saw, and about whose lofty dome the brightest seraphs of Heaven chanted their sweetest lays—that great temple around which clustered the hopes of the liberty-loving world, was threatened with destruction, and there can hardly be any excuse for him who, having the power to save, refused to adopt such decisive measures as were essential to salvation.

It is true that the Southern people had acted a very important part in the election of Mr. Buchanan, but it is very far from being true that a majority of these people were in favor of secession. The great Democratic party was not a party of traitors, either North or South. The masses of the people of the Southern States were by no means desirous of severing their connection with the Government of the United States, as was amply testified in the overwhelming Union majorities given in North Carolina, Tennessee, and other Southern States, even after South Carolina had sloughed off, and all the preliminary steps had been taken by the leading secessionists toward the formation of a Southern Confederacy. And there is no doubt that had Mr. Buchanan taken hold of the rebellion, while it was in the larva, with that determination to crush it which the great Jackson exhibited when South Carolina proposed her scheme of nullification, it had never seen its winged existence.

Buchanan's administration, in one respect, may possibly yet be productive of good, in that it may serve to impress the people with the importance of selecting a man for the chief magistracy who loves the right and dares to do it.

He only survived the close of the war about three years, as he died on the 1st of June, 1868, in the 77th year of his age.

Election for the Eighteenth Term, commencing March 4, 1857 and terminating March 3, 1861.

No. of Electors from each State.	STATES.	PRESIDENT.			VICE-PRES'T.		
		James Buchanan, of Pennsylvania.	John C. Fremont, of New York.	Millard Fillmore, of New York.	John C. Breckenridge, of Kentucky.	William L. Dayton, of New Jersey.	Andrew J. Donelson, of Tennessee.
8	Maine	....	8	....	....	8	....
5	New Hampshire	....	5	....	....	5	....
13	Massachusetts	....	13	....	....	13	....
4	Rhode Island	....	4	....	....	4	....
6	Connecticut	....	6	....	....	6	....
5	Vermont	....	5	....	....	5	....
35	New York	....	35	....	....	35	....
7	New Jersey	7	....	....	7	....	....
27	Pennsylvania	27	....	....	27	....	....
3	Delaware	3	....	....	3	....	....
8	Maryland	....	....	8	....	....	....
15	Virginia	15	....	....	15	....	8
10	North Carolina	10	....	....	10	....	....
8	South Carolina	8	....	....	8	....	....
10	Georgia	10	....	....	10	....	....
12	Kentucky	12	....	....	12	....	....
12	Tennessee	12	....	....	12	....	....
23	Ohio	....	23	....	....	23	....
6	Louisiana	6	....	....	6	....	....
7	Mississippi	7	....	....	7	....	....
3	Indiana	13	....	....	13	....	....
11	Illinois	11	....	....	11	....	....
19	Alabama	9	....	....	9	....	....
9	Missouri	9	....	....	9	....	....
4	Arkansas	4	....	....	4	....	....
6	Michigan	....	6	....	....	6	....
3	Florida	3	....	....	3	....	....
4	Texas	4	....	....	4	....	....
4	Iowa	....	4	....	....	4	....
5	Wisconsin*	....	5	....	....	5	....
4	California	4	....	....	4	....	....
296	No. of Electors	174	114	8	174	114	8
	Majority 149						

James Buchanan took the oath of office, as President, and entered upon his duties, March 4, 1857.

John C. Breckenridge took the oath of office, as Vice-President, and entered upon his duties, March 4, 1857.

*When the Electoral votes were being counted, in Joint Convention of the Senate and House of Representatives, objections were made to including the votes of Wisconsin, because the electors did not meet until the day after that prescribed by law The President of the Convention stated that he merely announced that James Buchanan had been elected President of the United States, without any reference to the contested votes, and declined expressing an opinion on the subject.

ABRAHAM LINCOLN,

THE FOURTEENTH PRESIDENT OF THE UNITED STATES,

Was born in Hardin County, Kentucky, February 12th, 1809. The record of his boyhood and youth, so far as we have been able to trace it, is not distinguished by any thing more remarkable than the usual experience of children of pioneers in a new country. In 1816, he removed with his parents to what is now Spencer County, Indiana. Here he enjoyed the advantages of a little schooling—less than a year, however, in all. Whatever else he afterward learned from books was without the aid of the school-master—the result of his own energy and indomitable perseverance.

In 1832, he served in the Black Hawk war, and, on his return from that service, was nominated for the Illinois Legislature from the county of Macon. In 1834, he was elected to the Legislature, and reëlected in 1836, 1838, and 1840. While in the Legislature, he placed himself on record against slavery; and it is but just to say that the principles which actuated him then are the moving principles of the great party he to-day represents as the executive of the nation.

For many years Mr. Lincoln was a prominent leader of the Whig party in Illinois, and was on the electoral ticket in several Presidential campaigns. In 1844, he canvassed the entire State for Henry Clay, of whom he was a sincere and enthusiastic friend, and exerted himself powerfully for the favorite of his party. In 1846, he was elected to Congress, and took his seat on the first Monday in December, 1847, the only Whig Representative from his State.

In November, 1860, he was elected President of the United States by the party known as Republicans.

On the 11th of February, 1861, he left his home in Springfield, Illinois, and proceeded to Washington, passing *en route* the cities of Toledo, Indianapolis, Cincinnati, Columbus, Steubenville, Pittsburgh, Cleveland, Buffalo, Albany, Poughkeepsie, New York, Trenton, Philadelphia, Harrisburg, and Baltimore—at all of which places, except the last, he was received with great cordiality, and addressed the people. At Baltimore a plot had been formed to assassinate him; and, in this affair, it seems that some of the most prominent citizens of that place were implicated. But Mr. Lincoln, by prompt, shrewd management, reached Washington uninjured, and, on the 4th of March, 1861, was duly inaugurated, and proceeded upon the duties of his office, notwithstanding the threats of Baltimoreans that he never should be installed. In his inaugural address, in view of the threatening attitude assumed by some of the Southern States, in consequence of the accession of a Republican administration, after declaring that there never had been any just cause for the apprehension that such an administration would encroach upon the constitutional rights of any State, he said that he had "no purpose, directly or indirectly, to interfere with the institution of slavery in the States where it existed; that he, as well as every Member of Congress, was sworn to support the whole Constitution, one of the provisions of which is, that 'no person held to service or labor in one State, under the laws thereof, escaping into another State, shall, in consequence of any law or regulation therein, be discharged from such service or labor, but shall be delivered up on claim of the party to whom such service or labor may be due;' that he took his oath to support the Constitution, without any mental reservation; that while he did not then choose to specify particular acts of Congress as proper to be enforced, he did suggest that it would be much safer for all, both in official and private stations, to conform to and abide by all those acts which stand unrepealed than to violate any of them, trusting to find impunity in having them held to be unconstitutional; that he held that, in the contemplation of universal law and of the Constitution, the union of the States is perpetual; that no State could, upon its own mere motion, get out of the Union; that acts of violence within any State or States against the authority of the United States are insurrectionary or revolutionary, and that he should, as the Constitution expressly enjoined upon him, take care that the laws of the Union should be executed in all the States; that while he should perform this duty perfectly, so far as practicable, unless restrained by his rightful masters, the

American people, he trusted the declaration so to do would not be regarded as a menace, but only as the express purpose of the Union to maintain itself."

The inaugural address, while considered as clear and explicit by many, was regarded as very obscure and unsatisfactory by others (the people of the South), and, on the 13th of April, 1861, Messrs. Preston, Stuart, and Randolph, appointed by the Virginia Convention, were formally received by the President, and presented resolutions requesting that, inasmuch as "great uncertainty prevailed in the public mind as to the policy" to be pursued by the Federal Executive, he should communicate to the Convention the course he intended to take in regard to the "Confederate States."

To this request the President replied that, while he was sorry that dangerous uncertainty should exist respecting his mode of procedure with the seceded States, he could give no clearer exposition of his policy than was given in his inaugural address, a careful consideration of which he recommended to the Virginia Convention.

Two days after this, Fort Sumter having been reduced by the Confederate Government, and other demonstrations of a revolutionary character having been made, the President issued a proclamation calling for 75,000 volunteers, for three months, to suppress the rebellion, and summoned Congress to assemble in extraordinary session. The call was heartily responded to, and, in a few days, a vastly greater number than had been requested offered themselves to their country. Meantime Washington was placed in a state of defense. Shortly after the commencement of hostilities, a blockade of all the Southern ports was declared. This was directly followed by a blockade of Virginia and North Carolina. On the 3d of May, 1861, the President issued a call for 42,034 additional volunteers for the term of three years. Congress having assembled, he addressed a message to that body, asking that at least 400,000 men and $400,000,000 be placed at his control, that the work of crushing the rebellion might be expedited. Congress readily complied, granting more men and money than had been askea.

On the 16th of August, 1861, the President issued a proclamation prohibiting all commercial intercourse between the loyal and seceded States. In the latter part of August, he modified a proclamation issued by General Fremont, which declared martial law in the State of Missouri, ordering the confiscation of the property of disloyal persons, and declaring their slaves free. The two latter of these measures Mr. Lincoln declared void. For this act he was blamed by many of his own party at the time.

Passing some other acts of less importance, we next notice the message addressed to Congress on the 6th of March, 1862, by the President, recommending that the Government coöperate with any State desiring a gradual emancipation of the slaves, by affording it such pecuniary aid as would enable it to "compensate for the inconveniences, public and private, produced by such change of system." This message was hailed by the radical antislavery party of the country as the initiatory step toward a final and total abolition of slavery; by conservative Union men, with indifference; and by the secessionists as a hostile encroachment upon State rights.

On the 11th of March, 1862, Mr. Lincoln assumed command of the Army and Navy of the United States, ordering a general movement of both, and confining General McClellan to the command of the Department of the Potomac.

April 16th, 1862, he approved and signed an act of Congress, abolishing the institution of slavery in the District of Columbia, which act "recognized and practically applied" the principles of compensation and colonization.

During the month of May, the President issued two proclamations, the one declaring the ports of Port Royal, Beaufort, and New Orleans open for trade, the other repudiating an order issued by General Hunter, emancipating all the slaves in Georgia, Florida, and South Carolina. This act also produced some dissatisfaction. During the years 1862–1863, Mr. Lincoln was actively employed in calling out and furnishing troops, and making important changes in the organization of the army. It was also during this period that he issued his general emancipation proclamations—the first on the 22d day of September, 1862, declaring that all slaves held in any State, or part of a State found in actual rebellion against the authority of the United States on the 1st day of January, 1863, should then and forever thereafter be free; the second, on the 1st of January, 1863, declaring that, in accordance with the first proclamation, slavery is abolished in all the States and counties then in armed rebellion against the Government.

These measures, while they greatly unpopularized the President with certain parties in the Northern and Southern border States, were regarded as the exponents of the true policy by the radicals. His suspension of the writ of *habeas corpus*, in certain cases, September 15th, 1863, also produced considerable stir in political circles.

At the Republican Convention which met at Baltimore, in January, 1864, Mr. Lincoln was re-nominated for the Presidency of the United States—was elected November 8th, and duly inaugurated March 4th, 1865.

The following note of his inaugural address is from an English journal. It speaks for itself:

"On the 4th instant, the day of inaugurating his second term, President Lincoln read a short State paper, which for political weight, moral dignity, and unaffected solemnity has had no equal in our time. His presidency began, he says, with the efforts of both parties to avoid war. 'To strengthen, perpetuate, and extend the slave interest was the object for which the insurgents would rend the Union by war, while the Government claimed the right to do no more than restrict the territorial enlargement of it.' Both parties 'read the same Bible and pray to the same God.' * * * * *

"The prayer of both can not be answered, that of neither has been answered fully, for the Almighty has his own purposes. Mr. Lincoln goes on to confess for the North its partnership in the original guilt of slavery: 'Woe unto the world because of its offenses, for it must needs be that offenses come; but woe unto that man by whom the offenses cometh! If we shall suppose American slavery one of the offenses which in the providence of God must needs come, but which, having continued through His appointed time,

He now wills to remove, and that He gives to both North and South this terrible war, as was due to those by whom the offense came, we will not discern that there is any departure from those divine attributes which believers in the living God always ascribe to Him. Fondly do we hope, fervently do we pray, that this mighty scourge of war may speedily pass away. Yet, if it be God's will that it continue till the wealth piled by bondsmen by two hundred and fifty years' unrequited toil shall be sunk, and till every drop of blood drawn with the lash shall be repaid by another drawn with the sword, as was said three thousand years ago, so still it must be said that the judgments of the Lord are true and righteous altogether. With malice toward none, with charity for all, with firmness in the right, as God gives us to see the light, let us strive on to finish the work we are in, to bind up the nation's wounds, to care for those who have borne the battle, and for their widows and orphans. And with all this let us strive after a just and lasting peace among ourselves and with all nations.' No statesman ever uttered words stamped at once with the seal of so deep a wisdom aud so true a simplicity. The 'village attorney,' of whom Sir G. C. Lewis and many other wise men wrote with so much scorn, in 1861, seems destined to be one of those 'foolish things of the world' which are destined to confound the wise, one of those weak things which shall 'confound the things that are mighty.'"

The rebel General Lee had surrendered. The war was apparently at an end. Abraham Lincoln, the honored and the great, looked forward to a speedy restoration of the Union. But while the storm lulled, the assassin did his work. J. Wilkes Booth shot Abraham Lincoln on the night of the 13th, and he died April 14th, 1865, honored and lamented by every true American. The world never before beheld such universal sorrow. A nation not merely mourned but was clad in the deepest mourning.

*Election for the Nineteenth Term, commencing **March** 4, 1861, and terminating **March** 3, 1865.*

No. of Electors from each State.	STATES.	PRESIDENT.				VICE PRESIDENT.			
		Abraham Lincoln, of Illinois.	Jno. C. Breckenridge, of Kentucky.	John Bell, of Tennessee.	Stephen A. Douglas, of Illinois.	Hannibal Hamlin, of Maine.	Joseph Lane, of Texas.	Edward Everett, of Massachusetts.	Herschel V. Johnson, of Georgia.
8	Maine	8	....	....	....	8	....	....	....
5	New Hampshire	5	....	....	....	5	....	....	....
13	Massachusetts	13	....	....	....	13	....	....	....
4	Rhode Island	4	....	....	....	4	....	....	....
6	Connecticut	6	....	....	....	6	....	....	....
5	Vermont	5	....	....	....	5	....	....	....
35	New York	35	....	....	....	35	....	....	....
7	New Jersey	4	....	....	3	4	....	....	3
27	Pennsylvania	27	....	....	....	27	....	....	....
3	Delaware	....	3	....	....	....	3	....	....
8	Maryland	....	8	....	....	....	8	....	....
15	Virginia	....	....	15	....	....	....	15	....
10	North Carolina	....	10	....	....	....	10	....	....
8	South Carolina	....	8	....	....	....	8	....	....
10	Georgia	....	10	....	....	....	10	....	....
12	Kentucky	....	....	12	....	....	....	12	....
12	Tennessee	....	....	12	....	....	....	12	....
23	Ohio	23	....	....	....	23	....	....	....
6	Louisiana	....	6	....	....	....	6	....	....
7	Mississippi	....	7	....	....	....	7	....	....
13	Indiana	13	....	....	....	13	....	....	....
11	Illinois	11	....	....	....	11	....	....	....
19	Alabama	....	9	....	....	....	9	....	....
9	Missouri	....	....	....	9	....	....	....	9
4	Arkansas	....	4	....	....	....	4	....	....
6	Michigan	6	....	....	....	6	....	....	....
3	Florida	....	3	....	....	....	3	....	....
4	Texas	....	4	....	....	....	4	....	....
4	Iowa	4	....	....	....	4	....	....	....
5	Wisconsin	5	....	....	....	5	....	....	....
4	California	4	....	....	....	4	....	....	....
4	Minnesota	4	....	....	....	4	....	....	....
3	Oregon	3	....	....	....	3	....	....	....
315	Whole No. of Electors	180	72	39	12	180	72	39	12
	Majority ... 157								

Abraham Lincoln took the oath of office as President, and entered upon his duties, March 4th, 1861. Hannibal Hamlin took the oath of office as Vice-President, and attended in the Senate as its President, on the 4th of March, 1861. The accession of Mr. Lincoln to the Presidency was made the pretext for the great rebellion of 1861.

Election for the Twentieth Term, commencing March 4, 1865, and terminating March 3, 1869.

No. of Electors from each State.	STATES.	PRESIDENT. Abraham Lincoln, of Illinois.	PRESIDENT. Geo. B. McClellan, of Ohio.	V. PRESIDENT. Andrew Johnson, of Tennessee.	V. PRESIDENT. Geo. H. Pendleton, of Ohio.
7	Maine	7	......	7	......
5	New Hampshire	5	......	5	......
12	Massachusetts	12	......	12	......
4	Rhode Island	4	......	4	......
6	Connecticut	6	......	6	......
5	Vermont	5	......	5	......
33	New York	33	......	33	......
7	New Jersey	......	7	......	7
26	Pennsylvania	26	......	26	......
3	Delaware	......	3	......	3
7	Maryland	7	......	7	......
15	Virginia	......	......	......	......
5	Western Virginia	5	......	5	......
8	South Carolina	......	......	......	......
10	North Carolina	......	......	......	......
10	Georgia	......	......	......	......
11	Kentucky	......	11	......	11
12	Tennessee	......	......	......	......
21	Ohio	21	......	21	......
6	Louisiana	......	......	......	......
7	Mississippi	......	......	......	......
13	Indiana	13	......	13	......
15	Illinois	15	......	15	......
19	Alabama	......	......	......	......
11	Missouri	11	......	11	......
4	Arkansas	......	......	......	......
8	Michigan	8	......	8	......
3	Florida	......	......	......	......
4	Texas	......	......	......	......
8	Iowa	8	......	8	......
8	Wisconsin	8	......	8	......
5	California	5	......	5	......
4	Minnesota	4	......	4	......
3	Oregon	3	......	3	......
3	Nevada	3	......	......	......
3	Kansas	3	......	3	......
331		212	21	213	21

Virginia, South Carolina, North Carolina, Georgia, Tennessee, Louisiana, Mississippi, Alabama, Arkansas, Florida and Texas, being in rebellion, did not vote for President and Vice President.

Whole number of Electoral votes cast were 233—for Lincoln and Johnson, 212; for McClellan and Pendleton, 21. Lincoln and Johnson's majority 191, the greatest majority attained since the organization of the Government.

Abraham Lincoln took the oath of office as President and entered upon his duties March 4, 1865.

Andrew Johnson took the oath of office as Vice President, and attended in the Senate as its President March 4, 1865.

ANDREW JOHNSON

Was born at Raleigh, North Carolina, December 29th, 1808, and is now in his sixtieth year. He lost his father when only four years old. At the age of ten he was apprenticed to a tailor in Raleigh, and served with him an apprenticeship of seven years. His mother was poor, and had been unable to give him any educational advantages; but young Andy, whose unconquerable spirit was not to be restrained by any disadvantages, became stimulated with a desire for knowledge. He acquired the alphabet with no other instructions than those obtained from the journeymen with whom he worked. He learned to read from an old volume of speeches, loaned him by a friend, and thenceforward, after ten hours' work with his goose, needle, and scissors, applied himself with vigor to study for three or four hours each evening. In 1824, having completed his apprenticeship, he went to Laurens Court-house, South Carolina, where he worked as journeyman for two years. In 1826, he set out for the West, taking his mother, whom already, at his early age, and with his scanty wages, he was supporting. He made his home at Greenville, Tennessee, where he remained, and commenced business, and where he became a thriving and popular man. With the indefatigable thirst for knowledge which had characterized his early career, he still pursued his studies, and, in the evenings which followed a day of labor, with his wife as instructress, pushed on in the road to knowledge.

He entered early into political life, being elected to the first office he ever held—that of Alderman of the village of Greenville—in 1828. He was reëlected to the same office in 1829. In 1830, he was elected Mayor, and retained that position for three years. In 1835, he was sent to the Legislature, where he chiefly distinguished himself by taking strong grounds against a scheme of internal improvements, which, he argued, was extravagant and useless. The measure was popular, however, and he was defeated in 1837. In 1838, he was a candidate again, and was this time successful. In 1840, he served as Presidential elector for the State at large on the Democratic ticket, and during the campaign rendered efficient service to the party as a stump speaker. In 1841, he was elected to the State Senate, and, in 1843, at the age of thirty-five, he was elected to Congress, where he held his seat, being four times reëlected, until 1853. During this time he was thoroughly identified with the old Democratic party, and supported all the party measures. In 1853, he was elected Governor, after a very exciting contest, over Gustavus A. Henry. He was reëlected in 1855, over Meredith P. Gentry, the Whig candidate. At the expiration of his Gubernatorial term, in 1857, he was chosen United States Senator by a Democratic majority in the Legislature of Tennessee. In that body he commanded the respect of all his compeers, as an able, eloquent, and patriotic statesman. At the breaking out of the rebellion, Senator Andrew Johnson still proclaimed his allegiance to the United States, and continued to hold his seat in the Senate, though his course subjected him to much unpopularity, and even danger.

When, in the spring of 1862, our army had penetrated Tennessee to Nashville, and the northern and central portions of the States were wrested from rebel control, the President desired the services of a wise and sagacious man, of unquestionable loyalty, to act as Military Governor of that State; and he did not have long to look—Andrew Johnson was at once recognized as the man for the place, and, being commissioned a Brigadier-General, he repaired to Nashville, where he for two years discharged the delicate and responsible duty of his charge with a degree of wisdom and efficiency which challenged general admiration. Under his administration, the rebellion had steadily been losing its hold in Tennessee, and loyalty was as constantly cultivated and developed.

He was nominated for the Vice-Presidency by the Union Convention at Baltimore, June 8th, 1864, and was elected November 8, 1864, and was sworn into office March 4th, 1865.

President Lincoln died April 15. Andrew Johnson was sworn into office as President of the United States, on the same day, by Chief Justice Chase.

Soon after entering upon the duties of his office, he vetoed the Civil Rights Bill, the Constitutional Amendment, the Military Government Bill, and all the important bills passed by Congress; also suspended Edwin M. Stanton, Secretary of War, from office, during the recess of Congress; on the assembling of which, he sent them his reasons for so doing. Upon considering which, they reinstated Secretary Stanton. Whereupon the President issued an order removing him, and ordering Major-General Thomas, Adjutant-General of the army, to act as Secretary *ad interim*—the same being done without the consent or advice of the Senate—for which and many other acts committed by him, and by Congress deemed unconstitutional, the House did, on the 25th of February, 1868, impeach Andrew Johnson of high crimes and misdemeanors; and he was accordingly tried for the same by the Senate—the result of which trial will be found in the Impeachment Act, on another page.

LIEUTENANT-GENERAL ULYSSES S. GRANT,

Was born at Mount Pleasant, Clermont county, Ohio. It seems that the only marked traits of character he exhibited in early boyhood were energy, industry, will. His educational advantages, at this period, were those of the common, country school —no more.

In the year 1839, at the age of seventeen, he entered the United States Military Academy at West Point, from which he graduated on the 30th day of January, 1843. During his stay t this Institution he manifested that untiring industry, close application and unconquerable will which distinguished his boyhood, and which have constituted so conspicuous an element of his military character. It appears, however, that he was never regarded as a genius; and the grade he sustained on the day of graduation—that of 21 in a class of about 42—would not indicate extraordinary advancement in the studies assigned him. But it was remarked by those who conducted him through his Academic course, as it has been by those who have observed his military career, that he never lost an inch of the ground gained at each successive step in his progress. At his graduation it is said he possessed a "practical knowledge of the use of the rifled musket, the field piece, mortar, siege, and sea-coast guns, small sword and bayonet, as well as the construction of field works, and the fabrication of all munitions and *materiel* of war."

At the close of his Academic course, he entered the United States regular army as a Brevet Second-Lieutenant of infantry. At this time, the United States being at peace with all nations, Grant was attached as a Supernumerary Lieutenant to the fourth infantry, then stationed on the frontier in Missouri and Missouri Territory, and engaged in keeping down the Indian tribes that at that time were very troublesome to the early settlers of that region. Here Grant had not been many months when he was ordered, with his regiment, to join the army of General Taylor, in Texas. Soon after this, Corpus Christi, an important port on the Texan shore, was taken possession of by the American army as a base of operations against the Mexicans, between whom and the United States disputes respecting certain imaginary boundary lines were fast ripening into a war; and it was here that Grant received his commission as full Second Lieutenant of Infantry. This commission dated from the 30th day of September, 1845. On the 8th day of May, 1846, he participated in the battle of Palo Alto, and although not noticed in the official reports, was spoken of by his comrades as having displayed great gallantry. He was likewise engaged in the subsequent brilliant operations of General Taylor along the banks of the Rio Grande. On the 23d of September, 1846, he took part, with great credit to himself, in the splendid affair at Monterey. It is a noteworthy fact that, although Grant's conduct in every one of these engagements was highly meritorious, he remained in the back ground, claiming no honors or promotions, but quietly biding his time.

After the formal declaration of war by the United States, against Mexico, he was transferred to the command of General Scott, and subsequently (March 29, 1847,) participated in the siege of Vera Cruz. Immediately after this affair, he was appointed the Quartermaster of his regiment, which office he retained throughout the Mexican campaign. He was, however, honored with the appointment, on the field, of First Lieutenant, to date from the 8th of September, 1847, for gallant and distinguished voluntary services rendered on that day in the famous battle of Molino del Ray. Congress afterwards wished to confirm the appointment as a mere brevet, but Grant refused to accept it under such circumstances.

On the 13th of September, 1847, he was made Brevet Captain of the regular army for gallant conduct in the battle of Chepultepec, which battle occurred on the preceding day. On the 16th of November, 1847, he was commissioned a First Lieutenant in the fourth regiment of regular infantry, still retaining his brevet rank of Captain.

At the close of the Mexican war, Grant, upon the distribution of his regiment in companies and sections among the various Northern frontier defences, along the borders of the States of Michigan and New York, took command of his company in one of these defences. His regiment having been afterwards consolidated and ordered to the Department of the Pacific, Grant, with his own and some other companies, was sent into Oregon to Fort Dallas. He received his full promotion to Captain of infantry, in August, 1853, and was, shortly afterwards, attached to the Department of the West; but, not regarding military so favorable to progress as civil life, he resigned his connection with the United States army on the 31st day of July, 1854, after which he resided near the city of St. Louis, Missouri, until the year 1859. Here he resided on a small farm, occupying himself in winter by hauling wood to the Carondelet market, and during the summer in the collection of debts, for which latter business, it is said, he had little capacity.

In the year 1859, he embarked in the leather trade with his father, the firm opening business in the city of Galena, Illinois. Grant continued in the leather business, driving a prosperous trade, up to the breaking out of the Rebellion in 1861, when he offered his services to his country, upon the first call for volunteers, and was appointed by Governor Yates as Commander-in Chief of the Illinois forces and mustering officer of Illinois volunteers. Desiring active service in the field, he resigned his appointment as mustering officer, and accepted the Colonelcy of the 21st regiment of Illinois volunteers, with a commission dating from June 15, 1861. In August, 1861, Colonel Grant was promoted to the rank of Brigadier General of volunteers, his commission dating from May 17, 1861.

Shortly after this he was appointed commandant of the post at Cairo—which post included the Missouri shore of the Mississippi river, from Cape Girardeau to New Madrid, and the opposite shore, to the point of land on which Cairo stands. This position Grant filled with great ability, checkmating, by his adroit maneuvering, the efforts of the rebels to occupy, permanently, southern Kentucky, and conducting those successful expeditions against Forts Henry and Donelson, which opened the way to the occupation of Western Tennessee.

On the 16th of February, 1862, the day after the surrender of Fort Donelson, he was appointed Major General of volunteers, and was placed in command of an expedition up the Tennessee river against the rebels in and about Corinth, under comman of Johnston and Beauregard. This expedition terminated in the great battle of Shiloh or Pittsburg Landing—which battle, occupying two days, (April 6th and 7th, 1862,) was one of the bloodiest of the war, and resulted in the defeat of the rebels and their retreat upon Corinth.

For the immense slaughter which attended this battle, General Grant was very severely censured by the people, generally, throughout the Western States.

Soon after this, General Halleck having assumed command of the army before Corinth, and that place having fallen into the hands of the United States forces by evacuation, an important change took place in the army, which resulted in the assignment of General Grant to the District of West Tennessee, and the promotion of General Halleck to the office of General-in-Chief. The former soon after formed the plan of opening the Mississippi river to its mouth. Memphis having been given up to our troops, the chief obstacle in the way of the prosecution of the design were Vicksburg and Port Hudson.

After a series of expeditions and battles, land and naval, in which the courage and fortitude of the Union troops were no less prominently exhibited than the superior engineering powers and unyielding stubbornness of General Grant, Vicksburg was reduced by siege, and was occupied by Grant on the 4th of July, 1863; and directly after this (July 8, 1863) followed the surrender of Port Hudson to General N. P. Banks.

On the 16th of October, 1863, the Departments of the Ohio, of the Cumberland, and of the Tennessee were formed into the Military Division of the Mississippi, under the command of

General Grant. The General, however, was not long in this position until, the grade of Lieutenant-General having been revived, he was promoted to that office—which office gave him control of the entire forces of the United States. This appointment was made in February, 1864, and was immediately followed by the most active, thorough preparations for a movement upon Richmond by the Army of the Potomac under the personal command of General Grant, and an expedition against Atlanta under command of General Sherman. After the battles of the Wilderness, Spottsylvania Court House and the siege of Petersburg, Lee's retreat was cut off by the rapid movements which Grant instituted, and on the 9th of April, just one week after the last great battle, the army of Northern Virginia capitulated. Soon after the rebel General Johnston surrendered to General Sherman, on the same terms granted by Grant to Lee, and the great civil war was ended. Grant was appointed Secretary of War *ad interim*, August 12th, 1867, and filled the office with distinction until January 14, 1868, at which time Secretary Stanton was reinstated by Congress. On the 21st of May, 1868, he was unanimously nominated for the Presidential chair by the Republican Convention, which met at Chicago.

Election for the Twenty-first Term, commencing March 4, 1869, and terminating March 3, 1873.

No. of Electors from each State.	STATES.	Ulysses S. Grant, of Illinois.	Horatio Seymour, of New York.	Schuyler Colfax, of Indiana.	Francis P. Blair, of Missouri.
7	Maine	7	....	7	....
5	New Hampshire	5	....	5	....
12	Massachusetts	12	....	12	....
4	Rhode Island	4	....	4	....
6	Connecticut	6	....	6	....
5	Vermont	5	....	5	....
33	New York	....	33	....	33
7	New Jersey	....	7	....	7
26	Pennsylvania	26	....	26	....
3	Delaware	....	3	....	3
7	Maryland	....	7	....	7
15	Virginia	....	....	....	....
5	West Virginia	5	....	5	....
6	South Carolina	6	....	6	....
9	North Carolina	9	....	9	....
9	Georgia	....	9	....	9
11	Kentucky	....	11	....	11
10	Tennessee	10	....	10	....
21	Ohio	21	....	21	....
6	Louisiana	....	6	....	6
7	Mississippi	....	....	....	....
13	Indiana	13	....	13	....
15	Illinois	15	....	15	....
9	Alabama	9	....	9	....
11	Missouri	11	....	11	....
5	Arkansas	5	....	5	....
8	Michigan	8	....	8	....
3	Florida	3	....	3	....
4	Texas	....	....	....	....
8	Iowa	8	....	8	....
8	Wisconsin	8	....	8	....
5	California	5	....	5	....
4	Minnesota	4	....	4	....
3	Oregon	....	3	....	3
3	Nevada	3	....	3	....
3	Kansas	3	....	3	....
316	Whole number of Electors.	211	79	211	79
159	Necessary to a choice.				

Virginia, Mississippi and Texas, did not vote, not having conformed to the reconstruction acts of Congress.

Election for the Twenty-second Term, commencing March 4, 1873, and terminating March 3, 1877.

No. of Electors from each State.	STATES.	Ulysses S. Grant, of Illinois.	Horace Greeley,* of New York.	Henry Wilson, of Massachusetts.	B. Gratz Brown, of Missouri.
10	Alabama	10		10	
6	Arkansas				
6	California	6		6	
6	Connecticut	6		6	
3	Delaware	3		3	
4	Florida	4		4	
11	Georgia †				8
21	Illinois	21		21	
15	Indiana	15		15	
11	Iowa	11		11	
5	Kansas	5		5	
12	Kentucky				12
8	Louisiana †				
7	Maine	7		7	
8	Maryland				8
13	Massachusetts	13		13	
11	Michigan	11		11	
5	Minnesota	5		5	
8	Mississippi	8		8	
15	Missouri				15
3	Nebraska	3		3	
3	Nevada	3		3	
5	New Hampshire	5		5	
9	New Jersey	9		9	
35	New York	35		35	
10	North Carolina	10		10	
22	Ohio	22		22	
3	Oregon	3		3	
29	Pennsylvania	29		29	
4	Rhode Island	4		4	
7	South Carolina	7		7	
12	Tennessee				12
8	Texas				8
5	Vermont	5		5	
11	Virginia	11		11	
5	West Virginia	5		5	
10	Wisconsin	10		10	

* Owing to the death of Horace Greeley, the vote of no Electoral College was given for him. The Democratic Electoral vote was for B. Gratz Brown, 18; Thomas A. Hendricks, 42; Charles J. Jenkins, 2; Davis Davis, 1.

† Not counted, 17; of these, three votes cast in Georgia for Horace Greeley were excluded, he having died before the votes were so cast—the House voting to exclude, the Senate to receive. The vote of Arkansas was rejected—the House voting to receive, the Senate to reject. The vote of Louisiana was rejected, both Houses concurring.

Total counted, 349—necessary to a choice, 175.

POPULAR VOTE FOR PRESIDENT, BY STATES.

STATES.	1824.*				1828.		1832.†		1836.	
	Adams.	Jackson.	Crawford.	Clay.	Adams.	Jackson.	Clay, *Nat'l Repub.*	Jackson, *Democrat.*	Harris'n, etc.‡ *Whig.*	Van Buren, *Democrat.*
Alabama	2416	9443	1680	67	1938	17138	No op	J'son.	15637	19068
Arkansas	....	....	....	....	....	....	....	....	1238	2400
California......	....	....	....	....	....	....	....	....	....	....
Connecticut ...	7587	—	1978	—	13829	4448	17755	11269	18466	19234
Delaware........	By	Legisl	ature	....	4769	4349	4276	4110	4738	4155
Florida	....	....	....	....	....	....	....	....	....	....
Georgia	By	Legisl	ature	....	—	18709	—	20750	24930	22126
Illinois	1542	1901	219	1047	1581	6763	5429	14147	14983	18097
Indiana	3095	7343	—	5315	17052	22237	15472	31552	41281	32480
Iowa..............	....	....	....	....	....	....	....	....	....	....
Kentucky	—	6453	—	16782	31172	39084	43396	36247	36955	33435
Louisiana	By	Legisl	ature	....	4097	4605	2528	4049	3383	3653
Maine	6870	2330	—	—	20773	13927	27204	33291	15239	22300
Maryland	14632	14523	3646	695	25759	24578	19160	19156	25852	22167
Massachusetts	30687	—	6616	—	29836	6019	33003	14545	41093	33501
Michigan........	....	....	....	....	....	....	....	....	4000	7360
Mississippi	1694	3234	119	—	1581	6763	—	5919	9638	9979
Missouri	311	987	—	1401	3422	8232	maj.	5192	8337	10995
N. Hampshire	4107	643	—	—	24076	20692	19010	25486	6228	18722
New Jersey ...	9110	10985	1196	—	23758	21950	23393	23856	26892	26347
New York......	By	Legisl	ature	....	135413	140763	154896	168497	138543	166815
NorthCarolina	—	20415	15621	—	13918	37857	4563	24862	23626	26910
Ohio	12280	18457	—	19255	63396	67597	76539	81246	105405	96948
Pennsylvania.	5440	36100	4206	1609	50848	101652	56716	90983	87111	91475
Rhode Island.	2145	—	200	—	2754	821	2810	2126	2710	2964
SouthCarolina	By	Legisl	ature	....	....	....	....	....	....	....
Tennessee	216	20197	312	—	2240	44090	1436	28740	35962	26120
Texas	....	....	....	....	....	....	....	....	....	....
Vermont	By	Legisl	ature	....	24784	8205	11152	7870	20991	14037
Virginia	3189	2861	8489	416	12101	26752	11451	33609	23368	30261
Wisconsin	....	....	....	....	....	....	....	....	....	....
Total.........	105321	155872	44282	46587	509097	647231	530189	687502	736656	761549

Jackson over Adams, in 1824, 50,551; over Adams in 1828, 138,134; over Clay, in 1832, 157,313. Van Buren over Harrison and all others, in 1836, 24,893.

*Neither candidate received a majority of the Electoral Vote, and the House of Representatives elected Mr. John Quincy Adams.

† William Wirt, of Maryland, ran as an Anti-Masonic candidate, in 1832, receiving a considerable vote in New England, New York and Pennsylvania, which is added to that of Mr. Clay in our tables. Mr. Wirt received the electoral vote of Vermont.

‡ The Opposition vote was divided between General William H. Harrison, of Ohio, Hugh L. White, of Tennessee, Willie P. Mangum, of North Carolina, and Daniel Webster, of Massachusetts.

POPULAR VOTE FOR PRESIDENT, BY STATES—Continued.

NAMES.	1840.			1844.			1848.		
	Harrison, *Whig.*	Van Buren, *Democrat.*	Birney, *Abolitionist.*	Clay, *Whig.*	Polk, *Democrat.*	Birney, *Abolitionist.*	Taylor, *Whig.*	Cass, *Democrat.*	Van Buren, *Free Dem.*
Alabama ...	28471	33991	—	26084	37740	—	30482	31363	—
Arkansas ...	5160	6766	—	5504	9546	—	7588	9300	—
California...	....	....	.....	....	....	....	....	....	....
Connectic't	31601	25296	174	32832	29841	1943	30314	27046	5005
Delaware ...	5967	4884	—	6278	5996	—	6421	5898	80
Florida	....	....	.....	....	....	....	3116	1847	—
Georgia	40261	31921	—	42100	44177	—	47544	44802	—
Illinois	45537	47476	149	45528	57920	3570	53047	56300	15774
Indiana......	65302	51604	—	67867	70181	2106	69907	74745	8100
Iowa.	....	....	.....	....	....	....	11084	12093	1126
Kentucky...	58489	32616	—	61255	51988	—	67141	49720	—
Louisiana...	11296	7616	—	13083	13782	—	18217	15370	—
Maine	46612	46201	194	34378	45719	4836	35125	39880	12096
Maryland...	33528	28752	—	35984	32676	—	37702	34528	125
Massach'tts	72874	51944	1621	67418	52846	10860	61070	35281	38058
Michigan ...	22933	21131	321	24337	27759	3632	23940	30687	10389
Mississippi.	19518	16995	—	19206	25126	—	25922	26537	—
Missouri	22972	29760	—	31251	41369	—	32671	40077	—
New Hamp.	26158	32761	126	17866	27160	4161	14781	27763	7560
New Jersey.	33351	31034	69	38318	37495	131	40015	36901	829
New York...	225817	212527	2798	232482	237588	15812	218603	114318	120510
N. Carolina	46376	33782	—	43232	39287	—	43550	34869	—
Ohio	148157	124782	903	155057	149117	8050	138360	154775	35354
Pennsylv'a.	144021	143672	343	161203	167535	3138	185513	171176	11263
Rhode Isl'd	5278	3301	42	7322	4867	107	6779	3646	730
S. Carolina.	....	....	.....	....	....	....	....	....	....
Tennessee ..	60391	48289	—	60030	59917	—	64705	58419	—
Texas.........	....	....	.....	....	....	....	4509	10668	—
Vermont.....	32440	18018	319	26770	18041	3954	23122	10948	13837
Virginia	42501	43893	—	43677	49570	—	45124	46586	9
Wisconsin ..	....	....	.....	....	....	....	13747	15001	10418
Total......	1275011	1122912	7059	1299062	1337243	62300	1360099	1220544	291263

Harrison over Van Buren, 145,999; over Van Buren and Birney, 138,940.
Polk over Clay, 38,181; Clay and Birney over Polk, 24,119.
Taylor over Cass, 139,555; Cass and Van Buren over Taylor, 151,700.

POPULAR VOTE FOR PRESIDENT, BY STATES—Continued.

STATES.	1852.			1856.		
	Scott, *Whig.*	Pierce, *Democrat.*	Hale, *Free Soil.*	Fremont, *Republican.*	Buchanan, *Democrat.*	Fillmore, *American.*
Alabama	15038	26881	—	—	46739	28552
Arkansas	7404	12173	—	—	21910	10787
California	35407	40626	100	20691	53365	36165
Connecticut	30357	33249	3160	42715	34995	2615
Delaware	6293	6318	62	308	8004	6175
Florida	2875	4318	—	—	6358	4833
Georgia	16660	34705	—	—	56578	42228
Illinois	64934	80597	9966	96189	105348	37444
Indiana	80901	95340	6929	94375	118670	22386
Iowa	15856	17763	1604	43954	36170	9180
Kentucky	57068	53806	—	314	74642	67416
Louisiana	17255	18647	—	—	22164	20709
Maine	32543	41609	8030	67379	39080	3325
Maryland	35066	40020	54	281	39115	47460
Massachusetts	52683	44569	28023	108190	39240	19626
Michigan	33859	41842	7237	71762	52136	1660
Mississippi	17548	26876	—	—	35446	24195
Missouri	29984	38353	—	—	58164	48524
New Hampshire	16147	29997	6695	38345	32789	422
New Jersey	38556	44305	350	28338	46943	24115
New York	234882	262083	25329	276007	195878	124604
North Carolina	39058	39744	—	—	48246	36886
Ohio	152526	169220	31682	187497	170874	28126
Pennsylvania	179174	198568	8525	147510	230710	82175
Rhode Island	7626	8735	644	11467	6680	1675
South Carolina	Electors	chosen	by Leg	islature.	....	....
Tennessee	58898	57018	—	—	73638	66178
Texas	4995	13552	—	—	31169	15639
Vermont	22173	13044	8621	39561	10569	545
Virginia	58572	73858	—	291	89706	60310
Wisconsin	22240	33658	8814	66090	52843	579
Total	1386580	1601274	155825	1341264	1838169	874534

Pierce over Scott, 214,694; over Scott and Hale, 58869.

Buchanan over Fremont, 496,905; Fremont and Fillmore over Buchanan, 377,629.

POPULAR VOTE FOR PRESIDENT, BY STATES—Continued.

STATES.	1860.				1864.		1868.	
	Lincoln.	Bell.	Douglas.	Breckinridge.	Lincoln.	McClellan.	Grant.	Seymour.
Maine	62811	2046	26693	6368	72278	47736	70433	42394
New Hampshire	37519	441	25881	2112	36595	33034	37718	30571
Massachusetts	106533	22331	34372	5939	126742	48745	136379	59408
Rhode Island	12244	....	*7707	....	14343	8718	12993	6548
Connecticut	43792	3291	15522	14641	44693	42288	49726	46381
Vermont	33808	1969	6849	218	42422	13325	44167	12045
New York	362646	....	*312510	....	368726	361986	419883	429883
New Jersey	58324	....	*62801	....	60723	68014	79871	82725
Pennsylvania	268030	12776	16785	*178871	296389	276308	342280	313382
Delaware	3815	3864	1023	7337	8155	8767	7615	10960
Maryland	2294	41760	5966	42482	40153	32739	30500	62275
Virginia	1929	74681	16290	74323	....	....	....	....
North Carolina	....	44990	2701	48539	....	....	96488	85311
South Carolina	No	popu	larvote	....	....	....	62300	45137
Georgia	....	42886	11590	51889	....	....	56935	102198
Kentucky	1364	66058	25651	53143	27786	64301	39566	115889
Tennessee	....	69274	11350	64709	....	....	90447	61948
Ohio	231610	12193	187232	11405	265154	205508	280222	239032
Louisiana	....	20204	7625	22681	....	....	27911	41358
Mississippi	....	25040	3283	40797	....	....	....	....
Indiana	139033	5306	115509	12295	150422	130233	176552	165480
Illinois	172161	4913	160215	2404	189487	158349	250293	199141
Alabama	....	27875	13651	48831	....	....	77366	72086
Missouri	17028	58372	58801	31317	72991	31026	95164	74976
Arkansas	....	20094	5227	28732	....	....	32513	28496
Michigan	88480	405	65057	805	85352	67370	128560	97068
Florida	....	5437	367	8543	....	....	....	....
Texas	....	*15438	....	47518	....	....	....	....
Iowa	70409	1763	55111	1048	87331	49260	120399	74128
Wisconsin	86110	161	65021	888	79564	63875	109444	84668
California	39173	6817	38516	34334	62134	43841	54589	54081
Minnesota	22069	62	11920	748	25060	17375	43566	28117
Oregon	5270	183	3951	5006	9888	8457	8926	9138
Kansas	Admitt	ed	since	1860.	14228	3871	29703	13408
West Virginia	Includ	ed in	Va.in	"	23223	10457	22146	12943
Nevada	Admitt	ed	since	"	9826	6594	8627	6791
Nebraska	"	"	"	"	....	....	9720	3429
Total	1866452	590631	1375157	847953	2213665	1802237	3053111	2714195

* Fusion ticket.

POPULAR VOTE FOR PRESIDENT, BY STATES—Continued.

STATES.	1872.	
	Republican. Grant.	Liberal and Democratic. Greeley.*
Alabama	90272	79444
Arkansas	41373	37927
California	54020	40718
Connecticut	50638	45880
Delaware	11115	10206
Florida	17763	15427
Georgia	62550	76356
Illinois	241944	184938
Indiana	186147	163632
Iowa	131566	71196
Kansas	67048	32970
Kentucky	88766	99995
Louisiana	71663	57029
Maine	61422	29087
Maryland	66760	67687
Massachusetts	133472	59260
Michigan	138455	78355
Minnesota	55117	34423
Mississippi	82175	47288
Missouri	119196	151434
Nebraska	18329	7812
Nevada	8413	6236
New Hampshire	37168	31424
New Jersey	91656	76456
New York	440736	387281
North Carolina	94769	70094
Ohio	281852	244321
Oregon	11819	7730
Pennsylvania	349589	212041
Rhode Island	13665	5329
South Carolina	72290	22703
Tennessee	85655	94391
Texas	47468	66546
Vermont	41481	10927
Virginia	93468	91654
West Virginia	32315	29451
Wisconsin	104997	86477
Total	3597132	2834125

* Chas. O'Conor, Straight Democrat, received 29,489 votes, and James Black, Temperance, 5,608.

THE MILITARY GOVERNMENT BILL.

AN ACT for the More Efficient Government of the Rebel States:

WHEREAS, No legal State government, or adequate protection for life, or property, now exists in the rebel States of Virginia, North Carolina, South Carolina, Georgia, Alabama, Louisiana, Florida, Texas, and Arkansas; and,

WHEREAS, It is necessary that peace and good order should be enforced in said States until loyal and republican State governments can be established; therefore,

Be it enacted, etc., That said rebel States shall be divided into military districts, and made subject to the military authority of the United States, as hereinafter prescribed; and for that purpose Virginia shall constitute the first district; North Carolina and South Carolina the second district; Georgia, Alabama, and Florida the third district; Mississippi and Arkansas the fourth district; Louisiana and Texas the fifth district.

SEC. 2. That it shall be the duty of the President to assign to the command of each of said districts an officer of the army, not below the rank of brigadier-general, and to detail a sufficient military force to enable such officer to perform his duties and enforce his authority within the district to which he is assigned.

SEC. 3. That it shall be the duty of each officer assigned, as aforesaid, to protect all persons in their rights of person and property; to suppress insurrection, disorder, and violence, and to punish, and cause to be punished, all disturbers of the public peace, and criminals; and to this end he may allow loyal civil tribunals to take jurisdiction of and try offenders; or, when in his judgment it may be necessary, for the trial of offenders, he shall have power to organize military commissions or tribunals for that purpose; and all interference under color of State authority with the exercise of military authority under this act shall be null and void.

SEC. 4. That all persons put under military arrest by virtue of this act shall be tried without unnecessary delay, and no cruel or unusual punishment shall be inflicted, and no sentence of any military commission or tribunal, hereby authorized, affecting the life or liberty of any person, shall be executed until it is approved by the officer in command of the district; and the laws and regulations for the government of the army shall not be affected by this act, except in so far as they may conflict with its provisions.

SEC. 5. That when the people of any one of said rebel States shall have formed a constitutional government, in conformity with the Constitution of the United States in all respects, framed by a convention of delegates elected by the persons who may vote upon the ratification or rejection thereof, as hereinafter provided; and when said constitution, so framed, shall have been ratified by a majority of the male citizens of said State, twenty-one years old and upward, of whatever race, color, or previous condition of servitude, who may have been resident in said State for one year previous to the day of voting on the question of ratifying such constitution, except such as may be disfranchised for participating in the rebellion, or for felony at common law; and when such constitution shall provide that the elective franchise shall be enjoyed by all such persons that have the qualifications herein stated, and shall have been submitted to Congress for examination, and Congress shall have approved the same; and when said State, by a vote of its legislature elected under said constitution, shall have adopted the amendment to the Constitution of the United States, proposed by the Thirty-ninth Congress, and known as article fourteen, and when said article shall become a part of the Constitution of the United States, such State shall be declared entitled to representation in Congress, and senators and representatives shall be admitted thereupon, on their taking the oath prescribed by the law; and then and thereafter the preceding sections of this bill shall be inoperative in said State.

SEC. 6, (proposed by Mr. Doolittle,) provides that the penalty of death shall not be inflicted by the military power without the approval of the President.

SEC. 7. (Shellabarger's amendment.) That until the people of said rebel States shall, by law, be admitted to representation in the Congress of the United States, the civil governments that may exist therein shall be deemed provisional only, and shall be in all respects subject to the paramount authority of the United States, which may at any time abolish, modify, control, and supersede the same, and in all elections to any office under such provisional governments all persons shall be entitled to vote, and none others, who are entitled to vote under the provisions of the fifth section of this act, and no person shall be eligible to any office under such provisional governments who would be disqualified from holding office under the provisions of the third article of said Constitutional Amendment.

SUPPLEMENT TO THE MILITARY GOVERNMENT BILL.

Passsd at the First Session of the Fortieth Congress.

AN ACT supplementary to an act entitled, "An act to provide for the more efficient government of the rebel States," passed March second, eighteen hundred and sixty-seven, and to facilitate restoration.

Be it enacted by the Senate and House of Representatives of the United States of America in Congress assembled, That before the first day of September, eighteen hundred and sixty-seven, the commanding general in each district defined by an act entitled, "An act to provide for the more efficient government of the rebel States," passed March second, eighteen hundred and sixty-seven, shall cause a registration to be made of the male citizens of the United States, twenty-one years of age and upward, resident in each county or parish in the State or States included in his district, which registration shall include only those persons who are qualified to vote for delegates by the act aforesaid, and who shall have taken and subscribed the following oath or affirmation: "I, ——, do solemnly swear, (or affirm,) in the presence of Almighty God, that I am a citizen of the State of ——; that I have resided in said State for —— months next preceding this day, and now reside in the county of ——, or the parish of ——, in said State, (as the case may be;) that I am twenty-one years old; that I have not been disfranchised for participation in any rebellion or civil war against the United States, nor for felony committed against the laws of any State or of the United States; that I have never been a member of any State legislature, nor held any executive or judicial office in any State, and afterward engaged in insurrection or rebellion against the United States, or given aid or comfort to the enemies thereof; that I have never taken an oath as a member of Congress of the United States, or as an officer of the United States, or as a member of any State legislature, or as an executive or judicial officer of any State, to support the Constitution of the United States, and afterward engaged in insurrection or rebellion against the United States, or given aid or comfort to the enemies thereof; that I will faithfully support the Constitution and obey the laws of the United States, and will, to the best of my ability, encourage others so to do, so help me God;" which oath or affirmation may be administered by any registering officer.

SEC. 2. *And be it further enacted*, That after the completion of the registration hereby provided for in any State, at such time and places therein as the commanding general shall appoint and direct, of which at least thirty days' public notice shall be given, an election shall be held of delegates to a convention for the purpose of establishing a constitution and civil government for such State loyal to the Union, said convention in each State, except Virginia, to consist of the same number of members as the most numerous branch of the State legislature of such State in the year eighteen hundred and sixty, to be apportioned among the several districts, counties, or parishes of such State by the commanding general, giving to each representation in the ratio of voters registered as aforesaid as nearly as may be. The convention in Virginia shall consist of the same number of members as represented the territory now constituting Virginia in the most numerous branch of the legislature of said State in the year eighteen hundred and sixty, to be apportioned as aforesaid.

SEC. 3. *And be it further enacted*, That at said election the registered voters of each State shall vote for or against a convention to form a constitution therefor under this act. Those voting in favor of such a convention shall have written or printed on the ballots by which they vote for delegates, as aforesaid, the words, "For a convention;" and those voting against such a convention shall have written or printed on such ballots the words, "Against a convention." The persons appointed to superintend said election, and to make return of the votes given thereat, as herein provided, shall count and make return of the votes given for and against a convention; and the commanding general to whom the same shall have been returned shall ascertain and declare the total vote in each State for and against a convention. If a majority of the votes given on that question shall be for a convention, then such convention shall be held as hereinafter provided; but if a majority of said votes shall be against a convention, then no such convention shall be held under this act: *Provided*, That such convention shall not be held unless a majority of all such registered voters shall have voted on the question of holding such convention.

SEC. 4. *And be it further enacted*, That the commanding general of each district shall appoint as many boards of registration as may be necessary, consisting of three loyal officers or persons, to make and complete the registration, superintend the election, and make return to him of the votes, list of voters, and of the persons elected as delegates, by a plurality of the votes cast at said election; and upon receiving said returns, he shall open the same, ascertain the persons elected as delegates, according to the returns of the officers who conducted said election, and make proclamation thereof; and if a majority of the votes given on that question shall be for a convention, the commanding general, within sixty days from the date of election, shall notify the delegates to assemble in convention, at a time and place to be mentioned in the notification; and said convention, when organized, shall proceed to frame a constitution and civil government according to the provisions of this act, and the act to which it is supplementary; and when the same shall have been so framed, said constitution shall be submitted by the convention for ratification to the persons registered under the provisions of this act, at an election to be conducted by the officers or persons appointed or to be appointed by the commanding general, as hereinbefore provided, and to be held after the expiration of thirty days from the date of notice thereof, to be given by said convention; and the returns thereof shall be made to the commanding general of the district.

SEC. 5. *And be it further enacted*, That if, according to said returns, the constitution shall be ratified by a majority of the votes of the registered electors qualified as herein specified, cast at said election, at least one-half of all the registered voters voting upon the question of such ratification, the president of the convention shall transmit a copy of the same, duly certified, to the President of the United States, who shall forthwith transmit the same to Congress, if then in session, and if not in session, then immediately upon its next assembling; and if it shall moreover appear to Congress that the election was one at which all the registered and qualified electors in the State had an opportunity to vote freely and without restraint, fear, or the influence of fraud, and if the Congress shall be satisfied that such constitution meets the approval of a majority of all the qualified electors in the State, and if the said constitution shall be declared by Congress to be in conformity with the provisions of the act to which this is supplementary, and the other provisions of said act shall have been complied with, and the said constitution shall be approved by Congress, the State shall be declared entitled to representation, and senators and representatives shall be admitted therefrom, as therein provided.

SEC. 6. *And be it further enacted*, That all elections in the States mentioned in the said "Act to provide for the more efficient government of the rebel States," shall, during the operation of said act, be by ballot; and all officers making the said registration of voters and conducting said elections shall, before entering upon the discharge of their duties, take and subscribe the oath prescribed by the act approved July second, eighteen hundred and sixty-two, entitled, "An act to prescribe an oath of office:" *Provided*, That if any person shall knowingly and falsely take and subscribe any oath in this act prescribed, such person so offending, and being thereof duly convicted, shall be subject to the pains, penalties, and disabilities which by law are provided for the punishment of the crime of willful and corrupt perjury.

SEC. 7. *And be it further enacted*, That all expenses incurred by the several commanding generals, or by virtue of any orders issued, or appointments made, by them, under or by virtue of this act, shall be paid out of any moneys in the treasury not otherwise appropriated.

SEC. 8. *And be it further enacted*, That the convention for each State shall prescribe the fees, salary, and compensation to be paid to all delegates and other officers and agents herein authorized or necessary to carry into effect the purposes of this act not herein otherwise provided for, and shall provide for the levy and collection of such taxes on the property in such State as may be necessary to pay the same.

SEC. 9. *And be it further enacted*, That the word "article," in the sixth section of the act to which this is supplementary, shall be construed to mean "section."

SCHUYLER COLFAX,
Speaker of the House of Representatives.
B. F. WADE,
President of the Senate *pro tempore*.

After the election which was held early in February, 1868, upon the ratification of a new Constitution for the State of Alabama, the law was so amended by Congress that a majority of the votes cast (instead of a majority of the registered voters) should be required to ratify or reject State constitutions in the seceded States.

THE AMNESTY ACT AS PASSED AND APPROVED.

Be it enacted, etc., (two thirds of each House concurring therein,) That all legal and political disabilities imposed by the third section of the fourteenth article of the amendments of the Constitution of the United States are hereby removed from all persons whomsoever, except Senators and Representatives of the Thirty-sixth and Thirty-seventh Congress, officers in the judicial, military, and naval service of the United States, heads of Departments, and foreign ministers of the United States.

Approved May 22, 1872.

HOMESTEAD LAW.

By act of Congress of May 20, 1862, any person who is the head of a family, or who has arrived at the age of twenty-one years, or has performed service in the army or navy, and is a citizen of the United States, or shall have filed his declaration of intention to become such, and has never borne arms against the Government of the United States, or given aid and comfort to its enemies, shall, from and after the 1st of January, 1863, be entitled to enter a quarter section (160 acres,) of unappropriated public land, upon which he or she may have already filed a pre-emption claim, or which is subject to pre-emption, at $1.25 per acre; or 80 acres of unappropriated lands, at $2.50 per acre. In order to make his or her title good to such lands, however, such person must make affidavit that such application is made for his or her exclusive use and benefit, and that said entry is made for the purpose of actual settlement and cultivation, and not, either directly or indirectly, for the use or benefit of any other person or persons whomsoever; and upon filing the affidavit, and paying the sum of ten dollars to the register or receiver, such person shall be allowed to enter the land specified; but no certificate or patent is issued for the land until five years from the date of such entry, and the land must, during that time, be improved and not alienated, (it can not be taken for debt). At any time within two years after the expiration of said five years, the person making the entry, or, in case of his or her death, his widow or heirs, may, on proof by two witnesses that he or she has cultivated or improved said land, has not alienated any part of it, and has borne true allegiance to the United States, be entitled to a patent, if at that time a citizen of the United States. In case of the abandonment of the lands by the person making the entry, for a period of more than six months at one time, they revert to the United States.

STATISTICAL VIEW OF THE STATES, ETC.,

Showing dates of acts creating Territories, and admitting States—Time of holding general elections—Number of Representatives in Congress—Date of general elections in the several States, with number of Representatives and Senators—Terms of office—Times of meeting—Location of capitals, etc.

States and Territories.	No. Members of Congress.	Settled—		Date of Creating—		Time of holding gen'l elections.	Representatives.		Senators.		Time of meeting of legislature.	Governor's term of office.	State Capitals.
		By whom.	Date.	Territory.	State.		Number.	Term.	Number.	Term.			
Alabama	8	French	1713	March 3, 1817	March 2, 1819	Tues. af. 1st Mon. Nov.	100	2	33	4	3d Monday in Nov.	2	Montgom'y.
Arkansas	4	"	1670	March 2, 1819	June 15, 1836	1st Monday in Nov.	93	2	31	4	November, 1876.†	4	Little Rock.
California	4	Span.	1769	....	Sept. 9, 1850	1st Wednesday in Sept.	80	2	40	4	1st Monday in Dec.†	4	Sacramento.
Connecticut*	4	Engl.	1633	....	....	1st Monday in April.	241	1	21	1	1st Wednesday in May.	1	Hartford.
Delaware*	1	Swedes	1627	....	....	1st Monday in Nov.	21	2	9	4	1st Tuesday in Jan. †	4	Dover.
Florida	2	Span.	1564	March 3, 1823	March 3, 1845	Tues. af. 1st Mon. Nov.	52	2	24	4	Tues. af. 1st Mon. Jan.	4	Tallahassee.
Georgia*	9	Engl.	1733	....	....	2d Wednesday in Oct.	175	2	44	4	2d Wedn'day in Jan.†	4	Atlanta.
Illinois	19	French	1749	Feb'y 3, 1809	Dec. 3, 1818	Tues. af. 1st Mon. Nov.	153	2	51	4	1st Monday in Jan.†	4	Springfield.
Indiana	13	"	1730	May 7, 1800	April 19, 1816	2d Tuesday in Oct.	100	2	50	4	" " " " †	4	Indian'polis.
Iowa	9	Amer's	1835	June 12, 1838	March 3, 1845	" " " "	100	2	50	4	2d " " " †	2	Des Moines.
Kansas	3	"	1850	May 30, 1854	Jan'y 29, 1861	Tues, af. 1st Mon. Nov.	107	2	33	2	2d Tuesday " "	2	Topeka.
Kentucky	10	Vir'ns	1775	....	June 1, 1792	1st Monday in August.	100	2	38	4	January, 1876. †	4	Frankfort.
Louisiana	6	French	1699	M'ch 26, 1804	Feb'y 20, 1811	" " " Nov.	111	2	36	4	1st Monday in Jan.	4	New Orl'ns.
Maine	5	Engl.	1630	....	M'ch 15, 1820	2d Monday in Sept'ber.	149	1	31	1	1st Wedn'day in Jan.	1	Augusta.
Maryland*	6	"	1634	....	....	Tues. af. 1st Mon. Nov.	85	2	26	4	" " " " †	4	Annapolis.
Massachusetts*	11	"	1620	....	....	" " " "	240	1	40	1	" " " "	1	Boston.
Michigan	9	French	1670	Jan'y 11, 1805	Jan'y 26, 1837	1st Monday in April.	100	2	32	2	" " " " †	2	Lansing.

Minnesota..........	3	Amer's	1847	March 3, 1849	May 14, 1858	Tues. af. 1st Mon. Nov.	106	1	41	2	Tues. af. 1st Mon. Jan.	2	St. Paul.
Mississippi..........	6	French	1716	April 7, 1798	Dec. 10, 1817	" " " "	112	2	34	4	" " " "	4	Jackson.
Missouri..............	13	"	1763	March 3, 1805	March 6, 1820	" " " "	131	2	33	4	Last Monday in Dec. †	2	Jefferson C'y.
New Hampshire*	3	Engl.	1623	....	....	2d Tuesday in March.	348	1	12	1	1st Monday in June.	1	Concord.
New Jersey*........	7	Swedes	1627	....	....	Tues' af. 1st Mon. Nov.	60	1	21	3	2d Tuesday in Jan.	3	Trenton.
New York*..........	33	Dutch	1613	....	....	" " " "	128	1	32	2	1st " "	2	Albany.
North Carolina*.	8	Engl.	1650	....	....	1st Monday in Nov.	118	2	50	2	3d Monday in Nov.†	4	Raleigh.
Nevada................	1	Amer's	1860	March 2, 1861	Oct. 31, 1864	Tues. af. 1st Mon. Nov.	50	2	25	4	1st Monday in Jan.†	2	Carson City.
Nebraska............	1	"	1850	May 30, 1854	March 4, 1867	2d Tuesday in October.	39	2	13	2	Thurs. af. 1. Mon. Jan.†	2	Lincoln.
Ohio.....................	20	V & N E	1788	July 13, 1787	April 30, 1802	" " " "	105	2	36	2	1st Monday in Jan.†	2	Columbus.
Oregon................	1	Engl.	1796	Aug. 14, 1848	Feb'y 12, 1859	1st Monday in June.	60	2	30	4	2d Monday in Sept.†	4	Salem.
Pennsylvania*....	27	"	1682	....	....	Tues. af. 1st Mon. Nov.	201	2	50	4	1st Tuesday in Jan.†	3	Harrisburg.
Rhode Island*.....	2	"	1631	....	....	1st Wedn'day in April.	72	1	36	4	May and June.	1	Newp't, Prov.
South Carolina*.	5	"	1689	....	....	Tues. af. 1st Mon. Nov.	124	2	33	4	4th Monday in Nov.†	2	Columbia.
Tennessee...........	10	N C & V	1765	May 26, 1790	June 1, 1796	" " " "	75	2	25	2	January, 1875.†	2	Nashville.
Texas	6	Span.	1690	....	Dec. 29, 1845	1st Tuesday in Dec.	90	2	30	4	2d Tuesday in Jan.†	4	Austin.
Vermont............	3	Engl.	1763	....	March 4, 1791	" " " Sept.	236	2	30	2	1st Wednesday in Oct.†	2	Montpelier.
Virginia*	9	"	1607	....		" " " Nov.	132	2	42	4	January, 1875.†	4	Richmond.
West Virginia.....	3	Amer's	......	....	Dec. 31, 1862	2d " " Oct.	65	1	24	2	2d Tuesday in Jan'y.†	4	Wheeling.
Wisconsin...........	8	"	1831	April 30, 1836	Aug. 6, 1846	Tues. af. 1st Mon. Nov.	100	1	33	2	1st Wedn'day in Jan.	2	Madison.
Colorado.............	1	"	1860	March 2, 1861	March 3, 1875	2d Tuesday in Sep'ber.	26	1	13	2	January, 1876.	4	Denver.
Arizona Ter'y.....	1	Amer's	......	Feb'y 24, 1863		Tues. af. 1st Mon. Nov.	18	1	9	2	January, 1877.†	4	Tucson.
Dakota Ter'y......	1	"	......	March 2, 1861		" " " "	26	1	13	2	December, 1876.†	4	Yankton.
Idaho Ter'y.........	1	"	......	March 3, 1863		" " " "	26	1	13	2	" " †	4	Boise City.
Montana Ter'y...	1	"	......	May 26, 1864		1st Monday in August.	26	1	13	2	December, 1875.	4	Virginia C'y.
Indian Ter'y.......		....	......	....		....	.....	..	...	..	....		Tahlaquah.
New Mexico T'y.	1	Span.	1598	Sept. 9, 1850		1st Monday in Sept.	26	1	13	2	December, 1876.†	4	Santa Fe.
Utah Ter'y...	1	Amer's	......	" " "		" " " Aug.	26	1	13	2	January, 1876.†	4	Salt Lake C'y.
Washington T'y.	1	"	......	March 2, 1853		Tues. af. 1st Mon. Nov.	30	1	9	3	October, 1875.†	4	Olympia.
Wyoming Ter'y...	1	"	......	July 25, 1868		1st Wedn'day in Sept.	13	1	9	2	November, 1875.†	4	Cheyenne.
Distr't Columbia		....	......	July 10, 1790		Three Commissioners.	.....	..	...	..	....		....
Alaska Ter'y......		....	......	....		....	.....	..	...	..	....		Sitka.

* One of the thirteen original States.

† Legislatures meet biennially.

[U. S. Senators serve six years, and each State is entitled to two.]

(a—h)

WEALTH, LOCAL DEBT, AND TAXATION

in the several States and Territories, by Census of 1850, 1860, *and* 1870.

STATES.	True Value of Real and Personal Estate.			State, County, Town, and City Taxation.		State, County, Town, and City Debt.
	1850.	1860.	1870.	1860.	1870.	1870.
Alabama...	$228,204,332	$495,237,078	$201,855,841	$851,171	$2,982,932	$13,277,154
Arkansas..	39,841,025	219,256,473	156,394,691	635,393	2,866,890	4,151,152
California.	22,161,872	207,874.613	638,767,017	2,981,122	7,817,115	18,089,082
Conn.........	155,707,980	444,274,114	774,631,524	1,015,037	6,064,843	17,088,906
Delaware..	21,062,556	46,242,181	97,180,833	(a) 205,891	418,092	526,125
Florida.....	22,862.270	73,101,500	44,163,655	159,112	496,166	2,185,838
Georgia.....	335,425,714	645,895,537	268,169,207	797,885	2,627,029	21,753,712
Illinois.....	156,265,006	871,860,282	2,121,680,579	6,121,766	21,825,008	42,191,869
Indiana....	202,650,264	528,835,371	1,268,180,543	3,701,352	10,791,121	7,818,710
Iowa.........	23,714,638	247,338,265	717,644,750	2,378,400	9,055,614	8,043,133
Kansas.....	....	31,327,895	188,892,014	195,857	2,673,992	6,442,282
Kentucky.	301,628,456	666,043,112	604,318,552	2,148,241	5,730,118	18,953,484
Louisiana.	233,998,764	602,118,568	323,125,666	4,960,780	7,060,722	53,087,441
Maine.......	122,777,571	190,211,600	348,155,671	2,257,213	5.348,645	16,624,624
Maryland.	219,217,364	376,919,944	643,748,976	2,158,895	6,632,842	29,032,577
Mass.........	573,342,286	815,237,433	2,132,148,741	7,436,578	24,922,900	69,211,538
Michigan..	59,787,255	257,163,983	719,208,118	1,766,694	5,412,957	6,725,231
Minnesota	....	52,294,413	228,909,590	666,007	2,648,372	2.788,797
Mississippi	228,951,130	607,324,911	209,197,345	954,806	3,736,432	2,594,415
Missouri...	137,247,707	501,214,398	1,284,922,897	4,109,653	13,908,498	46,909,865
Nebraska..	....	9,131,056	69,277,483	91,863	1,027,327	2,089,264
Nevada......	....	....	31,134,012	....	820,308	1,986,093
New Hamp	103,652,835	156,310,860	252,624,112	1,261,866	3,255,793	11,153,373
NewJersey	200,000,000	467,018,324	940,976,064	1,457,506	7,416,724	22,854,304
New York.	1,080,309,216	1,843,338,517	6,500,841,261	15,363,422	48,550,308	159,808,234
North Car.	226,800,472	358,739,399	260,757,244	1,044,732	2,352,809	32,474,036
Ohio.	504,726,120	1,193,898,422	2,235,430,300	9,611,021	23,526,548	22,241,988
Oregon......	5,063,474	28,930,637	51,558,932	199,056	580,956	218,486
Penna.......	722,486,120	1,416,501,818	3,808,340,112	8,729,736	21,531,397	89,027,131
R. Island..	80,508,794	135,337,588	296,965,646	686,133	2,170,152	5,938,642
South Car.	288,257,694	548,138,754	208,146,989	1,280,386	2,767,675	13,075,229
Tennessee.	201,246,686	493,903,892	498,237,724	1,102,793	3,381,579	48,827,191
Texas........	52,740,473	365,200,614	159,052,542	533,265	1,129,577	1,613,907
Vermont ..	92.205,049	122,477,170	235,349,553	908,080	2,135,919	3,594,700
Virginia ...	430,701,082	793,249,681	409,588,133	3,672,689	4,613,798	55,921,255
W. Va.......	....	....	190,651,491	....	1,722,158	561,767
Wisconsin	42,056,595	273,671,668	702,307,329	2,330,011	5,387,970	5,903,532
Total...	$7,115,000,800	$16,086,519,771	$29,822,535,140	$93,774,421	$278,391,286	$864,785,067
TERRITORIES.						
Arizona....	....	....	$3,440,791	....	$31,323	$10,500
Colorado...	....	....	20,243,303	....	362,197	681.158
Dakota	....	....	5,599,752	(b)	13,867	5,761
Dist. of C..	$14,018,874	$41,084,945	126,873,618	$260,218	1,581,569	2,596,515
Idaho........	....	....	6,552,681	....	174,711	222,621
Montana...	....	....	15,184,522	....	198,527	278,719
N. Mexico.	5,174,471	20,813,768	31,349,793	29,790	61,014	7,560
Utah	986,083	5,596,118	16,159,995	65,006	167,355	....
Wash'gton	....	5,601,466	13,562,164	57,311	163,992	88,827
Wyoming..	....	....	7,016,748	....	34,471	....
Total...	$20,179.428	$73,096,297	$245,983,367	$412,325	$2,789,026	$3,891,691
Gr'ndTot'l	$7,135,780,228	$16,159,616,068	$30,068,518,507	$94,186,746	$281,180,312	$868,676,758

(a) Returns of taxation at 1860 incomplete.
(b) No returns of taxation at 1860.

AGRICULTURAL STATISTICS.

Lands, Productions, etc.	1870.	1860.	1850.
Farm lands, improved, acres	188,921,099	163,110,720	113,032,614
Farm lands, woodland, acres	159,310,177	244,101,818	180,528,000
Farm lands, other, unimproved, acres	59,503,765		
Farms, cash value of	$9,262,803,861	$6,645,045,007	$3,271,575,426
Farming implem'ts & machinery, cash val	$336,878,429	$246,118,141	$151,587,638
Wages, including val. of board during year	$310,286,285	....	....
Total (estimated) value of all farm productions, including betterments and additions to stock	$2,447,538,658	....	....
Orchard products	$47,335,189	$19,991,885	$7,723,186
Produce of market gardens	$20,719,229	$16,159,498	$5,280,030
Forest products	$36,808,277	....	....
Value of home manufactures	$23,423,332	$24,546,876	$27,493,644
Value of animals slaughtered or sold for slaughter	$398,956,376	$213,618,692	$111,703,142
Value of all live stock	$1,525,276,457	$1,089,329,915	$544,180,516
Horses, number of	7,145,370	6,249,174	4,336,719
Mules and asses, number of	1,125,415	1,151,148	559,331
Milch cows, number of	8,935,332	8,585,735	6,385,094
Working oxen, number of	1,319,271	2,254,911	1,700,744
Other cattle, number of	13,566,005	14,779,373	9,693,069
Sheep, number of	28,477,951	22,471,275	21,723,220
Swine, number of	25,134,569	33,512,867	30,354,213
Wheat, spring, bushels	112,549,733	173,104,924	100,485,944
Wheat, winter, bushels	175,195,893		
Rye, bushels	16,918,795	21,101,380	14,188,813
Indian corn, bushels	760,944,549	838,792,742	592,071,104
Oats, bushels	282,107,157	172,643,185	146,584,179
Barley, bushels	29,761,305	15,825,898	5,167,015
Buckwheat, bushels	9,821,721	17,571,818	8,956,912
Rice, pounds	73,635,021	187,167,032	215,313,497
Tobacco, pounds	262,735,341	434,209,461	199,752,655
Cotton, bales	3,011,996	5,387,052	2,469,093
Wool, pounds	100,102,387	60,264,913	52,516,959
Peas and beans, bushels	5,746,027	15,061,995	9,219,901
Potatoes, Irish, bushels	143,337,473	111,148,867	65,797,896
Potatoes, sweet, bushels	21,709,824	42,095,026	38,268,148
Wine, gallons	3,092,330	1,627,192	221,249
Butter, pounds	514,092,683	459,681,372	313,345,306
Cheese, pounds	53,492,153	103,663,927	105,535,893
Milk sold, gallons	235,500,599	....	....
Hay, tons	27,316,048	19,083,896	13,838,642
Seed, clover, bushels	639,657	956,188	468,978
Seed, grass, bushels	583,188	900,040	416,831
Hops, pounds	25,456,669	10,991,996	3,497,029
Hemp, tons	12,746	74,493	34,871
Flax, pounds	27,133,034	4,720,145	7,709,676
Flax-seed, bushels	1,730,444	566,867	562,312
Silk cocoons, pounds	3,937	11,944	10,843
Sugar, cane, hogsheads	87,043	230,982	247,577
Sugar, sorghum, hogsheads	24	....	....
Sugar, maple, pounds	28,443,645	40,120,205	34,253,436
Molasses, cane, gallons	6,593,323	14,963,996	
Molasses, sorghum, gallons	16,050,089	6,749,123	12,700,896
Molasses, maple, gallons	921,057	1,597,589	
Beeswax, pounds	631,129	1,322,787	14,853,790
Bees' honey, pounds	14,702,815	23,366,357	

PUBLIC DEBT.

Being a statement of outstanding principal of the public debt of the United States, on the 1st day of July of each year, from 1857 to 1875, inclusive.

Year	Amount	Year	Amount
1857	$28,699,831 85	1867	$2,678,126,103 87
1858	44,911,881 03	1868	2,611,687,851 19
1859	58,496,837 88	1869	2,588,452,213 94
1860	64,842,287 88	1870	2,480,672,427 81
1861	90,580,873 72	1871	2,353,211,332 32
1862	524,176,412 13	1872	2,253,251,328 78
1863	1,119,772,138 63	1873	2,234,482,993 20
1864	1,815,784,370 57	1874	2,251,690,468 43
1865	2,680,647,869 74	1875	2,232,284,531 95
1866	2,773,236,173 69		

(*k*)

DEBT OF EACH ADMINISTRATION.

The public debt at the close of each Administration was: Washington, first term, ending 1793, $80,352,634 04; second term, $82,064,479 33; John Adams, $83,038,050 80; Jefferson, first term, $82,312,150 50; second term, $57,023,192 09; Madison, first term, $55,962,827 57; second term, $123,491,965 16; Monroe, first term, $89,987,427 66; second term, $83,788,432 71; John Quincy Adams, $58,421,413 67; Jackson, first term, $7,001,698 83; second term, $3,308,124 07; Van Buren, $13,594,480 73; Tyler, $15,925,303 01; Polk, $63,061,858 69; Fillmore, $59,803,117 70; Pierce, $28,699,831 85; Buchanan, $90,580,873 72; Lincoln, $2,680,647,869 74; Johnson, $2,588,452,213 94; Grant, first term, ending 1873, $2,234,482,993 20.

(*l*)

PUBLIC LANDS.

		ACRES.
Total number of acres of public lands of the United States, including those disposed of as well as those yet on hand		1,834,998,400.00
Quantity sold	161,766,426.46	
Entered under the homestead laws of 1860, 1864, & 1866.	20,500,216.69	
Granted for military services	62,115,202.03	
Granted for agricultural colleges:		
Selected in place	1,461,157.64	
Located with scrip	6,175,431.35	
Approved under grants in aid of railroads	26,027,673.52	
Approved swamp selections (given to the States)	48,775,990.05	
Quantity granted to the States and Territories for internal improvements	12,403,054.43	
Donations and grants for schools	67,983,922.00	
Donations and grants for universities	1,082,880.00	
Located with Indian scrip	732,165.21	
Located with float scrip under act of March 17, 1862	15,296.24	
Estimated quantity granted for wagon-roads	3,857,213.00	
Quantity granted for ship-canal	1,450,000.00	
Salines	514,485.00	
Seats of government and public buildings	146,860.00	
Granted to individuals and companies	2,482,861.32	
Granted for deaf and dumb asylums	44,971.11	
Reserved for benefit of Indians	13,280,699.94	
Reserved for companies, individuals, and corporations	8,955,383.75	
Confirmed private land claims	18,696,947.62	
Total disposed of		458,468,837.36
Remaining unsold and unappropriated June 30, 1870		1,376,529,562.64

(*m*)

REVENUES OF THE GOVERNMENT

For each fiscal year (ending June 30) from each source since 1859.

	1860.	1861.	1862.	1863.
Customs	$53,187,511 87	$39,582,125 64	$49,056,397 62	$69,059,642 40
Internal revenue	....	....	....	37,640,787 95
Direct taxes	....	....	1,795,331 73	1,485,103 61
Public lands	1,778,557 71	870,658 54	152,203 77	167,617 17
Miscellaneo's sources	1,088,530 25	1,023,515 31	915,327 97	3,741,794 38
Totals	$56,054,599 83	$41,476,299 49	$51,919,261 09	$112,094,945 51

	1864.	1865.	1866.	1867.
Customs	$102,316,152 99	$ 84,928,260 60	$179,046,651 58	$176,417,810 88
Internal revenue	109,741,134 10	209,464,215 25	309,226,813 42	266,027,537 43
Direct taxes	475,648 96	1,200,573 03	1,974,754 12	4,200,233 70
Public lands	588,333 29	996,553 31	665,031 03	1,163,575 76
Miscellaneo's sources	30,291,701 86	25,441,556 00	29,036,314 23	15,037,522 15
Totals	$243,412,971 20	$322,031,158 19	$519,949,564 38	$462,846,679 92

	1868.	1869.	1870.	1871.
Customs	$164,464,599 56	$180,048,426 63	$194,538.374 44	$206,270,408 05
Internal revenue	191,087,589 41	158,356,460 86	184,899,756 49	143,098,153 63
Direct taxes	1,788,145 85	765,685 16	229,102 88	580,355 37
Public lands	1,348,715 41	4,020,344 34	3,350,481 76	2,388,646 68
Miscellaneo's sources	17,745,403 59	13,997,338 65	12,942,118 30	22,093,541 21
Totals	$376,434,453 82	$357,188,255 64	$395,959,833 87	$374,431,104 94

	1872.	1873.	1874.
Customs	$216,370,286 77	$188,089,522 70	$163,103,833 69
Internal revenue	130,642,177 72	113,729,314 14	102,409,784 90
Direct taxes	....	315,254 51	....
Public lands	2,575,714 19	2,882,312 38	1,882,428 93
Miscellaneous sources	15,106,051 23	17,161,270 05	32,575,043 32
Totals	$364,694,229 91	$322,177,673 78	$299,941,090 84

EXPENDITURES OF THE GOVERNMENT

For each fiscal year (ending June 30) since 1859.

	1860.	1861.	1862.	1863.
Civil list	$6,148,655 41	$6,156,199 25	$5,939,009 29	$6,350,618 78
Foreign intercourse	1,163,207 15	1,142,973 41	1,339,710 35	1,231,413 06
Navy Department	11,514,649 83	12,387,156 52	42,640,353 09	63,261,235 31
War Department	16,472,202 72	23,001,530 67	389,173,562 29	603,314,411 82
Pensions	1,100,802 32	1,034,599 73	852,170 47	1,078,513 36
Indians	2,991,121 54	2,865,481 17	2,327,948 37	3,152,032 70
Miscellaneous	20,666,115 74	16,028,115 03	14,107,142 95	15,616,350 53
Totals	$60,056,754 71	$62,616,055 78	$456,379,896 81	$694,004,575 56
Int. on public debt	$3,144,120 94	$4,034,157 30	$13,190,344 84	$24,729,700 62

	1864.	1865.	1866.	1867.
Civil list	$8,059,177 23	$10,833,944 87	$12,287,828 55	$15,585,489 55
Foreign intercourse	1,290,691 92	1,260,818 08	1,338,388 18	1,548,589 26
Navy Department	85,704,963 74	122,617,434 07	43,363,654 17	31,034,011 04
War Department	690,391,048 66	1,030,690,400 06	286,776,456 13	95,224,415 63
Pensions	4,985,473 90	16,347,621 34	15,615,287 75	20,936,551 71
Indians	2,629,975 97	5,059,360 71	3,349,015 93	4,642,531 77
Miscellaneous	18,222,347 72	30,894,620 15	27.705,666 96	33,976,144 91
Totals	$811,283,679 14	$1,217,704,199 28	$390,436,297 67	$202,947,732 87
Int. on public debt	$53,685,421 69	$77,395,090 30	$133,070,513 39	$143,781,591 91

	1868.	1869.	1870.	1871.
Civil list	$11,950,156 58	$12,443,712 07	$19,031,283 56	$18.760,779 46
Foreign intercourse	1,441,344 05	8,365,416 77	1,490,776 25	1,604,373 87
Navy Department	25,775,502 72	20,000,757 97	21,780,229 87	19,431,027 21
War Department	123,236,648 62	78,501,990 61	57,655,675 40	35,799,991 82
Pensions	23,782,386 78	28,476,621 78	28,340,202 17	34,443,894 88
Indians	4,100,682 32	7,042,923 06	3,407,938 15	7,426,997 44
Miscellaneous	39,618,367 04	35,664,932 69	32,715,401 75	40,116,762 90
Totals	$229,915,088 11	$190,496,354 95	$164,421,507 15	$157,583,827 58
Int. on public debt	$140,424,045 71	$130,694,242 80	$129,235,498 00	$125,576,565 93

	1872.	1873.	1874.
Civil list	$16,187,059 20	$19,348,521 01	$17,627,115 09
Foreign intercourse	1,839,369 14	1,571,362 85	1,508,064 27
Navy Department	21,249,809 99	23,526,256 79	30,932,587 42
War Department	35,372,157 20	46,323,138 31	42,303,927 22
Pensions	28,533,402 76	29,359,426 86	29,038,414 66
Indians	7,061,728 82	7,951,704 88	6,692,462 09
Miscellaneous	42,958,329 08	52,408,226 20	85,141,593 61
Totals	$153,201,856 19	$180,488,636 90	$213,254,164 36
Int. on public debt	$117,357,839 72	$104,750,688 44	$107,119,815 21

(o)

MANUFACTURES.

Total value, gross productions, at the Censuses of 1850, 1860, and 1870.

STATES, ETC.	1870.	1860.	1850.
Alabama	$13,220,655	$10,588,566	$4,528,876
Arizona	185,410	....	....
Arkansas	7,699,676	2,880,576	537,908
California	73,116,756	68,253,328	12,862,522
Colorado	2,797,820	....	....
Connecticut	160,974,574	81,924,555	47,114,585
Dakota	178,570	....	....
Delaware	18,343,818	9,892,902	4,649,296
Dist. of Col.	9,294,489	5,412,102	2,690,258
Florida	4,707,908	2,447,969	668,335
Georgia	32,994,267	16,925,564	7,082,075
Idaho	1,047,624	....	....
Illinois	209,392,657	57,580,886	6,534,272
Indiana	109,120,684	42,803,469	8,725,423
Iowa	46,782,497	13,971,325	3,551,783
Kansas	11,798,353	4,357,408	....
Kentucky	54,149,043	37,931,240	21,710,212
Louisiana	45,737,346	15,587,473	6,779,417
Maine	79,822,005	38,193,254	24,661,057
Maryland	75,924,104	41,735,157	33,043,892
Massachusetts	551,805,067	255,545,922	157,743,994
Michigan	118,776,853	32,658,356	11,169,002
Minnesota	23,541,325	3,373,172	58,300
Mississippi	11,268,102	6,590,687	2,912,068
Missouri	206,687,354	41,782,731	24,324,418
Montana	2,494,511	....	....
Nebraska	5,892,512	607,328	....
Nêvada	15,870,539	....	....
N. Hampshire	71,678,013	37,586,453	23,164,503
New Jersey	169,969,895	76,306,104	39,851,256
New Mexico	1,489,868	1,219,123	249,010
New York	787,776,218	378,870,939	237,597,249
N'th Carolina	20,701,532	16,678,698	9,111,050
Ohio	280,969,151	121,691,148	62,692,279
Oregon	6,901,412	2,976,761	2,236,640
Pennsylvania	715,545,302	290,121,188	155,044,910
Rhode Island	110,469,650	40,711,296	22,117,688
S'th Carolina	13,438,226	8,615,195	7,045,477
Tennessee	38,587,953	17,987,225	9,725,608
Texas	15,369,731	6,577,202	1,168,538
Utah	2,351,011	900,153	291,220
Vermont	31,976,889	14,637,807	8,570,920
Virginia	38,496,077	} 50,652,124	29,602,507
West Virginia	24,169,051		
Washington	3,045,802	1,406,921	....
Wisconsin	78,606,308	27,849,467	9,293,068
Wyoming	765,424	....	....
Aggregate*	$4,305,932,032	$1,885,861,676	$1,019,106,616

* Increase: 1860 over 1850, 85 per cent.; 1870 over 1860, 128 per cent.; 1870 over 1850, 323 per cent.

(*q*)

GOLD FLUCTUATIONS.

PERIOD.	HIGHEST.											LOWEST.										
	1862.	1863.	1864.	1865.	1866.	1867.	1868.	1869.	1870.	1871.	1872.	1862.	1863.	1864.	1865.	1866.	1867.	1868.	1869.	1870.	1871.	1872.
First quarter	105	172½	169¾	234½	144⅝	140½	144	136¾	123¼	112¼	111	101⅛	134	151½	148⅛	125	132	133¼	130⅛	110¼	110⅛	108⅛
Second quarter	109½	159	251	160	167¾	141⅞	141¾	144¾	115⅝	113⅛	114¾	101½	140½	166¼	128⅝	125	132⅝	137¾	131⅜	110⅞	110⅛	109⅞
Third quarter	124	145	285	146½	155¾	146⅜	150	162½	122¾	115⅜	115⅝	109	122⅛	185	138	143¼	138⅜	140¼	130¾	111⅛	111⅝	112⅛
Fourth quarter	137	156¾	260	149	154⅜	145⅝	140½	131¾	114¼	115	115⅛	122	140⅜	189	144	131¼	133	132⅛	119½	110	108⅜	111⅜

(*p*)

DISTRIBUTION OF THE CURRENCY.

The acts of February 25, 1863, and June 3, 1864, and March 3, 1865 authorize the issue of three hundred millions of circulating notes to national banks, one hundred and fifty millions of which were to be "apportioned to associations in the States, in the District of Columbia, and the Territories, according to representative population, and the remainder among associations formed in the several States, the District of Columbia, and the Territories, having due regard to the existing capital, the resource and business of each State, District, and Territory." The whole amount of currency authorized by these acts was issued to national banks during the four years following.

The following is a statement, prepared by the Comptroller of the Currency, of the apportionment of $354,000,000 national bank circulation, upon the basis of population and wealth, as given in the Census of 1870, together with the amount outstanding July 1, 1874, and the excess and deficiency, to which has added the capital paid in:

STATES AND TERRITORIES.	Apportionment on population.	Apportionment on wealth.	Aggregate apportionment.	Circulation outstanding July 1, 1874.	Excess.	Deficiency.	Capital paid in.
Maine	$2,877,818	$2,053,200	$4,931,018	$8,006,582	$3,075,564	....	$9,540,000
New Hampshire	1,461,138	1,486,800	2,947,938	4,668,830	1,720,892	....	5,185,000
Vermont	1,517,376	1,380,600	2,897,976	6,973,115	4,075,139	....	8,335,012
Massachusetts	6,689,889	12,549,300	19,239,189	59,141,371	39,902,182	....	91,342,000
Rhode Island	997,747	1,752,300	2,750,047	13,376,290	10,626,243	....	20,504,800
Connecticut	2,467,152	4,566,600	7,033,752	17,962,178	10,928,426	....	25,384,620
Total	16,011,120	23,788,800	39,799,920	110,128,366	70,328,446	....	160,291,432
New York	20,118,813	38,267,400	58,386,213	60,138,568	1,752,355	....	110,654,691
New Jersey	4,159,382	5,540,100	9,699,482	11,125,000	1,425,518	....	13,958,350
Pennsylvania	16,167,317	22,425,900	38,593,217	42,166,895	3,573,678	....	53,510,240
Delaware	573,878	566,400	1,140,273	1,296,975	156,702	....	1,523,185
Maryland	3,584,651	3,787,800	7,372,451	9,250,147	1,877,696	....	13,640,203
Total	44,604,036	70,587,600	115,191,636	123,977,585	8,785,949	....	193,286,669
District of Columbia	604,560	743,400	1,347,960	1,491,191	143,231	....	1,652,000
Virginia	5,624,042	2,407,200	8,031,242	3,651,441	....	$4,379,801	4,185,000
West Virginia	2,029,041	1,115,100	3,144,141	2,380,440	....	763,701	2,596,000
North Carolina	4,918,022	1,539,900	6,457,922	1,754,985	....	4,702,937	2,100,000
South Carolina	3,239,045	1,221,300	4,460,345	2,208,400	....	2,251,945	3,170,000
Georgia	5,435,587	1,575,300	7,010,887	2,320,624	....	4,690,263	2,785,000
Florida	861,846	265,500	1,127,346	....	....	1,127,346	....
Alabama	4,576,646	1,185,900	5,762,546	1,347,183	....	4,415,363	1,569,300
Mississippi	3,800,529	1,239,000	5,039,529	4,876	....	5,034,653	....

Louisiana	3,336,863	1,893,900	5,230,763	3,513,454	....	1,717,309	5,250,000
Texas	3,757,640	938,100	4,695,740	748,410	....	3,947,330	995,000
Arkansas	2,223,936	920,400	3,144,336	189,955	....	2,954,341	205,000
Kentucky	6,064,027	3,557,700	9,621,727	7,309,241	....	2,312,486	8,263,700
Tennessee	5,777,118	2,938,200	8,715,318	3,027,591	....	5,687,527	3,520,481
Missouri	7,901,509	7,557,900	15,459,409	6,161,488	....	9,297,921	9,545,300
Total	60,150,411	29,098,800	89,249,211	36,109,319	143,231	53,283,123	45,836,781
Ohio	12,234,726	13,151,100	25,385 826	23,561,033	....	1,824,793	29,093,000
Indiana	7,714,871	7,469,400	15,184,271	14,560,850	....	623,421	17,611,800
Illinois	11,659,230	12,496,200	24,155,430	16,619,250	....	7,536,180	20,843,000
Michigan	5,435,357	4,230,300	9,665,657	7,333,063	....	2,332,594	9,763,500
Wisconsin	4,841,403	4,141,800	8,983,203	3,209,916	....	5,773,287	3,680,000
Iowa	5,481,081	4,230,300	9,711,381	5,473,115	....	4,238,266	6,017,000
Minnesota	2 018,445	1,345,200	3,363,645	3,297,521	....	66,124	4,173,700
Kansas	1,672,754	1,115,100	2,787,854	1,536,321	....	1,251,533	1,975,000
Nebraska	564,592	407,100	971,692	899,410	....	72,282	905,000
Total	51,622,459	48,586,500	100.208,959	76,490,479	....	23.718,480	94,062,000
Nevada	195,052	177,000	372,052	9,263	....	362,689	....
Oregon	417,377	300,900	718,277	224,100	....	494,177	250,000
California	2,571,783	3,752,400	6,324,183	....	....	6,324,183	....
Colorado	182,993	123,900	306,893	593,990	287,097	....	625,000
Utah	398,386	88,500	486,886	416,859	....	70,027	450,000
Idaho	68,852	35,400	104,252	90,000	....	14,252	100,000
Montana	94,540	88,500	183,040	271,895	88,855	....	350,000
Wyoming	41,855	35,400	77,255	54,000	....	23,255	125,000
New Mexico	421,742	194,700	616,442	269,000	....	347,442	300,000
Arizona	44,334	17,700	62,034	....	....	62,034	....
Dakota	65,096	35,400	100,496	45,000	....	55,496	50,000
Washington	109,964	88,500	198,464	....	....	198,464	....
Total	4,611,974	4,938,300	9,550,274	1,974,207	375,952	7,952,019	2,250,000
Grand Total	$177,000,000	$177,000,000	$354,000,000	348,679,956	$79,633,578	$84,953,622	$495,726,882
Add amount due banks for mutilated notes returned				1,271,068			
				$349,951,024			

The balance of the circulation, $4,048,976, has been assigned to banks organized and in process of organization in States deficient, but the necessary bonds have not yet been deposited.

* Capital paid in (gold banks), $3,200,000.

THE CIVIL RIGHTS BILL.

An Act to protect all persons in the United States in their civil rights, and furnish the means of their vindication.

Be it enacted, &c., That all persons born in the United States and not subject to any foreign power, excluding Indians, not taxed, are hereby declared to be citizens of the United States; and such citizens of every race and color, without regard to any previous condition of slavery or involuntary servitude, except as a punishment for crime whereof the party shall have been duly convicted, shall have the same right in every State and Territory in the United States to make and enforce contracts; to sue, be parties, and give evidence; to inherit, purchase, lease, sell, hold, and convey real and personal property; and to full and equal benefit of all laws and proceedings for the security of person and property as is enjoyed by white citizens, and shall be subject to like punishment, pains, and penalties, and to none other, any law, statute ordinance, regulation, or custom, to the contrary notwithstanding.

SEC. 2. That any person who, under color of any law, statute, ordinance, regulation, or custom, shall subject, or cause to be subjected, any inhabitant of any State or Territory to the deprivation of any right secured or protected by this act, or to different punishment, pains, or penalties on account of such person having at any time been held in a condition of slavery or involuntary servitude, except as a punishment for crime whereof the party shall have been duly convicted, or by reason of his color or race, than is prescribed for the punishment of white persons, shall be deemed guilty of a misdemeanor, and, on conviction, shall be punished by fine not exceeding one thousand dollars, or imprisonment not exceeding one year, or both, in the discretion of the court.

SEC. 3. That the district courts of the United States, within their respective districts, shall have, exclusively of the courts of the several States, cognizance of all crimes and offences committed against the provisions of this act, and also, concurrently with the circuit courts of the United States, of all causes, civil and criminal, affecting persons who are denied or cannot enforce in the courts or judicial tribunals of the State or locality where they may be any of the rights secured to them by the first section of this act; and if any suit or prosecution, civil or criminal, has been or shall be commenced in any State court against any such person, for any cause whatsoever, or against any officer, civil or military, or other person, for any arrest or imprisonment, trespasses, or wrongs done or committed by virtue or under color of authority derived from this act or the act establishing a bureau for the relief of freedmen and refugees, and all acts amendatory thereof, or for refusing to do any act upon the ground that it would be inconsistent with this act, such defendant shall have the right to remove such cause for trial to the proper district or circuit court in the manner prescribed by the "Act relating to *habeas corpus* and regulating judicial proceedings in certain cases," approved March three, eighteen hundred and sixty-three, and all acts amendatory thereof. The jurisdiction in civil and criminal matters hereby conferred on the district and circuit courts of the United States shall be exercised and enforced in conformity with the laws of the United States, so far as such laws are suitable to carry the same into effect; but in all cases where such laws are not adapted to the object, or are deficient in the provisions necessary to furnish suitable remedies and punish offences against law, the common law, as modified and changed by the constitution and statutes of the State wherein the court having jurisdiction of the cause, civil or criminal, is held, so far as the same is not inconsistent with the Constitution and laws of the United States, shall be extended to and govern said courts in the trial and disposition of such cause, and, if of a criminal nature, in the infliction of punishment on the party found guilty.

SEC. 4. That the district attorneys, marshals, and deputy marshals of the United States, the commissioners appointed by the circuit court and territorial courts of the United States, with power of arresting, imprisoning, or bailing offenders against the laws of the United States, the officers and agents of the Freedmen's Bureau, and every other officer who may be specially empowered by the President of the United States, shall be, and they are hereby, specially authorized and required, at the expense of the United States, to institute proceedings against all and every person who shall violate the provisions of this act, and cause him or them to be arrested and imprisoned, or bailed, as the case may be, for trial before such court of the United States or territorial court as by this act has cognizance of the offence. And with a view to affording reasonable protection to all persons in their constitutional rights of equality before the law, without distinction of race or color, or previous condition of slavery or involuntary servitude, except as a punishment for crime, whereof the party shall have been duly convicted, and to the prompt discharge of the duties of this act, it shall be the duty of the circuit courts of the United States and the superior courts of the Territories of the United States, from time to time, to increase the number of commissioners, so as to afford a speedy and convenient means for the arrest and examination of persons charged with a violation of this act. And such commissioners are hereby authorized and required to exercise and discharge all the powers and duties conferred on them by this act, and the same duties with regard to offences created by this act, as they are authorized by law to exercise with regard to other offences against the laws of the United States.

SEC. 5. That it shall be the duty of all marshals and deputy marshals to obey and execute all warrants and precepts issued under the provisions of this act, when to them directed; and should any marshal or deputy marshal refuse to receive such warrant or other process when tendered, or to use all proper means diligently to execute the same, he shall, on conviction thereof, be fined in the sum of one thousand dollars, to the use of the person upon whom the accused is alleged to have committed the offence. And the better to enable the said commissioners to execute their duties faithfully and efficiently, in conformity with the Constitution of the United States and the requirements of this act, they are hereby authorized and empowered, within their counties respectively, to appoint, in writing, under their hands, any one or more suitable persons, from time to time, to execute all such warrants and other process that may be issued by them in the lawful performance of their respective duties; and the persons so appointed to execute any warrant or process as aforesaid shall have authority to summon and call to their aid the bystanders or the *posse comitatus* of the proper county, or such portion of the land and naval forces of the United States, or of the militia, as may be necessary to the performance of the duty with which they are charged, and to insure a faithful observance of the clause of the Constitution which prohibits slavery, in conformity with the provisions of this act; and said warrants shall run and be executed by said officers anywhere in the State or Territory within which they are issued.

SEC. 6. That any person who shall knowingly and wilfully obstruct, hinder or prevent any officer, or other person charged with the execution of any warrant or process issued under the provisions of this act, or any person or persons lawfully assisting him or them, from arresting any person for whose apprehension such warrant or process may have been issued, or shall rescue or attempt to rescue such person from the custody of the officer, other person or persons, or those lawfully assisting as aforesaid, when so arrested pursuant to the authority herein given and declared, or shall aid, abet, or assist any person so arrested as aforesaid, directly or indirectly, to escape from the custody of the officer or other person legally authorized as aforesaid, or shall harbor or conceal any person for whose arrest a warrant or process shall have been issued as aforesaid, so as to prevent his discovery and arrest after notice or knowledge of the fact that a warrant has been issued for the apprehension of such person, shall, for either of said offences, be subject to a fine not exceeding one thousand dollars, and imprisonment not exceeding six months, by indictment and conviction before the district court of the United States for the district in which said offence may have been committed, or before the proper court of criminal jurisdiction, if committed within any one of the organized Territories of the United States.

Sec. 7. That the district attorneys, the marshals, their deputies, and the clerks of the said district and territorial courts shall be paid for their services the like fees as may be allowed to them for similar services in other cases; and in all cases where the proceedings are before a commissioner, he shall be entitled to a fee of ten dollars in full for his services in each case, inclusive of all services incident to such arrest and examination. The person or persons authorized to execute the process to be issued by such commissioners for the arrest of offenders against the provisions of this act shall be entitled to a fee of five dollars for each person he or they may arrest and take before any such commissioner as aforesaid, with such other fees as may be deemed reasonable by such commissioner for such other additional services as may be necessarily performed by him or them, such as attending at the examination, keeping the prisoner in custody, and providing him with food and lodging during his detention, and until the final determination of such commissioner, and in general for performing such other duties as may be required in the premises; such fees to be made up in conformity with the fees usually charged by the officers of the courts of justice within the proper district or county, as near as may be practicable, and paid out of the treasury of the United States on the certificate of the judge of the district within which the arrest is made, and to be recoverable from the defendant as part of the judgment in case of conviction.

Sec. 8. That whenever the President of the United States shall have reason to believe that offences have been, or are likely to be committed against the provisions of this act within any judicial district, it shall be lawful for him, in his discretion, to direct the judge, marshal, and district attorney of such district to attend at such place within the district, and for such time as he may designate, for the purpose of the more speedy arrest and trial of persons charged with a violation of this act; and it shall be the duty of every judge or other officer, when any such requisition shall be received by him, to attend at the place and for the time therein designated.

Sec. 9. That it shall be lawful for the President of the United States, or such person as he may empower for that purpose, to employ such part of the land or naval forces of the United States, or of the militia, as shall be necessary to prevent the violation and enforce the due execution of this act.

Sec. 10. That upon all questions of law arising in any cause under the provisions of this act, a final appeal may be taken to the Supreme Court of the United States.

The Bill passed in the Senate over the President's veto by the vote of 33 yeas to 15 nays, and in the House by 122 yeas to 41 nays.

THE TENURE-OF-OFFICE BILL.

(PASSED MARCH 2, 1867.)

Be it enacted by the Senate and House of Representatives of the United States of America in Congress assembled, That every person holding any civil office to which he has been appointed by and with the advice and consent of the Senate, and every person who shall hereafter be appointed to any such office, and shall become duly qualified to act therein, is, and shall be entitled to hold such office until a successor shall, in like manner, have been appointed and duly qualified, except as herein otherwise provided: *Provided,* That the Secretaries of State, of the Treasury, of War, of the Navy, and of the Interior, the Postmaster-General, and the Attorney-General shall hold their offices respectively for and during the term of the President by whom they may have been appointed, and for one month thereafter, subject to removal by and with the advice and consent of the Senate.

SEC. 2. That when any officer, appointed as aforesaid, excepting Judges of the United States Courts, shall, during a recess of the Senate, be shown, by evidence satisfactory to the President to be guilty of misconduct in office, or crime, or for any reason shall become incapable or legally disqualified to perform its duties, in such case, and in no other, the President may suspend such officer and designate some suitable person to perform temporarily the duties of such office until the next meeting of the Senate, and until the case shall be acted upon by the Senate, and such person so designated, shall take the oaths and give the bonds required by law to be taken and given by the person duly appointed to fill such office, and in such case it shall be the duty of the President, within twenty days after the first day of such next meeting of the Senate, to report to the Senate such suspension with the evidence and reasons for his actions in the case, and the name of the person so designated to perform the duties of such office. And if the Senate shall concur in such suspension, and advise and consent to the removal of such officer, they shall so certify to the President, who may thereupon remove such officer, and by and with the advice and consent of the Senate, appoint another person to such office. But if the Senate shall refuse to concur in such suspension, such officer so suspended shall forthwith resume the functions of his office, and the powers of the person so performing its duties in his stead shall cease, and the official salary and emoluments of such officer shall, during such suspension, belong to the person so performing the duties thereof, and not to the officer so suspended: *Provided, however*, That the President in case he shall become satisfied that such suspension was made on insufficient grounds shall be authorized at any time before reporting such suspension to the Senate, as above provided, to revoke such suspension and reinstate such officer in the performance of the duties of his office.

SEC. 3. That the President shall have power to fill all vacancies which may happen during the recess of the Senate by reason of death or resignation, by granting commissions which shall expire at the end of their next session thereafter. And if no appointment by and with the advice and consent of the Senate shall be made to such office so vacant or temporarily filled as aforesaid, during such next session of the Senate, such office shall remain in abeyance without any salary, fees, or emoluments attached thereto until the same shall be filled by appointment thereto by and with the advice and consent of the Senate, and during such time all the powers and duties belonging to such office shall be exercised by such other officer as may by law exercise such powers and duties in case of a vacancy in such office.

SEC. 4. That nothing in this act contained shall be construed to extend the term of any office, the duration of which is limited by law.

SEC. 5. That if any person shall, contrary to the provisions of this act, accept any appointment to, or employment in, any office, or shall hold or exercise, or attempt to hold or exercise any such office or employment, he shall be deemed, and is hereby declared to be guilty of a high misdemeanor, and upon trial and conviction thereof, he shall be punished therefor by a fine not exceeding ten thousand dollars, or by imprisonment not exceeding five years, or both said punishments, in the discretion of the court.

SEC. 6. That every removal, appointment, or employment made, had, or exercised contrary to the provisions of this act, and the making, signing, sealing, countersigning, or issuing of any commission or letter of authority for or in respect to any such appointment or employment, shall be deemed and are hereby declared to be high misdemeanors, and upon trial and conviction thereof, every person guilty thereof shall be punished by a fine not exceeding ten thousand dollars, or by imprisonment not exceeding five years, or both said punishments in the discretion of the court: *Provided*, That the President shall have power to make out and deliver after the adjournment of the Senate, commissions for all officers whose appointments shall have been advised and consented to by the Senate.

SEC. 7. That it shall be the duty of the Secretary of the Senate, at the close of each session thereof, to deliver to the Secretary of the Treasury, and to each of his assistants, and to each of the auditors, and to each of the comptrollers in the treasury, and to the treasurer and to the register of the treasury, a full and complete list, duly certified, of all the persons who shall have been nominated to and rejected by the Senate during such session, and a like list of all the offices to which nominations shall have been made and not confirmed and filled at such session.

SEC. 8. That whenever the President shall, without the advice and consent of the Senate, designate, authorize, or employ any person to perform the duties of any office, he shall forthwith notify the Secretary of the Treasury thereof, and it shall be the duty of the Secretary of the Treasury thereupon to communicate such notice to all the proper accounting and disbursing officers of his department.

SEC. 9. That no money shall be paid or received from the Treasury, or paid or received from or retained out of any public moneys or funds of the United States, whether in the Treasury or not to or by or for the benefit of any person appointed to or authorized to act in or holding or exercising the duties or functions of any office contrary to the provisions of this act, nor shall any claim, account, voucher, order, certificate, warrant, or other instrument providing for or relating to such payment, receipt, or retention, be presented, passed, allowed, approved, certified, or paid by any officer of the United States or by any person exercising the functions or performing the duties of any office or place of trust under the United States for or in respect to such office or the exercising or performing the functions or duties thereof; and every person who shall violate any of the provisions of this section, shall be guilty of a high misdemeanor, and upon trial and conviction thereof, shall be punished therefor by a fine not exceeding ten thousand dollars, or by imprisonment not exceeding ten years, or both said punishments in the discretion of the court.

PLATFORMS OF 1860-1864.

PLATFORM OF THE BRECKINRIDGE PARTY OF 1860.

Resolved, That the platform adopted by the Democratic party at Cincinnati be affirmed, with the following explanatory resolutions:

1. That the government of a territory organized by an act of Congress is provisional and temporary, and during its existence all citizens of the United States have an equal right to settle with their property in the territory, without their rights, either in person or property, being destroyed by congressional or territorial legislation.

2. That it is the duty of the Federal Government, in all its departments, to protect the rights of persons and property in the territories, and wherever else its constitutional authority extends.

3. That when the settlers in a territory, having an adequate population, form a State Constitution, the right of sovereignty commences, and being consummated by their admission into the Union, they stand on an equality with the people of other States, and a State thus organized ought to be admitted into the Federal Union, whether its constitution prohibits or recognizes the institution of slavery.

4. That the Democratic party are in favor of the acquisition of Cuba, on such terms as shall be honorable to ourselves and just to Spain, at the earliest practicable moment.

5. That the enactments of State Legislatures to defeat the faithful execution of the Fugitive Slave Law are hostile in character, subversive of the Constitution, and revolutionary in their effect.

6. That the Democracy of the United States recognize it as an imperative duty of the government to protect the naturalized citizen in all his rights, whether at home or in foreign lands, to the same extent as its native born citizens.

WHEREAS, One of the greatest necessities of the age, in a political, commercial, postal, and military point of view, is a speedy communication between the Pacific and Atlantic coasts; therefore, be it resolved,

7. That the National Democratic party do hereby pledge themselves to use every means in their power to secure the passage of some bill, to the extent of the Constitutional authority by Congress, for the construction of a railroad to the Pacific Ocean, at the earliest practicable moment.

PLATFORM OF THE DOUGLAS PARTY OF 1860.

Resolved, That we, the Democracy of the Union in Convention assembled, hereby declare our affirmation of the resolutions unanimiously adopted and declared as a platform of principles by the Democratic Convention at Cincinnati, in the year 1856, believing that Democratic principles are unchangable in their nature when applied to the same subject matter, and we recommend as our only further resolutions the following:

That inasmuch as differences of opinion exist in the Democratic party as to the nature and extent of the powers of a Territorial Legislature, and as to the powers and duties of Congress, under the Constitution of the United States, over the institution of slavery in the territories;

Resolved, That the Democratic party will abide by the decision of the Supreme Court of the United States over the institution of slavery in the territories.

Resolved, That it is the duty of the United States to afford ample and complete protection to all its citizens, at home or abroad, and whether native or foreign born.

Resolved, That one of the necessities of the age, in a military, commercial, and postal point of view, is a speedy communication between the Atlantic and Pacific States, and the Democratic party pledge such constitutional enactment as will insure the construction of a railroad to the Pacific coast at the earliest practical period.

Resolved, That the Democratic party are in favor of the acquisition of the Island of Cuba, on such terms as shall be honorable to ourselves and just to Spain.

Resolved, That the enactments of State Legislatures to defeat the faithful execution of the Fugitive Slave Law are hostile in character, subversive to the Constitution, and revolutionary in their effect.

Resolved, That it is in accordance with the Cincinnati Platform, that during the existence of Territorial Governments, the measure of restriction, whatever it may be, imposed by the Federal Constitution on the power of the Territorial Legislature over the subject of the domestic relations, as the same has been or shall hereafter be decided by the Supreme Court of the United States, should be respected by all good citizens, and enforced with promptness and fidelity by every branch of the General Government.

THE REPUBLICAN PLATFORM OF 1860.

Resolved, That we, the delegated representatives of the Republican electors of the United States, in Convention assembled, in the discharge of the duty we owe to our constituents and our country, unite in the following resolutions:

1. That the history of the nation during the last four years has fully established the propriety and necessity of the organization and perpetuation of the Republican party, and that the causes which called it into existence are permanent in their nature, and now, more than ever, demand its peaceful and constitutional triumph.

2. That the maintenance of the principles promulgated in the Declaration of Independence, and embodied in the Federal Constitution, that "all men are created equal; that they are endowed by their Creator with certain inalienable rights, among which are those of life, liberty and the pursuit of happiness, and that Governments are instituted among men to secure the enjoyment of these rights, deriving their just power from the consent of the governed"—are essential to the preservation of our republican institutions, and that the Federal Constitution, the rights of the States, and the union of the States, must and shall be preserved.

3. That to the union of the States this nation owes its unprecedented increase in population, its surprising developments of material resources; its rapid augmentation of wealth; its happiness at home and its honor abroad; and we hold in abhorrence all schemes for disunion, come from whatever source they may; and we congratulate the country that no Republican member of Congress has uttered or countenanced the threats of disunion as often made by the Democratic members of Congress, without rebuke and with applause from their political associates; and we denounce those threats of disunion in case of a popular overthrow of their ascendency, as denying the vital principles of a free Government, and as an avowal of contemplated treason which it is the imperative duty of an indignant people sternly to rebuke and forever silence.

4. That the maintenance inviolate, of the rights of the States, and especially of each State, to order and control its own domestic institutions according to its own judgment exclusively, is essential to that balance of power on which the perfection and endurance of our political fabric depends; and we denounce the lawless invasion by armed force of the soil of any State or

Territory, no matter under what pretext, as one of the gravest of crimes.

5. That the present Democratic Administration has far exceeded our worst apprehensions in the measureless subserviency to the exactions of a sectional interest, as especially evinced in its desperate exertions to force the infamous Lecompton Constitution upon the protesting people of Kansas, construing the relation between master and servant to involve an unqualified property in persons; in its attempted enforcement everywhere, on land and sea, through the intervention of Congress and of the Federal Courts, of the extreme pretensions of a purely local interest; and in its general and unvarying abuse of the power entrusted to it by a confiding people.

6. That the people justly view with alarm the reckless extravagance which pervades every department of the Federal Government. That a return to right economy and accountability is indispensible to arrest the plunder of the public treasury by favored partisans, while the recent startling developments of frauds and corruption at the Federal metropolis show that an entire change of administration is imperatively demanded.

7. That the new dogma that the Constitution of its own force carries slavery into any or all the Territories of the United States, is a dangerous political heresy, at variance with the explicit provisions of that instrument itself, with cotemporaneous exposition, and with legislative and judicial precedents, that it is revolutionary in its tendency and subversive of the peace and harmony of the country.

8. That the nominal condition of all the territory of the United States is that of freedom; that as our Republican fathers, when they had abolished slavery in all our national territory, ordained that no person should be deprived of life, liberty or property without due process of law, it becomes our duty by legislation, whenever such legislation is necessary, to maintain this provision of the Constitution against all attempts to violate it; and we deny the authority of Congress, or a Territorial Legislature, or of any individual, to give legal existence to slavery in any Territory of the United States.

9. That we brand the recent re-opening of the African Slave Trade, under the cover of our national flag, aided by perversions of judicial power, as a crime against humanity, and a burning shame to our country and age; and we call upon Congress to take prompt and efficient measures for the total and final suppression of that execrable traffic.

10. That in the recent vetoes by their Federal Governors of the acts of the Legislatures of Kansas and Nebraska, prohibiting slavery in these Territories, we find a practical illustration of the boasted Democratic principles of non-intervention and

Popular Sovereignty, embodied in the Kansas-Nebraska bill, and a demonstration of the deception and fraud involved therein.

11. That Kansas should, of right, be immediately admitted as a State under the Constitution recently formed and adopted by her people, and accepted by the House of Representatives.

12. That while providing revenue for the support of the General Government, by duties upon imports, sound policy requires such an adjustment of these imports as to encourage the development of the industrial interests of the whole country, and we commend that policy of National Exchange which secures to the working men liberal wages, agriculture remunerative prices, to merchants and manufacturers an adequate reward for their skill, labor and enterprise, and to the nation commercial prosperity and independence.

13. That we protest against any sale or alienation to others of the public lands held by actual settlers, and against any view of the free homestead policy, which regards the settlers as paupers or suppliants for public bounty, and we demand the passage by Congress of the complete and satisfactory homestead measure which has already passed the House.

14. That the National Republican party is opposed to any change in our naturalization laws, or any State Legislation, by which the rights of citizenship hitherto accorded to immigrants from foreign lands shall be abridged or impaired, and in favor of giving a full and efficient protection to the rights of all classes of citizens, whether native or naturalized, both at home and abroad.

15. That appropriations by Congress for river and harbor improvements of a national character, is required for the accommodation and security of an existing commerce, or authorized by the Constitution and justified by the obligation of the Government to protect the lives and property of its citizens.

16. That a railroad to the Pacific ocean is imperatively demanded by the interests of the whole country; and that the Federal Government ought to render immediate and efficient aid in its construction, and that preliminary thereto, a daily overland mail should be promptly established.

17. Finally, having thus set forth our distinctive principles and views, we invite the co-operation of all citizens, however differing in other questions, who substantially agree with us, in their affirmance and support.

PLATFORM OF THE NATIONAL CONSTITUTIONAL PARTY OF 1860.

The Union, the Constitution and the Laws.

UNION PLATFORM, ADOPTED AT BALTIMORE JUNE 8, 1864.

Resolved, That it is the highest duty of every American citizen to maintain against all its enemies, the integrity of the Union, and the paramount authority of the Constitution and laws of the United States, and that, laying all political opinions aside, we pledge ourselves, as Union men, animated by a common sentiment, and aiming at a common object, to do everything in our power to aid the Government in quelling, by force of arms, the rebellion now raging against its authority, and bringing to the punishment due to their crimes, the rebels and traitors arrayed against it.

Resolved, That we approve the determination of the Government of the United States not to compromise with rebels, or to offer any terms of peace, except such as may be based upon an unconditional surrender of their hostility, &c., and a return to their just allegiance to the Constitution and laws of the United States, and that we call upon the Government to maintain this position, and to prosecute the war with the utmost possible vigor to the complete suppression of the rebellion, in full reliance upon the self-sacrifices, the patriotism, the heroic valor, and the undying devotion of the American people to their country and its free institutions.

Resolved, That slavery was the cause and now constitutes the strength of the rebellion, and that as it must be always and everywhere hostile to the principles of Republican Governments, justice and the national safety demand its utter and complete extirpation from the soil of the Republic, and that we uphold and maintain the acts and proclamations, by which the Government, in its own defence, has aimed a death blow at this gigantic evil. We are in favor, furthermore, of such an amendment to the Constitution, to be made by the people in conformity with its provisions, as shall terminate and forever prohibit the existence of slavery within the limits of the jurisdiction of the United States.

Resolved, That the thanks of the American people are due to the soldiers and sailors of the army and navy, who have periled their lives in defence of their country, and in vindication of the honor of the flag; that the nation owes them some permanent recognition of their patriotism and their valor, and ample and permanent provision for those of their survivors who have received disabling and honorable wounds in the service of their country, and that the memories of those who have fallen in its defense shall be held in grateful and everlasting remembrance.

Resolved, That we approve and applaud the political wisdom, the unselfish patriotism and unswerving fidelity to the Constitution and the principles of American liberty with which

Abraham Lincoln has discharged, under circumstances of unparalelled difficulty, the great duties and responsibilities of the Presidential office; that we approve and endorse, as demanded by the emergency and essential to the preservation of the nation, and as within the Constitution, the measures and acts which he has adopted to defend the nation against its open and secret foes; especially the Proclamation of Emancipation, and the employment, as Union soldiers, of men heretofore held in slavery, and that we have full confidence in his determination to carry these and all other Constitutional measures, essential to the salvation of the country, into full and complete effect.

Resolved, That we deem it essential to the general welfare, that harmony should prevail in the national councils, and we regard as worthy of public confidence and official trust those only who cordially endorse the principle proclaimed in these resolutions, and which should characterize the administration of the Government.

Resolved, That the Government owes to all men employed in its armies, without distinction of color, the full protection of the laws of war, and any violation of these laws and of the usages of civilized nations in the time of war, by the rebels now in arms, should be made the subject of full and prompt redress.

Resolved, That the foreign immigration, which in the past has added so much to the wealth and development of resources and increase of power to this nation, the asylum of the oppressed of all nations, should be fostered and encouraged by a liberal and just policy.

Resolved, That we are in favor of the speedy construction of the railroad to the Pacific.

Resolved, That the national faith is pledged for the redemption of the public debt and must be kept inviolate; and that for this purpose we recommend economy and rigid responsibilities in the public expenditures, and a vigorous and just system of taxation; that it is the duty of every loyal State to sustain the use of the national currency.

Resolved, That we approve the position taken by the Government, that the people of the United States can never regard with indifference the attempt of European power to overthrow by force, or to supplant by fraud, the institutions of any Republican government on the Western Continent, and that they will view with extreme jealousy, as menacing to the peace and independence of this our country, the efforts of any such power to obtain new footholds for monarchical governments sustained by a foreign military force in near proximiry to the United States.

FREMONT PLATFORM, ADOPTED AT CLEVELAND, MAY 31, 1864.

1. That the Federal Union must be preserved.

2. That the Constitution and laws of the United States must be observed and obeyed.

3. That the rebellion must be suppressed by the force of arms, and without compromise.

4. That the rights of Free Speech, Free Press, and the Habeas Corpus must be held inviolate, save in districts where martial law has been proclaimed.

5. That the rebellion has destroyed slavery, and the Federal Constitution should be amended to prohibit its re-establishment.

6. That the right for asylum, except for crime, and subject to law, is a recognized principle—a principle of American liberty; that any violation of it must not be overlooked, and must not go unrebuked.

7. That the National policy known as the Monroe doctrine has become a recognized principle, and that the establishment of an anti-republican government on this continent by a foreign power can not be tolerated.

8. That the gratitude and support of the nation is due to the faithful soldiers, and the earnest leaders of the Union army and navy, for their heroic achievements and valor in defense of our imperiled country and of civil liberty.

9. That the one term policy for the Presidency adopted by the people is strengthened by the existing crisis, and shall be maintained by constitutional amendments.

10. That the constitution shall be so amended that the President and Vice President shall be elected by a direct vote of the people.

11. That the reconstruction of the rebellious States belongs to the people through their representatives in Congress, and not to the Executive.

12. That the confiscation of the lands of the rebels and their distribution among the soldiers and actual settlers is a measure of justice; that integrity and economy are demanded at all times in the measures of the government, and that now the want of this is criminal.

NATIONAL DEMOCRATIC PLATFORM
OF 1864.

Resolved, That in the future, as in the past, we will adhere with unswerving fidelity to the Union under the Constitution as the only solid foundation of our strength, security and happiness as a people, and as a framework of government equally conducive to the welfare and prosperity of all the States, both Northern and Southern.

Resolved, That this Convention does explicitly declare, as the sense of the American people, that after four years of failure to restore the Union by the experiment of war, during which, under the pretense of military necessity or war power higher than the Constitution, the Constitution itself has been disregarded in every part, and public liberty and private right alike trodden down, and the material prosperity of the country essentially impaired, justice, humanity, liberty and the public welfare demand that immediate efforts be made for a cessation of hostilities with a view to an ultimate convention of the States, or other peaceable means, to the end that at the earliest practical moment peace may be restored on the basis of the Federal Union of the States.

Resolved, That the direct interference of the military authorities of the United States in the recent elections held in Kentucky, Maryland, Missouri and Delaware was a shameful violation of the Constitution, and a repetition of such acts in the approaching election will be held as revolutionary, and resisted with all the means and power under our control.

Resolved, That the aim and object of the Democratic party is to preserve the Federal Union and the rights of the States unimpaired, and they hereby declare that they consider that the administrative usurpation of extraordinary and dangerous powers not granted by the Constitution, the subversion of the civil by military law in States not in insurrection, the arbitrary military arrest, imprisonment, trial and sentence of American citizens in States where the civil law exists in full force, the suppression of freedom of speech and of the press, the denial of the right of asylum, the open and avowed disregard of State rights, the employment of unusual test oaths, and the interference with, and denial of the right of the people to bear arms in their defense, is calculated to prevent a restoration of the Union and the perpetuation of the Government deriving its just powers from the consent of the governed.

Resolved, That the shameful disregard of the Administration to its duty in respect to our fellow-citizens who now are, and long have been, prisoners of war in a suffering condition, deserves the severest reprobation on the score alike of public policy and common humanity.

Resolved, That the sympathy of the Democratic party is heartily and earnestly extended to the soldiery of our army and sailors of our navy who are and have been in the field and on the sea, under the flag of their country, and in the event of its attaining power, they will receive all the care, protection and regard that the brave soldiers and sailors of the Republic have so nobly earned.

THE CHICAGO PLATFORM, 1868.

The following is the platform as adopted:

"The National Republican Party of the United States, assembled in National Convention, in the city of Chicago, on the 20th day of May, 1868, make the following declaration of principles:

"1. We congratulate the country on the assured success of the reconstruction policy of Congress, as evinced by the adoption, in the majority of the States lately in rebellion, of constitutions securing equal civil and political rights to all; and it is the duty of the Government to sustain those constitutions and to prevent the people of such States from being remitted to a state of anarchy.

"2. The guarantee by Congress of equal suffrage to all loyal men at the South was demanded by every consideration of public safety, of gratitude, and of justice, and must be maintained, while the question of suffrage in all the loyal States properly belongs to the people of those States.

"3. We denounce all forms of repudiation as a national crime, and the national honor requires the payment of the public indebtedness in the utmost good faith to all creditors at home and abroad, not only according to the letter but the spirit of the laws under which it was contracted.

"4. It is due to the labor of the nation that taxation should be equalized and reduced as rapidly as the national faith will permit.

"5. The national debt, contracted, as it has been, for the preservation of the Union for all time to come, should be extended over a fair period for redemption; and it is the duty of Congress to reduce the rate of interest thereon whenever it can be honestly done.

"6. That the best policy to diminish our burden of debt is to so improve our credit that capitalists will seek to loan us money at lower rates of interest than we now pay, and must continue to pay, so long as repudiation, partial or total, open or covert, is threatened or suspected.

"7. The Government of the United States should be administered with the strictest economy, and the corruptions which have been so shamefully nursed and fostered by Andrew Johnson call loudly for radical reform.

"8. We professedly deplore the untimely and tragic death of Abraham Lincoln, and regret the accession of Andrew Johnson to the Presidency, who has acted treacherously to the people who elected him, and the cause he was pledged to support—who has usurped high legislative and judicial functions—who has refused to execute the laws—who has used his high office to induce other officers to ignore and violate the laws—who has employed his executive powers to render insecure the property, the peace, liberty, and life of the citizen—who has abused the pardoning power—who has denounced the National Legislature as unconstitutional—persistently and corruptly resisted, by every measure in his power, every proper attempt at the reconstruction of the States lately in rebellion—who has perverted the public patronage into an engine of wholesale corruption, and who has been justly impeached for high crimes and misdemeanors, and properly pronounced guilty thereof by the vote of thirty-five Senators.

"9. The doctrine of Great Britain and other European Powers, that because a man is once a subject he is always so, must be resisted at every hazard by the United States as a relic of the feudal times, not authorized by the law of nations, and at war with our national honor and independence. Naturalized citizens are entitled to be protected in all their rights of citizenship as though they were native born; and no citizen of the United States, native or naturalized, must be liable to arrest and imprisonment by any foreign power for acts done or words spoken in this country; and if so arrested and imprisoned it is the duty of the Government to interfere in his behalf.

"10. Of all who were faithful in the trials of the late war there were none entitled to more especial honor than the brave soldiers and seamen who endured the hardships of campaign and cruise, and imperiled their lives in the service of the country. The bounties and pensions provided by the laws for these brave defenders of the nation are obligations never to be forgotten. The widows and orphans of the gallant dead are the wards of the people, a sacred legacy bequeathed to the nation's protecting care.

"11. Foreign emigration, which in the past has added so much to the wealth, development, and resources, and increase of power to this nation, the asylum of the oppressed of all nations, should be fostered and encouraged by a liberal and just policy.

"12. This Convention declares itself in sympathy with all the oppressed people which are struggling for their rights."

The following resolutions were also adopted unanimously, and are added to the declaration of principles:

"*Resolved*, That we highly commend the spirit of magnanimity and forgiveness with which the men who have served in the rebellion, but now frankly and honestly coöperate with us in restoring the peace of the country and reconstructing the Southern State governments upon the basis of impartial justice and equal rights, are received back into the communion of the loyal people. And we favor the removal of the disqualifications and restrictions placed upon the late rebels in the same measure as the spirit of loyalty will direct, and as may be consistent with the safety of the loyal people.

"*Resolved*, That we recognize the great principles laid down in the immortal Declaration of Independence as the true foundation of Democratic government: and we hail with gladness every effort toward making these principles a living reality on every inch of American soil."

DEMOCRATIC PLATFORM.

The Democratic party, in National Convention assembled, reposing its trust in the intelligence, patriotism, and discriminating justice of the people, standing upon the Constitution as the foundation and limitation of the powers of the Government and the guarantee of the liberties of the citizen, and recognizing the questions of slavery and secession as having been settled for all time to come by the war or the voluntary action of the Southern States in Constitutional Conventions assembled, and never to be revived or re-agitated, do, with the return of peace, demand:

1. The immediate restoration of all the States to their rights in the Union under the Constitution of the civil Government and the American people.

2. Amnesty for all past political offenses; the regulation of the elective franchise in the States by their citizens.

3. Payment of the public debt of the United States as rapidly as practicable, all money drawn from the people by taxation, except so much as is requisite for the necessities of the Government economically administered being honestly applied to such payment, and where the obligations of the Government do not expressly state upon their face or the law under which they were issued does not provide that they shall be paid in coin they ought, in right and in justice, to be paid in the lawful money of the United States.

4. Equal taxation of every species of property according to the value; reducing Government bonds and other public securities.

5. One currency for the Government and the people, the laborer and the office-holder, pensioner and the soldier, the producer and the bondholder.

6. Economy in the administration of the Government; the reduction of the standing army and navy; the abolition of the Freedmen's Bureau, and all political instrumentalities designed to secure negro supremacy; simplification of the system and discontinuance of inquisitorial modes of assessing and collecting internal revenue, that the burden of taxation may be equalized and lessened, and the credit of the Government and the currency made good; the repeal of all enactments for enrolling the State militia into a national force in time of peace; and a tariff for revenue upon foreign imports and such equal taxation under the internal revenue laws as will afford incidental protection to domestic manufactures as well, without impairing the revenue, impose the least

burden upon and best promote and encourage the great industrial interests of the country.

7. Reform of abuses in the Administration; the expulsion of corrupt men from office; the abrogation of useless offices; the restoration of the rightful authority to and the independence of the Executive and Judicial Departments of the Government; the subordination of the military to the civil power, to the end that the usurpation of Congress and the despotism of the sword may cease.

8. Equal rights and protection for naturalized and native born citizens at home and abroad; the assertion of American nationality, which will command the respect of foreign powers, furnish an example and encouragement to people struggling for national integrity, constitutional liberty, and individual rights; and the maintenance of the rights of naturalized citizens against the absolute doctrine of immutable allegiance and the claims of foreign powers to punish them for alleged crimes committed beyond their jurisdiction. In demanding these measures and reforms, we arraign the radical party for its disregard of right and the unparalleled oppression and tyranny which have marked its career, after the most solemn and unanimous pledge of both houses of Congress to prosecute the war exclusively for the maintenance of the Government and the preservation of the Union under the Constitution. It has repeatedly violated that most sacred pledge under which was rallied that noble volunteer army which carried our flag to victory. Instead of restoring the Union it has, so far as it is in its power, dissolved it, and subjected ten States in time of peace to military despotism and negro supremacy. It has nullified there the right of trial by jury; it has abolished the writ of habeas corpus, that most sacred writ of liberty; it has overthrown the freedom of speech and of the press; it has substituted arbitrary seizures and arrests, military trials, secret star chambers and inquisitions for constitutional tribunals; it has disregarded, in time of peace, the right of the people to be free from search and seizure; it has entered the post-office and telegraph office, and even the private rooms of individuals and seized there their private papers and letters, without any specification or notice of affidavit, as required by the organic law. It has converted the American Capitol into a bastile; it has established a system of spies and official espionage to which the constitutional monarchies of Europe never dare to resort. It has abolished the right of appeal on important constitutional questions to the supreme judicial tribunals, and threatens to curtail or destroy its original jurisdiction, which is irrevocably vested by the Constitution; while the learned Chief Justice has been subjected to the most atrocious calumnies merely because he would not prostitute his high office to the support of the false and partisan charges against the President. Its corruption and extravagance have exceeded any thing

known in history, and by its frauds and monopolies it has nearly doubled the burden of the debt created during the war. It has stripped the President of his Constitutional power of appointment even of his own Cabinet. Under its repeated assaults the pillars of the Government are rocking to their base; and should it succeed in November next, and inaugurate its President, we will meet as a subjected and conquered people amid the ruins of liberty and the scattered fragments of the Constitution; and we do declare and resolve that ever since the people of the United States threw off all subjection to the British crown, the privilege and trust of suffrage have belonged to the several States, and have been granted, regulated, and controlled exclusively by the political power of each State respectively, and any attempt by Congress, on any pretext whatever, to deprive any State of this right, or interfere with this exercise, is a flagrant usurpation of power which can find no warrant in the Constitution, and if sanctioned by the people will subvert our form of Government, and can only end in a single, centralized and consolidated Government, in which the separate existence of the States will be entirely absorbed, and an unqualified despotism then be established in place of a Federal Union of coequal States, and that we regard the reconstruction acts so-called of Congress such usurpations and unconstitutional, revolutionary and void: that our soldiers and sailors who carried the flag of our country to victory against a most gallant and determined foe must ever be gratefully remembered, and all the guarantees given in their favor must be faithfully carried into execution; that the public lands should be distributed widely among the people and should be disposed of either under the preëmption of the homestead lands and sold in reasonable quantities, and to none but actual occupants, at the price established by the Government. When the grants of the public lands may be allowed necessary for the encouragement of important public improvements, the proceeds of the sale of such lands, and not the lands themselves, should be so applied; that the President of the United States, Andrew Johnson, exercising the power of his high office in resisting the aggressions of Congress on the constitutional rights of the States and the people, is entitled to the gratitude of the whole American people, and on behalf of the Democratic party, we tender him our thanks for his patriotic efforts in that regard.

Upon this platform the Democratic party appeal to every patriot, including all the conservative element, and all who desire to support the Constitution and restore the Union, forgetting all past differences of opinion, to unite with us in the present great struggle for the liberties of the people; and that to all such, to whatever party they may have heretofore belonged, we extend the right hand of fellowship, and hail all such coöperating with us as friends and brothers.

"PLATFORMS OF 1872."

"REPUBLICAN PLATFORM."

The Republican party of the United States assembled in national convention in the city of Philadelphia on the 5th and 6th days of June, 1872, again declares its faith, appeals to its history, and announces its position upon the questions before the country:

1. During eleven years of supremacy it has accepted with grand courage the solemn duties of the time. It suppressed a gigantic rebellion, emancipated four millions of slaves, decreed the equal citizenship of all, and established universal suffrage. Exhibiting unparalleled magnanimity, it criminally punished no man for political offenses, and warmly welcomed all who proved loyalty by obeying the laws and dealing justly with their neighbors. It has steadily decreased with firm hand the resultant disorders of a great war, and initiated a wise and humane policy toward the Indians. The Pacific Railroad and similar vast enterprises have been generously aided and successfully conducted, the public lands freely given to actual settlers, immigration protected and encouraged, and a full acknowledgment of the naturalized citizen's rights secured from European powers. A uniform national currency has been provided, repudiation frowned down, the national credit sustained under the most extraordinary burdens, and new bonds negotiated at lower rates. The revenues have been carefully collected and honestly applied. Despite annual large reductions of the rates of taxation, the public debt has been reduced during General Grant's Presidency at the rate of a hundred millions a year, great financial crises have been avoided, and peace and plenty prevail throughout the land. Menacing foreign difficulties have been peacefully and honorably composed, and the honor and power of the nation kept in high respect throughout the

world. This glorious record of the past is the party's best pledge for the future. We believe the people will not intrust the government to any party or combination of men composed chiefly of those who have resisted every step of this beneficent progress.

2. The recent amendments to the national constitution should be cordially sustained because they are right, not merely tolerated because they are law, and should be carried out according to their spirit by appropriate legislation, the enforcement of which can safely be intrusted only to the party that secured those amendments.

3. Complete liberty and exact equality in the enjoyment of all civil, political, and public rights should be established and effectually maintained throughout the Union by efficient and appropriate State and Federal legislation. Neither the law nor its administration should admit any discrimination in respect of citizens by reason of race, creed, color, or previous condition of servitude.

4. The national government should seek to maintain honorable peace with all nations, protecting its citizens every-where and sympathizing with all peoples who strive for greater liberty.

5. Any system of the civil service under which the subordinate positions of the government are considered rewards for mere party zeal is fatally demoralizing, and we therefore favor a reform of the system by laws which shall abolish the evils of patronage and make honesty, efficiency, and fidelity the essential qualifications for public positions, without practically creating a life tenure of office.

6. We are opposed to further grants of the public lands to corporations and monopolies, and demand that the national domain be set apart for free homes for the people.

7. The annual revenue, after paying current expenditures, pensions, and the interest on the public debt, should furnish a moderate balance for the reduction of the principal, and that revenue, except so much as may be derived from a tax upon tobacco and liquors, should be raised by duties upon importations, the details of which should be so adjusted as to aid in securing remunerative wages to labor, and pro

mote the industries, prosperity, and growth of the whole country.

8. We hold in undying honor the soldiers and sailors whose valor saved the Union. Their pensions are a sacred debt of the nation, and the widows and orphans of those who died for their country are entitled to the care of a generous and grateful people. We favor such additional legislation as will extend the bounty of the government to all our soldiers and sailors who were honorably discharged, and who in the line of duty became disabled, without regard to the length of service or the cause of such discharge.

9. The doctrine of Great Britain and other European Powers concerning allegiance—"once a subject always a subject"—having at last through the efforts of the Republican party been abandoned, and the American idea of the individual's right to transfer allegiance having been accepted by European nations, it is the duty of our government to guard with jealous care the rights of adopted citizens against the assumption of unauthorized claims by their former governments, and we urge continued careful encouragement and protection of voluntary immigration.

10. The franking privilege ought to be abolished, and the way prepared for a speedy reduction in the rates of postage.

11. Among the questions which press for attention is that which concerns the relations of capital and labor, and the Republican party recognizes the duty of so shaping legislation as to secure full protection and the amplest field for capital, and for labor, the creator of capital, the largest opportunities and a just share of the mutual profits of these two great servants of civilization.

12. We hold that Congress and the President have only fulfilled an imperative duty in their measures for the suppression of violent and treasonable organizations in certain lately rebellious regions, and for the protection of the ballot-box; and therefore they are entitled to the thanks of the nation.

13. We denounce repudiation of the public debt, in any form or disguise, as a national crime. We witness with pride the reduction of the principal of the the debt, and

of the rates of interest upon the balance, and confidently expect that our excellent national curreney will be perfected by a speedy resumption of specie payment.

14. The Republican party is mindful of its obligations to the loyal women of America for their noble devotion to the cause of freedom. Their admission to wider fields of usefulness is viewed with satisfaction; and the honest demand of any class of citizens for additional rights should be treated with respectful consideration.

15. We heartily approve the action of Congress in extending amnesty to those lately in rebellion, and rejoice in the growth of peace and fraternal feeling throughout the land.

16. The Republican party proposes to respect the rights reserved by the people to themselves as carefully as the powers delegated by them to the State and to the Federal Government. It disapproves of the resort to unconstitutional laws for the purpose of removing evils, by interference with rights not surrendered by the people to either the State or National Government.

17. It is the duty of the General Government to adopt such measures as may tend to encourage and restore American commerce and ship-building.

18. We believe that the modest patriotism, the earnest purpose, the sound judgment, the practical wisdom, the incorruptible integrity, and the illustrious services of Ulysses S. Grant have commended him to the heart of the American people, and with him at our head we start to-day upon a new march to victory.

"LIBERAL REPUBLICAN PLATFORM."

We, the Liberal Republicans of the United States in national convention assembled at Cincinnati, proclaim the following principles as essential to just government:

1. We recognize the equality of all men before the law, and hold that it is the duty of Government, in its dealings with the people, to mete out equal and exact justice to all,

of whatever nativity, race, color, or persuasion, religious or political.

2. We pledge ourselves to maintain the Union of these States, emancipation, and enfranchisement, and to oppose any reopening of the questions settled by the thirteenth, fourteenth, and fifteenth amendments of the Constitution.

3. We demand the immediate and absolute removal of all disabilities imposed on account of the rebellion, which was finally subdued seven years ago, believeing that universal amnesty will result in complete pacification in all sections of the country.

4. Local self-government, with impartial suffrage, will guard the rights of all citizens more securely than any centralized power. The public welfare requires the supremacy of the civil over the military authority, and the freedom of person under the protection of the *habeas corpus*. We demand for the individual the largest liberty consistent with public order, for the State self-government, and for the nation a return to the methods of peace and the constitutional limitations of power.

5. The civil service of the government has become a mere instrument of partisan tyranny and personal ambition, and an object of selfish greed. It is a scandal and reproach upon free institutions, and breeds a demoralization dangerous to the perpetuity of republican government. We therefore regard a thorough reform of the civil service as one of the most pressing necessities of the hour; that honesty, capacity, and fidelity constitute the only valid claims to public employment; that the offices of the government cease to be a matter of arbitrary favoritism and patronage, and that public station shall become again a post of honor. To this end it is imperatively required that no President shall be a candidate for re-election.

6. We demand a system of Federal taxation which shall not unnecessarily interfere with the industry of the people, and which shall provide the means necessary to pay the expenses of the government, economically administered, the pensions, the interest on the public debt, and a moderate reduction annually of the principal thereof; and recognizing that there are in our midst honest but irrecon-

cilable difference of opinion with regard to the respective systems of protection and free trade, we remit the discussion of the subject to the people in their congressional districts and the decision of Congress thereon, wholly free from executive interference or dictation.

7. The public credit must be sacredly maintained, and we denounce repudiation in every form and guise.

8. A speedy return to specie payments is demanded alike by the highest considerations of commercial morality and honest government.

9. We remember with gratitude the heroism and sacrifices of the soldiers and sailors of the Republic, and no act of ours shall ever detract from their justly earned fame or the full rewards of their patriotism.

10. We are opposed to all further grants of lands to railroads or other corporations. The public domain should be held sacred to actual settlers.

11. We hold that it is the duty of the government, in its intercourse with foreign nations, to cultivate the friendships of peace by treating with all on fair and equal terms, regarding it alike dishonorable either to demand what is not right or submit to what is wrong.

12. For the promotion and success of these vital principles and the support of the candidates nominated by this convention, we invite and cordially welcome the co-operation of all patriotic citizens, without regard to previous political affiliations.

CINCINNATI, *May* 1–3.

"DEMOCRATIC PLATFORM."

We, the Democratic electors of the United States in convention assembled, do present the principles already adopted at Cincinnati, as essential to just government.

[See Liberal Republican Platform.]

BALTIMORE, July 9, 10.

"THE CIVIL SERVICE REGULATIONS."

1. No person will be appointed to any position in the civil service who shall not have furnished satisfactory evidence of his fidelity to the Union and the Constitution of the United States.

2. The evidence in regard to character, health, age, and knowledge of the English language, required by the first rule, shall be furnished in writing, and if such evidence shall be satisfactory to the head of the department in which the appointment is to be made, the applicant shall be notified when and where to appear for examination; but when the applicants are so numerous that the examination of all whose preliminary papers are satisfactory is plainly impracticable, the head of the department shall select for examination a practicable number of those who are apparently best qualified.

3. Examinations to fill vacancies in any of the Executive Departments in Washington shall be held not only at the city of Washington, but also, when directed by the head of the department in which the vacancy may exist, in the several States, either at the capital or other convenient place.

4. The appointment of persons to be employed exclusively in the secret service of the Government; also of persons to be employed as translators, stenographers, or private secretaries, or to be designated for secret service, to fill vacancies in clerkships in either of the Executive Departments at Washington, may be excepted from the operation of the rules.

5. When a vacancy occurs in a consular office, of which the lawful annual compensation is three thousand dollars or more, it will be filled at the discretion of the President, either by the transfer of some person already in the service or by a new appointment, which may be excepted from the operation of the rules. But if the vacancy occur in an

office of which the lawful annual compensation, by salary or by fees ascertained by the last official returns, is more than one thousand dollars and less than three thousand dollars, and it is not filled by transfer, applications will be addressed to the Secretary of State, inclosing proper certificates of character, responsibility, and capacity, and the Secretary will notify the applicant who, upon investigation, appears to be most suitable and competent, to attend for examination; and if he shall be found qualified, he will be nominated for confirmation; but if not found qualified, or if his nomination be not confirmed by the Senate, the Secretary will proceed in like manner with the other applicants who appear to him to be qualified. If, however, no applicants under this regulation shall be found suitable and qualified, the vacancy will be filled at discretion. The appointment of commercial agents and of consuls whose annual compensation is one thousand dollars or less (if derived from fees, the amount to be ascertained by the last official returns), of vice consuls, deputy consuls, and of consular agents and other officers who are appointed upon the nomination of the principal officer, and for whom he is responsible upon his official bond, may be, until otherwise ordered, excepted from the operation of the rules.

6. When a vacancy occurs in the office of collector of the customs, naval officer, appraiser, or surveyor of the customs, in the customs districts of New York, Boston, and Charlestown, Baltimore, San Francisco, New Orleans, Philadelphia, Vermont (Burlington), Oswego, Niagara, Buffalo Creek, Champlain, Portland, and Falmouth, Corpus Christi, Oswegatchie, Mobile, Brazos de Santiago, (Brownsville,) Texas, (Galveston, etc.,) Savannah, Charleston, Chicago, or Detroit, the Secretary of the Treasury shall ascertain if any of the subordinates in the customs district in which such vacancy occurs are suitable persons qualified to discharge efficiently the duties of the office to be filled, and, if such persons be found, he shall certify to the President the name or names of those subordinates, not exceeding three, who, in his judgment, are best qualified for the position, from which the President will make the nomination to fill the vacancy. But if no such subor-

dinate be found qualified, or if the nomination be not confirmed, the nomination will be made at the discretion of the President. Vacancies occuring in such positions in the customs service in the said districts as are included in the subjoined classification will be filled in accordance with the rules. Appointments to all other positions in the customs service in said districts may be, until otherwise ordered, excepted from the operation of the rules.

7. When a vacancy occurs in the office of collector, appraiser, surveyor, or other chief officer in any customs district not specified in the preceding regulation, applications in writing from any subordinate or subordinates in the customs service of the district, or from other person or persons residing within the said district, may be addressed to the Secretary of the Treasury, including proper certificates of character, responsibility, and capacity; and if any of the subordinates so applying shall be found suitable and qualified, the name or names, not exceeding three, of the best qualified shall be certified by the board of examiners to the Secretary, and from this list the nomination or appointments will be made. But if no such subordinate be found qualified, the said board shall certify to the Secretary the name or names, not exceeding three, of the best qualified among the other applicants, and from this list the nomination or appointment will be made. If, however, no applicants under this regulation shall be found suitable and qualified, the vacancy will be filled at discretion. Appointments to all other positions in the customs service in said districts may be, until otherwise ordered, excepted from the operation of the rules.

8. When a vacancy occurs in the office of postmaster, in cities having, according to the census of 1870, a population of twenty thousand or more, the Postmaster General shall ascertain if any of the subordinates in such office are suitable persons qualified to discharge efficiently the duties of postmaster, and, if such are found, he shall certify to the President the name or names of those subordinates, not exceeding three in number, who, in his judgment, are best qualified for the position, from which list the President will make the nomination to fill the vacancy. But

if no such subordinate be found so qualified, or if the nomination be not confirmed by the Senate, the nomination will be made at the discretion of the President. Vacancies occurring in such positions in the said post-offices as are included in the subjoined classification will be filled in accordance with the rules. Appointments to all other positions in the said post-offices may be, until otherwise ordered, excepted from the operation of the rules.

9. When a vacancy occurs in the office of postmaster, of a class not otherwise provided for, applications for the position from any subordinate or subordinates in the office, or from other persons residing within the delivery of the office, may be addressed to the Postmaster General, inclosing proper certificates of character, responsibility, and capacity; and if any of the subordinates so applying shall be found suitable and qualified, the name or names of the best qualified, not exceeding three, shall be certified by the board of examiners to the Postmaster General, and from them the nomination or appointment shall be made. But if no subordinate be found qualified, the said board shall certify to the Postmaster General the name or names, not exceeding three, of the best qualified among the other applicants, and from them the nomination or appointment shall be made. If, however, no applicants under this regulation shall be found suitable and qualified, the vacancy will be filled at discretion. Appointments to all other positions in the said post-offices may be, until otherwise ordered, excepted from the operation of the rules.

10. Special agents of the Post-office Department shall be appointed by the Postmaster General at discretion, from persons already in the postal service, and who shall have served therein for a period of not less than one year immediately preceding the appointment. But if no person within the service shall, in the judgment of the Postmaster General, be suitable and qualified, the appointment shall be made from all applicants under the rules.

11. Mail route messengers shall be appointed in the manner provided for the appointment of postmasters whose annual salary is less than two hundred dollars.

12. When a vacancy occurs in the office of register or receiver of the land office, or of pension agent, applications in writing from residents in the district in which the vacancy occurs may be addressed to the Secretary of the Interior, inclosing proper certificates of character, responsibility, and capacity; and if any of the applicants shall be found suitable and qualified, the name or names, not exceeding three, of the best qualified, shall be certified by the board of examiners to the Secretary, and from this list the nomination will be made. If, however, no applicants under this regulation shall be found suitable and qualified, the nomination will be made at discretion.

13. When a vacancy occurs in the office of United States marshal, applications in writing from residents in the district in which the vacancy occurs may be addressed to the Attorney General of the United States, inclosing proper certificates of character, responsibility, and capacity; and if any of the applicants shall be found suitable and qualified, the name or names, not exceeding three, of the best qualified, shall be certified by the board of examiners to the Attorney General, and from this list the nomination will be made. If, however, no applicants under this regulation shall be found suitable and qualified, the nomination will be made at discretion.

14. Appointments to fill vacancies occurring in offices in the several Territories, excepting those of judges of the United States courts, Indian agents and superintendents, will be made from suitable and qualified persons domiciled in the Territory in which the vacancy occurs, if any such are found.

15. It shall be the duty of the examining board in each of the departments to report to the advisory board such modifications in the rules and regulations as, in the judgment of such examining board, are required for appointments to certain positions, to which, by reason of distance, or of difficult access, or of other sufficient cause, the rules and regulations can not be applied with advantage; and if the reason for such modifications shall be satisfactory to the advisory board, said board will recommend them for approval.

16. Nothing in these rules and regulations shall prevent the reappointment at discretion of the incumbents of any office the term of which is fixed by law; and when such reappointment is made no vacancy within the meaning of the rules shall be deemed to have occurred.

17. Appointments to all positions in the civil service, not included in the subjoined classifications, nor otherwise specially provided for by the rules and regulations, may, until otherwise ordered, be excepted from the operation of the rules. [The Civil Service Regulations are practically discontinued in many departments, in consequence of a failure on the part of Congress to make appropriations for continuing them, though they are yet adhered to in some.]

RELATIONS OF THE UNITED STATES AND GREAT BRITAIN.

TREATY BETWEEN THE UNITED STATES AND GREAT BRITAIN — CLAIMS, FISHERIES, NAVIGATION OF THE ST. LAWRENCE, ETC., AMERICAN LUMBER ON THE RIVER ST. JOHN, BOUNDARY — CONCLUDED MAY 8, 1871; RATIFICATIONS EXCHANGED JUNE 17, 1871; PROCLAIMED JULY 4, 1871.

By the President of the United States of America.

A PROCLAMATION.

Whereas a treaty between the United States of America and her Majesty the Queen of the United Kingdom of Great Britain and Ireland, concerning the settlement of all causes of difference between the two countries, was concluded and signed at Washington by the high commissioners and plenipotentiaries of the respective Governments on the 8th day of May last; which treaty is, word for word, as follows:

The United States of America and her Britannic Majesty, being desirous to provide for an amicable settlement of all causes of difference between the two countries, have for that purpose appointed their respective plenipotentiaries, that is to say: the President of the United States has appointed, on the part of the United States, as commissioners in a joint high commission and plenipotentiaries, Hamilton Fish, Secretary of State; Robert Cumming Schenck, envoy extraordinary and minister plenipotentiary to Great Britain; Samuel Nelson, an associate justice of the Supreme Court of the United States; Ebenezer Rockwood Hoar, of Massachusetts; and George Henry Williams, of Oregon; and her Britanic Majesty, on her part, has appointed as her high commissioners and plenipotentiaries the right honorable George Frederick Samuel, Earl de Grey and Earl of Ripon, Viscount Goderich, Baron Grantham, a baronet, a peer of the United Kingdom, lord president of her Majesty's most honorable Privy Council, knight of the most noble order of the Garter, etc.; the right honorable Sir Stafford Henry Northcote, baronet, one of her Majesty's most honorable Privy Council, a member of Parliament, a companion of the most honorable order of the Bath, etc.; Sir Edward Thornton, knight commander of the most honorable order of the Bath, her Majesty's envoy extraordinary and minister plenipotentiary to the United States of America; Sir John Alexander Macdonald, knight commander of the most honorable order of the Bath, a member of her Majesty's Privy Council for Canada, and minister of justice and attorney-general of her Majesty's Dominion of Canada; and Montague Bernard, Esq., Chichele professor of international law in the University of Oxford.

And the said plenipotentiaries, after having exchanged their full powers, which were found to be in due and proper form, have agreed to and concluded the following articles:

ARTICLE I.

Whereas differences have arisen between the Government of the United States and the Government of her Britannic Majesty, and still exist, growing out of the acts committed by the several vessels which have given rise to the claims generically known as the "Alabama claims;"

And whereas her Britannic Majesty has authorized her high commissioners and plenipotentiaries to express, in a friendly spirit, the regret felt by her Majesty's Government for the escape, under whatever circumstances, of the Alabama and other vessels from British ports, and for the depredations committed by those vessels:

Now, in order to remove and adjust all complaints and claims on the part of the United States, and to provide for the speedy settlement of such claims which are not admitted by her Britannic Majesty's Government, the high contracting parties agree that all the said claims, growing out of acts committed by the aforesaid vessels and generically known as the "Alabama claims," shall be referred to a tribunal of arbitration, to be composed of five arbitrators, to be appointed in the following manner, that is to say: one shall be named by the President of the United States; one shall be named by her Britannic Majesty; his Majesty the King of Italy shall be requested to name one; the President of the Swiss Confederation shall be requested to name one; and his Majesty the Emperor of Brazil shall be requested to name one.

In case of the death, absence, or incapacity to serve of any or either of the said arbitrators, or, in the event of either of the said arbitrators omitting or declining or ceasing to act as such, the President of the United States, or her Britannic Majesty, or his Majesty the King of Italy, or the President of the Swiss Confederation, or his Majesty the Emperor of Brazil, as the case may be, may forthwith name another person to act as arbitrator in the place and stead of the arbitrator originally named by such head of a State.

And in the event of the refusal or omission for two months after receipt of the request from either of the high contracting parties of his Majesty the King of Italy, or the President of the Swiss Confederation, or his Majesty the Emperor of Brazil, to name an arbitrator either to fill the original appointment or in the place of one who may have died, be absent, or incapacitated, or who may omit, decline, or from any cause cease to act as such arbitrator, his Majesty the King of Sweden and Norway shall be requested to name one or more persons, as the case may be, to act as such arbitrator or arbitrators.

ARTICLE II.

The arbitrators shall meet at Geneva, in Switzerland, at the earliest convenient day after they shall have been named, and shall proceed impartially and carefully to examine and decide all questions that shall be laid before them on the part of the Governments of the United States and her Britannic Majesty respectively. All questions considered by the tribunal, including the final award, shall be decided by a majority of all the arbitrators.

Each of the high contracting parties shall also name one person to attend the tribunal as its agent to represent it generally in all matters connected with the arbitration.

ARTICLE III.

The written or printed case of each of the two parties, accompanied by the documents, the official correspondence, and other evidence on which each relies, shall be delivered in duplicate to each of the arbitrators and to the agent of the other party as soon as may be after the organization of the tribunal, but within a period not exceeding six months from the date of the exchange of the ratifications of this treaty.

ARTICLE IV.

Within four months after the delivery on both sides of the written or printed case, either party may, in like manner, deliver in duplicate to each of the said arbitrators, and to the agent of the other party, a counter case and additional documents, correspondence, and evidence, in reply to the case, documents, correspondence, and evidence so presented by the other party.

The arbitrators may, however, extend the time for delivering such counter case, documents, correspondence, and evidence, when, in their judgment, it becomes necessary, in consequence of the distance of the place from which the evidence to be presented is to be procured.

If in the case submitted to the arbitrators either party shall have specified or alluded to any report or document in its own exclusive possession without annexing a copy, such party shall be bound, if the other party thinks proper to apply for it, to furnish that party with a copy thereof; and either party may call upon the other, through the arbitrators, to produce the originals or certified copies of any papers adduced as evidence, giving in each instance such reasonable notice as the arbitrators may require.

ARTICLE V.

It shall be the duty of the agent of each party, within two months after the expiration of the time limited for the delivery of the counter case on both sides, to deliver in duplicate to each of the said arbitrators and to the agent of the other party a written or printed argument showing the points and referring to the evidence upon which his Government relies; and the arbitrators may, if they desire further elucidation with regard to any point, require a written or printed statement or argument, or oral argument by counsel upon it; but in such case the other party shall be entitled to reply either orally or in writing, as the case may be.

ARTICLE VI.

In deciding the matters submitted to the arbitrators, they shall be governed by the following three rules, which are agreed upon by the high contracting parties as rules to be taken as applicable to the case, and by such principles of international law not inconsistent therewith as the arbitrators shall determine to have been applicable to the case.

Rules.

A neutral Government is bound —

First, to use due diligence to prevent the fitting out, arming, or equipping, within its jurisdiction, of any vessel which it has reasonable ground to believe is intended to cruise or to carry on war against a Power with which it is at peace; and also to use like diligence to prevent the departure from its jurisdiction of any vessel intended to cruise or carry on war as above, such vessel having been specially adapted, in whole or in part, within such jurisdiction, to warlike use.

Secondly, not to permit or suffer either belligerent to make use of its ports or waters as the base of naval operations against the other, or for the purpose of the renewal or augmentation of military supplies or arms, or the recruitment of men.

Thirdly, to exercise due diligence in its own ports and waters, and, as to all persons within its jurisdiction, to prevent any violation of the foregoing obligations and duties.

Her Britannic Majesty has commanded her high commissioners and plenipotentiaries to declare that her Majesty's Government can not assent to the foregoing rules as a statement of principles of international law which were in force at the time when the claims mentioned in Article I arose, but that her Majesty's Government, in order to evince its desire of strengthening the friendly relations between the two countries, and of making satisfactory provision for the future, agrees that in deciding the questions between the two countries arising out of those claims the arbitrators should assume that her Majesty's Government had undertaken to act upon the principles set forth in these rules.

And the high contracting parties agree to observe these rules as between themselves in future, and to bring them to the knowledge of other maritime Powers, and to invite them to accede to them.

ARTICLE VII.

The decision of the tribunal shall, if possible, be made within three months from the close of the argument on both sides.

It shall be made in writing and dated, and shall be signed by the arbitrators who may assent to it.

The said tribunal shall first determine as to each vessel separately whether Great Britain has, by any act or omission, failed to fulfill any of the duties set forth in the foregoing three rules, or recognized by the principles of international law not inconsistent with such rules, and shall certify such fact as to each of the said vessels. In case the tribunal find that Great Britain has failed to fulfill any duty or duties as aforesaid, it may, if it think proper, proceed to award a sum in gross to be paid by Great Britain to the United States for all the claims referred to it; and in such case the gross sum so awarded shall be paid in coin by the Government of Great Britain to the Government of the United States, at Washington, within twelve months after the date of the award.

The award shall be in duplicate, one copy whereof shall be delivered to the agent of the United States for his Government, and the other copy shall be delivered to the agent of Great Britain for his Government.

ARTICLE VIII.

Each government shall pay its own agent and provide for the proper remuneration of the counsel employed by it, and for the arbitrator appointed by it, and for the expense of preparing and submitting its case to the tribunal. All other expenses connected with the arbitration shall be defrayed by the two Governments in equal moieties.

ARTICLE IX.

The arbitrators shall keep an accurate record of their proceedings, and may appoint and employ the necessary officers to assist them.

ARTICLE X.

In case the tribunal finds that Great Britain has failed to fulfill any duty or duties as aforesaid, and does not award a sum in gross, the high contracting parties agree that a board of assessors shall be appointed to ascertain and determine what claims are valid, and what amount or amounts shall be paid by Great Britain to the United States on account of the liability arising from such failure, as to each vessel, according to the extent of such liability as decided by the arbitrators.

The board of assessors shall be constituted as follows: one member thereof shall be named by the President of the United States, one member thereof shall be named by her Britannic Majesty, and one member thereof shall be named by the representative at Washington of his Majesty the King of Italy; and in case of a vacancy happening from any cause, it shall be filled in the same manner in which the original appointment was made.

As soon as possible after such nominations the board of assessors shall be organized in Washington, with power to hold their sittings there, or in New York, or in Boston. The members thereof shall severally subscribe a solemn declaration that they will impartially and carefully examine and decide, to the best of their judgment and according to justice and equity, all matters submitted to them, and shall forthwith proceed, under such rules and regulations as they may prescribe to the investigation of the claims which shall be presented to them by the Government of the United States, and shall examine and decide upon them in such order and manner as they may think proper, but upon such evidence or information only as shall be furnished by or on behalf of the Governments of the United States and of Great Britain, respectively. They shall be bound to hear on each separate claim, if required, one person on behalf of each Government, as counsel or agent. A majority of the assessors in each case shall be sufficient for a decision.

The decision of the assessors shall be given upon each claim in writing, and shall be signed by them respectively and dated.

Every claim shall be presented to the assessors within six months from the day of their first meeting, but they may, for good cause shown, extend the time for the presentation of any claim to a further period not exceeding three months.

The assessors shall report to each Government at or before the expiration of one year from the date of their first meeting the amount of claims decided by them up to the date of such report. If further claims then remain undecided, they shall make a further report at or before the expiration of two years from the date of such first meeting, and in case any claims remain undetermined at that time they shall make a final report within a further period of six months.

The report or reports shall be made in duplicate, and one copy thereof shall be delivered to the Secretary of State of the United States, and one copy thereof to the representative of her Britannic Majesty at Washington.

All sums of money which may be awarded under this article shall be payable at Washington, in coin, within twelve months after the delivery of each report.

The board of assessors may employ such clerks as they shall think necessary.

The expenses of the board of assessors shall be borne equally by the two Governments, and paid from time to time, as may be found expedient, on the production of accounts certified by the board. The remuneration of the assessors shall also be paid by the two Governments in equal moieties in a similar manner.

ARTICLE XI.

The high contracting parties engage to consider the result of the proceedings of the tribunal of arbitration and of the board of assessors, should such board be appointed, as a full, perfect, and final settlement of all the claims hereinbefore referred to; and further engage that every such claim, whether the same may or may not have been presented to the notice of, made, preferred, or laid before the tribunal or board shall, from and after the conclusion of the proceedings of the tribunal or board, be considered and treated as finally settled, barred, and thenceforth inadmissible.

ARTICLE XII.

The high contracting parties agree that all claims on the part of corporations, companies, or private individuals, citizens of the United States, upon the Government of her Britannic Majesty, arising out of acts committed against the persons or property of citizens of the United

States during the period between the 13th of April, 1861, and the 9th of April, 1865, inclusive, not being claims growing out of the acts of the vessels referred to in Article I of this treaty; and all claims, with the like exception, on the part of corporations, companies, or private individuals, subjects of her Britannic Majesty, upon the Government of the United States, arising out of acts committed against the persons or property of subjects of her Britannic Majesty during the same period which may have been presented to either Government for its interposition with the other, and which yet remain unsettled, as well as any other such claims which may be presented within the time specified in Article XIV of this treaty, shall be referred to three commissioners, to be appointed in the following manner, that is to say: one commissioner shall be named by the President of the United States, one by her Britannic Majesty, and a third by the President of the United States and her Britannic Majesty conjointly; and in case the third commissioner shall not have been so named within a period of three months from the date of the exchange of the ratifications of this treaty, then the third commissioner shall be named by the representative at Washington of his Majesty the King of Spain. In case of the death, absence, or incapacity of any commissioner, or in the event of any commissioner omitting or ceasing to act, the vacancy shall be filled in the manner hereinbefore provided for making the original appointment; the period of three months in case of such substitution being calculated from the date of the happening of the vacancy.

The commissioners so named shall meet at Washington at the earliest convenient period after they have been respectively named; and shall, before proceeding to any business, make and subscribe a solemn declaration that they will impartially and carefully examine and decide, to the best of their judgment and according to justice and equity, all such claims as shall be laid before them on the part of the Governments of the United States and of her Britannic Majesty, respectively; and such declaration shall be entered on the record of their proceedings.

ARTICLE XIII.

The commissioners shall then forthwith proceed to the investigation of the claims which shall be presented to them. They shall investigate and decide such claims in such order and such manner as they may think proper, but upon such evidence or information only as shall be furnished by or on behalf of the respective Governments. They shall be bound to receive and consider all written documents or statements which may be presented to them by or on behalf of the respective Governments in support of or in answer to any claim, and to hear, if required, one person on each side, on behalf of each Government, as counsel or agent for such Government, on each and every separate claim. A majority of the commissioners shall be sufficient for an award in each case. The award shall be given upon each claim in writing, and shall be signed by the commissioners assenting to it. It shall be competent for each Government to name one person to attend the commissioners as its agent, to present and support claims on its behalf, and to answer claims made upon it, and to represent it generally in all matters connected with the investigation and decision thereof.

The high contracting parties hereby engage to consider the decision of the commissioners as absolutely final and conclusive upon each claim decided upon by them, and to give full effect to such decisions without any objection, evasion, or delay whatsoever.

ARTICLE XIV.

Every claim shall be presented to the commissioners within six months from the day of their first meeting, unless in any case where reasons for delay shall be established to the satisfaction of the commissioners, and then, and in any such case, the period for presenting the claim may be extended by them to any time not exceeding three months longer.

The commissioners shall be bound to examine and decide upon every claim within two years from the day of their first meeting. It shall be competent for the commissioners to decide in each case whether any claim has or has not been duly made, preferred, and laid before them, either wholly or to any and what extent, according to the true intent and meaning of this treaty.

ARTICLE XV.

All sums of money which may be awarded by the commissioners on account of any claim shall be paid by the one Government to the other, as the case may be, within twelve months after the date of the final award, without interest, and without any deduction, save as specified in Article XVI of this treaty.

ARTICLE XVI.

The commissioners shall keep an accurate record, and correct minutes or notes of all their proceedings, with the dates thereof, and may appoint or employ a secretary, and any other necessary officer or officers to assist them in the transaction of the business which may come before them.

Each Government shall pay its own commissioner and agent or counsel. All other expenses shall be defrayed by the two Governments in equal moieties.

The whole expenses of the commission, including contingent expenses, shall be defrayed by a ratable deduction on the amount of the sums awarded by the commissioners, provided always that such deduction shall not exceed the rate of five per cent. on the sums so awarded.

ARTICLE XVII.

The high contracting parties engage to consider the result of the proceedings of this commission as a full, perfect, and final settlement of all such claims as are mentioned in Article XII of this treaty upon either Government; and further engage that every such claim, whether or not the same may have been presented to the notice of, made, preferred, or laid before the said commission, shall, from and after the conclusion of the proceedings of the said commission, be considered and treated as finally settled, barred, and thenceforth inadmissible.

ARTICLE XVIII.

It is agreed by the high contracting parties that in addition to the liberty secured to the United States fishermen by the convention between the United States and Great Britain, signed at London on the 20th day of October, 1818, of taking, curing, and drying fish on certain coasts of the British North American colonies therein defined, the inhabitants of the United States shall have, in common with the subjects of her Britannic Majesty, the liberty, for the term of years mentioned in Article XXXIII of this treaty, to take fish of every kind, except shell fish, on the sea-coasts and shores, and in the bays, harbors, and creeks of the provinces of Quebec, Nova Scotia, and New Brunswick, and the colony of Prince Edward's Island, and of the several islands thereunto adjacent, without being restricted to any distance from the shore, with permission to land upon the said coasts and shores and islands, and also upon the Magdalen Islands, for the purpose of drying their nets and curing their fish; provided that in so doing they do not interfere with the rights of private property, or with British fishermen in the peaceable use of any part of the said coasts in their occupancy for the same purpose.

It is understood that the above-mentioned liberty applies solely to the sea fishery, and that the salmon and shad fisheries, and all other fisheries in rivers and the mouth of rivers, are hereby reserved exclusively for British fishermen.

ARTICLE XIX.

It is agreed by the high contracting parties that British subjects shall have, in common with the citizens of the United States, the liberty, for the term of years mentioned in Article XXXIII of this treaty, to take fish of every kind, except shell-fish, on the eastern sea-coasts and shores of the United States north of the thirty-ninth parallel of north latitude, and on the shores of the several islands thereunto adjacent, and in the bays, harbors, and creeks of the said sea-coasts and shores of the United States and of the said islands, without being restricted to any distance from the shore, with permission to land upon the said coasts of the United States and of the islands aforesaid, for the purpose of drying their nets and curing their fish; provided that, in so doing, they do not interfere with the rights of private property, or with the fishermen of the United States in the peaceable use of any part of the said coasts in their occupancy for the same purpose.

It is understood that the above-mentioned liberty applies solely to the sea fishery, and that salmon and shad fisheries, and all other fisheries in rivers and mouth of rivers, are hereby reserved exclusively for fishermen of the United States.

ARTICLE XX.

It is agreed that the places designated by the commissioners appointed under the first article of the treaty between the United States and Great Britain, concluded at Washington on the 5th of June, 1854, upon the coasts of her Britannic Majesty's dominions and the United States, as places reserved from the common right of fishing under that treaty, shall be regarded as in like manner reserved from the common right of fishing under the preceding articles. In case any question should arise between the Governments of the United States and of her Britannic Majesty as to the common right of fishing in places not thus designated as reserved, it is agreed that a commission shall be appointed to designate such places, and shall be constituted in the same manner and have the same powers, duties, and authority as the commission appointed under the said first article of the treaty of the 5th of June, 1854.

ARTICLE XXI.

It is agreed that, for the term of years mentioned in Article XXXIII of this treaty, fish oil and fish of all kinds, (except fish of the inland lakes, and of the rivers falling into them, and except fish preserved in oil,) being the produce of the fisheries of the United States, or of the Dominion of Canada, or of Prince Edward's Island, shall be admitted into each country, respectively, free of duty.

ARTICLE XXII.

Inasmuch as it is asserted by the Government of her Britannic Majesty that the privileges accorded to the citizens of the United States under Article XVIII of this treaty are of greater value than those accorded by Articles XIX and XXI of this treaty to the subjects of her Britannic Majesty, and this assertion is not admitted by the Government of the United States, it is further agreed that commissioners shall be appointed to determine, having regard to the privileges accorded by the United States to the subjects of her Britannic Majesty, as stated in Articles XIX and XXI of this treaty, the amount of any compensation which, in their opinion, ought to be paid by the Government of the United States to the Government of her Britannic Majesty in return for the privileges accorded to the citizens of the United States under Article XVIII of this treaty; and that any sum of money which the said commissioners may so award shall be paid by the United States Government, in a gross sum, within twelve months after such award shall have been given.

ARTICLE XXIII.

The commissioners referred to in the preceding article shall be appointed in the following manner, that is to say: one commissioner shall be named by the President of the United States, one by her Britannic Majesty, and a third by the President of the United States and her Britannic Majesty conjointly, and in case the third commissioner shall not have been so named within a period of three months from the date when this article shall take effect, then the third commissioner shall be named by the representative at London of his Majesty the Emperor of Austria and King of Hungary. In case of the death, absence, or incapacity of any commissioner, or in the event of any commissioner omitting or ceasing to act, the vacancy shall be filled in the manner hereinbefore provided for making the original appointment, the period of three months in case of such substitution being calculated from the date of the happening of the vacancy.

The commissioners so named shall meet in the city of Halifax, in the province of Nova Scotia, at the earliest convenient period after they have been respectively named, and shall, before proceeding to any business, make and subscribe a solemn declaration that they will impartially and carefully examine the matters referred to them to the best of their judgment, and according to justice and equity; and such declaration shall be entered on the record of their proceedings.

Each of the high contracting parties shall also name one person to attend the commission as its agent, to represent it generally in all matters connected with the commission.

ARTICLE XXIV.

The proceedings shall be conducted in such order as the commissioners appointed under Articles XXII and XXIII of this treaty shall determine. They shall be bound to receive such oral or written testimony as either Government may present. If either party shall offer oral testimony, the other party shall have the right of cross-examination, under such rules as the commissioners shall prescribe.

If in the case submitted to the commissioners either party shall have specified or alluded to any report or document in its own exclusive possession, without annexing a copy, such party shall be bound, if the other party thinks proper to apply for it, to furnish that party with a copy thereof; and either party may call upon the other, through the commissioners, to produce the originals or certified copies of any papers adduced as evidence, giving in each instance such reasonable notice as the commissioners may require.

The case on either side shall be closed within a period of six months from the date of the organization of the commission, and the commissioners shall be requested to give their award as soon as possible thereafter. The aforesaid period of six months may be extended for three months in case of a vacancy occurring among the commissioners under the circumstances contemplated in Article XXIII of this treaty.

ARTICLE XXV.

The commissioners shall keep an accurate record and correct minutes or notes of all their proceedings, with the dates thereof, and may appoint and employ a secretary and any other necessary officer or officers to assist them in the transaction of the business which may come before them.

Each of the high contracting parties shall pay its own commissioner and agent or counsel; all other expenses shall be defrayed by the two Governments in equal moieties.

ARTICLE XXVI.

The navigation of the river St. Lawrence, ascending and descending, from the forty-fifth parallel of north latitude, where it ceases to form the boundary between the two countries, from, to, and into the sea, shall forever remain free and open for the purposes of commerce to the citizens of the United States, subject to any laws and regulations of Great Britain, or of the Dominion of Canada, not inconsistent with such privilege of free navigation.

The navigation of the rivers Yukon, Porcupine, and Stikine, ascending and descending, from, to, and into the sea, shall forever remain free and open for the purposes of commerce to the subjects of her Britannic Majesty and to the citizens of the United States, subject to any laws and regulations of either country within its own territory, not inconsistent with such privilege of free navigation.

ARTICLE XXVII.

The Government of her Britannic Majesty engages to urge upon the Government of the Dominion of Canada to secure to the citizens of the United States the use of the Welland, St. Lawrence, and other canals in the Dominion on terms of equality with the inhabitants of the Dominion; and the Government of the United States engages that the subjects of her Britannic Majesty shall enjoy the use of the St. Clair Flats canal on terms of equality with the inhabitants of the United States, and further engages to urge upon the State governments to secure to the subjects of her Britannic Majesty the use of the several State canals connected with the navigation of the lakes or rivers traversed by or contiguous to the boundary line between the possessions of the high contracting parties, on terms of equality with the inhabitants of the United States.

ARTICLE XXVIII.

The navigation of Lake Michigan shall also, for the term of years mentioned in Article XXXIII of this treaty, be free and open for the purposes of commerce to the subjects of her Britannic Majesty, subject to any laws and regulations of the United States or of the States bordering thereon, not inconsistent with such privilege of free navigation.

ARTICLE XXIX.

It is agreed that, for the term of years mentioned in Article XXXIII of this treaty, goods, wares, or merchandise arriving at the ports of New York, Boston, and Portland, and any other ports in the United States which have been or may, from time to time, be specially designated by the President of the United States, and destined for her Britannic Majesty's possessions in North America, may be entered at the proper custom-house and conveyed in transit, without the payment of duties, through the territory of the United States, under such rules, regulations, and conditions for the protection of the revenue as the Government of the United States may, from time to time, prescribe; and under like rules, regulations, and conditions, goods, wares, or merchandise may be conveyed in transit, without the payment of duties, from such possessions through the territory of the United States for export from the said ports of the United States.

It is further agreed that, for the like period, goods, wares, or merchandise arriving at any of the ports of her Britannic Majesty's possessions in North America, and destined for the United States, may be entered at the proper custom-house and conveyed in transit, without the payment of duties, through the said possessions, under such rules and regulations and conditions for the protection of the revenue as the Governments of the said possessions may, from time to time, prescribe; and, under like rules, regulations, and conditions, goods, wares, or merchandise may be conveyed in transit, without payment of duties, from the United States through the said possessions to other places in the United States, or for export from ports in the said possessions.

ARTICLE XXX.

It is agreed that, for the term of years mentioned in Article XXXIII of this treaty, subjects of her Britannic Majesty may carry in British vessels, without payment of duty, goods, wares, or merchandise from one port or place within the territory of the United States upon the St. Lawrence, the great lakes, and the rivers connecting the same, to another port or place within the territory of the United States as aforesaid; provided, that a portion of such transportation is made through the Dominion of Canada by land carriage and in bond, under such rules and regulations as may be agreed upon between the Government of her Britannic Majesty and the Government of the United States.

Citizens of the United States may, for the like period, carry in United States vessels, without payment of duty, goods, wares, or merchandise from one port or place within the possessions of her Britannic Majesty in North America to another port or place within the said possessions; provided, that a portion of such transportation is made through the territory of the United States by land carriage and in bond, under such rules and regulations as may be agreed upon between the Government of the United States and the Government of her Britannic Majesty.

The Government of the United States further engages not to impose any export duties on goods, wares, or merchandise carried under this article through the territory of the United States; and her Majesty's Government engages to urge the Parliament of the Dominion of Canada and the legislatures of the other colonies not to impose any export duties on goods, wares, or merchandise carried under this article; and the Government of the United States may, in case such export duties are imposed by the Dominion of Canada, suspend, during the period that such duties are imposed, the right of carrying granted under this article in favor of the subjects of her Britannic Majesty.

The Government of the United States may suspend the right of carrying granted in favor of the subjects of her Britannic Majesty, under this article, in case the Dominion of Canada should at any time deprive the citizens of the United States of the use of the canals in the said Dominion on terms of equality with the inhabitants of the Dominion, as provided in Article XXVII.

ARTICLE XXXI.

The Government of her Britannic Majesty further engages to urge upon the Parliament of the Dominion of Canada and the Legislature of New Brunswick that no export duty, or other duty, shall be levied on lumber or timber of any kind cut on that portion of the American territory in the State of Maine watered by the river St. John and its tributaries, and floated down that river to the sea, when the same is shipped to the United States from the province of New Brunswick. And in case any such export or other duty continues to be levied after the expiration of one year from the date of the exchange of the ratifications of this treaty, it is agreed that the Government of the United States may suspend the right of carrying hereinbefore granted under Article XXX of this treaty for such period as such export or other duty may be levied.

ARTICLE XXXII.

It is further agreed that the provisions and stipulations of Articles XVIII to XXV of this treaty, inclusive, shall extend to the colony of Newfoundland, so far as they are applicable. But if the Imperial Parliament, the Legislature of Newfoundland, or the Congress of the United States, shall not embrace the colony of Newfoundland in their laws enacted for carrying the foregoing articles into effect, then this article shall be of no effect; but the omission to make provision by law to give it effect, by either of the legislative bodies aforesaid, shall not in any way impair any other articles of this treaty.

ARTICLE XXXIII.

The foregoing Articles XVIII to XXV inclusive, and Article XXX of this treaty, shall take effect as soon as the laws required to carry them into operation shall have been passed by the Imperial Parliament of Great Britain, by the Parliament of Canada, and by the Legislature of Prince Edward's Island on the one hand, and by the Congress of the United States on the other. Such assent having been given, the said articles shall remain in force for the period of ten years from the date at which they may come into operation; and further, until the expiration of two years after either of the high contracting parties shall have given notice to the other of its wish to terminate the same, each of the high contracting parties being at liberty to give such notice to the other at the end of the said period of ten years, or at any time afterward.

ARTICLE XXXIV.

Whereas it was stipulated by Article I of the treaty concluded at Washington on the 15th of June, 1846, between the United States and her Britannic Majesty, that the line of boundary between the territories of the United States and those of her Britannic Majesty, from the point on the forty-ninth parallel of north latitude up to which it had already been ascertained, should be continued westward along the said parallel of north latitude "to the middle of the channel which separates the continent from Vancouver's Island, and thence southerly, through the middle of the said channel and of Fuca straits, to the Pacific ocean;" and whereas the commissioners appointed by the two high contracting parties to determine that portion of the boundary which runs southerly through the middle of the channel aforesaid were unable to agree upon the same; and whereas the Government of her Britannic Majesty claims that such boundary line should, under the terms of the treaty above recited, be run through the Rosario straits, and the Government of the United States claims that it should be run through the Canal de Haro, it is agreed that the respective claims of the Government of the United States and of the Government of her Britannic Majesty shall be submitted to the arbitration and award of his Majesty the Emperor of Germany, who, having regard to the above-mentioned article of the said treaty, shall decide thereupon, finally and without appeal, which of those claims is most in accordance with the true interpretation of the treaty of June 15, 1846.

ARTICLE XXXV.

The award of his Majesty the Emperor of Germany shall be considered as absolutely final and conclusive; and full effect shall be given to such award without any objection, evasion, or delay whatsoever. Such decision shall be given in writing and dated; it shall be in whatsoever form his Majesty may choose to adopt; it shall be delivered to the representatives or other public agents of the United States and of Great Britain, respectively, who may be actually at Berlin, and shall be considered as operative from the day of the date of the delivery thereof.

ARTICLE XXXVI.

The written or printed case of each of the two parties, accompanied by the evidence offered in support of the same, shall be laid before his Majesty the Emperor of Germany within six months from the date of the exchange of the ratifications of this treaty, and a copy of such case and evidence shall be communicated by each party to the other, through their respective representatives at Berlin.

The high contracting parties may include in the evidence to be considered by the arbitrator such documents, official correspondence, and other official or public statements bearing on the subject of the reference as they may consider necessary to the support of their respective cases.

After the written or printed case shall have been communicated by each party to the other, each party shall have the power of drawing up and laying before the arbitrator a second and definite statement, if it think fit to do so, in reply to the case of the other party so communicated, which definite statement shall be so laid before the arbitrator, and also be mutually communicated in the same manner as aforesaid, by each party to the other, within six months from the date of laying the first statement of the case before the arbitrator.

ARTICLE XXXVII.

If, in the case submitted to the arbitrator, either party shall specify or allude to any report or document in its own exclusive possession without annexing a copy, such party shall be bound, if the other party thinks proper to apply for it, to furnish that party with a copy thereof, and either party may call upon the other, through the arbitrator, to produce the originals or certified copies of any papers adduced as evidence, giving in each instance such reasonable notice as the arbitrator may require. And if the arbitrator should desire further elucidation or evidence with regard to any point contained in the statements laid before him, he shall be at liberty to require it from either party, and he shall be at liberty to hear one counsel or agent for each party, in relation to any matter, and at such time and in such manner as he may think fit.

ARTICLE XXXVIII.

The representatives or other public agents of the United States and of Great Britain at Berlin, respectively, shall be considered as the agents of their respective Governments to conduct their cases before the arbitrator, who shall be requested to address all his communications and give all his notices to such representatives or other public agents who shall represent their respective Governments, generally, in all matters connected with the arbitration.

ARTICLE XXXIX.

It shall be competent to the arbitrator to proceed in the said arbitration, and all matters relating thereto, as and when he shall see fit, either in person, or by a person or persons named by him for that purpose, either in the presence or absence of either or both agents, and either orally or by written discussion or otherwise.

ARTICLE XL.

The arbitrator may, if he think fit, appoint a secretary, or clerk, for the purposes of the proposed arbitration, at such rate of remuneration as he shall think proper. This, and all other expenses of and connected with the said arbitration, shall be provided for as hereinafter stipulated.

ARTICLE XLI.

The arbitrator shall be requested to deliver, together with his award, an account of all the costs and expenses which he may have been put to in relation to this matter, which shall forthwith be repaid by the two Governments in equal moieties.

ARTICLE XLII.

The arbitrator shall be requested to give his award in writing as early as convenient after the whole case on each side shall have been laid before him, and to deliver one copy thereof to each of the said agents.

ARTICLE XLIII.

The present treaty shall be duly ratified by the President of the United States of America, by and with the advice and consent of the Senate thereof, and by her Britannic Majesty; and the ratifications shall be exchanged either at Washington or at London within six months from the date hereof, or earlier if possible.

In faith whereof, we, the respective plenipotentiaries, have signed this treaty and have hereunto affixed our seals.

Done in duplicate at Washington the 8th day of May, in the year of our Lord 1871.

[L. S.] HAMILTON FISH.
[L. S.] ROBERT C. SCHENCK.
[L. S.] SAMUEL NELSON.
[L. S.] EBENEZER ROCKWOOD HOAR.
[L. S.] GEORGE H. WILLIAMS.
[L. S.] DE GREY & RIPON.
[L. S.] STAFFORD H. NORTHCOTE.
[L. S.] EDWARD THORNTON.
[L. S.] JOHN A. MACDONALD.
[L. S.] MOUNTAGUE BERNARD.

And whereas the said treaty has been duly ratified on both parts, and the respective ratifications of the same were exchanged in the city of London, on the 17th day of June, 1871, by Robert C. Schenck, envoy extraordinary and minister plenipotentiary of the United States, and

Earl Granville, her Majesty's principal Secretary of State for Foreign Affairs, on the part of their respective Governments:

Now, therefore, be it known that I, Ulysses S. Grant, President of the United States of America, have caused the said treaty to be made public, to the end that the same, and every clause and article thereof, may be observed and fulfilled with good faith by the United States and the citizens thereof.

In witness whereof, I have hereunto set my hand and caused the seal of the United States to be affixed.

Done at the city of Washington this 4th day of July, in the year of our Lord 1871, and of the Independence of the United States the ninety-sixth.

[SEAL.]

U. S. GRANT.

By the President:

HAMILTON FISH,
Secretary of State.

Arbitrator on the part of the United States—CHARLES FRANCIS ADAMS.

Arbitrator on the part of Great Britain—The Right Honorable Sir ALEXANDER COCKBURN, Baronet, Lord Chief Justice of England.

Arbitrator on the part of Italy—His Excellency Senator Count SCLOPIS.

Arbitrator on the part of Switzerland—Mr. JACOB STAMPFLI.

Arbitrator on the part of Brazil—Baron D'ITAJUBA.

Agent on the part of the United States—J. C. BANCROFT DAVIS.

Agent on the part of Great Britain—Right Honorable LORD TENTERDEN.

Counsel for the United States—CALEB CUSHING, WILLIAM M. EVARTS, MORRISON R. WAITE.

Counsel for Great Britain—Sir ROUNDELL PALMER.

Solicitor for the United States—CHARLES C. BEAMAN, Jr

ENFORCEMENT ACT.

An Act to enforce the right of citizens of the United States to vote in the several States of this Union, and for other purposes.

Be it enacted by the Senate and House of Representatives of the United States of America in Congress assembled, That all citizens of the United States who are or shall be otherwise qualified by law to vote at any election by the people in any State, Territory, district, county, city, parish, township, school district, municipality, or other territorial subdivision, shall be entitled and allowed to vote at all such elections, without distinction of race, color, or previous condition of servitude; any constitution, law, custom, usage, or regulation of any State or Territory, or by or under its authority, to the contrary notwithstanding.

Sec. 2. *And be it further enacted,* That if by or under the authority of the constitution or laws of any State, or the laws of any Territory, any act is or shall be required to be done as a prerequisite or qualification for voting, and by such constitution or laws persons or officers are or shall be charged with the performance of duties in furnishing to citizens an opportunity to perform such prerequisite, or to become qualified to vote, it shall be the duty of every such person and officer to give to all citizens of the United States the same and equal opportunity to perform such prerequisite, and to become qualified to vote without distinction of race, color, or previous condition of servitude; and if any such person or officer shall refuse or knowingly omit to give full effect to this section, he shall, for every such offense, forfeit and pay the sum of five hundred dollars to the person aggrieved thereby, to be recovered by an action on the case, with full costs and such allowance for counsel fees as the court shall deem just, and shall also, for every such offense, be deemed guilty of a misdemeanor, and shall, on conviction thereof, be fined not less than five hundred dollars, or be imprisoned not less than one month and not more than one year, or both, at the discretion of the court.

SEC. 3. *And be it further enacted,* That whenever, by or under the authority of the constitution or laws of any State, or the laws of any Territory, any act is or shall be required to [be] done by any citizen as a prerequisite to qualify or entitle him to vote, the offer of any such citizen to perform the act required to be done as aforesaid shall, if it fail to be carried into execution by reason of the wrongful act or omission aforesaid of the person or officer charged with the duty of receiving or permitting such performance or offer to perform or acting thereon, be deemed and held as a performance in law of such act; and the person so offering and failing as aforesaid, and being otherwise qualified, shall be entitled to vote in the same manner, and to the same extent, as if he had in fact performed such act; and any judge, inspector, or other officer of election whose duty it is or shall be to receive, count, certify, register, report, or give effect to the vote of any such citizen who shall wrongfully refuse or omit to receive, count, certify, register, report, or give effect to the vote of such citizen upon the presentation by him of his affidavit stating such offer and the time and place thereof, and the name of the officer or person whose duty it was to act thereon, and that he was wrongfully prevented by such person or officer from performing such act, shall for every such offense forfeit and pay the sum of five hundred dollars to the person aggrieved thereby, to be recovered by an action on the case, with full costs and such allowance for counsel fees as the court shall deem just, and shall also for every such offense be guilty of a misdemeanor, and shall, on conviction thereof, be fined not less than five hundred dollars, or be imprisoned not less than one month and not more than one year, or both, at the discretion of the court.

SEC. 4. *And be it further enacted,* That if any person, by force, bribery, threats, intimidation, or other unlawful means, shall hinder, delay, prevent, or obstruct, or shall combine and confederate with others to hinder, delay, prevent, or obstruct, any citizen from doing any act required to be done to qualify him to vote or from voting at any election as aforesaid, such person shall for every such offense forfeit and pay the sum of five hundred dollars to the person aggrieved thereby, to be recovered by an action on the case, with full costs and such allowance for counsel fees as the court shall deem just, and shall also for every such offense be guilty of a misdemeanor, and shall, on conviction thereof, be fined not less than five hundred dollars, or be imprisoned not less than one month and not more than one year, or both, at the discretion of the court.

SEC. 5. *And be it further enacted,* That if any person shall prevent, hinder, control, or intimidate, or shall attempt to prevent, hinder, control, or intimidate, any person from exercising or in exercising the right of suffrage, to whom the right of suffrage is secured or guaranteed by the fifteenth amendment to the Constitution of the United States, by means of bribery, threats, or threats of depriving such person of employment or occupation, or of ejecting such person from rented house, lands, or other property, or by threats of refusing to renew leases or contracts for labor, or by threats of violence to himself or family, such person so offending shall be deemed guilty of a misdemeanor, and shall, on conviction thereof, be fined not less than five hundred dollars, or be imprisoned not less than one month, and not more than one year, or both, at the discretion of the court.

SEC. 6. *And be it further enacted,* That if two or more persons shall band or conspire together, or go in disguise upon the public highway, or upon the premises of another, with intent to violate any provision of this act, or to injure, oppress, threaten, or intimidate any citizen with intent to prevent or hinder his free exercise and enjoyment of any right or privilege granted or secured to him by the Constitution or laws of the United States, or because of his having exercised the same, such persons shall be held guilty of felony, and, on conviction thereof, shall be fined or imprisoned, or both, at the discretion of the court—the fine not to exceed five thousand dollars, and the imprisonment not to exceed ten years—and shall, moreover, be thereafter ineligible to, and disabled from holding, any office or place of honor, profit, or trust created by the Constitution or laws of the United States.

SEC. 7. *And be it further enacted*, That if in the act of violating any provision in either of the two preceding sections, any other felony, crime, or misdemeanor shall be committed, the offender, on conviction of such violation of said sections, shall be punished for the same with such punishments as are attached to the said felonies, crimes, and misdemeanors by the laws of the State in which the offense may be committed.

SEC. 8. *And be it further enacted*, That the district courts of the United States, within their respective districts, shall have, exclusively of the courts of the several States, cognizance of all crimes and offenses committed against the provisions of this act, and also, concurrently with the circuit courts of the United States, of all causes, civil and criminal, arising under this act, except as herein otherwise provided, and the jurisdiction hereby conferred shall be exercised in conformity with the laws and practice governing United States courts; and all crimes and offenses committed against the provisions of this act may be prosecuted by the indictment of a grand jury, or, in cases of crimes and offenses not infamous, the prosecution may be either by indictment or information filed by the district attorney in a court having jurisdiction.

SEC. 9. *And be it further enacted*, That the district attorneys, marshals, and deputy marshals of the United States, the commissioners appointed by the circuit and territorial courts of the United States, with powers of arresting, imprisoning, or bailing offenders against the laws of the United States, and every other officer who may be specially empowered by the President of the United States, shall be, and they are hereby, specially authorized and required, at the expense of the United States, to institute proceedings against all and every person who shall violate the provisions of this act, and cause him or them to be arrested and imprisoned, or bailed, as the case may be, for trial before such court of the United States or territorial court as has cognizance of the offense. And with a view to afford reasonable protection to all persons in their constitutional right to vote without distinction of race, color, or previous condition of servitude, and to the prompt discharge of the duties of this act, it shall be the duty of the circuit courts of the United States, and the superior courts of the Territories of the United States, from time to time, to increase the number of commissioners, so as to afford a speedy and convenient means for the arrest and examination of persons charged with a violation of this act; and such commissioners are hereby authorized and required to exercise and discharge all the powers and duties conferred on them by this act, and the same duties with regard to offenses created by this act as they are authorized by law to exercise with regard to other offenses against the laws of the United States.

SEC. 10. *And be it further enacted*, That it shall be the duty of all marshals and deputy marshals to obey and execute all warrants and precepts issued under the provisions of this act, when to them directed; and should any marshal or deputy marshal refuse to receive such warrant or other process when tendered, or to use all proper means diligently to execute the same, he shall, on conviction thereof, be fined in the sum of one thousand dollars, to the use of the person deprived of the rights conferred by this act. And the better to enable the said commissioners to execute their duties faithfully and efficiently, in conformity with the Constitution of the United States and the requirements of this act, they are hereby authorized and empowered, within their districts respectively, to appoint, in writing, under their hands, any one or more suitable persons, from time to time, to execute all such warrants and other process as may be issued by them in the lawful performance of their respective duties, and the persons so appointed to execute any warrant or process as aforesaid shall have authority to summon and call to their aid the bystanders or posse comitatus of the proper county, or such portion of the land or naval forces of the United States, or of the militia, as may be necessary to the performance of the duty with which they are charged, and to insure a faithful observance of the fifteenth amendment to the Constitution of the

United States; and such warrants shall run and be executed by said officers anywhere in the State or Territory within which they are issued.

SEC. 11. *And be it further enacted,* That any person who shall knowingly and willfully obstruct, hinder, or prevent any officer or other person charged with the execution of any warrant or process issued under the provisions of this act, or any person or persons lawfully assisting him or them from arresting any person for whose apprehension such warrant or process may have been issued, or shall rescue or attempt to rescue such person from the custody of the officer or other person or persons, or those lawfully assisting as aforesaid, when so arrested pursuant to the authority herein given and declared, or shall aid, abet, or assist any person so arrested as aforesaid, directly or indirectly, to escape from the custody of the officer or other person legally authorized as aforesaid, or shall harbor or conceal any person for whose arrest a warrant or process shall have been issued as aforesaid, so as to prevent his discovery and arrest after notice or knowledge of the fact that a warrant has been issued for the apprehension of such person, shall, for either of said offenses, be subject to a fine not exceeding one thousand dollars, or imprisonment not exceeding six months, or both, at the discretion of the court, on conviction before the district or circuit court of the United States for the district or circuit in which said offense may have been committed, or before the proper court of criminal jurisdiction, if committed within any one of the organized Territories of the United States.

SEC. 12. *And be it further enacted,* That the commissioners, district attorneys, the marshals, their deputies, and the clerks of the said district, circuit, and territorial courts shall be paid for their services the like fees as may be allowed to them for similar services in other cases. The person or persons authorized to execute the process to be issued by such commissioners for the arrest of offenders against the provisions of this act shall be entitled to the usual fees allowed to the marshal for an arrest for each person he or they may arrest and take before any such commissioner as aforesaid, with such other fees as may be deemed reasonable by such commissioner for such other additional services as may be necessarily performed by him or them, such as attending at the examination, keeping the prisoner in custody, and providing him with food and lodging during his detention and until the final determination of such commissioner, and in general for performing such other duties as may be required in the premises; such fees to be made up in conformity with the fees usually charged by the officers of the courts of justice within the proper district or county as near as may be practicable, and paid out of the treasury of the United States on the certificate of the judge of the district within which the arrest is made, and to be recoverable from the defendant as part of the judgment in case of conviction.

SEC. 13. *And be it further enacted,* That it shall be lawful for the President of the United States to employ such part of the land or naval forces of the United States, or of the militia, as shall be necessary to aid in the execution of judicial process issued under this act.

SEC. 14. *And be it further enacted,* That whenever any person shall hold office, except as a member of Congress or of some State legislature, contrary to the provisions of the third section of the fourteenth article of amendment of the Constitution of the United States, it shall be the duty of the district attorney of the United States for the district in which such person shall hold office, as aforesaid, to proceed against such person, by writ of quo warranto, returnable to the circuit or district court of the United States in such district, and to prosecute the same to the removal of such person from office; and any writ of quo warranto so brought, as aforesaid, shall take precedence of all other cases on the docket of the court to which it is made returnable, and shall not be continued unless for cause proved to the satisfaction of the court.

SEC. 15. *And be it further enacted,* That any person who shall hereafter knowingly accept or hold any office under the United States, or any State to which he is ineligible under the third section of the fourteenth article of amendment of the Constitution of the United States, or who shall attempt to hold or exercise the duties of any such office, shall be deemed guilty of a misdemeanor against the United States, and upon conviction thereof before the circuit or district court of the United States, shall be imprisoned not more than one year, or fined not exceeding one thousand dollars, or both, at the discretion of the court.

SEC. 16. *And be it further enacted,* That all persons within the jurisdiction of the United States shall have the same right in every State and Territory in the United States to make and enforce contracts, to sue, be parties, give evidence, and to the full and equal benefit of all laws and proceedings for the security of person and property as is enjoyed by white citizens, and shall be subject to like punishment, pains, penalties, taxes, licenses, and exactions of every kind, and none other, any law, statute, ordinance, regulation, or custom to the contrary notwithstanding. No tax or charge shall be imposed or enforced by any State upon any person immigrating thereto from a foreign country which is not equally imposed and enforced upon every person immigrating to such State from any other foreign country; and any law of any State in conflict with this provision is hereby declared null and void.

SEC. 17. *And be it further enacted,* That any person who, under color of any law, statute, ordinance, regulation, or custom, shall subject, or cause to be subjected, any inhabitant of any State or Territory to the deprivation of any right secured or protected by the last preceding section of this act, or to different punishment, pains, or penalties on account of such person being an alien, or by reason of his color or race, than is prescribed for the punishment of citizens, shall be deemed guilty of a misdemeanor, and, on conviction, shall be punished by fine not exceeding one thousand dollars, or imprisonment not exceeding one year, or both, at the discretion of the court.

SEC. 18. *And be it further enacted,* That the act to protect all persons in the United States in their civil rights, and furnish the means of their vindication, passed April nine, eighteen hundred and sixty-six, is hereby re-enacted; and sections sixteen and seventeen hereof shall be enforced according to the provisions of said act.

SEC. 19. *And be it further enacted,* That if at any election for representative or delegate in the Congress of the United States any person shall knowingly personate and vote, or attempt to vote, in the name of any other person, whether living, dead, or fictitious; or vote more than once at the same election for any candidate for the same office; or vote at a place where he may not be lawfully entitled to vote; or vote without having a lawful right to vote; or do any unlawful act to secure a right or an opportunity to vote for himself or any other person; or by force, threat, menace, intimidation, bribery, reward, or offer, or promise thereof, or otherwise unlawfully prevent any qualified voter of any State of the United States of America, or of any Territory thereof, from freely exercising the right of suffrage, or by any such means induce any voter to refuse to exercise such right; or compel or induce by any such means, or otherwise, any officer of an election in any such State or Territory to receive a vote from a person not legally qualified or entitled to vote; or interfere in any manner with any officer of said elections in the discharge of his duties; or by any of such means, or other unlawful means, induce any officer of an election, or officer whose duty it is to ascertain, announce, or declare the result of any such election, or give or make any certificate, document, or evidence in relation thereto, to violate or refuse to comply with his duty, or any law regulating the same; or knowingly and willfully receive the vote of any person not entitled to vote, or refuse to receive the vote of any person entitled to vote; or aid, counsel, procure, or advise any such voter, person, or officer to do any act hereby made a crime, or to omit to do any duty the omission of which is hereby made a crime, or attempt to do so, every such person shall be deemed guilty of a crime, and shall for such crime be liable to prosecution in any court of the United States of competent jurisdiction, and, on conviction thereof, shall be punished by a fine not exceeding five hundred dollars, or by imprisonment for a term not exceeding three years, or both, in the discretion of the court, and shall pay the costs of prosecution.

SEC. 20. *And be it further enacted*, That if, at any registration of voters for an election for representative or delegate in the Congress of the United States, any person shall knowingly personate and register, or attempt to register, in the name of any other person, whether living, dead, or fictitious, or fraudulently register, or fraudulently attempt to register, not having a lawful right so to do; or do any unlawful act to secure registration for himself or any other person; or by force, threat, menace, intimidation, bribery, reward, or offer, or promise thereof, or other unlawful means, prevent or hinder any person having a lawful right to register from duly exercising such right; or compel or induce, by any of such means, or other unlawful means, any officer of registration to admit to registration any person not legally entitled thereto, or interfere in any manner with any officer of registration in the discharge of his duties, or by any such means, or other unlawful means, induce any officer of registration to violate or refuse to comply with his duty, or any law regulating the same; or knowingly and willfully receive the vote of any person not entitled to vote, or refuse to receive the vote of any person entitled to vote, or aid, counsel, procure, or advise any such voter, person, or officer to do any act hereby made a crime, or to omit any act, the omission of which is hereby made a crime, every such person shall be deemed guilty of a crime, and shall be liable to prosecution and punishment therefor, as provided in section nineteen of this act for persons guilty of any of the crimes therein specified: *Provided*, That every registration made under the laws of any State or Territory, for any State or other election at which such representative or delegate in Congress shall be chosen, shall be deemed to be a registration within the meaning of this act, notwithstanding the same shall also be made for the purposes of any State, territorial, or municipal election.

SEC. 21. *And be it further enacted*, That whenever, by the laws of any State or Territory, the name of any candidate or person to be voted for as representative or delegate in Congress shall be required to be printed, written, or contained in any ticket or ballot with other candidates or persons to be voted for at the same election for State, territorial, municipal, or local officers, it shall be sufficient prima facie evidence, either for the purpose of indicting or convicting any person charged with voting, or attempting or offering to vote, unlawfully under the provisions of the preceding sections, or for committing either of the offenses thereby created, to prove that the person so charged or indicted, voted, or attempted or offered to vote, such ballot or ticket, or committed either of the offenses named in the preceding sections of this act with reference to such ballot. And the proof and establishment of such facts shall be taken, held, and deemed to be presumptive evidence that such person voted, or attempted or offered to vote, for such representative or delegate, as the case may be, or that such offense was committed with reference to the election of such representative or delegate, and shall be sufficient to warrant his conviction, unless it shall be shown that any such ballot, when cast, or attempted or offered to be cast, by him, did not contain the name of any candidate for the office of representative or delegate in the Congress of the United States, or that such offense was not committed with reference to the election of such representative or delegate.

SEC. 22. *And be it further enacted*, That any officer of any election at which any representative or delegate in the Congress of the United States shall be voted for, whether such officer of election be appointed or created by or under any law or authority of the United States, or by or under any State, territorial, district, or municipal law or authority, who shall neglect or refuse to perform any duty in regard to such election required of him by any law of the United States, or of any State or Territory thereof; or violate any duty so imposed, or knowingly do any act thereby unauthorized, with intent to affect any such election, or the result thereof; or fraudulently make any false certificate of the result of such election in regard to such representative or delegate; or withhold, conceal, or destroy any certificate of record so required by law respecting, concerning, or pertaining to the election of any such representative or delegate; or neglect or refuse to make and return the same as so required by law; or aid, counsel, procure, or advise any voter, person, or officer to do any act by this or any of the preceding sections made a crime; or to omit to do any duty the omission of which is by this or any of said sections made a crime, or attempt to do so, shall be deemed guilty of a crime and shall be liable to prosecution and punishment therefor, as provided in the nineteenth section of this act for persons guilty of any of the crimes therein specified.

SEC. 23. *And be it further enacted*, That whenever any person shall be defeated or deprived of his election to any office, except elector of President or Vice-President, representative or delegate in Congress, or member of a State legislature, by reason of the denial to any citizen or citizens who shall offer to vote, of the right to vote, on account of race, color, or previous condition of servitude, his right to hold and enjoy such office, and the emoluments thereof, shall not be impaired by such denial; and such person may bring any appropriate suit or proceeding to recover possession of such office, and in cases where it shall appear that the sole question touching the title to such office arises out of the denial of the right to vote to citizens who so offered to vote, on account of race, color, or previous condition of servitude, such suit or proceeding may be instituted in the circuit or district court of the United States of the circuit or district in which such person resides. And said circuit or district court shall have, concurrently with the State courts, jurisdiction thereof so far as to determine the rights of the parties to such office by reason of the denial of the right guaranteed by the fifteenth article of amendment to the Constitution of the United States, and secured by this act.

Approved, May 31, 1870.

ENFORCEMENT LEGISLATION OF THE FORTY-FIRST CONGRESS.

AN ACT TO ENFORCE THE RIGHT TO VOTE.

AN ACT to amend an act approved May 31, 1870, entitled "An act to enforce the rights of citizens of the United States to vote in the several States of this Union, and for other purposes."

Be it enacted, etc., That section twenty of the "Act to enforce the rights of citizens of the United States to vote in the several States of this Union, and for other purposes," approved May 31, 1870, shall be, and hereby is, amended so as to read as follows:

"SEC. 20. That if any registration of voters for an election for Representative or Delegate in the Congress of the United States, any person shall knowingly personate and register, or attempt to register, in the name of any other person, whether living, dead, or fictitious, or fraudulently register, or fraudulently attempt to register, not having a lawful right so to do; or do any unlawful act to secure registration for himself or any other person; or by force, threat, menace, intimidation, bribery, reward, or offer, or promise thereof, or other unlawful means, prevent or hinder any person having a lawful right to register from duly exercising such right; or compel or induce by any of such means, or other unlawful means, any officer of registration to admit to registration any person not legally entitled thereto, or interfere in any manner with any officer of registration in the discharge of his duties, or by any such means, or other unlawful means, induce any officer of registration to violate or refuse to comply with his duty, or any law regulating the same; or if any such officer shall knowingly and willfully register as a voter any person not entitled to be registered, or refuse to so register any person entitled to be registered; or if any such officer, or other person whose duty it is to perform any duty in relation to such registration or election, or to ascertain, announce, or declare the result thereof, or give or make any certificate, document, or evidence in relation thereto, shall knowingly neglect or refuse to perform any duty required by law, or violate any duty imposed by law, or do any act unauthorized by law relating to or affecting such registration or election, or the result thereof, or any certificate, document, or evidence in relation thereto; or if any person shall aid, counsel, procure, or advise any such voter, person, or officer to do any act hereby made a crime, or to omit any act, the omission of which is hereby made a crime, every such person shall be deemed guilty of a crime, and shall be liable to prosecution and punishment therefor, as provided in section nineteen of said act of May 31, 1870, for persons guilty of any of the crimes therein specified: *Provided*, That every registration made under the laws of any State or Territory for any State or other election at which such Representative or Delegate in Congress shall be chosen shall be deemed to be a registration within the meaning of this act, notwithstanding the same shall also be made for the purposes of any State, Territorial, or municipal election."

SEC. 2. That whenever in any city or town having upward of twenty thousand inhabitants there shall be two citizens thereof who, prior to any registration of voters for an election for Representative or Delegate in the Congress of the United States, or prior to any election at which a Representative or Delegate in Congress is to be voted for, shall make known in writing, to the judge of the circuit court of the United States for the circuit wherein such city or town shall be, their desire to have said registration, or said election, or both, guarded and scrutinized, it shall be the duty of the said judge of the circuit court, within not less than ten days prior to said registration, if one there be, or, if no registration be required, within not less than ten days prior to said election, to open the said circuit court at the most convenient point in said circuit; and the said court, when so opened by said judge, shall proceed to appoint and commission, from day to day and from time to time, and under the hand of the said circuit judge, and under the seal of said court, for each election district or voting precinct in each and every such city or town as shall, in the manner herein prescribed, have applied therefor, and to revoke, change, or renew said appointment from time to time, two citizens, residents of said city or town, who shall be of different political parties, and able to read and write the English language, and who shall be known and designated as supervisors of election. And the said circuit court, when opened by the said circuit judge as required herein, shall therefrom and thereafter, and up to and including the day following the day of election, be always open for the transaction of business under this act, and the powers and jurisdiction hereby granted and conferred shall be exercised as well in vacation as in term time; and a judge sitting at chambers shall have the same powers and jurisdiction, including the power of keeping order and of punishing any contempt of his authority, as when sitting in court.

SEC. 3. That whenever, from sickness, injury, or otherwise, the judge of the circuit court of the United States in any judicial circuit shall be unable to perform and discharge the duties by this act imposed, it shall be his duty, and he is hereby required, to select and to direct and assign to the performance thereof in his place and stead such one of the judges of the district courts of the United States within his circuit as he shall deem best; and upon such selection and assignment being made it shall be lawful for, and shall be the duty of, the district judge so designated to perform and discharge, in the place and stead of the said circuit judge, all the duties, powers, and obligations imposed and conferred upon the said circuit judge by the provisions of this act.

SEC. 4. That it shall be the duty of the supervisors of election appointed under this act, and they and each of them are hereby authorized and required, to attend at all times and places fixed for the registration of voters who, being registered, would be entitled to vote for a Representative or Delegate in Congress, and to challenge any person offering to register; to attend at all times and places when the names of registered voters may be marked for challenge, and to cause such names registered as they shall deem proper to be so marked; to make, when required, the lists, or either of them, provided for in section thirteen of this act, and verify the same; and upon any occasion, and at any time when in attendance under the provisions of this act, to personally inspect and scrutinize such registry, and for purposes of identification to affix their or his signature to each and every page of the original list, and of each and every copy of any such list of registered voters, at such times, upon each day when any name may or shall be received, entered, or registered, and in such manner as will, in their or his judgment, detect and expose the improper or wrongful removal therefrom, or addition thereto, in any way, of any name or names.

SEC. 5. That it shall also be the duty of the said supervisors of election, and they, and each of them, are hereby authorized and required to attend at all times and places for holding elections of Representatives or Delegates in Congress, and for counting the votes cast at said elections; to challenge any vote offered by any person whose legal qualifications the supervisors, or either of them, shall doubt; to be and remain where the ballot-boxes are kept at all times after the polls are open until each and every vote cast at said time and place shall be counted, the canvass of all votes polled be wholly completed, and the proper and requisite certificates or returns made, whether said certificates or returns be required under any law of the United States, or any State, Territorial, or municipal law, and to personally inspect and scrutinize, from time to time, and at all times, on the day of election, the manner in which the voting is done, and the way and method in which the poll-books, registry-lists, and tallies or check-books, whether the same are required by any law of the United States, or any State, Territorial, or municipal law, are kept; and to the end that each candidate for the office of Representative or Delegate in Congress shall obtain the benefit of every vote for him cast, the said supervisors of election are, and each of them is, hereby required, in their or his respective election districts or voting precincts, to personally scrutinize, count, and canvass each and every ballot in their or his election district or voting precinct cast, whatever may be the indorsement on said ballot, or in whatever box it may have been placed or be found; to make and forward to the officer who, in accordance with the provisions of section thirteen of this act, shall have been designated as the chief supervisor of the judicial district in which the city or town wherein they or he shall serve shall be, such certificates and returns of all such ballots as said officer may direct or require, and to attach to the registry-list, and any and all copies thereof, and to any certificate, statement, or return, whether the same, or any part or portion thereof, be required by any law of the United States, or of any State, Territorial, or municipal law, any statement touching the truth or accuracy of the registry, or the truth or fairness of the election and canvass, which the said supervisors of election, or either of them, may desire to make or attach, or which should properly and honestly be made or attached, in order that the facts may become known, any law of any State or Territory to the contrary notwithstanding.

Sec. 6. That the better to enable the said supervisors of election to discharge their duties, they are, and each of them is, hereby authorized and directed, in their or his respective election districts or voting precincts, on the day or days of registration, on the day or days when registered voters may be marked to be challenged, and on the day or days of election, to take, occupy, and remain in such position or positions, from time to time, whether before or behind the ballot-boxes, as will, in their judgment, best enable them or him to see each person offering himself for registration or offering to vote, and as will best conduce to their or his scrutinizing the manner in which the registration or voting is being conducted; and at the closing of the polls for the reception of votes, they are, and each of them is, hereby required to place themselves or himself in such position in relation to the ballot-boxes for the purpose of engaging in the work of canvassing the ballots in said boxes contained as will enable them or him to fully perform the duties in respect to such canvass provided in this act, and shall there remain until every duty in respect to such canvass, certificates, returns, and statements shall have been wholly completed, any law of any State or Territory to the contrary notwithstanding.

SEC. 7. That if in any election district or voting precinct in any city, town, or village, for which there shall have been appointed supervisors of election for any election at which a Representative or Delegate in Congress shall be voted for, the said supervisors of election, or either of them, shall not be allowed to exercise or discharge, fully and freely, and without bribery, solicitation, interference, hinderance, molestation, violence, or threats thereof, on the part of or from any person or persons, each and every of the duties, obligations, and powers conferred upon them by this act and the act hereby amended, it shall be the duty of the supervisors of election, and each of them, to make prompt report, under oath, within ten days after the day of election, to the officer who, in accordance with the provisions of section thirteen of this act, shall have been designated as the chief supervisor of the judicial district in which the city or town wherein they or he served shall be, of the manner and means by which they were or he was not so allowed to fully and freely exercise and discharge the duties and obligations required and imposed by this act. And upon receiving any such report it shall be the duty of the said chief supervisor, acting both in such capacity and officially as a commissioner of the circuit court, to forthwith examine into all the facts thereof; to subpœna and compel the attendance before him of any witnesses; administer oaths and take testimony in respect to the charges made; and, prior to the assembling of the Congress for which any such Representative or Delegate was voted for, to have filed with the Clerk of the House of Representatives of the Congress of the United States all the evidence by him taken, all information by him obtained, and all reports to him made.

SEC. 8. That whenever an election at which Representatives or Delegates in Congress are to be chosen shall be held in any city or town of twenty thousand inhabitants or upward, the marshal of the United States for the district in which said city or town is situated shall have power, and it shall be his duty, on the application, in writing, of at least two citizens residing in any such city or town, to appoint special deputy marshals, whose duty it shall be, when required as provided in this act, to aid and assist the supervisors of election in the verification of any list of persons made under the provisions of this act, who may have registered, or voted, or either; to attend in each election district or voting precinct at the times and places fixed for the registration of voters, and at all times and places when and where said registration may by law be scrutinized, and the names of registered voters be marked for challenge; and, also, to attend, at all times for holding such elections, the polls of the election in such district or precinct. And the marshal and his general deputies, and such special deputies, shall have power, and it shall be the duty of such special deputies, to keep the peace, and support and protect the supervisors of elections in the discharge of their duties; preserve order at such places of registration and at such polls; prevent fraudulent registration and fraudulent voting thereat, or fraudulent conduct on the part of any officer of election, and immediately, either at said place of registration, or polling-place, or elsewhere, and either before or after registering or voting to arrest and take into custody, with or without process, any person who shall commit, or attempt or offer to commit, any of the acts or offenses prohibited by this act, or the act hereby amended, or who shall commit any offense against the laws of the United States: *Provided*, That no person shall be arrested without process for any offense not committed in the presence of the marshal or his general or special deputies, or either of them, or of the supervisors of election, or either of them; and, for the purposes of arrest or the preservation of the peace, the supervisors of election, and each of them, shall, in the absence of the marshal's deputies, or if required to assist said deputies, have the same duties and powers as deputy marshals: *And provided further*, That no person shall, on the day or days of any such election, be arrested without process for any offense committed on the day or days of registration.

SEC. 9. That whenever any arrest is made under any provision of this act, the person so arrested shall forthwith be brought before a commissioner, judge, or court of the United States for examination of the offenses alleged against him; and such commissioner, judge, or court shall proceed in respect thereto as authorized by law in cases of crimes against the United States.

SEC. 10. That whoever, with or without any authority, power, or process, or pretended authority, power, or process, of any State, Territorial, or muncipal authority, shall obstruct, hinder assault, or by bribery, solicitation, or otherwise, interfere with or prevent the supervisors of election, or either of them, or the marshal or his general or special deputies, or either of them, in the performance of any duty required of them, or either of them, or which he or they, or either of them, may be authorized to perform by any law of the United States, whether in the execution of process or otherwise, or shall, by any of the means before mentioned, hinder or prevent the free attendance and presence at such places of registration or at such polls of election, or full and free access and egress to and from any such place of registration or poll of election, or in going to and from any such place of registration or poll of election, or to and from any room where any such registration or election, or canvass of votes, or of making any returns or certificates thereof, may be had; or shall molest, interfere with, remove, or eject from any such place of registration or poll of election, or of canvassing votes cast thereat, or of making returns or certificates thereof, any supervisor of election, the marshal, or his general or special deputies, or either of them, or shall threaten, or attempt, or offer so to do, or shall refuse or neglect to aid and assist any supervisor of election, or the marshal, or his general or special deputies, or either of them, in the performance of his or their duties, when required by him or them, or either of them, to give such aid and assistance, he shall be guilty of a misdemeanor, and liable to instant arrest without process, and on conviction thereof shall be punished by imprisonment not more than two years, or by fine not more than three thousand dollars, or by both such fine and imprisonment, and shall pay the costs of the prosecution. Whoever shall, during the progress of any verification of any list of the persons who may have registered or voted, and which shall be had or made under any of the provisions of this act, refuse to answer, or refrain from answering, or answering shall knowingly give false information in respect to any inquiry lawfully made, such person shall be liable to arrest and imprisonment as for a misdemeanor, and on conviction thereof shall be punished by imprisonment not to exceed thirty days, or by fine not to exceed one hundred dollars, or by both such fine and imprisonment, and shall pay the costs of the prosecution.

SEC. 11. That whoever shall be appointed a supervisor of election or a special deputy marshal under the provisions of this act, and shall take the oath of office as such supervisor of election or such special deputy marshal, who shall thereafter neglect or refuse, without good and lawful excuse, to perform and discharge fully the duties, obligations, and requirements of such office until the expiration of the term for which he was appointed, shall not only be subject to removal from office with loss of all pay or emoluments, but shall be guilty of a misdemeanor, and on conviction shall be punished by imprisonment for not less than six months nor more than one year, or by fine not less than two hundred dollars and not exceeding five hundred dollars, or by both fine and imprisonment, and shall pay the costs of prosecution.

SEC. 12. That the marshal, or his general deputies, or such special deputies as shall be thereto specially empowered by him in writing under his hand and seal, whenever he, or his said general deputies, or his special deputies, or either or any of them, shall be forcibly resisted in executing their duties under this act, or the act hereby amended, or shall, by violence, threats, or menaces, be prevented from executing such duties, or from arresting any person or persons who shall commit any offense for which said marshal or his general or special deputies are authorized to make such arrest, are, and each of them is hereby, empowered to summon and call to his or their aid the bystanders or *posse comitatus* of his district.

SEC. 13. That it shall be the duty of each of the circuit courts of the United States in and for each judicial circuit, upon the recommendation, in writing, of the judge thereof, to name and appoint, on or before the first day of May, in the year 1871, and thereafter as vacancies may from any cause arise, from among the circuit court commissioners in and for each judicial district in each of said judicial circuits, one of such officers, who shall be known for the duties required of him under this act as the chief supervisor of elections of the judicial district in and for which he shall be a commissioner, and shall, so long as faithful and capable, discharge the duties in this act imposed, and whose duty it shall be to prepare and furnish all necessary books, forms, blanks, and instructions for the use and direction of the supervisors of election in the several cities and towns in their respective districts; to receive the applications of all parties for appointment to such positions; and upon the opening, as contemplated in this act, of the circuit court for the judicial circuit in which the commissioner so designated shall act, to present such applications to the judge thereof, and furnish information to said judge in respect to the appointment by the said court of such supervisors of election; to require of the supervisors of election, where necessary, lists of the persons who may register and vote, or either, in their respective election districts or voting precincts, and to cause the names of those upon any such list whose right to register or vote shall be honestly doubted to be verified by proper inquiry and examination at the respective places by them assigned as their residences; and to receive, preserve, and file all oaths of office of said supervisors of election, and of all special deputy marshals appointed under the provisions of this act, and all certificates, returns, reports, and records of every kind and nature contemplated or made requisite under and by the provisions of this act, save where otherwise herein specially directed. And it is hereby made the duty of all United States marshals and commissioners who shall in any judicial district perform any duties under the provisions of this act, or the act hereby amended, relating to, concerning, or affecting the election of Representatives or Delegates in the Congress of the United States, to, from time to time, and with all due diligence, forward to the chief supervisor in and for their judicial district all complaints, examinations, and records pertaining thereto, and all oaths of office by them administered to any supervisor of election or special deputy marshal, in order that the same may be properly preserved and filed.

SEC 14. That there shall be allowed and paid to each chief supervisor, for his services as such officer, the following compensation, apart from and in excess of all fees allowed by law for the performance of any duty as circuit court commissioner: for filing and caring for every return, report, record, document, or other paper required to be filed by him under any of the provisions of this act, ten cents; for affixing a seal to any paper, record, report, or instrument, twenty cents; for entering and indexing the records of his office, fifteen cents per folio; and for arranging and transmitting to Congress, as provided for in section seven of this act, any report, statement, record, return, or examination, for each folio, fifteen cents; and for any copy thereof, or of any paper on file, a like sum. And there shall be allowed and paid to each and every supervisor of election, and each and every special deputy marshal who shall be appointed and shall perform his duty under the provisions of this act, compensation at the rate of five dollars per day for each and every day he shall have actually been on duty, not exceeding ten days. And the fees of the said chief supervisors shall be paid at the Treasury of the United States, such accounts to be made out, verified, examined, and certified as in case of accounts of commissioners, save that the examination or certificate required may be made by either the circuit or district judge.

SEC. 15. That the jurisdiction of the circuit court of the United States shall extend to all cases in law or equity arising under the provisions of this act, or the act hereby amended; and if any person shall receive any injury to his person or property for or on account of any act by him done under any of the provisions of this act, or the act hereby amended, he shall be entitled to maintain suit for damages therefor in the district or circuit court of the United States in the district wherein the party doing the injury may reside or shall be found.

SEC. 16. That in any case where suit or prosecution, civil or criminal, shall be commenced in a court of any State against any officer of the United States, or other person, for or on account of any act done under the provisions of this act, or under color thereof, or for or on account of any right, authority, or title set up or claimed by such officer or other person under any of said provisions, it shall be lawful for the defendant in such suit or prosecution, at any time before trial, upon a petition to the circuit court of the United States in and for the district in which the defendant shall have been served with process, setting forth the nature of said suit or prosecution, and verifying the said petition by affidavit, together with a certificate signed by an attorney or counselor at law of some court of record of the State in which such suit shall have been commenced, or of the United States, setting forth that as counsel for the petition he has examined the proceedings against him, and has carefully inquired into all the matters set forth in the petition, and that he believes the same to be true, which petition, affidavit, and certificate shall be presented to the said circuit court, if in session, and, if not, to the clerk thereof at his office, and shall be filed in said office, and the cause shall thereupon be entered on the docket of said court, and shall be thereafter proceeded in as a cause originally commenced in that court; and it shall be the duty of the clerk of said court, if the suit was commenced in the court below by summons, to issue a writ of *certiorari* to the State court, requiring said court to send to the circuit court the record and proceedings in said cause; or, if it was commenced by *capias*, he shall issue a writ of *habeas corpus cum causa*, a duplicate of which said writ shall be delivered to the clerk of the State court, or left at his office by the marshal of the district, or his deputy, or some person duly authorized thereto; and thereupon it shall be the duty of the said State court to stay all further proceedings in such cause, and the said suit or prosecution, upon delivery of such process, or leaving the same as aforesaid, shall be deemed and taken to be moved to the said circuit court, and any further proceedings, trial, or judgment therein in the State court shall be wholly null and void; and any person, whether an attorney or officer of any State court, or otherwise, who shall thereafter take any steps, or in any manner proceed in the State court in any action so removed, shall be guilty of a misdemeanor, and liable to trial and punishment in the court to which the action shall have been removed, and upon conviction thereof shall be punished by imprisonment for not less than six months nor more than one year, or by fine not less than five hundred nor more than one thousand dollars, or by both such fine and imprisonment, and shall, in addition thereto, be amenable to the said court to which said action shall have been removed as for a contempt; and if the defendant in any such suit be in actual custody on *mesne* process therein, it shall be the duty of the marshal, by virtue of the writ of *habeas corpus cum causa*, to take the body of the defendant into his custody, to be dealt with in the said cause according to the rules of law and the order of the circuit court, or of any judge thereof in vacation. And all attachments made and all bail or other security given upon such suit or prosecution shall be, and continue in like force and effect, as if the same suit or prosecution had proceeded to final judgment and execution in the State court. And if, upon the removal of any such suit or prosecution, it shall be made to appear to the said circuit court that no copy of the record and proceedings therein in the State court can be obtained, it shall be lawful for the said circuit court to allow and require the plaintiff to proceed *de novo*, and to file a declaration of his cause of action, and the parties may thereupon proceed as in actions originally brought in said circuit court; and on failure of so proceeding judgment of *non prosequitur* may be rendered against the plaintiff, with costs for the defendant.

SEC. 17. That in any case in which any party is or may be by law entitled to copies of the record and proceedings in any suit or prosecution in any State court, to be used in any court of the United States, if the clerk of said court shall, upon demand and the payment or tender of the legal fees, refuse or neglect to deliver to such party certified copies of such record and proceedings, the court of the United States in which such record and proceedings may be needed, on proof, by affidavit, that the clerk of such State court has refused or neglected to deliver copies thereof on demand as aforesaid, may direct and allow such record to be supplied, by affidavit or otherwise, as the circumstances of the case may require and allow; and thereupon such proceeding, trial, and judgment may be had in the said court of the United States, and all such processes awarded as if certified copies of such records and proceedings had been regularly before the said court; and hereafter in all civil actions in the courts of the United States either party thereto may notice the same for trial.

SEC. 18. That sections five and six of the act of the Congress of the United States, approved July 14, 1870, and entitled "An act to amend the naturalization laws, and to punish crimes against the same," be, and the same are hereby, repealed; but this repeal shall not affect any proceeding or prosecution now pending for any offense under the said sections, or either of them, or any question which may arise therein respecting the appointment of the persons in said sections, or either of them, provided for, or the powers, duties, or obligations of such persons.

SEC. 19. That all votes for Representatives in Congress shall hereafter be by written or printed ballot, any law of any State to the contrary notwithstanding; and all votes received or recorded contrary to the provisions of this section shall be of none effect.

Approved February 28, 1871.

SUPPLEMENT.

The Act of February 28, 7871, has been supplemented and amended so as to further provide as follows:

That whenever, in any county or parish in any congressional district, there shall be ten citizens thereof of good standing who, prior to any registration of voters for an election for Representative in Congress, or prior to any election at which a Representative in Congress is to be voted for, shall make known, in writing, to the judge of the circuit court of the United States for the district wherein such county or parish is situate, their desire to have said registration or election both guarded and scrutinized, it shall be the duty of the said judge of the circuit court, within not less than ten days prior to said registration or election, as the case may be, to open the said court at the most convenient point in said district; and the said court, when so opened by said judge, shall proceed to appoint and commission, from day to day and from time to time, and under the hand of the said judge, and under the seal of said court, for such election district or voting precinct in said congressional district, as shall, in the manner herein prescribed, have been applied for, and to revoke, change, or renew said appointment from time to time, two citizens, residents of said election district or voting precinct in said county or parish, who shall be of different political parties, and able to read and write the English language, and who shall be known and designated as supervisors of election; and the said court, when so opened by the said judge as required herein, shall, therefrom and thereafter, and up to and including the day following the day of the election, be always open for the transaction of business under this act; and the powers and jurisdiction hereby granted and conferred shall be exercised as well in vacation as in term time; and a judge sitting at chambers shall have the same powers and jurisdiction, including the power of keeping order and of punishing any contempt of his authority, as when sitting in the court: *Provided*, That no compensation shall be allowed to the supervisors herein authorized to be appointed, except those appointed in cities or towns of twenty thousand or more inhabitants. And no person shall be appointed under this act as supervisor of election who is not at the time of his appointment a qualified voter of the county, parish, election district, or voting precinct for which he is appointed. And no person shall be appointed deputy marshal under the act of which this is amendatory who is not a qualified voter at the time of his appointment in the county, parish, district, or precinct in which his duties are to be performed. And section thirteen of the act of which this is an amendment shall be construed to authorize and require the circuit courts of the United States in said section mentioned to name and appoint, as soon as may be after the passage of this act, the commissioners provided for in said section in all cases in which such appointments have not already been made in conformity therewith. And the third section of the act to which this is an amendment shall be taken and construed to authorize each of the judges of the circuit courts of the United States to designate one or more of the judges of the district courts within his circuit to discharge the duties arising under this act or the act to which this is an amendment. And the words "any person," in section four of the act of May 31, 1870, shall be held to include any officer or other person having powers or duties of an official character under this act or the act to which this is an amendment: *Provided*, That nothing in this section shall be so construed as to authorize the appointment of any marshals or deputy marshals in addition to those heretofore authorized by law: *And provided further*, That the supervisors herein provided for shall have no power or authority to make arrests or to perform other duties than to be in the immediate presence of the officers holding the election and to witness all their proceedings, including the counting of the votes and the making of a return thereof. And so much of said sum herein appropriated as may be necessary for said supplemental and amendatory provisions is hereby appropriated from and after the passage of this act.

These provisions were inserted in the sundry civil bill, approved June 10, 1872.

"THE KU KLUX ACT."

An Act to enforce the provisions of the fourteenth amendment to the Constitution of the United States, and for other purposes.

Be it enacted, etc., That any person who, under color of any law, statute, ordinance, regulation, custom, or usage of any State, shall subject, or cause to be subjected, any person within the jurisdiction of the United States to the deprivation of any rights, privileges, or immunities secured by the Constitution of the United States, shall, any such law, statute, ordinance, regulation, custom, or usage of the State to the contrary notwithstanding, be liable to the party injured in any action at law, suit in equity, or other proper proceeding for redress; such proceeding to be prosecuted in the several district or circuit courts of the United States, with and subject to the same rights of appeal, review upon error, and other remedies provided in like cases in such courts, under the provisions of the act of the 9th of April, 1866, entitled "An act to protect all persons in the United States in their civil rights, and to furnish the means of their vindication;" and the other remedial laws of the United States which are in their nature applicable in such cases.

Sec. 2. That if two or more persons within any State or Territory of the United States shall conspire together to overthrow, or to put down, or to destroy by force the Government of the United States, or to levy war against the United States, or to oppose by force the authority of the Government of the United States; or by force, intimidation, or threat to prevent, hinder, or delay the execution of any law of the United States, or by force to seize, take, or possess any property of the United States contrary to the authority thereof; or by force, intimidation, or threat to prevent any person from accepting or holding any office, or trust, or place of confidence under the United States, or from discharging the duties thereof; or by force, intimidation, or threat to induce any officer of the United States to leave any State, district, or place where his duties as such officer might lawfully be performed, or to injure him in his person or property on account of his lawful discharge of the duties of his office, or to injure his person while engaged in the lawful discharge of the duties of his office, or to injure his property so as to molest, interrupt, hinder, or impede him in the discharge of his official duty; or by force, intimidation, or threat to deter any party or witness in any court of the United States from attending such court, or from testifying in any matter pending in such court fully, freely, and truthfully, or to injure any such party or witness in his person or property on account of his having so attended or testified; or by force, intimidation, or threat to influence the verdict, presentment, or indictment of any juror or grand juror in any court of the United States, or to injure such juror in his person or property on account of any verdict, presentment, or indictment lawfully assented to by him, or on account of his being or having been such juror; or shall conspire together, or go in disguise upon the public highway, or upon the premises of another, for the purpose, either directly or indirectly, of depriving any person or any class of persons of the equal protection of the laws, or of equal privileges or immunities under the laws, or for the purpose of preventing or hindering the constituted authorities of any State from giving or securing to all persons within such State the equal protection of the laws; or shall conspire together for the purpose of in any manner impeding, hindering, obstructing, or defeating the due course of justice in any State or Territory with intent to deny to any citizen of the United States the due and equal protection of the laws, or to injure any person in his person or his property for lawfully enforcing the right of any person or class of persons to the equal protection of the laws; or by force, intimidation, or threat to prevent any citizen of the United States lawfully entitled to vote from giving his support or advocacy in a lawful manner toward or in favor of the election of any lawfully qualified person as an elector of President or Vice-President of the United States, or as a member of the Congress of the United States, or to injure any such citizen in his person or property on account of such support or advocacy, each and every person so offending shall be deemed guilty of a high crime, and, upon conviction thereof in any district or circuit court of the United States or district or supreme court of any Territory of the United States having jurisdiction of similar offenses, shall be punished by a fine not less than five hundred dollars nor more than five thousand dollars, or by imprisonment, with or without hard labor, as the court may determine, for a period of not less than six months nor more than six years, or by both such fine and imprisonment as the court shall determine. And if any one or more persons engaged in any such conspiracy shall do, or cause to be done, any act in furtherance of the object of such conspiracy, whereby any person shall be injured in his person or property, or deprived of having and exercising any right or privilege of a citizen of the United States, the person so injured or deprived of such rights and privileges may have and maintain an action for the recovery of damages occasioned by such injury or deprivation of rights and privileges against any one or more of the persons engaged in such conspiracy, such action to be prosecuted in the proper district or circuit court of the United States, with and subject to the same rights of appeal, review upon error, and other remedies provided in like cases in such courts under the provisions of the act of April 9, 1866, entitled "An act to protect all persons in the United States in their civil rights, and to furnish the means of their vindication."

Sec. 3. That in all cases where insurrection, domestic violence, unlawful combinations, or conspiracies in any State shall so obstruct or hinder the execution of the laws thereof, and of the United States, as to deprive any portion or class of the people of such State of any of the rights, privileges, or immunities, or protection named in the Constitution and secured by this act, and the constituted authorities of such State shall either be unable to protect, or shall, from any cause, fail in or refuse protection of the people in such rights, such facts shall be deemed a denial by such State of equal protection of the laws to which they are entitled under the Constitution of the United States; and in all such cases, or whenever any such insurrection, violence, unlawful combination, or conspiracy shall oppose or obstruct the laws of the United States, or the due execution thereof, or impede or obstruct the due course of justice under the same, it shall be lawful for the President, and it shall be his duty, to take such measures, by the employment of the militia or the land and naval forces of the United States, or of either, or by other means as he may deem necessary for the suppression of such insurrection, domestic violence, or combinations; and any person who shall be arrested under the provisions of this and the preceding section shall be delivered to the marshal of the proper district to be dealt with according to law.

Sec. 4. That whenever in any State or part of a State the unlawful combinations named in the preceding section of this act shall be organized and armed, and so numerous and powerful as to be able by violence to either overthrow or set at defiance the constituted authorities of such State, and of the United States within such State; or when the constituted authorities are in complicity with or shall connive at the unlawful purposes of such powerful and armed combinations; and whenever, by reason of either or all of the causes aforesaid, the conviction of such offenders and the preservation of the public safety shall become in such district impracticable, in every such case such combinations shall be deemed a rebellion against the Government of the United States, and during the continuance of such rebellion, and within the limits of the district which shall be so under the sway thereof, such limits to be prescribed by proclamation, it shall be lawful for the President of the United States, when in his judgment the public safety shall require it, to suspend the privileges of the writ of *habeas corpus*, to the end that such rebellion may be overthrown: *Provided*, That all the provisions of the second section of an act entitled "An act relating to *habeas corpus*, and regulating judicial proceedings in certain cases," approved March 3, 1863, which relate to the discharge of prisoners other than prisoners of war, and to the penalty for refusing to obey the order of the court, shall be in full force so far as the same are applicable to the provisions of this section: *Provided further*, That the President shall first have made proclamation, as now provided by law, commanding such insurgents to disperse: *And provided also*, That the provisions of this section shall not be in force after the end of the next regular session of Congress.

SEC. 5. That no person shall be a grand or petit juror in any court of the United States upon any inquiry, hearing, or trial of any suit, proceeding, or posecution based upon or arising under the provisions of this act who shall, in the judgment of the court, be in complicity with any such combination or conspiracy; and every such juror shall, before entering upon any such inquiry, hearing, or trial, take and subscribe an oath in open court that he has never, directly or indirectly, counseled, advised, or voluntarily aided any such combination or conspiracy; and each and every person who shall take this oath, and shall therein swear falsely, shall be guilty of perjury, and shall be subject to the pains and penalties declared against that crime; and the first section of the act entitled "An act defining additional causes of challenge and prescribing an additional oath for grand and petit jurors in the United States courts,' approved June 17, 1862, be, and the same is hereby, repealed.

SEC. 6. That any person or persons, having knowledge that any of the wrongs conspired to be done and mentioned in the second section of this act are about to be committed, and having power to prevent or aid in preventing the same, shall neglect or refuse so to do, and such wrongful act shall be committed, such person or persons shall be liable to the person injured, or his legal representatives, for all damages caused by any such wrongful act which such first named person or persons by reasonable diligence could have prevented; and such damages may be recovered in an action on the case in the proper circuit court of the United States; and any number of persons guilty of such wrongful neglect or refusal may be joined as defendants in such action: *Provided*, That such action shall be commenced within one year after such cause of action shall have accrued; and if the death of any person shall be caused by any such wrongful act and neglect, the legal representatives of such deceased person shall have such action therefor, and may recover not exceeding five thousand dollars damages therein for the benefit of the widow of such deceased person, if any there be, or if there be no widow, for the benefit of the next of kin of such deceased person.

SEC. 7. That nothing herein contained shall be construed to supersede or repeal any former act or law except so far as the same may be repugnant thereto; and any offenses heretofore committed against the tenor of any former act shall be prosecuted, and any proceeding already commenced for the prosecution thereof shall be continued and completed the same as if this act had not been passed, except so far as the provisions of this act may go to sustain and validate such proceedings.

Approved April 20, 1871.

SALARY ACT OF 1873.

Be it enacted, etc., That, on and after the 4th day of March, A. D. 1873, the President of the United States shall receive in full for his services during the term for which he shall have been elected the sum of $50,000 per annum, to be paid monthly; the Vice-President of the United States shall receive in full for his services during the term for which he shall have been elected the sum of $10,000 per annum, to be paid monthly; and the Chief Justice of the Supreme Court of the United States shall receive the sum of $10,500 per annum, and the justices of the Supreme Court of the United States shall receive the sum of $10,000 per annum each, to be paid monthly; the Secretary of State, the Secretary of the Treasury, the Secretary of War, the Secretary of the Navy, the Secretary of the Interior, the Attorney-General, and the Postmaster-General shall receive $10,000 per annum each for their services, to be paid monthly; and each Assistant Secretary of the Treasury, State, and Interior Departments shall receive as annual compensation, to be paid monthly, $6,000; and the Speaker of the House of Represntatives shall, after the present Congress, receive in full for all his services compensation at the rate of $10,000 per annum; and Senators, Representatives, and Delegates in Congress, including Senators, Representatives, and Delegates in the Forty-second Congress, shall receive $7,500 per annum each, and this shall be in lieu of all pay and allowances; and all those holding such office at the passage of this act, and whose claim to a seat has not been adversely decided, shall receive $7,500 per annum each, and this shall be in lieu of all pay and allowances, except the actual individual traveling expenses from their homes to the seat of Government and return by the most direct route of usual travel, once for each session of the House to which such Senator, member, or Delegate belongs, to be certified to under his hand to the disbursing officer, and filed as a voucher: *Provided*, That, in settling the pay and allowances of Senators, members, and Delegates in the Forty-second Congress, all mileage shall be deducted, and no allowance made for expenses of travel. And there is hereby appropriated a sum sufficient to make the annual salaries of such of the clerks in the office of the Clerk of the House of Representatives as receive $2,500 and upward, and less than $3,000 (including the petition clerk and printing clerk), $3,000 each; and of such as receive $2,000 and upward, and less than $2,500, the sum of $2,500 each; and of such as receive $1,800 and upward, and less than $2,000, the sum of $2,000 each; and of the Secretary of the Senate and Clerk of the House of Representatives $5,000 each; and of the chief clerk and journal clerk of the House, while such positions are held by the present incumbents, and no longer, $3,600 each; and of the doorkeeper of the House and the assistant doorkeeper of the Senate, while the position is held by the present incumbents, and no longer, $3,000; and of the postmaster of the Senate, $2,592; assistant postmaster, $2,000; and of two mail carriers, $1,700; and of the superintendent and first assistant of the Senate document room, $2,500 each; and second assistant in said document room, $1,800; and of the additional compensation to the reporters of the House and Senate for the Congressional Globe, $1,500 each; and additional pay to the chief engineer of the House, $360 (so as to equalize his pay with that of the chief engineer of the Senate). And it is hereby provided that the increase of compensation to the officers, clerks, and others in the employ of the Senate and House of Representatives provided for in this act shall begin with the present Congress; and the pay of all the present employees of the Senate and House of Representatives, including the employees in the Library of Congress and those under the Committee on Public Buildings and Grounds, now employed in the Capitol building, and also the House reporters whose pay has not been specifically increased by this act, holding their places by appointment under the respective officers thereof, or by the authority of the Committee of Contingent Expenses of the Senate, or the Committee of Accounts of the House, be increased fifteen per cent. of their present compensation on the amount actually received and payable to them respectively from the beginning of the present Congress, or from the date of their appointment during the present Congress, and who shall be actually employed at the passage of this act. And the amounts of money necessary to carry the foregoing provisions into effect are hereby appropriated out of any monies in the Treasury not otherwise appropriated.

REPEAL OF THE SALARY ACT.

An Act repealing the increase of salaries of members of Congress and other officers.

Be it enacted by the Senate and House of Representatives of the United States of America in Congress assembled: That so much of the act of March 3, 1873, entitled "An act making appropriations for legislative, executive, and judicial expenses of the Government for the year ending June 30, 1874," as provides for the increase of the compensation of public officers and employees, whether members of Congress, Delegates, or others, except the President of the United States and the justices of the Supreme Court, be, and the same is hereby, repealed, and the salaries, compensation, and allowances of all said persons, except as aforesaid, shall be as fixed by the laws in force at the time of the passage of said act: *Provided*, That mileage shall not be allowed for the first session of the Forty-third Congress; that all monies appropriated as compensation to the members of the Forty-second Congress, in excess of the mileage and allowances fixed by law at the commencement of said Congress, and which shall not have been drawn by the members of said Congress respectively, or which, having been drawn, have been returned in any form to the United States, are hereby covered into the Treasury of the United States, and are declared to be the monies of the United States absolutely, the same as if they had never been appropriated as aforesaid.

Approved January 20, 1874.

GRANT'S VETO OF THE SENATE CURRENCY BILL, APRIL 22, 1874.

To the Senate of the United States:

Herewith I return Senate bill No. 617, entitled "An act to fix the amount of United States notes and the circulation of national banks, and for other purposes," without my approval.

In doing so I must express my regret at not being able to give my assent to a measure which has received the sanction of a majority of the legislators chosen by the people to make laws for their guidance, and I have studiously sought to find sufficient arguments to justify such assent, but unsuccessfully.

Practically, it is a question whether the measure under discussion would give an additional dollar to the irredeemable paper currency of the country or not, and whether, by requiring three-fourths of the reserves to be retained by the banks, and prohibiting interest to be received on the balance, it might not prove a contraction.

But the fact can not be concealed that, theoretically, the bill increases the paper circulation $100,000,000, less only the amount of reserves restrained from circulation by the provision of the second section. The measure has been supported on the theory that it would give increased circulation. It is a fair inference, therefore, that if in practice the measure should fail to create the abundance of circulation expected of it, the friends of the measure, particularly those out of Congress, would clamor for such inflation as would give the expected relief.

The theory, in my belief, is a departure from true principles of finance, national interest, national obligations to creditors, congressional promises, party pledges, on the part of both political parties, and of personal views and promises made by me in every annual message sent to Congress, and in each inaugural address.

In my annual message to Congress in December, 1869, the following passages appear:

"Among the evils growing out of the rebellion, and not yet referred to, is that of an irredeemable currency. It is an evil which I hope will receive your most earnest attention. It is a duty, and one of the highest duties, of Government to secure to the citizen a medium of exchange of fixed, unvarying value. This implies a return to specie basis; and no substitute for it can be devised. It should be commenced now, and reached at the earliest practicable moment consistent with a fair regard to the interests of the debtor class. Immediate resumption, if practicable, would not be desirable. It would compel the debtor class to pay, beyond their contracts, the premium on gold at the date of their purchase, and would bring bankruptcy and ruin to thousands. Fluctuation, however, in the paper value of the measure of all values (gold) is detrimental to the interests of trade. It makes the man of business an involuntary gambler; for in all sales where future payment is to be made, both parties speculate as to what will be the value of the currency to be paid and received. I earnestly recommend to you, then, such legislation as will insure a gradual return to specie payments and put an immediate stop to fluctuations in the value of currency."

I still adhere to the views then expressed.

As early as December 4, 1865, the House of Representatives passed a resolution, by a vote of 144 yeas to 6 nays, concurring "in the views of the Secretary of the Treasury in relation to the necessity of a contraction of the currency with a view to as early a resumption of specie payments as the business interests of the country will permit," and pledging "co-operative action to this end as speedily as possible."

The first act passed by the Forty-first Congress, on the 18th day of March, 1869, was as follows:

AN ACT TO STRENGTHEN THE PUBLIC CREDIT OF THE UNITED STATES.

Be it enacted, etc., That, in order to remove any doubt as to the purpose of the Government to discharge all its obligations to the public creditors, and to settle conflicting questions and interpretations of the law, by virtue of which such obligations have been contracted, it is hereby provided and declared that the faith of the United States is solemnly pledged to the payment in coin, or its equivalent, of all the obligations of the United States, and of all the interest-bearing obligations, except in cases where the law authorizing the issue of any such obligations has expressly provided that the same may be paid in lawful money, or in other currency than gold and silver; but none of the said interest-bearing obligations not already due shall be redeemed or paid before maturity, unless at such times as the United States notes shall be convertible into coin at the option of the holder, or unless at such time bonds of the United

States bearing a lower rate of interest than the bonds to be redeemed can be sold at par in coin. And the United States also solemnly pledges its faith to make provision, at the earliest practicable period, for the redemption of the United States notes in coin.

This act still remains as a continuing pledge of the faith of the United States "to make provision, at the earliest practicable moment, for the redemption of the United States notes in coin."

A declaration contained in the act of June 30, 1864, created an obligation that the total amount of United States notes issued, or to be issued, should never exceed $400,000,000. The amount in actual circulation was actually reduced to $356,000,000, at which point Congress passed the act of February 4, 1868, suspending the further reduction of the currency. The $44,000,000 have ever been regarded as a reserve, to be used only in case of emergency, such as has occurred on several occasions, and must occur when, from any cause, revenues suddenly fall below expenditures; and such a reserve is necessary, because the fractional currency, amounting to $50,000,000, is redeemable in legal tender on call. It may be said that such a return of fractional currency for redemption is impossible. But let steps be taken for a return to a specie basis, and it will be found that silver will take the place of fractional currency as rapidly as it can be supplied, when the premium on gold reaches a sufficiently low point.

With the amount of United States notes to be issued permanently fixed within proper limits, and the Treasury so strengthened as to be able to redeem them in coin on demand, it will then be safe to inaugurate a system of free banking, with such provisions as to make compulsory redemption of the circulating notes of the banks in coin, or in United States notes, themselves redeemable and made equivalent to coin.

As a measure preparatory to free banking, and for placing the Government in a condition to redeem its notes in coin "at the earliest practicable moment," the revenues of the country should be increased so as to pay current expenses, provide for the sinking fund required by law, and also a surplus, to be retained in the Treasury, in gold.

I am not a believer in any artificial method of making paper money equal to coin when the coin is not owned or held ready to redeem the promises to pay; for paper money is nothing more than promises to pay, and is valuable exactly in proportion to the amount of coin that it can be converted into. While coin is not used as a circulating medium, or the currency of the country is not convertible into it at par, it becomes an article of commerce as much as any other product. The surplus will seek a foreign market, as will any other surplus. The balance of trade has nothing to do with the question. Duties on imports being required in coin creates a limited demand for gold. About enough to satisfy that demand remains in the country. To increase this supply I see no way open but by the Government hoarding, through the means above given, and possibly by requiring the national banks to aid.

It is claimed by the advocates of the measure herewith returned that there is an unequal distribution of the banking capital of the country. I was disposed to give great weight to this view of the question at first, but on reflection it will be remembered that there still remain $4,000,000 of authorized bank-note circulation, assigned to States having less than their quota, not yet taken. In addition to this the States having less than their quota of bank circulation have the option of $25,000,000 more to be taken from those States having more than their proportion. When this is all taken up, or when specie payments are fully restored, or are in rapid process of restoration, will be the time to consider the question of "more currrency."

U. S. GRANT.

THE CURRENCY.

The following is the Dawes Compromise Bank Note Redemption, Inflation, Redistribution Bill, in full:

An Act fixing the amount of United States notes, providing for a redistribution of the national bank currency, and for other purposes.

Be it enacted by the Senate and House of Representatives of the United States of America in Congress assembled, That the act entitled "An act to provide a national currency secured by a pledge of the United States bonds, and to provide for the circulation and redemption thereof," approved June 3, 1864, shall hereafter be known as "the national bank act."

RELEASE OF RESERVES ON CIRCULATION. RESERVES ON DEPOSIT RETAINED.

Sec. 2. That section thirty-one of "the national bank act" be so amended that the several associations therein provided for shall not hereafter be required to keep on hand any amount of money whatever, by reason of the amount of their respective circulations; but the monies required by said section to be kept at all times on hand shall be determined by the amount of deposits in all respects, as provided for in the said section.

PROVISIONS FOR REDEMPTION OF BANK NOTES.

Sec. 3. That every association organized, or to be organized, under the provisions of the said act, and of the several acts amendatory thereof, shall at all times keep and have on deposit in the Treasury of the United States, in lawful money of the United States, a sum equal to five percentum of its circulation, to be held and used for the redemption of such circulation; which sum shall be counted as a part of its lawful reserve, as provided in section two of this act; and when the circulating notes of any such associations, assorted or unassorted, shall be presented for redemption, in sums of $1,000, or any multiple thereof, to the Treasurer of the United States, the same shall be redeemed in United States notes. All notes so redeemed shall be charged by the Treasurer of the United States to the respective associations issuing the same, and he shall notify them severally, on the first day of each month, or oftener, at his discretion, of the amount of such redemptions; and whenever such redemptions for any association shall amount to the sum of $500, such association so notified shall forthwith deposit with the Treasurer of the United States a sum in United States notes equal to the amount of its circulating notes so redeemed. And all notes of national banks worn, defaced, mutilated, or otherwise unfit for circulation, shall, when received by any assistant treasurer, or at any designated depository of the United States, be forwarded to the Treasurer of the United States for redemption, as provided herein. And when such redemptions have been so reimbursed, the circulating notes so redeemed shall be forwarded to the respective associations by which they were issued; but if any of such notes are worn, mutilated, defaced, or rendered otherwise unfit for use, they shall be forwarded to the Comptroller of the Currency, and destroyed and replaced, as now provided by law: *Provided*, That each of said associations shall reimburse to the Treasury the charges for transportation, and the costs for assorting such notes; and the associations hereafter organized shall also severally reimburse to the Treasury the cost of engraving such plates as shall be ordered by each association respectively; and the amount assessed upon each association shall be in proportion to the circulation redeemed, and be charged to the fund on deposit with the Treasurer: *And provided further*, That so much of section thirty-two of said national bank act requiring or permitting the redemption of its circulating notes elsewhere than at its own counter, except as provided for in this section, is hereby repealed.

WITHDRAWAL OF CIRCULATION.

SEC. 4. That any association organized under this act, or any of the acts of which this is an amendment, desiring to withdraw its circulating notes, in whole or in part, may, upon the deposit of lawful money with the Treasurer of the United States in sums of not less than $9,000, take up the bonds which said association has on deposit with the Treasurer for the security of such circulating notes; which bonds shall be assigned to the bank in the manner specified in the nineteenth section of the national bank act; and the outstanding notes of said association, to an amount equal to the legal tender notes deposited, shall be redeemed at the Treasury of the United States, and destroyed, as now provided by law: *Provided*, That the amount of the bonds on deposit for circulation shall not be reduced below $50,000.

CHARTER NUMBERS OF ASSOCIATIONS TO BE PRINTED ON NATIONAL BANK NOTES.

SEC. 5. That the Comptroller of the Currency shall, under such rules and regulations as the Secretary of the Treasury may prescribe, cause the charter numbers of the association to be printed upon all national bank notes which may be hereafter issued by him.

INCREASE OF THE LAWFUL LEGAL TENDER CIRCULATION.

SEC. 6. That the amount of United States notes outstanding and to be used as a part of the circulating medium, shall not exceed the sum of $382,000,000, which said sum shall appear in each monthly statement of the public debt, and no part thereof shall be held or used as a reserve.

WITHDRAWAL OF CURRENCY TO SECURE EQUITABLE DISTRIBUTION.

SEC. 7. That so much of the act entitled "An act to provide for the redemption of the three per centum temporary loan certificates, and for an increase of national bank notes," as provides that no circulation shall be withdrawn under the provisions of section six of said act, until after the $54,000,000 granted in section one of said act shall have been taken up, is hereby repealed; and it shall be the duty of the Comptroller of the Currency, under the direction of the Secretary of the Treasury, to proceed forthwith, and he is hereby authorized and required, from time to time, as applications shall be duly made therefor, and until the full amount of $55,000,000 shall be withdrawn, to make requisitions upon each of the national banks described in said section, and in the manner therein provided, organized in States having an excess of circulation, to withdraw and return so much of their circulation as by said act may be apportioned to be withdrawn from them, or, in lieu thereof, to deposit in the Treasury of the United States in lawful money sufficient to redeem such circulation; and upon the return of the circulation required, or the deposit of lawful money, as herein provided, a proportionate amount of the bonds held to secure the circulation of such association as shall make such return or deposit shall be surrendered to it.

DELINQUENT BANKS, HOW DEALT WITH.

SEC. 8. That upon the failure of national banks upon which requisition for circulation shall be made, or of any of them, to return the amount required, or to deposit in the Treasury lawful money to redeem the circulation required, within thirty days, the Comptroller of the Currency shall at once sell, as provided in section forty-nine of the national currency act, approved June 3, 1864, bonds held to secure the redemption of the circulation of the association or associations which shall so fail, to an amount sufficient to redeem the circulation required of such association or associations, and with the proceeds, which shall be deposited in the Treasury of the United States, so much of the circulation of such association or associations shall be redeemed as will equal the amount required and not returned; and if there be any excess of proceeds over the amount required for such redemption, it shall be returned to the association or associations whose bonds shall have been sold. And it shall be the duty of the Treasurer, assistant treasurers, designated depositaries, and national bank depositaries of the United States, who shall be kept informed by the Comptroller of the Currency of such associations as shall fail to return circulation as required, to assort and return to the Treasury for redemption the notes of such associations as shall come into their hands until the amount required shall be redeemed, and in like manner to assort and return to the Treasury for redemption the notes of such national banks as have failed, or gone into voluntary liquidation for the purpose of winding up their affairs, and of such as shall hereafter so fail or go into liquidation.

REDISTRIBUTION OF BANK NOTE CIRCULATION.

SEC. 9. That from and after the passage of this act it shall be lawful for the Comptroller of the Currency, and he is hereby required, to issue circulating notes without delay, as applications therefor are made, not to exceed the sum of $55,000,000, to associations organized, or to be organized, in those States and Territories having less than their proportion of circulation, under an apportionment made on the basis of population and of wealth, as shown by the returns of the census of 1870; and every association hereafter organized shall be subject to, and be governed by, the rules, restrictions, and limitations, and possess the rights, privileges, and franchises now or hereafter to be prescribed by law as to national banking associations, with the same power to amend, alter, and repeal provided by "the national bank act:" *Provided*, That the whole amount of circulation withdrawn and redeemed from banks transacting business shall not exceed $55,000,000, and that such circulation shall be withdrawn and redeemed as it shall be necessary to supply the circulation previously issued to the banks in those States having less than their apportionment: *And provided further*, That not more than $30,000,000 shall be withdrawn and redeemed, as herein contemplated, during the fiscal year ending June 30, 1875.

Approved June 20, 1874.

BANKRUPT BILL,

AS AMENDED 1875.

AN ACT to establish a uniform system of bankruptcy throughout the United States.

Be it enacted by the Senate and House of Representatives of the United States of America in Congress assembled, That the several district courts of the United States be, and they hereby are, constituted courts of bankruptcy, and they shall have original jurisdiction in their respective districts in all matters and proceedings in bankruptcy, and they are hereby authorized to hear and adjudicate upon the same according to the provisions of this act. The said courts shall be always open for the transaction of business under this act, and the powers and jurisdiction hereby granted and conferred shall be exercised as well in vacation as in term time; and a judge sitting at chambers shall have the same powers and jurisdiction, including the power of keeping order and of punishing any contempt of his authority, as when sitting in court. And the jurisdiction hereby conferred shall extend to all cases and controversies arising between the bankrupt and any creditor or creditors who shall claim any debt or demand under the bankruptcy; to the collection of all the assets of the bankrupt; to the ascertainment and liquidation of the liens and other specific claims thereon; to the adjustment of the various priorities and conflicting interests of all parties; and to the marshaling and disposition of the different funds and assets, so as to secure the rights of all parties and due distribution of the assets among all the creditors; and to all acts, matters, and things to be done under and in virtue of the bankruptcy, until the final distribution and settlement of the estate of the bankrupt, and the close of the proceedings in bankruptcy. The said courts shall have full authority to compel obedience to all orders and decrees passed by them in bankruptcy, by process of contempt and other remedial process, to the same extent that the circuit courts now have in any suit pending therein in equity. Said courts may sit for the transaction of business in bankruptcy at any place in the district, of which place, and the time of holding court, they shall have given notice, as well as at the places designated by law for holding such courts. The court having charge of the estate of any bankrupt may direct that any of the legal assets or debts of the bankrupt, as contradistinguished from equitable demands, shall, when such debt does not exceed five hundred dollars, be collected in the courts of the State where such bankrupt resides having jurisdiction of claims of such nature and amount.

SEC. 2. *And be it further enacted*, That the several circuit courts of the United States, within and for the districts where the proceedings in bankruptcy shall be pending, shall have a general superintendence and jurisdiction of all cases and questions arising under this act; and, except when special provision is otherwise made, may, upon bill, petition, or other proper process, of any party aggrieved, hear and determine the case as a court of equity. The powers and jurisdiction hereby granted may be exercised either by said court, or by any justice thereof, in term time or vacation. Said circuit courts shall also have concurrent jurisdiction with the district courts of any district, of all suits at law or in equity, which may or shall be brought by the assignee in bankruptcy against any person claiming an adverse interest, or owing any debt to such bankrupt, or by such person against such assignee, touching any property or rights of property of said bankrupt transferable to or vested in such assignee; but no suit at law or in equity shall, in any case, be maintainable by or against such assignee, or by or against any person claiming an adverse interest, touching the property and rights of property aforesaid, in any court whatsoever, unless the same shall be brought within two years from the time the cause of action accrued, for or against such assignee; *Provided*, That nothing herein contained shall revive a right of action barred at the time such assignee is appointed. The court may, in its discretion, on sufficient cause shown, and upon notice and hearing, direct the receiver or assignee to take possession of the property, and carry on the business of the debtor, or any part thereof, under the direction of the court, when, in its judgment, the interest of the estate as well as of the creditors will be promoted thereby, but not for a period exceeding nine months from the time the debtor shall have been declared a bankrupt: *Provided*, That such order shall not be made until the court shall be satisfied that it is approved by a majority in value of the creditors.

OF THE ADMINISTRATION OF THE LAW IN COURTS OF BANKRUPTCY.

SEC. 3. *And be it further enacted*, That it shall be the duty of the judges of the district courts of the United States within and for the several districts to appoint in each congressional district in said districts, upon the nomination and recommendation of the Chief Justice of the Supreme Court of the United States, one or more registers in bankruptcy, to assist the judge of the district court in the performance of his duties under this act. No person shall be eligible to such appointment unless he be a counsellor of said court, or of some one of the courts of record of the State in which he resides. Before entering upon the duties of his office, every person so appointed a register in bankruptcy shall give a bond to the United States, with condition that he will faithfully discharge the duties of his office, in a sum not less than one thousand dollars, to be fixed by said court, with sureties satisfactory to said court, or to either of the said justices thereof; and he shall, in open court, take and subscribe the oath prescribed in the act entitled "An act to prescribe an oath of office, and for other purposes," approved July second, eighteen hundred and sixty-two; and also that he will not, during his continuance in office, be, directly or indirectly, interested in or benefited by the fees or emoluments arising from any suit or matter pending in bankruptcy in either the district or circuit court in his district.

SEC. 4. *And be it further enacted*, That every register in bankruptcy so appointed and qualified, shall have power, and it shall be his duty, to make adjudication of bankruptcy, to receive the surrender of any bankrupt, to administer oaths in all proceedings before him, to hold and preside at meetings of creditors, to take proof of debts, to make all computations of dividends, and all orders of distribution, and to furnish the assignee with a certified copy of such orders, and of the schedules of creditors and assets filed in each case, to audit and pass accounts of assignees, to grant protection, to pass the last examination of any bankrupt in cases whenever the assignee or a creditor do not oppose, and to sit in chambers and dispatch there such part of the administrative business of the court and such uncontested matters as shall be defined in general rules and orders, or as the district judge shall in any particular matter direct; and he shall also make short memoranda of his proceedings in each case in which he shall act, in a docket to be kept by him for that purpose, and he shall forthwith, as the proceedings are taken, forward to the clerk of the district court a certified copy of said memoranda, which shall be entered by said clerk in the proper minute-book to be kept in his office, and any register of the court may act for any other register thereof: *Provided, however*, That nothing in this section contained shall empower a register to commit for contempt, or to hear a disputed adjudication, or any question of the allowance or suspension of an order of discharge; but in all matters where an issue of fact or of law is raised and contested by any party to the proceedings before him, it shall be his duty to cause the question or issue to be stated by the opposing parties in writing, and he shall adjourn the same into court for decision by the judge. No register shall be of counsel or attorney, either in or out of court, in any suit or matter pending in bankruptcy in either the circuit or district court of his district, nor in an appeal therefrom; nor shall he be executor, administrator, guardian, commissioner, appraiser, divider, or assignee, of or upon any estate within the jurisdiction of either of said courts of bankruptcy, nor be interested in the fees or emoluments arising from either of said trusts. The fees of said registers, as established by this act, and by the general rules and orders required to be framed under it, shall be paid to them by the parties for whom the services may be rendered in the course of proceedings authorized by this act.

SEC. 5. *And be it further enacted*, That the judge of the district court may direct a register to attend at any place within the district, for the purpose of hearing such voluntary applications under this act as may not be opposed, of attending any meeting of creditors, or receiving any proof of debts, and, generally, for the prosecution of any bankruptcy or other proceedings under this act; and the traveling and incidental expenses of such register, and of any clerk or other officer attending him, incurred in so acting, shall be settled by said court in accordance with the rules prescribed under the tenth section of this act, and paid out of the assets of the estate in respect of which such register has so acted; or if there be no such assets, or if the assets shall be insufficient, then such expenses shall form a part of the costs in the case or cases in which the register shall have acted in such journey, to be apportioned by the judge; and such register, so acting, shall have and exercise all powers, except the power of commitment, vested in the district court for the summoning and examination of persons or witnesses, and for requiring the production of books, papers, and documents: *Provided always*, That all depositions of persons and witnesses taken before said register, and all acts done by him, shall be reduced to writing and be signed by him, and shall be filed in the clerk's office as part of the proceedings. Such register shall be subject to removal by the judge of the [circuit] district court, and all vacancies occurring by such removal, or by resignation, change of residence, death, or disability, shall be promptly filled by other fit persons, unless said court shall deem the continuance of the particular office unnecessary.

SEC. 6. *And be it further enacted*, That any party shall, during the proceedings before a register, be at liberty to take the opinion of the district judge upon any point or matter arising in the course of such proceedings, or upon the result of such proceedings, which shall be stated by the register in the shape of a short certificate to the judge, who shall sign the same, if he approve thereof; and such certificate, so signed, shall be binding on all the parties to the proceeding; but every such certificate may be discharged or varied by the judge at chambers or in open court. In any baukruptcy, or in any other proceedings within the jurisdiction of the court under this act, the parties concerned, or submitting to such jurisdiction, may, at any stage of the proceedings, by consent, state any question or questions in a special case for the opinion of the court; and the judgment of the court shall be final, unless it be agreed and stated in such special case that either party may appeal, if, in such case, an appeal is allowed by this act. The parties may also, if they think fit, agree, that upon the question or questions raised by such special case being finally decided, a sum of money, fixed by the parties, or to be ascertained by the court, or in such manner as the court may direct, or any property, or the amount of any disputed debt or claim, shall be paid, delivered, or transferred by one of such parties to the other of them, either with or without costs.

SEC. 7. *And be it further enacted*, That parties and witnesses summoned before a register shall be bound to attend in pursuance of such summons at the place and time designated therein, and shall be entitled to protection, and be liable to process of contempt in like manner as parties and witnesses are now liable thereto in case of default in attendance under any writ of subpoena; and all persons willfully and corruptly swearing or affirming falsely before a register shall be liable to all the penalties, punishments, and consequences of perjury. If any person examined before a register shall refuse or decline to answer, or to swear to or sign his examination when taken, the register shall refer the matter to the judge, who shall have power to order the person so acting to pay the costs thereby occasioned, if such person be compellable by law to answer such question, or to sign such examination, and such person shall also be liable to be punished for contempt.

OF APPEALS AND PRACTICE.

SEC. 8. *And be it further enacted*, That appeals may be taken from the district to the circuit courts in all cases in equity, and writs of error may be allowed to said circuit courts from said district courts in cases at law under the jurisdiction created by this act when the debt or damages claimed amount to more than five hundred dollars; and any supposed creditor, whose claim is wholly or in part rejected, or an assignee who is dissatisfied with the allowance of a claim, may appeal from the decision of the district court to the circuit court for the same district; but no appeal shall be allowed in any case from the district to the circuit court unless it is claimed, and notice given thereof to the clerk of the district court, to be entered with the record of the proceedings, and also to the assignee or creditor, as the case may be, or to the defeated party in equity, within ten days after the entry of the decree or decision appealed from. The appeal shall be entered at the term of the circuit court which shall be first held within and for the district next after the expiration of ten days from the time of claiming the same. But if the appellant in writing waives his appeal before any decision thereon, proceedings may be had in the district court as if no appeal had been taken, and no appeal shall be allowed unless the appellant at the time of claiming the same shall give bond in manner now required by law in cases of such appeals. No writ of error shall be allowed unless the party claiming it shall comply with the statutes regulating the granting of such writs.

SEC. 9. *And be it further enacted*, That in cases arising under this act no appeal or writ of error shall be allowed in any case from the circuit courts to the Supreme Court of the United States unless the matter in dispute in such case shall exceed two thousand dollars.

SEC. 10. *And be it further enacted*, That the justices of the Supreme Court of the United States, subject to the provisions of this act, shall frame general orders for the following purposes:

For regulating the practice and procedure of the district

courts in bankruptcy, and the several forms of petitions, orders, and other proceedings to be used in said courts in all matters under this act;

For regulating the duties of the various officers of said courts;

For regulating the fees payable, and the charges and costs to be allowed, with respect to all proceedings in bankruptcy before said courts, not exceeding the rate of fees now allowed by law for similar services in other proceedings:

For regulating the practice and procedure upon appeals;

For regulating the filing, custody, and inspection of records;

And generally for carrying the provisions of this act into effect.

After such general orders shall have been so framed, they, or any of them, may be rescinded or varied, and other general orders may be framed in manner aforesaid, and all such general orders so framed shall, from time to time, be reported to Congress, with such suggestions as said justices may think proper.

VOLUNTARY BANKRUPTCY — COMMENCEMENT OF PROCEEDINGS.

SEC. 11. *And be it further enacted*, That if any person residing within the jurisdiction of the United States, owing debts provable under this act exceeding the amount of three hundred dollars, shall apply by petition, addressed to the judge of the judicial district in which such debtor has resided or carried on business for the six months next immediately preceding the time of filing such petition, or for the longest period during such six months, setting forth his place of residence, his inability to pay all his debts in full, his willingness to surrender all his estate and effects for the benefit of his creditors, and his desire to obtain the benefit of this act, and shall annex to his petition a schedule, verified by oath before the court, or before a register in bankruptcy, or before one of the commissioners of the Circuit Court of the United States, containing a full and true statement of all his debts, and, as far as possible, to whom due, with the place of residence of each creditor, if known to the debtor, and if not known the fact to be so stated, and the sum due to each creditor, also the nature of each debt or demand, whether founded on written security, obligation, contract, or otherwise, and also the true cause and consideration of such indebtedness in each case, and the place where such indebtedness accrued, and a statement of any existing mortgage, pledge, lien, judgment, or collateral or other security given for the payment of the same; and shall also annex to his petition an accurate inventory and valuation, verified in like manner, of all his estate, both real and personal, assignable under this act, describing the same, and stating where it is situated, and whether there are any, and if so, what incumbrances thereon, the filing of such petition shall be an act of bankruptcy, and such petitioner shall be adjudged a bankrupt: *Provided*, That all citizens of the United States petitioning to be declared bankrupt, shall, on filing such petition and before any proceedings thereon, take and subscribe an oath of allegience and fidelity to the United States, which oath shall be filed and recorded with the proceedings in bankruptcy. And the judge of the district court, or, if there be no opposing party, any register of said court, to be designated by the judge, shall forthwith, if he be satisfied that the debts due from the petitioner exceed three hundred dollars, issue a warrant, to be signed by such judge or register, directed to the marshal of said district, authorizing him forthwith, as messenger, to publish notices in such newspapers as the marshal shall select, not exceeding two; to serve written or printed notice, by mail or personally, on all creditors upon the schedule filed with the debtor's petition, or whose names may be given to him, in addition, by the debtor, and to give such personal or other notice to any persons concerned as the warrant specifies. But whenever the creditors of the bankrupt are so numerous as to make any notice now required by law to them, by mail or otherwise a great and disproportionate expense to the estate, the court may in lieu thereof, in its discretion, order such notice to be given by publication in a newspaper or newspapers to all such creditors whose claims as reported do not exceed the sums respectively of fifty dollars, which notice shall state—

First, That a warrant in bankruptcy has been issued against the estate of the debtor.

Second, That the payment of any debts and the delivery of any property belonging to such debtor to him or for his use, and the transfer of any property by him, are forbidden by law.

Third, That a meeting of the creditors of the debtor, giving the names, residences, and amounts, so far as known, to prove their debts and choose one or more assignees of his estate, will be held at a court of bankruptcy, to be holden at a time and place designated in the warrant, not less than ten nor more than ninety days after the issuing of the same.

OF ASSIGNMENTS AND ASSIGNEES.

SEC. 12. *And be it further enacted*, That at the meeting, held in pursuance of the notice, one of the registers of the court shall preside, and the messenger shall make return of the warrant and of his doings thereon; and if it appears that the notice to the creditors has not been as required in the warrant, the meeting shall forthwith be adjourned, and a new notice given as required. If the debtor dies after the issuing the warrant, the proceedings may be continued and concluded in like manner as if he had lived.

SEC. 13. *And be it further enacted*, That the creditors shall, at the first meeting held after due notice from the messenger, in presence of a register designated by the court, choose one or more assignees of the estate of the debtor; the choice to be made by the greater part in value and in number of the creditors who have proved their debts. If no choice is made by the creditors at said meeting, the judge, or, if there be no opposing interest, the register shall appoint one or more assignees. If an assignee, so chosen or appointed, fails within five days to express in writing his acceptance of the trust, the judge or register may fill the vacancy. All elections or appointments of assignees shall be subject to the approval of the judge; and when in his judgment it is for any cause needful or expedient, he may appoint additional assignees, or order a new election. The judge at any time may, and, upon the request in writing of any creditor who has proved his claim, shall require the assignee to give good and sufficient bond to the United States, with a condition for the faithful performance and discharge of his duties; the bond shall be approved by the judge or register by his indorsement thereon, shall be filed with the record of the case, and inure to the benefit of all creditors proving their claims, and may be prosecuted in the name and for the benefit of any injured party. If the assignee fails to give the bond within such time as the judge orders, not exceeding ten days after notice to him of such order, the judge shall remove him and appoint another in his place.

SEC. 14. *And be it further enacted,* That as soon as said assignee is appointed and qualified, the judge, or, where there is no opposing interest, the register shall, by an instrument under his hand, assign and convey to the assignee all the estate, real and personal, of the bankrupt, with all his deeds, books, and papers relating thereto, and such assignment shall relate back to the commencement of said proceedings in bankruptcy, and thereupon, by operation of law, the title to all such property and estate, both real and personal, shall vest in said assignee, although the same is then attached on mesne process as the property of the debtor, and shall dissolve any such attachment made within four months next preceding the commencement of said proceedings: *Provided, however,* That there shall be excepted from the operation of the provisions of this section the necessary household and kitchen furniture, and such other articles and necessaries of such bankrupt as the said assignee shall designate and set apart, having reference in the amount to the family, condition, and circumstances of the bankrupt, but altogether not to exceed in value, in any case, the sum of five hundred dollars; and also the wearing apparel of such bankrupt, and that of his wife and children, and the uniform, arms, and equipments of any person who is or has been a soldier in the militia or in the service of the United States; and such other property as now is, or hereafter shall be, exempted from attachment, or seizure, or levy on execution by the laws of the United States, and such other property not included in the foregoing exceptions as is exempted from levy and sale upon execution or other process or order of any court by the laws of the State in which the bankrupt has his domicile at the time of the commencement of the proceedings in bankruptcy, to an amount not exceeding that allowed by such State exemption laws in force in the year eighteen hundred and sixty-four: *Provided,* That the foregoing exception shall operate as a limitation upon the conveyance of the property of the bankrupt to his assignees, and in no case shall the property hereby excepted pass to the assignees, or the title of the bankrupt thereto be impaired or affected by any of the provisions of this act; and the determination of the assignee in the matter shall, on exception taken, be subject to the final decision of the said court: *And provided further,* That no mortgage of any vessel or of any other goods or chattels, made as security for any debt or debts, in good faith and for present considerations, and otherwise valid, and duly recorded, pursuant to any statute of the United States, or of any State, shall be invalidated or affected hereby; and all the property conveyed by the bankrupt in fraud of his creditors; all rights in equity, choses in action, patents and patent rights and copyrights; all debts due him, or any person for his use, and all liens and securities therefor; and all his rights of action for property or estate, real or personal, and for any cause of action which the bankrupt had against any person arising from contract or from the unlawful taking or detention of or injury to the property of the bankrupt; and all his rights of redeeming such property or estate, with the like right, title, power, and authority to sell, manage, dispose of, sue for, and recover or defend the same, as the bankrupt might or could have had if no assignment had been made, shall, in virtue of the adjudication of bankruptcy and the appointment of his assignee, be at once vested in such assignee; and he may sue for and recover the said estate, debts, and effects, and may prosecute and defend all suits at law or in equity, pending at the time of the adjudication of bankruptcy, in which such bankrupt is a party in his own name, in the same manner and with the like effect as they might have been presented or defended by such bankrupt; and a copy, duly certified by the clerk of the court under the seal thereof, of the assignment made by the judge or register, as the case may be, to him as assignee, shall be conclusive evidence of his title as such assignee to take, hold, sue for, and recover the property of the bankrupt, as hereinbefore mentioned; but no property held by the bankrupt in trust shall pass by such assignment. No person shall be entitled to maintain an action against an assignee in bankruptcy for any thing done by him as such assignee, without previously giving him twenty days' notice of such action, specifying the cause thereof, to the end that such assignee may have an opportunity of tendering amends, should he see fit to do so. No person shall be entitled, as against the assignee, to withhold from him possession of any books of account of the bankrupt, or claim any lien thereon; and no suit in which the assignee is a party shall be abated by his death or removal from office, but the same may be prosecuted and defended by his successor, or by the surviving or remaining assignee, as the case may be. The assignee shall have authority, under the order and direction of the court, to redeem or discharge any mortgage or conditional contract, or pledge or deposit, or lien upon any property, real or personal, whenever payable, and to tender due performance of the condition thereof, or to sell the same subject to such mortgage, lien, or other incumbrances. The debtor shall also, at the request of the assignee, and at the expense of the estate, make and execute any instruments, deeds, and writings which may be proper, to enable the assignee to possess himself fully of all the assets of the bankrupt. The assignee shall immediately give notice of his appointment, by publication at least once a week for three successive weeks, in such newspapers as shall, for that purpose, be designated by the court, due regard being had to their general circulation in the district, or in that portion of the district in which the bankrupt and his creditors shall reside, and shall, within six months, cause the assignment to him to be recorded in every registry of deeds or other office within the United

States where a conveyance of any lands owned by the bankrupt ought by law to be recorded; and the record of such assignment, or a duly certified copy thereof, shall be evidence thereof in all courts.

SEC. 15. *And be it further enacted,* That the assignee shall demand and receive from any and all persons holding the same all the estate assigned, or intended to be assigned, under the provisions of this act; that unless otherwise ordered by the court, the assignee shall sell the property of the bankrupt, whether real or personal, at public auction, in such parts or parcels and at such times and places as shall be best calculated to produce the greatest amount with the least expense. All notices of public sales under this act by any assignee or officer of the court shall be published once a week for three consecutive weeks in the newspaper or newspapers, to be designated by the judge, which, in his opinion, shall be best calculated to give general notice of the sale. And the court, on the application of any party in interest, shall have complete supervisory power over such sales, including the power to set aside the same and to order a re-sale, so that the property sold shall realize the largest sum. And the court may, in its discretion, order any real estate of the bankrupt, or any part thereof, to be sold for one-fourth cash at the time of sale, and the residue within eighteen months in such instalments as the court may direct, bearing interest at the rate of seven per centum per annum, and secured by proper mortgage or lien upon the property so sold. And it shall be the duty of every assignee to keep a regular account of all moneys received or expended by him as such assignee, to which account every creditor shall, at reasonable times, have free access. If any assignee shall fail or neglect to well and faithfully discharge his duties in the sale or disposition of property as above contemplated, it shall be the duty of the court to remove such assignee, and he shall forfeit all fees and emoluments to which he might be entitled in connection with such sale. And if any assignee shall, in any manner, in violation of his duty aforesaid, unfairly or wrongfully sell or dispose of, or in any manner fraudulently or corruptly combine, conspire, or agree with any person or persons, with intent to unfairly or wrongfully sell or dispose of the property committed to his charge, he shall, upon proof thereof, be removed, and forfeit all fees or other compensation for any and all services in connection with such bankrupt's estate, and, upon conviction thereof before any court of competent jurisdiction, shall be liable to a fine of not more than ten thousand dollars, or imprisonment in the penitentiary for a term of not exceeding two years, or both fine and imprisonment, at the discretion of the court. And any person so combining, conspiring, or agreeing with such assignee for the purpose aforesaid shall, upon conviction, be liable to a like punishment. That the assignee shall report, under oath, to the court, at least as often as once in three months, the condition of the estate in his charge, and the state of his accounts in detail, and at all other times when the court, on motion or otherwise, shall so order. And on any settlement of the accounts of any assignee, he shall be required to account for all interest, benefit, or advantage received, or in any manner agreed to be received, directly or indirectly, from the use, disposal, or proceeds of the bankrupt's estate. And he shall be required, upon such settlement, to make and file in court an affidavit declaring, according to the truth, whether he has or has not, as the case may be, received, or is or is not, as the case may be, to receive, directly or indirectly, any interest, benefit, or advantage from the use or deposit of such funds; and such assignee may be examined orally upon the same subject, and if he shall willfully swear falsely, either in such affidavit or examination, or to his report provided for in this section, he shall be deemed to be guilty of perjury, and, on conviction thereof, be punished by imprisonment in the penitentiary not less than one and not more than five years.

SEC. 16. *And be it further enacted,* That the assignee shall have the like remedy to recover all said estate, debts, and effects, in his own name, as the debtor might have had if the decree in bankruptcy had not been rendered and no assignment had been made. If, at the time of the commencement of proceedings in bankruptcy, an action is pending in the name of the debtor for the recovery of a debt or other thing which might or ought to pass to the assignee by the assignment, the assignee shall, if he requires it, be admitted to prosecute the action in his own name, in like manner and with like effect, as if it had been originally commenced by him. No suit pending in the name of the assignee shall be abated by his death or removal; but upon the motion of the surviving, or remaining, or new assignee, as the case may be, he shall be admitted to prosecute the suit, in like manner and with like effect as if it had been originally commenced by him. In suits prosecuted by the assignee, a certified copy of the assignment made to him by the judge or register shall be conclusive evidence of his authority to sue.

SEC. 17. *And be it further enacted*, That the assignee shall, as soon as may be after receiving any money belonging to the estate, deposit the same in some bank in his name as assignee, or otherwise keep it distinct and apart from all other money in his possession; and shall, as far as practicable, keep all goods and effects belonging to the estate separate and apart from all other goods in his possession, or designated by appropriate marks, so that they may be easily and clearly distinguished, and may not be exposed or liable to be taken as his property or for the payment of his debts. When it appears that the distribution of the estate may be delayed by litigation or other cause, the court may direct the temporary investment of the money belonging to such estate in securities to be approved by the judge or a register of said court, or may authorize the same to be deposited in any convenient bank, upon such interest, not exceeding the legal rate, as the bank may contract with the assignee to pay thereon. He shall give written notice to all known creditors, by mail or otherwise, of all dividends, and such notice of meetings, after the first, as may be ordered by the court. He shall be allowed, and may retain, out of money in his hands, all the necessary disbursements made by him in the discharge of his duty, and a reasonable compensation for his services, in the discretion of the court. He may, under the direction of the court, submit any controversy, arising in the settlement of demands against the estate, or of debts due to it, to the determination of arbitrators, to be chosen by him and the other party to the controversy, and may, under such direction, compound and settle any such controversy by agreement with the other party, as he thinks proper and most for the interest of the creditors.

SEC. 18. *And be it further enacted*, That the court, after due notice and hearing, may remove an assignee for any cause which, in the judgment of the court, renders such removal necessary or expedient. At a meeting called by order of the court in its discretion for the purpose, or which shall be called upon the application of a majority of the creditors in number and value, the creditors may, with consent of the court, remove any assignee by such a vote as is hereinbefore provided for the choice of assignee. An assignee may, with the consent of the judge, resign his trust and be discharged therefrom. Vacancies caused by death or otherwise in the office of assignee may be filled by appointment of the court, or, at its discretion, by an election by the creditors, in the manner hereinbefore provided, at a regular meeting, or at a meeting called for the purpose, with such notice thereof in writing to all known creditors, and by such person, as the court shall direct. The resignation or removal of an assignee shall in no way release him from performing all things requisite on his part for the proper closing up of his trust and the transmission thereof to his successors, nor shall it affect the liability of the principal or surety on the bond given by the assignee. When, by death or otherwise, the number of assignees is reduced, the estate of the debtor not lawfully disposed of shall vest in the remaining assignee or assignees, and the persons selected to fill vacancies, if any, with the same powers and duties relative thereto as if they were originally chosen. Any former assignee, his executors or administrators upon request, and at the expense of the estate, shall make and execute to the new assignee all deeds, conveyances, and assurances, and do all other lawful acts requisite to enable him to recover and receive all the estate. And the court may make all orders which it may deem expedient to secure the proper fulfillment of the duties of any former assignee, and the rights and interests of all persons interested in the estate. No person who has received any preference contrary to the provisions of this act shall vote for or be eligible as assignee; but no title to property, real or personal, sold, transferred, or conveyed by an assignee, shall be affected or impaired by reason of his ineligibility. An assignee refusing or unreasonably neglecting to execute an instrument when lawfully required by the court, or disobeying a lawful order or decree of the court in the premises, may be punished as for a contempt of court.

OF DEBTS AND PROOF OF CLAIMS.

SEC. 19. *And be it further enacted*, That all debts due and payable from the bankrupt at the time of the adjudication of bankruptcy, and all debts then existing but not payable until a future day, a rebate of interest being made when no interest is payable by the terms of contract, may be proved against the estate of the bankrupt. All demands against the bankrupt for or on account of any goods or chattels wrongfully taken, converted, or withheld by him, may be proved and allowed as debts to the amount of the value of the property so taken or withheld, with interest. If the bankrupt shall be bound as drawer, indorser, surety, bail, or guarantor upon any bill, bond, note, or any other specialty or contract, or for any debt of another person, and his liability shall not have become absolute until after the adjudication of bankruptcy, the creditor may prove the same, after such liability shall have become fixed, and before the final dividend shall have been declared. In all cases of contingent debts and contingent liabilities contracted by the bankrupt, and not herein otherwise provided for, the creditor may make claim therefor, and have his claim allowed, with the right to share in the dividends, if the contingency shall happen before the order for the final dividend; or he may at any time apply to the court to have the present value of the debt or liability ascertained and liquidatad, which shall then be done in such manner as the court shall order, and he shall be allowed to prove for the amount so ascertained. Any person liable as bail, surety, guarantor, or otherwise for the bankrupt, who shall have paid the debt or any part thereof in discharge of the whole, shall be entitled to prove such debt, or to stand in the place of the creditor if he shall have proved the same, although such payments shall have been made after the proceedings in bankruptcy were commenced. And any person so liable for the bankrupt, and who has not paid the whole of said debt, but is still liable for the same or any part thereof, may, if the creditor shall fail or omit to prove such debt, prove the same either in the name of the creditor or otherwise, as may be provided by the rules, and subject to such regulations and limitations as may be established by such rules. Where the bankrupt is liable to pay rent, or other debt falling due at fixed and stated periods, the creditor may prove for a proportionate part thereof up to the time of the bankruptcy, as if the same grew due from day to day, and not at such fixed and stated periods. If any bankrupt shall be liable for unliquidated damages arising out of any contract or promise, or on account of any goods or chattels wrongfully taken, converted, or withheld, the court may cause such damages to be assessed in such mode as it may deem best, and the sum so assessed may be proved against the estate. No debts other than those above specified shall be proved or allowed against the estate.

SEC. 20. *And be it further enacted*, That in all cases of mutual debts or mutual credits between the parties, the account between them shall be stated, and one debt set off against the other, and the balance only shall be allowed or paid, but no set-off shall be allowed of a claim in its nature not provable against the estate, or in cases of compulsory bankruptcy after the act of bankruptcy upon or in respect of which the adjudication shall be made, and with a view of making such set-off: *Provided*, That no set-off shall be allowed in favor of any debtor to the bankrupt of a claim purchased by or transferred to him after the filing of the petition. When a creditor has a mortgage or pledge of real or personal property of the bankrupt, or a lien thereon for securing the payment of a debt owing to him from the bankrupt, he shall be admitted as a creditor only for the balance of the debt after deducting the value of such property, to be ascertained by agreement between him and the assignee, or by a sale thereof, to be made in such manner as the court shall direct; or the creditor may release or convey his claim to the assignee upon such property, and be admitted to prove his whole debt. If the value of the property exceeds the sum for which it is so held as security, the assignee may release to the creditor the bankrupt's right of redemption therein on receiving such excess; or he may sell the property, subject to the claim of the creditor thereon; and in either case the assignee and creditor, respectively, shall execute all deeds and writings necessary or proper to consummate the transaction. If the property is not so sold or released and delivered up, the creditor shall not be allowed to prove any part of his debt.

SEC. 21. *And be it further enacted*, That no creditor proving his debt or claim shall be allowed to maintain any suit at law or in equity therefor against the bankrupt, but shall be deemed to have waived all right of action and suit against the bankrupt, and all proceedings already commenced, or unsatisfied judgments already obtained thereon, shall be deemed to be discharged and surrendered thereby. But a creditor proving his debt or claim shall not be held to have waived his right of action or suit against the bankrupt where a discharge has been refused, or the proceedings have been determined without a discharge; and no creditor whose debt is provable under this act shall be allowed to prosecute to final judgment any suit at law or in equity therefor against the bankrupt, until the question of the debtor's discharge shall have been determined; and any such suit or proceedings shall, upon the application of the bankrupt, be stayed to await the determination of the court in bankruptcy on the question of the discharge, provided there be no unreasonable delay on the part of the bankrupt in endeavoring to obtain his discharge, and provided, also, that if the amount due the creditor is in dispute, the suit, by leave of the court in bankruptcy, may proceed to judgment, for the purpose of ascertaining the amount due, which amount may be proved in bankruptcy, but execution shall be stayed as aforesaid. If any bankrupt shall, at the time of adjudication, be liable upon any bill of exchange, promissory note, or other obligation in respect of distinct contracts as a member of two or more firms carrying on separate and distinct trades, and having distinct estates to be wound up in bankruptcy, or as a sole trader and also as a member of a firm, the circumstance that such firms are in whole or in part composed of the same individuals, or that the sole contractor is also one of the joint contractors, shall not prevent proof and receipt of dividend in respect of such distinct contracts against the estates respectively liable upon such contracts.

SEC. 22. *And be it further enacted,* That all proofs of debts against the estate of the bankrupt, by or in behalf of creditors residing within the judicial district where the proceedings in bankruptcy are pending, shall be made before one of the registers of the court in said district, and by or in behalf of non-resident debtors before any register in bankruptcy in the judicial district where such creditors, or either of them, reside, or before any commissioner of the circuit court authorized to administer oaths in any district. To entitle a claimant against the estate of a bankrupt to have his demand allowed, it must be verified by a deposition in writing on oath or solemn affirmation before the proper register or commissioner, setting forth the demand, the consideration thereof, whether any and what securities are held therefor, and whether any and what payments have been made thereon; that the sum claimed is justly due from the bankrupt to the claimant; that the claimant has not, nor has any other person for his use, received any security or satisfaction whatever other than that by him set forth; that the claim was not procured for the purpose of influencing the proceedings under this act, and that no bargain or agreement, express or implied, has been made or entered into, by or on behalf of such creditor, to sell, transfer, or dispose of the said claim, or any part thereof, against such bankrupt, or take or receive, directly or indirectly, any money, property, or consideration whatever, whereby the vote of such creditor for assignee, or any action on the part of such creditor or any other person in the proceedings under this act, is or shall be in any way affected, influeuced, or controlled, and no claim shall be allowed unless all the statements set forth in such deposition shall appear to be true. Such oath or solemn affirmation shall be made by the claimant testifying of his own knowledge, unless he is absent from the United States or prevented by some other good cause from testifying, in which cases the demand may be verified in like manner by the attorney or authorized agent of the claimant testifying to the best of his knowledge, information, and belief, and setting forth his means of knowledge, or, if in a foreign country, the oath of the creditor may be taken before any minister, consul, or vice-consul of the United States; and the court may, if it shall see fit, require or receive further pertinent evidence, either for or against the admission of the claim. Corporations may verify their claims by the oath or solemn affirmation of their president, cashier, or treasurer. If the proof is satisfactory to the register or commissioner, it shall be signed by the deponent, and delivered or sent by mail to the assignee, who shall examine the same and compare it with the books and accounts of the bankrupt, and shall register, in a book to be kept by him for that purpose, the names of creditors who have proved their claims, in the order in which such proof is received, stating the time of receipt of such proof, and the amount and nature of the debts, which books shall be open to the inspection of all the creditors. The court may, on the application of the assignee, or of any creditor, or of the bankrupt, or without any application, examine upon oath the bankrupt, or any person tendering or who has made proof of claims, and may summon any person capable of giving evidence concerning such proof, or concerning the debt sought to be proved, and shall reject all claims not duly proved, or where the proof shows the claim to be founded in fraud, illegality, or mistake.

SEC. 23. *And be it further enacted,* That when a claim is presented for proof before the election of the assignee, and the judge entertains doubts of its validity, or of the right of the creditor to prove it, and is of opinion that such validity or right ought to be investigated by the assignee, he may postpone the proof of the claim until the assignee is chosen. Any person who, after the approval of this act, shall have accepted any preference, having reasonable cause to believe that the same was made or given by the debtor, contrary to any provision of this act, shall not prove the debt or claim on account of which the preference was made or given, nor shall he receive any dividend therefrom, until he shall first have surrendered to the assignee all property, money, benefit, or advantage, received by him under such preference. The court shall allow all debts duly proved, and shall cause a list thereof to be made and certified by one of the registers; and any creditor may act at all meetings by his duly constituted attorney the same as though personally present.

SEC. 24. *And be it further enacted*, That a supposed creditor who takes an appeal to the circuit court from the decision of the district court rejecting his claim, in whole or in part, shall, upon entering his appeal in the circuit court, file in the clerk's office thereof a statement in writing of his claim, setting forth the same, substantially, as in a declaration for the same cause of action at law, and the assignee shall plead or answer thereto in like manner, and like proceedings shall thereupon be had in the pleadings, trial, and determination of the cause, as in an action at law commenced and prosecuted, in the usual manner, in the courts of the United States, except that no execution shall be awarded against the assignee for the amount of a debt found due to the creditor. The final judgment of the court shall be conclusive, and the list of debts shall, if necessary, be altered to conform thereto. The party prevailing in the suit shall be entitled to costs against the adverse party, to be taxed and recovered as in suits at law; if recovered against the assignee they shall be allowed out of the estate. A bill of exchange, promissory note, or other instrument, used in evidence upon the proof of a claim, and left in court, or deposited in the clerk's office, may be delivered, by the register or clerk having the custody thereof, to the person who used it, upon his filing a copy thereof, attested by the clerk of the court, who shall indorse upon it the name of the party against whose estate it has been proved and the date and amount of any dividend declared thereon.

OF PROPERTY PERISHABLE AND IN DISPUTE.

SEC. 25. *And be it further enacted,* That when it appears to the satisfaction of the court that the estate of the debtor, or any part thereof, is of a perishable nature, or liable to deteriorate in value, the court may order the same to be sold, in such manner as may be deemed most expedient, under the direction of the messenger or assignee, as the case may be, who shall hold the funds received in place of the estate disposed of; and whenever it appears to the satisfaction of the court that the title to any portion of an estate, real or personal, which has come into possession of the assignee, or which is claimed by him, is in dispute, the court may, upon the petition of the assignee, and after such notice to the claimant, his agent or attorney, as the court shall deem reasonable, order it to be sold, under the direction of the assignee, who shall hold the funds received in place of the estate disposed of; and the proceeds of the sale shall be considered the measure of the value of the property in any suit or controversy between the parties in any courts. But this provision shall not prevent the recovery of the property from the possession of the assignee by any proper action commenced at any time before the court orders the sale.

EXAMINATION OF BANKRUPTS.

SEC. 26. *And be it further enacted,* That the court may, on the application of the assignee in bankruptcy, or of any creditor, or without any application, at all times require the bankrupt, upon reasonable notice, to attend and submit to an examination, on oath, upon all matters relating to the disposal or condition of his property, to his trade and dealings with others, and his accounts concerning the same, to all debts due to or claimed from him, and to all other matters concerning his property and estate and the due settlement thereof according to law, which examination shall be in writing, and shall be signed by the bankrupt and filed with the other proceedings; and the court may, in like manner, require the attendance of any other person as a witness, and if such person shall fail to attend, on being summoned thereto, the court may compel his attendance by warrant directed to the marshal, commanding him to arrest such person and bring him forthwith before the court, or before a register in bankruptcy, for examination as such witness. If the bankrupt is imprisoned, absent, or disabled from attendance, the court may order him to be produced by the jailer, or any officer in whose custody he may be, or may direct the examination to be had, taken, and certified, at such time and place and in such manner, as the court may deem proper, and with like effect as if such examination had been had in court. The bankrupt shall, at all times, until his discharge, be subject to the order of the court, and shall, at the expense of the estate, execute all proper writings and instruments, and do and perform all acts required by the court touching the assigned property or estate, and to enable the assignee to demand, recover, and receive all the property and estate assigned, wherever situated; and for neglect or refusal to obey any order of the court, such bankrupt may be committed and punished as for a contempt of court. If the bankrupt is without the district, and unable to return and personally attend at any of the times or do any of the acts which may be specified or required pursuant to this section, and if it appears that such absence was not caused by willful default, and if, as soon as may be after the removal of such impediment, he offers to attend and submit to the order of the court in all respects, he shall be permitted so to do, with like effect as if he had not been in default. He shall also be at liberty, from time to time, upon oath, to amend and correct his schedule of creditors and property, so that the same shall conform to the facts. For good cause shown the wife of any bankrupt may be required to attend before the court, to the end that she may be examined as a witness; and if such wife do not attend at the time and place specified in the order, the bankrupt shall not be entitled to a discharge unless he shall prove to the satisfaction of the court that he was unable to procure the attendance of his wife. No bankrupt shall be liable to arrest during the pendency of the proceedings in bankruptcy in any civil action, unless the same is founded on some debt or claim from which his discharge in bankruptcy would not release him. In all causes and trials arising or ordered under this act, the alleged bankrupt, and any party thereto, shall be a competent witness.

OF THE DISTRIBUTION OF THE BANKRUPT'S ESTATE.

SEC. 27. *And be it further enacted*, That all creditors whose debts are duly proved and allowed shall be entitled to share in the bankrupt's property and estate *pro rata*, without any priority or preference whatever, except that wages due from him to any operative, or clerk, or house servant, to an amount not exceeding fifty dollars, for labor performed within six months next preceding the adjudication of bankruptcy, shall be entitled to priority, and shall be first paid in full: *Provided*, That any debt proved by any person liable as bail, surety, guarantor, or otherwise, for the bankrupt shall not be paid to the person so proving the same until satisfactory evidence shall be produced of the payment of such debt by such person so liable, and the share to which such debt would be entitled may be paid into court, or otherwise held for the benefit of the party entitled thereto, as the court may direct. At the expiration of three months from the date of the adjudication of bankruptcy in any case, or as much earlier as the court may direct, the court, upon request of the assignee, shall call a general meeting of the creditors, of which due notice shall be given, and the assignee shall then report, and exhibit to the court and to the creditors just and true accounts of all his receipts and payments, verified by his oath, and he shall also produce and file vouchers for all payments for which vouchers shall be required by any rule of the court; he shall also submit the schedule of the bankrupt's creditors and property as amended, duly verified by the bankrupt, and a statement of the whole estate of the bankrupt as then ascertained, of the property recovered and of the property outstanding, specifying the cause of its being outstanding, also what debts or claims are yet undetermined, and stating what sum remains in his hands. At such meeting the majority in value of the creditors present shall determine whether any and what part of the net proceeds of the estate, after deducting and retaining a sum sufficient to provide for all undetermined claims which, by reason of the distant residence of the creditor, or for other sufficient reason, have not been proved, and for other expenses and contingencies, shall be divided among the creditors; but unless at least one-half in value of the creditors shall attend such meeting, either in person or by attorney, it shall be the duty of the assignee so to determine. In case a dividend is ordered the register shall within ten days after such meeting, prepare a list of creditors entitled to dividend, and shall calculate and set opposite to the name of each creditor who has proved his claim the dividend to which he is entitled out of the net proceeds of the estate set apart for dividend, and shall forward by mail to every creditor a statement of the dividend to which he is entitled, and such creditor shall be paid by the assignee in such manner as the court may direct.

SEC. 28. *And be it further enacted,* That the like proceedings shall be had at the expiration of the next three months, or earlier, if practicable, and a third meeting of creditors shall then be called by the court, and a final dividend then declared, unless any action at law or suit in equity be pending, or unless some other estate or effects of the debtor afterwards come to the hands of the assignee, in which case the assignee shall, as soon as may be, convert such estate or effects into money, and within two months after the same shall be so converted the same shall be divided in manner aforesaid. Further dividends shall be made in like manner as often as occasion requires; and after the third meeting of creditors no further meeting shall be called, unless ordered by the court. If at any time there shall be in the hands of the assignee any outstanding debts or other property, due or belonging to the estate, which can not be collected and received by the assignee without unreasonable or inconvenient delay or expense, the assignee may, under the direction of the court, sell and assign such debts or other property in such manner as the court shall order. No dividend already declared shall be disturbed by reason of debts being subsequently proved, but the creditors proving such debts shall be entitled to a dividend equal to those already received by the other creditors before any further payment is made to the latter. Preparatory to the final dividend, the assignee shall submit his account to the court and file the same, and give notice to the creditors of such filing, and shall also give notice that he will apply for a settlement of his account, and for a discharge from all liability as assignee, at a time to be specified in such notice; and at such time the court shall audit and pass the accounts of the assignee, and such assignee shall, if required by the court, be examined as to the truth of such account, and if found correct he shall thereby be discharged from all liability as assignee to any creditor of the bankrupt. The court shall thereupon order a dividend of the estate and effects, or of such part thereof as it sees fit, among such of the creditors as have proved their claims, in proportion to the respective amount of their said debts. In addition to all expenses necessarily incurred by him in the execution of his trust, in any case, the assignee shall be entitled to an allowance for his services in such case, on all moneys received and paid out by him therein, for any sum not exceeding one thousand dollars, five per centum thereon; for any larger sum, not exceeding five thousand dollars, two and a half per centum on the excess over one thousand dollars; and for any larger sum, one per centum on the excess over five thousand dollars; and if, at any time, there shall not be in his hands a sufficient amount of money to defray the necessary expenses required for the further execution of his trust, he shall not be obliged to proceed therein until the necessary funds are advanced or satisfactorily secured to him. If, by accident, mistake, or other cause, without fault of the assignee, either or both of the said second and third meetings should not be held within the times limited, the court may, upon motion of an interested party, order such meetings, with like effect as to the validity of the proceedings, as if the meeting had been duly held. In the order for a dividend, under this section, the following claims shall be entitled to priority or preference, and to be first paid in full in the following order:

First. The fees, costs, and expenses of suits, and the several proceedings in bankruptcy under this act, and for the custody of property, as herein provided.

Second. All debts due to the United States, and all taxes and assessments under the laws thereof.

Third. All debts due to the State in which the proceedings in bankruptcy are pending, and all taxes and assessments made under the laws of such State.

Fourth. Wages due to any operative, clerk, or house servant, to an amount not exceeding fifty dollars for labor performed within six months next preceding the first publication of the notice of proceedings in bankruptcy.

Fifth. All debts due to any persons who by the laws of the United States, are or may be entitled to a priority or preference, in like manner as if this act had not been passed: *Always provided,* That nothing contained in this act shall interfere with the assessment and collection of taxes by the authority of the United States or any State.

OF THE BANKRUPT'S DISCHARGE AND ITS EFFECT.

SEC. 29. *And be it further enacted,* That at any time after the expiration of six months from the adjudication of bankruptcy, or if no debts have been proved against the bankrupt, or if no assets have come to the hands of the assignee, at any time after the expiration of sixty days, and within one year from the adjudication of bankruptcy, the bankrupt may apply to the court for a discharge from his debts, and the court shall thereupon order notice to be given by mail to all creditors who have proved their debts, and by publication at least once a week in such newspapers as the court shall designate, due regard being had to the general circulation of the same in the district, or in that portion of the district in which the bankrupt and his creditors shall reside, to appear on a day appointed for that purpose, and show cause why a discharge should not be granted to the bankrupt. No discharge shall be granted, or, if granted, be valid, if the bankrupt has willfully sworn falsely in his affidavit annexed to his petition, schedule, or inventory, or upon any examination in the course of the proceedings in bankruptcy, in relation to any material fact concerning his estate or his debts, or to any other material fact; or if he has concealed any part of his estate or effects, or any books or writings relating thereto, or if he has been guilty of any fraud or negligence in the care, custody, or delivery to the assignee of the property belonging to him at the time of the presentation of his petition and inventory, excepting such property as he is permitted to retain under the provisions of this act, or if he has caused, permitted, or suffered any loss, waste, or destruction thereof; or if, within four months before the commencement of such proceedings, he has procured his lands, goods, money, or chattels to be attached, sequestered, or seized on execution; or if, since the passage of this act, he has destroyed, mutilated, altered, or falsified any of his books, documents, papers, writings, or securities, or has made or been privy to the making of any false or fraudulent entry in any book of account or other document, with intent to defraud his creditors; or has removed or caused to be removed any part of his property from the district, with intent to defraud his creditors; or if he has given any fraudulent preference contrary to the provisions of this act, or made any fraudulent payment, gift, transfer, conveyance, or assignment of any part of his property, or has lost any part thereof in gaming, or has admitted a false or fictitious debt against his estate; or if, having knowledge that any person has proved such false or fictitious debt, he has not disclosed the same to his assignee within one month after such knowledge; or if, being a merchant or tradesman, he has not, subsequently to the passage of this act, kept proper books of account; or if he, or any person in his behalf, has procured the assent of any creditor to the discharge, or influenced the action of any creditor at any stage of the proceedings, by any pecuniary consideration or obligation; or if he has, in contemplation of becoming bankrupt, made any pledge, payment, transfer, assignment, or conveyance of any part of his property, directly or indirectly, absolutely or conditionally, for the purpose of preferring any creditor or person having a claim against him, or who is or may be under liability for him, or for the purpose of preventing the property from coming into the hands of the assignee, or of being distributed under this act in satisfaction of his debts; or if he has been convicted of any misdemeanor under this act, or has been guilty of any fraud whatever contrary to the true intent of this act; and before any discharge is granted, the bankrupt shall take and subscribe an oath to the effect that he has not done, suffered, or been privy to any act, matter, or thing specified in this act as a ground for withholding such discharge, or as invalidating such discharge if granted.

SEC. 30. *And be it further enacted*, That no person who shall have been discharged under this act, and shall afterwards become bankrupt, on his own application shall be again entitled to a discharge, whose estate is insufficient to pay seventy per centum of the debts proved against it, unless the assent in writing of three-fourths in value of his creditors who have proved their claims is filed at or before the time of application for discharge. But a bankrupt who shall prove to the satisfaction of the court that he has paid all the debts owing by him at the time of any previous bankruptcy, or who has been voluntarily released therefrom by his creditors, shall be entitled to a discharge in the same manner and with the same effect as if he had not previously been bankrupt.

SEC. 31. *And be it further enacted*, That any creditor opposing the discharge of any bankrupt may file a specification in writing of the grounds of his opposition, and the court may in its discretion order any question of fact so presented to be tried at a stated session of the district court.

SEC. 32. *And be it further enacted*, That if it shall appear to the court that the bankrupt has in all things conformed to his duty under this act, and that he is entitled, under the provisions thereof, to receive a discharge, the court shall grant him a discharge from all his debts except as hereinafter provided, and shall give him a certificate thereof under the seal of the court, in substance as follows:

District Court of the United States, District of ——.

Whereas, ——, has been duly adjudged a bankrupt under the act of Congress establishing a uniform system of bankruptcy throughout the United States, and appears to have conformed to all requirements of law in that behalf, it is therefore ordered by the court that said ——, be forever discharged from all debts and claims which by said act are made provable against his estate, and which existed on the —— day of ——, on which day the petition for adjudication was filed by (or against) him; excepting such debts, if any, as are by said act excepted from the operation of a discharge in bankruptcy. Given under my hand and the seal of the court at ——, in the said district, this —— day of ——, A. D. ——.

[Seal.] ——, Judge.

SEC. 33. *And be it further enacted,* That no debt created by the fraud or embezzlement of the bankrupt, or by his defalcation as a public officer, or while acting in any fiduciary character, shall be discharged under this act; but the debt may be proved, and the dividend thereon shall be a payment on account of said debt; and no discharge granted under this act shall release, discharge, or affect any person liable for the same debt for or with the bankrupt, either as partner, joint contractor, indorser, surety, or otherwise.

That in cases of compulsory or involuntary bankruptcy, the provisions of said act, and any amendment thereof, or of any supplement thereto, requiring the payment of any proportion of the debts of the bankrupt, or the assent of any portion of his creditors, as a condition of his discharge from his debts, shall not apply; but he may, if otherwise entitled thereto, be discharged by the court in the same manner and with the same effect as if he had paid such per centum of his debts, or as if the required proportion of his creditors had assented thereto. And in cases of voluntary bankruptcy, no discharge shall be granted to a debtor whose assets shall not be equal to thirty per centum of the claims proved against his estate, upon which he shall be liable as principal debtor, without the assent of at least one-fourth of his creditors in number, and one-third in value.

SEC. 34. *And be it further enacted*, That a discharge duly granted under this act shall, with the exceptions aforesaid, release the bankrupt from all debts, claims, liabilities, and demands which were or might have been proved against his estate in bankruptcy, and may be pleaded, by a simple averment that on the day of its date such discharge was granted to him, setting the same forth in hæc verba, as a full and complete bar to all suits brought on any such debts, claims, liabilities, or demands, and the certificate shall be conclusive evidence in favor of such bankrupt of the fact and the regularity of such discharge: *Always provided*, That any creditor or creditors of said bankrupt, whose debt was proved or provable against the estate in bankruptcy, who shall see fit to contest the validity of said discharge on the ground that it was fraudulently obtained, may, at any time within two years after the date thereof, apply to the court which granted it to be set aside and annul the same. Said application shall be in writing, shall specify which, in particular, of the several acts mentioned in section twenty-nine it is intended to give evidence of against the bankrupt, setting forth the grounds of avoidance, and no evidence shall be admitted as to any other of the said acts; but said application shall be subject to amendment at the discretion of the court. The court shall cause reasonable notice of said application to be given to said bankrupt, and order him to appear and answer the same, within such time as to the court shall seem fit and proper. If, upon the hearing of said parties, the court shall find that the fraudulent acts, or any of them, set forth as aforesaid by said creditor or creditors against the bankrupt are proved, and that said creditor or creditors had no knowledge of the same until after the granting of said discharge, judgment shall be given in favor of said creditor or creditors, and the discharge of said bankrupt shall be set aside and annuled. But if said court shall find that said fraudulent acts, and all of them, set forth as aforesaid, are not proved, or that they were known to said creditor or creditors before the granting of said discharge, then judgment shall be rendered in favor of the bankrupt, and the validity of his discharge shall not be affected by said proceedings.

PREFERENCES AND FRAUDULENT CONVEYANCES DECLARED VOID.

SEC. 35. *And be it further enacted*, That if any person, being insolvent, or in contemplation of insolvency, within two months before the filing of the petition by or against him, with a view to give a preference to any creditor or person having a claim against him, or who is under any liability for him, procures any part of his property to be attached, sequestered, or seized on execution, or makes any payment, pledge, assignment, transfer, or conveyance of any part of his property either directly or indirectly, absolutely or conditionally, the person receiving such payment, pledge, assignment, transfer, or conveyance, or to be benefited thereby, or by such attachment, having reasonable cause to believe such person is insolvent, and knowing that such attachment, sequestration, seizure, payment, pledge, assignment, or conveyance is made in fraud of the provisions of this act, the same shall be void, and the assignee may recover the property, or the value of it, from the person so receiving it, or so to be benefited; and if any person being insolvent, or in contemplation of insolvency or bankruptcy, within three months before the filing of the petition by or against him, makes any payment, sale, assignment, transfer, conveyance, or other disposition of any part of his property to any person who then has reasonable cause to believe him to be insolvent, or to be acting in contemplation of insolvency, and knowing that such payment, sale, assignment, transfer, or other conveyance, is made with a view to prevent his property from coming to his assignee in bankruptcy, or to prevent the same from being distributed under tnis act, or to defeat the object of, or in any way impair, hinder, impede, or delay the operation and effect of, or to evade any of the provisions of this act, the sale, assignment, transfer, or conveyance shall be void, and the assignee may recover the property, or the value thereof, as assets of the bankrupt. And if such sale, assignment, transfer, or conveyance is not made in the usual and ordinary course of business of the debtor, the fact shall be prima facie evidence of fraud. Any contract, covenant, or security made or given by a bankrupt or other person with, or in trust for, any creditor for securing the payment of any money as a consideration for or with intent to induce the creditor to forbear opposing the application for discharge of the bankrupt, shall be void; and if any creditor shall obtain any sum of money or other goods, chattels, or security from any person as an inducement for forbearing to oppose, or consenting to such application for discharge, every creditor so offending shall forfeit all right to any share or dividend in the estate of the bankrupt, and shall also forfeit double the value or amount of such money, goods, chattels, or security so obtained, to be recovered by the assignee for the benefit of the estate. Nothing in this section shall be construed to invalidate any loan of actual value, or the security therefor made in good faith, upon a security taken in good faith on the occasion of the making of such loan.

BANKRUPTCY OF PARTNERSHIPS AND OF CORPORATIONS.

SEC. 36. *And be it further enacted,* That where two or more persons who are partners in trade shall be adjudged bankrupt, either on the petition of such partners or any one of them, or on the petition of any creditor of the partners, a warrant shall issue in the manner provided by this act, upon which all the joint stock and property of the copartnership, and also all the separate estate of each of the partners, shall be taken, excepting such parts thereof as are hereinbefore excepted; and all the creditors of the company, and the separate creditors of each partner, shall be allowed to prove their respective debts; and the assignee shall be chosen by the creditors of the company, and shall also keep separate accounts of the joint stock or property of the copartnership and of the separate estate of each member thereof; and after deducting out of the whole amount received by such assignee the whole of the expenses and disbursements, the net proceeds of the joint stock shall be appropriated to pay the creditors of the copartnership, and the net proceeds of the separate estate of each partner shall be appropriated to pay his separate creditors; and if there shall be any balance of the separate estate of any partner, after the payment of his separate debts, such balance shall be added to the joint stock for the payment of the joint creditors; and if there shall be any balance of the joint stock after payment of the joint debts, such balance shall be divided and appropriated to and among the separate estates of the several partners, according to their respective right and interest therein, and as it would have been if the partnership had been dissolved without any bankruptcy; and the sum so appropriated to the separate estate of each partner shall be applied to the payment of his separate debts; and the certificate of discharge shall be granted or refused to each partner as the same would or ought to be if the proceedings had been against him alone under this act; and in all other respects the proceedings against partners shall be conducted in the like manner as if they had been commenced and prosecuted against one person alone. If such copartners reside in different districts, that court in which the petition is first filed shall retain exclusive jurisdiction over the case.

SEC. 37. *And be it further enacted,* That the provisions of this act shall apply to all moneyed, business, or commercial corporations and joint-stock companies, and that upon the petition of any officer of any such corporation or company, duly authorized by a vote of a majority of the corporators present at any legal meeting called for the purpose, or upon the petition of any creditor or creditors of such corporation or company, made and presented in the manner hereinafter provided in respect to debtors, the like proceedings shall be had and taken as are hereinafter provided in the case of debtors; and all the provisions of this act which apply to the debtor, or set forth his duties in regard to furnishing schedules and inventories, executing papers, submitting to examinations, disclosing, making over, secreting, concealing, conveying, assigning, or paying away his money or property, shall in like manner, and with like force, effect, and penalties, apply to each and every officer of such corporation or company in relation to the same matters concerning the corporation or company, and the money and property thereof. All payments, conveyances, and assignments declared fraudulent and void by this act when made by a debtor, shall in like manner, and to the like extent, and with like remedies, be fraudulent and void when made by a corporation or company. No allowance or discharge shall be granted to any corporation or joint-stock company, or to any person or officer or member thereof: *Provided*, That whenever any corporation by proceedings under this act shall be declared bankrupt, all its property and assets shall be distributed to the creditors of such corporation in the manner provided in this act in respect to natural persons.

OF DATES AND DEPOSITIONS.

SEC. 38. *And be it further enacted*, That the filing of a petition for adjudication in bankruptcy, either by a debtor in his own behalf, or by any creditor against a debtor, upon which an order may be issued by the court, or by a register in the manner provided in section four, shall be deemed and taken to be the commencement of proceedings in bankruptcy under this act; the proceedings in all cases in bankruptcy shall be deemed matters of record, but the same shall not be required to be recorded at large, but shall be carefully filed, kept, and numbered in the office of the clerk of the court, and a docket only, or short memorandum thereof, kept in books to be provided for that purpose, which shall be open to public inspection. Copies of such records, duly certified under the seal of the court, shall in all cases be prima facie evidence of the facts therein stated. Evidence or examinations in any of the proceedings under this act may be taken before the court, or a register in bankruptcy, viva voce, or in writing, before a commissioner of the circuit court, or by affidavit, or on commission, and the court may direct a reference to a register in bankruptcy, or other suitable person, to take and certify such examination, and may compel the attendance of witnesses, the production of books and papers, and the giving of testimony, in the same manner as in suits in equity in the circuit court.

INVOLUNTARY BANKRUPTCY.

SEC. 39. *And be it further enacted,* That any person residing, and owing debts, as aforesaid, who, after the passage of this act, shall depart from the State, District, or Territory of which he is an inhabitant, with intent to defraud his creditors; or, being absent, shall, with such intent, remain absent; or shall conceal himself to avoid the service of legal process in any action for the recovery of a debt or demand provable under this act; or shall conceal or remove any of his property to avoid its being attached, taken, or sequestered on legal process; or shall make any assignment, gift, sale, conveyance, or transfer of his estate, properity, rights, or credits, either within the United States or elsewhere, with intent to delay, defraud, or hinder his creditors; or who has been arrested and held in custody under or by virtue of mesne process or execution, issued out of any court of the United States or of any State, District, or Territory within which such debtor resides or has property, founded upon a demand in its nature provable against a bankrupt's estate under this act, and for a sum exceeding one hundred dollars, and such process is remaining in force and not discharged by payment, or in any other manner provided by the law of the United States or of such State, District, or Territory, applicable thereto, for a period of twenty days, or has been actually imprisoned for more than twenty days in a civil action founded on contract for the sum of one hundred dollars or upward; or who, being bankrupt or insolvent, or in contemplation of bankruptcy or insolvency, shall make any payment, gift, grant, sale, conveyance, or transfer of money or other property, estate, rights, or credits, or confess judgment, or give any warrant to confess judgment, or procure his property to be taken on legal process, with intent to give a preference to one or more of his creditors, or to any person or persons who are or may be liable for him as indorsers, bail, sureties, or otherwise, or with the intent, by such disposition of his property, to defeat or delay the operation of this act; or who, being a bank, banker, broker, merchant, trader, manufacturer, or miner, has fraudulently stopped payment, or who being a bank, banker, broker, merchant, trader, manufacturer, or miner, has stopped or suspended and not resumed payment, within a period of forty days, of his commercial paper (made or passed in the course of his business as such), or who, being a bank or banker, shall fail for forty days to pay any depositor upon demand of payment lawfully made, shall be deemed to have committed an act of bankruptcy, and, subject to the conditions hereinafter prescribed, shall be adjudged a bankrupt on the petition of one or more of his creditors, who shall constitute one-fourth thereof, at least, in number, and the aggregate of whose debts provable under this act amounts to at least one-third of the debts so provable: *Provided:* That such petition is brought within six months after such act of bankruptcy shall have been committed. And the provisions of this section shall apply to all cases of compulsory or involuntary bankruptcy commenced since the first day of December, eighteen hundred and seventy-three, as well as to those commenced hereafter. And in all cases commenced since the first day of December, eighteen hundred and seventy-three, and prior to the passage of this act, as well as those commenced hereafter, the court shall, if such allegation as to the number or amount of petitioning creditors be denied by the debtor, by a statement in writing to that effect, require him to file in court forthwith a full list of his creditors, with their places of residence and the sums due them respectively, and shall ascertain, upon reasonable notice to the creditors, whether one-fourth in number and one-third in amount thereof, as aforesaid, have petitioned that the debtor be adjudged a bankrupt. But if such debtor shall, on the filing of the petition, admit in writing that the requisite number and amount of creditors have petitioned, the court (if satisfied that the admission was made in good faith,) shall so adjudge, which judgment shall be final, and the matter proceed without further steps on that subject. And if it shall appear that such number and amount have not so petitioned, the court shall grant reasonable time, not exceeding, in cases heretofore commenced, twenty days, and, in cases hereafter commenced, ten days, within which other creditors may join in such petition. And if, at the expiration of such time so limited, the number and amount shall comply with the requirements of this section, the matter of bankruptcy may proceed; but if, at the expiration of such limited time, such number and amount shall not answer the requirements of this section, the proceedings shall be dismissed, and, in cases hereafter commenced, with costs. And if such person shall be adjudged a bankrupt, the assignee may recover back the money or property so paid, conveyed, sold, assigned, or transferred contrary to this act: *Provided*, That the person receiving such payment or conveyance had reasonable cause to believe that the debtor was insolvent, and knew that a fraud on this act was intended; and such person, if a creditor, shall not, in cases of actual fraud on his part, be allowed to prove for more than a moiety of his debt; and this limitation on the proof of debts shall apply to cases of voluntary as well as involuntary bankruptcy. And the petition of creditors under this section may be sufficiently verified by the oaths of the first five signers thereof, if so many there be. And if any of said first five signers shall not reside in the district in which such petition is to be filed, the same may be signed and verified by the oath or oaths of the attorney or attorneys, agent or agents, of such signers. And in computing the number of creditors, as aforesaid, who shall join in such petition, creditors whose respective debts do not exceed two hundred and fifty dollars shall not be reckoned. But if there be no creditors whose debts exceed said sum of two hundred and fifty dollars, or if the requisite number of creditors holding debts exceeding two hundred and fifty dollars fail to sign the petition, the creditors having debts of a less amount shall be reckoned for the purposes aforesaid.

SEC. 40. *And be it further enacted*, That upon the filing of the petition authorized by the next preceding section, if it shall appear that sufficient grounds exist therefor, the court shall direct the entry of an order requiring the debtor to appear and show cause, at a court of bankruptcy to be holden at a time to be specified in the order, not less than five days from the service thereof, why the prayer of the petition should not be granted; and may also, by its injunction, restrain the debtor, and any other person, in the mean time, from making any transfer or disposition of any part of the debtor's property not excepted by this act from the operation thereof and from any interference therewith; and if it shall appear that there is probable cause for believing that the debtor is about to leave the district, or to remove or conceal his goods or chattels or his evidence of property, or make any fraudulent conveyance or disposition thereof, the court may issue a warrant to the marshal of the district, commanding him to arrest the alleged bankrupt and him safely keep, unless he shall give bail to the satisfaction of the court for his appearance from time to time, as required by the court, until the decision of the court upon the petition or the further order of the court, and forthwith to take possession provisionally of all the property and effects of the debtor, and safely keep the same until the further order of the court. A copy of the petition and of such order to show cause shall be served on such debtor by delivering the same to him personally, or leaving the same at his last or usual place of abode; or, if such debtor cannot be found, or his place of residence ascertained, service shall be made by publication, in such manner as the judge may direct. No further proceedings, unless the debtor appear and consent thereto, shall be had until proof shall have been given, to the satisfaction of the court, of such service or publication; and if such proof be not given on the return day of such order, the proceedings shall be adjourned and an order made that the notice be forthwith so served or published. And if, on the return-day of the order to show cause as aforesaid, the court shall be satisfied that the requirement of section thirty-nine of said act as to the number and amount of petitioning creditors has been complied with, or if, within the time provided for in section thirty-nine of this act, creditors sufficient in number and amount shall sign such petition so as to make a total of one-fourth in number of the creditors and one-third in the amount of the provable debts against the bankrupt, as provided in said section, the court shall so adjudge, which judgment shall be final; otherwise it shall dismiss the proceedings, and, in cases hereafter commenced, with costs.

SEC. 41. *And be it further enacted*, That on such return day or adjourned day, if the notice has been duly served or published, or shall be waived by the appearance and consent of the debtor, the court shall proceed summarily to hear the allegations of the petitioner and debtor, and may adjourn the proceedings from time to time, on good cause shown, and shall, if the debtor on the same day so demand in writing, order a trial by jury at the first term of the court at which a jury shall be in attendance, to ascertain the facts of such alleged bankruptcy. Or, at the election of the debtor, the court may, in its discretion, award a venire facias to the marshal of the district, returnable within ten days before him for the trial of the facts set forth in the petition, at which time the trial shall be had, unless adjourned for cause. And unless, upon such hearing or trial, it shall appear to the satisfaction of said court, or of the jury, as the case may be, that the facts set forth in said petition are true, or if it shall appear that the debtor has paid and satisfied all liens upon his property, in case the existence of such leins was the sole ground of the proceeding, the proceeding shall be dismissed, and the respondent shall recover costs; and all proceedings in bankruptcy may be discontinued on reasonable notice and hearing, with the approval of the court, and upon the assent, in writing, of such debtor, and not less than one half of his creditors in number and amount; or, in case all the creditors and such debtor assent thereto, such discontinuance shall be ordered and entered; and all parties shall be remitted, in either case, to the same rights and duties existing at the date of the filing of the petition for bankruptcy, except so far as such estate shall have been already administered and disposed of. And the court shall have power to make all needful orders and decrees to carry the foregoing provision into effect.

SEC. 42. *And be it further enacted,* That if the facts set forth in the petition are found to be true, or if default be made by the debtor to appear pursuant to the order, upon due proof of service thereof being made, the court shall adjudge the debtor to be a bankrupt, and, as such, subject to the provisions of this act, and shall forthwith issue a warrant to take possession of the estate of the debtor. The warrant shall be directed, and the property of the debtor shall be taken thereon, and shall be assigned and distributed in the same manner and with similar proceedings to those hereinbefore provided for the taking possession, assignment, and distribution of the property of the debtor upon his own petition. The order of adjudication of bankruptcy shall require the bankrupt forthwith, or within such number of days, not exceeding five after the date of the order or notice thereof, as shall by the order be prescribed, to make and deliver, and transmit by mail, post paid, to the messenger, a schedule of the creditors and an inventory and valuation of his estate in the form and verified in the manner required of a petitioning debtor by section thirteen. If the debtor has failed to appear in person, or by attorney, a certified copy of the adjudication shall be forthwith served on him by delivery or publication in the manner hereinbefore provided for the service of the order to show cause; and if the bankrupt is absent or cannot be found, such schedule and inventory shall be prepared by the messenger and the assignee from the best information they can obtain. If the petitioning creditor shall not appear and proceed on the return day, or adjourned day, the court may, upon the petition of any other creditor, to the required amount, proceed to adjudicate on such petition, without requiring a new service or publication of notice to the debtor.

OF SUPERSEDING THE BANKRUPT PROCEEDINGS BY ARRANGEMENT.

SEC. 43. *And be it further enacted,* That if at the first meeting of creditors, or at any meeting of creditor to be specially called for that purpose, and of which previous notice shall have been given for such length of time and in such manner as the court may direct, three-fourths in value of the creditors whose claims have been proved shall determine and resolve that it is for the interest of the general body of the creditors that the estate of the bankrupt should be wound up and settled, and distribution made among the creditors by trustees, under the inspection and direction of a committee of the creditors, it shall be lawful for the creditors to certify and report such resolution to the court, and to nominate one or more trustees to take and hold and distribute the estate, under the direction of such committee. If it shall appear to the court, after hearing the bankrupt and such creditors as may desire to be heard, that the resolution was duly passed and that the interests of the creditors will be promoted thereby, it shall confirm the same; and upon the execution and filing by or on behalf of three-fourths in value of all the creditors whose claims have been proved of a consent that the estate of the bankrupt be wound up and settled by said trustees according to the terms of such resolution, the bankrupt, or his assignee in bankruptcy, if appointed, as the case may be, shall, under the direction of the court, and under oath, convey, transfer, and deliver all the property and estate of the bankrupt to the said trustee or trustees, who shall, upon such conveyance and transfer, have and hold the same in the same manner, and with the same powers and rights, in all respects, as the bankrupt would have had or held the same if no proceedings in bankruptcy had been taken, or as the assignee in bankruptcy would have done had such resolution not been passed; and such consent and the proceedings thereunder shall be as binding in all respects on any creditor whose debt is proveable, who has not signed the same, as if he had signed it, and on any creditor, whose debt, if proveable, is not proved, as if he had proved it; and the court, by order, shall direct all acts and things needful to be done to carry into effect such resolution of the creditors, and the said trustees shall proceed to wind up and settle the estate under the direction and inspection of such committee of the creditors, for the equal benefit of all such creditors, and the winding up and settlement of any estate under the provisions of this section shall be deemed to be proceedings in bankruptcy under this act; and the said trustees shall have all the rights and powers of assignees in bankruptcy. The court, on the application of such trustees, shall have power to summon and examine, on oath or otherwise, the bankrupt, and any creditor, and any person indebted to the estate, or known or suspected of having any of the estate in his possession, or any other person whose examination may be material or necessary to aid the trustees in the execution of their trust, and to compel the attendance of such persons and the production of books and papers in the same manner as in other proceedings in bankruptcy under this act; and the bankrupt shall have the like right to apply for and obtain a discharge after the passage of such resolution and the appointment of such trustees as if such resolution had not been passed, and as if all the proceedings had continued in the manner provided in the preceding sections of this act. If the resolution shall not be duly reported, or the consent of the creditors shall not be duly filed, or if, upon its filing, the court shall not think fit to approve thereof, the bankruptcy shall proceed as though no resolution had been passed, aud the court may make all necessary orders for resuming the proceedings. And the period of time which shall have elapsed between the date of the resolution and the date of the order for resuming proceedings shall not be reckoned in calculating periods of time prescribed by this act.

COMPOSITION WITH CREDITORS.

That in all cases of bankruptcy now pending, or to be hereafter pending, by or against any person, whether an adjudication in bankruptcy shall have been had or not, the creditors of such alleged bankrupt may, at a meeting called under the direction of the court, and upon not less than ten days' notice to each known creditor of the time, place, and purpose of such meeting, such notice to be personal or otherwise, as the court may direct, resolve that a composition proposed by the debtor shall be accepted in satisfaction of the debts due to them from the debtor. And such resolution shall, to be operative, have been passed by a majority in number and three-fourths in value of the creditors of the debtor assembled at such meeting either in person or by proxy, and shall be confirmed by the signatures thereto of the debtor and two-thirds in number and one-half in value of all the creditors of the debtor. And in calculating a majority for the purposes of a composition under this section, creditors whose debts amount to sums not exceeding fifty dollars shall be reckoned in the majority in value, but not in the majority in number; and the value of the debts of secured creditors above the amount of such security, to be determined by the court, shall, as nearly as circumstances admit, be estimated in the same way. And creditors whose debts are fully secured shall not be entitled to vote upon or to sign such resolution without first relinquishing such security for the benefit of the estate.

The debtor, unless prevented by sickness or other cause satisfactory to such meeting, shall be present at the same, and shall answer any inquiries made of him; and he, or, if he is so prevented from being at such meeting, some one in his behalf, shall produce to the meeting a statement showing the whole of his assets and debts, and the names and addresses of the creditors to whom such debts respectively are due.

Such resolution, together with the statement of the debtor as to his assets and debts, shall be presented to the court; and the court shall, upon notice to all the creditors of the debtor of not less than five days, and upon hearing, inquire whether such resolution has been passed in the manner directed by this section; and if satisfied that it has been so passed, it shall, subject to the provisions hereinafter contained, and upon being satisfied that the same is for the best interest of all concerned, cause such resolution to be recorded and statement of assets and debts to be filed; and until such record and filing shall have taken place, such resolution shall be of no validity. And any creditor of the debtor may inspect such record and statement at all reasonable times.

The creditors may, by resolution passed in the manner and under the circumstances aforesaid, add to, or vary the provisions of, any composition previously accepted by them, without prejudice to any persons taking interests under such provisions who do not assent to such addition or variation. And any such additional resolution shall be presented to the court in the same manner and proceeded with in the same way and with the same consequences as the resolution by which the composition was accepted in the first instance. The provisions of a composition accepted by such resolution in pursuance of this section shall be binding on all the creditors whose names and addresses and the amounts of the debts due to whom are shown in the statement of the debtor produced at the meeting at which the resolution shall have been passed, but shall not affect or prejudice the rights of any other creditors.

Where a debt arises on a bill of exchange or promissory note, if the debtor shall be ignorant of the holder of any such bill of exchange or promissory note, he shall be required to state the amount of such bill or note, the date on which it falls due, the name of the acceptor and of the person to whom it is payable, and any other particulars within his knowledge respecting the same; and the insertions of such particulars shall be deemed a sufficient description by the debtor in respect to such debt.

Any mistake made inadvertently by a debtor in the statement of his debts may be corrected upon reasonable notice, and with the consent of a general meeting of his creditors.

Every such composition shall, subject to priorities declared in said act, provide for a pro-rata payment or satisfaction, in money, to the creditors of such debtor in proportion to the amount of their unsecured debts, or their debts in respect to which any such security shall have been duly surrendered and given up.

The provisions of any composition made in pursuance of this section may be enforced by the court, on motion made in a summary manner by any person interested, and on reasonable notice; and any disobedience of the order of the court made on such motion shall be deemed to be a contempt of court. Rules and regulations of court may be made in relation to proceedings of composition herein provided for in the same manner and to the same extent as now provided by law in relation to proceedings in bankruptcy.

If it shall at any time appear to the court, on notice, satisfactory evidence, and hearing, that a composition under this section can not, in consequence of legal difficulties, or for any sufficient cause, proceed without injustice or undue delay to the creditors or to the debtor, the court may refuse to accept and confirm such composition, or may set the same aside; and, in either case, the debtor shall be proceeded with as a bankrupt in conformity with the provisions of law, and proceedings may be had accordingly; and the time during which such composition shall have been in force shall not, in such case, be computed in calculating periods of time prescribed by said act.

PENALTIES AGAINST BANKRUPTS.

SEC. 44. *And be it further enacted,* That from and after the passage of this act, if any debtor or bankrupt shall, after the commencement of proceedings in bankruptcy, secrete or conceal any property belonging to his estate, or part with, conceal, or destroy, alter, mutilate, or falsify, or cause to be concealed, destroyed, altered, mutilated, or falsified, any book, deed, document, or writing relating thereto, or remove, or cause to be removed, the same or any part thereof, out of the district, or otherwise dispose of any part thereof, with intent to prevent it from coming into the possession of the assignee in bankruptcy, or to hinder, impede, or delay either of them in recovering or receiving the same, or make any payment, gift, sale, assignment, transfer, or conveyance of any property belonging to his estate with the like intent, or spends any part thereof in gaming; or shall, with intent to defraud, wilfully and fraudulently conceal from his assignee or omit from his schedule any property or effects whatsoever; or if, in case of any person having, to his knowledge or belief, proved a false or fictitious debt against his estate, he shall fail to disclose the same to his assignee within one month after coming to the knowledge or belief thereof, or shall attempt to account for any of his property by fictitious losses or expenses; or shall, within three months before the commencement of proceedings in bankruptcy, under the false color and pretence of carrying on business and dealing in the ordinary course of trade, obtain on credit from any person any goods or chattels with intent to defraud; or shall, with intent to defraud his creditors, within three months next before the commencement of proceedings in bankruptcy, pawn, pledge, or dispose of, otherwise than by bona fide transactions in the ordinary way of his trade, any of his goods or chattels which have been obtained on credit and remain unpaid for, he shall be deemed guilty of a misdemeanor, and upon conviction thereof in any court of the United States, shall be punished by imprisonment, with or without hard labor, for a term not exceeding three years.

PENALTIES AGAINST OFFICERS.

SEC. 45. *And be it further enacted,* That if any judge, register, clerk, marshal, messenger, assignee, or any other officer of the several courts of bankruptcy, shall, for any thing done or pretended to be done under this act, or under color of doing any thing thereunder, wilfully demand or take, or appoint or allow any person whatever to take for him or on his account, or for or on account of any other person, or in trust for him or for any other person, any fee, emolument, gratuity, sum of money, or any thing of value whatever, other than is allowed by this act, or which shall be allowed under the authority thereof, such person, when convicted thereof, shall forfeit and pay the sum of not less than three hundred dollars, and not exceeding five hundred dollars, and be imprisoned not exceeding three years.

SEC. 46. *And be it further enacted,* That if any person shall forge the signature of a judge, register, or other officer of the court, or shall forge or counterfeit the seal of the court, or knowingly concur in using any such forged or counterfeit signature or seal, for the purpose of authenticating any proceeding or document, or shall tender in evidence any such proceeding or document with a false or counterfeit signature of any such judge, register, or other officer, or a false or counterfeit seal of the court, snbscribed or attached thereto, knowing such signature or seal to be false or counterfeit, any such person shall be guilty of felony, and upon conviction thereof shall be liable to a fine of not less than five hundred dollars, and not more than five thousand dollars, and to be imprisoned not exceeding five years, at the discretion of the court.

FEES AND COSTS.

SEC. 47. *And be it further enacted*, That in each case there shall be allowed and paid, in addition to the fees of the clerk of the court as now established by law, or as may be established by general order, under the provisions of this act, for fees in bankruptcy, the following fees, which shall be applied to the payment for the services of the registers:

For issuing every warrant, two dollars.

For each day in which a meeting is held, three dollars.

For each order for a dividend, three dollars.

For every order substituting an arrangement by trust deed for bankruptcy, two dollars.

For every bond with sureties, two dollars.

For every application for any meeting in any matter under this act, one dollar.

For every day's service while actually employed under a special order of the court, a sum not exceeding five dollars, to be allowed by the court.

For taking depositions, the fees now allowed by law.

For every discharge when there is no opposition, two dollars.

Such fees shall have priority of payment over all other claims out of the estate, and before a warrant issues the petitioner shall deposit with the senior register of the court, or with the clerk, to be delivered to the register, fifty dollars as security for the payment thereof; and if there are not sufficient assets for the payment of the fees, the person upon whose petition the warrant is issued shall pay the same, and the court may issue an execution against him to compel payment to the register.

Before any dividend is ordered the assignee shall pay out of the estate to the messenger the following fees, and no more:

First. For service of warrant, two dollars.

Second. For all necessary travel, at the rate of five cents a mile, each way.

Third. For each written note to creditor named in the schedule, ten cents.

Fourth. For custody of property, publication of notices, and other services, his actual and necessary expenses upon returning the same in specific items, and making oath that they have been actually incurred and paid by him, and are just and reasonable, the same to be taxed or adjusted by the court, and the oath of the messenger shall not be conclusive as to the necessity of said expenses.

For cause shown, and upon hearing thereon, such further allowance may be made as the court, in its discretion, may determine.

The enumeration of the foregoing fees shall not prevent the judges, who shall frame general rules and orders in accordance with the provisions of section ten, from prescribing a tariff of fees for all other services of the officers of courts of bankruptcy, or from reducing the fees prescribed in this section in classes of cases to be named in their rules and orders.

Sec. 48. *And be it further enacted*, That the word "assignee" and the word "creditor" shall include the plural also; and the word "messenger" shall include his assistant or assistants, except in the provision for the fees of that officer. The word "marshal" shall include the marshal's deputies, the word "person" shall also include "corporation," and the word "oath" shall include "affirmation." And in all cases in which any particular number of days is prescribed by this act, or shall be mentioned in any rule or order of court or general order which shall at any time be made under this act, for the doing of any act, or for any other purpose, the same shall be reckoned, in the absence of any expression to the contrary, exclusive of the first and inclusive of the last day, unless the last day shall fall on a Sunday, Christmas day, or on any day appointed by the Presdent of the United States as a day of public fast or thanksgiving, or on the Fourth of July, in which case the time shall be reckoned exclusive of that day also.

SEC. 49. *And be it further enacted,* That all the jurisdiction, power, and authority conferred upon and vested in the district court of the United States by this act in cases in bankruptcy are hereby conferred upon and vested in the supreme court of the District of Columbia, and in and upon the district courts of the several Territories of the United States, subject to the general superintendence and jurisdiction conferred upon circuit courts by section two of said act, when the bankrupt resides in the said District of Columbia or in either of the said Territories. And in those judicial districts which are not within any organized circuit of the United States the power and jurisdiction of a circuit court in bankruptcy may be exercised by the district judge.

SEC. 50. *And be it furher enacted,* That this act shall commence and take effect as to the appointment of the officers created hereby, and the promulgation of rules and general orders, from and after the date of its approval: *Provided,* That no petition or other proceeding under this act shall be filed, received, or commenced before the first day of June, anno Domini eighteen hundred and sixty-seven.

That from and after the passage of this act the fees, commissions, charges, and allowances, excepting actual and necessary disbursements, of, and to be made by the officers, agents, marshals, messengers, assignees, and registers in cases of bankruptcy, shall be reduced to one half of the fees, commissions, charges, and allowances heretofore provided for or made in like cases: *Provided,* That the preceding provision shall be and remain in force until the justices of the Supreme Court of the United States shall make and promulgate new rules and regulations in respect to the matters aforesaid, under the powers conferred upon them by sections ten and forty-seven of said act, and no longer, which duties they shall perform as soon as may be. And said justices shall have power under said sections, by general regulations, to simplify and, so far as in their judgment will conduce to the benefit of creditors, to consolidate the duties of the register, assignee, marshal, and clerk, and to reduce fees, costs, and charges, to the end that prolixity, delay, and unnecessary expenses may be avoided. And no register or clerk of court, or any partner or clerk of such register or clerk of court, or any person having any interest with either in any fees or emoluments in bankruptcy, or with whom such register or clerk of court shall have any interest in respect to any matter in bankruptcy, shall be of council, solicitor, or attorney, either in or out of court, in any suit or matter pending in bankruptcy in either the circuit or district court of his district, or in an appeal therefrom. Nor shall they, or either of them, be executor, administrator, guardian, commissioner, appraiser, divider, or assignee of or upon any estate within the jurisdiction of either of said courts of bankruptcy; nor be interested, directly or indirectly, in the fees or emoluments arising from either of said trusts.

That it shall be the duty of the marshal of each district, in the month of July of each year, to report to the clerk of the district court of such district, in a tabular form, to be prescribed by the justices of the Supreme Court of the United States, as well as such other or further information as may be required by said justices.

First, The number of cases in bankruptcy in which the warrant prescribed in section eleven of said act has come to his hands during the year ending June thirtieth, preceding;

Secondly, how many such warrants were returned, with the fees, costs, expenses, and emoluments thereof, respectively and separately;

Thirdly, the total amount of all other fees costs, expenses, and emoluments, respectively and separately, earned or received by him during such year from or in respect of any matter in bankruptcy;

Fourthly, a summarized statement of such fees, costs, and emoluments, exclusive of actual disburements in bankruptcy received or earned for such year;

Fifthly, a summarized statement of all actual disbursements in such cases for such year.

And in like manner, every register shall, in the same month and for the same year, make a report to such clerk of—

First, the number of voluntary cases in bankruptcy coming before him during said year;

Secondly, the amount of assets and liabilities, as nearly as may be, of the bankrupts;

Thirdly, the amount and rate per centum of all dividends declared;

Fourthly, the disposition of all such cases;

Fifthly, the number of compulsory cases in bankruptcy coming before him, in the same way;

Sixthly, the amount of assets and liabilities, as nearly as may be, of such bankrupt;

Seventhly, the disposition of all such cases;

Eighthly, the amounts and rate per centum of all dividends declared in such cases;

Ninthly, the total amount of fees, charges, costs, and emoluments of every sort, received or earned by such register during said year in each class of cases above stated.

And in like manner, every assignee shall, during said month, make like return to such clerk of—

First, the number of voluntary and compulsory cases, respectively and separately, in his charge during said year.

Secondly, the amount of assets and liabilities therein, respectively and separately;

Thirdly, the total receipts and disbursements therein, respectively and separately;

Fourthly, the amount of dividends paid or declared, and the rate per centum thereof, in each class, respectively and separately;

Fifthly, the total amount of all his fees, charges, and emoluments, of every kind therein, earned or received;

Sixthly, the total amount of expenses incurred by him for legal proceedings and counsel fees;

Seventhly, the disposition of the cases respectively;

Eightly, a summarized statement of both classes as aforesaid.

And in like manner, the clerk of said court, in the month

of August in each year, shall make up a statement for such year, ending June thirtieth, of—

First, all cases in bankruptcy pending at the beginning of the said year;

Secondly, all of such cases disposed of;

Thirdly, all dividends declared therein;

Fourthly, the number of reports made from each assignee therein;

Fifthly, the disposition of all such cases;

Sixthly, the number of assignees' accounts filed and settled;

Seventhly, whether any marshal, register, or assignee has failed to make and file with such clerk the reports by this act required, and, if any have failed to make such reports, their respective names and residences.

And such clerk shall report in respect of all cases begun during said year.

And he shall make a classified statement, in tabular form, of all his fees, charges, costs, and emoluments, respectively, earned or accrued during said year, giving each head under which the same accrued, and also the sum of all moneys paid into and disbursed out of court in bankruptcy, and the balance in hand or on deposit.

And all the statements and reports herein required shall be under oath, and signed by the persons respectively making the same.

And said clerk shall, in the said month of August, transmit every such statement and report so filed with him, together with his own statement and report aforesaid, to the Attorney-General of the United States.

Any person who shall violate the provisions of this section shall, on motion made, under the direction of the Attorney-General, be by the district court dismissed from his office, and shall be deemed guilty of a misdemeanor, and, on conviction thereof, be punished by a fine of not more than five hundred dollars, or by imprisonment not exceeding one year.

That in addition to the officers now authorized to take proof of debts against the estate of a bankrupt, notaries public are hereby authorized to take such proof, in the manner and under the regulations provided by law; such proof to be certified by the notary and attested by his signature and official seal.

That all acts and parts of acts inconsistent with the provisions of this act be, and same are hereby, repealed.

RESUMPTION OF SPECIE PAYMENT.

AN ACT to provide for the resumption of specie payments.

Be it enacted by the Senate and House of Representatives of the United States of America in Congress assembled, That the Secretary of the Treasury is hereby authorized and required, as rapidly as practicable, to cause to be coined at the mints of the United States, silver coins of the denominations of ten, twenty-five, and fifty cents, of standard value, and to issue them in redemption of an equal number and amount of fractional currency of similar denominations, or, at his discretion, he may issue such silver coins through the mints, the sub-treasuries, public depositaries, and post-offices of the United States; and, upon such issue, he is hereby authorized and required to redeem an equal amount of such fractional currency, until the whole amount of such fractional currency outstanding shall be redeemed.

SEC. 2. That so much of section three thousand five hundred and twenty-four of the Revised Statutes of the United States as provides for a charge of one-fifth of one per centum for converting standard gold bullion into coin is hereby repealed, and hereafter no charge shall be made for that service.

SEC. 3. That section five thousand one hundred and seventy-seven of the Revised Statutes of the United States, limiting the aggregate amount of circulating-notes of national banking-associations, be, and is hereby repealed; and each existing banking-association may increase its circulating-notes in accordance with existing law without respect to said aggregate limit; and new banking-associations may be organized in accordance with existing law without respect to said aggregate limit; and the provisions of law for the withdrawal and redistribution of national-bank currency among the several States and Territories are hereby repealed. And whenever, or so often, as circulating-notes shall be issued to any such banking-association, so increasing its capital or circulating notes, or so newly organized as aforesaid, it shall be the duty of the Secretary of the Treasury to redeem the legal-tender United States notes in excess only of three hundred million of dollars, to the amount of eighty per centum of the sum of national-bank notes so issued to any such banking-association as aforesaid, and to continue such redemption as such circulating-notes are issued until there shall be outstanding the sum of three hundred million dollars of such legal-tender United States notes, and no more. And on and after the first day of January, Anno Domini eighteen hundred and seventy-nine, the Secretary of the Treasury shall redeem, in coin, the United States legal-tender notes then outstanding on their presentation for redemption, at the office of the assistant treasurer of the United States in the city of New York, in sums of not less than fifty dollars. And to enable the Secretary of the Treasury to prepare and provide for the redemption in this act authorized or required, he is authorized to use any surplus revenues, from time to time, in the Treasury not otherwise appropriated, and to issue, sell, and dispose of, at not less than par, in coin, either of the descriptions of bonds of the United States described in the act of Congress approved July fourteenth, eighteen hundred and seventy, entitled, "An act to authorize the funding of the national debt," with like qualities, privileges, and exemptions, to the extent necessary to carry this act into full effect, and to use the proceeds thereof for the purposes aforesaid. And all provisions of law inconsistent with the provisions of this act are hereby repealed.

Approved, January 14, 1875.

GENEVA AND SAN JUAN AWARDS.

THE GENEVA AWARD, SEPT. 14, 1872.

Decision and award made by the tribunal of arbitration constituted by virtue of the first article of the treaty concluded at Washington, the 8th of May, 1871, between the United States and Great Britain.

The United States of America and Her Britannic Majesty having agreed, by article I of the treaty concluded and signed at Washington, the 8th of May, 1871, to refer all the claims, "generically known as the Alabama claims," to a tribunal of arbitration, to be composed of five arbitrators, named; one by the President of the United States, one by Her Britannic Majesty, one by His Majesty the King of Italy, one by the President of the Swiss Confederation, one by His Majesty the Emperor of Brazil.—And the President of the United States, Her Britannic Majesty, His Majesty the King of Italy, the President of the Swiss Confederation, and His Majesty the Emperor of Brazil having respectively named their arbitrators, to-wit: The President of the United States, Charles Francis Adams, Esq.; Her Britannic Majesty, Sir Alexander James Edmund Cockburn, baronet, a member of Her Majesty's privy council, lord chief justice of England; His Majesty the King of Italy, His Excellency Count Frederick Sclopis, of Salerano, a knight of the Order of the Annunciata, minister of state, senator of the Kingdom of Italy; the President of the Swiss Confederation, M. James Stämpfli; His Majesty the Emperor of Brazil, His Excellency Marcos Antonio d'Araujó, Viscount d'Itajubá, a grandee of the Empire of Brazil, member of the council of His Majesty the Emperor of Brazil, and his envoy extraordinary and minister plenipotentiary in France.—And the five arbitrators above named having assembled at Geneva (in Switzerland), in one of the chambers of the Hotel de Ville, on the 15th of December, 1871, in conformity with the terms of the second article of the Treaty of Washington, of the 8th of May of that year, and having proceeded to the inspection and verification of their respective powers, which were found duly authenticated, the tribunal of arbitration was declared duly organized.

The agents named by each of the high contracting parties, by virtue of the same article II, to-wit: For the United States of America, John C. Bancroft Davis, Esq.; and for Her Britannic Majesty, Charles Stuart Aubrey, Lord Tenterden, a peer of the United Kingdom, companion of the Most Honorable Order of the Bath, assistant under secretary of state of foreign affairs, whose powers were found likewise duly authenticated,—then delivered to each of the arbitrators the printed case prepared by each of the two parties, accompanied by the documents, the official correspondence, and other evidence on which each relied, in conformity with the terms of the third article of the said treaty.

In virtue of the decision made by the tribunal at its first session, the counter case and additional documents, correspondence, and evidence referred to in article IV of the said treaty were delivered by the respective agents of the two parties to the secretary of the tribunal on the 15th of April, 1872, at the chamber of conference, at the Hotel de Ville of Geneva.

The tribunal, in accordance with the vote of adjournment passed at their second session, held on the 16th of December, 1871, reassembled at Geneva on the 15th of June, 1872, and the agent of each of the parties duly delivered to each of the arbitrators, and to the agent of the other party, the printed argument referred to in article V of the said treaty.

The tribunal having since fully taken into their consideration the treaty, and also the cases, counter cases, documents, evidence, and arguments, and likewise all other communications made to them by the two parties during the progress of their sittings, and having impartially and carefully examined the same, has arrived at the decision embodied in the present award.

Whereas, having regard to the sixth and seventh articles of the said treaty, the arbitrators are bound, under the terms of the said sixth article, "in deciding the matters submitted to them, to be governed by the three rules therein specified, and by such principles of international law, not inconsistent therewith, as the arbitrators shall determine to have been applicable to the case;"

And whereas the "due diligence" referred to in the first and third of the said rules ought to be exercised by neutral Governments in exact proportion to the risks to which either of the belligerents may be exposed, from a failure to fulfill the obligations of neutrality on their part;

And whereas the circumstances out of which the facts constituting the subject matter of the present controversy arose, were of a nature to call for the exercise on the part of Her Britannic Majesty's Government of all possible solicitude for the observance of the rights and the duties involved in the proclamation of neutrality issued by Her Majesty on the 13th day of May, 1861;

And whereas the effects of a violation of neutrality committed by means of the construction, equipment, and armament of a vessel are not done away with by any commission which the Government of the belligerent power, benefited by the violation of neutrality, may afterward have granted to that vessel; and the ultimate step, by which the offense is completed, can not be admissible as a ground for the absolution of the offender, nor can the consummation of the fraud become the means of establishing his innocence;

And whereas the privilege of exterritoriality accorded to vessels of war has been admitted into the law of nations, not as an absolute right, but solely as a proceeding founded on the principle of courtesy and mutual deference between different nations, and therefore can never be appealed to for the protection of acts done in violation of neutrality;

And whereas the absence of a previous notice can not be regarded as a failure in any consideration required by the law of nations, in those cases in which a vessel carries with it its own condemnation;

And whereas in order to impart to any supplies of coal a character inconsistent with the second rule, prohibiting the use of neutral ports or waters as a base of naval operations for a belligerent, it is necessary that the said supplies should be connected with special circumstances of time, of persons, or of place, which may combine to give them such character;

And whereas, with respect to the vessel called the "Alabama," it clearly results from all the facts relative to the construction of the ship at first designated by the number "290" in the port of Liverpool, and its equipment and armament in the vicinity of Terceira, through the agency of the vessels called the "Agrippina" and the "Bahama," dispatched from Great Britain to that end, that the British Government failed to use due diligence in the performance of its neutral obligations; and especially that it omitted, notwithstanding the warnings and official representations made by the diplomatic agents of the United States during the construction of the said number "290," to take in due time any effective measures of prevention, and that those orders which it did give at last, for the detention of the vessel, were issued so late that their execution was not practicable;

And whereas, after the escape of that vessel, the measures taken for its pursuit and arrest were so imperfect as to lead to no result, and therefore can not be considered sufficient to release Great Britain from the responsibility already incurred;

And whereas, in despite of the violations of the neutrality of Great Britain committed by the "290," this same vessel, later known as the Confederate cruiser Alabama, was on several occasions freely admitted into the ports of colonies of Great Britain, instead of being proceeded against as it ought to have been in any and every port within British jurisdiction in which it might have been found;

And whereas the Government of Her Britannic Majesty can not justify itself for a failure in due diligence on the plea of insufficiency of the legal means of action which it possessed.

Four of the arbitrators, for the reasons above assigned, and the fifth for reasons separately assigned by him, are of opinion that Great Britain has in this case failed, by omission, to fulfill the duties prescribed in the first and the third of the rules established by the sixth article of the treaty of Washington.

And whereas, with respect to the vessel called the "Florida," it results from all the facts relative to the construction of the "Oreto" in the port of Liverpool, and to its issue therefrom, which facts failed to induce the authorities in Great Britain to resort to measures adequate to prevent the violation of the neutrality of that nation, notwithstanding the warnings and repeated representations of the agents of the United States, that Her Majesty's Government has failed to use due diligence to fulfill the duties of neutrality;

And whereas it likewise results from all the facts relative to the stay of the Oreto at Nassau, to her issue from that port, to her enlistment of men, to her supplies, and to her armament, with the co-operation of the British vessel "Prince Alfred," at Green Bay, that there was negligence on the part of the British colonial authorities;

And whereas, notwithstanding the violation of the neutrality of Great Britain committed by the Oreto, this same vessel, later known as the Confederate cruiser "Florida," was, nevertheless, on several occasions, freely admitted into the ports of British colonies;

And whereas the judicial acquittal of the Oreto at Nassau can not relieve Great Britain from the responsibility incurred by her under the principles of international law; nor can the fact of the entry of the Florida into the Confederate port of Mobile, and of its stay there during four months, extinguish the responsibility previously to that time incurred by Great Britain.

For these reasons, the tribunal, by a majority of four voices to one, is of opinion, that Great Britain has in this case failed, by omission, to fulfill the duties prescribed in the first, in the second, and in the third of the rules established by article VI of the treaty of Washington.

And whereas, with respect to the vessel called the "Shenandoah," it results from all the facts relative to the departure from London of the merchant vessel the "Sea King," and to the transformation of that ship into a Confederate cruiser under the name of the "Shenandoah," near the island of Madeira, that the Government of Her Britannic Majesty is not chargeable with any failure, down to that date, in the use of due diligence to fulfill the duties of neutrality;

But whereas it results from the facts connected with the stay of the Shenandoah at Melbourne, and especially with the augmentation which the British Government itself admits to have been clandestinely effected of her force, by the enlistment of men within that port, that there was negligence on the part of the authorities at that place;

For these reasons, the tribunal is unanimously of opinion, that Great Britain has not failed, by any act or omission, "to fulfill any of the duties prescribed by the three rules of article VI in the treaty of Washington, or by the principles of international law not inconsistent therewith," in respect to the vessel called the Shenandoah, during the period of time anterior to her entry into the port of Melbourne;

And, by a majority of three to two voices, the tribunal decides that Great Britain has failed, by omission, to fulfill the duties prescribed by the second and third of the rules aforesaid, in the case of this same vessel, from and after her entry into Hobson's Bay, and is therefore responsible for all acts committed by that vessel after her departure from Melbourne, on the 18th day of February, 1865.

And so far as relates to the vessels called the "Tuscaloosa" (tender to the Alabama), the "Clarence," the "Tacony," and the "Archer" (tenders to the Florida), the tribunal is unanimously of opinion, that such tenders or auxiliary vessels, being properly regarded as accessories, must necessarily follow the lot of their principals, and be submitted to the same decision which applies to them respectively.

And so far as relates to the vessel called "Retribution," the tribunal, by a majority of three to two voices, is of opinion, that Great Britain has not failed, by any act or omission, to fulfill any of the duties prescribed by the three rules of article VI in the treaty of Washington, or by the principles of international law not inconsistent therewith.

And so far as relates to the vessels called the "Georgia," the "Sumter," the "Nashville," the "Tallahassee," and the "Chickamauga," respectively, the tribunal is unanimously of opinion, that Great Britain has not failed, by any act or omission, to fulfill any of the duties prescribed by the three rules of article VI in the treaty of Washington, or by the principles of international law not inconsistent therewith.

And so far as relates to the vessels called the "Sallie," the "Jefferson Davis," the "Music," the "Boston," and the "V. H. Joy," respectively, the tribunal is unanimously of opinion, that they ought to be excluded from consideration for want of evidence.

And whereas, so far as relates to the particulars of the indemnity claimed by the United States, the costs of pursuit of the Confederate cruisers are not, in the judgment of the tribunal, properly distinguishable from the general expenses of the war carried on by the United States. The tribunal is, therefore, of opinion, by a majority of three to two voices, that there is no ground for awarding to the United States any sum by way of indemnity under this head.

And whereas prospective earnings can not properly be made the subject of compensation, inasmuch as they depend in their nature upon future and uncertain contingencies, the tribunal is unanimously of opinion that there is no ground for awarding to the United States any sum by way of indemnity under this head.

And whereas, in order to arrive at an equitable compensation for the damages which have been sustained, it is necessary to set aside all double claims for the same losses, and all claims for "gross freights," so far as they exceed "net freights;"

And whereas it is just and reasonable to allow interest at a reasonable rate;

And whereas, in accordance with the spirit and letter of the treaty of Washington, it is preferable to adopt the form of adjudication of a sum in gross, rather than to refer the subject of compensation for further discussion and deliberation to a board of assessors, as provided by article X of the said treaty.

The tribunal, making use of the authority conferred upon it by article VII of the said treaty, by a majority of four voices to one, awards to the United States a sum of $15,500,000 in gold, as the indemnity to be paid by Great Britain to the United States, for the satisfaction of all the claims referred to the consideration of the tribunal, conformably to the provisions contained in article VII of the aforesaid treaty.

And, in accordance with the terms of article XI of the said treaty, the tribunal declares that "all the claims referred to in the treaty as submitted to the tribunal are hereby fully, perfectly, and finally settled."

Furthermore it declares, that "each and every one of the said claims, whether the same may or may not have been presented to the notice of, or made, preferred, or laid before the tribunal, shall henceforth be considered and treated as finally settled, barred, and inadmissible."

In testimony whereof this present decision and award has been made in duplicate, and signed by the arbitrators who have given their assent thereto, the whole being in exact conformity with the provisions of article VII of the said treaty of Washington.

Made and concluded at the Hotel de Ville of Geneva, in Switzerland, the 14th day of the month of September, in the year of our Lord one thousand eight hundred and seventy-two.

CHARLES FRANCIS ADAMS.
FREDERICK SCLOPIS.
STAMPFLI.
VICOMPTE D'ITAJUBA.

Under the act approved June 23, 1874, creating a "Court of Commissioners of Alabama Claims," for the distribution of the award, its jurisdiction is thus defined in sections 11 and 12:

SEC. 11. That it shall be the duty of said court to receive and examine all claims admissible under this act that may be presented to it, directly resulting from damage caused by the so-called insurgent cruisers "Alabama," "Florida," and their tenders, and also all claims admissible under this act directly resulting from damage caused by the so-called insurgent cruiser "Shenandoah" after her departure from Melbourne on the eighteenth day of February, eighteen hundred and sixty-five, and to decide upon the amount and validity of such claims, in conformity with the provisions hereinafter contained, and according to the principles of law and the merits of the several cases. All claims shall be verified by oath of the claimant, and filed in said court within six months next after the organization thereof, as provided in section eight of this act; and no claim shall be received, docketed, or considered that shall have not been so filed within the time aforesaid; but every such unrepresented claim shall be deemed and held to be finally and conclusively waived and barred.

SEC. 12. That no claim shall be admissible or allowed by said court for any loss or damage for or in respect to which the party injured, his assignees or legal representative, shall have received compensation or indemnity from any insurance company, insurer or otherwise; but if such compensation or indemnity so received shall not have been equal to the loss or damage so actually suffered, allowance may be made for the difference. And in no case shall any claim be admitted or allowed for or in respect to unearned freights, gross freights, prospective profits, freights, gains, or advantages, or for wages of officers or seamen for a longer time than one year next after the breaking up of a voyage by the acts aforesaid. And no claim shall be admissible or allowed by said court by or in behalf of any insurance company or insurer, either in its or his own right, or as assignee, or otherwise, in the right of a person or party insured as aforesaid, unless such claimant shall show, to the satisfaction of said court, that during the late rebellion the sum of its or his losses, in respect to its or his war risks, exceeded the sum of its or his premiums or other gains upon or in respect to such war risks; and in case of any such allowance, the same shall not be greater than such excess of loss. And no claim shall be admissible or allowed by said court arising in favor of any insurance company not lawfully existing at the time of the loss under the laws of some one of the United States. And no claim shall be admissible or allowed by said court arising in favor of any person not entitled at the time of his loss to the protection of the United States in the premises, nor arising in favor of any person who did not at all times during the late rebellion bear true allegiance to the United States.

Provision is made for retaining in the Treasury, as a special fund, subject to future action, the amount which may be undisposed of under this act. And if the sum of all the judgments rendered by the court, together with interest, should exceed the amount of the award, provision is made for ratable reductions of the judgment claims.

THE SAN JUAN BOUNDARY AWARD.

We, William, by the grace of God, German Emperor, King of Prussia, etc., etc., etc.,

After examination of the treaty concluded at Washington on the 6th of May, 1871, between the governments of Her Britannic Majesty and of the United States of America, according to which the said governments have submitted to our arbitrament the question at issue between them, whether the boundary line which, according to the treaty of Washington of June 15, 1846, after being carried westward along the forty-ninth parallel of northern latitude to the middle of the channel which separates the continent from Vancouver's Island is thence to be drawn southerly through the middle of the said channel and of the Fuca Straits to the Pacific Ocean, should be drawn through the Rosario Channel, as the Government of Her Britannic Majesty claims, or through the Haro Channel, as the Government of the United States claims; to the end that we may finally and without appeal decide which of these claims is most in accordance with the true interpretation of the treaty of June 15, 1846.

After hearing the report made to us by the experts and jurists upon the contents of the interchanged memorials and their appendices,—

Have decreed the following award:

Most in accordance with the true interpretations of the treaty concluded on the 15th of June, 1846, between the governments of Her Britannic Majesty and of the United States of America, is the claim of the Government of the United States that the boundary line between the territories of Her Britannic Majesty and the United States should be drawn through the Haro Channel.

Authenticated by our autographic signature and the impression of the imperial green seal.

Given at Berlin, October the 21st, 1872.

[L. S] WILLIAM.

POLAND'S GAG LAW.

An Act conferring jurisdiction upon the criminal court of the District of Columbia, and for other purposes.

Be it enacted by the Senate and House of Representatives of the United States of America in Congress assembled, That the criminal court of the District of Columbia shall have jurisdiction of all crimes and misdemeanors committed in said District, not lawfully triable in any other court, and which are required by law to be prosecuted by indictment or information.

SEC. 2. That the provisions of the thirty-third section of the judiciary act of seventeen hundred and eighty-nine shall apply to courts created by act of Congress in the District of Columbia.

Approved, June 22, 1874.

CIVIL RIGHTS BILL OF 1875.

SECTION 1. That all the persons within the jurisdiction of the United States shall be entitled to the full and equal enjoyment of the accommodations, advantages, facilities, and privileges of insurances, public conveyances on land and water, theatres, and other places of public amusement, subject only to the conditions and limitations established by law, and applicable alike to the citizens of every race and color, regardless of any previous condition of servitude.

SEC. 2. That any person who shall violate the foregoing section by denying to any citizen, except for reasons by law applicable to the citizens of every race and color, and regardless of any previous condition of servitude, the full enjoyment of any of the accommodations, advantages, facilities, or privileges in said section enumerated, or by aiding or inciting, shall for every such offense forfeit and pay the sum of five hundred dollars to the person aggrieved thereby, to be recovered in an action of debt, with full costs, and shall also, for every such offense, be deemed guilty of a misdemeanor, and upon conviction thereof be fined not less than five hundred nor more than one thousand dollars, or shall be imprisoned not less than thirty days nor more than one year; provided that all persons may elect to sue for the penalty aforesaid, or to proceed under their rights at common law and by State statutes, and having so elected to proceed in the one mode or the other: their right to proceed in the other jurisdiction shall be barred; but this proviso shall not apply to criminal proceedings either under this act or the criminal law of any State: and provided further that the judgment for the penalty in favor of the party aggrieved, or a judgment upon an indictment, shall be a bar to either prosecution respectively.

SEC. 3. That the District and Circuit Courts of the United States shall have, exclusively of the courts of the several States, cognizance of all the crimes and offenses against and violations of the provisions of this act, and actions for the penalty given by the preceding section, may be prosecuted in a Territorial district or circuit court of the United States wherever the dependent may be found, without regard to the other party; and the district attorneys, marshals, and deputy marshals of the United States, and commissioners appointed by the circuit and territorial courts of the United States, with powers of arresting and imprisoning or bailing offenders against the law of the United States, are hereby especially authorized and required to institute proceedings against every person who shall violate the provisions of this act, and cause him to be arrested and imprisoned, or bailed, as the case may be, for trial before such court of the United States or Territorial court as by law has cognizance of the offense, except in respect of the right of action accruing to the person aggrieved, and such district attorney shall cause such proceedings to be prosecuted to their termination, as in other cases, provided nothing contained in this section shall be construed to deny or defeat any right of civil action accruing to any person, whether by reason of this act or otherwise; and any district attorney who shall willfully fail to institute and prosecute the proceedings herein referred to shall for every offense forfeit and pay the sum of five hundred dollars to the party aggrieved thereby, to be recovered by an action of debt, with costs, and shall on conviction thereof be deemed guilty of a misdemeanor, and be fined not less than one thousand nor more than five thousand dollars; and provided further that a judgment for the penalty in favor of the party aggrieved against any such district attorney, or a judgment upon an indictment against any such district attorney, shall be a bar to either prosecution respectively.

SEC. 4. That no citizen, possessing all other qualifications which are or may be prescribed by law, shall be disqualified for the service of a grand or petit juror in any court of the United States, or of any State, on account of race, color, or previous condition of servitude; and any officer or other person charged with any duty of the selection or summoning of jurors, who shall exclude or fail to summon any citizen for the cause aforesaid, shall, on conviction thereof, be deemed guilty of a misdemeanor and be fined not more than five thousand dollars.

SEC. 5. That all cases arising under the provisions of this act in the courts of the United States shall be reviewable by the Supreme Court of the United States, without regard to the sum in controversy, under the same provisions and regulations as are now provided by law for review of other causes in said court.

PARLIAMENTARY RULES

FOR THE GOVERNMENT OF PUBLIC ASSEMBLIES.

A knowledge of the rules which regulate the formation and order of business in public assemblies, is essential to every well informed citizen. Every citizen is obliged, at some time, to take part in the primary assemblies of the people. These are constantly held, not merely for political purposes, but for those of business—commercial, literary, benevolent, or religious. In addition to these primary assemblies, there are various and numerous organized associations, with some one or more of which almost every citizen is connected. The rules for the transaction of business in the assemblies, or associations, are substantially the same in all of them, the most important of which are substantially as follows:

ORGANIZATION.

1. In regularly *organized* bodies, such as Congress, the State Legislature, religious, political, or other associations, the constitution under which they act usually designates the title of their presiding officer, defines his duties, and provides for the mode of his appointment.

2. When a *primary assembly* of the people, or of any part of them, is called together for any purpose, the first thing to be done is to choose a presiding officer, usually designated as *chairman.*

3. At the proper time some one rises, and moves that A. B. be appointed chairman of the meeting. When this is seconded *the person making the motion* puts the question, and if it be carried, A. B. takes the chair as presiding officer.

4. Regularly every public assembly should have a *secretary,* who is chosen in such manner as the body may direct.

5. The assembly may appoint such other officers as is deemed expedient; and on important occasions there are usually appointed several vice-presidents and additional secretaries.

6. In deliberate bodies composed of delegates, it is usual to effect a *primary organization* as above; then appoint a committee on "permanent organization," who *nominate* permanent officers for the assembly; and a committee on "credentials," who prepare a list of those entitled to take part in the proceedings.

7. Immediately before or after (usually after) the permanent organization there is appointed committees on order of business, resolutions, address, and such others as the case may require.

DUTIES OF OFFICERS.

8. The *presiding officer* opens each sitting of the body by taking the chair and calling the members to order; he announces the business in order; receives all communications, messages, motions, and propositions; puts to vote all questions coming before the body for their decision; and enforces the rules of order. He may read sitting, but should rise to state a motion or put a question.

9. The *secretary* keeps a record of the proceedings of the body; reads all papers as ordered; calls the roll of members, and records their vote during a call for the ayes and nays; notifies committees of their appointment, and the business referred to them; and takes charge of all papers and documents belonging to the assembly.

10. The *vice-president* takes the chair in the absence of the presiding officer, or when he leaves the chair to take part in the proceedings of the meeting.

11. When other officers are chosen their duties are set forth in the resolution appointing them, or in the by-laws of the association.

ORDER.

12. In all assemblies any member may at any time rise to a point of order. He must distinctly state his question or objection, which the presiding officer will decide.

13. Any member dissatisfied with the ruling of the chair may appeal to the assembly; and the presiding officer may call upon the house to sustain him in preserving order. The decision of the meeting is final.

14. Every member must treat every other member with respect and decorum; and especially must he acknowledge the dignity of the body at large, and of the officers thereof.

15. The chairman of an assembly can not regularly speak to any thing but a point of order, or a question of fact.

16. In general the chairman has his own vote no more, but in primary meetings he is usually entitled to the casting vote.

17. If two persons rise to speak together, the chairman determines which shall have precedence; it may, however, be referred to the house.

18. A person speaking can not regularly mention another member of the assembly by name. He must describe him as "the gentleman who has just sat down," "the gentleman on the other side of the question," etc.

19. When a person rises to speak, he must address the presiding officer, who should call him by name, that the assembly may know who he is.

20. The person speaking should confine himself to the question under debate, and avoid personality. If he transgress the rules of order, he may be called to order by the presiding officer, or any member.

21. No one should be interrupted while speaking, except he be out of order, or to ask, or to make an explanation.

22. A speaker may allow others to ask questions or make explanations; but if he yield the floor, he can not claim it again as his right.

ORDER OF BUSINESS.

23. All business should be presented by a motion—and in writing, if so required—the motion to be made by one member and seconded by another.

24. A question is not to be discussed until it is moved, seconded, and distinctly stated by the presiding officer.

25. A question before the meeting can not be withdrawn, except by unanimous consent.

26. A motion should contain but one distinct proposition, or question. If it contains more than one, it may be divided at the request of any member, and the questions acted on separately.

27. A motion before the meeting must be put to vote, unless withdrawn, laid on the table, or postponed.

28. A motion lost should not be renewed at the same meeting, unless under circumstances of peculiar necessity.

29. While a motion is under debate, no other motion can be allowed, except

THE PRIVILEGED QUESTIONS.

1. To adjourn.
2. To lay on the table.
3. For the previous question.
4. To postpone to a day certain.
5. To commit or amend.

6. To postpone indefinitely.

Which several motions shall have precedence in the order in which they are arranged; and no motion to postpone to a day certain, to commit, or to postpone indefinitely, being decided, shall be again allowed on the same day, and of the same stage of the proposition.

30. Motions to adjourn, to lay on the table, for the previous question, to commit, and to indefinitely postpone, are not debatable. But when they are modified by some condition of *time*, *place*, or *purpose*, they become debatable, and subject to the rules of other motions.

31. A motion to *adjourn* is always in order, except while the body is engaged in voting, on another question, or while a member is speaking.

32. A body may adjourn to specified time. But if no time is mentioned, then it is understood to be adjourned to the time of its next meeting; or if it have no other fixed time for meeting, then an adjournment without date is equivalent to a dissolution.

33. If a meeting votes to adjourn at a specified hour, no vote is requisite when that hour arrives. The chair simply announces that the meeting stands adjourned.

34. By adjournment the condition of things is not changed; and when the body meet again, every thing is renewed at the point where it was left.

35. Immediate and decisive action, on any question, may be deferred by a vote to *lay* the resolution pending *on the table*, whence it can be ordered up when it suits the convenience of the assembly.

36. When any question is before the house, any member may move the *previous question*, which is: "Shall the main question be now put." If it pass, then the main question is to be put immediately, without debate or amendment; but if lost, then the main question is not put, and the discussion goes on.

37. A postponement to *a day certain*, is used when a proposition is made which it is proper to act on—but information is wanted, or something more pressing claims present attention.

38. An *indefinite postponement* is considered equivalent to a final dismissal of the question.

39. The meeting may decide to take up some particular business at a special time. That business becomes the *order of the day*, and when the hour specified arrives the chair announces the order of the day and other business is suspended.

40. Questions relating to the *rights* and *privileges* of the meeting, and of its members, are of primary importance, and for the time take precedence of all other business, and supersede all other motions, except that of adjournment.

41. When a question has been decided it is in order for any member who voted with the majority to move at the same or next succeeding sitting of the body for a *reconsideration* thereof. A question reconsidered is placed again before the body for action.

COMMITTEES.

42. All committees shall be appointed by the presiding officer, unless otherwise directed. If voted for by the body it requires a majority (in the absence of any other rule) of all the votes cast to elect.

43. The first one named in the appointment of a committee is, by courtesy, considered the chairman; but the committee have the right to appoint their own chairman.

44. Any subject in debate, or matter of business, may be referred to a committee, with or without instructions; the committee to report the result of their investigation to the meeting.

45. The report of a committee is accepted by a vote, which simply acknowledges the service of the committee, and places their report before the meeting for its action. Afterwards, any distinct proposition or recommendation contained in the report is separately acted on, and may be *adopted* or *rejected*.

46. A majority of a committee constitutes a *quorum* for business, who may meet where they please, but they can not act except when together; and nothing can be the report of the committee except what is agreed upon in committee.

AMENDMENTS.

47. Amendments may be made to motions by omitting, adding, or substituting, words or sentences, and amendments to amendments, are in order.

48. The amendment should be discussed and voted on first, and then the original resolution, as amended.

49. No amendment should be made, which essentially changes the nature or design of the original resolution.

50. But a *substitute* may be offered for any motion or amendment under debate, which may or may not change the design of the motion.

51. It is in order to move an amendment to strike out certain words and insert others; this being rejected, it is in order to move to strike out, and insert a different set of words; this being rejected, it is in order to move to strike out the same words, and insert nothing; because each of these is a distinct proposition differing from the others. But it must be recollected, that it is *not in order*, if the motion to strike out and insert A. *is*

carried, to move an amendment to *strike out* A. and *insert* B. To avoid this dilemma, the mover of B. must *give notice*, pending the motion to insert A., that he intends to move the insertion of B., in which case he will gain the votes of all who prefer the amendment B. to the amendment A., in opposition to A. But, after A. *is inserted*, it is in order to move an amendment by striking out the whole or part of the *original paragraph, including* A.; for this is essentially *a different proposition* from that to strike out A. merely.

QUORUM.

52. In every constitutionally organized body there must be some number fixed which are sufficient to do business. This number is called a *quorum*, and is usually designated in the constitution under which the body acts. Sometimes a quorum consists of a definite number of members; sometimes of two-thirds of all the members; but usually, as in congress, of a majority of the members.

53. When a quorum is necessary to do business, in general, the chair should not be taken by the presiding officer till *that quorum* is present. And whenever, in the progress of business, it is observed that a quorum is not present, any member may call for a count of the house; and a quorum being found wanting, business must be suspended.

54. In primary assemblies of the people there is, of course, no number requisite to constitute a quorum, and it frequently happens that a very small number of persons act for a large community.

MISCELLANEOUS.

55. The question is *first* put on the *affirmative*, and then on the *negative* side; till which, it is not a full question; but in the cases of small matters, such as receiving reports, petitions, reading papers, etc., the presiding officer may presume consent unless some objection be formally made; which saves the time of taking votes on matters of mere routine.

56. In putting a question the presiding officer declares whether the yeas or nays have it by the *sound* if he be himself satisfied; if he be not satisfied, or if any member express dissatisfaction, the body is divided, usually by rising. The ayes first rise, and are counted standing in their places, by the chair or by tellers, as the case may be, then they sit; and the noes rise, and are counted in the same manner.

57. If the result be a *tie* (unless the chair give the casting vote, or if his vote make the tie) *the motion is lost.*

58. A *mistake* in the announcement of a vote may be rectified after the result is announced.

59. There is precedent that a member may change his vote if it be done before any other business is taken up.

60. Where different numbers are suggested for *filling blanks*, the highest number, greatest distance, and longest time, are usually voted on first.

61. A rule of order may be *suspended*, by a vote of the meeting, to allow of transacting business which could not otherwise be done.

62. The chair has a right to name any one to act for him; but this substitution does not extend beyond the first adjournment.

PAY OF OFFICERS OF THE UNITED STATES.

EXECUTIVE DEPARTMENT.

President	per annum	$50,000
Private Secretary	"	3,500
Assistant Secretary	"	2,500
Executive Clerks	"	2,300
Vice-President	"	8,000

HEADS OF DEPARTMENTS.

Secretary of State	per annum	$8,000
Secretary of the Treasury	"	8,000
Secretary of War	"	8,000
Secretary of the Navy	"	8,000
Secretary of the Interior	"	8,000
Postmaster General	"	8,000
Attorney General	"	8,000

LEGISLATIVE DEPARTMENT.

Speaker of House of Representatives, (mileage, 20 cents per mile,)	per annum	$8,000
United States Senators, Members of Congress, and Delegates from Territories	"	5,000

JUDICIARY (SUPREME COURT OF UNITED STATES).

Chief Justice	per annum	$10,500
Associate Justices, (eight in number ; court meets 1st Monday in December)	"	10,000

MINISTERS AND DIPLOMATIC AGENTS OF THE UNITED STATES IN FOREIGN COUNTRIES—ENVOYS EXTRAORDINARY AND MINISTERS PLENIPOTENTIARY.

Minister to Great Britain	per annum	$17,500
Minister to Russia	"	17,500
Minister to France	"	17,500
Minister to Germany	"	17,500
Minister to Spain	"	12,000
Minister to Austria	"	12,000
Minister to Italy	"	12,000
Minister to China	"	12,000
Minister to Mexico	"	12,000
Minister to Brazil	"	12,000
Minister to Japan	"	12,000
Minister to Chili	"	10,000
Minister to Peru	"	10,000
Minister to Central America	"	10,000

MINISTERS RESIDENT.

Minister in Portugal	per annum	$7,500
Minister in Belgium	"	7,500
Minister in Netherlands	"	7,500
Minister in Denmark	"	7,500
Minister in Sweden and Norway	"	7,500
Minister in Switzerland	"	7,500
Minister in Turkey	"	7,500
Minister in Venezuela	"	7,500
Minister in Ecuador	"	7,500
Minister in Argentine Confederation	"	7,500
Minister in Hawaiian Islands	"	7,500
Minister in Greece	"	7,500
Minister in Columbia	"	7,500
Minister in Bolivia	"	7,500

WAR DEPARTMENT.

Secretary of War	per annum	$8,000
General	"	13,500
Adjutant General	"	5,500
Assistant Adjutant General	"	3,500
Second Assistant Adjutant General	"	3,000
Third Assistant Adjutant General	"	3,000
Fourth Assistant Adjutant General	"	3,000
Chief Clerk Adjutant General's Bureau	"	2,000
Inspector General	"	3,500
Judge Advocate General	"	5,500
Assistant Judge Advocate	"	3,500
Quartermaster General	"	5,500
Deputy Quartermaster General	"	3,000
Assistant Quartermaster	"	3,500
Chief Clerk Quartermaster's Bureau	"	2,000
Chief of Engineers' Bureau	"	5,500
Chief Clerk of Engineers' Bureau	"	2,000
Surgeon General	"	5,500
Assistant Surgeon General	"	3,500
Chief Clerk Surgeon General's Bureau	"	2,000
Chief of Ordnance	"	5,500
Chief Clerk of Ordnance	"	2,000
Paymaster General	"	3,500
Deputy Paymaster General	"	3,000
Assistant Paymaster General	"	3,500
Chief Clerk Paymaster General's Bureau	"	2,000
Commissary General of Subsistence	"	5,500
Assistant Commissary General	"	3,500
Chief Clerk Commissary General's Bureau	"	2,000

GENERAL OFFICERS.

Lieutenant General	per month	$916 67
Aids-de-camp	according to rank.	
Major General	per month	$625 00
Brigadier General	"	458 33

ADJUTANT GENERAL'S DEPARTMENT.

Adjutant General—Brigadier General	per month	$458 33
Assistant Adjutant General—Colonel	"	291 67
Assistant Adjutant General—Lieutenant Colonel	"	250 00
Assistant Adjutant General—Major	"	208 33
Judge Advocate General—Colonel	"	291 67
Judge Advocate—Major	"	208 33

INSPECTOR GENERAL'S DEPARTMENT.

Inspector General—Colonel	per month	$291 67
Assistant Inspector General—Major	"	208 33

SIGNAL DEPARTMENT.

Signal Officer—Colonel	per month	$291 67

PAY DEPARTMENT.

Paymaster General	per month	$291 67
Deputy Paymaster General	"	250 50
Paymaster	"	208 33

OFFICERS OF THE CORPS OF ENGINEERS, TOPOGRAPHICAL ENGINEERS, AND ORDNANCE DEPARTMENT.

Chief of Ordnance—Brigadier General	per month	$453 83
Colonel	"	291 67
Lieutenant Colonel	"	250 00
Major	"	208 33
Captain	"	150 00
First Lieutenant	"	125 00
Second Lieutenant	"	116 67

OFFICERS OF MOUNTED DRAGOONS, CAVALRY, RIFLEMEN, AND LIGHT ARTILLERY.

Colonel	per month	$291 67
Lieutenant Colonel	"	250 00
Major	"	208 33
Captain	"	166 67
First Lieutenant	"	133 33
Second Lieutenant	"	125 00

QUARTERMASTER'S DEPARTMENT.

Quartermaster General—Brigadier General	per month	$458 33
Assistant Quartermaster General—Colonel	"	291 61
Deputy Quartermaster General—Lieuten't Colonel	"	250 00
Quartermaster—Major	"	208 33
Assistant Quartermaster—Captain	"	166 67

SUBSISTENCE DEPARTMENT.

Commissary General of Subsistence—Brigadier General	per month	$458 33
Assistant Commissary General—Colonel	"	291 67
Commissary of Subsistence—Major	"	208 33
Commissary of Subsistence—Captain	"	150 00

MEDICAL DEPARTMENT.

Surgeon General—Brigadier General	per month	$458 33
Assistant Surgeon General	"	291 67
Chief Medical Purveyor	"	291 67
Assistant Medical Purveyor	"	250 00
Surgeons—Majors	"	208 33
Assistant Surgeons—Captains	"	150 00
Adjutant Regimental Quartermaster	"	150 06

OFFICERS OF ARTILLERY AND INFANTRY.

Colonel	per month	$291 67
Lieutenant Colonel	"	250 00
Major	"	208 33
Captain	"	150 00
First Lieutenant	"	125 00
Second Lieutenant	"	116 67

MONTHLY PAY OF ENLISTED MEN OF THE UNITED STATES ARMY—FIRST ENLISTMENT.

COMPANY.

Private—Artillery, Cavalry, and Infantry	per month	$13 00
Private, 2d class—Engineers and Ordnance	"	13 00
Musician—Engineers, Artillery, and Infantry	"	13 00
Trumpeter—Cavalry	"	13 00
Wagoner—Artillery, Cavalry, and Infantry	"	14 00
Artificer—Artillery and Infantry	"	15 00
Corporal—Artillery, Cavalry, and Infantry	"	15 00
Blacksmith and Farrier—Cavalry	"	15 00
Saddler—Cavalry	"	15 00
Quartermaster Sergeant	"	17 00
Sergeant—Artillery, Cavalry, and Infantry	"	17 00
Private, 1st Class—Engineers and Ordnance	"	17 00
Corporal—Engineers and Ordnance	"	20 00
First Sergeant—Artillery, Cavalry and Infantry	"	22 00
Saddler—Sergeant—Cavalry	"	22 00
Sergeant—Engineers and Ordnance	"	34 00

REGIMENT.

Chief Trumpeter—Cavalry	per month	$22 00
Principal Musician—Artillery and Infantry	"	22 00
Chief Musician—Artillery, Cavalry, and Infantry	"	60 00
Sergeant Major—Artillery, Cavalry, and Infantry	"	23 00
Quartermaster Sergeant—Artillery, Cavalry, and Infantry	"	23 00
Sergeant Major and Quartermaster Sergeant—Engineers	"	36 00
Veterinary Surgeon—Senior	"	100 00
Veterinary Surgeon—Junior	"	75 00

POST.

Hospital Matron	per month	$10 00
Hospital Steward—1st class	"	30 00
Hospital Steward—2d class	"	22 00
Hospital Steward—3d class	"	20 00
Ordnance Sergeant	"	34 00
Commissary Sergeant	"	34 00

N.B.—The pay of enlisted men, excepting the wagoner, artificer, quartermaster sergeant, chief musician, veterinary surgeons, and hospital matron, during first enlistment increases $1 per annum after the second year. First re-enlistment pay is increased $2, and $1 for second, third, and fourth re-enlistment, and is uniform in each.

SAPPERS AND MINERS, AND PONTOONIERS.

Sergeant	per month	$34 00
Corporal	"	20 00
Private—1st class	"	17 00
Private—2d class	"	13 00
Musician	"	13 00

PAY OF THE NAVY OF THE UNITED STATES.

OFFICERS.	PER ANNUM.		
	On Sea.	On Shore.	On Orders.
Admiral	$13000	....	....
Vice Admiral	9000	$8000	$6000
Rear Admirals	6000	5000	4000
Commodores	5000	4000	3000
Captains	4500	3500	2800
Commanders	3500	3000	2300
Lieut. Commanders—1st four years of commission	2800	2400	2000
" " —after four years	3000	2600	2200
Lieutenants—1st five years of commission	2400	2000	1600
" —after five years	2600	2200	1800
Masters—1st five years of commission	1400	1200	1000
" —after five years	1800	1500	1200
Ensigns—1st five years of commission	1200	1000	800
" —after five years	1400	1200	1000
Midshipmen	1000	800	600
Fleet Surgeons—Medical and Pay Directors	4400	....	....
Medical and Pay Inspectors, and Chief Engineers	4400	....	....
Surgeons—1st five years of commission	2800	2400	2000
" —2d " " " "	3200	2800	2400
" —3d " " " "	3500	3200	2600
" —4th " " " "	3700	3600	2800
" —after twenty years	4200	4000	3000
Past Assistant Surgeons—1st five years of commission	2000	1800	1500
" " " —after five years	2200	2000	1700
Assistant Surgeons—1st five years of commission	1700	1400	1000
" " —after five years	1900	1600	1200
Paymasters—same as Surgeons.	....	....	....
Past Assistant Paymasters—same as P. A. Surgeons.	....	....	....
Assistant Paymasters—1st five years of commission	1700	1400	1000
" " —after five years	1900	1600	1200
Chaplains—1st five years of commission	2500	2000	1600
" —after five years	2800	2300	1900
Professors of Mathematics—1st five years of commis'n	2400	2400	1500
" " " —2d " " " "	2700	2700	1800
" " " —3d " " " "	3000	3000	2100
" " " —after fifteen years	3500	3500	2600
Boatswains—Gunners—Carpenters	1200	900	700
Sailmakers—1st three years of commission	1200	900	700
" —2d " " " "	1300	1000	800
" —3d " " " "	1400	1300	900
" —4th " " " "	1600	1300	1000
" —after twelve years	1800	1600	1200
Naval Contractors—1st five years of commission	....	3200	2200
" " —2d " " " "	....	3400	2400
" " —3d " " " "	....	3700	2700
" " —4th " " " "	....	4000	3000
" " —after twenty years	....	4200	3200
Assistant Naval Contractors—1st four years of com'n	....	2000	1500
" " " —2d " " " "	....	2200	1700
" " " —after eight years	....	2600	1900

OFFICERS OF THE NAVY—*Continued.*

Chief Engineers—same as Surgeons.
Past Assistant Engineers—same as P. A. Surgeons.
Assistant Engineers—same as Assistant Surgeons.

Secretaries to Admiral and Vice Admiral	per annum	$2500
" " Commanders of Squadrons	"	2000
Clerks to Commanders of Squadrons	"	750
" " " " Vessels	"	750
" at Navy Yards—Boston and New York	"	1600
" " " " —Washington	"	1600
" " " " —Philadelphia	"	1600
" " " " —Mare Island	"	1800
Yeomen—first and second rate	per month	$61 50
" —third rate	"	56 50
" —fourth rate	"	51 50
Armorers—first rate	"	36 50
" —second, third, and fourth rate	"	31 50
Boatswain's Mate and Gunners, each	"	28 50
Carpenters	"	31 50
Sailmaker's Mate	"	26 50
Masters-at-arms—first and second rate	"	61 50
" —third rate	"	56 50
" —fourth rate	"	51 50
Ship's Corporals	"	23 50
Coxswains, Quartermasters, Quarter Gunners	"	26 50
Captains of Forecastle, Tops, Afterguard, and Hold	"	26 50
Coopers	"	23 50
Painters—first class	"	26 50
" —second class	"	23 50
Stewards—of Cabin	"	36 50
" —of Ward Room	"	31 50
" —of Steerage	"	21 50
" —of Warrant Officers	"	19 50
Nurses—complement less than 200—one nurse	"	15 50
" — " over 200—two nurses	"	15 50
Cooks—Cabin	"	31 50
" —Ward Room	"	26 50
" —Steerage	"	19 50
" —Warrant Officers	"	15 50
Musicians—Masters of Band	"	51 50
" —first class	"	36 50
" —second class	"	31 50
Seamen	"	21 50
" —Ordinary	"	17 50
Landsmen	"	15 50
Firemen—first class	"	31 50
" —second class	"	26 50
Coal Heavers	"	21 50
Marine Corps—Brigadier General	per annum	$5500
" " —Ass't Quartermaster, captain's rank	"	2000
" " —Colonel	"	3500
" " —Lieutenant Colonel	"	3000
" " —Major	"	2500
" " —Captain	"	1800
" " —1st Lieutenant and Aid-de-camp	"	1750
" " —1st Lieutenant	"	1500
" " —2d "	"	1400

N.B.—All officers on retired list receive 75 or 50 per cent. of their sea pay, according as they are retired for long and faithful service or for other causes.

SCHEDULE OF STAMP DUTIES.

REVISED AND CORRECTED TO DATE.

STAMP DUTIES UNDER SCHEDULE B.

	Stamp Duty.
BANK CHECK, draft, order, or voucher for the payment of any sum of money whatever drawn upon any bank, banker, or trust company, at sight or on demand........	02
BILL OF EXCHANGE (foreign), or letter of credit drawn in but payable out of the United States. If drawn singly, same rates of duty as inland bills of exchange or promissory notes.	
If drawn in sets of three or more, for every bill of each set, where the sum made payable shall not exceed $100 or the equivalent thereof in any foreign currency........	02
And for every additional $100, or fractional part thereof in excess of $100........	02

CANCELLATION.

In all cases where adhesive stamps are used for denoting the tax upon an instrument, the person or party using or affixing them must so affix them that the entire surface of each and every stamp shall be exposed to view, and must cancel them by writing or imprinting upon each stamp *with ink* the initials of his name, and the date (year, month, and day) on which the same is attached or used, or by cutting and canceling the same by a machine which shall affix the date, and so cut and deface the stamp as to render it manifestly unfit for re-use, and at the same time shall not so deface the stamp as to prevent its denomination and genuineness from being readily determined.

When the stamps are printed upon checks, etc., so that in filling up the instrument the face of the stamp is, and must necessarily be, written across, no other cancellation will be required.

PENALTIES.

A penalty of $50 is imposed upon every person who makes, signs, or issues, or who causes to be made, signed, or issued, any paper of any kind or description whatever, or who accepts, negotiates, or pays, or who causes to be accepted, negotiated, or paid, any check, draft, order, or voucher drawn upon any bank, banker, or bank company for the payment of any sum of money whatever, without the same being duly stamped, or having thereupon an adhesive stamp for denoting the tax chargeable thereon, canceled in the manner required by law, with intent to evade the provisions of the revenue act. (Sec. 3422 R. S.)

A penalty of $50 is imposed upon every person who fraudently makes use of an adhesive stamp to denote the duty required by the revenue act, without effectually canceling and obliterating the same in the manner required by law. (Sec. 3422 R. S.)

No bank check, draft, or order required by law to be stamped, which is issued without being stamped, shall be admitted or used in evidence in any court until a legal stamp denoting the amount of tax is applied thereto, as provided by law.

It is not lawful to record any instrument, document, or paper, required by law to be stamped, or any copy thereof, unless a stamp or stamps of the proper amount have been affixed and canceled in the manner required by law; and such instrument or copy and the record thereof are utterly null and void, and can not be used or admitted as evidence in any court until the defect has been cured, as provided in section 3422 R. S.

GENERAL REMARKS REFERRING TO SCHEDULE B.

Revenue stamps may be used indiscriminately upon any of the matters or things enumerated in Schedule B, except proprietary and playing card stamps, for which a special use has been provided.

Postage stamps can not be used in payment of the duty chargeable on instruments.

The law does not designate which of the parties to an instrument shall furnish the necessary stamp, nor does the commissioner of internal revenue assume to determine that it shall be supplied by one party rather than by another; but if an instrument subject to stamp duty is issued without having the necessary stamp affixed thereto, it can not be recorded, or admitted, or used as evidence in any court, until a legal stamp or stamps, denoting the amount of tax, shall have been affixed as prescribed by law, and the person who thus issues it is liable to a penalty if he omits the stamps with an attempt to evade the provisions of the internal revenue act.

STAMP DUTIES UPON ARTICLES IN SCHEDULE C.

	Stamp Duty.
PROPRIETARY MEDICINES AND PREPARATIONS. For and upon every packet, box, bottle, pot, phial, or other enclosure, containing any pills, powders, tinctures, troches, lozenges, sirups, cordials, bitters, anodynes, tonics, plasters, liniments, salves, ointments, pastes, drops, waters, essences, spirits, oils, or other medicinal preparations or compositions whatsoever, sold, offered, or exposed for sale, or removed for consumption and sale, by any person or persons whatever, where such packet, box, etc., with its contents, does not exceed, at retail price or value, the sum of twenty-five cents	$0 01
Exceeding twenty-five and not exceeding fifty cents	02
Exceeding fifty and not exceeding seventy-five cents	03
Exceeding seventy-five cents and not exceeding one dollar	04
Exceeding one dollar, for every additional fifty cents, or fractional part thereof in excess of one dollar	02
Officinal preparations, and medicines mixed or compounded specially for any person according to the written recipe or prescription of any physician or surgeon	Exempt.
PERFUMERY AND COSMETICS. For and upon every packet, box, bottle, pot, phial, or other enclosure containing any essence, extract, toilet-water, cosmetic, hair-oil, pomade, hair-dressing, hair-restorative, hair.dye, tooth-wash, dentifrice, tooth-paste, aromatic cachous, or any similar articles, by whatsoever name the same heretofore have been, now are, or may hereafter be called, known or distinguished, used or applied, or to be used or applied, as perfumes or applications to the hair, mouth, or skin, sold, offered for sale, or removed for consumption and sale, the same rates per package, etc., as for medicines and preparations.	
FRICTION MATCHES. For and upon every parcel or package of 100 or less	01
More than 100 and not more than 200	02
For every additional 100 or fractional part thereof.	01

	Stamp Duty.
WAX TAPERS, double the rates for friction matches.	
CIGAR LIGHTS, made in part of wood, wax, glass, paper, or other materials, in parcels or packages, containing twenty-five lights or less in each parcel or package	01
When in parcels or packages containing more than twenty-five and not more than fifty lights..	02
For every additional twenty-five lights, or fractional part of that number, one cent additional.	......
PLAYING CARDS. For and upon every pack not exceeding fifty-two cards in number, irrespective of price or value	05

GENERAL REMARKS ON SCHEDULE C.

Perfumery and cosmetics are liable to stamp duty whether sold with the bottle or other enclosure containing them, or in bottles, etc., furnished by the purchaser.

Stamps appropriated to denote the duty charged upon articles named in Schedule C, and in the amendments thereto, can not be used for any other purpose, nor can stamps appropriated to denote the duty upon instruments to be used in payment of the duties upon articles enumerated in this schedule.

Any person who offers or exposes for sale any of the articles named in Schedule C, or in any of the amendments thereto, whether they are imported or of foreign or domestic manufacture, is to be deemed the manufacturer thereof and subject to all the duties, liabilities, and penalties imposed by law in regard to the sale of domestic articles without the use of the proper stamp or stamps for denoting the tax paid thereon. The stamp tax upon such articles imported or of foreign manufacture is in addition to the import duties.

HISTORY OF THE NATIONAL BANKS.

DIGEST OF THE LAW, ETC.

Be it enacted by the Senate and House of Representatives of the United States of America in Congress assembled, That there shall be established in the Treasury Department a separate Bureau, the chief officer of which shall be denominated the Comptroller of the Currency, who shall be under the general direction of the Secretary of the Treasury.

SEC. 5. That associations for carrying on the business of banking may be formed by any number of persons, not less in any case than five, who shall enter into articles of association, which shall specify in general terms the object for which the association is formed, and may contain any other provisions, not inconsistent with the provisions of this act, which the association may see fit to adopt for the regulation of the business of the association and the conduct of its affairs, which said articles shall be signed by the persons uniting to form the association, and a copy of them forwarded to the Comptroller of the Currency, to be filed and preserved in his office.

SEC. 6. That the persons uniting to form such an association shall, under their hands, make an organization certificate, which shall specify—

First. The name assumed by such association, which name shall be subject to the approval of the Comptroller.

Second. The place where its operations of discount and deposit are to be carried on, designating the State, Territory, or District, and also the particular county and city, town or village.

Third. The amount of its capital stock, and the number of shares into which the same shall be divided.

Fourth. The names and places of residence of the shareholders, and the number of shares held by each of them.

Fifth. A declaration that said certificate is made to enable such persons to avail themselves of the advantages of this act.

The said certificate shall be acknowledged before a judge of some court of record or a notary public, and such certificate, with the acknowledgment thereof authenticated by the seal of such court or notary, shall be transmitted to the Comptroller of the Currency, who shall record and carefully preserve the same in his office. Copies of such certificate, duly certified by the Comptroller and authenticated by his seal of office, shall be legal and sufficient evidence in all courts and places within the United States, or the jurisdiction of the Government thereof, of the existence of such association, and of every other matter or thing which could be proved by the production of the original certificate.

SEC. 7. That no association shall be organized under this act, with a less capital than one hundred thousand dollars, nor in a city whose population exceeds fifty thousand persons, with a less capital than two hundred thousand dollars: *Provided*, That banks with a capital of not less than fifty thousand dollars may, with the approval of the Secretary of the Treasury, be organized in any place, the population of which does not exceed six thousand inhabitants.

SEC. 8. That every association formed, pursuant to the provisions of this act, shall, from the date of the execution of its organization certificate, be a body-corporate, but shall transact no business except such as may be incidental to its organization and necessarily preliminary, until authorized by the Comptroller of the Currency to commence the business of banking. Such association shall have power to adopt a corporate seal, and shall have succession by the name designated in its organization certificate, for the period of twenty years from its organization, unless sooner dissolved according to the provisions of its articles of association, or by the act of its shareholders owning two-thirds of its stock, or unless the franchise shall be forfeited by a violation of this act; by such name it may make contracts, sue and be sued, complain and defend, in any court of law and equity as fully as natural persons; it may elect or appoint directors, and by its board of directors appoint a president, vice-president, cashier, and other officers, define their duties, require bonds of them, and fix the penalty thereof, dismiss said officers or any of them at pleasure, and appoint others to fill their places, and exercise under this act all such incidental powers as shall be necessary to carry on the business of banking by discounting and negotiating promissory notes, drafts, bills of exchange, and other evidences of debt; by receiving deposits; by buying and selling exchange, coin, and bullion; by loaning money on personal security; by obtaining, issuing, and circulating notes according to the provisions of this act; and its board of directors shall also have power to define and regulate by by-laws, not inconsistent with the provisions of this act, the manner in which its stock shall be transferred, its directors elected or appointed, its officers appointed, its property transferred, its general business conducted, and all the privileges granted by this act to associations organized under it shall be exercised and enjoyed; and its usual business shall be transacted at an office or banking-house located in the place specified in its organization certificate.

SEC. 9. That the affairs of every association shall be managed by not less than five directors, one of whom shall be the president. Every director shall, during his whole term of service, be a citizen of the United States; and at least three-fourths of the directors shall have resided in the State, Territory, or District in which such association is located one year next preceding their election as directors, and be residents of the same during their continuance in office. Each director shall own, in his own right, at least ten shares of the capital stock of the association of which he is a director.

SEC. 11. That in all elections of directors, and in deciding all questions at meetings of shareholders, each shareholder shall be entitled to one vote on each share of stock held by him. Shareholders may vote by proxies duly authorized in writing; but no officer, clerk, teller, or book-keeper of such association shall act as proxy; and no shareholders, whose liability is past due and unpaid, shall be allowed to vote.

SEC. 12. That the capital stock of any association formed under this act shall be divided into shares of one hundred dollars each, and be deemed personal property and transferable on the books of the association; and every person becoming a shareholder by such transfer shall, in proportion to his shares, succeed to all the rights and liabilities of the prior holder of such shares, and no change shall be made in the articles of association by which the rights, remedies, or security of the existing creditors of the association shall be impaired. The shareholders of each association formed under the provisions of this act, and of each existing bank or banking association that may accept the provisions of this act, shall be held individually responsible, equally and ratably, and not one for another, for all contracts, debts, and engagements of such association to the extent of amount of their stock therein at the par value thereof, in addition to the amount invested in such shares; except that shareholders of any banking association now existing under State laws, having not less than five millions of dollars of capital actually paid in, and a surplus of twenty per centum on hand, both to be determined by the Comptroller of the Currency, shall be liable only to the amount invested in their shares; and such surplus of twenty per centum shall be kept undiminished, and be in addition to the surplus provided for in this act; and if at any time there shall be a deficiency in said surplus of twenty per centum, the said banking association shall not pay any dividends to its shareholders until such deficiency shall be made good; and in case of such deficiency, the Comptroller of the Currency may compel said banking association to close up its business and wind up its affairs under the provisions of this act. And the Comptroller shall have authority to withhold from an association his certificate authorizing the commencement of business, whenever he shall have reason to suppose that the shareholders thereof have formed the same for any other than the legitimate objects contemplated by this act.

SEC. 13. That it shall be lawful for any association formed under this act, by its articles of association to provide for an increase of its capital from time to time, as may be deemed expedient, subject to the limitations of this act: *Provided*, That the maximum of such increase in the articles of association shall be determined by the Comptroller of the Currency; and no increase of capital shall be valid until the whole amount of such increase shall be paid in, and notice thereof shall have been transmitted to the Comptroller of the Currency, and his certificate obtained specifying the amount of such increase of capital stock, with his approval thereof, and that it has been duly paid in as part of the capital of such association. And every association shall have power, by the vote of shareholders owning two-thirds of its capital stock, to reduce the capital of such association to any sum not below the amount required by this act in the formation of associations: *Provided*, That by no such reduction shall its capital be brought below the amount required by this act for its outstanding circulation, nor shall any such reduction be made until the amount of the proposed reduction has been reported to the Comptroller of the Currency and his approval thereof obtained.

SEC. 14. That at least fifty per centum of the capital stock of every association shall be paid in before it shall be authorized to commence business; and the remainder of the capital stock of such association shall be paid in installments of at least ten per centum each on the whole amount of the capital as frequently as one installment at the end of each succeeding month from the time it shall be authorized by the Comptroller to commence business; and the payment of each installment shall be certified to the Comptroller, under oath, by the president or cashier of the association.

SEC. 16. That every association, after having complied with the provisions of this act, preliminary to the commencement of banking business under its provisions, and before it shall be authorized to commence business, shall transfer and deliver to the Treasurer of the United States any United States registered bonds bearing interest to an amount not less than thirty thousand dollars nor less than one-third of the capital stock paid in, which bonds shall be deposited with the Treasurer of the United States, and by him safely kept in his office until the same shall be otherwise disposed of, in pursuance of the provisions of this act; and the Secretary of the Treasury is hereby authorized to receive and cancel any United States coupon bonds, and to issue in lieu thereof registered bonds of like amount, bearing a like rate of interest, and having the same time to run; and the deposit of bonds shall be, by every association, increased as its capital may be paid up or increased, so that every association shall at all times have on deposit with the Treasurer registered United States bonds to the amount of at least one-third of its capital stock actually paid in:

Provided, That nothing in this section shall prevent an association that may desire to reduce its capital or to close up its business and dissolve its organization from taking up its bonds upon returning to the Comptroller its circulating notes in the proportion hereinafter named in this act, nor from taking up any excess of bonds beyond one-third of its capital stock, and upon which no circulating notes have been delivered.

SEC. 17. That whenever a certificate shall have been transmitted to the Comptroller of the Currency, as provided in this act, and the association transmitting the same shall notify the Comptroller that at least fifty per centum of its capital stock has been paid in as aforesaid, and that such association has complied with all the provisions of this act as required to be complied with before such association shall be authorized to commence the business of banking, the Comptroller shall examine into the condition of such association, ascertain especially the amount of money paid in on account of its capital, the name and place of residence of each of the directors of such association, and the amount of the capital stock of which each is the bona fide owner, and generally whether such association has complied with all the requirements of this act to entitle it to engage in the business of banking; and shall cause to be made and attested by the oaths of a majority of the directors and by the president or cashier of such association, a statement of all the facts necessary to enable the Comptroller to determine whether such association is lawfully entitled to commence the business of banking under this act.

SEC. 19. That all transfers of United States bonds which shall be made by any association under the provisions of this act shall be made to the Treasurer of the United States in trust for the association, with a memorandum written or printed on each bond, and signed by the cashier or some other officer of the association making the deposit, a receipt therefor to be given to said association, or by the Comptroller of the Currency, or by a clerk appointed by him for that purpose, stating that it is held in trust for the association on whose behalf such transfer is made, and as a security for the redemption and payment of any circulating notes that may have been or may be delivered to such association. No assignment or transfer of any such bonds by the Treasurer shall be deemed valid or of binding force and effect unless countersigned by the Comptroller of the Currency. It shall be the duty of the Comptroller of the Currency to keep in his office a book in which shall be entered the name of every association from whose accounts such transfer of bonds is made by the Treasurer, and the name of the party to whom such transfer is made; and the par value of the bonds so transferred shall be entered therein; and it shall be the duty of the Comptroller, immediately upon countersigning and entering the same, to advise by mail the association from whose account such transfer was made of the kind and numerical designation of the bonds and the amount thereof so transferred.

SEC. 21. That upon the transfer and delivery of bonds to the Treasurer, as provided in the foregoing section, the association making the same shall be entitled to receive from the Comptroller of the Currency circulating notes of different denominations, in blank, registered and countersigned, as hereinafter provided, equal in amount to ninety per centum of the current market value of the United States bonds so transferred and delivered, but not exceeding ninety per centum of the amount of said bonds at the par value thereof, it bearing interest at a rate not less than five per centum per annum; and the amount of such circulating notes to be furnished to each association shall be in proportion to its paid-up capital, as follows, and no more: To each association whose capital shall not exceed five hundred thousand dollars, ninety per centum of such capital; to each association whose capital exceeds five hundred thousand dollars, but does not exceed one million dollars, eighty per centum of such capital; to each association whose capital exceeds one million dollars, but does not exceed three millions of dollars, seventy-five per centum of such capital; to each association whose capital exceeds three millions of dollars, sixty per centum of such capital. And that one hundred and fifty millions of dollars of the entire amount of circulating notes authorized to be issued shall be apportioned to associations in the States, in the District of Columbia, and in the Territories, according to representative population, and the remainder shall be apportioned by the Secretary of the Treasury among associations formed in the several States, in the District of Columbia, and in the Territories, having due regard to the existing banking capital, resources, and business of such State, District, and Territory. (Act as amended and approved, March 3, 1865.)

SEC. 22. That the entire amount of notes for circulation to be issued under this act shall not exceed three hundred millions of dollars. In order to furnish suitable notes for circulation, the Comptroller of the Currency is hereby authorized and required, under the direction of the Secretary of the Treasury, to cause plates and dies to be engraved, in the best manner, to guard against counterfeiting and fraudulent alterations, and to have printed therefrom, and numbered, such quantity of circulating notes, in blank, of the denominations of one dollar, two dollars, three dollars, five dollars, ten dollars, twenty dollars, fifty dollars, one hundred dollars, five hundred dollars, and one thousand dollars, as may be required to supply, under this act, the associations entitled to receive the same; which notes shall express upon their face that they are secured by United States bonds, deposited with the Treasurer of the United States by the written or engraved signatures of the Treasurer and Register, and by the imprint of the seal of the Treasury; and

44

shall also express upon their face the promise of the association receiving the same to pay on demand, attested by the signatures of the president or vice-president and cashier. And the said notes shall bear such devices and such other statements, and shall be in such form as the Secretary of the Treasury shall, by regulation, direct: *Provided*, That not more than one-sixth part of the notes furnished to an association shall be of a less denomination than five dollars, and that after specie payments shall be resumed no association shall be furnished with notes of a less denomination than five dollars.

SEC. 23. That after any such association shall have caused its promise to pay such notes on demand to be signed by the president or vice-president, and cashier thereof, in such manner as to make them obligatory promissory notes, payable on demand, at its place of business, such association is hereby authorized to issue and circulate the same as money; and the same shall be received at par in all parts of the United States in payment of taxes, excises, public lands, and all other dues to the United States, except for duties on imports; and also for all salaries and other debts and demands owing by the United States to individuals, corporations, and associations within the United States, except interest on the public debt, and in redemption of the national currency. And no such association shall issue post notes or any other notes to circulate as money than such as are authorized by the foregoing provisions of this act.

SEC. 24. That it shall be the duty of the Comptroller of the Currency to receive worn-out or mutilated circulating notes issued by any such banking association, and also, on due proof of the destruction of any such circulating notes, to deliver in place thereof to such association other blank circulating notes to an equal amount. And such worn-out or mutilated notes, after a memorandum shall have been entered in the proper books, in accordance with such regulations as may be established by the Comptroller, as well as all circulating notes which shall have been paid or surrendered to be canceled, shall be burned to ashes in the presence of four persons, one to be appointed by the Secretary of the Treasury, one by the Comptroller of the Currency, one by the Treasurer of the United States, and one by the association, under such regulations as the Secretary of the Treasury may prescribe. And a certificate of such burning, signed by the parties so appointed, shall be made in the books of the Comptroller, and a duplicate thereof forwarded to the association whose notes are thus cancelled.

SEC. 26. That the bonds transferred to and deposited with the Treasurer of the United States, as hereinbefore provided, by any banking association for the security of its circulating notes, shall be held exclusively for that purpose, until such notes shall be redeemed, except as provided in this act; but the Comptroller of the Currency shall give to any such banking association powers of attorney to receive and appropriate to its own use the interest on the bonds which it shall have so transferred to the Treasurer; but such powers shall become inoperative whenever such banking association shall fail to redeem its circulating notes as aforesaid. Whenever the market or cash value of any bonds deposited with the Treasurer of the United States, as aforesaid, shall be reduced below the amount of the circulation issued for the same, the Comptroller of the Currency is hereby authorized to demand and receive the amount of such depreciation in other United States bonds at cash value, or in money, from the association receiving said bills, to be deposited with the Treasurer of the United States as long as such depreciation continues. And said Comptroller, upon the terms prescribed by the Secretary of the Treasury, may permit an exchange to be made of any of the bonds deposited with the Treasurer by an association for other bonds of the United States authorized by this act to be received as security for circulating notes: *Provided*, that the remaining bonds which shall have been transferred by the banking association offering to surrender circulating notes shall be equal to the amount required for the circulating notes not surrendered by such banking association, and that the amount of bonds in the hands of the Treasurer shall not be diminished below the amount required to be kept on deposit with him by this act: *And provided*, That there shall have been no failure by such association to redeem its circulating notes, and no other violation by such association of the provisions of this act, and that the market or cash value of the remaining bonds shall not be below the amount required for the circulation issued for the same.

SEC. 27. That it shall be unlawful for any officer acting under the provisions of this act to countersign or deliver to any association, or to any other company or person, any circulating notes contemplated by this act, except as hereinbefore provided, and in accordance with the true intent and meaning of this act.

SEC. 28. That it shall be lawful for any such association to purchase, hold, and convey real estate as follows:

First. Such as shall be necessary for its immediate accommodation in the transaction of its business.

Second. Such as shall be mortgaged to it in good faith by way of security for debts previously contracted.

Third. Such as shall be conveyed to it in satisfaction of debts previously contracted in the course of its dealings.

Fourth. Such as it shall purchase at sales under judgments, decrees, or mortgages held by such association, or shall purchase to secure debts due to said association.

Such association shall not purchase or hold real estate in any other case or for any other purpose than as specified in this section. Nor shall it hold the possession of any real estate under mortgage, or hold the title and possession of any real estate purchased to secure any debts due to it for a longer period than five years.

SEC. 29. That the total liabilities to any association, of any person, or of any company, corporation, or firm for money borrowed, including in the liabilities of a company or firm the liabilities of the several members thereof, shall at no time exceed one-tenth part of the amount of the capital stock of such association actually paid in: *Provided*, That the discount of bona fide bills of exchange drawn against actually existing values, and the discount of commercial or business paper actually owned by the person or persons, corporation, or firm negotiating the same shall not be considered as money borrowed.

SEC. 30. That every association may take, receive, reserve, and charge on any loan or discount made, or upon any note, bill of exchange, or other evidences of debt, interest at the rate allowed by the laws of the State or Territory where the bank is located, and no more, except that where by the laws of any State a different rate is limited for banks of issue organized under State laws, the rate so limited shall be allowed for associations organized in any such State under this act. And when no rate is fixed by the laws of the State or Territory, the bank may take, receive, reserve, or charge a rate not exceeding seven per centum, and such interest may be taken in advance, reckoning the days for which the note, bill, or other evidence of debt has to run. And the knowingly taking, receiving, reserving, or charging a rate of interest greater than aforesaid shall be held and adjudged a forfeiture of the entire interest which the note, bill, or other evidence of debt carries with it, or which has been agreed to be paid thereon. And in case a greater rate of interest has been paid, the person or persons paying the same, or their legal representatives, may recover back, in any action of debt twice the amount of the interest thus paid from the association taking or receiving the same: *Provided*, That such action is commenced within two years from the time the usurious transaction occurred. But the purchase, discount, or sale of a bona fide bill of exchange, payable at another place than the place of such purchase, discount, or sale, at not more than the current rate of exchange for sight drafts, in addition to the interest, shall not be considered as taking or receiving a greater rate of interest.

SEC. 31. That every association in the cities hereinafter named shall, at all times, have on hand, in lawful money of the United States, an amount equal to at least twenty-five per centum of the aggregate amount of its notes in circulation and its deposits; and every other association shall, at all times, have on hand, in lawful money of the United States, an amount equal to at least fifteen per centum of the aggregate amount of its notes in circulation and of its deposits. And whenever the lawful money of any association in any of the cities hereinafter named shall be below the amount of twenty-five per centum of its circulation and deposits, and whenever the lawful money of any other association shall be below fifteen per centum of its circulation and deposits, such association shall not increase its liabilities by making any new loans or discounts, otherwise than by discounting or purchasing bills of exchange payable at sight, nor make any dividend of its profits until the required proportion between the aggregate amount of its outstanding notes of circulation and deposits and its lawful money of the United States shall be restored: *Provided*, That three-fifths of said fifteen per centum may consist of balances due to an association available for the redemption of its circulating notes from associations approved by the Comptroller of the Currency, organized under this act, in the cities of Saint Louis, Louisville, Chicago, Detroit, Milwaukee, New Orleans, Cincinnati, Cleveland, Pittsburg, Baltimore, Philadelphia, Boston, New York, Albany, Leavenworth, San Francisco, and Washington City: *Provided, also*, That clearing-house certificates, representing specie or lawful money specially deposited for the purpose of any clearing-house association, shall be deemed to be lawful money in the possession of any association belonging to such clearing-house holding and owning such certificate, and shall be considered to be a part of the lawful money which such association is required to have under the foregoing provisions of this section: *Provided*, That the cities of Charleston and Richmond may be added to the list of cities in the national associations, of which other associations may keep three-fifths of their lawful money, whenever, in the opinion of the Comptroller of the Currency, the condition of the Southern States will warrant it. And it shall be competent for the Comptroller of the Currency to notify any association, whose lawful money reserve as aforesaid shall be below the amount to be kept on hand as aforesaid, to make good such reserve; and if such association shall fail for thirty days thereafter, so as to make good its reserve of lawful money of the United States, the Comptroller may, with the concurrence of the Secretary of the Treasury, appoint a receiver to wind up the business of such association, as provided in this act.

SEC. 32. That each association organized in any of the cities named in the foregoing section shall select, subject to the approval of the Comptroller of the Currency, an association in the city of New York, at which it will redeem its circulating notes at par. And each of such associations may keep one-half of its lawful money reserve in cash deposits in the city of New York. And each association, not organized within the cities named in the preceding section, shall select, subject to the approval of the Comptroller of the Currency, an association in either of the cities named in the preceding section, at which it will redeem its circulating notes at par. And every association formed or existing under the provisions of this act shall take and receive at par, for any debt or liability to said association, any and all notes or bills issued by any association existing under and by virtue of this act.

SEC. 35. That no association shall make any loan or discount on the security of the shares of its own capital stock, nor be the purchaser or holder of any such shares, unless such security or purchase shall be necessary to prevent loss upon a debt previously contracted in good faith; and stock so purchased or acquired, shall, within six months from the time of its purchase, be sold or disposed of at public or private sale, in default of which a receiver may be appointed to close up the business of the association, according to the provisions of this act.

SEC. 36. That no association shall, at any time, be indebted, or in any way liable, to an amount exceeding its capital stock at such time actually paid in and remaining undiminished by losses or otherwise, except on the following accounts; that is to say:

First. On account of its notes of circulation.

Second. On account of moneys deposited with, or collected by, such association.

Third. On account of bills of exchange or drafts drawn against money actually on deposit to the credit of such association, or due thereto.

Fourth. On account of liabilities to its stockholders for dividends and reserved profits.

Sec. 37. That no association shall, either directly or indirectly, pledge or hypothecate any of its notes of circulation, for the purpose of procuring money to be paid in on its capital stock, or to be used in its banking operations, or otherwise; nor shall any association use its circulating notes, or any part thereof, in any manner or form, to create or increase its capital stock.

SEC. 38. That no association or any member thereof, shall, during the time it shall continue its banking operations, withdraw, or permit to be withdrawn, either in forms of dividends or otherwise, any portion of its capital. And if losses shall at any time have been sustained by any such association equal to or exceeding its dividend profits then on hand, no dividend shall be made; and no dividend shall ever be made by any association while it shall continue its banking operations, to an amount greater than its net profits then on hand, deducting therefrom its losses and bad debts. And all debts due to any association on which interest is past due and unpaid for a period of six months, unless the same shall be well secured, and shall be in process of collection, shall be considered bad debt, within the meaning of this act: *Provided*, That nothing in this section shall prevent the reduction of the capital stock of the association under the thirteenth section of this act.

SEC. 39. That no association shall at any time pay out on loans or discounts, or in purchasing drafts or bills of exchange, or in payment of deposits, or in any other mode pay or put in circulation the notes of any bank or banking association which shall not, at any such time, be receivable, at par on deposit and in payment of debts by the association so paying out or circulating such notes, nor shall it knowingly pay out or put in circulation any notes issued by any bank or banking association, which, at the time of such paying out or putting in circulation, is not redeeming its circulating notes in lawful money of the United States.

SEC. 41. And in lieu of all existing taxes, every association shall pay to the Treasurer of the United States, in the months of January and July, a duty of one-half of one per centum each half year from and after the first day of January, eighteen hundred and sixty-four, upon the average amount of its notes in circulation, and a duty of one-quarter of one per centum each half year upon the average amount of its deposits, and a duty of one quarter of one per centum each half year, as aforesaid, on the average amount of its capital stock beyond the amount invested in United States bonds. And it shall be the duty of each association, within ten days from the first days of January and July of each year, to make a return under the oath of its president or cashier, to the Treasurer of the United States, in such form as he may prescribe, of the average amount of its notes in circulation, and of the average amount of its deposits, and of the average amount of its capital stock beyond the amount invested in United States bonds, for the six months next preceding said first days of January and July as aforesaid: *Provided*, That nothing in this act shall be construed to prevent all the shares in any of the said associations, held by any person or body corporate from being included in the valuation of the personal property of such person or corporation in the assessment of taxes imposed by or under State authority at the place where such bank is located, and not elsewhere, but not at a greater rate than is assessed upon other moneyed capital in the hands of individual citizens of such State: *Provided further*, That the tax so imposed under the laws of any State upon the shares of any of the associations authorized by this act shall not exceed the rate imposed upon the shares in any of the banks organized under authority of the State where such association is located: *Provided, also*, That nothing in this act shall exempt the real estate of associations from either State, county, or municipal taxes to the same extent, according to its value, as other real estate is taxed.

SEC. 42. That any association may go into liquidation and be closed by the vote of its shareholders owning two-thirds of its stock. And whenever such vote shall be taken it shall be the duty of the board of directors to cause notice of this fact to be certified, under the seal of the association, by its president or cashier, to the Comptroller of the Currency, and publication thereof to be made for a period of two months in a newspaper, published in the city of New York, and also in a newspaper published in a city or town in which the association is located; and one year after that time the outstanding notes of said association shall be redeemed at the Treasury of the United States, and the said association and the shareholders thereof shall be discharged from all liabilities therefor

SEC. 44. That any bank incorporated by special law, or any banking institution organized under a general law of any State, may, by authority of this act, become a national association under its provisions, by the name prescribed in its organization certificate; and in such case the articles of association and the organization certificate required by this act may be executed by a majority of the directors of the bank or banking institution; and said certificate shall declare that the owners of two-thirds of the capital stock shall have authorized the directors to make such certificate and to change and convert the said bank or banking institution into a national association under this act. And a majority of the directors, after executing said articles of association and organization certificate, shall have power to execute all other papers, and to do whatever may be required to make its organization perfect and complete as a national association. The shares of any such bank may continue to be for the same amount each as they were before said conversion, and the directors aforesaid may be the directors of the association until others are elected or appointed in accordance with the provisions of this act; and any State bank which is a stockholder in any other bank, by authority of State laws, may continue to hold its stock, although either bank, or both, may be organized under and have accepted the provisions of this act. When the Comptroller shall give to such association a certificate, under his hand and official seal, that the provisions of this act have been complied with, and that it is authorized to commence the business of banking under it, the association shall have the same powers and privileges, and shall be subject to the same duties, responsibilities and rules, in all respects as are prescribed in this act for other associations organized under it, and shall be held and regarded as an association under this act: *Provided, however*, That no such association shall have a less capital than the amount prescribed for banking associations under this act.

SEC. 45. That all associations under this act, when designated for that purpose by the Secretary of the Treasury, shall be depositaries of public money, except receipts from customs, under such regulations as may be prescribed by the Secretary; and they may also be employed as financial agents of the Government; and they shall perform all such reasonable duties, as depositaries of public moneys and financial agents of the Government, as may be required of them. And the Secretary of the Treasury shall require of the associations thus designated satisfactory security, by the deposit of United States bonds and otherwise, for the safe keeping and prompt payment of the public money deposited with them, and for the faithful performance of their duties as financial agents of the Government: *Provided*, That every association which shall be selected and designated as receiver or depositary of the public money, shall take and receive at par all of the national currency bills, by whatever association issued, which have been paid in to the Government for internal revenue, or for loans or stocks.

SEC. 46. That if any such association shall at any time fail to redeem, in the lawful money of the United States, any of its circulating notes, when payment thereof shall be lawfully demanded during the usual hours of business, at the office of such association, or at its place of redemption aforesaid, the holder may cause the same to be protested, in one package, by a notary public, unless the president or cashier of the association, whose notes are presented for payment, or the president or cashier of the association at the place at which they are redeemable, shall offer to waive demand and notice of the protest, and shall, in pursuance of such offer, make, sign, and deliver to the party making such demand, an admission in writing, stating the time of the demand, the amount demanded, and the fact of the non-payment thereof; and such notary public, on making such protest, or upon receiving such admission, shall forthwith forward such admission or notice of protest to the Comptroller of the Currency, retaining a copy thereof. And after such default, on examination of the facts by the Comptroller, and notice by him to the association, it shall not be lawful for the association suffering the same to pay out any of its notes, discount any notes or bills, or otherwise prosecute the business of banking, except to receive and safely keep money belonging to it, and to deliver special deposits. *Provided*, That if satisfactory proof be produced to such notary public, that the payment of any such notes is restrained by order of any court of competent jurisdiction, such notary public shall not protest the same; and when the holder of such notes shall cause more than one note or package to be protested on the same day, he shall not receive pay for more than one protest.

SEC. 56. That all suits and proceedings arising out of the provisions of this act, in which the United States or its officers or agents shall be parties, shall be conducted by the district attorneys of the several districts, under the direction and supervision of the Solicitor of the Treasury.

SEC. 57. That suits, actions, and proceedings against any association under this act, may be had in any circuit, district, or territorial court of the United States held within the district in which such association may be established; or in any State, county, or municipal court in the county or city in which said association is located, having jurisdiction in similar cases: *Provided, however*, That all proceedings to enjoin the Comptroller under this act shall be had in a circuit, district, or territorial court of the United States, held in the district in which the association is located.

SEC. 58. That every person who shall mutilate, cut, deface, disfigure, or perforate with holes, or shall unite or cement together, or do any other thing to any bank bill, draft, note, or other evidence of debt, issued by any such association, or shall cause or procure the same to be done, with intent to render such bank bill, draft, note, or other evidence of debt unfit to be reissued by said association, shall, upon conviction, forfeit fifty dollars to the association who shall be injured thereby, to be recovered by action in any court having jurisdiction.

SEC. 61. That it shall be the duty of the Comptroller of the Currency to report annually to Congress at the commencement of its session—

First. A summary of the state and condition of every association from whom reports have been received the preceding year at the several dates to which such reports refer, with an abstract of the whole amount of banking capital returned by them, of the whole amount of their debts and liabilities, the amount of circulating notes outstanding, and the total amount of means and resources, specifying the amount of lawful money held by them at the times of their several returns, and such other information in relation to said associations as, in his judgment may be useful.

SEC. 110. That there shall be levied, collected, and paid a duty of one twenty-fourth of one per centum each month upon the average amount of the deposits of money, subject to payment by check or draft, or represented by certificates of deposit or otherwise, whether payable on demand or at some future day, with any person, bank, association, company or corporation engaged in the business of banking; and a duty of one twenty-fourth of one per centum each month, as aforesaid, upon the average amount of the capital of any bank, association, company or corporation, or person engaged in the business of banking, beyond the amount invested in United States bonds; and a duty of one-twelfth of one per centum each month upon the average amount of circulation issued by any bank, association, corporation, company or person, including as circulation all certified checks and all notes and other obligations circulated or intended to circulate, or to be used as money, but not including that in the vault of the bank, or redeemed and on deposit for said bank, and an additional duty of one-sixth of one per centum each month upon the average amount of such circulation, issued as aforesaid, beyond the amount of ninety per centum of the capital of any such bank, association, corporation, company or person, and upon any amount of such circulation beyond the average amount of the circulation that had been issued as aforesaid by any such bank, association, corporation, company or person, for the six months preceding the first day of July, eighteen hundred and sixty-four. And on the first Monday of August next, and of each month thereafter, a true and accurate return of the amount of circulation, of deposit and of capital, as aforesaid, for the previous month, shall be made and rendered in duplicate by each of such banks, associations, corporations, companies or persons, to the assessor of the district in which any such bank, association, corporation or company may be located, or in which such person may reside, with a declaration annexed thereto, and the oath or affirmation of such person, or the president or cashier of such bank, association, corporation or company, in such form and manner as may be prescribed by the Commissioner of Internal Revenue, that the same contains a true and faithful statement of the amount of circulation, deposits, and capital, as aforesaid, subject to duty as aforesaid, and shall transmit the duplicate of said return to the Commissioner of Internal Revenue, and within twenty days thereafter shall pay to the said Commissioner of Internal Revenue the duties hereinbefore prescribed upon the said amount of circulation, of deposits and of capital, as aforesaid.

Old debt	Unclaimed dividends upon debt created prior to 1800, and the principal and interest of the outstanding debt created during the war of 1812, and up to 1837.
Treasury notes prior to 1846.	The acts of October 12, 1837, (5 Statutes, 201;) May 21, 1838, (5 Statutes, 228;) March 31, 1840, (5 Statutes, 370;) February 15, 1841, (5 Statutes, 411;) January 31, 1842, (5 Statutes, 469;) August 31, 1842, (5 Statutes, 581;) and March 3, 1843, (5 Statutes, 614;) authorized the issue of Treasury notes in various amounts, and with interest at rates named therein, from 1 mill to 6 per centum per annum.
Treasury notes of 1846	The act of July 22, 1846, (9 Statutes, 39;) authorized the issue of Treasury notes in such sums as the exigencies of the Government might require: the amount outstanding at any one time not to exceed $10,000,000, to bear interest at not exceeding 6 per centum per annum, redeemable one year from date. These notes were receivable in payment of all debts due the United States, including customs-duties.
Mexican indemnity	A proviso in the civil and diplomatic appropriation act of August 10, 1846, (9 Statutes, 94,) authorized the payment of the principal and interest of the fourth and fifth installments of the Mexican indemnities due April and July, 1844, by the issue of stock, with interest at 5 per centum, payable in five years.
Treasury notes of 1847	The act of January 28, 1847, (9 Statutes, 118,) authorized the issue of $23,000,000 Treasury notes, with interest at not exceeding 6 per centum per annum, or the issue of stock for any portion of the amount, with interest at 6 per centum per annum. The Treasury notes under this act were redeemable at the expiration of one or two years, and the interest was to cease at the expiration of sixty days' notice. These notes were receivable in payment of all debts due the United States, including customs-duties.
Loan of 1847	The act of January 28, 1847, (9 Statutes, 118,) authorized the issue of $23,000,000 Treasury notes, with interest at not exceeding 6 per centum per annum, or the issue of stock for any portion of the amount, with interest at 6 per centum per annum, re-imbursable after December 31, 1867. Section 14 authorized the conversion of Treasury notes under this or any preceding act into like stock, which accounts for the apparent overissue.
Bounty land scrip	The 9th section of the act of February 11, 1847, (9 Statutes, 125,) authorized the issue of land warrants to soldiers of the Mexican war, or scrip, at the option of the soldiers, to bear 6 per centum interest per annum, redeemable at the pleasure of the Government, by notice from the Treasury Department. Interest ceases July 1, 1849.
Texan indemnity stock	The act of September 9, 1850, (9 Statutes, 447,) authorized the issue of $10,000,000 stock, with interest at 5 per centum per annum, to the State of Texas, in satisfaction of all claims against the United States arising out of the annexation of the said State. This stock was to be redeemable at the end of fourteen years.
Treasury notes of 1857	The act of December 23, 1857, (11 Statutes, 257,) authorized the issue of $20,000,000 in Treasury notes, $6,000,000 with interest at not exceeding 6 per centum per annum, and

Legal Tender Notes, etc., of the Century.

Length of loan.	When redeemable.	Rates of interest.	Price at which sold.	Amount authorized.	Amount issued.	Amount outstanding.
....	On demand	5 and 6 per cent.	....	....	....	$57,665 00
1 & 2 years	1 & 2 years from date.	1 mill to 6 per cent.	Par.	....	....	82,575 35
1 year.	1 year from date.	6 per cent.	Par.	$10,000,000 00	....	6,000 00
5 years.	April and July, 1849.	5 per cent.	Par.	350,000 00	$303,573 92	1,104 91
1 & 2 years	After 60 days' notice	6 per cent.	Par.	23,000,000 00	....	950 00
20 years.	Jan. 1, 1868.	6 per cent.	Par.	23,000,000 00	28,207,000 00	1,250 00
Indefinite.	July 1, 1849.	6 per cent.	Par.	Indefinite.	....	3,400 00
14 years.	Jan. 1, 1865.	5 per cent.	Par.	10,000,000 00	5,000,000 00	174,000 00
1 year.	60 days' notice.	5 & 5½ per cent.	Par.	20,000,000 00	20,000,000 00	2,000 00

	the remainder with interest at the lowest rates offered by bidders, but not exceeding 6 per centum per annum. These notes were redeemable at the expiration of one year, and interest was to cease at the expiration of sixty days' notice after maturity. They were receivable in payment of all debts due the United States, including customs-duties.
Loan of 1858	The act of June 14, 1858, (11 Statutes, 365,) authorized a loan of $20,000,000, with interest at not exceeding 5 per centum per annum, and redeemable any time after January 1, 1874.
Loan of 1860	The act of June 22, 1860, (12 Statutes, 79,) authorized a loan of $21,000,000, (to be used in redemption of Treasury notes,) with interest at not exceeding 6 per centum per annum, redeemable in not less than ten nor more than twenty years.
Loan of February, 1861 (1881s.)	The act of February 8, 1861, (12 Statutes, 129,) authorized a loan of $25,000,000, with interest at not exceeding 6 per centum per annum, reimbursable in not less than ten nor more than twenty years from the date of the act.
Treasury Notes of 1861.	The act of March 2, 1861, (12 Statutes, 178,) authorized a loan of $10,000,000, with interest at not exceeding 6 per centum per annum, redeemable on three months' notice after July 1, 1871, and payable July 1, 1881. If proposals for the loan were not satisfactory, authority was given to issue the whole amount in Treasury notes, with interest at not exceeding 6 per centum per annum. The same act gave authority to substitute Treasury notes for the whole or any part of loans authorized at the time of the passage of this act. These notes were to be received in payment of all debts due the United States, including customs-duties, and were redeemable at any time within two years from the date of the act.
Oregon war debt	The act of March 2, 1861, (12 Statutes, 198,) appropriated $2,800,000 for the payment of expenses incurred by the Territories of Washington and Oregon in the suppression of Indian hostilities in the years 1855 and 1856. Section 4 of the act authorized the payment of these claims in bonds redeemable in twenty years, with interest at 6 per centum per annum.
Loan of July and August, 1861 (1881s.)	The act of July 17, 1861, (12 Statutes, 259), authorized the issue of $250,000,000 bonds, with interest at not exceeding 7 per centum per annum, redeemable after twenty years. The act of August 5, 1861, (12 Statutes, 331,) authorized the issue of bonds, with interest at 6 per centum per annum, payable after twenty years from date, in exchange for 7-30 notes issued under the act of July 17, 1861. None of such bonds were to be issued for a sum less than $500, and the whole amount of them was not to exceed the whole amount of 7-30 notes issued under the above act of July 17. The amount issued in exchange for 7-30s was $139,321,200.
Old demand notes	The act of July 17, 1861, (12 Statutes, 259,) authorized the issue of $50,000,000 Treasury notes, not bearing interest, of a less denomination than fifty dollars and not less than ten dollars, and payable on demand by the assistant treasurers at Philadelphia, New York, or Boston. The act of August 2, 1861, (12 Statutes, 313,) authorized the issue of these notes in denominations of five dollars; it also added the assistant treasurer at Saint Louis and the designated depositary at Cincinnati to the places where these notes were made payable. The act of February 12, 1862, (12 Statutes, 338,) increased the amount of demand notes authorized $10,000,000.
Seven-thirties of 1861	The act of July 17, 1861, (12 Statutes, 259,) authorized a

Length of loan.	When redeemable.	Rates of interest.	Price at which sold.	Amount authorized.	Amount issued.	Amount outstanding.
15 years.	Jan. 1, 1874.	5 per cent.	Par.	$20,000,000 00	$20,000,000 00	$394,000 000
10 years.	Jan. 1, 1871.	5 per cent.	Par.	21,000,000 00	7,022,000 00	10,000 00
10 or 20 yrs	Jan. 1, 1881.	6 per cent.	Par.	25,000,900 00	18,415,000 00	18,415,000 00
2 years.	2 yrs. after date.	6 per cent.	Par.	22,468,100 00 12,896,350 00	35,364,450 00	3,150 00
60 days.	60days after date.	6 per cent.	Par.	22,468,100 00 12,896,350 00	35,364,450 00	3,150 00
20 years.	July 1, 1881.	6 per cent.	Par.	2,800,000 00	1,090,850 00	945,000 00
20 years.	July 1, 1881.	6 per cent.	Par.	250,000,000 00	50,000,000 00 139,321,200 00	189,321,350 00
....	On demand	None.	Par.	60,000,000 00	60,000,000 00	76,732 50
3 years.	Aug. 19 and Oct. 1, 1864.	7 3-10 p. c.	Par.	140,094,750 00	140,094,750 00	19,200 00

	loan of $250,000,000, part of which was to be in Treasury notes, with interest at 7 3-10 per centum per annum, payable three years after date.
Five-twenties of 1862....	The act of February 25, 1862, (12 Statutes, 345,) authorized a loan of $500,000,000, for the purpose of funding the Treasury notes and floating debt of the United States, and the issue of bonds therefor, with interest at 6 per centum per annum. These bonds were redeemable after five and payable twenty years from date. The act of March 3, 1864, (13 Statutes, 13,) authorized an additional issue of $11,000,000 of bonds to persons who subscribed for the loan on or before January 21, 1864. The act of January 28, 1865, (13 Statutes, 425,) authorized an additional issue of $4,000,000 of these bonds and their sale in the United States or Europe.
Legal tender notes.......	The act of February 25, 1862, (12 Statutes, 345,) authorized the issue of $150,000,000 United States notes, not bearing interest, payable to bearer, at the Treasury of the United States, and of such denominations, not less than five dollars, as the Secretary of the Treasury might deem expedient, $50,000,000 to be in lieu of demand notes authorized by the act of July 17, 1861,—these notes to be a legal tender. The act of July 11, 1862, (12 Statutes, 532,) authorized an additional issue of $150,000,000 United States Treasury notes, of such denominations as the Secretary of the Treasury might deem expedient; but no such note should be for a fractional part of a dollar, and not more than $35,000,000 of a lower denomination than five dollars;—these notes to be a legal tender. The act of March 3, 1863, (12 Statutes, 710,) authorized an additional issue of 8150,000,000 United States notes, payable to bearer, of such denominations, not less than one dollar, as the Secretary of the Treasury might prescribe; which notes were made a legal tender. The same act limited the time at which Treasury notes might be exchanged for United States bonds to July 1, 1863. The amount of notes authorized by this act were to be in lieu of $100,000,000 authorized by the resolution of January 17, 1863, (12 Statutes, 822.)
Temporary loan............	The act of February 25, 1862, (12 Statutes, 346,) authorized temporary loan deposits of $25,000,000 for not less than thirty days, with interest at 5 per centum per annum, payable after ten days' notice. The act of March 17, 1862, (12 Statutes, 370,) authorized the increase of temporary loan deposits to $50,000,000. The act of July 11, 1862, (12 Statutes, 532,) authorized a further increase of temporary loan deposits to $100,000,000. The act of June 30, 1864, (13 Statutes, 218,) authorized a further increase of temporary loan deposits to not exceeding $150,000,000, and an increase of the rate of interest to not exceeding 6 per centum per annum, or a decrease of the rate of interest on ten days' notice, as the public interest might require.
Certificates of indebtedness.	The act of March 1, 1862, (12 Statutes, 352,) authorized the issue of certificates of indebtedness to public creditors who might elect to receive them, to bear interest at the rate of 6 per centum per annum, and payable one year from date, or earlier, at the option of the Government. The act of May 17, 1862, (12 Statutes, 370,) authorized the issue of these certificates in payment of disbursing officers' checks. The act of March 3, 1863, (12 Statutes, 710,) made the interest payable in lawful money.
Fractional currency....	The act of July 17, 1862, (12 Statutes, 592,) authorized the use of postal and other stamps as currency, and made them receivable in payment of all dues to the United

Length of loan.	When redeemable.	Rates of interest.	Price at which sold.	Amount authorized.	Amount issued.	Amount outstanding.
5 or 20 yrs	May 1, 1867.	6 per cent.	Par.	$515,000,000 00	$514,771,600 00	$169,516,150 00
....	On demand	None.	Par.	450,000,000 00	915,420,031 00	382,000,000 00
Not less than 30 days.	After 10 days' notice	4, 5, & 6 per cent.	Par.	150,000,000 00	....	78,560 00
1 year.	1 year after date.	6 per cent.	Par.	No limit.	561,753,211 65	5,000 00
....	On presentation.	None.	Par.	50,000,000 00	223,625,663 45	45,881,295 67

	States less than five dollars. The 4th section of the act of March 3, 1863, (12 Statutes, 711,) authorized the issue of fractional notes in lieu of postal and other stamps and postal currency; made them exchangeable in sums not less than three dollars for United States notes, and receivable for postage and revenue stamps, and in payment of dues to the United States, except duties on imports, less than five dollars; and limited the amount to $50,000,000. The 5th section of the act of June 30, 1864, (13 Statutes, 220,) authorized an issue of $50,000,000 in fractional currency, and provided that the whole amount of these notes outstanding at any one time should not exceed this sum.
Loan of 1863	The act of March 3, 1863, (12 Statutes, 709,) authorized a loan of $900,000,000, and the issue of bonds, with interest at not exceeding 6 per centum per annum, and redeemable in not less than ten nor more than forty years, principal and interest payable in coin. The act of June 30, 1864, (13 Statutes, 219,) repeals so much of the preceding act as limits the authority thereunder to the current fiscal year, and also repeals the authority altogether except as relates to $75,000,000 of bonds already advertised for.
One-year notes of 1863	The act of March 3, 1863, (12 Statutes, 710,) authorized the issue of $400,000,000 Treasury notes, with interest at not exceeding 6 per centum per annum, redeemable in not more than three years, principal and interest payable in lawful money, to be a legal tender for their face value.
Two-year notes of 1863	The act of March 3, 1863, (12 Statutes, 710,) authorized the issue of $400,000,000 Treasury notes, with interest at not exceeding 6 per centum per annum, redeemable in not more than three years, principal and interest payable in lawful money, to be a legal tender for their face value.
Coin certificates	The 5th section of the act of March 3, 1863, (12 Statutes, 711,) authorized the deposit of gold coin and bullion with the Treasurer or any assistant treasurer, in sums not less than twenty dollars, and the issue of certificates therefor in denominations the same as United States notes; also authorized the issue of these certificates in payment of interest on the public debt. It limits the amount of them to not more than 20 per centum of the amount of coin and bullion in the Treasury, and directs their receipt in payment for duties on imports.
Compound interest notes.	The act of March 3, 1863, (12 Statutes, 709,) authorized the issue of $400,000,000 Treasury notes, with interest at not exceeding 6 per centum per annum, in lawful money, payable not more than three years from date, and to be a legal tender for their face value. The act of June 30, 1864, (13 Statutes, 218,) authorized the issue of $200,000,000 Treasury notes, of any denomination not less than ten dollars, payable not more than three years from date, or redeemable at any time after three years, with interest at not exceeding 7 3-10 per centum, payable in lawful money at maturity, and made them a legal tender for their face value to the same extent as United States notes; $177,045,770 of the amount issued was in redemption of 5 per cent. notes.
Ten-forties of 1864	The act of March 3, 1864, (13 Statutes, 13,) authorized the issue of $200,000,000 bonds, at not exceeding 6 per centum per annum, redeemable after five and payable not more than forty years from date, in coin.
Five-twenties of March 1864.	The act of March 3, 1864, (13 Statutes, 13,) authorized the issue of $200,000,000 bonds, at not exceeding 6 per centum

Length of loan.	When redeemable.	Rates of interest.	Price at which sold.	Amount authorized.	Amount issued.	Amount outstanding.
17 years.	July 1, 1881.	6 per cent.	Average prem. of 4,13.	$75,000,000 00	$75,000,000 00	$75,000,000 00
1 year.	1 year after date.	5 per cent.	Par.	400,000,000 00	44,520,000 00	74,775 00
2 years.	2 yrs. after date.	5 per cent.	Par.	400,000,000 00	166,480,000 00	52,850 00
....	On demand	None.	Par.	Indefinite.	562,776,400 00	22,825,100 00
3 years.	June 10, 1867 & May 15, 1868.	6 per cent., compound	Par.	400,000,000 00	266,595,440 00	415,210 00
10 or 40 yrs	March 1, 1874.	5 per cent.	Par to 7 p. c. prem.	200,000,000 00	196,117,300 00	194,567,300 00
5 or 20 yrs.	Nov. 1, 1869.	6 per cent.	Par.	....	3,882,500 00	946,600 00

	per annum, redeemable after five and payable not more than forty years from date, in coin.
Five-twenties of June, 1864.	The act of June 30, 1864, (13 Statutes, 218,) authorized a loan of $400,000,000, and the issue therefor of bonds redeemable at not less than five nor more than thirty (or forty, if deemed expedient) years from date, with interest at not exceeding 6 per centum per annum, payable semi-annually in coin.
Seven-thirties of 1864 & 1865.	The act of June 30, 1864, (13 Statutes, 218), authorized the issue of $200,000,000 Treasury notes, of not less than ten dollars each, payable at not more than three years from date, or redeemable at any time after three years, with interest at not exceeding 7 3-10 per centum per annum. The act of March 3, 1865, (13 Statutes, 468,) authorized a loan of $600,000,000, and the issue therefor of bonds or Treasury notes; the notes to be of denominations of not less than fifty dollars, with interest in lawful money at not more than 7 3-10 per centum per annum.
Navy pension fund.......	The act of July 1, 1864, (13 Statutes, 414,) authorized the Secretary of the Navy to invest in registered securities of the United States so much of the Navy pension fund in the Treasury January 1 and July 1 in each year as would not be required for the payment of naval pensions. Section 2 of the act of July 23, 1868, (15 Statutes, 170,) makes the interest on this fund 3 per centum per annum, in lawful money, and confines its use to the payment of naval pensions exclusively.
Five-twenties of 1865....	The act of March 3, 1865, (13 Statutes, 468,) authorized the issue of $600,000,000 of bonds or Treasury notes in addition to amounts previously authorized; the bonds to be for not less than fifty dollars, payable not more than forty years from date of issue, or after any period not less than five years; interest payable semi-annually at not exceeding 6 per centum per annum when in coin, or 7 3-10 per centum per annum when in currency. In addition to the amount of bonds authorized by this act, authority was also given to convert Treasury notes or other interest-bearing obligations into bonds authorized by it. The act of April 12, 1866, (14 Statutes, 31.) construed the above act to authorize the Secretary of the Treasury to receive any obligations of the United States, whether bearing interest or not, in exchange for any bonds authorized by it, or to sell any of such bonds, provided the public debt is not increased thereby.
Consols of 1865..............	The act of March 3, 1865, (13 Statutes, 468,) authorized the issue of $600,000,000 of bonds or Treasury notes in addition to amounts previously authorized; the bonds to be for not less than fifty dollars, payable not more than forty years from date of issue, or after any period not less than five years; interest payable semi-annually, at not exceeding 6 per centum per annum when in coin, or 7 3-10 per centum per annum when in currency. In addition to the amount of bonds authorized by this act, authority was also given to convert Treasury notes or other interest-bearing obligations into bonds authorized by it. The act of April 12, 1866, (14 Statutes, 31.) construed the above act to authorize the Secretary of the Treasury to receive any obligations of the United States, whether bearing interest or not, in exchange for any bonds authorized by it, or to sell any of such bonds, provided the public debt is not increased thereby.
Consols of 1867..............	The act of March 3, 1865, (13 Statutes, 468,) authorized the issue of $600,000,000 of bonds or Treasury notes in addition to amounts previously authorized; the bonds to be for not less than fifty dollars, payable not more than

Length of loan.	When redeemable.	Rates of interest.	Price at which sold.	Amount authorized.	Amount issued.	Amount outstanding.
5 or 20 yrs.	Nov. 1, 1869.	6 per cent.	Par.	$400,000,000 00	$125,561,300 00	$58,046,200 00
3 years.	Aug. 15, 1867 June 15, 1868 July 15, 1868	7 3-10 p. c.	Par.	800,000,000 00	829,992,500 00	228,450 00
Indefinite.	....	3 per cent.	Par.	Indefinite.	14,000,000 00	14,000,000 00
5 or 20 yrs.	Nov. 1, 1870.	6 per cent.	Par.	203,327,250 00	203,327,250 00	152,534,350 00
5 or 20 yrs.	July 1, 1870.	6 per cent.	Par.	332,998,950 00	332,998,950 00	202,663,100 00
5 or 20 yrs.	July 1, 1872.	6 per cent.	Par.	379,602,350 00	37[illegible],616,[illegible]50 00	31[illegible],624,400 00

	forty years from date of issue, or after any period not less than five years; interest payable semi-annually, at not exceeding 6 per centum per annum when in coin, or 7 3-10 per centum per annum when in currency. In addition to the amount of bonds authorized by this act, authority was also given to convert Treasury notes or other interest-bearing obligations into bonds authorized by it. The act of April 12, 1866, (14 Statutes, 31,) construed the above act to authorize the Secretary of the Treasury to receive any obligations of the United States, whether bearing interest or not, in exchange for any bonds authorized by it, or to sell any of such bonds, provided the public debt is not increased thereby.
Consols of 1868	The act of March 3, 1865, (13 Statutes, 468,) authorized the issue of $600,000,000 of bonds or Treasury notes in addition to amounts previously authorized: the bonds to be for not less than fifty dollars, payable not more than forty years from the date of issue, or after any period not lees than five dollars; interest payable semi-annually, at not exceeding 6 per centum per annum when in coin, or 7 3-10 per centum per annum when in currency. In addition to the amount of bonds authorized by this act, authority was also given to convert Treasury notes or other interest-bearing obligations into bonds authorized by it. The act of April 12, 1866, (14 Statutes, 31,) construed the above act to authorize the Secretary of the Treasury to receive any obligations of the United States, whether bearing interest or not, in exchange for any bonds authorized by it, or to sell any of such bonds, provided the public debt is not increased thereby.
Three per cent. certificates.	The act of March 3, 1867, (14 Statutes, 558,) authorized the issue of $50,000,000 in temporary loan certificates of deposit, with interest at 3 per centum per annum, payable in lawful money, on demand, to be used in redemption of compound interest notes. The act of July 25, 1868, (15 Statutes, 183,) authorized $25,000,000 additional of these certificates, for the sole purpose of redeeming compound interest notes.
Certificates of indebtedness of 1870.	The act of July 8, 1870, (16 Statutes, 197,) authorized the issue of certificates of indebtedness, payable five years after date, with interest at 4 per centum per annum, payable semi-annually, principal and interest, in lawful money, to be hereafter appropriated and provided for by Congress. These certificates were issued, one-third to the State of Maine and two-thirds to the State of Massachusetts, both for the use and benefit of the European and North American Railway Company, and were in full adjustment and payment of any and all claims of said States or railway company for moneys expended, or interest thereon, by the State of Massachusetts on account of the war of 1812-15.
Funded loan of 1881	The act of July 14, 1870, (16 Statutes, 272,) authorizes the issue of $200,000,000 at 5 per centum, $300,000,000 at 4½ per centum, and $1,000,000,000 at 4 per centum, principal and interest payable in coin of the present standard value, at the pleasure of the United States Government, after ten years for the 5 per cents, after fifteen years for the 4½ per cents, and after thirty years for the 4 per cents; these bonds to be exempt from the payment of all taxes or duties of the United States, as well as from taxation in any form by or under State, municipal, or local authority. Bonds and coupons payable at the Treasury of the United States. This act not to authorize an increase of the bonded debt of the United States. Bonds to be sold at not less than par in coin, and the proceeds

Length of loan.	When redeemable.	Rates of interest.	Price at which sold.	Amount authorized.	Amount issued.	Amount outstanding.
5 or 20 yrs.	July 1, 1873.	6 per cent.	Par.	$42,539,350 00	$42,539,350 00	$37,474,000 00
Indefinite.	On demand	3 per cent.	Par.	75,000,000 00	85,150,000 00	5,000 00
5 years.	Sep. 1, 1875.	4 per cent.	Par.	678,362 41	678.362 41	678,000 00
10 years.	May 1, 1881.	5 per cent.	Par.	500,000,000 00	200,000,000 00	315,800,750 00

	to be applied to the redemption of outstanding 5-20s, or to be exchanged for said 5-20s par for par. Payment of these bonds, when due, to be made in order of dates and numbers, beginning with each class last dated and numbered. Interest to cease at the end of three months from notice of intention to redeem. The act of January 20, 1871, (16 Statutes, 399,) increases the amount of 5 per cents to $500,000,000, provided the total amount of bonds issued shall not exceed the amount originally authorized, and authorizes the interest on any of these bonds to be paid quarterly.
Certificates of deposit...	The act of June 8, 1872, (17 Statutes, 336,) authorizes the deposit of United States notes without interest, by banking associations, in sums not less than $10,000, and the issue of certificates therefor in denominations of not less than $5,000; which certificates shall be payable on demand, in United States notes, at the place where the deposits were made. It provides that the notes so deposited in the Treasury shall not be counted as a part of the legal reserve, but that the certificates issued therefor may be held and counted by the national banks as part of their legal reserve, and may be accepted in the settlement of clearing-house balances at the places where the deposits therefor were made, and that the United States notes for which such certificates were issued, or other United States notes of like amount, shall be held as special deposits in the Treasury, and used only for the redemption of such certificates.

Length of loan.	When redeemable.	Rates of interest.	Price at which sold.	Amount authorized.	Amount issued.	Amount outstanding.
Indefinite.	On demand	None.	Par.	No limit.	$137,675,000 00	$58,760,000 00
						2,251,690,468 43